Le monde francophone

La France : les régions / les départements
LA MER DU NORD
N
L'ANGLETERRE
L'ALLEMAG
LA BELGIQUE
LE LUXEMBOURG
LA MANCHE
L'OCÉAN ATLANTIQUE
LA SUIS
L'ITA
L'ANDORRE
L'ESPAGNE
LA MER MÉDITERRANÉE
NORD-PAS DE CALAIS
Lille
Pas-de-Calais
Arras
Nord
Somme
Amiens
PICARDIE
Charleville-Mézières
Laon
Aisne
Ardennes
Seine-Maritime
Rouen
HAUTE-NORMANDIE
Beauvais
Oise
Pontoise
Val-d'Oise
Manche
Saint-Lo
Caen
Calvados
BASSE-NORMANDIE
Orne
Evreux
Eure
Yvelines
Versailles
Paris
ILE-DE-FRANCE
Évry
Essonne
Melun
Seine-et-Marne
LORRAINE
Metz
Meuse
Moselle
Marne
Châlons-sur-Marne
Bar-le-Duc
Nancy
Meurthe-et-Moselle
ALSACE
Bas-Rhin
Str
Finistère
St-Brieuc
Côtes-du-Nord
BRETAGNE
Quimper
Morbihan
Vannes
Rennes
Ille-et-Vilaine
Alençon
Chartres
Mayenne
Laval
Le Mans
Eure-et-Loir
CHAMPAGNE-ARDENNE
Troyes
Chaumont
Aube
Epinal
Vosges
Colmar
Haut-Rhin
PAYS DE LA LOIRE
Sarthe
Orléans
Loiret
Blois
Auxerre
Yonne
Haute-Marne
Territoire de Belfort
Loire-Atlantique
Angers
Maine-et-Loire
Tours
Loir-et-Cher
Côte-d'Or
Dijon
Vesoul
Haute-Saône
Doubs
Besançon
Nantes
Indre-et-Loire
CENTRE
Bourges
Cher
Nièvre
Nevers
BOURGOGNE
FRANCHE-COMTÉ
La Roche-sur-Yon
Vendée
Deux-Sèvres
Poitiers
Vienne
Châteauroux
Indre
Moulins
Allier
Saône-et-Loire
Lons-le-Saunier
Jura
Niort
La Rochelle
POITOU-CHARENTES
Haute-Vienne
Guéret
Creuse
AUVERGNE
Mâcon
Bourg-en-Bresse
Ain
Haute-Savoie
Annecy
Charente-Maritime
Charente
Limoges
Clermont-Ferrand
Rhône
Loire
Lyon
RHÔNE-ALPES
Chambéry
Angoulême
LIMOUSIN
Puy-de-Dôme
Isère
Savoie
Périgueux
Tulle
Corrèze
Cantal
Haute-Loire
St.-Étienne
Grenoble
Bordeaux
AQUITAINE
Dordogne
Aurillac
Le Puy
Valence
Gironde
Lot
Privas
Ardèche
Drôme
Gap
Hautes-Alpes
Lot-et-Garonne
Cahors
Mende
Aveyron
Lozère
Rodez
Landes
Agen
Tarn-et-Garonne
MIDI-PYRÉNÉES
Gard
Vaucluse
Digne
Alpes-Maritimes
Alpes de Haute-Provence
Mont-de-Marsan
Gers
Montauban
Albi
Tarn
Nîmes
Avignon
Nice
Mo
Auch
Toulouse
Montpellier
Hérault
Bouches-du-Rhône
PROVENCE-ALPES-CÔTE-D'AZUR
Pyrénées-Atlantiques
Pau
Tarbes
Haute-Garonne
Carcassonne
LANGUEDOC-ROUSSILLON
Marseille
Var
Toulon
Hautes-Pyrénées
Foix
Ariège
Aude
Perpignan
Pyrénées-Orientales
Seine-Saint-Denis
Nanterre
Bobigny
Paris
Hauts-de-Seine
Créteil
Val-de-Marne
Bastia
Haute-Corse
CORSE
Ajaccio
Corse-du-Sud
Limite départementale
Limite régionale
Ardèche Nom du département
CENTRE Nom de la région
200 kilomètres
200 milles

Part of the award-winning MyLanguageLabs suite of online learning and assessment systems for basic language courses, MyFrenchLab brings together—in one convenient, easily navigable site—a wide array of language-learning tools and resources, including an interactive version of the *Points de départ* student text, an online Student Activities Manual, and all materials from the audio and video programs. Chapter Practice Tests, tutorials, and English grammar Readiness Checks personalize instruction to meet the unique needs of individual students. Instructors can use the system to make assignments, set grading parameters, listen to student-created audio recordings, and provide feedback on student work. MyFrenchLab can be packaged with the text at a substantial savings. For more information, visit us online at http://www.mylanguagelabs.com/books

A GUIDE TO Points de départ ICONS		
	Text Audio Program	This icon indicates that recorded material to accompany *Points de départ* is available in MyFrenchLab (www.mylanguagelabs.com), on Audio CD, or on the Companion Website (www.pearsonhighered.com/pointsdedepart)
	Pair Activity	This icon indicates that the activity is designed to be done by students working in pairs.
	Group Activity	This icon indicates that the activity is designed to be done by students working in small groups or as a whole class.
	Video	This icon indicates that a video episode is available for the video that accompanies the *Points de départ* program. The video is available on DVD and in MyFrenchLab.
	Student Activities Manual	This icon indicates that there are practice activities available in the *Points de départ* Student Activities Manual. The activities may be found either in the printed version of the manual or in the interactive version available through MyFrenchLab. Activity numbers are indicated in the text for ease of reference.

ANNOTATED INSTRUCTOR'S EDITION

SECOND EDITION

Points de départ

Mary Ellen Scullen

University of Maryland, College Park

Cathy Pons

University of North Carolina, Asheville

Albert Valdman

Indiana University, Bloomington

PEARSON

Prentice Hall

Boston Columbus Indianapolis
New York San Francisco Upper Saddle River
Amsterdam Cape Town Dubai London
Madrid Milan Munich Paris Montreal Toronto
Delhi Mexico City São Paulo Sydney
Hong Kong Seoul Singapore Taipei Tokyo

Executive Acquisitions Editor: *Rachel McCoy*
Editorial Assistant: *Lindsay Miglionica*
Publishing Coordinator: *Regina Rivera*
Executive Marketing Manager: *Kris Ellis-Levy*
Marketing Assistant: *Michele Marchese*
Senior Managing Editor for Product Development: *Mary Rottino*
Associate Managing Editor: *Janice Stangel*
Production Project Manager: *Manuel Echevarria*
Executive Editor, MyLanguageLabs: *Bob Hemmer*
Senior Media Editor: *Samantha Alducin*
MyLanguageLabs Development Editor: *Bill Bliss*
Procurement Manager: *Mary Fischer*
Senior Art Director: *Maria Lange*
Senior Operations Specialist: *Alan Fischer*
Cover Designer: *Liz Harasymczuk Design*
Interior Designer: *Delgado & Company*
Project Manager: *Francesca Monaco*
Composition: *Preparé, Inc.*
Printer/Binder: *RR Donnelley/Willard*
Cover Printer: *Lehigh/Phoenix Color*
Cover Image: *Travelpix Ltd /Getty Images*
Publisher: *Phil Miller*

This book was set in Palatino 10.

10 9 8 7 6 5 4 3 2 1

Prentice Hall
is an imprint of

www.pearsonhighered.com

Student Edition
ISBN-10: 0-205-78840-8
ISBN-13: 978-0-205-78840-8

Annotated Instructor's Edition
ISBN-10: 0-205-79626-5
ISBN-13: 978-0-205-79626-7

Brief Contents

Scope & Sequence

Scope & Sequence

Chapitre 6
Nous sommes chez nous 176

Chapitre 7
La santé et le bien-être 204

Scope & Sequence

Preface

Points de départ, Second Edition is a complete, versatile program for introductory college and university French courses. It has been conceived for use in accelerated, intensive, and review programs; in hybrid courses incorporating distance learning; and in courses with limited contact time, i.e., three or fewer hours per week over an academic year. Developed by the authors of the extremely successful *Chez nous* French program, **Points de départ**, **Second Edition** incorporates many of the innovative features of that text while maintaining a focus on the essential content of an introductory course.

WHAT'S NEW IN THIS EDITION?

1. **Substantive new content.** Language use and cultural realities are constantly changing, and this is reflected in **Points de départ, Second Edition**.
   - Vocabulary presentations (**Points de départ**) have been significantly updated. For example, presentations related to the topics of education, health, media, and technology have been revised, along with their corresponding art.
   - Approximately one-third of the cultural notes (**Vie et culture**) are new or revised to include additional topics (such as small town life) or updated information, offering a more contemporary and nuanced picture of France and the Francophone world.
   - More than one-third of the skill-building activities (**Lisons, Écoutons, Observons, Parlons, Écrivons**) are new or revised for this edition, introducing new texts, video clips, and authentic tasks.
2. **Further refinement of the cyclical scope and sequence.** Users' feedback has led to additional modification of the scope and sequence for enhanced linguistic effectiveness and flexibility in the classroom. Some highlights include the following:
   - The preliminary chapter has been streamlined to a single **Leçon préliminaire**; this allows instructors to cover a few essential topics while demonstrating the principal lesson components before beginning the first full chapter.
   - The chapter treating food and its related grammatical content has been moved to the first half of the book (**Chapitre 5**); this allows for earlier treatment of useful vocabulary and structural features such as the partitive.
   - The chapter on studies and professions has been moved to the second half of the book (**Chapitre 8**); this means that students have more language to handle education and workplace topics.
3. **Sons et lettres sections in every chapter**. Pronunciation is now treated throughout the book.
4. **Increased attention to the development of learner strategies.**
   - **Écrivons** sections now target explicit writing strategies, and a four-step process now encourages students to draft and revise their writing, focusing first on content and then on form.
   - A new feature, **Fiche pratique**, outlines practical strategies to help students learn specific lesson content (for example, showing them ways to organize the new material, how to interact with native speakers using new content or structures, or how to test themselves).
5. **Comprehension before production.** Within many of the **Formes et fonctions** practice sections, new comprehension-based activities allow students to make an initial form-meaning link as they learn grammatical structures.

6. **Incorporation of the Orthographic Reform.** Although championed in Canada, the Orthographic Reform of 1990 has met with limited success in France. **Points de départ, Second Edition** incorporates a few of the most widely accepted elements of the Reform. Notably, changes related to the use of the **accent grave** have been implemented, affecting some verb conjugations in the future and conditional (for verbs like **préférer**) as well as the spelling of individual lexical items, such as **crèmerie** and **évènement**. Also, all numbers are now written with connecting hyphens, eliminating ambiguity and simplifying the learner's task: **cinq-mille-deux-cent-soixante-et-onze**, for example.
7. **Focus on learner outcomes.** Chapter openers now provide an overview of expected learner outcomes with a self-assessment checklist that encourages students to take stock of what they have learned to do.
8. **Revised testing package.** A completely revised testing program includes a test bank with exercises testing listening, reading, writing, and cultural knowledge. Instructors can select activities from the test bank to create their own tests, and exercises can be adapted for use in specific courses. We also provide fully constructed sample tests and special format tests for speaking. Complete grading guides are included.
9. **New design and art.** An entirely new design increases the book's user-friendliness. More abundant photos offer a richer depiction of the Francophone world and combine with updated line art to enhance the contemporary focus and visual appeal.

Points de départ, Second Edition stands apart from other first-year French texts by:

- Carefully selecting lexical and cultural content for broad coverage within a highly disciplined framework
- Streamlining grammatical presentations and reducing coverage of complex grammar points such as the subjunctive and the conditional
- Eliminating other complex and less-frequent grammatical features (for example, double-pronoun substitution, *plus-que-parfait, passé du conditionnel, futur antérieur*)
- Streamlining exercise sequences to suit the needs of a course intended to develop basic language proficiency
- Weaving cultural content into skills development activities that are fully integrated within each lesson
- Presenting concisely the fundamentals of the French sound system
- Limiting the number of chapters to ten

Points de départ, Second Edition also is distinguished by key features that enable it to be used on a highly flexible basis in a variety of contexts:

- **To maximize self-instruction:** Rich visuals, recordings, grammar explanations in English, reference sections, and online resources provide students with tools for self-instruction or preparation for focused in-class practice. Also, a process or discovery approach makes it possible for students to prepare vocabulary, culture, grammar, and skills sections on their own if necessary, for quick verification or more extended practice in class.
- **To tailor student practice:** Instructors can pick and choose among many types of practice available in the textbook, the Student Activities Manual, and **MyFrenchLab™** with the aim of providing immediate feedback to students or facilitating extensive instructor-student interaction. In turn, expansion and enrichment activities provide a challenge for motivated students.
- **To use classroom time efficiently:** The abundant visual aids, extensive annotations, and careful progression of activities designed for oral practice make class preparation simple and help teachers make the most of in-class time. Novice instructors will learn solid pedagogical skills, and experienced teachers will find a satisfying array of tools and techniques.

The National Standards for Foreign Language Learning for the 21st Century. With its disciplined yet flexible focus on the essential content of an introductory course and the incorporation of features long a hallmark of the *Chez nous* program, **Points de départ, Second Edition** provides a richly nuanced focus on the Francophone world through a highly integrative, process-oriented approach to the development of language skills. This approach is consistent with the **National Standards for Foreign Language Learning for the 21st Century**, widely recognized as a set of desired outcomes for foreign language instruction. Rather than functioning as discrete and occasional influences on the text, the National Standards constitute an essential underlying principle of the program as a whole. The "**Five C's,**" as defined by the National Standards, are directly embodied in essential aspects of the **Points de départ, Second Edition** program. The National Standards also constitute a subtext throughout the program—for example, many practice activities introduce cultural realities from across the French-speaking world, and culture is explored through skill-using activities and discovery methods of language learning.

Points de départ, Second Edition addresses the Five C's:

- Emphasizing **communication** developed through authentic language samples and tasks
- Encouraging cultural **comparisons**
- Presenting a broad cross section of French-speaking **communities**
- Fostering **connections** by guiding students through a variety of disciplines, including history, geography, art, and literature
- Promoting skill development within a distinctive **cultural** framework

HALLMARK PEDAGOGICAL FEATURES

While much is new in **Points de départ, Second Edition**, we remain committed to the hallmark features that distinguish this program from all others:

- **Innovative treatment of grammar.** Structures are presented in the context of authentic communicative use of the language; i.e., the periphrastic future (**aller** plus the infinitive) is not the notional equivalent of the inflected future (**le futur simple**), and this distinction is clearly made in the presentation and in practice activities. Grammar treatments, reflecting the spoken language, make important generalizations about the structure of French. For example, the presentation of adjectives is based on the concept that the masculine form of variable adjectives is derived from the longer feminine form by dropping the final pronounced consonant (**grande/grand**). Similarly, students learn that verbs with two stems have a longer stem in the plural, from which the singular can be derived by this general rule of final consonant deletion (**partent/part**).

  Use of a cyclical syllabus facilitates language acquisition by allowing the instructor to gradually develop students' understanding of complex topics. For example, we first present the **imparfait** as a means of making suggestions. We then treat the more frequent, complex uses of the **imparfait**, describing situations or habitual actions in the past. Finally, we contrast uses of the **passé composé** and the **imparfait**.
- **Process orientation to skills development.** The receptive skills (listening and reading) are developed using authentic materials that are just beyond students' productive skill level. Preview activities provide or activate background knowledge and introduce comprehension strategies; listening and reading activities guide and check comprehension as students encounter the material; and follow-up activities encourage them to reflect on what they have read or heard. The productive skills (speaking and writing) are likewise practiced via carefully sequenced activities that emphasize carrying out authentic tasks through a process approach. Pre-speaking and pre-writing preparation ready students to carry out the assigned tasks; frameworks for the actual speaking and writing assignments are provided; and thoughtful follow-up is encouraged. Through this process approach to developing the four skills, students gradually become confident and proficient at carrying out a wide variety of communicative tasks.
- **Pervasive and highly nuanced treatment of French and Francophone cultures.** Throughout each chapter, thematically interrelated lessons closely integrate the presentation of lexical and grammatical content within interesting and culturally authentic contexts. Nuanced cultural presentations also explicitly encompass the breadth and richness of the Francophone world, leading students to a deeper analysis and understanding of the diverse cultures of France and the French-speaking world.
- **Authentic texts and tasks.** Authentic texts and tasks form the basis for developing students' language skills in **Points de départ, Second Edition.** Listening activities and models for speaking reflect the everyday language of young people. Varied readings and writing tasks help students develop an awareness of appropriate style as they are exposed to a wide variety of Francophone writers. Throughout the textbook and supplements, practice of vocabulary and grammar is oriented toward real situations and authentic tasks.

ORGANIZATION OF THE TEXT

Points de départ, Second Edition consists of a brief introductory lesson plus ten full-length chapters. Each chapter is built around a cultural theme reinforced by informative photographs, line drawings, and realia. The user-friendly organization divides each chapter into three lessons that feature integrated lexical and grammatical presentations, sequenced practice, cultural information, and a culturally based skills activity.

Each lesson typically includes the following components:

Points de départ. Reflecting the chapter theme, this opening section presents vocabulary through varied and appealing visuals and language samples representing authentic everyday contexts. Recordings of the language samples are available on the Audio CDs to accompany the text, on the Companion Website, and through **MyFrenchLab™**. The **Points de départ** section includes related and up-to-date cultural notes in the **Vie et culture** section, written initially in English, then (beginning in Chapter 5) in French. The notes incorporate video, photos, and realia that students must analyze in order to discover features of French culture and make cross-cultural comparisons. Each **Points de départ** section offers sequenced practice (**À vous la parole**) through clearly labeled whole-class, paired, and small-group activities. Extensive marginal annotations make it easy for the instructor to present and practice the material in class.

Sons et lettres. This section presents the main phonetic features of French, so that students can incorporate them into their speech. It emphasizes the sound contrasts that determine differences in meaning, the major differences between French and English, and the relationship between sounds and spellings. Practice exercises from the text (**À vous la parole**) are available on the Audio CDs to accompany the text, on the Companion Website, and through **MyFrenchLab™**.

Formes et fonctions. Concise, clearly written grammar explanations in English focus on authentic usage and point out features of the spoken and written language. Numerous examples are provided and, where appropriate, color-coded charts summarize the forms. This section includes class-friendly exercises (**À vous la parole**) that provide a full range of practice—from form-based to meaningful and personalized activities—incorporating the theme and the vocabulary of the lesson. Icons clearly indicate pair and small-group activities.

Lisons, Observons, Écoutons, Parlons, Écrivons. Each lesson concludes with one of these culturally rich, thematically linked skills activities, helping students put into practice the vocabulary and grammar acquired in the lesson as they explore the chapter theme. Through work with an authentic text or task in a reading, listening, speaking, or writing activity, students are guided in their development of receptive and productive skills.

Vocabulaire. At the end of each chapter, a comprehensive list summarizes vocabulary targeted for students' productive use. Words and phrases are grouped semantically by lesson, and English equivalents are provided. Recordings of these words and expressions are available on **MyFrenchLab™**.

Appendices. Located at the end of the text, these include the **International Phonetic Alphabet** with key words from the early lessons; **verb charts** for regular and irregular verbs; **French-English** and **English-French glossaries**; and an **Index** of grammar, vocabulary, and cultural topics found in the book.

Finally, a series of colorful updated **maps** is included in the front and back of the book.

PROGRAM COMPONENTS

Student Resources

Text Audio. Students and instructors have access to extensive audio resources. Each chapter's **Points de départ**, **Sons et lettres**, and **Écoutons** sections have been recorded, as well as several texts from the **Lisons** sections. These are available on Audio CDs and the Companion Web Site; **MyFrenchLab™** also includes all of these recordings as well as the end-of-chapter Vocabulary.

Student Activities Manual (SAM). The Student Activities Manual is available in two formats. The traditional paper format is available with an optional separate Answer Key. For those using the paper format, audio files are available on Audio CDs. The SAM is also available in an electronic format via **MyFrenchLab™**, which includes all audio and video files and provides immediate correction for most activities. In both formats, the SAM features exercises that provide meaningful and communicative writing and listening practice, incorporating the vocabulary and structures introduced in each chapter and offering additional skill-using activities. The oral exercises stress authentic speech and real-life tasks and feature native speakers of French. There are also video activities that complement the listening practice provided in the textbook using additional video clips on DVD or via **MyFrenchLab™**.

Answer Key to Accompany the Student Activities Manual. This Answer Key is available for optional inclusion in course packages; it includes answers for all discrete and short answer exercises in the SAM.

Video Program. The beautifully produced video, shot on location, introduces native speakers from across the Francophone world, who address the topics and themes of each chapter in varied settings and contexts. Carefully integrated with the **Points de départ, Vie et culture, and Observons** sections through explicit activities and extensive annotations to the instructor, the video is easy to incorporate into daily lesson plans. In each chapter, the textbook's **Observons** exercise and the video activities in the SAM take a process-oriented approach to the development of viewing skills. The video is available via DVD and incorporated into MyFrenchLab™.

Instructor Resources

Instructor's Resource Manual. An extensive introduction to the components of the **Points de départ** program is included in the Instructor's Resource Manual (IRM). The IRM is available in a downloadable format via the Instructor's Resource Center (described below) and MyFrenchLab™. Sample syllabi for one-, two-, and three-term course sequences are outlined, along with numerous sample lesson plans. The extensive cultural annotations are a unique feature of this IRM, providing further information about topics introduced in the textbook. Information-gap activities, ready for classroom use, are also provided for each chapter. In addition, the IRM provides the scripts for the audio exercises in the SAM and the video clips on the DVD.

Testing Program. A highly flexible testing program allows instructors to customize tests by selecting the modules they wish to use or changing individual items. This complete testing program, available in a downloadable electronic format (via the Instructor's Resource Center and MyFrenchLab™), includes sample chapter tests and comprehensive examinations that test listening, reading, and writing skills as well as cultural knowledge. Special formats to test listening and speaking skills are also included.

Audio for the Testing Program. All aural sections are recorded for the instructor's use in a classroom or laboratory setting. The audio is available on CD and **MyFrenchLab™**. For all elements in the testing program, detailed grading guidelines are provided.

Online Resources

Companion Website. The Companion Website contains the audio from the Text Audio CDs and SAM Audio CDs. www.pearsonhighered.com/pointsdedepart

Instructor's Resource Center. The IRC is located on *www.pearsonhighered.com* and provides password-protected instructor access to all the IRM resources. This material is also available electronically for downloading.

MyFrenchLab™. **The moment you know.** Educators know it. Students know it. It's that inspired moment when something that was difficult to understand suddenly makes perfect sense. Pearson's MyLab products have been designed and refined with a single purpose in mind—to help educators create that moment of understanding for their students. MyLanguageLabs deliver **proven results** in helping individual students succeed. They provide **engaging experiences** that personalize, stimulate, and measure learning for each student. And, they come from a **trusted partner** with educational expertise and an eye on the future. MyLanguageLabs can be linked out to any learning management system. To learn more about how the MyLanguageLabs combine proven learning applications with powerful assessment, visit http://www.mylanguagelabs.com. MyLanguageLabs—the moment you know.

TO THE STUDENT

Why did you choose to study French? Most students of French want to develop basic language skills that they can put to practical use and to learn about how the lives of French-speaking people compare to their own. The **Points de départ, Second Edition** program is designed to help you meet those goals. Specifically, with the aid of this textbook and the accompanying materials, you can expect to accomplish the following:

- Become familiar with many features of everyday life and culture in France and in the three dozen countries where French is spoken. You will have the opportunity to reflect on how your life in North America and your values compare with those of French speakers across the globe.

- Speak French well enough to get around in a country where French is spoken. You should be able to greet people, ask for directions, cope with everyday needs, give basic information about yourself, and talk about things that are important to you. You should also be able to assist French-speaking visitors in this country.
- Understand French well enough to get the main ideas and some details from a news broadcast, lecture, or conversation that you hear. You should understand French speakers quite well when they speak slowly about topics with which you are familiar.
- Read French web sites as well as newspaper and magazine articles dealing with current events or other familiar topics. With the help of a dictionary, you should be able to read more specialized material in fields of interest. You should also be able to enjoy short and simple pieces of literature in French.
- Write French well enough to take notes, write messages and letters for various purposes, and fill out forms.
- Gain an understanding of the structure of the French language: its pronunciation, grammar, and vocabulary. You will also gain insight into how languages function in societies. These insights may even help you understand your native language better!

Assuring Your Success

Whether or not you have already studied French, you bring some knowledge of that language to your study. Many words of French origin are used in English (**soufflé**, **croissant**, and **diplomat,** for example). You also bring to the study of French your knowledge of the world in general and of specific events, which you can use to predict what you will read or hear. You can use your knowledge of a particular topic, as well as accompanying photos or titles, to predict what will come next. Finally, the reading and listening skills you have learned for your native language will also prove useful as you study a foreign language.

Many of the materials found in **Points de départ, Second Edition** will seem challenging to you because you will not be able to understand every word you hear or read. That is to be expected—the readings in the textbook were written for native speakers, and listening exercises approximate native speech. The language used in **Points de départ, Second Edition** is real and the topics current. You should use your background knowledge and prediction skills to make intelligent guesses about what you are hearing and reading. In this way, you can get the main ideas and some details, a good first step toward real communication in a foreign language.

Since access to native French speakers is limited in most parts of the United States, the classroom offers an important opportunity for you to practice your listening and speaking skills. Unless your instructor indicates otherwise, keep your book closed. Since what you are learning is explained in the textbook, you will not need to take notes during class. Instead, it is important that you *participate* as much as possible in classroom activities.

Adequate preparation is another key to success. Prepare each lesson as directed by your instructor before going to class. Be sure to complete assignments made by your instructor and review regularly, not just for an exam.

Points de départ, Second Edition and its accompanying materials will provide you with opportunities to develop your French language skills—listening, reading, speaking, and writing—by exposing you to authentic French and encouraging you to express yourself on a variety of topics. It will also introduce you to Francophone cultures around the world and invite you to reflect on your own culture. As you begin this endeavor, we wish you « **Bon début !** »

Acknowledgments

The publication of the second edition of **Points de départ** represents the accumulated experience of many years of classroom instruction and continual fine-tuning, to which many instructors and students have contributed. We wish to thank our colleagues and students for their participation in this process, for their comments, and for their encouragement.

We extend our sincere thanks and appreciation to the colleagues who reviewed the manuscript at various stages of development. We gratefully acknowledge their participation and candor:

Julie Baker, University of Richmond
Debbie Bell, University of Georgia
Elizabeth Blood, Salem State College
Jana Alena Brill, Georgetown College
Frances Chevalier, Norwich University
Michelle Cheyne, University of Massachusetts – Dartmouth
Marie-Laure Hinton, Long Beach Community College
Amy Hubbell, Kansas State University
Aparna Nayak-Guercio, California State University – Long Beach
Atiyeh Showrai, University of Southern California
Karen Jane Taylor, Morehead State University
Madeline Turan, State University of New York – Stony Brook
Kimberly van Noort, University of Texas – Arlington
Françoise Vionnet-Bracher, Texas A&M University
Violette Vornicel-Guthmann, Fullerton College
Carolyn Woolard, Milligan College

We thank the following colleagues for their important contributions, without which the second edition would be incomplete: Virginie Cassidy of Georgetown College, for revisions to the Student Activities Manual; Elizabeth Schneider, for revisions to the Testing Program; Kathryn Lorenz, for the Instructor's Resource Manual. We would also like to thank Veronica Oliva for her meticulous and tireless work in securing permissions. At the University of Maryland, College Park, Mel is particularly grateful to all of you who go out of your way to provide material, answer questions, offer suggestions, and keep her up-to-date with the latest technology crazes. And to her group of language experts, *un énorme merci* for responding to an endless stream of random e-mail queries with patience, good humor, and insightful responses. *Merci encore Eva, Caroline, Cybèle, Dorothée, Marilyn, Cécile, Sarah, Valérie et Pierre.*

At the University of North Carolina, Asheville, Cathy wishes to thank supportive colleagues and cooperative students who tried out new texts and activities and offered helpful comments and enthusiastic encouragement. Special thanks go to her colleagues in French, Sandra Malicote and Ellen Bailey.

We would also like to acknowledge the many people on our Pearson team who contributed their ideas, talents, time, and publishing experience to this project. Thanks to Publisher for World Languages, Phil Miller, for his continuing support and for assembling a top-notch team. Many thanks to Rachel McCoy, Executive Acquisitions Editor, for her energy, enthusiasm, miles logged, and continual encouragement and faith in us. Our special thanks go to our Development Editor, Barbara Lyons, whose professionalism and exacting standards have once again improved our work in ways great and small. Copy Editor Pat Ménard patiently reviewed author queries and prepared the manuscript for production, and we greatly appreciate her help. The contributions of our proofreader, Katherine Gilbert, came relatively late in the process of putting together this book, but her contributions have been enormous. For your eagle eye and unwavering attention to the smallest detail, we thank you sincerely. We are indebted to the wonderful production crew both in Upper Saddle River and in Battipaglia. Mary Rottino, Senior Managing Editor for Product Development: Janice Stangel, Associate Managing Editor, and Manuel Echevarria, Production Editor, have trained us well. Many thanks to Frank Weihenig, Production Supervision, and Francesca Monaco, Editor, of Emilcomp/Preparé, who meticulously oversaw every detail to bring the second edition through production. *Grazie mille* especially to Francesca, whose endless supply of patience and good humor were much appreciated at every stage of the production process.

We would also like to thank Bob Hemmer, Executive Editor, MyLanguageLabs, and Samantha Alducin, Senior Media Editor, for their continued implementation of **MyFrenchLab**™. Thanks also to Bill Bliss, Developmental Editor for MyLanguageLabs, for carefully overseeing the preparation of the revised Student Activities Manual and Testing Program, and to Lindsay Miglionica, Editorial Assistant, for helping coordinate the revision of all components. Our thanks go on to Kris Ellis-Levy, Executive Marketing Manager, and Michele Marchese, Marketing Assistant, for their energy and innovative ideas. Thanks also go to Annette Linder for her assistance with photo research and to Steve Mannion for his clear and appealing line art, which has greatly enriched the book.

We wish to thank our families for their continued support, encouragement, patience, and good cheer as we worked on this edition during some particularly challenging times. We love you all and never take you for granted.

Finally, we would like to dedicate this edition to our editor Barbara Lyons, who has been an indispensable colleague as well as a dear and trusted friend through multiple editions of this book and *Chez nous*. When we began working together many years ago, our children were small, our concerns were different, and we spent a lot of time working things out on the phone and via second-day delivery of drafts. How times have changed. Most of the children are now young adults; we work through issues via cell phone and e-mail; and drafts are sent and received instantaneously via electronic media. Through it all, Barbara's careful reading, high standards, useful suggestions, and precise turns of phrase have been a constant and have proven invaluable to us in every aspect of our mutual projects. In addition to Barbara's consummate professionalism and dedication, we have enjoyed her moral support, encouragement, and understanding. We hope these few words (unedited by Barbara for a change) serve to express our deep gratitude and unending thanks.

Leçon Préliminaire

Présentons-nous !

What does the photo tell you about where these French speakers are? What might their gestures tell you about their relationship?

1. Première Partie
2. Seconde Partie

After completing this lesson, you should be able to:

- ❑ Greet people, make introductions, and say good-bye, using typical French gestures
- ❑ Identify objects in the classroom
- ❑ Follow classroom instructions
- ❑ Spell words in French
- ❑ Identify places throughout the world where French is spoken

1 Première Partie

POINTS DE DÉPART

Moi, je parle français

Chloé :	Salut ! Je m'appelle Chloé. Et toi, comment tu t'appelles ?
Alex :	Je m'appelle Alex.
Chloé :	Tu es de Paris ?
Alex :	Non, moi, je suis de Montréal.

le prof :	Bonjour, mademoiselle, bonjour, monsieur.
Chloé et Alex :	Bonjour, madame.
le prof :	Comment vous appelez-vous ?
Chloé :	Je m'appelle Chloé Lafont.
le prof :	Et vous ?
Alex :	Paradis, Alex Paradis.

Fiche pratique

As you begin your study of French, you will rely on a number of fixed expressions to help you navigate situations such as greeting people. Memorize these expressions in their entirety rather than trying to translate them literally.

Presentation: Present some of the material inductively by circulating around the room, shaking students' hands, greeting them, and introducing yourself using expressions from the dialogues. You might prepare blank name tags for students to fill out. Include phrases such as *Bonjour, je m'appelle...* and *Je suis de...* on the name tags to help students respond to you.

Next, you may wish to show the dialogues and related drawings as you present them one by one (MFL, Instructor's Resources). Ask students to describe what's going on in each conversation. Point out the learning strategy (**Fiche pratique**) and provide some examples. Check comprehension and have students repeat key phrases. To conclude, show the illustrations without the dialogues and let students supply sample exchanges. As you work through the exchanges, discuss the cultural notes (**Vie et culture**) and have students: 1) point out differences between the first two dialogues; 2) make a list of possible responses to the question *Comment ça va ?*; 3) make a list of ways to say "good-bye." Note that to say "good-bye," French Canadians often use *Bonjour* instead of *Au revoir*.

You might also use the opening montage of the ***Points de départ*** video to introduce students to the notion of the Francophone world as a focus of study; this is a colorful and exciting way to begin the course.

Chloé : Salut, Jean-Louis ! Comment ça va ?
Jean-Louis : Ça va. Et toi ?
Chloé : Pas mal.
Jean-Louis : Bonjour, madame. Comment allez-vous ?
le prof : Très bien, merci. Et vous ?
Jean-Louis : Bien aussi, merci.

Note: Although *la prof* is heard in conversational French and in Canada, it is more correct in Standard French to say *le prof*, even when referring to a woman.

Chloé : Madame, je vous présente Jean-Louis Richard. Jean-Louis, Madame Dupont.
Jean-Louis : Enchanté, madame.
le prof : Bonjour, Jean-Louis.
Chloé : Alex, voici mon ami Jean-Louis. Jean-Louis, voici mon camarade de classe, Alex.
Alex : Salut, Jean-Louis.
Jean-Louis : Salut.

Jean-Louis : Bon, au revoir, Chloé, au revoir, Alex.
Chloé : Salut, Jean-Louis.
Alex : À bientôt... Au revoir, madame.
le prof : Au revoir, Alex. À demain.

POUR SALUER ET RÉPONDRE

Comment ça va ?	*How are you?*
Très bien, merci.	*Very well, thanks.*
Ça va.	*Fine.*
Pas mal.	*Not bad.*
Comme ci, comme ça.	*So-so.*
Ça ne va pas.	*Things aren't going well.*

Vie et culture

Bonjour !

0P-33

Look at the photos here and watch the video segment *Bonjour*, in which people are greeting each other: what gestures and phrases do you notice?

When French people meet someone they know, or make contact with a stranger (for example, sales, office, or restaurant personnel), they always greet that person upon arriving and say good-bye when leaving. If the speakers are not on a first-name basis, the greeting includes an appropriate title, and the last name is not used. Usually a woman is addressed as **madame** unless she is very young:

Bonjour, monsieur.
Bonsoir, madame.
Au revoir, mademoiselle.

When they meet or say good-bye, French people who know each other almost always shake hands, using the right hand. Good friends and family members kiss each other lightly on each cheek. When talking together, the French stand or sit closer to each other than Americans do. A French person would be offended if you kept moving away as he or she attempted to maintain normal conversational distance.

Tu et *vous*

When addressing another person in French, you must choose between **tu** and **vous**, which both mean *you*. Use **tu** to address a family member, a child, a close friend, or another student. Use **vous** to address someone with whom you have a more formal relationship or to whom you wish to show respect. For example, use **vous** with people you do not know well, with older people, and with those in a position of authority, such as your teachers. Always use **vous** to address more than one person. Do the people in the video clip use **tu** or **vous**?

ET VOUS ?

1. Think of how you typically greet people each day. Although we do not make a distinction in English like the **tu/vous** distinction in French, how do we vary our forms of address?
2. What do the practices of shaking hands and kissing on the cheek tell you about the importance of close physical contact in French culture? Would you feel comfortable with these practices? Why or why not? Compare your answers to these questions with those of your classmates. How would you explain any differences?
3. View the video segment again, paying close attention to the ways in which people greet each other; what can you conclude about their relationship in each case?

Implementation: Before going over **Vie et culture**, ask students to make inferences about the use of *tu* and *vous* based on the dialogues in the **Points de départ**. Test their understanding of the differences in usage by suggesting various people and letting students tell which form of address they would use for example, with a police officer, a pet, a grandparent, their best friend's mother, etc. Americans are generally considered very informal by the French, but French speakers are also becoming less formal, using the first name and *tu* more frequently among colleagues and acquaintances.

0P-01
to
0P-04

À vous la parole

P-1 Le mot juste. Give an appropriate response. *Answers may vary.*

MODÈLE Comment vous appelez-vous ?
• Morin, Nicolas Morin.

1. Bonjour, mademoiselle. Bonjour, madame/mademoiselle/monsieur.
2. Comment tu t'appelles ? Je m'appelle...
3. Tu es de Montréal ? Non, je suis de...
4. Ça va ? Ça va.
5. Comment allez-vous ? Très bien, merci.
6. Comment ça va ? Pas mal.
7. Voici mon ami David. Enchanté/e.
8. Je vous présente mon amie Claire. Bonjour, Claire.
9. Au revoir, monsieur. Au revoir, madame/mademoiselle/monsieur.
10. Bon, à demain ! À demain/À bientôt.

Implementation: P-2 Students can work in small groups to prepare exchanges, then act out their variations. You might also bring in photos/drawings of people greeting each other and have students create the dialogues. Use the drawings and photos in this lesson for the same purpose.

P-2 Le savoir-faire. What would you say and do in the following situations? Act out each one with classmates.

MODÈLE You meet a very good friend.

É1 Salut, Anne ! Ça va ? (faire la bise)
É2 Ça va, et toi ?
É1 Pas mal.

1. You and a friend run into your instructor on campus.
2. You sit down in class next to someone you do not know.
3. You are with your roommate when a new friend joins you.
4. You run into your friend's mother while doing errands.
5. You are standing near a new teacher who does not yet know your name.
6. Class is over, and you are saying good-bye to a close friend.
7. Class is over, and you are saying good-bye to your teacher.

Implementation: P-3 Use as a mixing activity at the end of class. Have students report back the names of people they met. You may wish to adapt this activity and use it a second time by passing out cards with French names written on them and having students introduce themselves to each other with their new identities.

P-3 Faisons connaissance. Imagine that you are at a party with your classmates. Greet and introduce yourself to as many people as possible, and make introductions when others do not know each other. Tell what city you are from, then ask what city your classmates are from.

MODÈLE É1 Bonjour, je m'appelle Sean. Et toi ?
É2 Je m'appelle Natasha. Voici mon ami, Jérémie.
É1 Salut, Jérémie.
É3 Bonjour. Je suis de Chicago, et toi ?
É1 Moi, je suis de Lafayette, et toi, Natasha ?

FORMES ET FONCTIONS

Les pronoms sujets et le verbe *être*

Presentation: Present inductively by questioning students about the city they are from: *Je suis de Chicago — et vous ? Vous êtes de... ? Elle est de... — et vous aussi ?* Model the various verb forms in this way, then ask students to summarize meaning and forms. Display the chart. Point out that subject-verb agreement takes place in English as well: *I am, she is, we are.* Explain the organization of the verb chart, with singular forms on the left and plural forms on the right, and the division into first/second/third-person forms. Ask students to provide the meanings for each form. Use the textbook examples to illustrate the various points as students help you explain.

***Les pronoms sujets et le verbe* être**

SINGULIER			PLURIEL		
je	**suis**	*I am*	nous	**sommes**	*we are*
tu	**es**	*you are*	vous‿**êtes**		*you are*
il	**est**	*he is*	ils	**sont**	*they are*
elle	**est**	*she is*	elles	**sont**	*they are*
on	**est**	*we/they are*			

- The verb **être** means *to be*. This form is called the *infinitive*; it is the form you find in the dictionary listing for the verb. Notice that a specific form of **être** corresponds to each subject. Because these forms do not follow a regular pattern, **être** is called an *irregular verb*.

- A subject pronoun can be used in place of a noun as the subject of a sentence:

—**Alex** est de Paris ?	—*Alex is from Paris?*
—Non, **il** est de Montréal.	—*No, he's from Montreal.*

As you have learned, use **tu** with a person you know very well; otherwise use **vous**. Use **vous** also when speaking to more than one person, even if they are your friends. Pronounce the final **-s** of **vous** as /z/ if the word following it begins with a vowel sound, and link it to that word:

Olivier, **tu** es de Paris ?	*Olivier, are you from Paris?*
Madame, **vous**‿êtes de Liège ?	*Madame, are you from Liege?*
Audrey et Fred, **vous**‿êtes de Genève ?	*Audrey and Fred, are you from Geneva?*

On is an indefinite pronoun that can mean *one, they,* or *people,* depending on the context. In conversational French, **on** is often used instead of **nous** to mean *we*. **On** always takes the singular form, **est**.

Nous, on est de Lille.	*We are from Lille.*

Elles refers to more than one female person or to a group of feminine nouns. **Ils** refers to more than one male person, to a group of masculine nouns, or to a group that includes both males and females or both masculine and feminine nouns.

Anne et Sophie, **elles** sont en forme.	*Anne and Sophie are fine.*
Jean-Luc et Rémi, **ils** sont stressés.	*Jean-Luc and Rémi are stressed out.*
Julie et Damien, **ils** sont occupés.	*Julie and Damien are busy.*

- Use a form of the verb **être** in descriptions or to indicate a state of being.

Elle **est** occupée.	*She's busy.*
Tu **es** malade ?	*Are you sick?*
Je **suis** stressé.	*I'm stressed out.*

- The final **-t** of **est** and **sont** is usually pronounced before a word beginning with a vowel sound.

Il est‿en forme.	*He's fine.*
Il est malade.	*He's sick.*
Elles sont‿en forme.	*They're fine.*
Elles sont stressées.	*They're stressed out.*

Presentation: Have students repeat the expressions in the shaded box; these provide vocabulary for use with *être.* This treatment does not create a problem for oral practice, since the adjectives have identical masculine and feminine spoken forms. Written adjective agreement is treated in Ch. 1, L. 1.

Initial practice: Begin practice with a discrimination drill to ensure that students hear crucial distinctions: one, or more than one? *Il est fatigué. Elles sont en forme. C'est un professeur. Ce sont des étudiants. Elle est stressée. Ils sont malades. Ce sont des profs. Elle est occupée.* Follow up with a simple substitution drill: *Je suis en forme; vous → Vous êtes en forme,* etc. The spoken forms of these adjectives are identical, so students will never be wrong when they say these phrases. Exercises in the textbook with these adjectives should not be assigned as written work since students will not be able to produce the correct forms.

COMMENT ÇA VA ?

Je suis en forme.	*I am fine.*
... fatigué/e.	. . . *tired.*
... stressé/e.	. . . *stressed.*
... très occupé/e.	. . . *very busy.*
... malade.	. . . *sick.*

- Use **c'est** and **ce sont** to identify people and things:

C'est Madame Dupont ?	*That's Madame Dupont?*
C'est un étudiant.	*This is a (male) student.*
Ce sont M. et Mme Lafarges.	*This is Mr. and Mrs. Lafarges.*
Ce sont des étudiantes.	*These are (female) students.*

À vous la parole

OP-05 to OP-09

Implementation: P-4 You may wish to point out that the verb *aller* is used in the questions *Ça va ?* and *Comment allez-vous ?* and that some answers to these questions would require using a form of *aller*, such as *Je vais bien* (that is, students cannot say, **Je suis bien*). The verb *aller* is presented in Ch. 2, L. 3.

This exercise can be cued with photos/drawings. This oral exercise does not require students to make written agreement of adjectives such as *occupé/e/s.*

P-4 Comment ça va ? Tell how everyone is feeling today.

MODÈLE Moi ? Fatigué/e.
- Je suis fatigué/e.

1. Madame Hébert ? En forme. Elle est en forme.
2. Toi ? Fatigué/e. Tu es fatigué/e.
3. Adrien ? Très occupé. Il est très occupé.
4. Cécile ? Malade. Elle est malade.
5. Mathieu et toi ? En forme. Vous êtes en forme.
6. Julien ? Stressé. Il est stressé.
7. Nous ? Fatigués. Nous sommes fatigués.
8. Vous ? Stressés. Vous êtes stressés.

P-5 Qui est-ce ? Identify the celebrities pictured below who are speakers of French.

Expansion: P-5 Find pictures online of other well-known celebrities who speak French.

MODÈLE C'est Johnny Depp.

1.

C'est Halle Berry.

2.

Ce sont Angelina Jolie et Brad Pitt.

3.

C'est Gwyneth Paltrow.

4.

Ce sont John Travolta et Kelly Preston.

5.

C'est Orlando Bloom.

6.

C'est Andie MacDowell.

7.

C'est Sting.

P-6 Identité mystérieuse. Take on a new identity! Your instructor will give you a new name and city of origin, or you can invent one yourself. Circulate around the room and introduce yourself to at least three people. Be prepared to introduce someone you have met to the rest of the class!

MODÈLE É1 Bonjour, je m'appelle Mathilde.
É2 Tu es de Paris ?
É1 Non, je suis de Québec. Et toi ?
É2 Je m'appelle Louis-Jean, je suis de Port-au-Prince, à Haïti.

Implementation: P-6 Put names and cities on index cards to pass out (you can take these back and re-use them). You might also participate to provide students with practice using the *vous* form. Impose a time limit, and follow up by having students identify the people they met. Suggested names/cities: for women: Julie/Montréal, Marie-Claire/Marseille, Amira/Casablanca, Annick/Bruxelles, Honorée/Dakar, Kalida/Alger, Jennifer/Baton Rouge, Fatima/Paris, Jeanne-Marie/Port-au-Prince, Jamila/Tunis, Marine/Genève, Laura/Québec
For men: Kevin/Lafayette, Abir/Tunis, Farid/Rabat, Benjamin/Nice, Badu/Tombouctou, Louis-Jean/Port-au-Prince, Habib/Beyrouth, Daniel/Louvain, Grégory/Dijon, Bakari/Kinshasa, Paul/Québec, Alex/Paris

Preparation: P-7 To prepare this activity, pronounce for the class the name of each of the people shown, then pronounce the place names and languages listed in French. The entire **Observons** clip introduces nine speakers; only the first six are treated here. The remaining speakers are introduced in the SAM/MFL. You might complete this exercise in class and assign the remaining introductions as homework, with students completing the activities in the SAM/MFL. Point out that these speakers appear in other video clips. Be sure to explain the meaning of each subheading for the activity, because these are used consistently throughout the textbook.

OP-34 to OP-36

Script: Observons

ÉDOUARD : Bonjour, je suis Édouard Fleuriau-Château. J'ai vingt-quatre ans, euh, je parle l'anglais, le français, l'espagnol ... et bien sûr je suis français.

MARIE ÉLINE : Bonjour, je m'appelle Marie Éline Louis. Je suis de Port-au-Prince, Haïti, mais j'habite ici aux États-Unis. À la maison, on parle créole. Je parle aussi français et anglais.

FADOUA : Bonjour, je m'appelle Fadoua Bennani. J'ai vingt-cinq ans et j'habite à Nice. Mes parents vivent au Maroc. Euh, moi, je parle français et un peu arabe. Mon père il est marocain, donc lui il parle beaucoup plus arabe que moi, et ma mère est française.

BIENVENU : Je m'appelle Bienvenu Akpakla. Je suis du Bénin. Je parle le français, ma langue maternelle fongbé et l'anglais. Voici mon épouse, elle se présente.

HONORINE : Je m'appelle Honorine Akpakla, je viens du Congo. Je parle le français, ma langue maternelle et l'anglais.

MARIE-JULIE : Alors, je m'appelle Marie-Julie Keraro, je suis québécoise. Je suis originaire de Rimouski. J'habite les États-Unis depuis quelques années. Avant de venir ici, je parlais anglais, ce qui m'a aidé beaucoup.

Observons

P-7 Je me présente.

A. Avant de regarder. What information do people generally give when they introduce themselves? What expressions have you learned that people might use to provide this information in French?

B. En regardant. Watch and listen as the people shown introduce themselves, telling where they are from and what language(s) they speak. Match their photos with the places they come from and then find those places on the map inside the cover of your textbook. You can expect to listen more than once.

1. Vous avez compris ?
   a. Who is from . . .
      le Bénin ? Bienvenu
      le Congo ? Honorine
      la France ? Édouard
      Haïti ? Marie Éline
      le Maroc ? Fadoua
      le Québec ? Marie-Julie
   b. How many people are from places where languages other than French are spoken? all of them

Édouard FLEURIAU-CHÂTEAU

Marie Éline LOUIS

Fadoua BENNANI

Bienvenu et Honorine AKPAKLA

Marie-Julie KERHARO

2. Which of the following languages are mentioned?

   ✓ Arabic / l'arabe
   ✓ Creole / le créole
   ✓ English / l'anglais
   ✓ Fongbé / le fongbé
   ✓ Spanish / l'espagnol

C. Après avoir regardé. Discuss the following questions with your classmates.

1. What differences do you notice in the way these people look, dress, and speak?
2. What do these observations tell you about the Francophone world?

Expansion: You might also ask students to listen for expressions used to tell one's name: *je suis, je m'appelle;* to tell where you're from: *je suis de, j'habite, je suis né/e;* and to tell what language you speak: *je parle.* Regular *-er* verbs are introduced in Ch. 1, L. 3.

2 Seconde Partie

Presentation: You may wish to divide the material into two sections. First, focus on classroom objects and the mini-dialogues. Continue with the **Vie et culture** notes and Ex. P-8 and P-9. In a subsequent class or later in the same period, present the classroom expressions and commands. Follow with Ex. P-10 and P-11. To present, describe the classroom, showing the labeled art (MFL, Instructor's Resources) or real objects in the classroom. You can also bring in a specially prepared backpack or bag filled with various items (e.g., *une règle, un stylo, une craie, un livre, un DVD*). Use items in the bag to present the vocabulary or as an identification drill. Students can take turns reaching into the bag, drawing out an item and saying what it is. Using the unlabeled art (MFL, Instructor's Resources) or objects in the classroom, check comprehension by having students point to objects you name. Drill using either/or questions to practice pronunciation: *C'est une porte ou une fenêtre ?* Other simple drills: 1) draw one of the items and let others guess what it is; 2) find the "odd word out" in a list of three or four items: *une craie, un stylo, une règle, un crayon... (une règle)*; 3) associations: What word do you associate with each of the following? *un professeur ? —un étudiant ; une craie ? —un tableau*, etc.

POINTS DE DÉPART

La salle de classe

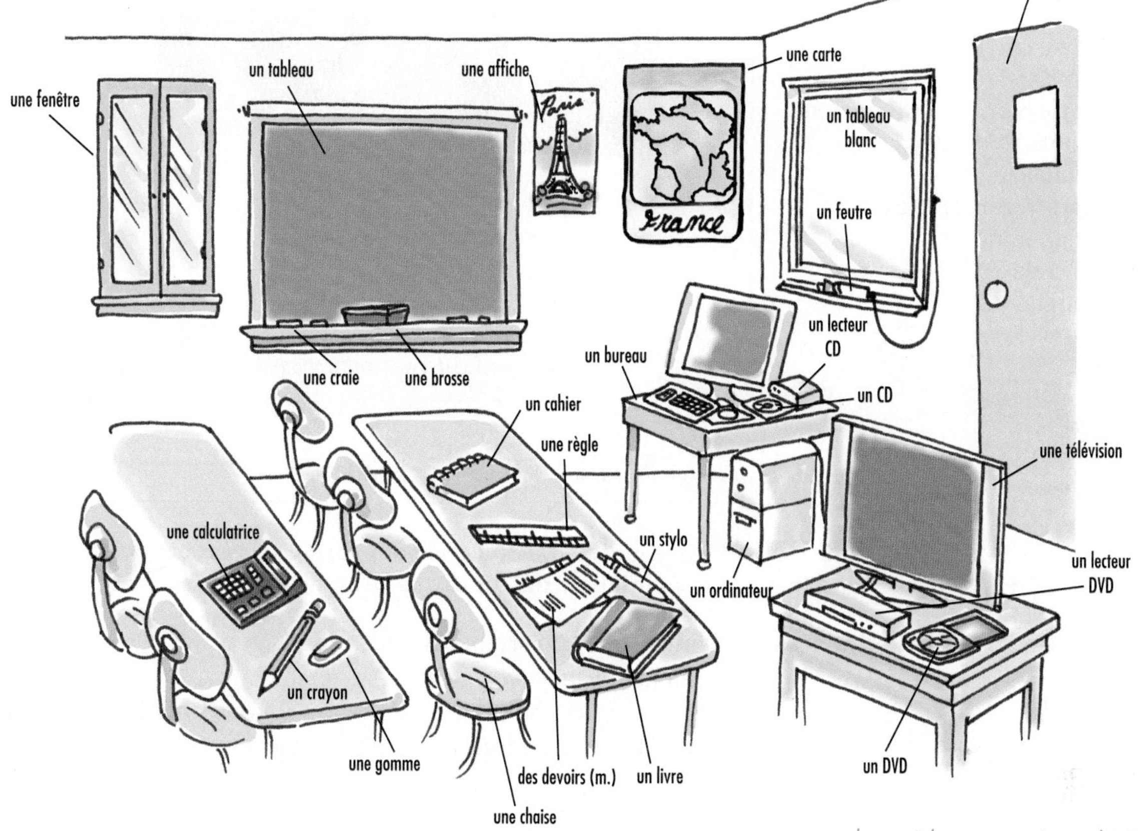

—Il y a un crayon sur le bureau ?
—Non, il n'y a pas de crayon, mais il y a un stylo. Voilà.
—Il y a des affiches dans la salle de classe ?
—Non, il n'y a pas d'affiches.

Presentation: Present the mini-dialogues, using examples of classroom objects; then move directly to the exercises. We avoid the traditional *voici/voilà* distinction because native speaker usage is highly variable. *Voilà* is the neutral term, acceptable in a wider variety of contexts. We present *voici* in the context of introductions: *Voici mon ami Jean-Louis,* since native speakers are consistent in their use of *voici* in this context. *Il n'y a pas de* is taught here as a lexical item; negation is treated productively in Ch. 1, L. 3.

Presentation: Use the standard TPR (Total Physical Response) sequence to introduce and practice classroom commands: 1) demonstrate; 2) hesitate as students respond; 3) have students perform alone; 4) introduce novel combinations and series of commands; finally, if you wish, 5) reverse roles, letting students give commands. For more information on TPR techniques, see MFL, Instructor's Resources. The goal of this treatment of commands is for students to be able to function in an all-French classroom and to follow basic classroom instructions; the forms of the imperative for productive control are treated in Ch. 2, L. 3. We assume that the instructor will use the polite form with students. You may wish to introduce the familiar forms as well.

LE PROFESSEUR DIT :

Écoutez bien, s'il vous plaît !
Regardez le tableau !
Levez-vous !
Allez au tableau !
Allez à la porte !
Ouvrez la fenêtre !
Fermez le livre !
Montrez-moi votre livre !
Montrez Paris sur la carte !
Ne parlez pas anglais !
Prenez un stylo !
Écrivez votre nom et votre prénom !
Lisez les mots au tableau !
Effacez le tableau !
Écoutez sans regarder le livre !
Répondez en français !
Donnez la craie à Marie-Laure !
Rendez-moi les devoirs !
Asseyez-vous !
Merci.
De rien.

LES ÉTUDIANTS RÉPONDENT :

Pardon ? Je ne comprends pas.
Répétez, s'il vous plaît !
Parlez plus fort !
Comment dit-on « *whiteboard* » en français ?

Note: Here we teach only *De rien*, but you might introduce other expressions: *Je vous/t'en prie*, *Il n'y a pas de quoi*, *Bienvenue* (Can.).

0P-13 to 0P-17

À vous la parole

P-8 Voilà ! As your instructor asks about various classroom objects, hand them over, point them out, or say there aren't any.

MODÈLES Donnez-moi un stylo, s'il vous plaît !
- Voilà (*and you hand over a pen*).

Montrez-moi une carte de France, s'il vous plaît !
- Voilà (*and you point to a map of France*).

Il y a des affiches ici ?
- Oui, voilà des affiches (*and you point to some posters*).

OU
- Non, il n'y a pas d'affiches.

Implementation: P-8 This focuses on comprehension and repetition of the classroom vocabulary and allows students to use *voilà* in an authentic context.
Suggestions: *Donnez-moi un stylo, un crayon, une craie, un livre, un cahier, une règle, une gomme. Montrez-moi une fenêtre, le tableau, la porte, un ordinateur, un bureau, une chaise, un étudiant. Il y a une carte ici ? un lecteur CD ? des règles ? un lecteur DVD ? des affiches ? des cahiers ?*

Modify by responding *Merci* each time a student gives you an object and suggesting that students reply appropriately.

To simplify, break down into two parts: 1) have students hand over or point out objects (*Donnez-moi... /Montrez-moi...*); 2) have students respond with *Il y a... /Il n'y a pas de...*

P-9 Dans la salle de classe. Write down as many different classroom objects as you can see. Now compare your list with that of a classmate. Cross off the items that are common to both lists, then give yourself a point for each item on your list that your partner did not name. Who has the most points?

MODÈLE É1 ~~un bureau~~, ~~une fenêtre~~, un livre, ~~une carte~~, une affiche, une télé
É2 ~~un bureau~~, un tableau, une craie, ~~une fenêtre~~, une porte, ~~une carte~~, un cahier

É1 = 3 pts, É2 = 4 pts

Variation: P-9 Make this a timed exercise so that students must write quickly; spelling is not critical as long as students have attempted the word. Follow up by finding out which students had the most points, then have the top two compare lists to declare a winner.

Exercice de mémoire: Have students look at a (complex) picture and then write down as many things as they can remember having seen; or display and then hide actual items.

 **P-10 C'est logique.** With a partner, complete each command in as many logical ways as possible. *Answers may vary.*

MODÈLE Ouvrez ...
• Ouvrez la fenêtre.
OU • Ouvrez le livre.

1. Regardez... le tableau
2. Écoutez... le professeur/bien
3. Rendez-moi... les devoirs
4. Montrez-moi... les devoirs/la carte de France
5. Fermez... la porte/le livre
6. Effacez... le tableau/le tableau blanc
7. Répondez... en français/s'il vous plaît
8. Allez... au tableau/à la porte
9. Écrivez... votre nom
10. Prenez... un stylo/votre livre

Variation: P-10 Students are required to demonstrate comprehension of the verbs by adding an appropriate completion. To simplify, give students a list of possible completions from which they must choose.

Additional practice: Put students in pairs or small groups and ask them to show each other what they have brought with them to class. For example, *Voilà un livre, un cahier, un stylo, un crayon et une gomme.* Alternatively, put several classroom objects into a bag and have students guess what is inside by asking questions: *Il y a un stylo ? — Non, il n'y a pas de stylo.* or *Oui, il y a un stylo. Voilà.* Turn this into a pair or small group activity by asking students to prepare bags with three items and having their classmates guess what's inside.

P-11 Qu'est-ce que vous dites ?
What could you say in each situation? *Answers may vary.*

MODÈLE You want the teacher to speak up.
• Parlez plus fort, s'il vous plaît !

1. You want to interrupt the teacher. Pardon.
2. You want the teacher to repeat. Répétez, s'il vous plaît.
3. You don't understand. Je ne comprends pas.
4. You ask how to say *door* in French. Comment dit-on « door » en français ?
5. You want to thank someone. Merci.
6. You can't hear what's being said. Parlez plus fort, s'il vous plaît./Répétez, s'il vous plaît.
7. You don't know how to say *please* in French. Comment dit-on « please » en français ?
8. Someone says **Merci !** to you. De rien.

Sons et lettres

L'alphabet et les accents

Here are the letters of the alphabet together with their pronunciation in French.

a	(a)	j	(ji)	s	(ès)
b	(bé)	k	(ka)	t	(té)
c	(sé)	l	(èl)	u	(u)
d	(dé)	m	(èm)	v	(vé)
e	(eu)	n	(èn)	w	(double vé)
f	(èf)	o	(o)	x	(iks)
g	(jé)	p	(pé)	y	(i grec)
h	(ach)	q	(ku)	z	(zèd)
i	(i)	r	(èr)		

Note: This presentation focuses on orthography rather than pronunciation, so the International Phonetic Alphabet is not taught here. IPA symbols, along with key words in French, are provided in Appendix 1.

Presentation: You may want to present the alphabet to your students in phonetic groups:
/ e / : b c d g p t v w
/ ɛ / : f l m n r s z
/ i / : i j x y
/ a / : a k h
/ y / : q u
Ce qui reste : e, o
First spell words and let students write them, then have students spell their name or another word that you provide. You may wish to teach students to say *deux èls*, etc., for double letters.

Accents and other diacritical marks are an integral part of French spelling.

- **L'accent aigu** is used with **e** to represent the vowel /e/ of **stressé**:

  André   Québec   stressé   répétez

- **L'accent grave** is used with **e** to represent the vowel /ɛ/ of **la règle**:

  la règle   le modèle   très   Genève

  It is also used with **a** and **u** to differentiate words:

  la *the* vs. là *there*   ou *or* vs. où *where*

- **L'accent circonflexe** can be used with all five vowel letters. It often marks the loss of the sound /s/ at an earlier stage of French. The **s** is still present in English words borrowed from French before that loss occurred.

  être   s'il vous plaît   bientôt
  la hâte *haste*   l'hôpital *hospital*   coûter *to cost*

- **Le tréma** indicates that vowel letters in a group are pronounced individually:

  toi vs. Loïc /lo-ik/   Claire vs. Haïti /a-i-ti/

- **La cédille** indicates that **c** is to be pronounced as /s/ rather than /k/ before the vowel letters **a**, **o**, or **u**:

  ça   français   Françoise

0P-18 to 0P-19

À vous la parole

P-12 Les sigles. Practice saying each French acronym, then match it with its full form. Can you provide the English equivalent for each?

c 1. l'ONU   a. l'Union européenne
e 2. l'OEA   b. les États-Unis d'Amérique
f 3. l'OTAN   c. l'Organisation des Nations unies
a 4. l'UE   d. le syndrome d'immunodéficitaire acquise
d 5. le SIDA   e. l'Organisation des États américains
b 6. les USA   f. l'Organisation du traité de l'Atlantique Nord

P-13 Qu'est-ce que c'est ? Reorder the letters to identify things you find in the classroom, and spell the correct word aloud.

MODÈLES LYSTO
- S-T-Y-L-O, stylo.

NORACY
- C-R-A-Y-O-N, crayon.

1. LERVI livre
2. TAREC carte
3. LATAUBE tableau
4. ICASHE chaise
5. TROPE porte
6. VISODER devoirs
7. DAUNITETÉ étudiante
8. CIERA craie

P-14 Les accents. Correct the following words or phrases by adding the missing accents and other diacritics, then spell each word aloud. (The asterisk indicates that these words are spelled incorrectly.)

1. le *francais français
2. une *regle règle
3. une *fenetre fenêtre
4. le verbe *etre être
5. *repondez répondez
6. *bientot bientôt
7. *repetez répétez
8. *voila voilà

Presentation: You may wish to divide the material into two sections. First, present the notion of gender along with the indefinite and definite articles. Practice using Ex. P-15 through #5 of P-17. In a subsequent class or later in the same period, present plurals. Follow up with #6–9 of Ex P-17 and P-18. To present the indefinite articles, begin with a series of either/or questions: *C'est un livre ou un cahier ? une affiche ou une carte ?*; then move to open-ended questions — *Qu'est-ce que c'est ?*— that require students to answer using familiar vocabulary and the indefinite article. Ask students how they decide whether to use *un* or *une* in their response. Their answers will help summarize the information provided in the textbook. Display the chart listing forms, and provide simple practice: *Un ou une ? livre, ordinateur, porte, bureau, fenêtre*, etc. Follow the same process for the definite article.

FORMES ET FONCTIONS

Le genre, le nombre et les articles

All French nouns are assigned to one of two noun classes—*feminine* or *masculine*—and are therefore said to have a *gender*. Nouns designating females are usually feminine and nouns designating males are usually masculine; however, for many objects, the assignment of gender is arbitrary and must be memorized. Knowing the gender of a noun is important, because it determines the form of other words that accompany it—for example, articles and adjectives.

- **The indefinite article**

  The indefinite articles **un** and **une** correspond to *a* or *an* in English. **Une** is used with feminine nouns and **un** with masculine nouns. **Un** or **une** can also mean *one*:

Voilà **un** bureau.	*Here's a desk.*
Donnez-moi **une** chaise.	*Give me a chair.*
Il y a **une** fenêtre dans la salle de classe.	*There's one window in the classroom.*

  Before a vowel sound, **un** ends with an /n/ sound that is pronounced a if it were part of the next word: **un‿**ami, **un‿**ordinateur.

  In negative sentences, the indefinite article is replaced by **de/d'**:

Il n'y a pas **de** lecteur DVD.	*There's no DVD player.*
Il n'y a pas **d'**ordinateur dans la salle de classe.	*There's no computer in the classroom.*

- **The definite article**

  There are three forms of the singular definite article, corresponding to *the* in English: **la** is used with feminine nouns, **le** with masculine nouns, and **l'** with all nouns beginning with a vowel sound. As in English, the definite article is used to indicate a previously mentioned or specified noun.

Voilà **la** carte.	*Here's the map.*
C'est **le** professeur.	*That's the professor.*
Donnez-moi **l'**affiche.	*Give me the poster.*

  In French the definite article also designates a noun used in a general or abstract sense. In such cases, no article is used in English.

J'aime **le** football.	*I like soccer.*
Ma sœur adore **la** musique.	*My sister loves music.*

Fiche pratique

It is a good idea to learn a new noun with the indefinite article, so you can remember the gender. For example, learn **une affiche** rather than **affiche** or **l'affiche**.

Note: You might share the following information on gender prediction: the names of languages are masculine; words recently borrowed from other languages are generally masculine; and some endings are good predictors of gender (*-isme, -age, eau, -o* are masculine; *-ion, -té* are feminine).

Presentation: For an inductive presentation, use written examples to elicit plural forms: *un livre, deux livre_ ? un bureau, deux bureau_ ? un cours, deux cours_ ?* Ask students to provide written plurals. Then contrast singular and plural forms to show that there is no difference in pronunciation of the noun, using first the noun alone, then the noun accompanied by a number or article: *bureau, bureaux ; un bureau, trois bureaux ; livre, livres ; le livre, les livres.*

- **Plurals of nouns**

Most French nouns are made plural by adding a written letter **-s**:

un livre	*a book*	deux livre**s**	*two books*
une fenêtre	*one window*	trois fenêtre**s**	*three windows*

Singular nouns that end in a written **-s** do not change in the plural; nouns ending in **-eau** add the letter **-x**:

un cours	*a course*	deux cours	*two courses*
un bureau	*one desk*	trois bureau**x**	*three desks*

Although a letter **-s** or **-x** is added to written words to indicate the plural, it is not pronounced. You must listen for a preceding word, usually a number or an article, to tell whether a noun is plural or singular.
A few nouns in French are invariable and have the same form in the singular and in the plural.

un CD	*one CD*	deux CD	*two CDs*
un DVD	*a DVD*	trois DVD	*three DVDs*

Note: Stress the pronunciation of the full vowel of the article in order to distinguish between singular and plural nouns.

- **Plurals of articles**

The plural form of the definite article is always **les**, which is pronounced /le/:

le livre	*the book*	**les** livres	*the books*
la chaise	*the chair*	**les** chaises	*the chairs*

The plural form of the indefinite article is always **des**, which is pronounced /de/:

un cahier	*a notebook*	**des** cahiers	*notebooks, some notebooks*
une porte	*a door*	**des** portes	*doors, some doors*

In English, plural nouns often appear without any article; in French, an article almost always accompanies the noun:

Il y a **des** livres ici.	*There are books here.*
J'aime **les** affiches.	*I like posters.*

Before a vowel sound, the **-s** of **les** and **des** is pronounced as /z/:

les chaises vs. **les**‿images /z/ des bureaux vs. **des**‿ordinateurs /z/

Les articles

	SINGULIER		PLURIEL
	MASCULIN	FÉMININ	MASCULIN ET FÉMININ
INDÉFINI	**un** cahier	**une** règle	**des** cahiers, **des** règles
	un‿ordinateur	**une** affiche	**des**‿ordinateurs
			des‿affiches
DÉFINI	**le** livre	**la** carte	**les** livres, **les** cartes
	l'ordinateur	**l'**affiche	**les**‿ordinateurs
			les‿affiches

À vous la parole

P-20 to P-24

P-15 Qu'est-ce qu'il y a ? Look carefully at the list of classroom objects below. Note the form of the article in each case to determine if this object is found in the classroom or not.

MODÈLES

	Il y a...	Il n'y a pas...	
	____	✓	...de carte.
	✓	____	...un tableau blanc.
1.	____	✓	...d'ordinateur.
2.	✓	____	...un bureau.
3.	✓	____	...une affiche.
4.	____	✓	...de télévision.
5.	✓	____	...un livre de français.
6.	____	✓	...de lecteur CD.
7.	✓	____	...une calculatrice.

In your opinion, what one object most needs to be added to make this a well-equipped classroom, and why?

Implementation: P-15 Begin practice with this comprehension-based exercise. To focus on form, use a discrimination drill: *masculin ou féminin ? Voici un ordinateur, une affiche, un stylo, une chaise, un crayon, une gomme, un crayon, une calculatrice.* Do the same for the definite article: *Voici la porte, le livre, le cahier, la brosse, le bureau, la télévision, le DVD, la règle.*

Follow with substitution drills, having students change first from the indefinite to the definite article (*Voilà un stylo → Voilà le stylo ; une gomme, un étudiant, une affiche, un crayon, un livre, une chaise*), then from the definite to the indefinite article (*Voilà le professeur → Voilà un professeur ; le livre, le bureau, la brosse, le cahier, la calculatrice, la gomme, l'ordinateur*).

Next, practice plurals with a discrimination drill: one, or more than one? *Voici une chaise, des ordinateurs, un crayon, une brosse, des devoirs, des cahiers, une affiche, des stylos, un livre, une gomme.* Follow with a simple transformation drill, singular to plural: *Voici une chaise → Voici des chaises,* then plural to singular (which is more difficult, since students need to produce the appropriate gender).

P-16 Dans la salle de classe. What can you name in this classroom?

MODÈLE • Il y a un bureau, des livres ...

Key: P-16 Answers may vary. *Il y a un tableau blanc, une fenêtre, des chaises, des étudiants, un ordinateur, un stylo, une règle, un lecteur CD, une carte, des devoirs, une calculatrice*

Implementation: P-16 If you are using this exercise after presenting singular forms only, modify the model to include only singular forms. If you have presented both singular and plural articles, encourage students to produce examples of both, e.g., *il y a des chaises, il y a des étudiantes, il y a une règle...*

Implementation: P-17 Be sure to bring some of the items to class and have them prominently displayed. To incorporate the idea of possession, place items on students' desks throughout the room.

P-17 Voilà ! Ask a classmate whether each of the objects listed can be found in your classroom. He or she can respond by indicating to whom they belong.

MODÈLES un lecteur CD ?

É1 Il y a un lecteur CD ?

É2 Oui, voilà le lecteur CD de Vincent.

des stylos ?

É1 Il y a des stylos ?

É2 Oui, voilà les stylos de Danielle.

1. un cahier
2. une carte
3. une calculatrice
4. un bureau
5. un feutre
6. des livres
7. des gommes
8. des devoirs
9. des crayons

Stratégie

Look for *cognates* (**des mots apparentés**) as you read a text. Cognates are words whose form and meaning are very similar in French and English. Focusing on cognates can help you grasp the general meaning of a text.

P-18 Sur mon bureau. In groups of three, compare what is on your desk at home by naming at least three items that are on it. What do you have on your desk that your partners don't have?

MODÈLE É1 Sur mon bureau, il y a un ordinateur, des livres et une photo.

É2 Et sur mon bureau, il y a...

É3 Sur mon bureau, il y a...

Lisons

Presentation: P-19 We recommend that you treat this first reading in class to introduce students to the techniques used in this process approach. Be sure to explain the meaning of each subheading for the activity, because these are used consistently throughout the textbook.

P-19 Titres de journaux.

A. Avant de lire. Here is a series of headlines from the French-language press. As you read them, you will find that you are able to grasp their general meaning because they include a number of cognates. For example, you can guess that the article entitled **Dossier Beauté : Écolo Cosméto** probably has to do with cosmetics and ecology because of the words **Écolo** and **Cosméto**. What cognates can you find in the subtitle that help to confirm this guess?

1.

Le vaccin antigrippal serait utile

La nouvelle vaccination réduit de 48 % le risque de décès chez les personnes qui ont plus de 65 ans et de 27 % les risques d'hospitalisation pour pneumonie ou grippe pour tous, d'après une étude de l'Université du Minnesota à Minneapolis.

Le Soir en ligne (Bruxelles)

2.

Un dinosaure rare découvert à Lisbonne

Un paléontologue français a découvert des morceaux de mâchoire d'un étrange dinosaure carnivore avec des dents « de crocodile ». C'est le baryonyx.

Le Soir en ligne (Bruxelles)

3.

DOSSIER BEAUTÉ : ÉCOLO COSMÉTO

La cosmétologie se met à l'heure écolo. Shampooings biodégradables, crèmes aux plantes, aérosols sans fréon...

20 ans (Paris)

Implementation: *Avant de lire* As you focus on the reading strategy, looking for cognates, ask why there are so many similar words in French and English. You may explain that after the arrival of William the Conquerer (*Guillaume le Conquérant*) in England in 1066, many of the English nobles and middle class people began to use French as their everyday language. Gradually, many French words found their way into the English language.

4.

CATASTROPHES NATURELLES

Cayes - inondations : 3.000 familles sinistrées

Est-ce la manifestation du changement climatique ?

La ville des Cayes, troisième ville d'Haïti comptant 100.000 habitants, était en partie sous les eaux mardi…

Haïti en marche (Miami)

5.

Politique québécoise

L'Assemblée nationale reprend ses travaux sur fond d'économie

Plusieurs dossiers économiques majeurs attendent le gouvernement Charest cet automne.

The Canadian Press

Implementation: *En regardant de plus près* This activity focuses on developing decoding techniques, so that students learn to rely on prior knowledge and contextual guessing rather than searching through a dictionary to discover the meaning of unfamiliar words and expressions. It is meant to build students' confidence. Work through the questions with them.

Show students how they use contextualized guessing in their native language, with examples such as the following: "Jancis, get the besom and sweep out my room a bit." "You did light a fire as will be hard to dout." In the first sentence, knowing what one does with a "besom" tells us what it must be: a broom. In the second, "dout" is something you do to a fire, clearly the opposite of "light." The examples are taken from *Precious Bane* by Mary Webb, which contains many examples of Welsh dialect that can be used to exemplify reading strategies for students.

Help students practice additional decoding strategies related to each headline: 1) the many cognates along with contextualized guessing and background knowledge can help students decide that *la grippe* is "influenza/flu"; have students also analyze the meaning of percentages used in the headline; 2) ask students to find the name of the dinosaur discovered and to identify the different nationalities involved in the story (French, Portuguese); 3) mention the tendency in French to abbreviate words (as in *métro, resto, McDo*); 4) help students discover what the proper name *Cayes* refers to; point out that words that appear to be cognates can also be *faux amis*, such as *sinistrées* (which here means "threatened"); relate the French word *inondations* to the English expression "to be inundated"; 5) have students find the name of the legislative body; 6) have students find the artist's full name and the city where the Kodak Awards were presented (*Arles* is a significant location, as Vincent van Gogh painted there).

6.

Voirol ou le regard émerveillé d'un môme photographe

… Portraitiste subtil, photoreporter nominé à l'European Kodak Award d'Arles, Xavier Voirol reste viscéralement attaché à son indépendance. Il travaille en freelance depuis 20 ans ….

L'Express (Neuchâtel)

B. En lisant. Watching for cognates, decide which headline/s deal/s with . . .

1. art 6
2. medical news 1
3. politics 5
4. a natural disaster 4
5. a scientific discovery 2
6. the economy 5
7. the environment 3, 4

Implementation: *En lisant* as you work with the headlines, point out to students that they can also use context to guess the meaning of unfamiliar words. For example, in the phrase **aérosols sans fréon**, they might guess that the word **sans** means *without*, since that would be an ecological improvement!

How did you make your decision in each case?

C. En regardant de plus près. Now look more closely at these features of the headlines. *Answers may vary.*

1. Point out at least one cognate in each headline. *vaccin, dinosaure, beauté, catastrophes, politique, photographe*
2. Based on the context and use of cognates, indicate what the following words or expressions mean:
   a. Le vaccin antigrippal (#1) the flu vaccine
   b. des dents « de crocodile » (#2) "crocodile" teeth
   c. Écolo cosméto ; crèmes aux plantes, aérosols sans fréon (#3) Eco-cosmetology: plant-based creams, aerosols without freon
   d. le changement climatique (#4) climate change/global warming
   e. Il travaille en freelance (#6) He works freelance

D. Après avoir lu. For each headline, the source has been indicated. What does this tell you about where French is used in the world today? Can you explain why French is used all over the world?

Note: *Après avoir lu* According to the *Organisation internationale de la Francophonie* (*l'OIF*), the continent with the largest percentage of French speakers is Africa — 11% of the total population. The regions with the highest percentages of French speakers (more than 15% of the total population) are the Maghreb, the Indian Ocean, and western Europe. The ten countries with the greatest number of French speakers are: France, Algeria, Canada, Morocco, Belgium, the Ivory Coast, Tunisia, Cameroon, the Republic of Congo, and Switzerland.

1 Première Partie

pour vous présenter	*to introduce yourself*
Comment tu t'appelles ?	*What is your name?*
Comment vous appelez-vous ?	*What is your name?*
Je m'appelle Chloé.	*My name is Chloé.*
Je vous présente Jean-Louis.	*I introduce/present Jean-Louis to you.*
Voici...	*This is/Here is/are . . .*
Enchanté/e.	*Delighted.*
Je suis de Montréal.	*I am from Montreal.*

pour saluer	*to greet someone*
Bonjour.	*Hello.*
Bonsoir.	*Good evening.*
Comment allez-vous ?	*How are you?*
Très bien, merci.	*Very well, thank you.*
Bien aussi.	*Fine, also.*
Salut.	*Hi.*
Comment ça va ?	*How's it going?*
Ça va, et toi ?/et vous ?	*Fine, and you?*
Pas mal.	*Not bad.*
Comme ci, comme ça.	*So-so.*
Ça ne va pas.	*Things aren't going well.*

pour prendre congé	*to take leave*
Au revoir.	*Good-bye.*
À bientôt.	*See you soon.*
À demain.	*See you tomorrow.*
Salut.	*'Bye.*

des personnes	*people*
Madame (Mme)	*Mrs./Ma'am/Ms.*
Mademoiselle (Mlle)	*Miss*
Monsieur (M.)	*Mr./Sir*
un/e ami/e	*friend*
un/e camarade de classe	*classmate*
moi	*me*

quelques expressions avec le verbe *être*	*a few expressions with the verb* to be
être en forme	*to be fine*
être fatigué/e	*to be tired*
être malade	*to be sick*
être occupé/e	*to be busy*
être stressé/e	*to be stressed out*
c'est/ce sont...	*this is/these are . . .*

autres mots utiles	*other useful words*
oui	*yes*
non	*no*
ou	*or*

2 Seconde Partie

dans la salle de classe	*in the classroom*
une affiche	*poster*
une brosse	*eraser (for chalk- or whiteboard)*
un bureau	*desk*
un cahier	*notebook*
une carte	*map*
une calculatrice	*calculator*
un CD (inv.)	*CD, compact disk*
une chaise	*chair*
une craie	*piece of chalk*
un crayon	*pencil*
des devoirs (m. pl.)	*homework*
un DVD (inv.)	*DVD*
une fenêtre	*window*
un feutre	*felt-tipped marker*
une gomme	*eraser (for pencil)*
un lecteur CD	*CD player*
un lecteur DVD	*DVD player*
un livre	*book*
un ordinateur	*computer*
une porte	*door*
une règle	*ruler*
un stylo	*pen*
un tableau	*chalkboard*
un tableau blanc	*whiteboard*
une télé(vision)	*television*

des expressions pour la salle de classe	*classroom expressions*
Allez à la porte !	*Go to the door!*
Allez au tableau !	*Go to the board!*
Asseyez-vous !	*Sit down!*
Donnez la craie à Marie-Laure !	*Give the piece of chalk to Marie-Laure!*
Écoutez bien, s'il vous plaît !	*Listen carefully, please!*
Écoutez sans regarder le livre !	*Listen without looking at the book!*
Écrivez votre nom et votre prénom !	*Write down your last name and your first name!*
Effacez le tableau !	*Erase the board!*
Fermez le livre !	*Close the book!*
Levez-vous !	*Get up/stand up!*
Lisez les mots au tableau !	*Read the words on the board!*
Montrez-moi votre livre !	*Show me your book!*

Montrez Paris sur la carte !	*Point to Paris on the map!*
Ne parlez pas anglais !	*Don't speak English!*
Ouvrez la fenêtre !	*Open the window!*
Prenez un stylo !	*Take a pen!*
Regardez le tableau !	*Look at the board!*
Rendez-moi les devoirs !	*Hand in your homework!*
Répondez en français !	*Answer in French!*
Pardon ?	*Excuse me?*
Je ne comprends pas.	*I don't understand.*
Répétez, s'il vous plaît.	*Repeat, please.*
Parlez plus fort !	*Speak louder!*
Comment dit-on « board » en français ?	*How do you say "board" in French?*

Voilà...	*Here/There is/are . . .*
Il y a...	*There is/are . . .*
...(mais) il n'y a pas de...	*. . . (but) there isn't/aren't any . . .*

pour remercier quelqu'un	*to thank someone*
Merci.	*Thank you.*
De rien.	*Not at all./You're welcome.*

des personnes	*people*
un/e étudiant/e	*student*
un professeur	*teacher*
une dame	*lady*
un monsieur	*man*

Vocabulaire

What kind of occasion is shown here? Who are the people involved? Does this remind you of similar events in your own experience?

1 Ma famille et moi

After completing this chapter, you should be able to:

- Talk about and describe family members
- Count from 0 to 100, state dates, and tell how old someone is
- Describe everyday activities
- Ask simple questions
- Talk about changing family structures across the French-speaking world

Leçon 1 Voici ma famille

POINTS DE DÉPART

Preparation: Preview Ch. 1 by showing the video montage *La famille dans le monde francophone.* Ask students to guess what the various family relationships depicted might be. What do they notice about the interactions they observe?

Ma famille

Salut, je m'appelle Éric Brunet. Voici ma famille :

D'abord il y a mes grands-parents Brunet — ce sont les parents de mon père. Mon père a une sœur ; elle s'appelle Annick Roy. Paul Roy est son mari. Ma tante est divorcée et remariée. Loïc est le fils de son premier mari mais Marie-Hélène est la fille de son deuxième mari, Paul Roy.

Ma mère est d'une famille nombreuse. Elle a deux frères et trois sœurs. Alors, j'ai beaucoup d'oncles, de tantes, de cousins et de cousines. Ma grand-mère Kerboul habite chez mon oncle ; mon grand-père Kerboul est décédé.

Dans ma famille, nous sommes trois enfants : deux garçons et une fille. Ma grande sœur Fabienne est fiancée. J'ai aussi un petit frère, Stéphane. Chez nous il y a des animaux familiers. Nous avons un chien, César, deux chats, Minou et Cédille, et trois oiseaux.

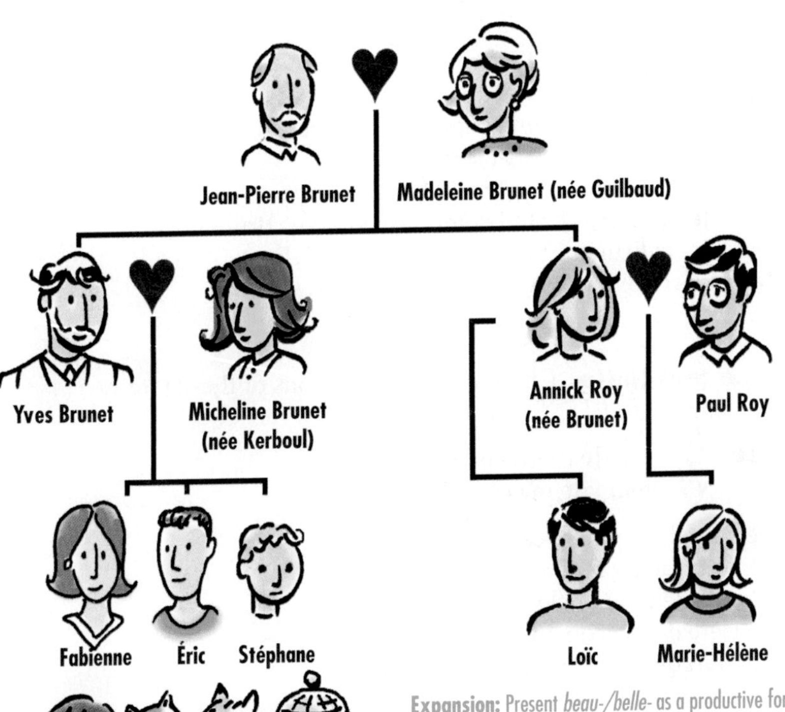

Expansion: Present *beau-/belle-* as a productive form for step- and in-law relationships (note the exception, *le gendre*, "son-in-law"). Additional useful vocabulary for students may include: *un fils/une fille unique, des jumeaux/des jumelles, des triplés.*

Presentation: Begin by having students listen to Éric's description of his family while they look at his family tree (MFL, Instructor's Resources), thereby presenting some of the vocabulary inductively. Next present kinship terms more systematically. First have students pronounce all the names. Then begin: *Voici Éric. La mère d'Éric s'appelle Micheline. Comment s'appelle la mère de Marie-Hélène ? la mère d'Annick ?*, etc. You might add labels (*la mère/le père*) as you go along. Not all terms need to be presented on the first day of the lesson.

Fiche pratique

As you learn new vocabulary, it can be helpful to organize words and expressions into pairs of logical opposites or counterparts, for example: **la mère et le père ; la sœur et le frère**.

Presentation: As you introduce the family's names, point out the frequent use of hyphenated names in French; most are composed with *Jean* or *Marie.* Explain that, as in English, some names can be either masculine or feminine: *Claude, Dominique, Pascal/e.* Other names have both a masculine and a feminine spoken form: *Simon, Simone ; Jean, Jeanne ; François, Françoise.* If you or your students are interested in learning more about popular names in France and Quebec, there are web sites available with this information.

Note: The word *les parents* means both "parents" and "relatives." For example: *Mes parents habitent aux États-Unis* refers to the speaker's mother and father; *J'ai des parents au Canada* refers to other relatives.

Initial practice: Show the Brunet family tree (MFL, Instructor's Resources) as you practice the vocabulary. Begin with a comprehension drill: *Nommez la mère d'Éric, la fille d'Yves et de Micheline Brunet, le grand-père d'Éric,* etc. Follow with true/false statements that students must correct: *Annick Roy est la sœur d'Éric. —Non, c'est la tante d'Éric,* etc. Finally, have students describe each person in as many ways as possible: *Micheline Brunet ? C'est la femme d'Yves Brunet, la mère de Fabienne, d'Éric et de Stéphane,* etc. Point out the learning strategy and practice opposite relationships: *C'est le père de Marie. — C'est la mère de Marie,* etc. The chart organizes the vocabulary into opposites.

LA FAMILLE

les parents		**les grands-parents**	
le père	la mère	le grand-père	la grand-mère
le beau-père	la belle-mère		
les enfants		**les petits-enfants**	
le fils	la fille	le petit-fils	la petite-fille
d'autres rapports familiaux			
le mari	la femme	l'oncle	la tante
le frère	la sœur	le neveu	la nièce
le demi-frère	la demi-sœur	le cousin	la cousine

l'état civil

célibataire — fiancé/e — marié/e — divorcé/e — décédé/e

01-01 to 01-04

À vous la parole

Key: 1-1 1) C'est le demi-frère de Marie-Hélène ; c'est le cousin d'Éric. 2) C'est la sœur d'Yves Brunet ; c'est la femme de Paul Roy. 3) C'est la fille de Madeleine Brunet ; c'est la tante de Fabienne. 4) C'est le neveu d'Yves Brunet ; c'est le petit-fils de Jean-Pierre Brunet. 5) C'est la nièce d'Annick Roy ; c'est la cousine de Marie-Hélène. 6) C'est le petit-fils de Jean-Pierre et Madeleine Brunet ; c'est le fils d'Yves Brunet. 7) C'est la mère d'Yves Brunet ; c'est la grand-mère d Marie-Hélène. 8) C'est le père d'Annick Roy ; c'est le grand-père de Fabienne.

1-1 Relations multiples. Describe the relationships among the various members of Éric's family.

MODÈLE Paul Roy : Annick Roy, Éric
• Paul Roy ? C'est le mari d'Annick Roy ; c'est l'oncle d'Éric.

1. Loïc : Marie-Hélène, Éric
2. Annick Roy : Yves Brunet, Paul Roy
3. Annick Roy : Madeleine Brunet, Fabienne
4. Loïc : Yves Brunet, Jean-Pierre Brunet
5. Fabienne : Annick Roy, Marie-Hélène
6. Éric : Jean-Pierre et Madeleine Brunet, Yves Brunet
7. Madeleine Brunet : Yves Brunet, Marie-Hélène
8. Jean-Pierre Brunet : Annick Roy, Fabienne

1-2 Le mot juste. Complete the definitions of these family relationships.

MODÈLE La mère de ma cousine est ma…
• La mère de ma cousine est ma tante.

1. Le père de ma mère est mon… grand-père
2. La sœur de mon père est ma… tante
3. La fille de mon oncle est ma… cousine
4. Le frère de ma cousine est mon… cousin
5. Le mari de ma tante est mon… oncle
6. La mère de mon père est ma… grand-mère
7. Le fils de mon frère est mon… neveu
8. La fille de ma sœur est ma… nièce

Variation: 1-2 This exercise includes *mon/ma* for receptive control; it can serve as an inductive presentation for the possessive adjectives. To simplify, complete the sentence and have students decide whether it is true or false. For a more challenging exercise, once possessives have been introduced have students provide the definition: *ma nièce ? — C'est la fille de mon frère ou de ma sœur.*

Implementation: The marriage rate in France is approximately half the rate in the United States. The reading in the SAM/MFL includes an example of a couple announcing their *PACS*; generally couples refer to their relationship by saying, *Nous sommes pacsés*. If you have not done so already, show the video montage *La famille dans le monde francophone* to provide an overview of Francophone families. You might pause and have students describe each family pictured.

Vie et culture

La famille en France

The family is changing in France. Today, nine out of ten couples begin their relationship by living together. It is common for unmarried couples to have children: 60% of all first-time births are to unmarried women. It is also not unusual for couples to marry after the birth of one or more children. Today's couples tend to marry later and have fewer children than in the past. Typically, French men marry at age 32 and French women, at age 30. Although the marriage rate is declining in France, 80% of couples sharing a household are married. The divorce rate, however, is rising: half of all marriages now end in divorce. Since the creation of the **Pacte Civil de Solidarité (le PACS)** in 1999, unmarried couples living together, whether of the same or opposite sex, can legalize their union. Each year, increasing numbers choose to do so: in 2008, there were almost half as many PACS formed as marriages.

Although the family is changing, relations among family members still tend to be close and to have a strong influence in a French person's life. Young people have frequent contact with their extended family. They also tend to remain in their parents' home longer: two thirds of French young people aged 20–24 live with their parents.

How does the typical French family compare to the typical North American family, and to your own? Is the role of the family similar in France and in the United States, in your opinion?

  Les animaux familiers

01-53

Pets are often an important part of the French family. Look at the video segment, *Les animaux familiers*, and identify the types of animals you see and where you see them—are there any places that surprise you? How would you feel about dining in a restaurant where pets are allowed? What does this custom suggest about differences in French and American attitudes toward public spaces?

Implementation: The French have approximately 10.7 million cats, 7.8 million dogs, 36.4 million fish, 3.5 million birds, and 3.2 million hamsters, rabbits, mice, etc.; 51.2% of households have a pet (statistics from Mermet, *Francoscopie*, 2010, p. 199). Ask students why they think cats outnumber dogs in France—it may be a function of urban living and smaller spaces; in fact, more dogs are found in rural than in urban areas.

Expansion: 1-3 Use other works of art that show families. Some examples include: Henri Rousseau, « *La carriole du père Junier* », Musée de l'Orangerie des Tuileries, Paris ; Frédéric Bazille, « *La réunion de famille* », Musée d'Orsay, Paris ; Pablo Picasso, « *Famille de saltimbanques* », National Gallery of Art, Washington, D.C. Personalized practice for presenting and describing one's family follows in the **Formes et fonctions** section on possessive adjectives.

1-3 Portrait d'une famille. Look at the family portrait by Post-Impressionist painter Henri Rousseau. The title of the painting is ***La noce*** and it depicts a wedding party. With a partner, identify the members of the wedding party.

MODÈLE Voilà le grand-père et la grand-mère…

Henri Rousseau, « La noce », C. Jean/Réunion des Musées Nationaux/Art Resource, NY.

FORMES ET FONCTIONS

1. Les adjectifs possessifs à un possesseur

Presentation: Present possessive forms inductively in class, using the Brunet family tree (MFL, Instructor's Resources): *Voici Éric. Son père s'appelle Yves Brunet. Comment s'appelle son grand-père ? Sa sœur s'appelle Fabienne. Comment s'appelle sa mère ? Ma mère s'appelle Pauline. Et ta mère ?* Ask students to summarize the rules, then display the chart.

- Possessive adjectives indicate ownership or other types of relationships.

Voilà **ma** mère.	*There's my mother.*
C'est **ton** frère ?	*Is that your brother?*
Ce sont **tes** crayons ?	*Are these your pencils?*

SINGULIER			PLURIEL
masculin + consonne	*masc./fém. + voyelle*	*féminin + consonne*	
mon frère	**mon**‿oncle	**ma** tante	**mes** cousins
ton père	**ton**‿ami/e	**ta** mère	**tes** parents
son cousin	**son**‿ami/e	**sa** sœur	**ses**‿amis

- The form of the possessive adjective depends on the gender and number of the noun that it modifies, not on the gender of the possessor, which is the case in English.

—C'est **le frère** de Sarah ?	—Oui, c'est **son** frère.	*Yes, it's her brother.*
—C'est **la tante** de Simon ?	—Oui, c'est **sa** tante.	*Yes, it's his aunt.*
—Voilà **les cousins** de Cédric.	—Voilà **ses** cousins.	*There are his cousins.*

- Use **mon**, **ton**, and **son** before any singular noun beginning with a vowel, and link the sound /n/ to the word that follows:

C'est **mon**‿amie Sandrine. — *This is my friend Sandrine.*
C'est **ton**‿oncle ? — *Is that your uncle?*

- For plural nouns beginning with a vowel, the **-s** of **mes**, **tes**, and **ses** is pronounced as /z/:

Voilà **ses**‿amies. — *There are his/her friends.*
Ce sont **mes**‿oncles. — *These are my uncles.*

Initial practice: Begin with discrimination drills to ensure that students hear meaningful distinctions before having to produce them: is the form students hear masculine or feminine? *C'est mon oncle. C'est ma sœur. C'est son prof. C'est ton bureau. C'est mon chien. C'est son ordinateur. C'est ta cousine. C'est mon livre. C'est sa règle. C'est ma tante.* Singular or plural? *Voilà mes cousins. Voilà son frère. Voilà ma sœur. Voilà mes tantes. Voilà ses devoirs. Voilà mon cahier. Voilà tes oncles.* Follow up with substitution (*Voilà ma cousine ; père. — Voilà mon père,* etc.) and transformation drills (*Voilà ma tante. — Voilà mes tantes,* and vice versa).

01-05 to 01-08

À vous la parole

1-4 C'est qui ? Imagine you are at a family gathering with a friend. Answer his or her questions about the other guests.

MODÈLES É1 Ce sont tes cousins ?
É2 Oui, ce sont mes cousins.
É1 C'est le frère de ton père ?
É2 Oui, c'est son frère.

1. C'est ta mère ? Oui, c'est ma mère.
2. Ce sont tes grands-parents ? Oui, ce sont mes grands-parents.
3. C'est ton frère ? Oui, c'est mon frère.
4. C'est ton oncle ? Oui, c'est mon oncle.
5. Ce sont ton cousin et ta cousine ? Oui, ce sont mes cousins.
6. C'est la sœur de ta mère ? Oui, c'est sa sœur.
7. C'est le mari de ta sœur ? Oui, c'est son mari.
8. Ce sont ta nièce et tes neveux ? Oui, ce sont ma nièce et mes neveux.

Implementation: 1-4 Go over the models carefully, demonstrating in particular how the second model elicits the third person forms *sa/son/ses.*

1-5 Tu as ça ? Is your partner well-equipped for class? Ask if he or she has each of the items listed.

MODÈLES É1 Tu as ton livre de français ?
É2 Oui, voilà mon livre.
É1 Tu as ton cahier ?
É2 Non, pas aujourd'hui (*not today*).

1. livre de français
2. cahier
3. devoirs
4. stylo
5. calculatrice
6. ordinateur
7. règle
8. photos

Implementation: 1-5 This activity allows for recycling of classroom vocabulary. Complete in pairs, then compare responses for the class as a whole.

Implementation: 1-6 Model for students by having them ask you questions as one student draws your family tree on the board. Students can work at their seats or at the board; as a follow-up, have some describe their partner's family while a third person draws the tree on the board. Encourage students to follow the model and use the question *Comment s'appelle/nt…* to elicit the information they need. You may want to introduce the expression *Je n'ai pas de…* as a lexical item.

Additional practice: Have students bring in a photo of family and/or friends to describe; bring in your own photo to serve as a model.

1-6 Un arbre généalogique. Ask your partner questions so that you can draw his/her family tree.

MODÈLE É1 Paul, comment s'appellent tes grands-parents ?
É2 Mes grands-parents s'appellent Smith, ce sont les parents de ma mère.
É1 Et comment s'appelle ta mère ?
É2 Ma mère s'appelle Anne.
É1 Comment s'appelle ton père ?
É2 Mon père s'appelle David.
É1 Et tes frères et sœurs ? …

2. Les adjectifs invariables

sympa(thique) ≠ désagréable

optimiste ≠ pessimiste

Presentation: Use the labeled illustrations of opposite traits (MFL, Instructor's Resources). Remind students of the learning strategy for learning vocabulary using logical opposites; the presentation and the practice activities in this **Formes et fonctions** follow this strategy. Once several sets of opposites have been introduced, switch to the images without labels (MFL, Instructor's Resources) to check students' comprehension (you might add names to the visual): *Il est optimiste ? — Non.* Or, *Nommez une personne qui est calme.* Follow comprehension checks with choral and individual repetitions of the vocabulary (*Il est optimiste ou pessimiste ?*), then go on to the exercises in **À vous la parole**.

sociable ≠ réservé/e

dynamique ≠ timide

idéaliste ≠ réaliste

disciplinė/e ≠ indiscipliné/e

conformiste ≠ individualiste

raisonnable ≠ têtu/e

calme ≠ stressé/e

- Adjectives are used to describe a person, place, or thing. French adjectives agree in gender and number with the noun they modify. Look at the adjective endings in the examples below. Note the addition of **-e** for the feminine forms (unless the adjective already ends in **-e**) and **-s** for the plural.

SINGULIER	*f.*	Claire est	calme	et	réservé**e**.
	m.	Jordan est	calme	et	réservé.
PLURIEL	*f.*	Mes amies sont	calme**s**	et	réservé**es**.
	m.	Mes cousins sont	calme**s**	et	réservé**s**.

- All forms of adjectives like **calme** and **réservé**, whose masculine singular form ends in a written vowel, are pronounced alike. Because they have only one spoken form, they are called *invariable*. The feminine ending **-e** and the plural ending **-s** are only apparent in the written forms.
- Most French adjectives follow the noun they modify.

Sarah est une étudiante **sociable**.	*Sarah is a friendly student.*
Damien est un enfant **raisonnable**.	*Damien is a reasonable child.*

Adjectives are also used in sentences with the verb **être**, where they modify the subject.

Laurent est **optimiste**.	*Laurent is optimistic.*
Marie-Louise est **calme**.	*Marie-Louise is calm.*

- With a mixed group of feminine and masculine nouns, the masculine plural form of the adjective is used.

Lucie et Madeleine sont **têtues**.	*Lucie and Madeleine are stubborn.*
Romain et Grégorie sont **réservés**.	*Romain and Gregory are reserved.*
Alexandre et Marie sont **disciplinés**.	*Alexander and Marie are disciplined.*

The French often express a negative trait or thought by using its opposite in a negative sentence:

Elle n'est pas très sympa !	*She's not very nice!*
instead of	
Elle est désagréable !	*She's disagreeable!*

01-09 to 01-12

À vous la parole

Implementation: 1-7 This comprehension-based activity focuses students' attention on the written cues to number and gender. Emphasize, by modeling pronunciation, that there is no difference in the spoken form for masculine/feminine, singular/plural. Have students discuss the follow-up question to bring the focus back to how form informs meaning.

1-7 Des jumeaux. Look at the adjectives below and decide whether they refer to Justine, to Jonathon, or to both twins.

		Justine	Jonathon
MODÈLES	sympathiques	✓	✓
	réservée	✓	
1.	indiscipliné		✓
2.	individualistes	✓	✓
3.	stressée	✓	
4.	têtu		✓
5.	disciplinée	✓	
6.	réalistes	✓	✓

Are the twins similar or different? Why?

Implementation: 1-8 This exercise allows students to practice the learning strategy presented earlier in the lesson.

1-8 Le contraire. Answer each question using the opposite adjective.

MODÈLE Ces étudiantes sont disciplinées ?
- Non, elles sont indisciplinées.

1. Ces femmes sont calmes ? Non, elles sont stressées.
2. Ces professeurs sont idéalistes ? Non, ils sont réalistes.
3. Ces enfants sont sociables ? Non, ils sont réservés.
4. Ces filles sont têtues ? Non, elles sont raisonnables.
5. Ces familles sont conformistes ? Non, elles sont individualistes.
6. Ces étudiants sont pessimistes ? Non, ils sont optimistes.
7. Ces étudiantes sont timides ? Non, elles sont dynamiques.

1-9 Contrastes. Compare your ideas with those of a classmate.

MODÈLE le frère/la sœur idéal/e

É1 Pour moi, le frère idéal est calme et réservé.

É2 Pour moi, le frère idéal est calme aussi, mais il est sociable.

1. le frère/la sœur idéal/e
2. le parent idéal
3. le professeur idéal
4. l'étudiant/e typique
5. le/la partenaire idéal/e

Implementation: 1-9, 1-10 Have students work in pairs and report back to the group. For **1-10**, have students suggest other people to describe, perhaps specific members of the class or celebrities.

POUR UNE DESCRIPTION PLUS PRÉCISE

un peu (*a little*) **assez** (*rather*) **très** (*very*) **vraiment** (*really*) **trop** (*too*)

1-10 Descriptions. Describe each of the following people to a classmate.

MODÈLE ton/ta camarade de classe

- Mon camarade de classe, Teddy, est un peu indiscipliné, mais il est très sympathique.

1. ton/ta camarade de classe
2. ton professeur préféré
3. ton/ta meilleur/e (*best*) ami/e
4. ton frère ou ta sœur
5. ton père ou ta mère

Script: *Observons*

PAULINE : Toute ma famille habite à Paris. Euh, c'est-à-dire, euh, mes parents, mes frères, mes grands-parents, mes oncles, mes tantes, absolument tout le monde. Euh j'ai donc, euh, j'ai deux frères qui s'appellent Maxime et Clément. Ils sont plus jeunes que moi. Euh, moi, je suis née en 1976. J'ai vingt-sept ans donc, et mes frères, euh, ont vingt-et-un ans et vingt-trois ans.

BRUNO : Bonjour, je m'appelle Bruno. J'ai sept ans. Voici mes deux sœurs, Claire et Diane.

DIANE : Bonjour, je m'appelle Diane. J'ai onze ans et demi. Voici ma grande sœur et mon petit frère.

CLAIRE : Tandis que moi, je m'appelle Claire. J'ai treize ans et j'ai un petit frère et une petite sœur qui s'appellent Diane et Bruno. Donc je suis la plus grande de toute la famille. Voilà.

MARIE-JULIE : Je vous présente ma fille, Laura. Laura est québécoise, française et elle est née américaine. Et voici mon mari, Patrick. Il est français d'origine, à moitié breton, à moitié du Midi.

Implementation: 1-11 This exercise treats the first three interviews in the clip. Additional interviews are treated in the SAM/MFL. You might ask students to complete those activities on their own.

Observons

1-55 to 1-57

1-11 C'est ma famille.

A. Avant de regarder. You will see three short interviews in which people describe their family. Watch the video clip a first time without sound. Try to determine which members of the family are being described by each speaker, and write down the relationships in French.

	without sound	**with sound**
Speaker(s)	relatives inferred	relatives described
Pauline :		
Bruno, Diane et Claire :		
Marie-Julie :	*son mari, sa fille*	

Marie-Julie et sa famille

B. En regardant. Now watch the video clip with sound and see if your list is correct and complete. Can you add to the list of family relationships based on what you hear?

Implementation: *Après avoir regardé.* Allow students to work in pairs, then follow up to compare opinions. Find out what questions students would ask, and compare partial family trees and descriptions of the photos.

C. Après avoir regardé. Discuss the following questions with a partner.

1. How are these Francophone families similar to, or different from, North American families?
2. Can you draw at least a partial family tree for each speaker? What information is still missing? What additional questions might you ask each speaker?
3. Now describe the Francophone families pictured below, using the video clips as a model.

une famille polynésienne

une famille sénégalaise

une famille marocaine

Leçon 2 Les dates importantes

POINTS DE DÉPART

Les fêtes et les anniversaires

Presentation: Show the illustrations of holidays and point out the significance of each date: *la fête nationale ; Noël ; la fête du travail ; l'Armistice* (MFL, Instructor's Resources). On May 1, France celebrates International Workers' Day: schools and workplaces are closed, and workers' unions organize parades and *manifestations*. Use the calendar to continue practice with months (MFL, Instructor's Resources).

Note: Days of the week are taught in L. 3 of this chapter; seasons in Ch. 4, L. 1. Liaison with numbers is treated in this lesson.

C'est le quatorze juillet.

C'est le vingt-cinq décembre.

C'est le premier mai.

C'est le onze novembre.

Presentation: Point out that months are not capitalized, and that the order day-month (*14/9, le quatorze septembre*) is used to write dates. Note the exception *le premier septembre* and that no elision is made before a date: *le onze novembre*.

LES MOIS DE L'ANNÉE

janvier	avril	juillet	octobre
février	mai	août	novembre
mars	juin	septembre	décembre

septembre

L	Ma	Me	J	V	S	D
1	2	3	4	5	6	7
8	9	10	11	12	13	14
15	16	17	18	19	20	21
22	23	24	25	26	27	28
29	30					

LES NOMBRES CARDINAUX DE 0 À 31

0 zéro	1 un	11 onze	21 vingt-et-un	31 trente-et-un
	2 deux	12 douze	22 vingt-deux	
	3 trois	13 treize	23 vingt-trois	
	4 quatre	14 quatorze	24 vingt-quatre	
	5 cinq	15 quinze	25 vingt-cinq	
	6 six	16 seize	26 vingt-six	
	7 sept	17 dix-sept	27 vingt-sept	
	8 huit	18 dix-huit	28 vingt-huit	
	9 neuf	19 dix-neuf	29 vingt-neuf	
	10 dix	20 vingt	30 trente	

Presentation: French speakers begin with their thumb when counting on their fingers. Show how the numbers 1–9 are typically written. Model pronunciation, then test comprehension: students write the number or date you say; they identify a) the higher or b) the lower of two numbers. Simple production drills: students say the number or date you write; count in even numbers (*les nombres pairs*), odd numbers (*impairs*), and backward (*à rebours*).

Note: Based on the orthographic reform of 1990, all numbers are linked by hyphens. This reform makes the writing of numbers more consistent and eliminates ambiguity. Students may see numbers such as *vingt et un* written without hyphens, since the reform is not uniformly followed.

01-16 to 01-19

À vous la parole

Expansion: 1-12 Have students provide additional groupings of numbers that form a series.

1-12 Complétez la série.

With a partner, take turns reading aloud each series of numbers and adding a number to complete it.

MODÈLE 2, 4, 6,...
É1 deux, quatre, six,...
É2 deux, quatre, six, huit

1. 1, 3, 5,... 7
2. 7, 14, 21,... 28
3. 6, 12, 18,... 24
4. 2, 4, 8,... 16
5. 5, 10, 15,... 20
6. 25, 27, 29,... 31
7. 31, 30, 29,... 28
8. 28, 26, 24,... 22

Implementation: 1-13 Begin with addition and give several models. Have one student state the problem and designate another student to answer. You may have the second student write the problem on the board. The first student then judges the correctness of the response. When the student responds correctly, he/she then asks the next question. You might focus only on addition at first, then review and add problems using subtraction, multiplication, and division.

1-13 Cours de mathématiques.

Create math problems to test your classmates!

MODÈLE É1 10 + 2 = ? (Dix et deux/Dix plus deux, ça fait combien ?)
É2 Ça fait douze.
É3 20 – 5 = ? (Vingt moins cinq, ça fait combien ?)
É4 Ça fait quinze.

1-14 Associations.

What number do you associate with the following? *Answers may vary.*

MODÈLE la superstition
- treize

1. le vote 18
2. une paire 2
3. l'alphabet 26
4. le premier 1
5. un imbécile 0
6. la chance 2, 7, or 11
7. l'indépendance 4, 14, 18, or 21
8. Noël 24 or 25

Expansion: 1-15 Have students work with a calendar to find other holidays and saints' days.

1-15 C'est quelle date ? What date corresponds to each holiday?

MODÈLE Noël
- C'est le 25 décembre.

1. le jour de l'An C'est le premier janvier.
2. la Saint-Valentin C'est le 14 février.
3. la fête du travail C'est le premier mai.
4. la fête nationale américaine C'est le 4 juillet.
5. la fête nationale française C'est le 14 juillet.
6. la Toussaint C'est le premier novembre.
7. l'Armistice C'est le onze novembre.

Implementation: 1-16 In a class of 20 students, the probability is high that two will share the same birthday. Many students will not have a saint's day. Follow up by having students report back and listing dates of birthdays and saints' days on the board. Also list names without a corresponding saint's day. Remind students that French first names have traditionally been influenced by Catholic tradition.

1-16 Votre anniversaire et votre fête. Find a partner and ask each other when your birthday is and when your saint's day is. Share what you have learned about your partner with the class.

MODÈLE É1 Ton anniversaire, c'est quel jour ?
É2 C'est le 30 août. Et toi ?
É1 C'est le 9 mai.
É2 Et ta fête, Tom ?
É1 C'est le 3 juillet. Et toi, Jenna ?
É2 Il n'y a pas de « Sainte Jenna ».

Vie et culture

Bon anniversaire et bonne fête !

Take a look at the French calendar below. How is it similar to the calendar you use? How is it different? Notice that some dates are highlighted in color. With a partner, make a list of these dates and try to determine the significance of each. Do some dates coincide with important dates on your own calendar? Also, note that a name is listed alongside most dates. Many French people celebrate two special days a year, their *birthday* (**Bon anniversaire !**) and their *saint's day* (**Bonne fête !**), the day associated in the Catholic tradition with the saint for whom they are named.

2014

JANVIER		
1	M	Jour de l'an
2	J	Basile
3	V	Geneviève
4	S	Odilon
5	D	Edouard
6	L	Mélaine
7	M	Raymond
8	M	Lucien
9	J	Alix
10	V	Guillaume
11	S	Pauline
12	D	Tatiana
13	L	Yvette
14	M	Nina
15	M	Rémi
16	J	Marcel
17	V	Roseline
18	S	Prisca
19	D	Marius
20	L	Sébastien
21	M	Agnès
22	M	Vincent
23	J	Barnard
24	V	Fr. de Sales
25	S	Conv. S. Paul
26	D	Paule
27	L	Angèle
28	M	Th. d'Aquin
29	M	Gildas
30	J	Martine
31	V	Marcelle

FÉVRIER		
1	S	Ella
2	D	Présentation
3	L	Blaise
4	M	Véronique
5	M	Agathe
6	J	Gaston
7	V	Eugénie
8	S	Jacqueline
9	D	Apolline
10	L	Arnaud
11	M	ND de Lourdes
12	M	Félix
13	J	Béatrice
14	V	Valentin
15	S	Claude
16	D	Julienne
17	L	Alexis
18	M	Bernadette
19	M	Gabin
20	J	Aimée
21	V	Damien
22	S	Isabelle
23	D	Lazare
24	L	Modeste
25	M	Roméo
26	M	Nestor
27	J	Honorine
28	V	Romain

MARS		
1	S	Aubin
2	D	Ch. le Bon
3	L	Guénolé
4	M	Casimir
5	M	Olive
6	J	Colette
7	V	Félicité
8	S	Jean de Dieu
9	D	Françoise
10	L	Vivien
11	M	Rosine
12	M	Justine
13	J	Rodrigue
14	V	Mathilde
15	S	Louise
16	D	Bénédicte
17	L	Patrice
18	M	Cyrille
19	M	Joseph
20	J	Printemps
21	V	Clémence
22	S	Léa
23	D	Victorien
24	L	Catherine
25	M	Annonciation
26	M	Larissa
27	J	Habib
28	V	Gontran
29	S	Gwladys
30	D	Amédée
31	L	Benjamin

AVRIL		
1	M	Hugues
2	M	Sandrine
3	J	Richard
4	V	Isidore
5	S	Irène
6	D	Marcellin
7	L	J.-B. de la S.
8	M	Julie
9	M	Gautier
10	J	Fulbert
11	V	Stanislas
12	S	Jules
13	D	Ida
14	L	Maxime
15	M	Paterne
16	M	B.-Joseph
17	J	Anicet
18	V	Parfait
19	S	Emma
20	D	Pâques
21	L	L. de Pâques
22	M	Alexandre
23	M	Georges
24	J	Fidèle
25	V	Marc
26	S	Alida
27	D	Zita
28	L	Valérie
29	M	Cath. de Si.
30	M	Robert

MAI		
1	J	Fête du travail
2	V	Boris
3	S	Phil., Jacq.
4	D	Sylvain
5	L	Judith
6	M	Prudence
7	M	Gisèle
8	J	Victoire 1945
9	V	Pacôme
10	S	Solange
11	D	Estelle
12	L	Achille
13	M	Rolande
14	M	Matthias
15	J	Denise
16	V	Honoré
17	S	Pascal
18	D	Eric
19	L	Yves
20	M	Bernardin
21	M	Constantin
22	J	Emile
23	V	Didier
24	S	Donatien
25	D	Sophie
26	L	Bérenger
27	M	Augustin
28	M	Germain
29	J	Ascension
30	V	Ferdinand
31	S	Visitation

JUIN		
1	D	Justin
2	L	Blandine
3	M	Kévin
4	M	Clotilde
5	J	Igor
6	V	Norbert
7	S	Gilbert
8	D	Pentecôte
9	L	L. de Pentecôte
10	M	Landry
11	M	Barnabé
12	J	Guy
13	V	Antoine de P.
14	S	Elisée
15	D	Germaine
16	L	J.-F. Régis
17	M	Hervé
18	M	Léonce
19	J	Romuald
20	V	Silvère
21	S	Eté
22	D	Alban
23	L	Audrey
24	M	Jean-Baptiste
25	M	Prosper
26	J	Anthelme
27	V	Fernand
28	S	Irénée
29	D	Pierre, Paul
30	L	Martial

JUILLET		
1	M	Thierry
2	M	Martinien
3	J	Thomas
4	V	Florent
5	S	Antoine
6	D	Mariette
7	L	Raoul
8	M	Thibault
9	M	Amandine
10	J	Ulrich
11	V	Benoît
12	S	Olivier
13	D	Henri, Joël
14	L	Fête Nationale
15	M	Donald
16	M	ND Mt Carmel
17	J	Charlotte
18	V	Frédéric
19	S	Arsène
20	D	Marina
21	L	Victor
22	M	Marie-Mad.
23	M	Brigitte
24	J	Christine
25	V	Jacques
26	S	Anne, Joachim
27	D	Nathalie
28	L	Samson
29	M	Marthe
30	M	Juliette
31	J	Ignace de L.

AOÛT		
1	V	Alphonse
2	S	Julien Eym.
3	D	Lydie
4	L	J.-M. Vianney
5	M	Abel
6	M	Transfiguration
7	J	Gaétan
8	V	Dominique
9	S	Amour
10	D	Laurent
11	L	Claire
12	M	Clarisse
13	M	Hippolyte
14	J	Evrard
15	V	Assomption
16	S	Armel
17	D	Hyacinthe
18	L	Hélène
19	M	Jean-Eudes
20	M	Bernard
21	J	Christophe
22	V	Fabrice
23	S	Rose de Lima
24	D	Barthélémy
25	L	Louis
26	M	Natacha
27	M	Monique
28	J	Augustin
29	V	Sabine
30	S	Fiacre
31	D	Aristide

SEPTEMBRE		
1	L	Gilles
2	M	Ingrid
3	M	Grégoire
4	J	Rosalie
5	V	Raïssa
6	S	Bertrand
7	D	Reine
8	L	Nativité
9	M	Alain
10	M	Inès
11	J	Adelphe
12	V	Apollinaire
13	S	Aimé
14	D	La Croix
15	L	Roland
16	M	Edith
17	M	Renaud
18	J	Nadège
19	V	Emilie
20	S	Davy
21	D	Matthieu
22	L	Maurice
23	M	Automne
24	M	Thècle
25	J	Hermann
26	V	Côme, Damien
27	S	Vincent de P.
28	D	Venceslas
29	L	Michel
30	M	Jérôme

OCTOBRE		
1	M	Thér. de l'E.
2	J	Léger
3	V	Gérard
4	S	Fr. d'Assise
5	D	Fleur
6	L	Bruno
7	M	Serge
8	M	Pélagie
9	J	Denis
10	V	Ghislain
11	S	Firmin
12	D	Wilfried
13	L	Géraud
14	M	Juste
15	M	Thér. d'Avila
16	J	Edwige
17	V	Baudouin
18	S	Luc
19	D	René
20	L	Adeline
21	M	Céline
22	M	Elodie
23	J	Jean de C.
24	V	Florentin
25	S	Crépin
26	D	Dimitri
27	L	Emeline
28	M	Jude
29	M	Narcisse
30	J	Bienvenu
31	V	Quentin

NOVEMBRE		
1	S	Toussaint
2	D	Défunts
3	L	Hubert
4	M	Charles
5	M	Sylvie
6	J	Bertille
7	V	Carine
8	S	Geoffroy
9	D	Théodore
10	L	Léon
11	M	Armist. 1918
12	M	Christian
13	J	Brice
14	V	Sidoine
15	S	Albert
16	D	Marguerite
17	L	Elisabeth
18	M	Aude
19	M	Tanguy
20	J	Edmond
21	V	Prés. de Marie
22	S	Cécile
23	D	Clément
24	L	Flora
25	M	Catherine
26	M	Delphine
27	J	Sévrin
28	V	Jacq. de la M.
29	S	Saturnin
30	D	André

DÉCEMBRE		
1	L	Florence
2	M	Viviane
3	M	Fr.-Xavier
4	J	Barbara
5	V	Gérald
6	S	Nicolas
7	D	Ambroise
8	L	Im. Concept.
9	M	Pierre Fourier
10	M	Romaric
11	J	Daniel
12	V	Jean. F. de C.
13	S	Lucie
14	D	Odile
15	L	Ninon
16	M	Alice
17	M	Gaël
18	J	Gatien
19	V	Urbain
20	S	Théophile
21	D	Hiver
22	L	Fr.-Xavière
23	M	Armand
24	M	Adèle
25	J	Noël
26	V	Etienne
27	S	Jean
28	D	Innocents
29	L	David
30	M	Roger
31	M	Sylvestre

Implementation: We use authentic documents to help students learn about culture through discovery techniques. Show students how to analyze the calendar, using the visual and discussion questions provided (MFL, Instructor's Resources). Point out that the French week runs from Monday to Sunday. Although France is *un état laïque*, the calendar is heavily influenced by the traditional religion, Catholicism. Most French are not devout, however. Religious holidays include: *Pâques* (Easter), *l'Ascension* (the ascent of Christ to heaven), *la Pentecôte* (the descent of the Holy Spirit upon the apostles), *l'Assomption* (the assumption of Mary into Heaven), and *la Toussaint* (All Saints' Day, November 1). Legal holidays include: *la fête du travail* (Labor Day, May 1), *le jour de la Victoire 1945* ou *la fin de la Seconde Guerre mondiale en Europe* (commemorating the Allies' victory over Nazi Germany in World War II, May 8), and *l'Armistice* (celebrating the signing of the armistice to end World War I, November 11).

Although church and state are separate in France, the religious holidays listed above are also legal holidays, as are the Mondays following *Pâques* and *la Pentecôte*.

When a legal holiday occurs on a Tuesday or a Thursday, many schools, businesses, and government offices opt to *faire le pont* ("make a bridge"), taking the extra day off to make a long weekend. Ask students which holidays on the calendar pictured here offer that possibility.

Sons et lettres

La prononciation des chiffres

numeral alone	before a consonant	before a vowel
un	un jour	un‿an
une	une fille	une affiche
deux	deux cousins	deux‿amis /z/
trois	trois frères	trois‿oncles /z/
quatre	quatre profs	quatre‿étudiants
cinq	cinq filles	cinq‿enfants
six /sis/	six tantes	six‿oncles /z/
sept	sept livres	sept‿images
huit	huit cahiers	huit‿affiches
neuf	neuf cousines	neuf‿amies
dix /dis/	dix mois	dix‿ans /z/
vingt	vingt crayons	vingt‿affiches

In general, final consonant letters are not pronounced in French, for example: **le chat, mes parents**.

The numbers 1–10 are exceptions. Their pronunciation depends on whether they occur by themselves, as in counting (**un, deux, trois**…), or whether they are followed by another word (**un‿ami, deux‿enfants, six chiens**).

Except for **sept**, all numbers have two or three spoken forms. **Neuf** has a special form before the words **ans** and **heures; f** is pronounced /v/:

Il a neuf ans.	*He is nine years old.*
Il est neuf heures.	*It's nine o'clock.*

Note: In normal conversational style, *quatre* is pronounced /kat/ before a consonant and in final position. Although there is some generational variation, *cinq* has a pronounced final consonant in most contexts; an exception is the expression *cinq cent(s)*, where the /k/ is never pronounced. There is also a tendency among native speakers to pronounce the final consonant of *six, huit,* and *dix* before a consonant in dates: *le huit* /t/ *mars.* In contrast, the final *t* of *quatre-vingt-un,* etc., is never pronounced.

À vous la parole

1-17 À la réunion de la famille Brunet. Repeat each expression.
Il y a…

un grand-père	un arrière-grand-père (*great-grandfather*)
trois tantes	trois oncles
dix filles	dix enfants
huit garçons	huit étudiants
cinq cousins	cinq animaux familiers

01-20 to 01-21

Initial practice: Begin with a discrimination drill. Give students a list of nouns and have them write in the number you call out (as if you were taking inventory). Begin student production with substitution drills, changing either the number or the noun: *Il a dix ans ; six. —Il a six ans,* etc . ; *Elle a cinq frères ; oncles. —Elle a cinq oncles,* etc. To practice the isolation form, use the following exercise:

É1 Il a six euros.
É2 Combien ?
É1 Six.

1-18 Une comptine. Repeat the following counting rhyme.

Un, deux, trois, nous irons au bois,
Quatre, cinq, six, cueillir des cerises.
Sept, huit, neuf, dans mon panier neuf.
Dix, onze, douze, elles seront toutes rouges.

Implementation: 1-18 Point out that *nous irons au bois* means "we'll go to the woods"; *cueillir des cerises,* "to gather cherries"; *dans mon panier neuf,* "in my new basket"; *elles seront toutes rouges,* "they'll all be red." Explain to students that *neuf* is a homonym that means "nine" and "new." Refer students to the SAM/MFL for a French Canadian version of this counting rhyme.

Additional practice: For further practice with numbers, have students tell each other the number of people or animals there are in their families in the following categories: *grands-parents ; petits-enfants ; étudiants ; arrière-grands-parents ; garçons ; enfants ; cousins ; oncles ; chats ; chiens.* For example, *— Il y a deux grands-parents.* If there is no one in a given category, students should use the structure *Il n' y a pas de....* For example, *— Il n'y a pas de grands-parents.*

Implementation: Have students examine the photo and explain what is pictured and for what occasion it was created. Is the person for whom is was made a girl or a boy?

FORMES ET FONCTIONS

1. Le verbe *avoir* et l'âge

- The irregular verb **avoir** (*to have*) is used to indicate possession and other relationships:

J'**ai** une sœur.	*I have a sister.*
Tu **as** un crayon ?	*Do you have a pencil?*

Presentation: Remind students that subject-verb agreement takes place in English as well: "I have," "she has." Remind them of the use of *avoir* in the idiomatic expression *il y a,* "there is/are."

Presentation: Review numbers 0–39 with a quick round of math problems on the day you plan to treat this topic. Display the numbers and ask students to look for patterns. The pattern of counting in 20s is a relic of the Gaulish language spoken in France before the arrival of Julius Caesar and Latin; the same pattern is found today in Celtic languages. In some dialects of eastern France, as well as in Belgium, French-speaking Switzerland, Democratic Republic of the Congo, and Rwanda, 70 is *septante* and 90 is *nonante;* 80 is *huitante* in some parts of Switzerland. Model pronunciation and test comprehension by having students write the number you say. Note that the final *-t* of *quatre-vingts* is never pronounced. When no other number follows, *quatre-vingts* ends in the letter *-s;* this *-s* can be heard in liaison when it is followed by a vowel: *quatre-vingts‿ans.*

Note: Based on the orthographic reform of 1990, all numbers are linked by hyphens. This reform makes the writing of numbers more consistent and eliminates ambiguity.

- **Avoir** is also used to indicate age. The word **ans** must always follow the number when indicating someone's age:

Vous **avez** vingt ans ?	*Are you 20 years old?*
Mon grand-père **a** cent ans.	*My grandfather is a hundred.*

In addition to the numbers you already know, the following numbers are useful for talking about ages:

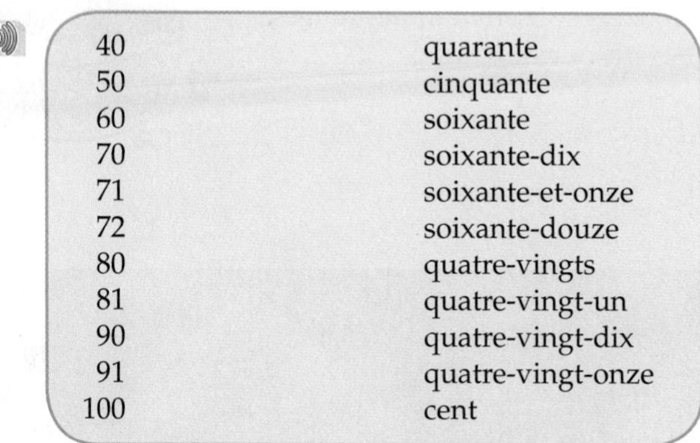

40	quarante
50	cinquante
60	soixante
70	soixante-dix
71	soixante-et-onze
72	soixante-douze
80	quatre-vingts
81	quatre-vingt-un
90	quatre-vingt-dix
91	quatre-vingt-onze
100	cent

Presentation: Point out the following about pronunciation:
The first person singular form is pronounced /e/ : *j'ai*
The other singular forms are pronounced /a/ : *tu as, il a*
Be sure students pronounce liaison /z/ for all the plural forms: *nous‿avons, vous‿avez, elles‿ont.*

Note: A more detailed treatment of negation with *ne… pas* is presented in L. 3 of this chapter.

- Here are the forms of **avoir**, shown with the subject pronouns. Notice that the subject pronoun **je** becomes **j'** before a vowel. Pronounce the final **-s** of **nous, vous,** and **ils/elles** as /z/, and link it to the plural form of **avoir** that follows.

AVOIR ***to have***

SINGULIER			PLURIEL		
j'	**ai**	*I have*	nous‿	**avons**	*we have*
tu	**as**	*you have*	vous‿	**avez**	*you have*
il	**a**	*he/it has*	ils‿	**ont**	*they have*
elle	**a**	*she/it has*	elles‿	**ont**	*they have*
on	**a**	*we/they have*			

- Use **ne… pas de** to express the idea of *not having any*. Notice that both **ne** and **de** drop their final **-e** before a vowel sound.

Je **n'**ai **pas de** sœurs.	*I don't have any sisters.*
Nous **n'**avons **pas d'**oncle.	*We don't have an uncle.*

À vous la parole

Initial practice: Begin with a discrimination exercise to ensure that students hear meaningful distinctions: one person, or more than one? *Ils ont un chien. Elle a un chat. Elles ont deux frères. Ils ont trois sœurs. Il a quinze ans. Elle a deux oiseaux. Ils ont dix-neuf ans. Elle n'a pas de chat. Ils n'ont pas de sœurs,* etc. Follow with a substitution drill: *J'ai un chat ; nous. — Nous avons un chat,* etc.

01-22 to 01-25

1-19 Qu'est-ce que vous avez ? Compare with a partner what you brought to class today, and report back to your classmates. See how many different items you can name.

MODÈLE • Ben et moi, on a des cahiers. J'ai aussi un stylo et un livre. Ben a un crayon et son ordinateur.

1-20 La famille Brunet. Tell how old each of the Brunet family members is.

Implementation: 1-20 You might use the diagram of the Brunet family tree to cue this exercise (MFL, Instructor's Resources). Add ages to the image before showing it.

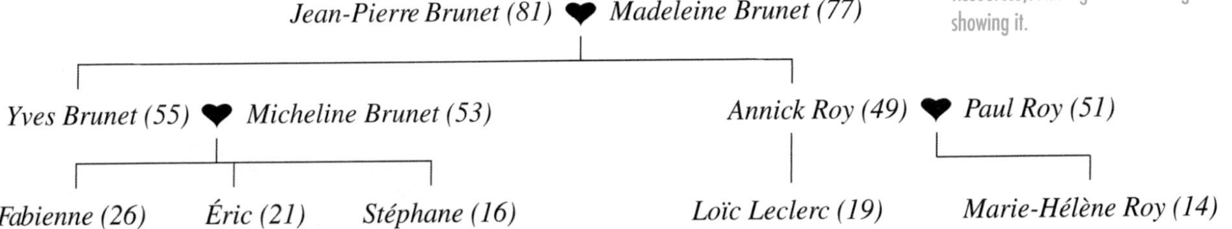

MODÈLE Quel âge ont les enfants de Jean-Pierre Brunet ?
- Yves Brunet a cinquante-cinq ans et Annick Roy a quarante-neuf ans.

1. Quel âge a la mère de Loïc ? Annick Roy a quarante-neuf ans.
2. Quel âge a le père de Marie-Hélène ? Paul Roy a cinquante-et-un ans.
3. Quel âge a la sœur d'Éric ? Fabienne a vingt-six ans.
4. Quel âge ont les parents d'Yves Brunet ? Jean-Pierre Brunet a quatre-vingt-un ans, et Madeleine Brunet a soixante-dix-sept ans.
5. Quel âge ont les enfants d'Annick Roy ? Loïc a dix-neuf ans, et Marie-Hélène a quatorze ans.
6. Quel âge a la femme d'Yves Brunet ? Micheline Brunet a cinquante-trois ans.
7. Quel âge ont les neveux de Paul Roy ? Fabienne a vingt-six ans, Éric a vingt-et-un ans, et Stéphane a seize ans.

1-21 Et ta famille ? Ask a classmate how old various members of his or her family are.

MODÈLES ta mère ?

É1 Quel âge a ta mère ?

É2 Ma mère a quarante-huit ans.

tes frères ?

É1 Quel âge ont tes frères ?

É2 Mon frère Robert a douze ans. Mon frère Kevin a quinze ans.

1. ta mère ?
2. ton père ?
3. tes frères ?
4. tes sœurs ?
5. tes grands-parents ?
6. tes nièces ?
7. tes neveux ?
8. tes cousins ?
9. tes animaux ?

Additional practice: The following exercise may be cued with visuals:

Qu'est-ce qu'ils ont ? Tell what each person has.

MODÈLES je/1 chat
- J'ai un chat.

nous/2 chiens
- Nous avons deux chiens.

1) les Marchand/5 filles
2) vous/6 amis
3) Stéphane et Pierre/3 sœurs
4) je/8 cahiers
5) tu/4 CD
6) nous/12 DVD
7) vous/1 ordinateur
8) Fanny/10 affiches

2. Les adjectifs possessifs à plusieurs possesseurs

Presentation: Review the singular-reference possessives, taught in Ch. 1, L. 1, before presenting the new forms. Use the Brunet family tree (MFL, Instructor's Resources) to present these forms inductively: *Voici Fabienne, Éric et Stéphane. Leur père s'appelle Yves Brunet. Comment s'appelle leur mère ?* Similarly, model the three children describing their family: *Notre mère s'appelle Micheline.* You may prefer to present these forms in the same manner using personal family portraits or magazine photos of well-known families. Summarize forms, using the chart that is part of this grammar presentation.

- Corresponding to the subjects **nous**, **vous**, and **ils/elles** are the following possessive adjectives:

Voici **notre** père.	*Here's our father.*
C'est **votre** mère ?	*Is that your mother?*
C'est **leur** tante.	*That's their aunt.*

Remember that **vous/votre** can refer to one person (*formal*) or more than one.

- There is no distinction between masculine and feminine for **notre**, **votre**, and **leur**.

- For the plural forms, pronounce the final **-s** as /z/ before a vowel:

Ce sont **nos**‿oncles.	*These are our uncles.*
Voici **vos**‿affiches.	*Here are your posters.*
Ce sont **leurs**‿amis.	*These are their friends.*

SINGULIER			PLURIEL
masculin + consonne	*masc./fém. + voyelle*	*féminin + consonne*	
mon frère	**mon**‿oncle	**ma** tante	**mes** cousins
ton père	**ton**‿ami/e	**ta** mère	**tes** parents
son cousin	**son**‿ami/e	**sa** sœur	**ses**‿amis
notre mère			**nos** cousines
votre oncle			**vos**‿amis
leur père			**leurs**‿oncles

01-26 to 01-29

À vous la parole

Initial practice: Begin with a transformation drill, singular ⟶ plural: *Voici notre tante* ⟶ *Voici nos tantes*, etc.

1-22 C'est logique. Use the possessive adjective to point out the person(s) indicated.

MODÈLE Nous avons une fille.
- Voici notre fille.

1. Nous avons deux fils. Voici nos fils.
2. Vous avez un neveu. Voici votre neveu.
3. Vous avez trois cousins. Voici vos cousins.
4. Ils ont une nièce. Voici leur nièce.
5. Ils ont trois enfants. Voici leurs enfants.
6. Nous avons une tante. Voici notre tante.
7. Nous avons deux oncles. Voici nos oncles.

Additional practice: At this point in the lesson, students generally know the Brunet family tree well. For a lively exercise using possessive adjectives, have class members take on the roles of various members of the Brunet family and test their memory of the family tree. Provide students with name tags and have them circulate in class asking each other questions such as [*à Fabienne, Éric et Stéphane Brunet*]: *Comment s'appelle votre mère ?* or *Comment s'appellent vos grands-parents ?* Students playing the role of these family members would respond: *—Notre mère s'appelle Micheline.* or *—Nos grands-parents s'appellent Jean-Pierre et Madeleine Brunet.* As an alternative, give students a card with their name on it, and have them circulate and ask questions to find their nuclear family: *Vous avez des enfants ? Combien ?* or *Je m'appelle Fabienne. Vous êtes ma mère ?*

1-23 Décrivons la famille Brunet. With a partner, describe the family from the point of view indicated.

Implementation: 1-23 If this proves difficult for students, display the Brunet family tree (MFL, Instructor's Resources).

MODÈLE pour Annick Roy
É1 Ses parents s'appellent Jean-Pierre et Madeleine.
É2 Sa nièce s'appelle Fabienne.

1. pour Fabienne Brunet
2. pour Jean-Pierre et Madeleine Brunet
3. pour Annick et Paul Roy
4. pour Loïc Leclerc et Marie-Hélène Roy
5. pour Yves Brunet
6. pour Fabienne, Éric et Stéphane Brunet

1-24 Encore la famille. Take turns asking and answering questions with a partner to describe your family.

MODÈLE des frères et des sœurs
É1 Tu as des frères et des sœurs ?
É2 Oui, j'ai deux frères.
É1 Comment s'appellent tes frères ?
É2 Mes frères s'appellent Chris et Alex.

1. des frères et des sœurs
2. des parents
3. des nièces et des neveux
4. des cousins
5. des grands-parents
6. des tantes et des oncles
7. des animaux

Lisons

Stratégie

Use accompanying graphic elements to help understand a text. Often a graph or table, for example, will summarize at a glance the main points made in the text, serving as a useful point of reference both before and as you read.

1-25 La famille au Québec.

A. Avant de lire. This reading about families in Quebec is accompanied by a table that presents census statistics about married and unmarried couples in the province. Examining the table beforehand can help you better understand the related text. Consider the following questions:

1. What types of family structure are referred to in the table? The key expressions here are: **avec enfants, sans enfants**, and **en union libre**. Can you explain the meaning of each? Notice that the footnotes provide additional information.
2. The far right column provides comparative data; what information is being compared?
3. What general conclusions might the statistics in the table lead you to make about the family in Quebec? Work with a partner to make a list.

Implementation: *Avant de lire.* The table does not duplicate the text information exactly. Display the table and work through it with students, using the questions provided; point out how large numbers and percentages are expressed, using spacing and commas. When students have developed their lists of preliminary conclusions, have them share these with the class as a whole. Note that the Canadian census is taken every five years, whereas in the U.S. it is every ten years. To learn more about the latest census figures for Quebec families, see *MyFrenchLab* for links to the Statistics Canada website.

Familles comptant un couple selon la présence d'enfants, chiffres de 2006, pour le Québec

Structure de la famille :		Variation 2001–2006 :
Nombre total de couples	1 768 785	5,0 %
Couples mariés avec enfants[1]	522 100	–12,3 %
Couples mariés sans enfants[2]	634 825	9,4 %
Couples en union libre avec enfants[1]	308 170	19,2 %
Couples en union libre sans enfants[2]	303 685	21,4 %

[1]un couple avec au moins un enfant âgé de moins de 25 ans
[2]un couple et enfants âgés de 25 ans et plus

Source : Statistique Canada, Familles et les ménages – Faits saillants en tableaux, Recensement de 2006, catalogue 97-553-XWF2006002, Date de parution 12 septembre 2007. http://www12.statcan.ca/censusrecensement/index-fra.cfm

Implementation: *En lisant.* You may wish to read the text aloud, asking students to circle the statistics. Do not ask students to read the text aloud, as it contains many unfamiliar words and large numbers. Afterward, review the statistics and have students explain their significance. Then address question #3, following up on the initial task and seeing whether students were able to draw correct conclusions. For #4, students should notice that information about same-sex couples is included in the 2006 census.

B. En lisant. The essential information in the text below, as in the preceding table, is statistical.

1. As you read, circle each statistic and focus on discovering its significance.
2. Which statistics are related to those in the preceding table?
3. Which of your preliminary conclusions based on analysis of the table can you now confirm?
4. What new information does the text provide about how couples are defined by the census?

Québec : le nombre d'unions libres continue de monter

Au Québec, un grand nombre de couples vivent[1] ensemble sans être mariés, selon le Recensement de 2006. De 2001 à 2006, le nombre d'unions libres a augmenté de 20,3 % au Québec pour atteindre[2] 611 900.

Les couples mariés représentent seulement[3] 54,5 % des familles comptées en 2006. C'est une baisse par rapport à[4] la proportion de 58 % enregistrée[5] en 2001. Parallèlement, la proportion de couples vivant en union libre a augmenté considérablement, passant de 25 % à 34,6 %.

En 2006, seulement 3 familles sur 10 (29,5 %) au Québec sont des couples mariés avec des enfants de 24 ans et moins à la maison.

Le Recensement de 2006 fournit[6] aussi des données[7] sur les couples de même[8] sexe. Un total de 13 700 couples se sont identifiés comme étant[9] des couples de même sexe. En mars 2004, le Québec est la troisième province à légaliser les mariages entre conjoints de même sexe. Au Recensement de 2006, on constate que 9,2 % des couples de même sexe au Canada sont mariés.

Statistique Canada, Portrait de famille : continuité et changement dans les familles et les ménage du Canada en 2006, Recensement de 2006, catalogue 97-553-XWF2006001, Date de parution 12 septembre 2007. http://www12.statcan.ca/francais/census06/analysis/famhouse/index.cfm

[1]habitent [2]*reach* [3]*only* [4]*in comparison with* [5]*recorded* [6]donne [7]*facts* [8]*same* [9]*as being*

C. En regardant de plus près. Find the French words in the text corresponding to the following words and expressions in English.

1. according to the Census selon le Recensement
2. to increase monter, augmenter
3. a decline une baisse
4. living together without being married vivant en union libre
5. same-sex partners conjoints de même sexe

D. Après avoir lu. Think about and then discuss the following questions with classmates.

1. What seems to be the primary trend in Quebec family life, as indicated by the statistics given in the text and illustrated by the related table? Based on what you have learned about current family life in France, is this trend similar to or different from what is happening in France? In what way? Are the trends similar in your own community? Explain your answer.
2. What options are available to same-sex couples in Quebec? How is this similar to, or different from, the options in France? How does it compare to where you live?

Leçon 3 Nos activités

POINTS DE DÉPART

Une semaine typique

Presentation: Present the vocabulary inductively, using the visual of the Dupont family's activities (MFL, Instructor's Resources). First describe the activities, then test students' comprehension: *Qui travaille dans le jardin ?*, etc. Use either/or questions to elicit repetitions: *M. Dupont joue au tennis ou il joue au golf ?*, etc. Follow up with open-ended questions: *Qu'est-ce qu'Émilie fait le samedi matin ?* At this point, other visuals could be introduced, such as magazine photos, to elicit the new vocabulary. Contracted forms of *à* and *de* plus definite articles are presented here as lexical items for students to memorize. These forms are treated in Ch. 2, L. 2.

Implementation: For the **Points de départ**, do not present forms of *-er* verbs, rather use the base form (*regarde/nt, joue/nt, écoute/nt*) with an appropriate subject to teach the lexical items. Point out that *rester* is a *faux ami.* The conjugation of *-er* verbs is presented later in this lesson, in **Formes et fonctions**.

C'est une semaine typique chez les Dupont. Le lundi matin, M. Dupont travaille normalement au bureau et Mme Dupont travaille dans le jardin. Leur fils Simon a 12 ans ; il est au collège. Et leur fille Émilie a 16 ans ; elle est au lycée.

Aujourd'hui, c'est mardi. Mme Dupont parle au téléphone maintenant ; elle invite ses parents à déjeuner dimanche.

Le mercredi, après-midi, Simon n'a pas d'école. Il joue au foot avec ses copains.

Le jeudi après-midi, M. Dupont joue souvent au golf ; il aime le sport.

Le vendredi soir, Simon ne travaille pas, il écoute de la musique ou regarde la télé.

Le samedi, il n'y a pas d'école. Les enfants restent à la maison. Émilie joue du piano et elle prépare sa leçon de chant.

Dimanche, les grands-parents arrivent, et la famille déjeune ensemble.

Implementation: In this chapter, students have learned the terms *lycée, collège,* and *école.* Ask them to analyze the document: How is the information organized? What are the main headings? What vocabulary is used to identify the various levels of instruction? Highlight the terms *école, collège,* and *lycée* and discuss their equivalents in North American educational systems. Can students guess at meaning based on cognates, context, and their knowledge of the real world? Point out that *6ème* is roughly equivalent to sixth grade in the United States. Encourage cross-cultural comparisons: for what ages is school attendance mandatory? When do children generally begin school? At what age do they complete their secondary education? Note that almost 100% of French children are enrolled in school by age three. This may be in part explained by the high percentage of women who work: 83% of women aged 25–49 (*Francoscopie 2010*, p. 278).

Vie et culture

La scolarité en France

This chart provides an overview of the French school system. As you examine the chart, answer the following questions.

1. What general information is provided about public schools in France?
2. Find the words **école**, **collège**, and **lycée** in the chart. To what levels of instruction do these terms correspond?
3. How does the French school system compare to the school system where you grew up?
4. Nearly all French children are enrolled in school by age three. Why do you think this might be the case?

LIRE EN PARTANT DU BAS DU TABLEAU

En France, la scolarité est obligatoire de 6 à 16 ans. L'école est publique, laïque et gratuite.

Enseignement supérieur	UNIVERSITÉS ou ÉCOLES SUPÉRIEURES			
Enseignement secondaire 2°	LYCÉE GÉNÉRAL, TECHNOLOGIQUE ou PROFESSIONNEL	Terminale pour Bac général ou Bac technologique	Bac professionnel (en 2 ans)	
		1ère	brevet d'études professionnelles ou certificat d'aptitude professionnelle	
		2ème	2ème professionnelle	
	COLLÈGE	3ème		14 – 15 ans
		4ème		13 – 14 ans
		5ème		12 – 13 ans
		6ème		11 – 12 ans
Enseignement primaire 1°	ÉCOLE ÉLÉMENTAIRE	cours moyen 2	Cycle 3	10 – 11 ans
		cours moyen 1		9 – 10 ans
		cours élémentaire 2		8 – 9 ans
		cours élémentaire 1	Cycle 2	7 – 8 ans
		cours préparatoire		6 – 7 ans
	ÉCOLE MATERNELLE	Grande section		5 – 6 ans
		Moyenne section	Cycle 1	4 – 5 ans
		Petite section		3 – 4 ans 2 – 3 ans

Presentation: Using the text in the **Points de départ** (MFL, Instructor's Resources), have students pick out which activities take place on a regular basis and which activities are one-time events. Make sure students notice that activities that happen on a regular basis use *le.* Point out that in contrast to English, a preposition is never used with the days of the weeks or times: *le lundi* or *le soir,* in contrast to "*on* Monday(s), *in* the evening." Point out the use of *maintenant* to express an action occurring now.

LES PARTIES DE LA JOURNÉE

le matin l'après-midi le soir

LES JOURS DE LA SEMAINE

lundi mardi mercredi jeudi vendredi samedi dimanche

DES ACTIVITÉS

arriver déjeuner dîner écouter inviter jouer à/de parler
préparer regarder rester réviser téléphoner travailler

The definite article **le** is used with days of the week or times of day to refer to an activity that always happens on that particular day of the week or at that particular time:

Le lundi, je travaille à la maison.	*Mondays, I work at home.*
Le samedi, on dîne au restaurant.	*On Saturdays, we eat out.*
Le soir, je regarde la télé.	*In the evening, I watch TV.*

Compare these examples with the sentences below, which do not use an article with the days of the week because they refer to specific, non-repeated activities.

Je joue au tennis avec des amis **mardi**.	*I'm playing tennis with friends on Tuesday.*
Dimanche, je déjeune avec ma mère.	*Sunday, I'm having lunch with my mother.*

À vous la parole

Implementation: Students have not yet learned to conjugate *-er* verbs; follow the exercise as written and do not expand by asking students to supply full sentences. This exercise can be recycled once *-er* verbs have been treated.

33
36

1-26 Associations de mots. What words do you associate with each of the verbs listed? Work with a partner to find as many answers as possible. *Answers may vary.*

MODÈLE regarder
- la télé, un film, le tableau

1. écouter de la musique, le prof
2. jouer au tennis, au golf
3. rester à la maison, dans le jardin
4. préparer les devoirs, le déjeuner
5. parler au téléphone, français
6. travailler au bureau, dans le jardin
7. aimer la musique, le sport
8. inviter les grands-parents, des amis

Key: 1-27 Jeudi après-midi, elle déjeune avec Alex. Jeudi soir, elle prépare un examen de maths. Elle a son examen vendredi matin. Vendredi après-midi, elle joue au tennis avec Julie. Samedi matin, elle travaille dans le jardin avec sa maman. Elle regarde un film avec Alex samedi soir.

Implementation: 1-27 To prepare, have students repeat the names of the days of the week. Drill by having them name the day after (*mardi ? —mercredi*) or the day before (*vendredi ? —jeudi*). This allows for practice of the vocabulary out of sequence. Then complete the exercise using Sophie's agenda (MFL, Instructor's Resources). Students produce only the third person form of *-er* verbs, which is the base form. Note use of the 24-hour clock. Time is presented only for receptive control here; students should merely recognize whether an activity takes place in the morning, afternoon, or evening. Telling time is treated in Ch. 3, L. 2. At the end of the exercise, let students speculate on who "Alex" might be.

1-27 L'agenda de Sophie. Tell what Sophie has written in her pocket calendar for Thursday through Saturday.

MODÈLE
- Jeudi matin, elle a rendez-vous avec un professeur.

Jeudi 18 (09) SEPTEMBRE Ste. Nadège	Vendredi 19 (09) SEPTEMBRE Ste. Emilie	Samedi 20 (09) SEPTEMBRE S. Davy
9 h rendez-vous avec prof d'anglais	10 h examen de maths	9 h travailler dans le jardin avec maman
13 h déjeuner avec Alex	16 h jouer au tennis avec Julie	
19 h préparer examen de maths		20 h regarder un film avec Alex

1-28 Qu'est-ce que vous faites le samedi ? Use the elements from each column to tell a classmate what you typically do on Saturday.

MODÈLE le matin/je révise/mes leçons
- Le matin je révise mes leçons.

le matin	je travaille	le dîner
l'après-midi	j'écoute	mes copains à dîner
le soir	je joue	au tennis
	je révise	la télé, un film
	je regarde	à la maison
	j'invite	de la musique
		mes leçons

Expansion: 1-28 Ask what students are doing tonight.

Sons et lettres

Les modes articulatoires du français : la tension et le rythme

Vowel tension and rhythm are distinctive qualities of spoken French.

Presentation: To present this information, have students discriminate between similar names spoken in English and French (Phillip/*Philippe*, Alice/*Alice*, *Paul*/Paul, Thomas/*Thomas*, Guy/*Guy*, *Jacques*/Jack, *Simone*/Simone, Juliet/*Juliette*. etc). Ask students how they could tell which language was used. Usually students mention stress/rhythm and vowel tenseness.

Presentation: Have students compare the pronunciation of English "say" and French *c'est* with a hand under their chin; in the first case, the chin will drop; in the second, it should not, and the lips should be spread. Use the hand under the chin as a way of monitoring production of a tense, unglided vowel. To help students produce /i/ and /u/ correctly, use rising intonation with /i/, falling intonation with /u/.

- **Pronouncing French vowels**

At the end of a syllable, French vowels are pronounced with lips and jaws tense. French vowels are usually shorter than corresponding English vowels, and the lips and jaws do not move as they are produced. In contrast, when you pronounce English vowels, your chin often drops or your lips move, and a glided vowel results.

- French /i/, as in **Mimi**, is pronounced with the lips smiling and tense. The sound produced is high-pitched.
- French /u/, as in **Doudou**, is pronounced with the lips rounded, tense, and projected forward. The sound produced is low-pitched and very different from the vowel of English *do*, because for the French /u/ the tongue is further back in the mouth.

- **Rhythm**

French speech is organized in rhythmic groups, short phrases usually two to six syllables long. Each syllable within a rhythmic group has the same strength; each receives the same degree of stress. The last syllable tends to be longer than the others.

In English, some syllables within words are stronger than others. Consider the pronunciation of the following words:

re***peat*** ***lis***ten Chi***ca***go Minne***a***polis

The syllables that are not stressed are usually short, and their vowel is a short, indistinct one. In French, each syllable and therefore each vowel is pronounced evenly and distinctly.

Listen to the pronunciation of the following English and French words. Then, as you pronounce each French word yourself, count out the rhythm or tap it out with your finger.

1-2		1-2-3		1-2-3-4	
English	**French**	**English**	**French**	**English**	**French**
Phillip	*Philippe*	Canada	*Canada*	Alabama	*Alabama*
machine	*machine*	alphabet	*alphabet*	Francophony	*francophonie*
madam	*madame*	Isabel	*Isabelle*	introduction	*introduction*

À vous la parole

01-37 to 01-38

1-29 Les animaux familiers. At a pet show, owners are calling their cats. Repeat what they say, paying particular attention to the /u/ and /i/ sounds.

Note: 1-29 The names provided are typical names for felines and, like many pet names and nicknames in French, often involve reduplication (*Mimi, Foufou*).

1. Ici (*here*), Mistigri !
2. Ici, Minouche !
3. Ici, Mimi !
4. Ici, Foufou !
5. Ici, Loulou !
6. Ici, Fifine !
7. Ici, Cachou !
8. Ici, Minette !

1-30 Slogan. In a French school zone you will find a sign urging motorists to drive slowly. Practice reading the warning aloud.

Pensez à nous ! Roulez tout doux ! *Think of us! Drive very slowly!*

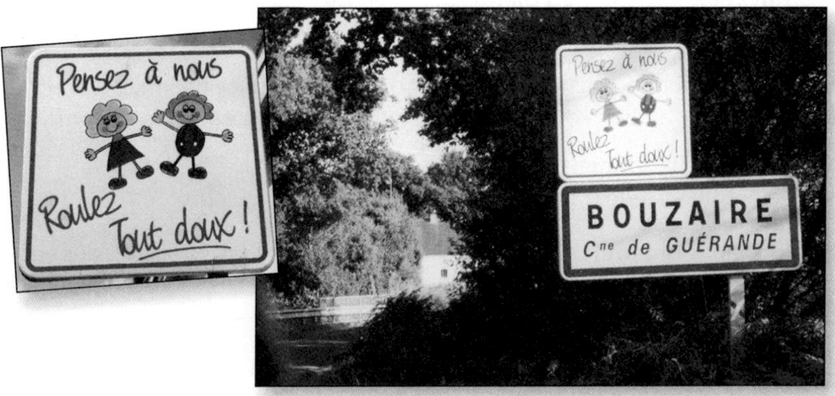

1-31 Répétez. Practice pronouncing the following sentences with even rhythm. Count out the rhythm of each rhythmic group. The last syllable of each rhythmic group is printed in boldface characters.

1. 1-2/1-2 — Bon**jour**/ma**dame**.
2. 1-2/1-2-3 — Voi**ci**/Fati**ma**.
3. 1-2-3/1-2 — Il s'ap**pelle**/Pa**trick**.
4. 1-2-3-4/1-2-3-4 — C'est mon am**ie**/Sylvie Da**vy**.

Presentation: Present the verb paradigm inductively using a personalized story: *Le week-end, je ne travaille pas à la fac. Avec ma fille, on joue au tennis et on travaille dans le jardin. Et vous, vous travaillez ou vous regardez la télé habituellement le week-end ?* etc. Ask students to provide the infinitive forms of verbs you use, and to identify the various spoken forms. Remind students that English verbs also vary according to the subject: "I watch, he/she watches." Stress the fact that regular *-er* verbs in French have three spoken forms (and five written forms). As pointed out in the **Fiche pratique**, these verbs show a boot pattern: the third-person plural form is pronounced the same as the three singular forms.

FORMES ET FONCTIONS

1. Le présent des verbes en *-er* et la négation

Regular French verbs are classified according to the ending of their infinitive. Most have an infinitive form that ends in **-er**. To form the present tense of an **-er** verb, drop the **-er** from the infinitive and add the appropriate endings according to the pattern shown.

REGARDER *to look at, to watch*

SINGULIER		PLURIEL	
je	regard**e**	nous	regard**ons**
tu	regard**es**	vous	regard**ez**
il / elle / on	regard**e**	ils / elles	regard**ent**

- Verbs ending in **-er** have three spoken forms. All singular forms and the **ils/elles** plural forms are pronounced alike. Their endings are important written signals, but they are not pronounced. The only endings that represent sounds are **-ons** and **-ez**, which correspond to the subject pronouns **nous** and **vous**.

Fiche pratique

Sometimes grammatical forms have a distinct visual pattern. For example, if you draw a box around the forms in the **-er** verb chart that are pronounced alike, you will see the shape of a boot. Think of the boot to remind yourself which forms have the same spoken form.

Can you provide the missing form of *jouer*?

- When a verb begins with a consonant, there is no difference in the pronunciation of singular and plural for **il/s** and **elle/s**. Use the context to decide whether the speaker means one person or more than one:

Mon cousin, il joue du piano.	*My cousin, he plays piano.*
Mes frères, ils jouent au foot.	*My brothers, they play soccer.*

- When the verb begins with a vowel sound, pronounce the final **-s** in **ils/elles** as /z/. This allows you to distinguish the singular form from the plural.

il aime vs. ils‿aiment	*he likes, they like*
elle habite vs. elles‿habitent	*she lives, they live*

- **On** is an indefinite pronoun that can mean *one, they,* or *people,* depending on the context. In conversational French, **on** is often used instead of **nous**.

On parle français ici.	*They speak French here.*
On joue au foot ?	*Shall we play soccer?*

- In French the present tense is used to talk about a state of being or a habitual action:

Je **parle** français.	*I speak French.*
Il **travaille** le week-end.	*He works on weekends.*

- It is also used to talk about an action taking place while one is speaking:

On **regarde** la télé.	*We're watching TV.*

- To make a sentence negative, put **ne** (or **n'**) before the verb and **pas** after it:

Je **ne** travaille **pas**.	*I'm not working.*
Nous **n'**aimons **pas** le golf.	*We don't like golf.*

- In casual spoken French, native speakers often drop the **ne**, so you may hear French speakers say sentences such as:

J'écoute **pas**.	*I'm not listening.*
Ils téléphonent **pas** ?	*They're not calling?*

Note: Although *ne* deletion is extremely common in spoken French, we advocate teaching students to consistently use the two-part negative to avoid their being perceived negatively by native speakers.

Initial practice: Begin with a discrimination drill highlighting the presence or absence of liaison as a cue for number: one person, or more than one? *Ils habitent un appartement. Elle aime le rock. Ils écoutent de la musique. Elles arrivent. Il invite son ami. Elles aiment le sport,* etc. Follow with substitution drills: *Je joue au tennis ; nous. —Nous jouons au tennis,* etc. *J'aime la musique ; vous. —Vous aimez la musique,* etc.; *Je ne travaille pas ; nous. —Nous ne travaillons pas,* etc.

01-39 to 01-42

Implementation: 1-32 Display the images illustrating the Dupont family's weekly activities, used to present *-er* verb vocabulary (MFL, Instructor's Resources).

À vous la parole

1-32 Une semaine chez les Dupont. Imagine that you're Mme Dupont, and describe your family's activities throughout the week.

MODÈLE lundi matin : Mme Dupont
- Je travaille dans le jardin. *Answers may vary.*

1. lundi matin : M. Dupont, les enfants Il travaille au bureau ; ils travaillent à l'école.
2. mardi : Mme Dupont Je téléphone à mes parents.
3. mercredi après-midi : Simon Il joue au foot.
4. jeudi après-midi : M. Dupont Il joue au golf.
5. vendredi soir : Simon Il écoute de la musique ou regarde la télé.
6. samedi matin : les enfants Ils restent à la maison/Émilie joue du piano et prépare sa leçon de chant.
7. dimanche : les grands-parents, la famille Ils arrivent, et on déjeune ensemble.

1-33 Vos habitudes. With a partner, take turns explaining when you or the people you know typically do the things listed.

MODÈLES vous / regarder la télé

- Je regarde la télé le vendredi soir.

OU
- Je ne regarde pas la télé.

vos parents / téléphoner aux enfants

- Ils téléphonent aux enfants le week-end.

1. vos amis / préparer leurs leçons
2. vous / regarder un film
3. vous et vos amis / jouer au tennis
4. votre père / préparer le dîner
5. vous / écouter la radio
6. votre frère ou sœur / téléphoner aux parents
7. vos parents / travailler
8. vous / rester à la maison

Additional practice: Put students in pairs and have them tell each other one thing they are and are not doing this evening. Begin by modeling with a student: *Ce soir, je travaille à la maison. Je ne regarde pas la télé.* Student: *—Moi non plus, je ne regarde pas la télé. Je joue au tennis.* (*Moi non plus* is provided here as a lexical item.) Follow up by having students report back to the class: *Nous ne regardons pas la télé. Chris joue au tennis, et moi, je travaille.*

1-34 Cette semaine. With a classmate, take turns telling some of the things you'll be doing later this week.

MODÈLE
- Jeudi soir, je révise mes leçons ; vendredi soir, je regarde un film avec mes copains ; samedi, je parle au téléphone avec mes parents…

Then report back to the class what you learned about your partner.

2. Les questions

There are two types of questions in English and French: *yes-no questions*, which require confirmation or denial, and *information questions*, which contain words such as **qui** (*who*) or **comment** (*how*) and ask for specific information.

Presentation: Information questions are presented in Ch. 2, L. 1. Introduce this topic by having students identify, by raising their hand, which of your utterances are questions: *Je m'appelle Sylvie. Elle s'appelle Nicole ? Comment ça va ? Ça va. Est-ce que tu habites Montréal ?*, etc. After many examples, ask students to explain how they identified these as questions. Students should then be able to provide additional examples.

- The simplest way to form yes-no questions in French is to raise the pitch level of your voice at the end of the sentence. These questions are said to have a rising intonation:

Émilie est ta cousine ?	*Emily is your cousin?*
Tu t'appelles Anne ?	*Your name is Anne?*

Another way of asking a yes-no question is by putting **est-ce que/qu'** at the beginning of the sentence. These questions are usually pronounced with a falling voice pitch:

Presentation: Show students that *est-ce que* functions like "do/does" in English: signaling a question, but not carrying meaning in itself.

Est-ce que vous parlez français ?	*Do you speak French?*
Est-ce qu'il joue au foot ?	*Does he play soccer?*

- If a question is phrased in the negative, and you want to contradict it, use **si** in your response:

—Tu n'es pas mariée ? —**Si**, voilà mon mari.	*—You're not married?* *—Yes (I am), there's my husband.*
—Tu n'aimes pas le français ? —**Si**, j'aime le français.	*—You don't like French?* *—Yes, I do like French.*

Presentation: To practice the use of *si* ; ask a series of questions and have students contradict you in every case, using *non* or *si* : *Vous jouez au foot ? —Non. Vous ne parlez pas français ? —Si*, etc. Follow up using the family tree and asking questions that require the answers *oui/non/si*. End with personalized questions.

- When French speakers think they already know the answer to a question, they sometimes add **n'est-ce pas** to the end of the sentence for confirmation.

Vous êtes de Paris, **n'est-ce pas** ?	*You're from Paris, aren't you?*
Ton père parle français, **n'est-ce pas** ?	*Your father speaks French, doesn't he?*

However, be careful. French speakers do not use **n'est-ce pas** as frequently as American speakers use tag questions such as *aren't you? doesn't he? didn't you?*

01-43 to 01-46

À vous la parole

Additional practice: Use the following exercise as a mixing activity. Have students get up and circulate around the room, asking each person no more than two questions. When a person answers yes, his/her name is written down beside that activity. Give students about five minutes; they will probably not complete the list. As a follow-up, have them ask questions to complete their list: *Qui joue de la guitare ?* A student who found the response can then answer: *Jean joue de la guitare.* Other information can then be elicited: what type of music?, for example. At this point, treat the expressions *jouer de la guitare, jouer du piano, jouer au golf/tennis/foot* as lexical chunks for students to memorize. The distinction between *jouer à* and *jouer de* as well as contractions with these prepositions and the definite articles is treated in Ch. 2, L. 2.

Un remue-ménage ! Circulate around the classroom, asking your classmates questions to find out who does what. Limit your questions to two per person, write down your classmate's name when you get a positive response, and be ready to compare notes with the class as a whole.

MODÈLE *jouer de la guitare*
É1 Est-ce que tu joues de la guitare ?
É2 Non, je joue du piano, mais pas de la guitare.

1) jouer de la guitare 2) travailler le week-end 3) rester à la maison le week-end 4) préparer le dîner 5) danser la salsa 6) travailler dans le jardin 7) écouter de la musique classique 8) ne pas regarder la télé 9) ne pas écouter de rap 10) jouer au golf

1-35 Encore la famille Brunet ! Ask for confirmation from your classmates concerning the members of the Brunet family.

MODÈLE La mère d'Éric s'appelle Micheline.
É1 Est-ce que la mère d'Éric s'appelle Micheline ?
OU É1 La mère d'Éric s'appelle Micheline ?
É2 Oui, sa mère s'appelle Micheline.

1. Éric a une sœur.
2. Sa sœur s'appelle Fabienne.
3. Il a deux cousins.
4. Ses grands-parents sont Jean-Pierre et Madeleine Brunet.
5. Il n'a pas de frère.
6. Sa tante est divorcée et remariée.
7. Elle a deux enfants.
8. La demi-sœur de Loïc s'appelle Marie-Hélène.
9. Annick Roy a un frère.
10. Le mari de Micheline s'appelle Yves.

Implementation: 1-35 Use the Brunet family tree (MFL, Instructor's Resources) to provide visual support; encourage students to invent other questions.

Expansion: 1-35 Other visuals—the classroom (MFL, Instructor's Resources), the Dupont family's activities (MFL, Instructor's Resources)—can be used as a point of departure for students' questions.

1-36 C'est bien ça ? Draw a picture on the board. Your classmates will try to guess what it is.

MODÈLE (Vous dessinez un crayon.)
É1 Est-ce que c'est un stylo ?
É2 C'est une craie ?
É3 Ah, c'est un crayon !

Variation: 1-36 Common objects can be hidden in a bag (Kim's game), and students must ask, *Est-ce qu'il y a un cahier ?*, etc.

1-37 Une interview. Interview a member of your class whom you do not know very well to find out more about him or her. Use the suggested topics, and report to the class something you have learned about your partner.

Variation: 1-37 You might arrange for another teacher, a Francophone, or an advanced student to visit your class and be interviewed.

MODÈLE avoir des frères ou des sœurs
É1 Est-ce que tu as des frères ou des sœurs ?
É2 J'ai une sœur, mais je n'ai pas de frère.

1. avoir des des frères ou des sœurs
2. avoir des animaux familiers

3. travailler beaucoup
4. jouer du piano ou de la guitare
5. jouer au football ou au tennis
6. regarder la télé
7. préparer le dîner
8. regarder des films
9. inviter des copains à dîner

Écrivons

1-38 Une famille louisianaise.

A. Avant d'écrire. Read Amélie Ledet's description of her family's origins. Her family is typical of many in southwest Louisiana: some of her ancestors are of Acadian origin, others came directly from western France, and still others were earlier German settlers who were assimilated into the French-speaking population. Based on her description, and focusing on the key terms for family members, sketch the part of Amélie's family tree that she describes.

A Louisiana family checks their fishing nets in the waters of the Atchafalaya swamp.

Mon nom, c'est Amélie Ledet. J'ai 22 ans et j'habite à Montagut dans la paroisse Lafourche. Mon arrière-arrière-arrière-grand-père du côté de mon père s'appelle Jules Desormeaux. Il est né[1] à Grand Pré, en Acadie, en 1745 et il est décédé en 1806. Sa femme s'appelle Marie Landry. Mon arrière-arrière-arrière-grand-mère est née à Port-Royal, Acadie, en 1751 et elle est décédée en 1810. Du côté de ma mère, mon arrière-arrière-arrière-grand-père s'appelle Pierre Arceneaux. Il est né près de La Rochelle, en France, en 1772. Il est décédé en Louisiane en 1840. Sa femme, Louise La Branche (Zweig), est née au Lac des Allemands, en Louisiane, en 1780. Elle est décédée en 1845.

[1] *was born*

Stratégie

Before you write a description, you may find it helpful to organize your thoughts using a chart or a diagram. You can then refer to it as you write to be sure you are following your plan and presenting your ideas in an orderly way.

B. En écrivant.

1. Sketch your own family tree.
2. Now write a paragraph describing your family origins. Use Amélie's description as a model, incorporating vocabulary and expressions that she uses into your own writing.

C. En révisant. As you re-read your paragraph, think about the following questions and make any necessary changes.

1. Analyze the content: does your description match the family tree you drew?
2. Look at the style and form of your paragraph: did you use the appropriate kinship terms and possessives (*mon, ma, mes*)? Did you incorporate expressions from the model to tell where your relatives come from, when they were born, and when they died?

D. Après avoir écrit. Share your paragraph with your classmates to get a sense of the diversity within your own class.

Implementation: *Avant d'écrire* Use a map to show where Amélie lives and where her ancestors came from. You might explain that the Cajun "myth" traces the ancestors of the Cajuns to Acadia, today New Brunswick. The Acadians were expelled after the British took control, in a movement known as **le Grand Dérangement**. Longfellow's epic poem, *Evangeline*, recounts this story. The reality is much more complex, however, with settlers of many ethnic origins mixing over the years. Call attention to the writing strategy, and have students brainstorm to anticipate the types of information that might be provided in Amélie's description of her origins.

If your own family has an interesting multi-ethnic origin, provide a family tree and a brief description as another model for students. Note that drawing the family tree first acts as another advance organizer.

Leçon 1

les relations familiales	*family relations*
un beau-père	*stepfather, father-in-law*
une belle-mère	*stepmother, mother-in-law*
un/e cousin/e	*cousin*
un demi-frère	*half brother, stepbrother*
une demi-sœur	*half sister, stepsister*
un/e enfant	*child*
une famille nombreuse	*big family*
une femme	*wife, woman*
une fille	*daughter, girl*
un fils	*son*
un frère	*brother*
un garçon	*boy*
une grand-mère	*grandmother*
un grand-père	*grandfather*
des grands-parents (m.)	*grandparents*
un mari	*husband*
une mère	*mother*
un neveu	*nephew*
une nièce	*niece*
un oncle	*uncle*
des parents (m.)	*parents, relatives*
un père	*father*
une petite-fille, des petites-filles	*granddaughter, granddaughters*
un petit-fils, des petits-fils	*grandson, grandsons*
des petits-enfants (m.)	*grandchildren*
une sœur	*sister*
une tante	*aunt*

l'état civil	*marital status*
célibataire	*single*
décédé/e	*deceased*
divorcé/e	*divorced*
fiancé/e	*engaged*
marié/e	*married*
remarié/e	*remarried*

des animaux familiers	*pets*
un animal familier	*pet*
un chat	*cat*
un chien	*dog*
un oiseau	*bird*

le caractère	*disposition, nature, character*
calme	*calm*
conformiste	*conformist*
désagréable	*disagreable*
discipliné/e	*disciplined*
dynamique	*dynamic*
idéaliste	*idealistic*
indiscipliné/e	*undisciplined*
individualiste	*individualistic*
optimiste	*optimistic*
pessimiste	*pessimistic*
raisonnable	*reasonable*
réaliste	*realistic*
réservé/e	*reserved*
sociable	*outgoing*
stressé/e	*stressed out*
sympa(thique)	*nice*
têtu/e	*stubborn*
timide	*shy*

pour exprimer l'intensité	*to express intensity*
assez	*rather*
beaucoup	*a lot*
un peu	*a little*
très	*very*
trop	*too (much)*
vraiment	*really*

autres mots utiles	*other useful words*
chez	*at the home of*
chez nous	*at our place*
deuxième	*second*
habiter	*to live*
un homme	*man*
premier	*first*

Leçon 2

les mois (m.) de l'année (f.)	*the months of the year*
janvier	*January*
février	*February*
mars	*March*
avril	*April*
mai	*May*
juin	*June*
juillet	*July*
août	*August*
septembre	*September*
octobre	*October*
novembre	*November*
décembre	*December*
Quelle est la date …de ton anniversaire (m.) ?	*What is the date . . . of your birthday?*

C'est le premier mai.	*It's May 1.*
C'est le 4 septembre.	*It's September 4.*

l'âge (m.)	*age*
un an	*one year*
avoir	*to have*
Quel est ton/votre âge ?	*What is your age?*
Quel âge as-tu ?/ Quel âge avez-vous ?	*How old are you?*
J'ai 19 ans.	*I am 19 years old.*

les nombres cardinaux de 0 à 100

(see p. 33 for 0 to 31 and p. 38 for 40 to 100)

Leçon 3

pour dire quand	*to say when*
lundi	*Monday*
mardi	*Tuesday*
mercredi	*Wednesday*
jeudi	*Thursday*
vendredi	*Friday*
samedi	*Saturday*
dimanche	*Sunday*
la semaine	*week*
le jour	*day*
le matin	*morning*
l'après-midi (m.)	*afternoon*
le soir	*evening*
aujourd'hui	*today*
maintenant	*now*
le week-end	*weekend*

les activités	*activities*
aimer	*to like, to love*
arriver	*to arrive*
déjeuner	*to have breakfast/lunch*
dîner	*to have dinner*
écouter la radio/ de la musique	*to listen to the radio/music*
inviter	*to invite*
jouer au foot/du piano	*to play soccer/the piano*
ne… pas (Je ne joue pas.)	*not (I'm not playing/ I don't play.)*
parler au téléphone	*to talk on the phone*
préparer le dîner	*to fix dinner*
regarder un film/ la télé/des photos	*to watch a movie/TV/ look at photos*
rester à la maison	*to stay home*
réviser la leçon	*to review the lesson*
téléphoner à quelqu'un	*to call somebody*
travailler dans le jardin	*to work in the garden/yard*

quelques lieux	*some places*
au bureau	*at the office*
à l'école	*at school*
au collège	*in middle school*
au lycée	*in high school*
à la maison	*at home*
au restaurant	*at the restaurant*

la musique	*music*
la musique classique	*classical music*
une guitare	*a guitar*

quelques sports	*some sports*
le foot(ball)	*soccer*
le golf	*golf*
le tennis	*tennis*

autres mots utiles	*other useful words*
avec	*with*
un copain/une copine	*friend*
ensemble	*together*
une leçon de chant	*singing lesson*
normalement	*normally*
si	*yes (after a negative question)*
typique	*typical*

Vocabulaire

Who are the people shown here, and what are they doing? Does this remind you of experiences you've had with people you know?

2 Voici mes amis

After completing this chapter, you should be able to:

- ❑ Describe people's appearance and personality
- ❑ Talk about sports and leisure activities
- ❑ Ask for information
- ❑ Compare French and American leisure activities, small towns, and notions of friendship

Leçon 1 Mes amis et moi

POINTS DE DÉPART

Elles sont comment ?

Denise et Marie regardent un album de photos.

DENISE : C'est toi sur la photo là, avec le chapeau ?
MARIE : Bien sûr !
DENISE : Tu es jolie ! Qui sont les autres filles ?
MARIE : Ce sont mes amies du collège.
DENISE : Comment s'appelle l'autre fille avec un chapeau ?
MARIE : Ça c'est Diane ; elle est maintenant à la fac avec moi. C'est ma colocataire. Elle est très intelligente et ambitieuse. Mais elle est amusante aussi ; elle adore les histoires drôles.
DENISE : Et la grande fille mince et rousse ?
MARIE : C'est Clara. Elle est très élégante. Elle travaille avec les personnes âgées ; c'est une fille gentille et généreuse.
DENISE : Et la blonde ?
MARIE : C'est Anne-Laure. Elle est super-sportive et sociable ; pas du tout paresseuse, elle !
DENISE : Pas comme toi, donc !
MARIE : Arrête !

Preparation: Provide an overview of the lesson by showing the Ch. 2 video segment *Les amis*. Have students listen and watch, then describe the activities friends are sharing. This video clip may also be shown in conjunction with the **Vie et culture** section.

Presentation: Only feminine forms of variable adjectives are presented here, since in most cases the masculine spoken form can be easily derived from the feminine. This derivation rule is taught in the **Formes et fonctions** section of this lesson. To present this vocabulary, use the girls' photo and the dialogue, as well as the boxed list of adjectives. Read or play the recorded dialogue, pointing out each person as she is described. Point out that *la fac(ulté)* refers to the university. In addition to *colocataire*, a roommate who shares an apartment or house, you may wish to introduce the expression *camarade de chambre*, a dormitory roommate. Test comprehension by asking *Qui est blonde ?*, etc., or by creating statements that students must identify as true or false. Next, use either/or questions to elicit repetitions: *Clara est blonde ou rousse ?* Finally, have students provide opposites for adjectives: *Elle est grande ? — Non, elle est petite.* As follow-up, have students describe magazine photos of interesting-looking women.

Note: Adjectives like *châtain*, derived from nouns, are invariable in spelling and never add an *e* or an *s*.

POUR DÉCRIRE LES FEMMES

jeune	d'un certain âge		âgée
belle	jolie		moche
grande	de taille moyenne		petite
maigre	mince	forte	grosse
blonde	rousse	châtain	brune
élégante			
gentille			méchante
généreuse			égoïste
intelligente			bête
ambitieuse	énergique		paresseuse
sportive			pantouflarde
sérieuse		drôle	amusante

02-01 to 02-04

À vous la parole

Implementation: 2-1 This allows students to practice creating more nuanced descriptions by using the negative and the qualifying adverbs taught in Ch. 1, L. 1.

Additional practice: Ask students to describe one of the women in your class so that classmates can guess who it is. For example, *É1 Elle est d'un certain âge. Elle est blonde, grande et assez mince. É2 C'est le professeur ? É1 Oui.* Be aware that some students are sensitive about physical descriptions. As an alternative, you might bring in magazine photos and have students work in pairs to create a description; post all the photos, then have the class guess which one is being described.

2-1 En d'autres termes. Describe each young woman using other words. *Answers may vary.*

MODÈLE Clara n'est pas égoïste.
- Clara est généreuse.

1. Clara n'est ni (*neither*) brune, ni blonde, ni châtain. Clara est rousse.
2. Clara n'est pas petite. Clara est grande/de taille moyenne.
3. Clara n'est pas méchante. Clara est gentille.
4. Diane n'est pas très mince. Diane est un peu forte.
5. Diane n'est pas petite. Diane est grande/de taille moyenne.
6. Diane n'est ni blonde, ni rousse, ni châtain. Diane est brune.
7. Diane n'est pas bête. Diane est intelligente.
8. Anne-Laure n'est pas paresseuse. Anne-Laure est ambitieuse/énergique.
9. Anne-Laure n'est pas grande, mais elle n'est pas petite non plus. Anne-Laure est de taille moyenne.
10. Anne-Laure n'est pas pantouflarde. Anne-Laure est sportive.

Implementation: 2-2 Offer a few examples, then have students work in pairs or small groups to prepare a description. Each group gives out its information bit by bit; they receive one point for each statement they make before class members guess correctly.

2-2 Une personne connue. Describe a well-known girl or woman, real or imaginary, and have your classmates guess who it is.

MODÈLE É1 Elle est très jeune ; elle a environ (*about*) douze ans. Elle est petite, mince et rousse. Elle n'a pas de parents, mais elle a un chien, Sandy.

É2 C'est Annie, la petite orpheline.

Expansion: 2-3 To follow up, display all pictures in the classroom. As individual students share their description with the class, classmates listen to determine which person is being described.

2-3 Voici une amie/mes amies. Bring in a photo of a female friend or friends to describe to a partner.

MODÈLE
- Voici la photo d'une de mes amies. Elle s'appelle Julie. Elle est grande et blonde. Elle est intelligente et très énergique. Elle aime le tennis.

Vie et culture

Presentation: If you have not yet shown it, use the Ch. 2 video segment, *Les amis*, to lead into this section or to follow up during discussion.

Les amis

Whom do we call a "friend"? Concepts of friendship vary from culture to culture. In France, friendships are usually formed slowly, over many years. Once established, they tend to last a lifetime. American visitors and exchange students in France sometimes find it difficult to form friendships with French peers because of the brevity of their stays. French exchange students and visitors to the United States, on the other hand, often report that Americans make friends very quickly and seem to refer to many people as "my friend." This contrasts sharply with French usage, where the word **ami** is reserved for those people with whom a strong bond of friendship has been established. In *Cultural Misunderstandings: The French-American Experience*, Raymonde Carroll, a French anthropologist living in the United States, explains the use of the word "friend" in American English: "For an American, . . . this is merely a verbal shortcut which saves the trouble of explaining the differences between 'friend' and all the other terms available (acquaintance, vague acquaintance, buddy, pal, chum, roommate, housemate, classmate, schoolmate, teammate, playmate, companion, co-worker, colleague, childhood friend, new friend, old friend, very old friend, family friend, close friend, very close friend, best friend, girlfriend, boyfriend, etc.)."*However, Americans' casual use of the word "friend" leads French observers to conclude that their own concept of friendship is more durable and considerably more nuanced.

Key: *Et vous ?* Point out the tendency for Americans to use first names immediately on meeting someone, to invite people into their homes very soon after they have met, and even to hug or kiss business associates. Suggest to students that because Americans tend to change jobs and move frequently, often far from family and childhood friends, there is perhaps more of a necessity to form new friendships quickly and the potential to lose contact with old friends.

* Carroll, Raymonde. *Cultural Misunderstandings: The French-American Experience*. Trans. Carol Volk. Chicago: University of Chicago Press: 1990, p. 77

ET VOUS ?

1. What behaviors or features of American society might promote the perception among the French that friendships are formed quickly?
2. Think about the contexts in which you would refer to someone as "my friend." Do you agree with Carroll's observation that Americans tend to use the word *friend* rather loosely? What advantages and disadvantages are there to using *friend* to refer to a wide range of relationships?
3. Do you agree with the judgment that American friendships are less durable and less nuanced than French friendships? Explain your response.

Voici deux amis.

Sons et lettres

La détente des consonnes finales

As a general rule, final consonant letters are not pronounced in French:

l'enfant   elle est   nous sommes   très jeunes   beaucoup

Presentation: Present this topic in conjunction with *Les adjectifs variables.*

However, there are four final consonant letters that are generally pronounced: **-c**, **-r**, **-f**, and **-l**. To remember them, think of the English word *careful*.

la fa**c**   pou**r**   neu**f**   Danie**l**

Note: Currently, there is a tendency to insert a final vowel ([œ]) after certain words ending in a pronounced -r: *alors, bonjour*. This should be avoided in teaching the language at the elementary level.

An exception is the letter **-r** in the infinitive ending **-er** and in words ending in **-er** and **-ier**:

écout**er**   dans**er**   le dîn**er**   le prem**ier**   janv**ier**

The letter **n** is seldom pronounced at the end of a word. Together with the preceding vowel letters it represents a nasal vowel sound:

m**on** cop**ain**   le chi**en**   l'**en**f**ant**

Initial practice: Reinforce with a discrimination drill to ensure that students hear pronounced final consonants: *un homme ou une femme ? Michel est amusant. Michèle est intelligente. Dominique est sérieuse. Dominique est généreux. Claude est grande. Daniel est petit. André est roux. Renée est élégante. Pascal est méchant. Danielle est ambitieuse.*

At the end of a word, one or more consonant letters followed by **-e** always stand for a pronounced consonant. These consonants must be clearly articulated, for they mark important grammatical distinctions such as feminine versus masculine forms of adjectives. The final written **-e** doesn't represent any sound.

	Danielle est	intelligen**te**	amusan**te**	sérieu**se**
vs.	Daniel est	intelligent	amusant	sérieux

À vous la parole

02-05 to 02-06

Implementation: **2-4** First have students go through and underline pronounced final consonants; draw a line through silent final consonants.

2-4 Prononcer ou ne pas prononcer ? In which words should you pronounce the final consonant?

avec Robert   il aime danser   s'il vous plaît   pour ma sœur
neuf cahiers   le jour de Noël   le Québec   le singulier

2-5 Contrastes. Read each pair of sentences aloud and note the contrasts.

C'est Denise. / C'est Denis.
Voilà Françoise. / Voilà François.
Pascale est amusante. / Pascal est amusant.
Michèle est blonde. / Michel est blond.

FORMES ET FONCTIONS

1. Les adjectifs variables

- You have learned that adjectives agree in gender and number with the noun they modify. *Invariable* adjectives have only one spoken form. The feminine ending **-e** and the plural ending **-s** show up only in the written forms.

Ma sœur est têtu**e**.	Mes amies sont têtu**es**.
Mon frère est discipliné.	Mes amis sont disciplinés.
Mon père est calme.	Mes parents sont calme**s**.

- *Variable* adjectives have masculine and feminine forms that differ in pronunciation. Their feminine form ends in a pronounced consonant. To pronounce the masculine, drop the final consonant sound. The written letter **-s** or **-x** at the end of plural adjectives is not generally pronounced.

SINGULIER	*f.*	Anne est	amusan**te**	et	généreu**se**.
	m.	Cédric est	amusan**t̸**	et	généreu**x̸**.
PLURIEL	*f.*	Mes amies sont	amusan**tes̸**	et	généreu**ses̸**.
	m.	Mes copains sont	amusan**t̸s̸**	et	généreu**x̸**.

The feminine form of variable adjectives always ends in the letter **-e**. The final **-e** is dropped in the masculine form; therefore, the final consonant sound that is heard in the feminine form is also dropped. Although some variable adjectives have spelling irregularities, this pronunciation rule still applies. For example, in the feminine form **généreuse** [ʒenerøz], the final consonant is pronounced, but it is dropped in the masculine form **généreux** [ʒenerø]. In the written form, the final **-e** is dropped in the masculine and the final **-s** is changed to **-x**. Other regular variable adjectives that show spelling changes include:

rou**sse** → roux   gro**sse** → gros   genti**lle** → gentil

- Adjectives whose masculine singular form ends in **-x** do not change in the masculine plural form.

Laurent est roux.	Laurent et Matthieu sont roux.

- As you have learned, with a mixed group of feminine and masculine nouns, the plural form of the adjective is always the masculine form.

Jessica et Laure sont **brunes**.	*Jessica and Laure are brunettes.*
Kevin et Marc sont **blonds**.	*Kevin and Marc are blonds.*
Max et Sylvie sont **roux**.	*Max and Sylvie are redheads.*

- Note the following irregular forms:

FÉMININ	MASCULIN
belle	beau
brune	brun
sportive	sportif

Presentation: What we call *invariable* adjectives have a single spoken form, but some have distinct written masculine and feminine forms as well as distinct plural written forms. This presentation focuses on spoken forms and is reinforced by the **Sons et lettres** treatment. Exercises in the SAM/MFL focus on the written forms of invariable and variable adjectives. To present variable adjectives, prepare a series of parallel examples describing *le couple idéal*, where the two members of the couple have identical personality and physical traits. Arrange the examples in two columns with *Elle est...* on the top of the first column and *Il est...* on the top of the second column. Then fill in the columns with examples such as: *élégante, élégant ; grande, grand ; ambitieuse, ambitieux ; brune, brun ; intelligente, intelligent ; amusante, amusant ; gentille, gentil ; généreuse, généreux.* As you read and display the forms, have students explain the written forms, then see whether they can give the rule for deriving the masculine spoken form from the feminine. Finish by asking students, *Est-ce que ce couple est vraiment un couple idéal ? Pourquoi ?*

Note: Point out that the irregularities involve changes in the final written consonant: *-ss* → *-x; -ll* → *-l;* etc.

Note: You may wish to point out that several frequently used adjectives precede the noun. These include *belle, grande, jeune, jolie,* and *petite,* all of which were presented in the **Points de départ**. Prenominal adjectives will be treated in Ch. 3, L. 3.

Note: Point out that *belle* and *brune* involve vowel changes (i.e., from [ɛ] to [o] for *belle-beau* and from [y] to [ɛ̃] for *brune-brun)* as well as the loss of the final consonant; *sportive* shows a final consonant change from [v] to [f].

À vous la parole

Initial practice: Begin with a discrimination drill, as in the **Sons et lettres**, so that students hear both masculine and feminine forms of adjectives: *Michel est amusant. Michèle est intelligente. Pascal est sportif. Pascale est ambitieuse. Claude est blonde. Claude est petit. René est gros. Renée est élégante.*, etc. Continue with a simple substitution exercise, such as the following:

Des jumeaux. Julien and Juliette are twins. Tell how they are alike: *Juliette est grande. — Et Julien est grand aussi ; elle est rousse ; elle est un peu forte ; elle est assez amusante ; elle est très intelligente ; elle est vraiment gentille ; elle est très élégante ; elle est généreuse.* Next reverse the direction of derivation by providing the masculine form and having students respond with the feminine. Stress the importance of over-articulating the final consonant, since it contains the signal for the gender: *Julien est très élégant. — Sa sœur, Juliette, est très élégante aussi. Il est sportif ; il est assez ambitieux ; il est très sérieux ; il est beau.*

02-07 to 02-10

2-6 Pas mes amis ! Your friends are quite different from what your mother thinks. Tell how. *Answers may vary.*

Implementation: 2-6 This exercise recycles some of the *adjectifs invariables* presented in Ch. 1. You may wish to review them with your class before completing this exercise.

MODÈLE Tes amies sont paresseuses !
- Ah non, elles sont énergiques.

1. Tes amis sont méchants ! Ah non, ils sont gentils.
2. Tes amis sont trop pantouflards ! Ah non, ils sont sportifs.
3. Tes amies sont moches ! Ah non, elles sont jolies/belles.
4. Tes amis sont trop conformistes ! Ah non, ils sont individualistes.
5. Tes amis sont trop bêtes ! Ah non, ils sont intelligents.
6. Tes amis sont égoïstes ! Ah non, ils sont généreux.
7. Tes amies sont trop sérieuses ! Ah non, elles sont drôles/amusantes.
8. Tes amis sont tous (*all*) pessimistes ! Ah non, ils sont optimistes.

2-7 Les amis. Describe the appearance and personality of this group of friends to your partner.

MODÈLE • Il y a trois femmes qui sont assez jeunes, une femme d'un certain âge et un homme…

Expansion: 2-7 You may also bring large photos, such as those found in fine art reproductions, catalogs, or magazines, into class. Put students into pairs to work out their description, then bring all the photos to the front of the class. As each pair describes their person, the other students try to guess to which photo the description corresponds. You may wish to introduce expressions such as *avoir les cheveux courts/longs/bouclés/blonds*, as appropriate.

Expansion: 2-8 To follow up, have each pair report back to the class and see how many people in the class have similar descriptions.

2-8 Le monde idéal. Ideally, what are the following people and pets like? Describe them to your partner.

MODÈLE le chien idéal

É1 Pour moi, le chien idéal est petit, gentil et intelligent.

É2 Pour moi aussi, le chien idéal est gentil et intelligent, mais il est grand.

1. le père idéal
2. la mère idéale
3. l'enfant idéal
4. le/la colocataire idéal/e
5. le professeur idéal
6. l'étudiant idéal
7. l'ami/e idéal/e
8. le chat idéal

2. Les adverbes interrogatifs

- To ask a question requesting specific information, it is necessary to use some type of interrogative word or expression. The interrogative word or expression usually comes at the beginning of the question and is followed by **est-ce que/qu'**:

Où est-ce que tes amis travaillent ? *Where do your friends work?*
Quand est-ce que sa copine arrive ? *When does his girlfriend arrive?*

Some of the words or expressions frequently used to ask questions are:

comment	*how*	**Comment est-ce que** tu t'appelles ?
où	*where*	**Où est-ce qu'**il travaille ?
quand	*when*	**Quand est-ce que** tu arrives ?
pourquoi	*why*	**Pourquoi est-ce que** tu ne travailles pas ?
combien de	*how many*	**Combien d'**étudiants **est-ce qu'**il y a ?

The question **pourquoi ?** can be answered in two ways:

—**Pourquoi est-ce que** tu aimes tes amis ? —*Why do you like your friends?*
—**Parce qu'**ils sont très amusants. —*Because they're lots of fun.*
—**Pourquoi est-ce que** tu téléphones ? —*Why are you calling?*
—**Pour** inviter mes amis à dîner. —*To invite my friends to dinner.*

When used to ask *how many*, **combien** is linked to the noun by **de/d'**:

Combien de frères est-ce que tu as ? *How many brothers do you have?*
Combien d'enfants est-ce qu'ils ont ? *How many children do they have?*

- Another question construction, called *inversion*, is used in writing, in formal conversation, and in a few fixed expressions. In questions with a pronoun subject using inversion, the subject follows the verb and is connected to it with a hyphen. Notice that when the verb form ends in a vowel, the letter **-t-** is inserted before the pronoun and linked to it with a hyphen.

Comment **vas-tu** ? *How are you?*
Comment **allez-vous** ? *How are you?*
Comment vous **appelez-vous** ? *What is your name?*
Quel âge **as-tu** ? *How old are you?*
Quel âge **a-t-il** ? *How old is he?*

Inversion is also more generally used with the verbs **aller** and **être** when the subject is a noun.

Comment **vont tes parents** ? *How are your parents?*
Où **est ta sœur** ? *Where is your sister?*

Presentation: Review formation of yes/no questions and the use of *si*, taught in Ch. 1, L. 3, before teaching this material; use modified exercises from those earlier sections. Present the new expressions inductively using multiple-choice questions: *Quand est-ce que nous avons notre cours de français ? le matin ? l'après-midi ? le soir ? Où est-ce que nous avons notre cours de français ? au café ? à la maison ? à la fac ? Combien d'étudiants est-ce qu'il y a dans notre classe ? vingt-deux ? vingt ? Comment est-ce que le prof de français s'appelle ? M. X ? Mme Y ? Mlle Z ?*

Note: Remind students that they have learned to form some information questions using simply a question word without rising intonation: *Comment tu t'appelles ? Il a quel âge ?*, but that this is a very informal way of asking a question.

Note: Questions using *quel* are treated in Ch. 4, L. 2; *qui, que,* and *quoi* are treated in Ch. 5, L. 2.

Presentation: To show the two possible answers for *pourquoi*, display a humorous exchange such as: *Pourquoi est-ce que vous parlez anglais ? — Parce que nous sommes américains ; — Pour frustrer le prof.*

Note: At this level, questions with inversion are presented largely for receptive control. Students should be able to recognize these questions and be able to use them in limited, fixed expressions such as *Quel âge avez-vous ? Comment vas-tu ?* Be sure to focus, in particular, on the questions *Quel âge as-tu ? / Quel âge avez-vous ?* since they feature in the exercises in this section. Apart from these limited fixed expressions, students should be encouraged to form their questions with intonation or *est-ce que*, and instructors should also make an effort to produce these types of questions in their spoken and written interactions with students.

Note: The verb *aller* is presented in L. 3 of this chapter.

02-11
to
02-14

À vous la parole

2-9 Pardon ? You can't quite hear all that your instructor says, so use a question word or expression to ask for the missing information.

MODÈLE J'ai cinq cahiers. *Answers may vary.*
• Combien ?

1. Nous travaillons dans la salle de classe. Où ?
2. Il y a un examen mardi. Quand ?
3. Il y a trois étudiants français. Combien ?
4. Jacques est absent parce qu'il est malade. Pourquoi ?
5. Elle s'appelle Chloé. Comment ?
6. Elle a deux sœurs. Combien ?
7. Nous ouvrons le livre pour réviser un exercice. Pourquoi ?

Implementation: 2-9 To make the exercise more realistic, read each of the instructor's statements out loud, replacing the underlined material with static-like noise. For further practice, repeat this exercise and have students provide the complete questions.

Additional practice: The following exercise is good preparation for playing the game called *Jeopardy!*, in which students earn points by providing the question that elicits the information given:
Au service des rencontres. Sandrine has called a dating service. As you listen in on her end of the phone conversation, imagine the questions she is being asked.

MODÈLE Je m'appelle Sandrine Trembley.
• Comment vous appelez-vous, mademoiselle ?

1. J'ai vingt-deux ans.
2. Mon anniversaire, c'est le 20 janvier.
3. J'habite à Ottawa.
4. Oui, j'ai un chien.
5. Je travaille le samedi et le dimanche.
6. Parce que je suis étudiante.
7. J'ai des cours (*classes*) le lundi, le mercredi et le vendredi.
8. Je travaille dans un bureau.

2-10 À propos de Thomas. Your friend is telling you about her new boyfriend, Thomas, and you want more details. *Answers may vary.*

MODÈLE Thomas a deux colocataires.
• Ah bon ? Comment est-ce qu'ils s'appellent ?
• Ah bon ? Est-ce qu'ils sont aussi étudiants ?

1. Il est assez jeune. Quel âge a-t-il ?
2. Il n'habite pas la résidence (*dorm*). Où est-ce qu'il habite ?
3. Il est d'une famille nombreuse. Combien de frères et sœurs est-ce qu'il a ?
4. Il travaille le week-end. Où est-ce qu'il travaille ?
5. Il arrive bientôt. Quand est-ce qu'il arrive ?
6. Il n'est pas en forme. Pourquoi est-ce qu'il n'est pas en forme ?
7. Il n'aime pas le sport. Pourquoi est-ce qu'il n'aime pas le sport ?
8. Il a des chiens. Combien de chiens est-ce qu'il a ? / Comment est-ce qu'ils s'appellent ?

Implementation: 2-10 Demonstrate an exaggerated pronunciation of *Ah bon ?*, and make sure students understand what it means. Challenge them to be expressive as they complete the exercise. You might put students in pairs to complete the activity.

2-11 Questions indiscrètes ? Interview one of your classmates, asking him/her questions about the following subjects. Report back to the class what you learned about your partner.

MODÈLES la famille
• Est-ce que tu as des frères ou des sœurs ?
• Où est-ce qu'ils habitent ? …

la musique
• Est-ce que tu aimes la musique ?
• Quand est-ce que tu aimes écouter de la musique ? …

(*you report back*) Voici Ian. Il a un frère. Il habite à Baltimore. Ian n'aime pas le sport mais…

1. la famille
2. les animaux
3. les amis
4. la musique
5. le sport

Expansion: 2-11 You might offer to let students ask you any questions they wish, or bring in a Francophone visitor to be interviewed.

Lisons

2-12 Les Misérables.

A. Avant de lire. You are about to read an excerpt from the opening paragraphs of the novel *Les Misérables* by Victor Hugo, a well-known nineteenth-century French novelist, playwright, and poet. *Les Misérables* has been translated into many languages, has served as the basis for many films, and has been a major musical.

Three characters are introduced in the beginning of the novel: the Bishop of Digne and the two women in his household. Look at the illustrations of these three characters created by Georges Jeanniot for the first edition of *Les Misérables*. Then make lists of adjectives you know in French that could be used to describe each person. Using the illustrations to make preliminary assumptions about these characters can help you follow the author's descriptions, even if you cannot understand every word.

L'évêque

Mme Magloire, Mlle Baptistine, Jean Valjean et l'évêque

Stratégie

Use illustrations to predict content. To anticipate and better understand an author's descriptions in a text, make preliminary assumptions by studying the illustrations.

Préparation: 2-12 If your students are not familiar with ***Les Misérables***, there are many online resources for both the show and the novel. To prepare for the reading (and the **Après avoir lu**), you could have students look for the synopsis and some details about the main characters on the Web. You may also wish to show a short excerpt from one of the many films based on ***Les Misérables***. In particular, before completing **Avant de lire**, you might show the scene where Valjean arrives at the Bishop's house; ask students to describe the characters they see.

Implementation: *Avant de lire.* You might have students work alone or in pairs. When everyone has come up with adjectives, lists could be compared in groups or though a whole-class discussion. Check to see whether some students are familiar with the story and know how these characters—especially the bishop, who is a key figure in Jean Valjean's life—fit into the plot.

B. En lisant. As you read the descriptions of the Bishop, Mlle Baptistine, and Mme Magloire, focus on getting a general sense of the passage. Note that the author incorporates a number of adjectives into his description of the two women and gives an indication of each person's age. Then look for the answers to the following specific questions:

1. How old is the Bishop, M. Myriel? 75
2. Knowing that **moins** means *less*, indicate how old his sister is. 65
3. What is the name of the Bishop's sister? Mlle Baptistine
4. What is the name of their household servant? Mme Magloire
5. Give two adjectives in English to describe each woman. Mlle Baptistine : tall, thin, pale, gentle; Mme Magloire : large, fat, busy, old, white-haired.

En 1815, M. Charles-Francois-Bienvenu Myriel était[1] évêque de Digne. C'était un vieillard[2] d'environ soixante-quinze ans…

M. Myriel était arrivé[3] à Digne accompagné d'une vieille fille[4], Mlle Baptistine, qui était sa sœur et qui avait[5] dix ans de moins que lui.

Ils avaient[6] pour tout domestique une servante appelée Mme Magloire.

Mlle Baptistine était une personne longue, pâle, mince, douce[7]. Elle n'avait jamais[8] été jolie…

Mme Magloire était une petite vieille, blanche, grasse, replète[9], affairée, toujours haletante, à cause de son activité d'abord, ensuite à cause d'un asthme.

[1]*past tense of the verb* être [2]une personne âgée [3]*had arrived* [4]une femme d'un certain âge qui est célibataire [5]*past tense of the verb* avoir, sg. [6]*past tense of the verb* avoir, pl. [7]*gentle* [8]*never* [9]grosse

C. En regardant de plus près. Take a closer look at the following features of the text.

1. There are two words in the text that are synonyms and mean "household worker." What are they?
2. Mlle Baptistine is described with the adjective **longue**. Can you provide a synonym in French for this word? What point do you think the author is trying to make with the choice of this particular adjective?
3. Look at the adjective **affairée**. This is an adjective used to describe a very busy person. Do you know any other adjectives in French that could be used to indicate the same idea?
4. Mme Magloire is described as **haletante**. The rest of the sentence explains why she is described in this way. Given this context, and the illustration of Mme Magloire, what do you think the adjective **haletante** means?

D. Après avoir lu. How successful are the author's brief descriptions in painting a portrait of each of the three characters? Look back at the lists of adjectives you drew up in preparation for reading. How closely do your predictions coincide with what you read? Is there anything you would change in the illustrations, based on the descriptions in the text?

Key: ***En regardant de plus près.*** *Answers may vary.* 1) *domestique, servante* 2) *grande*; the author is probably stressing how tall and thin she is 3) *occupé/e*, maybe *stressé/e* 4) *à cause de son activité d'abord*—heavy people who are busy get out of breath easily; *ensuite à cause d'un asthme*—people with asthma sometimes have difficulty breathing.

Expansion: Help students to see how the two female characters differ in looks and manner. You could have them make a list of adjectives for each in French and identify the opposites.

Expansion: The central characters in ***Les Misérables***, who are not introduced in these opening lines, include *Jean Valjean, l'Inspecteur Javert, Fantine, Marius*, and *Cosette*. You might ask whether any students have read the novel or seen a movie version or the musical and have them tell about it. As a follow-up assignment, ask students to work with a partner to prepare a two- or three-sentence description of one of the main characters mentioned above. Have them start by making a list of adjectives in French that fit the character. They should also indicate the person's age. Students may also describe the relationships between their character and other characters listed. After writing, groups may take turns sharing their description with the class; see if others can guess whom they have described.

Leçon 2 Nos loisirs

Presentation: Present this vocabulary by showing and describing the leisure activities (MFL, Instructor's Resources). Test comprehension by showing the unlabeled images (MFL, Instructor's Resources) and having students point to or mime the activity named. Use either/or questions to elicit repetitions of key vocabulary: *Il fait des courses ou il fait la cuisine ?* Have students repeat the new vocabulary, including the expressions in the boxed list. Then use visuals or miming (by the teacher or students) to get the class to recall the new vocabulary and identify activities. Use a quick substitution drill to review the forms of *-er* verbs like *jouer : Je joue au foot ; nous. —Nous jouons au foot,* etc.

POINTS DE DÉPART

Nos activités

Moi, je fais du sport ; je joue au foot avec des amis. On a un match tous les samedis.

Mes copains font de la musique. Ils jouent dans un groupe. Ils donnent un concert samedi soir. Mamadou joue de la guitare et Valentin joue du piano.

François et Léa organisent une fête. François fait les courses et Léa fait la cuisine.

Ma copine Amélie ne fait pas grand-chose ; elle reste à la résidence et elle regarde un film. Ses amies Vanessa et Anne-Laure jouent aux échecs.

Nathalie est super-sprotive ; elle fait de la natation. Elle fait du vélo aussi.

Benjamin fait du bricolage et son amie Élodie fait du jardinage.

Presentation: Students have already seen the verb *faire* in expressions such as *Qu'est-ce qu'il fait ?* and *Deux et deux, ça fait quatre.* Limit practice here to the singular forms, *fais/fait;* the complete paradigm for *faire* is treated in the **Formes et fonctions** for this lesson.

Note: The forms *le football, le basket-ball,* and *le volley-ball* are often abbreviated to *le foot, le basket,* and *le volley.* This is frequent in spoken French, particularly among students. Note that in Canada, *le football* is referred to as *le soccer, le football américain* as *le football,* and *le basket-ball* as *le ballon-panier.*

Fiche pratique

Some French verbs require a preposition. For example, the verb **jouer** is followed by the preposition **à** or the preposition **de**, plus the definite article. To remember that **jouer** is followed by **à** for sports and games, and by **de** for musical instruments, memorize a couple of sentences that are personally meaningful. For example, you might come up with: **Je joue au foot** and **Mon frère joue de la guitare**.

DES LOISIRS

On fait… du sport de la natation, du vélo, du jogging, de la gym	On joue… au football, au basket-ball, au tennis, au golf, au football américain, au rugby, au volley-ball, au hockey
On fait… de la musique	On joue… du piano, de la guitare, de l'harmonica, du saxophone, de la batterie de la musique classique, du jazz, du rock
On fait… des courses, la cuisine, du bricolage, du jardinage	On joue… aux cartes, aux échecs, au Scrabble, au loto, aux jeux de société

02-18 to 02-21

À vous la parole

2-13 On joue ? Based on the drawings, what is everyone doing this afternoon?

Implementation: 2-13 Show the visual cues for this exercise (MFL, Instructor's Resources).

MODÈLE • On joue au tennis.

1\.

On joue au basket(-ball).

2\.

On joue au golf.

3\.

On joue au foot(-ball).

4\.

On joue aux échecs.

5\.

On joue du piano.

6\.

On joue de la guitare.

7\.

On joue aux cartes.

8\.

On joue au football américain.

2-14 Chacun à son goût. Based on the descriptions, figure out with a partner what these friends probably do in their spare time.

MODÈLE É1 Margaux est très réservée.
É2 Elle ne fait pas grand-chose ; elle reste à la maison et regarde un film.

Answers may vary.

1. Charlotte est très sociable. Elle organise une fête.
2. Loïc est super sportif. Il joue au foot/au basket/au golf/au tennis.
3. Delphine est une bonne musicienne. Elle fait de la musique./Elle joue du piano/de la guitare…
4. Florian adore le cinéma. Il regarde un film.
5. Laurent est fanatique de jazz. Il fait de la musique./Il joue du saxophone./Il écoute de la musique.
6. Céline aime préparer le dîner. Elle fait des courses./Elle fait la cuisine.
7. Alex préfère les jeux de société. Il joue au Scrabble/aux jeux de société.
8. Rachid est très actif. Il fait du sport./Il fait du jogging.
9. Anaïs est bricoleuse. Elle fait du bricolage.

Implementation: All information is adapted from the 2010 edition of ***Francoscopie*** by Gérard Mermet and statistical data from a 2003 INSEE survey on the practice of sporting and cultural activities by those age 15 and older. Point out that *musculation* is related to the English word "muscles" and refers to strength training, and note that *gymnastique* in French may refer to gymnastics but also refers to any type of physical exercises or stretching. Help students figure out the meaning of *faire de la marche*, which means to walk for exercise. This expression is presented in the **Formes et fonctions** of this lesson.

Vie et culture

Les loisirs des Français

The French devote more than one-third of their waking hours to leisure activities, about seven hours per day on average. They now enjoy the shortest workweek of any European country, 35 hours, and have five weeks of paid vacation each year. Typically, about twenty percent of the total household budget is used for leisure activities.

The chart indicates the percentage of French people who participated in various leisure time activities at least once in the course of a year. Examine the chart with a partner: How many activities can you identify? How do these activities compare with your own leisure activities and those of the people you know? How do you think a chart drawn up for North Americans would differ from this one?

Additional practice: Use the following activity to carry out a classroom poll about leisure activities. Divide students into groups to make the data collection easier and allow more students the opportunity to participate. You may wish to postpone this activity until you have presented the conjugated forms of the verb *faire* in **Formes et fonctions** 2 of this lesson to allow students to report back sentences such as *Cinq étudiants font du vélo.*

Un sondage. Poll your classmates to find out what percentage participate in each of the activities included in the chart in the **Vie et culture**. Designate one student in your group to ask the questions, and another to keep track of responses on the board. Compare your percentages with those presented for the French. What are your conclusions?

1. Posez des questions.

   MODÈLE • Qui fait du vélo ? (*raise your hand if you do*)
   • Qui joue d'un instrument de musique ? (*raise your hand if you do*)

2. Comptez les réponses.
3. Annoncez les résultats.

   MODÈLE • Quatre étudiants font du vélo ; c'est 40 pour cent (*if your group has 10 members*). Deux étudiants jouent du piano ; c'est 20 pour cent.

Une année de loisirs

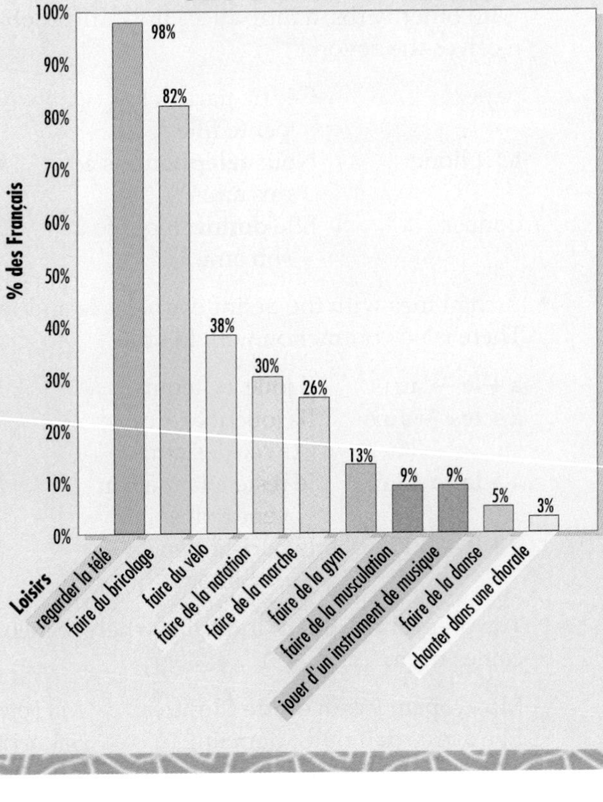

 **2-15 Et toi ?** With the person sitting beside you, take turns telling three things you typically do on the weekend. Use only words and expressions that you know. Then share with your classmates what you have learned about your partner.

MODÈLE É1 Le week-end, je travaille un peu, je joue au basket et je fais la cuisine. Et toi ?
É2 Je ne fais pas grand-chose ; je reste à la maison et je prépare mes cours.

Presentation: To present this topic inductively, use examples with *jouer à, jouer de,* and *faire*. For example: *J'aime le tennis. Je joue au tennis. Ma mère adore la natation. Elle fait de la natation le lundi et le mercredi. Mon père aime bien le golf. Il joue au golf le week-end. Ma sœur adore la musique, surtout la guitare. Elle joue de la guitare dans un groupe.* Using sentences with the definite article in the presentation allows students to discover that *à* and *de* form contractions with the definite articles *le, la,* and *les*. After providing numerous examples, both orally and in written form, ask students whether they can explain the rules, and display a simple graphic with the contractions as illustrated here.

Presentation: Point out that French and English differ with regard to the types of objects used with verbs: *téléphoner à* (+ indirect object) vs. *écouter* (+ direct object). You might also want to contrast *parler à* and *parler de*.

FORMES ET FONCTIONS

1. Les prépositions *à* et *de*

- The preposition **à** generally indicates location or destination and has several English equivalents.

Elle habite **à** Paris.	*She lives* **in** *Paris.*
Il est **à** la maison.	*He's* **at** *the house.*
Elle va **à** un concert.	*She's going* **to** *a concert.*

As you've seen, the preposition **à** is also used in the expression **jouer à**, *to play sports or games.*

Nous jouons **au** tennis le lundi.	*We play tennis on Mondays.*
Ils jouent **aux** cartes le samedi soir.	*They play cards on Saturday evenings.*

With other verbs, **à** introduces the indirect object, usually a person who receives the action.

parler	Cédric **parle à** la petite fille.	*Cédric's speaking to the little girl.*
téléphoner	Nous **téléphonons à** nos amis.	*We're phoning our friends.*
donner	Elle **donne** la photo **à** son ami.	*She gives her boyfriend the photo.*

- **À** combines with the definite articles **le** and **les** to form contractions. There is no contraction with **la** or **l'**.

à + le → au	Il joue **au** tennis.	*He plays tennis.*
à + les → aux	Ils jouent **aux** cartes avec des amis.	*They play cards with friends.*
à + la → à la	Je reste **à la** maison vendredi soir.	*I'm staying home on Friday evening.*
à + l' → à l'	Je parle **à l'**oncle de Simon.	*I'm talking to Simon's uncle.*

Fiche pratique

Note that although one meaning of the preposition **à** is "at": **Je travaille à la bibliothèque**, French has a special preposition to indicate "at home" or "at the home of." You have already learned this preposition, **chez : Je suis chez moi. Le dimanche, elle déjeune chez ses parents**.

- The preposition **de/d'** indicates where someone or something comes from.

Mon copain Justin est **de** Montréal.	*My boyfriend Justin is from Montreal.*
Elle arrive **de** France demain.	*She arrives from France tomorrow.*

As you've seen, **de** is also used in the expression **jouer de,** *to play music or a musical instrument* and in many expressions with the verb **faire**.

Son ami joue **du** piano dans un groupe.	*Her friend plays piano in a group.*
Lui, il joue **de l'**harmonica.	*He plays the harmonica.*
Je fais **des** courses l'après-midi.	*I'm running errands in the afternoon.*

De/d' also is used to indicate possession or other close relationships.

C'est le frère **du** professeur.	*He's the teacher's brother.*
Voilà le livre **de** Kelly.	*There's Kelly's book.*

- **De** combines with the definite articles **le** and **les** to form contractions. There is no contraction with **la** or **l'**.

de + le → du	Mon amie fait **du** jogging.	*My girlfriend goes jogging.*
de + les → des	On parle **des** projets pour le week-end.	*We're talking about plans for the weekend.*
de + la → de la	Moi, je joue **de la** guitare.	*I play the guitar.*
de + l' → de l'	Il joue **de l'**accordéon.	*He plays the accordion.*

À vous la parole

-22 to -25

2-16 Ça cause. Tell what today's subjects of conversation are for Camille and her friends.

Initial practice: Begin practice with simple substitution drills: *Il joue au foot ; loto. —Il joue au loto ; échecs ; basket ; cartes ; tennis ; jeux de société,* etc. ; *Je joue du piano ; guitare. —Je joue de la guitare ; batterie ; harmonica ; saxophone ; musique classique ; jazz,* etc.

MODÈLE la copine de Bruno
- Elles parlent de la copine de Bruno.

1. le professeur de français ...du professeur de français
2. le match de basket le week-end dernier (*last*) ...du match de basket le week-end dernier
3. les problèmes du campus ...des problèmes du campus
4. la nouvelle (*new*) colocataire de Camille ...de la nouvelle colocataire de Camille
5. l'oncle d'Antoine ...de l'oncle d'Antoine
6. les devoirs d'anglais ...des devoirs d'anglais
7. le concert samedi soir ...du concert samedi soir

2-17 Des célébrités. What do these famous people do?

2-17 Variation: Have students suggest other famous athletes and musicians.

MODÈLE LeBron James *Answers may vary.*
- Il joue au basket-ball.

1. Taylor Swift Elle joue de la guitare./Elle chante.
2. Lance Armstrong Il fait du vélo.
3. David Beckham Il joue au foot.
4. Paula Dean Elle fait la cuisine.
5. Serena Williams Elle joue au tennis.
6. Alicia Keys Elle joue du piano./Elle chante.
7. John Coltrane Il joue du saxophone.
8. Michelle Wie Elle joue au golf.

Implementation: 2-18 Use as a mixing activity; impose a time limit, then have students ask questions to get missing information: *Qui joue de l'harmonica ?* Ask follow-up questions: *Tu joues dans un groupe ?*, etc.

2-18 Trouvez une personne qui... Circulate in the classroom to find someone who does each of the things listed. You may have to speak to several people in each instance, so keep moving! When your instructor calls time, compare notes to see who came closest to completing the list.

MODÈLE joue de l'harmonica

É1 Est-ce que tu joues de l'harmonica ?
É2 Non. (*Ask another person the same question.*)
OU Oui. (*You write down this person's name and move on to the next question.*)

1. fait du vélo
2. fait de la natation
3. est d'une grande ville, par exemple de Chicago ou de New York
4. joue au golf le week-end
5. joue du piano
6. téléphone à ses parents le week-end
7. parle au professeur en français
8. joue du saxophone
9. joue souvent (*often*) aux cartes
10. fait du jardinage

Presentation: Present the verb inductively through a short narrative: *Le week-end, je fais des courses et je fais du jardinage. Mon mari/Ma femme fait du bricolage ; les enfants font du sport, etc. Et vous, vous faites du sport ?* Ask students to summarize the forms, and display the verb chart, re-modeling pronunciation. Remind students of where they have seen this verb before: in arithmetic problems and the question, *Qu'est-ce qu'il fait ?*, as well as in the lexical items taught in the **Points de départ.**

2. Le verbe *faire*

- The verb **faire** (*to make, to do*) is used in a wide variety of expressions. Here are the forms of this irregular verb.

FAIRE *to make, to do*

SINGULIER		PLURIEL	
je	fais	nous	**faisons**
tu	fais	vous	**faites**
il / elle / on	fait	ils / elles	**font**

- A question using **faire** does not necessarily require **faire** in the answer.

—Qu'est-ce que tu **fais** samedi ? *—What are you doing on Saturday?*
—Je joue au golf. *—I'm playing golf.*

- As you have learned, a form of the preposition **de** is used with the verb **faire** in some expressions.

—Elle fait **du** sport. *—She plays sports.*
—Moi aussi, je fais **de la** natation. *—Me too, I swim.*

- **Faire** is used in many idiomatic expressions related to everyday activities; it is one of the most common and useful French verbs.

Tu fais de la gym ?	*Do you work out?*
Nous faisons une promenade.	*We're taking a walk.*
On fait de la marche.	*We walk (for exercise).*
Elle aime faire la cuisine.	*She likes to cook.*
Il fait des courses.	*He's running errands.*
Ils font du jogging le matin.	*They jog in the morning.*
Vous faites de la danse ?	*Do you study dance?*
Je fais du français.	*I study French.*

Note: The expressions *faire une promenade* and *faire de la marche* can both be translated into English as "to take a walk," however, the nuances are quite different; *une promenade* is a leisurely walk or stroll, whereas *la marche* refers to vigorous walking, such as for exercise.

Ils font une promenade le dimanche après-midi. Est-ce que vous faites une promenade le week-end ?

À vous la parole

2-26 to 2-30

2-19 Suite logique. Based on their interests, what are these people doing in their spare time? *Answers may vary.*

MODÈLE Sylvie aime le ballet.
- Elle fait de la danse.

1. Nous arrivons au supermarché. Nous faisons des courses.
2. Florent et Hamid aiment la nature. Ils font une promenade./Ils font de la marche.
3. Tu adores préparer le dîner. Tu fais la cuisine.
4. Vous êtes fanatique de jazz. Vous faites de la musique.
5. Ludovic aime travailler dans le jardin. Il fait du jardinage.
6. Hélène et Béa sont vraiment sportives. Elles font du jogging./Elles font du sport.
7. J'aime travailler à la maison. Je fais du bricolage.
8. David et moi sommes très paresseux. Nous ne faisons pas grand-chose.

Initial practice: Begin with a discrimination drill: one person, or more than one? *Elle fait des courses. Ils font une promenade. Il fait de l'anglais. Elles font du français. Elles font la cuisine. Elle fait du vélo. Ils font du jogging. Il fait du sport. Elles font de la musique*, etc. Follow up with a simple substitution drill: *Je fais du foot ; vous ; toi ; eux*, etc.

Implementation: 2-20 Point out the use of *pas de* in negative expressions, as shown in the model. Have students report back what they found out from their partner. Compare answers for all class members. As an additional exercise, put up a frequency scale and let students indicate how often they do the things you ask about.

Implementation: *Avant de regarder.* Do not provide answers for the previewing activity; instead, let students make guesses and see whether they are confirmed by the clip. This activity is based on the first three interviews in the clip; two additional interviews are treated in the SAM/MFL.

Script: *Observons* Note that the elements in brackets reflect standard usage and have been added to the written transcripts. They were not pronounced by the speaker(s) in question.

HERVÉ-THOMAS : Je suis professeur de littérature et d'histoire de France, mais j'aime aussi le sport. Je fais beaucoup de sport : je joue beaucoup au tennis. Euh, en général, je joue au tennis le lundi, le mercredi et le samedi.

CAROLINE : En dehors de l'école on a un emploi de [du] temps très chargé, exemple : le mercredi,…j'ai une heure et demie de piano…

CATHERINE : Et moi, c'est le lundi.

CAROLINE : Le vendredi, on a deux heures d'athlétisme…et voici nos maillots. On en est fières.

CATHERINE : Très fières.

CAROLINE : Le samedi, on fait une heure et demie de danse. Voici les…chaussons de danse…les pointes.

CATHERINE : Et le dimanche, moi, je fais du tennis avec mon grand-père quand je peux. Parce que des fois il pleut, mais la plupart du temps je fais avec lui.

FADOUA : Donc je fais [de] la danse orientale à la faculté de Nice. Donc on…nous avons un gymnase où on peut faire [de] la danse ; nous avons un professeur qui est d'origine algérienne. Elle s'appelle Yamina. En fait j'aime bien faire [de] la danse orientale parce que ça me permet d'avoir un [une] attache…à mon pays.

2-20 Et vous ? Discuss with a partner your usual activities for each of the categories proposed.

MODÈLE la musique

É1 Je ne fais pas de musique, mais j'ai un iPod et beaucoup de chansons (*songs*) ; j'aime le jazz.

É2 Je fais de la musique ; je joue du piano et de la guitare. J'ai un concert ce week-end.

1. la musique
2. le sport
3. les jeux
4. la cuisine
5. les travaux à la maison

02-55 to 02-57

Observons

2-21 Nos passe-temps.

A. Avant de regarder. In this clip, several speakers describe their sports and cultural activities. Look at the list below of activities they mention; can you guess—in cases where you don't already know—what each of these activities might involve?

l'athlétisme   la danse classique   la danse orientale   le piano   le tennis

As you watch this video segment, look for any clues that might support your guesses about unfamiliar activities.

B. En regardant. Who does which activities? Each speaker is listed in order; fill in the activities each person mentions.

personne	activité/s	jour/s
Hervé-Thomas	*tennis*	le lundi, le mercredi, le samedi
Caroline	1. piano	le mercredi
	2. athlétisme	le vendredi
	3. danse	le samedi
Catherine (sa sœur)	1. piano	le lundi
	2. athlétisme	le vendredi
	3. danse	le samedi
	4. tennis	le dimanche
Fadoua	danse orientale	le lundi

Several of the speakers specify the days on which they participate in various activities; listen again and note those days on the chart.

C. Après avoir regardé. What is your impression of the types and number of activities in which these speakers are involved? How do their habits compare with your own habits and those of your family and friends?

Leçon 3 Où est-ce qu'on va ce week-end ?

POINTS DE DÉPART

Presentation: Present the vocabulary showing the labeled drawing of the small town (MFL, Instructor's Resources); play the recording, read aloud, or paraphrase the **Points de départ** text. Have students help describe in simple terms activities at each location, using *-er* verbs they know. Check comprehension by having students point to the places you name or describe. Have students repeat key words (as you point to the drawing): *C'est la librairie ou la bibliothèque ? —C'est la librairie.* The Ch. 6 **Observons** video segment (*Visitons Seillans*) features a visit to a small town; play this sequence without sound to allow students to see what a small town in France looks like. Point out that the verbs *manger* and *nager* have a spelling peculiarity in the first-person plural, reflecting the pronunciation: *nous mangeons, nous nageons.*

Destinations diverses

Le week-end, qu'est-ce que tu fais ? Tu aimes nager ? Alors tu vas probablement à la piscine. Tu pratiques un autre sport ? Alors tu vas peut-être au stade, au gymnase ou au parc. Tu aimes les activités culturelles ? Tu vas peut-être voir un film au cinéma ou une exposition au musée ; ou bien tu assistes à une pièce ou un ballet au théâtre. Tu cherches un livre ? Voilà la bibliothèque ou bien la librairie. Tu ne fais pas la cuisine ? Alors va au restaurant, au café ou chez des amis pour manger.

Note: Point out to students that the word *église* in French usually refers to a Catholic church; a Protestant church is *un temple.* Jewish people worship in *une synagogue* and Muslims in *une mosquée.*

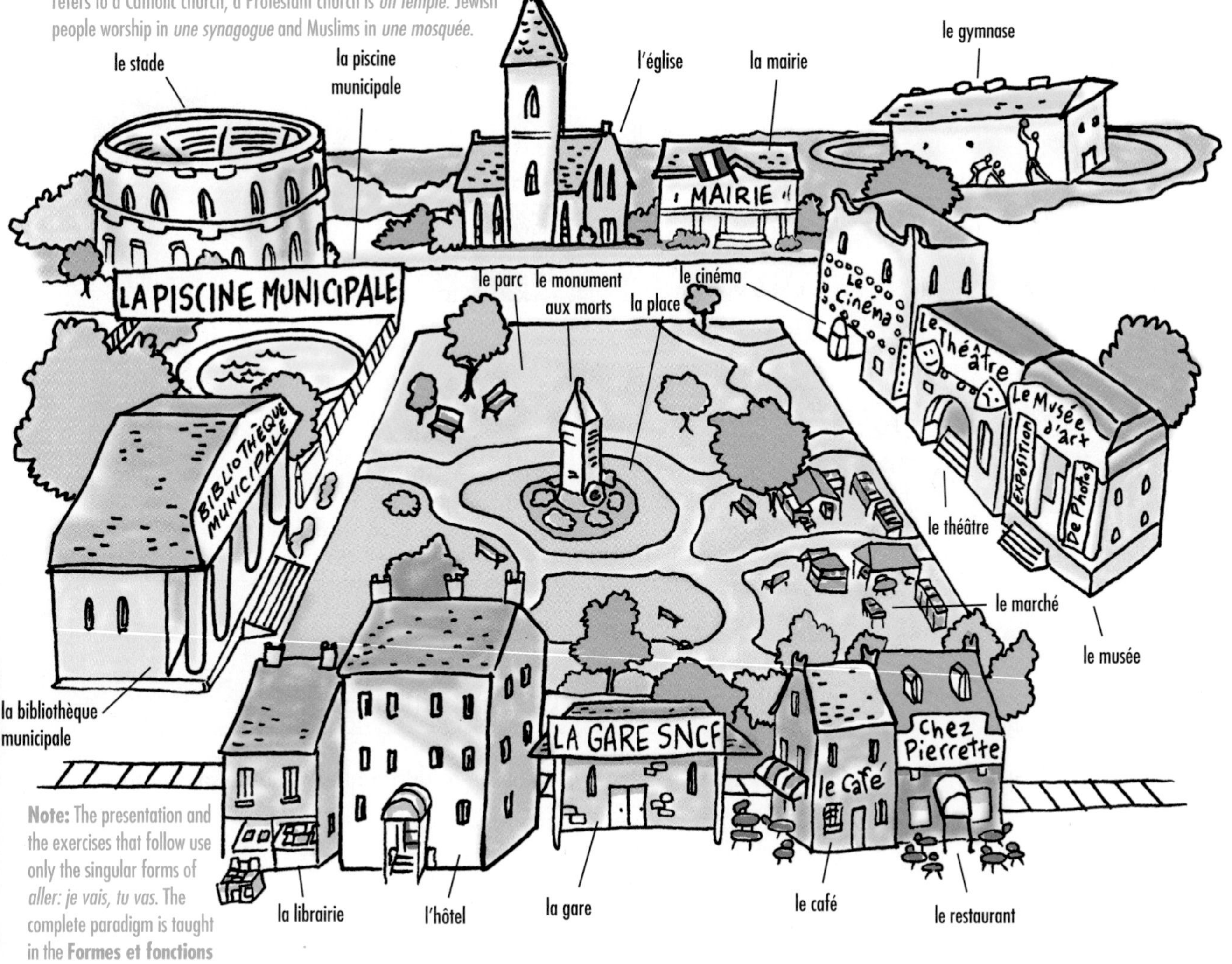

Note: The presentation and the exercises that follow use only the singular forms of *aller: je vais, tu vas.* The complete paradigm is taught in the **Formes et fonctions** section of this lesson.

Vie et culture

Presentation: Help students use cognates and their world knowledge to figure out other locations on the map such as *l'Office de Tourisme* and *la Poste*. To encourage cross-cultural comparisons, ask students how this layout corresponds to the layout of a small town that they may know or have visited. The town of Richelieu, located in the *département d'Indre et Loire*, was built under the direction of the Cardinal Richelieu between 1631 and 1642 by the same architect, Jacques Lemercier, who designed *la Sorbonne* and *le Palais-Royal* in Paris. Cardinal Richelieu was the powerful prime minister to Louis XIII. Point out the symmetry and other unique features of this town.

Les petites villes

Small towns in France have a traditional structure. At the center is the Catholic church; a square, often with a veterans' memorial, is nearby. This is usually the location for the open-air market. The town hall is also in a central location. Older towns and villages often still have small merchants clustered around this central area. In many cases, a train station and a modest hotel are close to the town center. Most communities provide municipal sports centers for their residents. Young people and adults can swim at **la piscine municipale**, play basketball or take an exercise class at a local **gymnase**, or watch soccer games at **le stade municipal**.

Initial practice: Before beginning the exercises, review the preposition *à* using a quick substitution drill: *Il est au café ; piscine. — Il est à la piscine ; stade ; mairie ; théâtre ; église ; gare ; parc,* etc.

02-34 to 02-37

À vous la parole

2-22 Dans quel endroit ? Where would you hear people saying this?

MODÈLE Du rosbif, s'il vous plaît. *Answers may vary.*
- au restaurant

Implementation: 2-22 This exercise can be completed with books closed; have students listen and respond with an appropriate place name as you read each sentence, exaggerating the pronunciation to fit the situation.

1. Tu nages bien, toi ! à la piscine
2. Le match commence dans dix minutes. au stade/au gymnase
3. Regarde, la mariée et le marié arrivent. à la mairie/à l'église

Key: *Et vous ?* In many small towns in the U.S., the county courthouse is located in the center of town and the downtown is arranged around this square. In the east, small towns often include a central green space, referred to as the mall or the commons. In the Midwest, small towns are laid out in a grid. The layout of many towns probably followed the principles of organization that the settlers brought with them from their home countries. For example, towns in the original thirteen colonies tend to resemble towns in England.

Look at the map and corresponding photo of the town of Richelieu, population 1,971. Locate the following places: **l'église, la mairie, la bibliothèque, le parc, le musée, le cinéma, la piscine, la Place du Marché**. What other places indicated on the map can you identify?

ET VOUS ?

1. Is there a traditional structure for small towns in North America? Does this vary from region to region? Why do you think North American towns tended to evolve as they did? Compare your ideas with those of a partner.
2. What basic similarities and differences can you identify in the layout of traditional town centers in North America and France? How would you explain them?

Ville de Richelieu, vue aérienne. Est-ce que vous pouvez idéntifier la Place du Marché ? le cinéma ? la Place Louis XIII ?

4. C'est mon ballet préféré. au théâtre
5. Où sont les biographies, s'il vous plaît ? à la bibliothèque/à la librairie
6. On regarde la télé ce soir ? à l'hôtel/chez un ami/à la maison
7. La musique est excellente ce soir. au théâtre/au parc
8. Encore un café ? au café/au restaurant/chez un ami
9. J'aime beaucoup cette statue. au musée/au parc
10. C'est combien pour ces deux livres et un cahier ? à la librairie

2-23 Votre itinéraire. With your partner, take turns telling where you're going and what you're doing this weekend. Then summarize your plans for your classmates.

MODÈLE É1 Ce week-end, je vais au restaurant. Mon copain et moi, nous dînons ensemble. Et toi ?
É2 Moi, je vais au musée. Il y a une exposition de photos.

2-24 Vos endroits préférés. Discuss with a partner your favorite place for each activity listed. How similar—or dissimilar—are your preferences?

MODÈLE pour dîner ?
É1 Moi, j'aime dîner chez ma mère. Et toi ?
É2 Moi, j'aime dîner au restaurant.

1. pour dîner ?
2. pour travailler ?
3. pour voir un film ?
4. pour discuter avec des amis ?
5. pour pratiquer un sport ?
6. pour écouter de la musique ?

FORMES ET FONCTIONS

1. Le verbe *aller* et le futur proche

Presentation: To present this verb inductively, provide a personal narrative and ask students questions about where they go: *Le week-end, je fais beaucoup de choses. Le matin, je vais au marché et après au café. L'après-midi, je vais au stade pour regarder un match de foot et quelquefois à la piscine pour nager. Et samedi soir, je vais souvent au ciné ; et vous ? Vous allez au marché ? au café ? au stade ? à la bibliothèque ? Et le soir ?,* etc. Have students summarize forms and display forms and sample sentences. You may wish to present the verb *aller* in its simple construction first and then present its use in the *futur proche* later in the day's lesson or on the next day.

- The irregular verb **aller** means *to go.*

Je **vais** à la librairie.	*I'm going to the bookstore.*
Tu **vas** au ciné avec nous ?	*You're going to the movies with us?*

- You have already used **aller** in greetings and commands.

Comment ça **va** ?	*How are things?*
Comment **allez**-vous ?	*How are you?*
Allez au tableau !	*Go to the board!*

ALLER ***to go***

SINGULIER		PLURIEL	
je	**vais**	nous‿**allons**	
tu	**vas**	vous‿**allez**	
il / elle / on	**va**	ils / elles	**vont**

Presentation: To introduce the *futur proche*, tell students what you are going to do this afternoon, this evening, or this weekend. Ask them if you are speaking about the past, the present, or the future; then have them identify the forms that are used to express the notion of future, and ask them to explain how it is formed in French.

- To express future actions that are intended or certain to take place, use the present tense of **aller** and an infinitive. This construction is called **le futur proche** (*the immediate future*). In negative sentences, place **ne… pas** around the form of **aller**; the infinitive does not change.

Je **vais travailler** ce soir.	*I'm going to work this evening.*
Il **va téléphoner** à son père.	*He's going to call his father.*
Tu **ne vas pas danser** ?	*You're not going to dance?*

- To express a future action you may also simply use the present tense of a verb and an adverb referring to the future.

Mon copain arrive **demain**.	*My friend arrives tomorrow.*
Tu joues **ce soir** ?	*Are you playing tonight?*

Here are some useful expressions referring to the immediate future:

ce soir	*tonight*
demain	*tomorrow*
ce week-end	*this weekend*
bientôt	*soon*
la semaine prochaine	*next week*
le mois prochain	*next month*
l'été prochain	*next summer*
l'année prochaine	*next year*

Presentation: Present these expressions by asking students to provide relevant examples for each, based on the actual date. For example, if you present this on Tuesday, October 3, for *ce soir* you could write *mardi 3 octobre à 18 heures ; demain* would be *mercredi 4 octobre*, and so forth.

Note: Ex. 2-25 is a comprehension-based activity focusing on the difference in the use of *aller* to express the present and the *futur proche*. It should be used as the initial exercise after presenting the use of *aller* in the *futur proche* construction, whether this is day 2 of your lesson or during the same day *aller* is presented. The marginal note, **Initial practice**, provides activities to begin practice after the present-tense forms of *aller* have been presented. Ex. 2-26 practices the present tense of *aller*, and 2-27 targets the *futur proche*. The additional activity, **Quoi faire ?** suggested in the marginal notes may be used after 2-25 or 2-26 to prepare students for 2-27.

À vous la parole

-38 to -42

2-25 Maintenant ou plus tard ? Look at these statements about the activities of Sévérine, Yann, and their friends and decide if each activity is occurring now (**maintenant**) or will occur later (**plus tard**).

	Maintenant, ils	Plus tard, ils
MODÈLE …vont à la bibliothèque.	✓	
1. …vont nager un peu.		✓
2. …vont manger.		✓
3. …vont au gymnase.	✓	
4. …vont au cinéma.	✓	
5. …vont travailler toute la journée (*all day*)		✓
6. …vont faire du jogging.		✓
7. …vont au parc.	✓	
8. …vont voir un film.		✓

Based on your answers, are the friends busier now, or will they be busier later?

2-26 Où aller ? Based on their interests, where are these people probably going? *Answers may vary.*

MODÈLE Anne adore nager.
- Elle va à la piscine.

1. Rémi aime le basket. Il va au gymnase.
2. Nous aimons les films. Nous allons au cinéma.
3. Tu désires manger des spaghettis. Tu vas au restaurant.
4. M. et Mme Dupont aiment l'art moderne. Ils vont au musée.
5. Vous adorez les concerts de jazz. Vous allez au stade/au parc.
6. Sandrine aime les livres historiques. Elle va à la bibliothèque/à la librairie.
7. J'aime beaucoup parler avec mes amis. Je vais au café/chez un/e ami/e.
8. Sophie et Angélique adorent faire de la marche le matin. Elles vont au parc/au stade.

Initial practice: Practice forms of *aller* with a discrimination drill: one person, or more than one? *Il va au ciné. Elles vont chez elles. Elles vont à la bibliothèque. Ils vont à l'hôtel. Il va au parc. Elle va au gymnase. Ils vont au théâtre. Elles vont au restaurant*, etc. Follow with a substitution drill: *Je vais bien ; vous. —Vous allez bien*, etc., and then complete exercise 2-26 to practice *aller* in the present tense.

Additional practice: Use this simple exercise after 2-25 or 2-26. Here students repeat the subject and the verb and add an infinitive to practice the *futur proche*. **Quoi faire ?** Based on where they're going, tell what these people are going to do.

MODÈLE Je vais à la bibliothèque.
Je vais travailler.

1. Nous allons à la piscine.
2. Tu vas au stade ?
3. Elles vont au restaurant.
4. Vous allez à la résidence.
5. Christine va au ciné.
6. Je vais au bureau du professeur.
7. Marc va au gymnase.
8. Jean et Louise vont au musée.

Implementation: 2-27 As time permits, this activity can either be used as an extended interview, or you may limit it to one or two items for students to discuss, then report back to the class as a whole.

2-27 Vos projets. Interview a partner about his/her plans, and report back to the class what you have found out.

MODÈLE cet après-midi

É1 Qu'est-ce que tu vas faire cet après-midi ?
É2 Cet après-midi je vais travailler. Et toi ?
É1 Mon camarade et moi, on va jouer au tennis.

1. cet après-midi
2. ce soir
3. demain
4. ce week-end
5. le semestre/trimestre prochain
6. l'été prochain
7. l'année prochaine

Presentation: To present, review by having students carry out classroom commands, using first the *vous* form; next, call on students individually and use the *tu* form. Have students explain the difference in the two forms. Display examples of the imperative forms, and point out the written forms.

Note: The imperative forms for *être* and *avoir* are irregular and relatively infrequent. We suggest not presenting these forms here; students will see them used with expressions of emotion in Ch. 7, L. 3 and when the subjunctive of irregular verbs is presented in Ch. 9, L. 3.

Note: Although the *nous* form of the imperative is used to make a suggestion for a group of which one is a member, this is a rather direct and infrequent way to do so in spoken French. For example, *On y va ?* is used more than *Allons-y !* Likewise, French speakers would tend to say: *Alors, on joue aux cartes ?* or *Si on jouait aux cartes ?* instead of *Jouons aux cartes.* The use of the imperfect to make a suggestion is treated in Ch. 6, L. 3.

Initial practice: Begin practice with a discrimination drill: have students decide whether they hear a command to one person or to a group: *Ferme la porte ! Parlez français ! Écoutez le professeur ! Travaille plus ! Va à la bibliothèque ! Mangez à la cafétéria ! Ne parlez pas anglais ! Écrivez le devoir en français !*, etc. Follow with a substitution drills, singular to plural: *Va au bureau ! —Allez au bureau !* In another simple exercise, have students associate verbs in the command form with nouns: *la fenêtre ? —Fermez la fenêtre ! Ouvrez la fenêtre !*

2. L'impératif

- To make a suggestion or a request, or to tell someone to do something, the *imperative* forms of a verb—without subject pronouns—may be used.

  To address someone with whom you are on informal terms, the imperative is the same as the **tu** form of the verb in the present tense. Note, however, that for **-er** verbs (including **aller**), the final **-s** is dropped in the written forms.

Ferme la porte !	*Shut the door!*
Va au tableau !	*Go to the blackboard!*
Écris ton nom !	*Write your name!*
Fais tes devoirs !	*Do your homework!*

  To address more than one person or someone with whom you are on formal terms, the imperative is the same as the **vous** form of the verb in the present tense.

Parlez plus fort !	*Speak louder!*
Écoutez-moi !	*Listen to me!*
Lisez à haute voix !	*Read aloud!*
Dites-moi votre nom !	*Tell me your name!*

  To make a suggestion to a group of which you are part, the imperative is the same as the **nous** form of the verb in the present tense.

Jouons aux cartes.	*Let's play cards.*
Allons au cinéma.	*Let's go to the movies.*
Faisons une promenade.	*Let's go for a walk.*

- To be more polite, add **s'il te plaît** or **s'il vous plaît** as appropriate:

Ouvrez la fenêtre, **s'il vous plaît**.	*Open the window, please.*
Parle plus fort, **s'il te plaît**.	*Please speak louder.*

- To tell someone not to do something, put **ne** (**n'**) before the verb and **pas** after it:

Ne regarde **pas** la télé !	*Don't watch TV!*
N'écris **pas** en anglais !	*Don't write in English!*
N'oubliez **pas** vos devoirs !	*Don't forget your homework!*

À vous la parole

-43 :o -46

2-28 Impératifs. Use appropriate forms of the imperative to make requests to your friends and your instructor.

MODÈLE Dites à un/e ami/e de ne pas regarder la télé.
- Ne regarde pas la télé !

Dites à un/e ami/e…

1. d'écouter le professeur Écoute le professeur !
2. de fermer la porte Ferme la porte !
3. de ne pas parler anglais Ne parle pas anglais !
4. de ne pas manger en classe Ne mange pas en classe !

Demandez à votre professeur (n'oubliez pas d'être poli/e !)…

5. de répéter Répétez s'il vous plaît !
6. de parler plus fort Parlez plus fort s'il vous plaît !
7. de ne pas fermer la porte Ne fermez pas la porte s'il vous plaît !
8. de ne pas lire en anglais Ne lisez pas en anglais s'il vous plaît !

Proposez à vos amis…

9. de jouer au basket Jouons au basket.
10. de faire du jogging Faisons du jogging.

2-29 Pourquoi pas ? You'd like to do something different in French class today. What can you suggest to your instructor? Choose from this list of possibilities and include some of your own ideas as well: **aller**, **écouter**, **écrire**, **faire**, **jouer**, **oublier**, **parler**, **regarder**. *Answers may vary.*

MODÈLE écrire
- Écrivons un poème.

Allons au café/au cinéma. Écoutons de la musique française. Faisons de la natation. Jouons au Scrabble. Oublions l'examen. Parlons en anglais. Regardons un film/la télé.

Implementation: 2-29 Students can first work in pairs to come up with ideas. Variations: give advice to a fellow student who wants to improve his/her grade; give advice to someone who wants to relax over the weekend.

2-30 Situations. With a partner, give examples of a request or suggestion you'd be likely to hear in each situation. How many examples can you come up with? *Answers may vary.*

MODÈLE une mère à son enfant
- Écoute, mon chéri (*dear*).
- Fais tes devoirs.

1. un professeur aux étudiants Faites vos devoirs !
2. une étudiante à un/e ami/e Allons au cinéma. / Faisons des courses.
3. un étudiant au professeur Répétez, s'il vous plaît ! / Parlez plus fort s'il vous plaît !
4. un étudiant à son copain Allons au café. /Jouons au basket.
5. un entraîneur (*coach*) de basket à ses joueurs Allez ! Travaillez plus !
6. votre professeur, à vous Répétez s'il vous plaît ! / Répondez en français s'il vous plaît !
7. vos parents, à vous Travaille bien ! / N'oublie pas tes devoirs ! / Téléphone à tes grands-parents !

Variation: 2-30 As a fun variation, sit down in a chair facing your class. Tell students that they should give you commands. Students enjoy turning the tables and having the teacher do the things that they are frequently asked to do.

Préparation: Preview this activity by finding out what sports events in the Francophone world and which Francophone athletes students are already familiar with—have any of them watched the World Cup, the French Open (*le Roland-Garros*), or the *Tour de France*, have they heard of Zinédine Zidane, do they know that Tony Parker of the San Antonio Spurs is French? Show the video montage (*Vive le sport !*); have students identify the various sports being practiced in this fast-paced segment.

Script: *Écoutons* Thierry Henry joue au football pour l'équipe de France et l'équipe de Red Bulls à New York. Il est né à Paris en 1977. Sa famille vient des Antilles, sa mère est de Martinique et son père est de Guadeloupe. Il est mince et assez grand. Il est intelligent, ambitieux et très rapide. Quand il ne joue pas au football, il aime regarder le basket. Il est divorcé et il a une fille qui s'appelle Téa.

Sandrine Gruda est une Française qui joue au basket en WNBA. Elle est née en 1987 à la Martinique. Elle est brune et très grande. Sandrine est très sportive. Elle aime regarder les matchs de tennis et de foot et aussi les compétitions de natation. Son père a joué au basket pour l'équipe de France.

Guillaume Latendresse joue au hockey pour l'équipe de Minnesota. C'est un jeune joueur québécois ; il est né le 24 mai 1987 à Sainte-Catherine au Québec. Il est blond, grand, musclé et très fort. Il est motivé et sérieux. Il aime beaucoup jouer au hockey et passer du temps avec sa famille. Son frère aîné, qui s'appelle Oliver, joue au hockey aussi.

Écoutons

2-31 Des portraits d'athlètes.

A. Avant d'écouter. Look at the photos of three Francophone athletes. Which sport does each play? Can you think of two or three adjectives to describe each athlete? Have you ever seen any of these athletes in person or on television?

Thierry HENRY

Sandrine GRUDA

Guillaume LATENDRESSE

B. En écoutant. Listen to the descriptions of the three athletes and fill in the missing information in the chart.

Note that birthdates are provided in the age column as this answer will change from year to year. *Answers may vary.*

name	sport	age	appearance	favorite activities and family information
Thierry HENRY	soccer	(1977)	slim, fairly tall, intelligent, ambitious, fast	likes to watch basketball, divorced and has a daughter, Téa
Sandrine GRUDA	basketball	(1987)	very tall, dark hair	likes tennis, soccer, and swimming, father played for France's national basketball team
Guillaume LATENDRESSE	hockey	(1987)	blond, tall, very muscular	playing hockey, spending time with family, brother Oliver plays hockey

C. Après avoir écouté. From Marseille to Madagascar, from Martinique to the Ivory Coast, sports are a unifying element in Francophone life. Throughout the year, people watch their favorite sporting events on television, listen to soccer matches on the radio, and follow their favorite athletes through stories in the Francophone press and on the Internet. Are sports a unifying element in North America, as they are in Francophone countries? Are victories a source of national pride? Are there sports and sporting events in North America whose popularity rivals that of soccer in the Francophone world? If so, which ones? Discuss with a partner.

Les Bleues (l'Équipe de France Féminine de football) fêtent leur victoire le 7 juillet 2011 contre l'Angleterre en quarts de finale de la Coupe du Monde Féminine.

Des supporteurs (*fans*) enthousiastes lors de la victoire historique des Bleues contre l'Angleterre et leur première qualification pour les demi-finales de la Coupe du Monde.

Leçon 

le caractère	*disposition, nature, character*
ambitieux/-euse	*ambitious*
amusant/e	*funny*
bête	*stupid*
drôle	*amusing, funny*
égoïste	*selfish*
énergique	*energetic*
généreux/-euse	*generous, warm-hearted*
gentil/le	*kind, nice*
intelligent/e	*intelligent, smart*
méchant/e	*mean, naughty*
pantouflard/e	*homebody, stay-at-home*
paresseux/-euse	*lazy*
sérieux/-euse	*serious*
sportif/-ive	*athletic*

le physique	*physical traits*
âgé/e	*aged, old*
beau/belle	*handsome, beautiful*
blond/e	*blond/e*
brun/e	*dark-haired, brunette*
châtain	*chestnut colored hair*
de taille moyenne	*of medium height*
d'un certain âge	*middle-aged*
élégant/e	*elegant*
fort/e	*strong, stout*
grand/e	*tall*
gros/se	*fat*
jeune	*young*
joli/e	*pretty*
maigre	*skinny*
mince	*thin, slender*
moche	*ugly*
petit/e	*short, little*
roux/-sse	*redhead, redhaired*

pour poser une question	*to ask a question*
combien de	*how many*
comment	*how*
où	*where*
parce que	*because*
pourquoi	*why*
quand	*when*
qui	*who*

autres mots utiles	*other useful words*
adorer	*to adore, love*
arrête !	*stop it!*
autre	*other, another*
bien sûr	*of course*
un chapeau	*hat*
un/e coloc(ataire)	*roommate*
comme	*like, as*
un copain/une copine	*friend, boyfriend/girlfriend*
donc	*then, therefore, so*
une fac(ulté)	*college, university*
une histoire drôle	*joke*
peut-être	*maybe*
une photo	*photo*
pour	*for, in order to*

Leçon 2

quelques sports (m.)	*some sports*
le basket(-ball)	*basketball*
le football américain	*football*
le *hockey	*hockey*
un match	*game (sports)*
le rugby	*rugby*
le volley(-ball)	*volleyball*

quelques jeux (m.)	*some games*
les cartes (f.)	*cards*
les échecs (m.)	*chess*
un jeu	*game*
un jeu de société	*board game*
le loto	*lottery*

la musique	*music*
le jazz	*jazz*
le rock	*rock*
une batterie	*percussion, drum set*
un concert	*concert*
donner un concert	*to give a concert*
un harmonica	*harmonica*
un saxophone	*saxophone*

d'autres activités	*other activities*
bricoler	*to carry out do-it-yourself projects*
les loisirs (m.)	*leisure-time activities*
organiser une fête	*to plan a party*
rester à la résidence	*to stay in the dorm*

*Some words in French that begin with a silent h behave as if they begin with a pronounced consonant: that is, there is no elision (*le hockey*) or liaison (*les héros*). These words are marked in the glossary with an asterisk.

quelques expressions avec *faire*	*expressions using* faire
faire du bricolage	*to carry out do-it-yourself projects*
faire des courses	*to run errands, to shop*
faire la cuisine	*to cook*
faire de la danse	*to dance, to study dance*
faire du français	*to study French*
faire de la gym	*to work out*
faire du jardinage	*to garden*
faire du jogging	*to go jogging*
faire de la marche	*to walk (for exercise)*
faire de la musique	*to play (make) music*
faire de la natation	*to swim*
faire une promenade	*to take a walk*
faire du sport	*to play sports*
faire du vélo	*to go biking*
ne pas faire grand-chose	*to not do much*

Leçon 3

en ville	*in town*
une bibliothèque (municipale)	*(municipal) library*
un café	*café*
un cinéma	*movie theater*
une église	*(Catholic) church*
une gare	*train station*
un gymnase	*gym*
un hôtel	*hotel*
une librairie	*bookstore*
la mairie	*town hall*
un marché	*market*
un monument aux morts	*veterans' memorial*
un musée	*museum*
un parc	*park*
une piscine (municipale)	*(municipal) swimming pool*
une place	*square (in a town)*
un restaurant	*restaurant*
un stade	*stadium*
un théâtre	*theatre*

activités culturelles	*cultural activities*
assister à…	*to attend . . .*
un ballet	*a ballet*
voir…	*to see . . .*
une exposition	*exhibition*
un film	*film (at a movie theater)*
une pièce	*a play (theater)*

pour parler de l'avenir	*to talk about the future*
aller (Je vais manger.)	*to go (I'm going to eat./ I will eat.)*
l'année (f.) prochaine	*next year*
bientôt	*soon*
ce soir	*tonight*
ce week-end	*this weekend*
demain	*tomorrow*
l'été (m.) prochain	*next summer*
le mois prochain	*next month*
la semaine prochaine	*next week*

autres mots utiles	*other useful words*
alors	*so*
chercher	*to look for*
dites-moi !	*tell me!*
manger	*to eat*
nager	*to swim*
oublier	*to forget*

Vocabulaire

Where are these people and where are they going, in your opinion? How do they seem to be feeling?

3 Métro, boulot, dodo

After completing this chapter, you should be able to:

- ❑ Talk about your daily routine
- ❑ Tell time
- ❑ Describe people, places, and activities
- ❑ Describe clothing
- ❑ Compare daily routines and fashion in places where French is spoken

Leçon 1 La routine de la journée

POINTS DE DÉPART

La routine du matin

Il est huit heures du matin. La journée commence !

Chez les Bouchard, Thomas se réveille ; il va bientôt se lever.

Sa petite sœur Vanessa est déjà debout dans sa chambre ; elle se coiffe. Monsieur Bouchard est en train de se raser. Après, il va prendre un bain.

Madame Bouchard se maquille et elle s'habille pour aller au travail. Le bébé s'endort de nouveau.

Dans son appartement, Caroline se dépêche ; elle va bientôt à la fac. Elle se lave les mains et la figure, et elle se brosse les dents.

Chez les Morin, Madame Morin se douche et se lave les cheveux ; après, elle s'essuie. Son mari rentre à la maison. Lui, il travaille tard la nuit, donc il rentre tôt le matin pour se coucher. Il se déshabille, et il se couche.

Presentation: Use the cross section of the apartment building (MFL, Instructor's Resources) to present the new vocabulary. Describe the activities pictured, using the textbook description as a model. Test comprehension by having students tell who is doing what: *Qui se lave la figure ?*, etc. Have students repeat key phrases using either/or questions (*Il se douche ou il se rase ?*), then mime, or have students mime, activities while others guess what's being done. The verb *prendre* appears in this chapter in the expressions *prendre une douche, prendre le métro, prendre un café*. Treat these as lexical items and do not ask students to conjugate the verb, although you may wish to introduce the form *je prends une douche*. The full conjugation of *prendre* is presented in Ch. 5, L. 1.

Note: Native speakers use the expressions *se doucher/prendre une douche, se laver les dents/se brosser les dents* interchangeably. The only forms practiced here are the third-person singular and the infinitive; the focus is on learning the meaning of the vocabulary. The forms of reflexive verbs are treated in the **Formes et fonctions** for this lesson.

Presentation: Use the video clip *La routine du matin* to help introduce or reinforce some of the new vocabulary; note that it is incorporated in the **Vie et culture** on the following page. Alternatively, the video can serve as an inductive presentation for **Formes et fonctions 1**. Note that in this segment, the two sisters use the form *nous nous levons*, etc., to describe their morning routine.

Vie et culture

Presentation: The SAM/MFL includes further activities to treat this video clip. You may wish to make a slide or a handout of the activities to use in class or assign as homework.

03-52

Métro, boulot, dodo

The expression **métro, boulot, dodo** epitomizes the daily routine of most Parisians. In the morning, many people take the **métro** (the highly efficient Paris subway), go to their **boulot** (a slang word for **un emploi/un travail**), then return home at night and crawl into bed to **faire dodo** (a child's expression for **se coucher/dormir**). In English, we often call this routine *the daily grind*.

What does the expression **métro, boulot, dodo** lead you to believe about life in Paris?

Describe a person whose daily routine could be summarized by this expression. Would this expression apply also to the daily routine of North Americans who live in big cities? Would it apply to life in your hometown?

Now watch the video clip *La routine du matin* as two girls describe their morning routine. Make a list of their activities, for example: **Elles se réveillent**. Is there anything that surprises you about their routine, or does it seem very familiar and logical?

Expansion: As a follow-up, ask students to come up with three words in French to evoke their own daily routine, perhaps words that describe their mornings, days, and evenings, respectively. Provide the following models: *Ma routine, c'est manger, étudier, dormir.* Or: *Ma routine, c'est pizza, télé, bibliothèque !*

Presentation: Bring in items to illustrate toiletries; for example, show toothpaste and shampoo containers with labels in French, and an actual *gant de toilette.* Use the visual of toiletry items (MFL, Instructor's Resources) to present additional items and test comprehension: have students point to items you name, then repeat by identifying items: *C'est un peigne ou une brosse à dents ?* Associate each item with an activity: *avec un rasoir ? — On se rase* ; or, *Qu'est-ce qu'il faut : pour se raser? — un rasoir*, etc.

du maquillage
un savon
un gant de toilette
une brosse à dents
un lavabo
du shampooing
un peigne
une brosse à cheveux
du dentifrice
un rasoir
une serviette de toilette

Les articles de toilette

À vous la parole

03-01 to 03-04

3-1 Ordre logique. In what order do most people complete the following activities? *Answers may vary.*

MODÈLE on se coiffe, on se douche

- On se douche, et après on se coiffe.

Note: Ex. 3-1 to 3-3 can serve as an inductive presentation of pronominal verbs, treated in this lesson. Verbs in *-ir* like *dormir, partir,* and *sortir* are treated in Ch. 3, L. 2.

1. on se lave, on s'habille *On se lave, et après on s'habille.*
2. on se lave les cheveux, on se coiffe *On se lave les cheveux, et après on se coiffe.*
3. on se lève, on se réveille *On se réveille, et après on se lève.*
4. on se déshabille, on se couche *On se déshabille, et après on se couche.*
5. on mange, on se brosse les dents *On mange, et après on se brosse les dents.*
6. on se couche, on se lave les dents *On se lave les dents, et après on se couche.*
7. on se couche, on s'endort *On se couche, et après on s'endort.*
8. on s'essuie, on se lave *On se lave, et après on s'essuie.*

3-2 Suite logique. Tell what these people are going to do next, choosing a verb from the list.

se coiffer	s'essuyer	se laver les cheveux
se coucher	s'habiller	se lever
s'endormir	se laver	se raser

MODÈLE Margaux a un tee-shirt et un jean.
- Elle va s'habiller. *Answers may vary.*

1. Adrien a un rasoir. *Il va se raser.*
2. Olivier va dans sa chambre. *Il va se déshabiller/se coucher/s'endormir.*
3. Julie cherche le shampooing. *Elle va se laver les cheveux.*
4. Fanny est très fatiguée. *Elle va se coucher/s'endormir.*
5. Damien entend sa mère qui dit : « Allez, debout ! C'est l'heure. » *Il va se lever.*
6. Grégory va prendre une douche. *Il va se déshabiller/se laver.*
7. Delphine termine sa douche. *Elle va s'essuyer/ s'habiller.*
8. Sandrine a un peigne. *Elle va se coiffer.*

3-3 Un questionnaire. Do you pay attention to how you look? A little? Too much? Not enough? Ask your partner the following questions and then add up the points. What are your conclusions?

Expansion: 3-3 Follow up by asking how many students are in each of the point ranges.

1.	Vous prenez une douche ou un bain tous les jours ?	**oui**	**non**
2.	Vous vous lavez les cheveux tous les jours ?	**oui**	**non**
3.	Vous vous brossez les dents après chaque repas *(meal)* ?	**oui**	**non**
4.	Vous vous coiffez trois ou quatre fois pendant la journée ?	**oui**	**non**
5.	Vous vous habillez différemment chaque jour ?	**oui**	**non**
6.	Vous vous maquillez/vous vous rasez tous les jours ?	**oui**	**non**
7.	Vous vous mettez du parfum/de l'eau de Cologne ?	**oui**	**non**
8.	Vous faites très attention de ne jamais grossir *(gain weight)* ?	**oui**	**non**

Maintenant, marquez un point pour les réponses « oui », zéro pour les réponses « non » et ensuite additionnez vos points :

- Si vous avez 7 ou 8 points, vous vous intéressez peut-être un peu trop à votre apparence physique. Pensez un peu aux choses plus sérieuses.
- Si vous avez de 3 à 6 points, c'est bien. Vous faites attention à votre présentation, mais vous n'exagérez pas.
- Si vous avez moins de 3 points, attention ! Vous risquez de vous négliger.

Fiche pratique

The reflexive construction is used much more frequently in French than in English. In French, a reflexive verb is always accompanied by a reflexive pronoun. To remember that a verb is used reflexively, memorize its infinitive form along with the reflexive pronoun **se**. For example, learn **se laver** (*to wash oneself*) and **se raser** (*to shave*).

Presentation: Remind students that they have seen reflexive pronouns used with the verb *s'appeler*. Although this presentation does not treat forms of the verbs used reciprocally, you might wish to introduce here the notion of reciprocal pronominal verbs, corresponding to English "each other": *Ils s'embrassent, Ils se téléphonent, Ils se parlent souvent*, etc. Idiomatic pronominal verbs, such as *se fâcher* and *s'entendre* are presented in Ch. 7, L. 3. You may also wish to use the video segment *La routine du matin* as you present this topic.

Presentation: Point out the following irregularities: *lever/lève, essuyer/essuie* (the latter with loss of stem-final /j/). Full conjugations are in Appendix 2.

Presentation: You may wish to delay presentation of the imperative forms and the accompanying Ex. 3-8 until day 2 of the lesson, so students can assimilate and practice verbs with reflexive pronouns before being confronted with the syntactic changes in the imperative.

FORMES ET FONCTIONS

1. Les verbes pronominaux et les pronoms réfléchis

- Verbs like **se laver** (*to wash oneself*) and **s'essuyer** (*to dry oneself off*) include a reflexive pronoun as part of the verb: this pronoun indicates that the action is reflected on the subject. In English, the word *-self* is sometimes used to express this idea.

Je **m'essuie**.	*I'm drying myself off.*
On **se lave**.	*We're washing ourselves.*
Tu **te lèves** ?	*Are you getting up?*

Here are the reflexive pronouns, shown with the verb **se laver**.

SE LAVER ***to wash oneself***

SINGULIER			PLURIEL		
je	**me**	lave	nous	**nous**	lav**ons**
tu	**te**	lave**s**	vous	**vous**	lav**ez**
il / elle / on	**se**	lave	ils / elles	**se**	lav**ent**

- Some verbs may be used both with and without a reflexive pronoun. Compare:

Elle **lave** la figure de sa fille.	*She is washing her daughter's face.*
Elle **se lave** la figure.	*She is washing her (own) face.*

The use of the reflexive pronoun means that the subject is acting upon himself or herself.

- Before a vowel sound, **me**, **te**, and **se** become **m'**, **t'**, **s'**.

Je **m'**essuie les mains.	*I'm drying my hands.*
Tu **t'**habilles ?	*Are you getting dressed?*
Il **s'**essuie la figure.	*He wipes his face.*

- Note that reflexive pronouns always maintain their position near the verb, even in the negative and the immediate future.

Il ne **se** lave pas.	*He's not washing up.*
Je ne vais pas **m'**habiller.	*I'm not going to get dressed.*

- When a part of the body is specified, the definite article is used, since the reflexive pronoun already indicates whose body part is affected.

Elle se lave **la** figure.	*She's washing her face.*
Ils se brossent **les** dents.	*They're brushing their teeth.*

- In an affirmative command, the reflexive pronoun follows the verb and is connected to it by a hyphen. Note the use of the stressed form **toi**. In negative commands, the reflexive pronoun precedes the verb.

Lave-**toi** les mains !	Ne **te** lave pas les mains !
Dépêchez-**vous** !	Ne **vous** dépêchez pas !

À vous la parole

-05
-09

3-4 C'est qui ? Read the sentences below and indicate if the action Mathilde is performing in each case refers to herself (**elle-même**) or to someone else (**quelqu'un d'autre**).

Implementation: 3-4 This comprehension-based activity focuses students' attention on the presence or absence of a reflexive pronoun. Have students discuss the follow-up question to bring the focus back to how form informs meaning and then continue with a substitution drill to practice forms: *Je me lave ; nous. —Nous nous lavons*, etc. Provide additional drills for the negative: *Elle ne se dépêche pas ; moi. —Je ne me dépêche pas*, etc., and *futur proche : Tu vas te coucher ; lui. —Il va se coucher*, etc.

Mathilde est très occupée ce matin. Elle…

	elle-même	quelqu'un d'autre
MODÈLE … s'habille	✓	
1. … se lave	✓	
2. … se coiffe	✓	
3. … réveille son petit frère		✓
4. … coiffe sa sœur		✓
5. … se dépêche	✓	
6. … brosse le chat		✓

Based on your responses, did Mathilde spend more time today on herself or helping others?

3-5 Qu'est-ce qu'on fait ? Explain how people use the objects mentioned. *Answers may vary.*

MODÈLE Moi, le shampooing ?
• Je me lave les cheveux.

1. Les enfants, le savon et un gant de toilette ? Ils se lavent.
2. Jules, son rasoir ? Il se rase.
3. Vous, la serviette de toilette ? Vous vous essuyez.
4. Toi, le pull-over ? Tu t'habilles.
5. Moi, le dentifrice ? Je me lave/me brosse les dents.
6. Nous, le peigne ? Nous nous coiffons./On se coiffe.
7. Julie, le maquillage ? Elle se maquille.

3-6 Fais ta toilette ! Your partner always has an excuse! Take turns asking and answering questions and making comments about grooming.

Initial practice: Begin practice of command forms with simple transformation drills: 1) singular to plural, and vice versa: *Réveille-toi ! —Réveillez-vous !* 2) affirmative to negative, and vice versa: *Réveille-toi ! —Ne te réveille pas !*

MODÈLE se raser
É1 Tu te rases ?
É2 Non, je n'ai pas de rasoir.
É1 Tiens, voilà un rasoir ; rase-toi donc !

Implementation: 3-6 Use objects if possible to make the exercise more realistic.

1. se laver les mains
2. se laver la figure
3. s'essuyer les mains
4. se laver les cheveux
5. se brosser les dents
6. se coiffer

Implementation: 3-7 First go over the questions in the exercise to verify comprehension of key expressions such as *en premier* and *tous les jours*, taught in the next **Formes et fonctions** section.

3-7 La routine chez vous. At your house or in your family, who does the following things? Compare your answers with those of a partner.

MODÈLE se lève en premier ?

É1 Qui se lève en premier chez toi ?
É2 Ma mère se lève en premier. Et chez toi ?
É1 Moi, je me lève en premier.

Additional practice: Ask students to describe three types of days to a partner: *une journée typique, une journée idéale, une journée horrible*. Provide a model such as this one for *une journée typique : Je me lève pour aller à mes cours. Je me lave et je m'habille, et je vais en classe. Après je vais manger. … Et toi ?*

1. se lève en premier ?
2. se douche en premier ?
3. se maquille tous les jours ?
4. s'habille avec beaucoup d'attention ?
5. se lave les cheveux tous les jours ?
6. se couche tard le soir ?
7. s'endort devant la télé ?

2. Les adverbes : intensité, fréquence, quantité

- The adverbs listed below indicate to what degree something occurs.

↑↓		
trop	Elle travaille **trop**.	*She works too much.*
beaucoup	Elle se douche **beaucoup**.	*She showers a lot.*
assez	Nous mangeons **assez**.	*We eat enough.*
un peu	Je me dépêche **un peu**.	*I hurry a little.*
ne… pas	Il **ne** se rase **pas**.	*He doesn't shave.*

- These same adverbs, followed by **de/d'** plus a noun, indicate quantities.

↑↓		
trop de	Il prend **trop de** douches.	*He takes too many showers.*
beaucoup de	Elle a **beaucoup d'**amis.	*She has lots of friends.*
assez de	Vous avez **assez d'**argent ?	*Do you have enough money?*
peu de	J'ai **peu de** maquillage chez moi.	*I don't have much makeup at my house.*
ne… pas de	Tu **n'**as **pas de** rasoir ?	*Don't you have a razor?*

Presentation: Provide examples of longer adverbs at the beginning or end of a sentence: *Tu travailles ici quelquefois ? Normalement il travaille chez lui.*

- Other adverbs indicate frequency, how often something is done. Notice that these adverbs generally follow the verb, like those you learned in the first section above. Longer adverbial expressions can be placed at the end or the beginning of a sentence.

↑↓		
tous les…	Je me lave les cheveux **tous les** jours.	*I wash my hair every day.*
toutes les…	**Toutes les** semaines, nous avons un match.	*Every week, we have a game.*
toujours	Je me lève **toujours** en premier.	*I always get up first.*
souvent	Il prend **souvent** le métro.	*He often takes the metro.*
quelquefois	Tu travailles **quelquefois** ici ?	*Do you work here sometimes?*
rarement	Elle se maquille **rarement**.	*She rarely wears makeup.*
ne… jamais	Il **ne** se coiffe **jamais**.	*He never combs his hair.*

- Another useful expression to indicate frequency is formed with the noun **fois** followed optionally by **par** and a time expression.

Il se rase **une fois par semaine**.	*He shaves once a week.*
Je me lave les dents **deux fois par jour**.	*I brush my teeth twice a day.*
Ma petite sœur prend une douche **trois fois par semaine**.	*My little sister takes a shower three times a week.*

-10
:o
-13

À vous la parole

Implementation: 3-8, 3-9 To assist students, show the scales from the first and third points as they complete Ex. 3-8; show the scale from the second point for Ex. 3-9.

3-8 Vos habitudes. Be precise! Compare your habits with those of your partner.

MODÈLE travailler le week-end
É1 Moi, je travaille beaucoup le week-end.
É2 Par contre, moi, je travaille rarement le week-end.

1. travailler le week-end
2. se réveiller tôt le matin
3. se brosser les dents
4. parler français
5. jouer au Scrabble
6. regarder la télé
7. faire la cuisine
8. se coucher de bonne heure (= tôt)

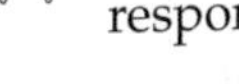

3-9 Combien ? How much or how many do you have? Compare your responses with those of your partner.

MODÈLE des livres
É1 J'ai beaucoup de livres.
É2 Moi, j'ai peu de livres.

1. des livres
2. des CD
3. des rasoirs
4. des serviettes
5. des peignes
6. du maquillage
7. des amis
8. de l'argent
9. des problèmes

3-10 Stéréotypes et réalité. What is the stereotype, and what is the reality? Compare ideas with your partner.

Implementation: 3-10 You might also ask students to generate additional examples.

MODÈLE les Américains : manger au McDo ?
É1 Les Américains mangent très souvent au McDo.
É2 Mais moi, je ne mange jamais au McDo.

1. les Américains : manger dans des fast-food ?
2. les Américains : se dépêcher ?
3. les Africains : être décontractés (*relaxed*) ?
4. les Suisses : avoir beaucoup d'argent ?
5. les Français : jouer au football ?
6. les Français : manger de la quiche ?
7. les étudiants : se coucher tard ?
8. les étudiants : travailler ?
9. les professeurs : se lever tôt ?
10. les professeurs : donner des devoirs ?

Stratégie

Pay attention to both the meaning and form of the text when you read a poem. In an effective poem, form and meaning work together, so that variations in form—the poem's rhythm or structure, for example—contribute to the impact of its message.

Lisons

3-11 Familiale.

A. Avant de lire. Jacques Prévert (1900–1977) has probably been the most popular and widely read French poet since Victor Hugo. Prévert's first book of poetry, *Paroles* (*Lyrics*), appeared in late 1945, just as World War II was ending. The poem you are about to read is taken from that collection.

In *Familiale*, Prévert uses the simple language of everyday life to make a profound statement about war and loss. He indicates in a matter-of-fact way what the three members of a family do:

La mère fait du tricot./Elle tricote.	*The mother knits.*
Le père fait des affaires.	*The father does business.*
Le fils fait la guerre.	*The son wages war.*

Note: This change in structure might reflect the banalization of war, the routinized, rapid descent toward the destruction of a moral society that gives no thought to the consequences of its actions. War is "business as usual."

As the poem reaches its climax, the poet's simple statements about the family members' lives are interrupted. The rhythm changes and verbs ultimately disappear from the narrative. Consider, as you read the poem, how these structural changes help to evoke and reinforce the poet's troubling message.

Key: *En lisant.* 1) The characters all live routinized, monotonous lives. 2) The climax comes with the line, *Le fils est tué il ne continue plus*—the parents continue their routine, but incorporate the cemetery into it; meanwhile, everything around them disintegrates.

B. En lisant. As you read the poem, answer these questions.

1. What is the nature of the characters' everyday life as conveyed in the first nine lines of the poem?
2. Like a play or a film, the poem builds to a climax. What is that climax? What happens afterward?

Key: *En regardant de plus près.* 1) *Elle/il trouve ça tout naturel* ; it is somewhat shocking that the parents consider their trips to the cemetery *tout naturel* ; repetition intensifies at the end of the poem to emphasize the machine-like life the family lives, unthinkingly. 2) The verb *faire*, a very non-specific verb that can be used in many contexts, is repeated throughout the poem—again, this produces a routinized, machine-like effect; when a new verb appears, *le fils est tué*, it brings the routine to a halt; but then verbs disappear altogether, speeding up the tempo and suggesting little thought behind the actions. 3) Chart the rhyme scheme with students and show how it is simple and repetitive, reinforcing the notion of machine-like adherence to convention that Prévert wants to convey. 4) The line is ironic and reinforces the writer's view that the society's reaction to war is not normal.

C. En regardant de plus près. Now look more closely at the structure of the poem.

1. The poem uses repetition to produce an effect and to convey meaning. For example, with what repeated phrase does Prévert suggest the characters' attitude toward their daily life? When this phrase recurs the third time, it has taken on new meaning and become associated with a terrible irony. Why? Can you point out some other instances of repetition that are significant in the poem?
2. What verb is used most frequently in the poem? What effect does this produce, and what is the effect when another verb is used instead? At what point do verbs disappear altogether?
3. Poetry is often characterized by a rhyme scheme. How would you describe the rhyme scheme in this poem? What might this type of rhyme scheme symbolize?
4. Look at the final line of the poem. How would you explain the seeming contradiction of the poet's reference to *"La vie avec le cimetière?"*

Note: Students may notice that very traditional roles have been assigned to the parents; they may be surprised that the son's role is to go to war, but remind them of the date of publication of this collection — the poem was written during World War II, and it is a social commentary that places some blame for the war on the bourgeoisie. Students who have read Dickens may pick up on the literary allusion of the mother knitting (as in *A Tale of Two Cities*).

FAMILIALE°

La mère fait du tricot
Le fils fait la guerre
Elle trouve° ça tout naturel la mère
Et le père qu'est-ce qu'il fait le père ?
Il fait des affaires
Sa femme fait du tricot
Son fils la guerre
Lui des affaires
Il trouve ça tout naturel le père
Et le fils et le fils
Qu'est-ce qu'il trouve le fils ?
Il ne trouve rien° absolument rien le fils
Le fils sa mère fait du tricot son père des affaires lui
  la guerre
Quand il aura fini° la guerre
Il fera° des affaires avec son père
La guerre continue la mère continue elle tricote
Le père continue il fait des affaires
Le fils est tué° il ne continue plus°
Le père et la mère vont au cimetière
Ils trouvent ça tout naturel le père et la mère
La vie continue la vie avec le tricot la guerre les affaires
Les affaires la guerre le tricot la guerre
Les affaires les affaires et les affaires
La vie avec le cimetière.

Family Life; *thinks*; *nothing*; *finishes*; *will do*; *killed; no longer*

"Familiale" from *Paroles* by Jacques Prévert

D. Après avoir lu. Now discuss the following questions with your classmates.

1. Poetry is meant to be read aloud. With a partner, or with your class as a whole, practice reading aloud *Familiale*. Does this help you appreciate Prévert's efforts to convey meaning through the form and rhythm of his poem as well as through the words themselves?
2. Work with a partner to translate the poem. How can you use the structure and rhythm of the poem in English to help convey Prévert's message?
3. Good literature has a timeless quality; readers in many different contexts can relate it to their circumstances. Do you believe Prévert's poem has this quality?

Leçon 2 À quelle heure ?

Presentation: Describe Delphine's day, using the illustrations (MFL, Instructor's Resources). Point out the expressions *Super !*, *Zut (alors) !*, *Mince !* *Ouf !* Encourage students to build up their own collection of such expressions and use them in appropriate contexts while speaking.

POINTS DE DÉPART

Je n'arrête pas de courir !

Presentation: Point out that *commencer*, like *manger* and *nager*, has a spelling change in the first-person plural: *nous commençons*. Explain that this change reflects the pronunciation. Full conjugations are in Appendix 2.

Delphine parle de sa journée :

Mon radio-réveil sonne à sept heures du matin. Mon premier cours commence à neuf heures, alors je quitte ma chambre à huit heures et demie pour aller à la fac.

J'arrive en classe à neuf heures moins le quart. Super ! Je suis en avance ; je vais trouver une bonne place.

Le professeur arrive toujours à l'heure ; il entre dans la classe vers neuf heures moins cinq et il commence à parler.

À dix heures et quart, je regarde ma montre. Zut alors ! encore un quart d'heure ! Le cours continue jusqu'à dix heures et demie.

À onze heures moins vingt je prends un café. Je parle avec des camarades de classe pendant vingt minutes. Je regarde l'horloge. Mince, je suis en retard ! J'arrive au deuxième cours à onze heures dix. J'ai dix minutes de retard.

Entre midi et une heure de l'après-midi, je déjeune au resto U avec un ami, Jean-Baptiste.

L'après-midi, nous allons voir le nouveau film de Gérard Depardieu. On va à la séance de 14 h 55. C'est moins cher, et ça fait une petite pause dans une journée mouvementée. Ouf !

Vous avez l'heure ?

Presentation: Drill the main divisions of the hour using a clock face with moveable hands, or the multiple images (MFL, Instructor's Resources). Describe your own daily activities, incorporating each of the time expressions. At the end of the narrative, summarize expressions. Then test student comprehension by having them draw (for an analog) or write (for a digital clock) the times you give.

Il est deux heures et quart de l'après-midi. (Il est quatorze heures quinze.)

21:30 — Il est neuf heures et demie du soir. (Il est vingt-et-une heures trente.)

23:45 — Il est minuit moins le quart. (Il est vingt-trois heures quarante-cinq.)

00:00 — Il est minuit. (Il est zéro heure.)

01:45 — Il est deux heures moins le quart du matin. (Il est une heure quarante-cinq.)

Note: *Demie* is written with a final *e* in all time expressions except *midi et demi, minuit et demi.* In the other forms, *demie* is an adjective modifying the feminine *heure.*

Key: 3-12 À onze heures moins le quart, elle a rendez-vous avec son prof d'anglais ; À onze heures et demie, elle mange au restaurant avec Lucie ; À deux heures de l'après-midi, elle travaille à la bibliothèque ; À quatre heures et demie, elle joue au tennis avec Jean-Claude ; À huit heures du soir, elle dîne avec sa maman ; À neuf heures, elle travaille chez Christine.

À vous la parole

17

20

3-12 Une journée bien mouvementée. Look at Sophie's agenda and tell what she is doing today.

MODÈLE • À neuf heures du matin, elle a son cours de littérature.

Implementation: 3-12 Ask students to convert to the informal system of telling time.

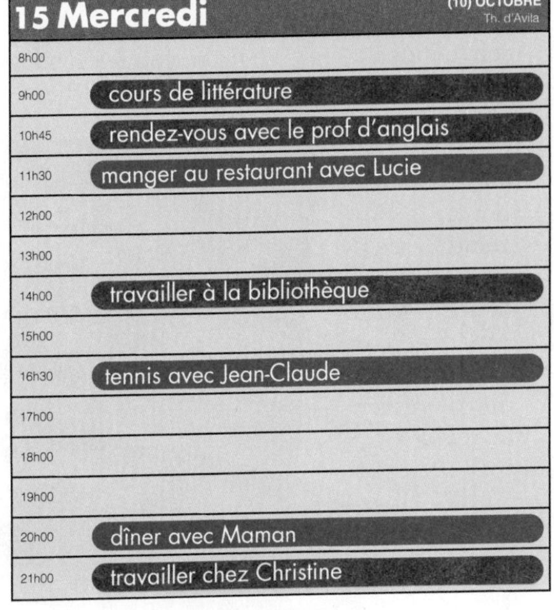

15 Mercredi — (10) OCTOBRE — Th. d'Avila

8h00	
9h00	cours de littérature
10h45	rendez-vous avec le prof d'anglais
11h30	manger au restaurant avec Lucie
12h00	
13h00	
14h00	travailler à la bibliothèque
15h00	
16h30	tennis avec Jean-Claude
17h00	
18h00	
19h00	
20h00	dîner avec Maman
21h00	travailler chez Christine

3-13 Dans le monde francophone. Look at the map below showing world time zones and tell what time it is in each of the Francophone cities shown. Then, based on the time, indicate what people are most likely to be doing.

MODÈLE À Paris. On mange ou on se couche ?
• À Paris il est midi. On mange.

1. À La Nouvelle-Orléans. On se lève ou on travaille ?
2. À Cayenne. Les étudiants vont en classe ou ils rentrent chez eux ?
3. À Dakar. On va bientôt déjeuner ou on va bientôt dîner ?
4. À Marseille. On rentre à la maison pour manger ou on travaille ?
5. À Djibouti. On fait la sieste ou on mange ?
6. À Mahé. On nage ou on rentre à la maison pour dormir ?
7. À Nouméa. On se couche ou on joue au football ?

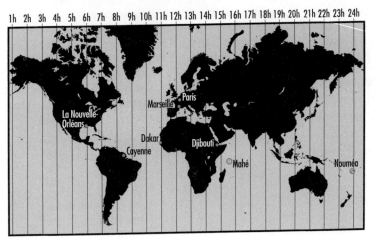

1h 2h 3h 4h 5h 6h 7h 8h 9h 10h 11h 12h 13h 14h 15h 16h 17h 18h 19h 20h 21h 22h 23h 24h

La Nouvelle-Orléans
Marseille
Paris
Dakar
Cayenne
Djibouti
Mahé
Nouméa

Key: 3-13 1) À La Nouvelle-Orléans il est six heures du matin. On se lève. 2) À Cayenne il est huit heures du matin. Les étudiants vont en classe. 3) À Dakar il est onze heures du matin. On va bientôt déjeuner. 4) À Marseille il est midi. On rentre à la maison pour manger. 5) À Djibouti il est deux heures de l'après-midi. On fait la sieste. 6) À Mahé il est trois heures de l'après-midi. On nage. 7) À Nouméa il est minuit. On se couche.

Vie et culture

Le système des 24 heures

In this lesson you have already seen examples of the 24-hour clock (sometimes called *military time* in English). What might be the advantage of using the 24-hour clock? The expressions **et quart**, **et demie**, and **moins le quart** are not used when reporting times using the 24-hour clock. Instead, give the exact number of minutes after the hour: for example, **15 h 15** is read as **quinze heures quinze**.

Find examples of the 24-hour clock in the photos. Can you restate the equivalents in conventional time? What can you learn about typical business hours in France from these photos? In what ways are these hours similar to and different from business hours in North America? Which system do you prefer and why?

DU MARDI AU SAMEDI

DE 9 H 00 A 12 H 00
ET 14 H 00 A 19 H 00

LE LUNDI

DE 14 H 00 A 19 H 00

fnac.com
HORAIRES D'OUVERTURE
le lundi de 13h00 à 19h00
du mardi au vendredi
de 10h00 à 19h00
le samedi
de 9h30 à 19h00
www.fnac.com

OUVERT
Du lundi au samedi
de 7H à 21H
le Dimanche
de 9H à 13H

Presentation: In many countries, the 24-hour clock is used to avoid ambiguity in published schedules for classes, transportation, television programming, and public events. Compare the use of the 24-hour clock with the use of A.M. and P.M. in Anglophone countries. Students should be able to explain conversion from one system to the other. They should be able to deduce from the photos regular store hours. You may wish to point out that the A.M./P.M. system is also operative in France in ordinary conversations where people use the expressions *du matin* and *de l'après-midi* or *du soir* to situate the time. Using the photos, help students discover that most shops and businesses are closed on Sunday in France (with the exception of small grocery stores, which are often open on Sunday mornings), and that many shops, banks, and businesses close for lunch, typically between the hours of noon and two P.M.

Implementation: 3-14 You could use this as a means of finding out how "compatible" partners are: could they function as roommates? If not, have them circulate to try to find a more compatible partner.

3-14 Votre journée typique. What do you typically do at the times specified below? Share your responses with a partner, using some of the boxed suggestions. How similar—or dissimilar—are your responses?

aller en cours/au labo
faire…
jouer à…
manger…
parler à…
regarder la télé
se coucher
se lever
téléphoner à…
travailler

MODÈLE à huit heures du matin

É1 Normalement, à huit heures du matin, je me lève. Et toi ?

É2 Moi, à huit heures, je suis en classe.

1. à huit heures du matin
2. à dix heures du matin
3. à midi et demi
4. à quatre heures de l'après-midi
5. à six heures du soir
6. à huit heures du soir
7. à minuit
8. à deux heures du matin

Sons et lettres

L'enchaînement et la liaison

In French, consonants that occur within a rhythmic group tend to be linked to the following syllable. This is called **enchaînement**. Because of this feature of French pronunciation, most syllables end in a vowel sound:

Presentation: As you present this topic, review the notion of rhythmic groups.

il a /i la/ sept amis /sɛ ta mi/ Élise arrive /e li za riv/

Some final consonants are almost always pronounced; these include final **-c**, **-r**, **-f**, **-l**, and all consonants followed by the written letter **-e**:

Éri**c** ma sœu**r** neu**f** l'éco**le** arrê**te** sei**ze** il ai**me**

Note that final **-f** is pronounced as a /v/ in the expressions **neuf ans** and **neuf heures** :

Elle a neu**f** ans. /ɛ la nœ vɑ̃/ *She is nine years old.*
Il est neu**f** heures. /i le nœ vœr/ *It's nine o'clock.*

Other final consonants are pronounced only when the following word begins with a vowel. These are called *liaison consonants*, and the process that links the liaison consonant to the beginning of the next syllable is called *liaison*. Liaison consonants are usually found in grammatical endings and words such as pronouns, articles, possessive adjectives, prepositions, and numbers. You have seen the following liaison consonants:

Note: Point out that liaison is never made with the final *-t* of the word *et*.

- **-s**, **-x**, **-z** (pronounced /z/): vou**s**‿avez, le**s**‿enfants, no**s**‿amis, au**x**‿échecs, trè**s**‿aimable, si**x**‿heures, che**z**‿eux
- **-t** : c'es**t**‿un chapeau, elles son**t**‿énergiques
- **-n** : o**n**‿a, u**n**‿oncle, mo**n**‿ami

When you pronounce a liaison consonant, articulate it as part of the next word:

deux‿oncles /dø zɔ̃kl/ *not* */døz ɔ̃kl/
on‿a /ɔ̃ na/ *not* */ɔ̃n a/
il est‿ici /i le ti si/ *not* */il et i si/

Note: The asterisk in the examples is a linguistic convention used to show that this form is not part of a native speaker's repertoire.

À vous la parole

3-15 Contrastes : sans et avec enchaînement. Pronounce each pair of phrases. Be sure to link the final consonant of the first word to the following word when it begins with a vowel.

une copine / une amie
pour Bertrand / pour Albert
Luc parle / Luc écoute
neuf minutes / neuf heures
quel jour / quelle heure
elle préfère ça / elle aime ça

3-16 Liaisons. Pronounce the liaison consonants in the following phrases. Be sure to link the consonant with the following word.

nous‿allons	vous‿écoutez
on‿a	un‿an
ils‿arrivent à neuf heures	elles‿habitent en ville
elles sont‿au bureau	elles vont‿à la maison
son petit‿ami	il a vingt‿ans
ton‿amie	son‿enfant

FORMES ET FONCTIONS

1. Les verbes en *-ir* comme *dormir, sortir, partir*

Presentation: Before presenting this topic, review *-er* verbs to highlight the differences. Stress the importance of a clear articulation of the final consonant in the third person plural; it is this final consonant that distinguishes the singular from the plural in speech. Note that *courir* does not have the same pattern as *dormir*, since *courir* has only one stem and thus three spoken forms in the present tense. The conjugation for *courir* is in Appendix 2.

- You have learned that regular **-er** verbs have one stem and three spoken forms in the present indicative. Unless the verb begins with a vowel sound, you must use the context to tell the difference between the third-person singular and plural:

Mon frère ? **Il regarde** la télé.	*My brother? He's watching TV.*
Mes amis ? **Ils regardent** le match de foot.	*My friends? They are watching the soccer game.*
Ma sœur ? **Elle écoute** son iPod.	*My sister? She's listening to her iPod.*
Ses amies ? **Elles‿écoutent** un CD. /z/	*Her friends? They are listening to a CD.*

- Verbs like **dormir** (*to sleep*) have two stems—one for the plural forms and one for the singular forms—and four spoken forms. The shorter stem for the singular forms is derived by dropping the final consonant sound of the long stem used for the plural forms. For these verbs, the singular written endings are **-s**, **-s**, **-t**; these letters are usually silent.

dormir (*to sleep*)	Ils dor**m**ent tard.	Il dor~~t~~ debout.
sortir (*to go out*)	Elles sor**t**ent souvent.	Elle sor~~t~~ le week-end.

DORMIR *to sleep*

SINGULIER		PLURIEL	
je	dors	nous	dorm**ons**
tu	dors	vous	dorm**ez**
il / elle / on	dor**t**	ils / elles	dorm**ent**

IMPÉRATIF : Dors bien ! Dorm**ez** tard ! Dorm**ons** ici !

- Here is a list of verbs conjugated like **dormir**, along with the prepositions often used with these verbs.

dormir jusqu'à	Je **dors jusqu'à** huit heures.	*I sleep until eight o'clock.*
s'endormir	Ils **s'endorment** tout de suite.	*They go to sleep right away.*

mentir à	Il **ment à** ses parents.	*He's lying to his parents.*
partir avec	Je **pars avec** mes parents.	*I'm leaving with my parents.*
de	Nous **partons de** Montréal.	*We're leaving from Montreal.*
pour	Vous **partez pour** la France ?	*Are you leaving for France?*
sortir avec	Elle **sort avec** ses amies.	*She goes out with her girl friends.*
	Elle **sort avec** David.	*She's dating David.*
de	Les étudiants **sortent du** labo.	*The students are leaving the lab.*
servir	Qu'est-ce qu'on **sert** ce soir ?	*What are they serving tonight?*

- Note that the verb **courir** (*to run*) has the same endings as the other **-ir** verbs; however, it has only one stem and therefore three spoken forms, like regular **-er** verbs.

Elle **court** pour arriver à l'heure.	*She hurries to arrive on time.*
Nous **courons** tout le temps.	*We are always running/in a hurry.*
Pourquoi est-ce que vous **courez** ?	*Why are you running?*

À vous la parole

-23 to -26

3-17 On sort. Based on the description, what building are these people going out of? *Answers may vary.*

MODÈLE Laurent apporte des livres ; il…
- Il sort de la bibliothèque.

1. Laure apporte un ballon de basket ; elle… sort du gymnase
2. Gilles et toi, vous avez un programme ; vous… sortez du théâtre
3. Mes amis et moi apportons des bagages ; nous… sortons de l'hôtel/de la gare
4. Mes parents ont une pizza ; ils… sortent du restaurant
5. Karine apporte un ballon de foot ; elle… sort du stade
6. Tu as des cahiers, des livres et des DVD ; tu… sors de la librairie
7. Mes amis ont des belles affiches de Picasso ; ils… sortent du musée

Initial practice: Begin with a discrimination drill: one person, or more than one? *Ils dorment très tard. Elle sert du café. Elles partent demain. Il sort ce soir. Elles dorment tard le week-end. Il sort souvent. Ils s'endorment tout de suite. Elle part en France. Ils servent du rosbif*, etc. Follow up with a simple substitution drill. Start first with the contrast third-person plural vs. third-person singular by visual cuing: *Ils partent ce soir ;* (show one finger) *—Il part ce soir.* Then proceed with the other forms. *Nous partons demain ; je —Je pars demain.*

3-18 Je n'arrête pas de courir. Compare your weekly routine with your partner's. Then tell the class what you've learned.

MODÈLE Pendant la semaine, je dors jusqu'à…

É1 Moi, pendant la semaine, je dors jusqu'à 7 h.

É2 Moi, je dors jusqu'à 8 h 30 ; mon premier cours commence à 9 h.

É1 (*aux autres*) Moi, pendant la semaine, je dors jusqu'à 7 h, mais Julie dort jusqu'à 8 h 30.

1. Pendant la semaine, je dors jusqu'à…
2. Le week-end, je dors jusqu'à…
3. Le matin, je pars pour mon premier cours à…
4. Souvent, je cours pour…
5. Je sors avec mes amis…
6. Je ne sors pas quand…
7. Le soir, je m'endors vers…

3-19 Nos habitudes. Try to find someone who does each of the things listed. When your instructor calls time, compare notes with classmates.

MODÈLE dormir l'après-midi

É1 Est-ce que tu dors l'après-midi ?

É2 Oui, je dors quelquefois l'après-midi.

1. s'endormir pendant les cours
2. sortir pendant la semaine
3. partir pour le week-end
4. servir le dîner dans un restaurant
5. dormir très tard le matin
6. mentir quelquefois à ses parents
7. partir de chez lui/elle très tôt le matin
8. dormir l'après-midi
9. partir en vacances
10. courir au parc le week-end

2. Le verbe *mettre*

Presentation: This presentation focuses on the basic meaning of *mettre*, "to put," and its use with time expressions. Ch. 3, L. 3 recycles *mettre* with clothing. Present the verb inductively by modeling numerous examples (and perhaps demonstrating with actual objects): *J'ai un programme très chargé aujourd'hui. Dans mon sac, je mets mon ordinateur. À midi, je vais être dans mon bureau, alors je mets aussi mon déjeuner dans mon sac. Après, je vais aller au gymnase, donc j'y mets des baskets, etc. Qu'est-ce que vous mettez dans votre sac typiquement ? Les étudiants y mettent toujours leur iPod ?* Ask students the meaning of the verb, and how many spoken forms they hear. See whether they can conjugate the forms orally. Then display the verb chart and examples to illustrate the various meanings of *mettre*. Other verbs that pattern like *mettre* (*promettre, permettre, remettre,* and *transmettre*) are not introduced because they generally occur in constructions with indirect objects.

- The verb **mettre** (*to put, to put on*) has a wide range of meanings.

Mettez vos livres sur le bureau ! — *Put your books on the desk!*
Tu **mets** un jean ? — *Are you putting on jeans?*
Tu peux **mettre** la table ? — *Can you set the table?*
Nous **mettons** une heure pour arriver là. — *It takes us one hour to get there.*

- Here are the forms of the verb **mettre**.

METTRE ***to put, to put on***

SINGULIER		PLURIEL	
je	mets	nous	mett**ons**
tu	mets	vous	mett**ez**
il / elle / on	met	ils / elles	mett**ent**

IMPÉRATIF : Mets la table ! Mett**ez** un jean ! Mett**ons** nos livres là !

- As is the case for all two-stem verbs, you can tell if someone is talking about one person or more than one person, since the plural form ends in a pronounced consonant.

Ils me**tt**ent des sandales. — Elle me~~t~~ son jean.

Initial practice: Begin with a discrimination drill: one person, or more than one? *Elle met un jean. Elles mettent des sandales. Ils mettent une heure pour arriver. Elle met la table. Elles mettent quinze minutes pour y aller. Ils mettent des livres sur le bureau. Il met l'ordinateur sur le bureau. Elles mettent deux heures pour arriver*, etc. Follow with a simple substitution drill: *Je mets un jean ; vous. —Vous mettez un jean*, etc.

Expansion: Ask students to summarize; this will allow them to use more verb forms: *Moi, je mets… Lui, il met… Nous, nous mettons…*

Expansion: Survey the class and compare responses given by students.

À vous la parole

03-27 to 03-30

3-20 Où est-ce que vous mettez ça ? Tell your partner where you normally put the items listed: **dans votre chambre**, **dans votre sac à dos** (*backpack*) ou **dans la voiture** (*car*).

MODÈLE tes lunettes de soleil (*sunglasses*)

É1 Où est-ce que tu mets tes lunettes de soleil ?

É2 Je mets mes lunettes dans la voiture.

1. tes CD préférés
2. ton dictionnaire
3. ton manuel de français
4. ta photo préférée
5. ton jean préféré
6. ton iPod
7. ton agenda

3-21 Vous mettez combien de temps ? In groups of three, ask your partners how much time it takes them for the trips listed: **quinze minutes ? deux heures ?** Then, compare your responses; are they similar or different?

MODÈLE pour aller à la fac le matin

É1 Combien de temps est-ce que vous mettez pour aller à la fac le matin ?
É2 Je mets quinze minutes pour aller à la fac. Et toi ?
É3 Moi, je mets trente minutes.
É1 Et moi aussi, trente minutes.
É3 Nous deux, nous mettons trente minutes, mais lui, il met quinze minutes.

1. pour aller à la fac le matin
2. pour aller à la bibliothèque
3. pour aller en ville
4. pour rentrer chez vous le soir
5. pour aller chez vos parents

Script: *Écoutons*
JÉRÉMIE : Alors, qu'est-ce que tu fais ce week-end ? On sort ensemble ?
CÉLINE : Oui, pourquoi pas ? On va voir un film ? ou bien jouer au tennis ?
JÉRÉMIE : Jouer au tennis plutôt ; j'aime faire du sport le week-end. Samedi matin, ça va pour le tennis ?
CÉLINE : Non, ce n'est pas possible, je vais au marché avec Maman à dix heures. L'après-midi, peut-être ?
JÉRÉMIE : Je travaille l'après-midi, de midi à dix-neuf heures. Mais je suis libre le soir, donc pourquoi pas voir un film après tout ?
CÉLINE : Ah non ; je vais au concert de jazz avec Mélanie samedi à vingt heures. Dimanche après-midi, c'est possible ?
JÉRÉMIE : Oh, dimanche, c'est le baptême de ma nièce ; nous partons tous en famille pour Dijon. Et vendredi soir ?
CÉLINE : C'est moi qui travaille à la librairie de six heures jusqu'à neuf heures ce soir-là.
JÉRÉMIE : Eh bien, ma grande, tu as un week-end très mouvementé !
CÉLINE : C'est vrai, je n'arrête pas de courir.
JÉRÉMIE : Alors, ce sera pour la semaine prochaine peut-être.

Écoutons

3-22 Pour fixer rendez-vous.

A. Avant d'écouter. Céline and Jérémie are good friends and want to get together this weekend. As they compare their schedules, think about the kinds of obligations that might keep them from seeing each other.

B. En écoutant. Indicate on the calendar the times when neither Céline nor Jérémie is free and why. Do they manage to find a time that works for both of them? What do they plan to do?

	VENDREDI	SAMEDI	DIMANCHE
8h00			J : au baptême
9h00			
10h00		C : au marché	
11h00			
12h00		J : au travail	
13h00			
14h00			
15h00			
16h00			
17h00			
18h00	C : au travail		
19h00			
20h00		C : au concert	
21h00			

C. Après avoir écouté. Now work with a classmate to find a time this week when both of you are available for one of the following activities: **réviser le cours de français, regarder un film français sur DVD, manger dans un restaurant français**.

MODÈLE É1 Allons manger au restaurant Bouchon !
É2 D'accord ; mercredi soir, c'est bon ?
É1 Non, j'ai un cours à 18 h 00 le mercredi soir. Pourquoi pas samedi ?
É2 Je travaille le samedi jusqu'à 19 h 00 – à 20 h 00, ça va ?
É1 C'est parfait, les Français dînent tard.

Implementation: *Après avoir écouté.* You might give students a sample page from a French desk calendar on which they can take notes as they work. To follow up, find out how many pairs managed to agree on a day and time, and what they agreed to do. For a more challenging activity, put students in groups of three or four to find a time that is mutually convenient.

Leçon 3 Qu'est-ce qu'on met ?

Presentation: This vocabulary is best presented over two days. On day 1, present sportswear and outerwear along with colors and the accompanying cultural notes. Review and present more formal clothes and the dialogue on day 2.

For the initial presentation, describe the articles of clothing using visuals (MFL, Instructor's Resources). Present only a few items at a time before checking students' comprehension: have them come up to the screen and point to the article that you name, using the unlabeled visual (MFL, Instructor's Resources); you may also ask, *Qui porte un tee-shirt ?*, etc.

To further test comprehension, use *la chasse à l'intrus : Quel mot ne va pas avec les autres ? un polo, un jean, un pantalon ; des chaussettes, des baskets, des gants ; un manteau, un imperméable, un short*, etc.

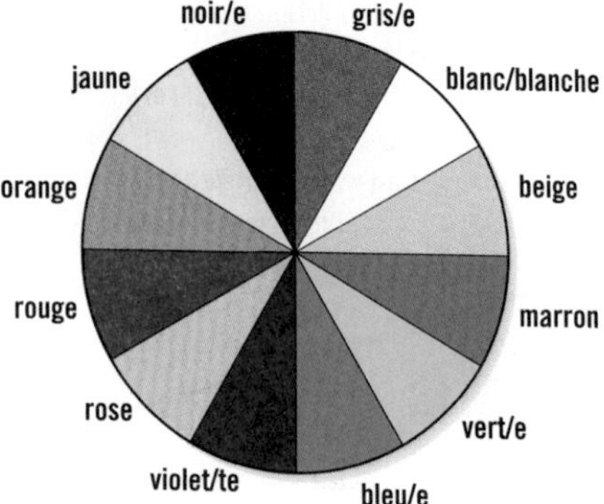

Presentation: Point out that when a color is paired with a noun, agreement is made, but when used alone, the color name takes the masculine form: *J'aime le vert* = "I like the color green" or "I like the green one." *Marron* and *orange* are unlike other color names. They are derived from the name of the fruit, *une orange*, and the nut, *un marron*, "chestnut." These two adjectives never vary in spelling; the same is not true of *rose*, which adds an *-s* in the plural. Point out the idiosyncratic spelling for *blanche* ; the masculine oral form is derived in normal fashion from the feminine, i.e., by the loss of the final consonant sound. Model pronunciation for the colors, then test comprehension; ask, *Qu'est-ce qui est bleu ?* Students can name an item of clothing from the visuals or something in the classroom.

To further practice colors, have students name the colors for: *le drapeau américain ; le drapeau français ; un pingouin ; une tulipe ; une banane ; une craie ; un éléphant ; un océan ; une plante ; un tigre ; un zèbre.*

For additional productive practice on day 1, ask *Qui porte du rouge ?* and have students respond with, for example: *Moi, je porte un polo rouge.* Ex. 3-23 can also be used on day 1.

POINTS DE DÉPART

Les vêtements et les couleurs

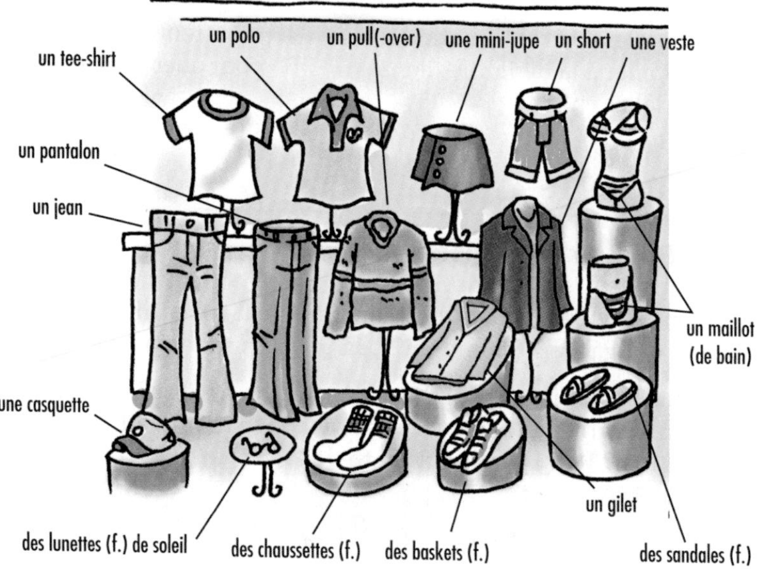

Vêtements de sport

Vêtements d'extérieur

Vêtements pour hommes et femmes

Presentation: On day 2, review sportswear and outerwear before presenting formal wear and the dialogue. You might bring in a suitcase filled with various clothing items, or encourage your students to "dress up" in interesting ways. Follow the same procedures as suggested for day 1 to present the new clothing items. Ex. 3-24 and 3-25 can be used on day 2.

Presentation: Have students listen to the dialogue. Point out the expression *avoir envie de* and ask students for a synonym in French (*désirer*). Point out *il faut* as a way of expressing necessity. Mention that both expressions can be followed by a noun or a verb. (*J'ai envie d'une belle robe noire. J'ai envie d'acheter la robe. Il faut des lunettes de soleil, il faut acheter le chemisier.*) Treat the verb *acheter* as a lexical item; the conjugation is introduced in Ch. 4, L. 3. Use the dialogue as the basis for simple role-play using the visuals or actual articles of clothing you have brought in.

Deux amies regardent des vêtements dans la vitrine d'un grand magasin :

MANON : Je vais à un mariage dans quinze jours, et j'ai envie d'acheter la belle robe noire en soie.

AUDREY : Dis donc, elle est chère ; regarde le prix ! Mais regarde le joli chemisier blanc ; si tu mets ta petite jupe bleue, ça va faire un bel ensemble.

MANON : Tu as raison ; il faut faire des économies ! J'ai aussi une nouvelle paire de chaussures à talons.

AUDREY : Voilà, ma belle, tu vas être très élégante !

Initial practice: 3-23 Before completing this exercise with the verb *mettre*, review forms with a simple substitution drill: *Je mets un pull ; vous. – Vous mettez un pull*, etc.

À vous la parole

34 37 **3-23 Comment s'habiller ?** Tell how people normally dress for each of the following occasions.

MODÈLE Pour aller en classe, je…
- Pour aller en classe, je mets un jean, un polo et des baskets.

1. Pour aller en classe, mes amis… mettent
2. Pour courir dans un marathon, tu… mets
3. Pour faire des courses, ma mère… met
4. Pour travailler dans le jardin, mes parents… mettent
5. Pour faire du ski, je… mets
6. Pour nager, elles… mettent
7. Pour manger au restaurant, vous… mettez
8. Pour sortir avec des amis, on… met

Additional practice:

1) Tell students: Find a partner, and take a minute to look at each other. Now stand back-to-back with your partner. (Wait until they have complied before continuing.) Describe what the other person is wearing today; no looking allowed! Provide a model such as:

É1 Tu portes un tee-shirt bleu et blanc ?
É2 Oui.
É1 Et un pantalon noir ?
É2 Non, mon pantalon est gris.

2) Ask students to close their eyes. Describe someone in the class by the clothes that he/she is wearing and have the class guess whom you are describing.

3) Ask one student to leave the classroom and stand in the hallway. While that person is gone, ask his/her classmates to describe what he/she is wearing. Bring the student back and compare the actual outfit to the students' recollections.

Presentation: Les compliments. Students should notice that in each case, the response does not imply agreement with the compliment, but rather a modest acceptance or even a denial. Ask students whether they often compliment people on their appearance. Also, is a compliment perceived differently depending on whether it is made to a person of the same, or the opposite, sex?

Vie et culture

Les compliments

The French do not usually compliment people they do not know well on their personal appearance. Among friends, the compliments and responses below are typical. What do you notice about the nature of the response in each case? How do you typically respond to compliments? Would you feel comfortable responding to compliments as the French do?

—Il est chic, ton pantalon !	—*Your pants are really stylish!*
—Tu trouves ?	—*Do you think so?*
—Elle est très jolie, ta robe !	—*Your dress is very pretty!*
—Oh, elle n'est pas un peu démodée ?	—*Oh, isn't it a little old-fashioned?*
—Tu parles très bien le français.	—*You speak French really well.*
—Ah ! pas toujours !	—*Oh! not always!*

La semaine de la mode à Dakar en 2010 : ce manneqin porte une création de la styliste sénégalaise, Éva Gabara.

03-53

La haute couture

Paris has long been an international fashion center with worldwide influence. When you think of French fashion, what images come to your mind? Watch the video clip *La mode*, and see how many designers and styles you can recognize. Did you see the names of such great designers as Coco Chanel, Pierre Cardin, and Christian Lacroix?

Paris is not the only center of **la haute couture** in the Francophone world. Since 1998, **FIMA (le Festival International de la Mode Africaine)** has been held in Niger and features the largest fashion shows of African designers. In 1997 in Senegal, Oumou Sy launched **SIMOD (la Semaine Internationale de la Mode à Dakar)**, which has since become the annual Dakar Fashion Week. These events present the creations of African designers such as Adama Paris, Diouma Dieng Diakhaté, Ndiaga Diaw, and Oumou Sy, who showcase traditional African styles alongside European styles.

Jean-Paul Gautier présente sa collection prêt-à-porter 2011 pour la maison Hermès à Paris.

Presentation: La haute couture. Students may mention outrageous styles, high prices, top models, luxurious materials, and the names of specific designers when they think of French fashion. Women's fashion magazines, many men's magazines, and department store sales flyers often carry ads by some of the designers shown in the video montage and named here. Bring ads to class, or ask your students to bring them, to enrich the presentation visually. You might link to designers' web sites or to the *FIMA* site for additional visuals. Video sharing sites also have clips from the latest edition of *FIMA* if you search by designer name or using the key word *FIMA*.

3-24 Marier les vêtements. What goes well with each of the items mentioned? Work with a partner to decide.

MODÈLE avec une robe bleue en soie ?

É1 Avec une robe bleue en soie, on met un foulard bleu et vert.

É2 Et des chaussures à talons.

É1 Oui, c'est bien, ça fait un joli ensemble.

1. avec une mini-jupe rouge ?
2. avec un costume bleu marine ?
3. avec un pantalon bleu ?
4. avec une veste noire ?
5. avec une belle jupe multicolore en soie ?
6. avec un tailleur marron ?
7. avec un jean ?
8. avec un pantalon noir en cuir ?

Variation: 3-25 Have students prepare and then read their lists, letting classmates guess their probable destination.

3-25 Préparez la valise. Imagine that you and the members of your group have just won a trip to one of the destinations indicated. Decide what items you will pack, and make a list.

MODÈLE huit jours à Tahiti

- trois maillots de bain, deux paires de sandales, des baskets, cinq shorts, sept tee-shirts, des lunettes de soleil

1. un long week-end à Québec, pour le Carnaval de Québec en février
2. quatre jours à Lafayette, en Louisiane, en juillet
3. huit jours à Grenoble, dans les Alpes, en janvier
4. six jours à Cannes, pour le Festival International du Film en mai
5. cinq jours à Dakar, au Sénégal
6. huit jours à Paris, en avril

Note: Consistent with the presentation of variable adjectives in Ch. 2, L. 1, this presentation focuses on the spoken forms of adjectives, and assumes the feminine as the base form, with a regular rule of final consonant deletion to derive the masculine. Plural forms are treated in the next **Formes et fonctions** section.

Presentation: First show students contrasting examples illustrating the position of adjectives: *C'est un pantalon noir ; C'est un beau pantalon.* Call attention to the learning strategy, and point out that the boxed list of adjectives is arranged according to the mnemonic. Some mnemonic devices used in English include: "Thirty days hath September,…" (the French count knuckles and the spaces between them); "A rat in Tom's house might eat Tom's ice cream" (to spell "arithmetic"). Then display and read aloud the sentence examples for prenominal adjectives, asking students how many different spoken forms these adjectives have. Ask specifically what they notice about the pronunciation of the masculine form before a vowel sound, versus before a consonant sound. Point out differences in written forms as well.

FORMES ET FONCTIONS

1. Les adjectifs prénominaux au singulier

- Most adjectives follow the noun in French. A few, however, are placed before the noun.

LES ADJECTIFS PRÉNOMINAUX

jolie/joli	
belle/bel/beau	
première/premier	dernière/dernier
jeune	vieille/vieil/vieux
nouvelle/nouvel/nouveau	
bonne/bon	mauvaise/mauvais
petite/petit	grande/grand
	grosse/gros

- In the singular, **jeune** and **joli/e** each have a single spoken form. For **joli**, add **-e** for the feminine written form: **jolie**.

une jeune étudiante	un jeune professeur
une jolie robe	un joli manteau

Fiche pratique

Use a mnemonic device to help you remember facts that you must learn by rote memory. For example, the list of adjectives that precede the noun is easy to remember if you use the acronym BRAGS as a reminder of their meaning—**b**eauty, **r**ank, **a**ge, **g**oodness, **s**ize. Can you think of mnemonic devices that you have used in English?

Presentation: These examples allow you to demonstrate that the cue to knowing whether a word is masculine or feminine is found consistently in the indefinite article, *un/une*, and sometimes at the end of the noun (compare *étudiant–étudiante* with *ami–amie*). In presenting feminine and masculine forms followed by a word beginning with a vowel sound, stress that the pronounced final consonant forms a syllable with the next word (*enchaînement*) : *un mauvais hôtel* /mo vɛ zo tɛl/.

- Most of the other adjectives that are placed before the noun have two spoken forms in the singular. Like other adjectives you know, the masculine form ends in a vowel sound and the feminine form ends in a pronounced consonant. However, because of liaison, the masculine form sounds just like the feminine form when followed by a word beginning in a vowel sound.

C'est une petite jupe.	C'est un peti**t**‿anorak. C'est un petit chemisier.
C'est une mauvaise étudiante.	C'est un mauvai**s**‿étudiant. C'est un mauvais prof.
C'est la première boutique.	C'est le premie**r**‿hôtel. C'est le premier magasin.

- **Belle**, **nouvelle**, and **vieille** also have two spoken forms in the singular. The feminine form and the masculine form used before a word beginning with a vowel sound end in the same pronounced consonant. (Note that the masculine form has a special written form.) However, when followed by a consonant, the masculine form is irregular.

C'est une belle écharpe.	C'est un **bel**‿anorak. C'est un **beau** costume.
C'est une nouvelle veste.	C'est un **nouvel**‿imperméable. C'est un **nouveau** pantalon.
C'est une vieille cravate.	C'est un **vieil**‿imper. C'est un **vieux** parapluie.

Presentation: Demonstrate the pronunciation difference between *grand* [grɑ̃], *grand* [grɑ̃t] and *grande* [grɑ̃d], and *gros* [gro], *gros* [groz], and *grosse* [gros], when these words are followed respectively by masculine nouns beginning with a consonant, masculine nouns beginning with a vowel sound, and feminine nouns beginning with either a vowel or a consonant.

- The adjectives **grande** and **grosse** have three spoken forms in the singular. When followed by a word beginning with a vowel sound, the masculine form has a final consonant sound different from the feminine form.

C'est une grande boutique. /d/	C'est un gran**d**‿hôtel. /t/ C'est un grand magasin.
Regarde la grosse veste ! /s/	Regarde le gros‿anorak ! /z/ Regarde le gros pull !

Variation: 3-26 Suggest additional emphatic statements: *Ah oui/Mais oui/C'est vrai, c'est un vieux pantalon.*

03-38 to 03-41

À vous la parole

Initial practice: Begin practice with a discrimination drill, having students write or select the appropriate form of the adjective they hear: *Voilà un nouvel anorak ; une nouvelle écharpe ; un nouveau manteau.* Point out the importance of the article in providing gender cues when the form of the adjective is ambiguous. Follow with simple substitution drills: *C'est une belle jupe ; chemise ; chemisier ; blouson ; casquette ; imperméable, manteau,* etc. *C'est un bon imperméable ; nouveau ; vieux ; gros ; beau ; mauvais ; grand,* etc.

3-26 Tout à fait d'accord ! Indicate that you agree.

MODÈLE Le magasin est bon ?
- Oui, c'est un bon magasin.

1. L'hôtel est mauvais ? Oui, c'est un mauvais hôtel.
2. La robe est nouvelle ? Oui, c'est une nouvelle robe.
3. L'imperméable est bon ? Oui, c'est un bon imperméable.
4. Le parapluie est grand ? Oui, c'est un grand parapluie.
5. L'anorak est nouveau ? Oui, c'est un nouvel anorak.
6. Le maillot est nouveau ? Oui, c'est un nouveau maillot.
7. L'imper est beau ? Oui, c'est un bel imper.
8. La jupe est jolie ? Oui, c'est une jolie jupe.

3-27 Ce n'est pas vrai ! Contradict your partner!

MODÈLE É1 C'est un vieux pantalon.
É2 Mais non, c'est un nouveau pantalon !

1. C'est un mauvais magasin. Mais non, c'est un bon magasin.
2. C'est un vieil anorak. ..., c'est un nouvel anorak.
3. C'est le premier hôtel. ..., c'est le dernier hôtel.
4. C'est un gros manteau. ..., c'est un petit manteau.
5. C'est la dernière boutique. ..., c'est la première boutique.
6. C'est un petit gilet. ..., c'est un grand gilet.
7. C'est un bon prix. ..., c'est un mauvais prix.
8. C'est un nouvel imper. ..., c'est un vieil imper.

Variation: 3-27 Suggest additional emphatic statements: *Ah non ! Au contraire, c'est un joli pull.* Encourage students to be expressive as they complete the exercise.

3-28 Trouvez une personne qui... Find someone in your class who. . .

MODÈLE a un gros parapluie
É1 Est-ce que tu as un gros parapluie ?
É2 Non, je n'ai pas de parapluie. (*you ask another person*)
É1 Est-ce que tu as un gros parapluie?
É3 Oui, j'ai un gros parapluie ; il est blanc et vert. (*you write down the name of this student*)

1. a un gros parapluie
2. a une belle écharpe
3. a un nouvel anorak
4. a son premier cours à huit heures du matin
5. a son dernier cours tard le soir
6. a un gros manteau
7. a un beau costume
8. a une nouvelle montre
9. a une grande télé
10. a un vieil imper

Implementation: 3-28 Use as a mixing activity and have students report back what they learned. Expand on each item, for example, asking all students: *Qui a une belle écharpe ? De quelle couleur ?*

2. Les adjectifs prénominaux au pluriel

- You have learned that the following adjectives precede the noun in French.

MASCULIN SG.		MASCULIN PL.	FÉMININ SG.	FÉMININ PL.
jeune		jeunes	jeune	jeunes
joli		jolis	jolie	jolies
petit		petits	petite	petites
bon		bons	bonne	bonnes
mauvais		mauvais	mauvaise	mauvaises
premier		premiers	première	premières
dernier		derniers	dernière	dernières
grand		grands	grande	grandes
gros		gros	grosse	grosses
+CONSONNE	+VOYELLE			
beau	bel	beaux	belle	belles
nouveau	nouvel	nouveaux	nouvelle	nouvelles
vieux	vieil	vieux	vieille	vieilles

Presentation: To introduce the new material, review adjective placement and singular prenominal adjective forms. Whereas the previous chart was meaning-based (using the BRAGS mnemonic), focus is on form in the chart provided here. Adjectives are grouped and shaded by the number of spoken forms when liaison is taken into account (2, 4, and 5) and number of written forms. Note that *grand* and *gros* have four written forms, but five spoken forms; *beau, nouveau,* and *vieux* have five written forms, but four spoken forms (like *petit, bon,* etc.). To present, read a number of examples aloud and have students choose the appropriate form from a list, analyzing why they made the choice they did: *Voici des petits oiseaux : petit, petits, petites.* Summarize rules using the examples provided.
Remind students that although *-s* or *-x* is generally added to written words to form the plural in French, this final letter is usually not pronounced. One must listen for a preceding word, usually a number or an article, to tell whether a noun is singular or plural. If the noun begins with a vowel, liaison can provide an additional clue: *les_anoraks, un_imper, mes_écharpes.* Stress the importance of articles and liaison in signaling gender and number, since, for example, /ptit/ is both masculine (before a vowel) and feminine, singular and plural (feminine before a consonant).
Point out that *mauvais* and *gros* do not change spelling in the masculine plural. We are using the more frequent plural variant for the indefinite determiner: *des nouveaux imperméables* instead of *de nouveaux imperméables,* even though some conservative speakers might consider the latter form more "correct."

- The final letter of the plural form of these adjectives is usually not pronounced.

des jolies filles	des jeunes filles

However, when these adjectives precede a noun beginning with a vowel sound, you hear the liaison /z/.

des beaux‿enfants	des jeunes‿amis

For **jeune** and **joli**, there are two spoken forms in the plural. For all the other prenominal adjectives you have learned, there are four spoken forms in the plural, for example:

des grands parapluies	des grands‿anoraks
des grandes bottes	des grandes‿écharpes
des petits shorts	des petits‿impers
des petites montres	des petites‿horloges

When the plural forms occur before a word beginning with a vowel, pronounce the liaison /z/.

03-42 to 03-45

À vous la parole

Initial practice: Begin practice with a discrimination drill similar to that used for the presentation: *Voici des vieilles bottes : viel, vieille, vieilles.* Follow up with substitution drills: *Voici des vieux manteaux ; bottes ; chaussettes ; gants*, etc.

3-29 Dans l'armoire. Respond affirmatively to the following questions.

MODÈLE Les bottes sont nouvelles ?
- Oui, ce sont des nouvelles bottes.

1. Les gants sont vieux ? Oui, ce sont des vieux gants.
2. Les parapluies sont bons ? Oui, ce sont des bons parapluies.
3. Les impers sont nouveaux ? Oui, ce sont des nouveaux impers.
4. Les sandales sont vieilles ? Oui, ce sont des vieilles sandales.
5. Les costumes sont beaux ? Oui, ce sont des beaux costumes.
6. Les manteaux sont gros ? Oui, ce sont des gros manteaux.
7. Les chaussures sont belles ? Oui, ce sont des belles chaussures.
8. Les écharpes sont nouvelles ? Oui, ce sont des nouvelles écharpes.

Variation: 3-30 Begin by having students read the text; then vary this activity by having students adapt the passage to their own personal situation.

Key: 3-30 J'habite une *vieille* maison. J'ai une *petite* chambre au *dernier* étage. Dans ma chambre, j'ai des *vieux* vêtements. Dans l'armoire, j'ai un *petit* manteau. Il y a aussi des *petites* bottes. Il y a des *vieux* pull-overs et une *nouvelle* casquette. J'ai des *grandes* vestes aussi.

3-30 C'est le contraire ! Change the following narrative by substituting adjectives that have the opposite meaning.

MODÈLE J'habite une *nouvelle* maison.
- J'habite une *vieille* maison.

J'habite une *nouvelle* maison. J'ai une *grande* chambre au *premier* étage. Dans ma chambre, j'ai des *nouveaux* vêtements. Dans l'armoire (*wardrobe*), j'ai un *gros* manteau. Il y a aussi des *grandes* bottes. Il y a des *nouveaux* pull-overs et une *vieille* casquette. J'ai des *petites* vestes aussi.

Implementation: 3-31 This exercise recycles the vocabulary of places from Ch. 2, L. 3. Point out that the adjectives are listed according to the BRAGS mnemonic to reinforce the use of this learning strategy. As a model, you might have the class as a whole describe the town where your university is located. Then put students into pairs to describe their hometown. Have them report back and briefly describe some aspect of their partner's hometown.

3-31 Votre ville natale. Describe your hometown to a classmate, commenting on the features outlined below. Use the correct form of adjectives from this list: **jolie, belle, première, dernière, jeune, nouvelle, vieille, bonne, mauvaise, petite, grande, grosse.**

MODÈLE des parcs
• Dans ma ville natale, il y a des jolis parcs…

1. une mairie
2. des parcs
3. des hôtels
4. des piscines municipales
5. des universités
6. des cinémas
7. des maisons
8. des appartements

Implementation: Point out the use of the slang term *boulot* for *travail* and the use of Canadian expressions such as *le soulier à talons* instead of *les chaussures à talons* and *la tuque* instead of *le bonnet*.

Observons

Note: See the SAM/MFL for video activities related to two additional speakers from Morocco and Paris who describe typical clothing.

3-32 Mon style personnel.

A. Avant de regarder. In this video clip, watch as two women from different parts of the world describe the ways in which they dress for different situations and the ways in which they express their own style through their choice of clothing. Do you dress the same each day of the week? Make a list in French of the things you normally wear in a work situation and in a more casual situation.

B. En regardant. As you watch, look for answers to the following questions.

1. Marie-Julie describes the clothes she typically wears in three different contexts; list the contexts and the articles of clothing she names:

   Context #1: work clothing: suit, blouse, long skirt, high heels
   Context #2: weekend clothing: slacks, jeans, tee-shirt, pullover, socks
   Context #3: Quebec clothing: hat, mittens, scarf, boots, down coat

2. What article of clothing does she most enjoy personalizing? How would you describe her choices for this item of clothing? her socks; colorful, patterned
3. Honorine and her friend model typical women's clothing from Bénin. She specifies that women dressed like this are . . .

   a. stared at b. imitated (c. respected)

4. In her country, women do not typically wear . . . slacks
5. She demonstrates how to use an item of clothing called . . .

   (a. un pagne) b. un boubou c. une chemise batik

Honorine est bien habillée.

C. Après avoir regardé. Now discuss the following questions with your classmates.

1. In this video clip Marie-Julie and Honorine model and talk about their clothing. Does either woman also make a personal statement through her clothing? How?
2. Is it more typical to dress like Marie-Julie or Honorine where you live? Do you ever see women dressed like Honorine? If so, where, and in what situations? What do you typically wear in such situations?
3. In French there is a proverb, **L'habit ne fait pas le moine** (*monk*). Do you know a similar proverb in English? How is it different from the French example?

Note: Students who live in areas with African heritage communities may see women dressed like Honorine for special occasions, celebrations, and to attend religious services. Ask students how they dress for formal occasions. Does their ethnic heritage play a role in how they or people they know dress for such occasions? The corresponding English proverb is "Clothes make the man," which expresses the opposite idea. However, students often cite the proverb, "Don't judge a book by its cover," which corresponds nicely to the French saying. Students may also think of "First impressions are lasting ones," since this can be related to appearance.

Script: *Observons.* The elements in brackets reflect standard usage and have been added to the written transcripts. They were not pronounced by the speaker(s) in question.

MARIE-JULIE : Pour le boulot, je préfère des vêtements beaucoup plus habillés : le tailleur, le chemisier, la jupe longue, le soulier à talons. Euh mais par contre, le week-end, je préfère [un style] un peu plus décontracté, c'est-à-dire, le pantalon ample, le jean, parfois même le tee-shirt, lorsqu'il fait un peu plus froid c'est le pull-over, mais surtout j'adore porter mes chaussettes rigolotes. Alors elles sont à braque et à bran, elles ont toutes sortes de petits motifs rigolos, et bon, quand je vais au Québec, il faut s'habiller un peu plus chaudement, il faut porter la tuque, les mitaines, le foulard, les bottes surtout et le manteau en duvet.

HONORINE : Et si on sort comme ça, on est [plus] respecté que de porter [des] pantalons comme ici, chez nous, on ne [les] porte pas. Les femmes ne portent pas [de] pantalon, c'est comme ça que nous nous habillons. Ici sur la tête, c'est un autre morceau de de ce pagne, là. On a beaucoup de manières pour [l']attacher. Voilà, je peux faire comme ça. Ça dépend de ce que tu veux. Voilà. C'est comme ça que nous nous habillons chez nous.

Leçon 1

la routine de la journée	*the daily routine*
être debout	*to be up*
prendre une douche, un bain	*to take a shower, a bath*
se brosser les dents	*to brush one's teeth*
se coiffer	*to fix one's hair*
se coucher	*to go to bed*
se dépêcher	*to hurry*
se déshabiller	*to undress*
se doucher	*to shower*
s'endormir	*to fall asleep*
s'essuyer	*to dry off, to wipe off*
s'habiller	*to get dressed*
se laver les cheveux (m.), les dents (f.), la figure, les mains (f.)	*to wash one's hair, one's teeth, one's face, one's hands*
se lever	*to get up*
se maquiller	*to put on makeup*
se raser	*to shave*
se réveiller	*to wake up*
rentrer	*to return home*

les articles de toilette	*toiletries*
une brosse à dents/ à cheveux	*toothbrush/hairbrush*
du dentifrice	*toothpaste*
un gant de toilette	*wash mitt*
du maquillage	*makeup*
un peigne	*comb*
un rasoir	*razor*
un savon	*soap*
une serviette de toilette	*towel*
du shampooing	*shampoo*

pour exprimer la fréquence	*to express frequency*
toujours	*always, still*
tous les... /toutes les...	*every ...*
souvent	*often*
quelquefois	*sometimes*
rarement	*rarely*
ne... jamais	*never*
deux fois (f.) par jour	*twice a day*

autres mots utiles	*other useful words*
un appartement	*apartment*
l'argent (m.)	*money*
assez	*enough*
une chambre	*bedroom*
déjà	*already*
de nouveau	*again*
être en train de (+ infinitif)	*to be busy (doing something)*
une journée	*day*
le lavabo	*bathroom sink*
la nuit	*at night*
tôt	*early*
tard	*late*

Leçon 2

pour parler de l'heure	*to talk about the time*
une horloge	*clock*
une montre	*watch*
un (radio-) réveil	*alarm clock (clock radio)*
être à l'heure (pour le cours)	*to be on time (for class)*
être en avance	*to be early*
être en retard	*to be late*
Vous avez l'heure ?	*What time is it?*
pendant	*during, for*
jusqu'à	*until*
encore (un quart d'heure)	*another (quarter of an hour)*
entre	*between*
vers	*around, toward*
Il est une heure, huit heures.	*It is one o'clock, eight o'clock.*
et quart	*00:15*
et demi/e	*00:30*
moins vingt	*00:40*
moins le quart	*00:45*
du matin	*in the morning,* A.M.
de l'après-midi	*in the afternoon,* P.M.
du soir	*in the evening,* P.M.
midi	*noon*
minuit	*midnight*

quelques expressions utiles	*some useful expressions*
Mince !	*Shoot!*
Super !	*Great!*
Ouf !	*Whew!*
Zut (alors) !	*Darn!*

quelques verbes utiles	*some useful verbs*
commencer	*to begin*
courir	*to run*
dormir	*to sleep*
mentir	*to tell a lie*
mettre	*to put/place, to put on (clothing), to set (the table), to take (time)*

partir	*to leave*
quitter (ma chambre)	*to leave (my room)*
servir	*to serve*
sonner	*to ring*
sortir	*to go out*
trouver	*to find*

Leçon 3

les vêtements (m.) de sport et d'extérieur	*sportswear and outerwear*
un anorak	*ski jacket, parka*
des baskets (f.)	*sports shoes*
un bonnet de laine	*knit/wool winter hat*
des bottes (f.)	*boots*
une casquette	*baseball cap*
un chapeau	*hat*
des chaussettes (f.)	*socks*
une écharpe	*scarf*
des gants (m.)	*gloves*
un gilet	*cardigan sweater*
un imper(méable)	*raincoat*
un jean	*jeans*
des lunettes (f.) (de soleil)	*(sun)glasses*
un maillot (de bain)	*swimsuit*
un manteau	*overcoat*
une (mini-)jupe	*(mini)skirt*
un pantalon	*slacks*
un parapluie	*umbrella*
un polo	*polo shirt*
un pull(-over)	*pullover sweater*
des sandales (f.)	*sandals*
un short	*shorts*
un tee-shirt	*T-shirt*
une veste	*jacket, suit coat*

les vêtements pour femmes	*women's clothing*
des chaussures (f.) à talons	*high-heeled shoes*
un chemisier	*blouse*
un collant	*pantyhose*
un foulard	*silk scarf*
une jupe	*skirt*
une robe	*dress*
un sac	*purse*
un tailleur	*woman's suit*

les vêtements pour hommes	*men's clothing*
une chemise	*man's shirt*
un costume	*man's suit*
une cravate	*tie*
des mocassins (m.)	*loafers*

les tissus (m.) et les matières (f.)	*fabrics and materials*
le coton	*cotton*
le cuir	*leather*
la laine	*wool*
la soie	*silk*

les couleurs	*colors*
Voir à la page 102	*See page 102*

au (grand) magasin	*at the (department) store*
avoir envie de (+ nom, + infinitif)	*to want (something, to do something)*
avoir raison	*to be right*
cher/chère	*expensive*
un ensemble	*outfit*
faire des économies	*to save money*
il faut	*it's necessary*
une paire de...	*a pair of . . .*
le prix	*price*
la vitrine	*display window*

adjectifs prénominaux	*adjectives that precede the noun*
beau/bel/belle	*beautiful, handsome*
bon/bonne	*good*
dernier/dernière	*last*
grand/e	*tall*
gros/se	*big, fat*
jeune	*young*
joli/e	*pretty*
mauvais/e	*bad*
nouveau/nouvel/nouvelle	*new*
petit/e	*small, short*
premier/première	*first*
vieux/vieil/vieille	*old*

Vocabulaire

Regardez ces deux amis : où sont-ils ? Qu'est-ce qu'ils font aujourd'hui ?

4 Activités par tous les temps

After completing this chapter, you should be able to:

- Talk about the weather and vacation activities
- Extend, accept, and refuse invitations
- Tell about past actions or events
- Ask for specific information
- Identify vacation spots and cultural activities in places where French is spoken

Leçon 1 Il fait quel temps ?

Presentation: Provide an overview of the chapter using the video montage *Vive les vacances !* See whether students can identify the places, activities, and seasons. Use the weather visuals (MFL, Instructor's Resources) and brief descriptions to present the new vocabulary. Once you have presented a few items, show an image without labels (MFL, Instructor's Resources) and test comprehension by having students point to a picture that illustrates the weather you describe. Next, have students repeat key expressions, using either/or questions: *Il fait beau ou il fait mauvais ?*, etc. Emphasize the use of *il fait* for most expressions, except for *il pleut* and *il neige*. Point out that the pronoun *il* is used in an impersonal way and does not refer to a person. Point out near-equivalent expressions, for example, *il y a des nuages, le ciel est couvert*. Finally, treat the first **Vie et culture** note and check comprehension: *Il fait 30°C. —Il fait très chaud*, etc. We suggest that you review this new vocabulary on day 2 of the lesson and then present the seasons, continuing with the exercises that follow. If you live in the Snow Belt, you may wish to introduce some Québec French weather expressions such as *neigeasser* 'to be snowing lightly,' *une poudrerie* 'blowing snow,' or *de la sloche* 'slush.'

POINTS DE DÉPART

Le temps à toutes les saisons

En été, il fait chaud et lourd.

Il fait beau. Il y a du soleil et le ciel est bleu. Il fait bon aussi, pas trop chaud : il fait 23 degrès.

Le ciel est couvert ; il y a des nuages. Il va pleuvoir.

Au printemps, il fait frais et il y a du vent.

En automne, il fait mauvais. Il pleut et il y a du brouillard.

Note: In case students are interested in the formula: to convert from Celsius to Fahrenheit, divide by 5, multiply by 9 and add 32. To convert from Fahrenheit to Celsius, subtract 32, multiply by 5 and divide by 9.

Il y a un orage : il y a des éclairs et du tonnerre.

En hiver, il gèle ; il y a du verglas.

Il fait froid et il neige. Il fait moins cinq degrès.

Implementation: Practice these expressions using the weather art (MFL, Instructor's Resources); for each image, have students decide which expression would be more appropriate: *j'ai chaud/j'ai froid.*

Fiche pratique

In Francophone countries and throughout much of the world, temperature is measured in degrees Celsius. To make things easy, just remember a few key expressions that correspond to certain temperatures. For example, look at the thermometer and associate the various temperatures with the listed expressions.

To indicate that a person feels cold or hot, use the verb **avoir**:

Il fait 30°C ; j'**ai** très **chaud**.	*It's 86 degrees; I'm very hot.*
Il commence à neiger ; nous **avons froid**.	*It's starting to snow; we're cold.*

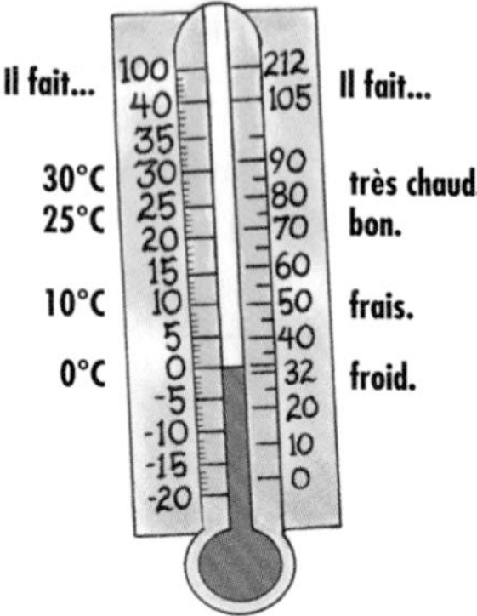

Implementation: Ask students to locate the *DOM-COM* on a map (MFL, Instructor's Resources) and speculate about what the climate would be like and what activities would be likely. *Les COM — Saint-Pierre-et-Miquelon, Saint-Barthélemy* et *Saint-Martin, Wallis-et-Futuna, la Polynésie française* (including *Tahiti*), *la Nouvelle-Calédonie*, and *les Terres australes et antarctiques françaises (TAAF)* — were formerly referred to as *les TOM* (*territoires d'outre-mer*). Under the constitutional revision in March 2003 and corresponding legislation passed in July 2003 and July 2007, *la Nouvelle-Calédonie* and *la Polynésie française* (including *Tahiti*) are considered *pays d'outre-mer; Wallis-et-Futuna, une collectivité d'outre-mer;* and *les TAAF, un territoire d'outre-mer*. For more information, visit the web site for the *Ministère de l'Outre-mer* or the *Aménagement* section of the *Trésor de la langue française du Québec* web site. Complete the questions in *Et vous ?* in small groups or as a whole class activity.

Compare *DOM* and *COM* with the status of Hawaii and Alaska versus Puerto Rico and the American Virgin Islands. Note the influences of colonial practices and the slave trade in the history of France.

Vie et culture

La France d'outre-mer

France is divided into 101 administrative units, or **départements**, and 22 **régions**. Five of these are **départements** (and **régions) d'outre-mer** (**DOM**): **la Guadeloupe, la Martinique, la Guyane, Mayotte**, and **la Réunion**. Former French colonies established in the seventeenth and eighteenth centuries, they are today an integral part of France, and their inhabitants are French citizens. French is the oficial language, but local varieties of Creole are also spoken. Because of their tropical climate, Guadeloupe, Martinique, and Réunion are prime vacation destinations for the French. A few other former colonies, known as **collectivités d'outre-mer (COM)**, continue their political association with France but have greater autonomy; French is also their official language. The largest and best known of these territories, **la Nouvelle-Calédonie** and **Tahiti**, are located in the Pacific Ocean.

ET VOUS ?

1. Find the **départements (régions) et collectivités d'outre-mer** on the map at the beginning of your textbook. As you can see, France has territories throughout the world. Is this an advantage for France? Explain your answer.
2. Is it also advantageous for these territories to have close links to France? Why, in your opinion?
3. Does the United States have territories comparable to the **DOM** and the **collectivités d'outre-mer**?

Il fait beau et très chaud à la Guadeloupe, un département et région d'outre-mer.

À vous la parole

4-1 Quel temps fait-il ?

According to the newspaper, what is the weather like today in these Francophone cities? *Answers may vary.*

Implementation: 4-1 Use a map (MFL/Instructor's Resources) to show the location of cities. Note the distinction between *la France métropole* and *la France d'outre-mer*—refer back to the **Vie et Culture** and ask students which cities are found in the *DOM* and *COM*. To review clothing, have students describe what they would wear in each city and why.

MODÈLE Paris
- À Paris, il fait assez frais et le ciel est couvert.

1. Cayenne … il fait assez chaud et il pleut.
2. Alger … il fait un peu frais et il y a du soleil.
3. Dakar … il fait assez chaud et il y a des orages.
4. Montréal … il fait très froid et il neige.
5. Nice … il fait frais et il y du soleil et du vent.
6. La Nouvelle-Orléans … il fait bon et il y a du soleil.
7. Papeete … il fait très chaud et il pleut.
8. Fort-de-France … il fait chaud et il y a du soleil.
9. Tunis … il fait assez chaud et il pleut.

PRÉVISIONS POUR LE 2 AVRIL

Ville par ville, les minima/maxima de température et l'état du ciel.
S : soleil ; C : couvert ; P : pluie ; V : vent fort ; O : orages ; N : neige

AMÉRIQUES		
BRASILIA	19/28	S
CHICAGO	7/21	S
MEXICO	10/24	S
MONTRÉAL	−6/0	N
NEW YORK	5/14	C
LA NOUVELLE-ORLÉANS	10/26	S
TORONTO	2/13	C

FRANCE métropole		
AJACCIO	9/19	S
BIARRITZ	8/16	P
CAEN	3/10	C
LILLE	3/11	C
NICE	9/16	S,V
PARIS	3/12	C

FRANCE d'outre-mer		
CAYENNE	23/27	P
FORT-DE-FR.	23/28	S
PAPEETE	25/31	P

AFRIQUE		
ALGER	13/21	S
DAKAR	20/26	O
KINSHASA	23/29	P
LE CAIRE	16/27	S
TUNIS	15/26	P

4-2 Prévisions météorologiques.

Ask your partner what the forecast is for the cities listed. He or she should refer to the weather map to respond.

Implementation: 4-2 Show the weather map (MFL, Instructor's Resources) and go over the city codes and weather symbols before completing the exercise.

Variation: 4-2 As an alternative, have students (in pairs or small groups) describe the weather in famous paintings you display as posters or slides. Some examples of good paintings to use include: *Rue de Paris, jour de pluie* ; *Toits sous la neige, Paris*, Gustave Caillebotte ; *La neige à Louveciennes* ; *Printemps aux environs de Paris, pommiers en fleurs*, Alfred Sisley ; *Coquelicots* ; *Promenade près d'Argenteuil* ; *Effet de vent, série des Peupliers* ; *Le Déjeuner*, Claude Monet ; *Les Boulevards extérieurs, effet de neige* ; *Arbres en fleurs*, Camille Pissarro ; *La Méridienne ou La Sieste (d'après Millet)*, Vincent van Gogh ; *Les parapluies*, Auguste Renoir.

MODÈLE à Lyon

É1 Quel temps est-ce qu'il va faire à Lyon ?
É2 À Lyon, il va pleuvoir.
É1 Et la température ?
É2 Il va faire onze degrés, donc il va faire assez frais.

1. à Paris
2. à Bordeaux
3. à Perpignan
4. à Brest
5. à Nice
6. à Grenoble
7. à Lille
8. à Strasbourg
9. à Bastia

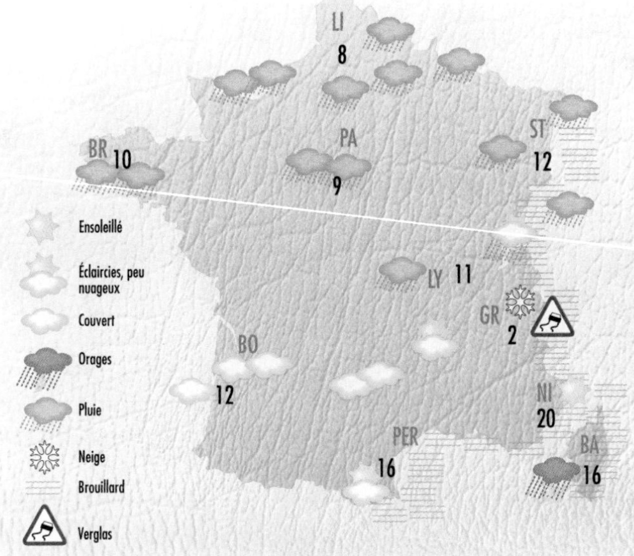

Implementation: **4-3** Follow up by having the class compare responses for each item.

Presentation: You may wish to present this vocabulary on day 2. Have students describe the weather in each photo. Ask what month they think it is, and present the seasons. Point out that the preposition *en* is used with all months of the year and all seasons except *le printemps* (*au printemps*).

4-3 Vos préférences. Find out your partner's preference in each case.

MODÈLE É1 Quand est-ce que tu n'aimes pas aller en classe ?
É2 Je n'aime pas aller en classe quand il neige beaucoup ou quand il y a un orage.

1. Quand est-ce que tu aimes rester dans le jardin ?
2. Quand est-ce que tu n'aimes pas faire du shopping ?
3. Quand est-ce que tu aimes faire du sport ?
4. Quand est-ce que tu préfères rester chez toi ?
5. Quand est-ce que tu aimes aller au cinéma ?
6. Quand est-ce que tu n'aimes pas voyager ?

LES SAISONS DE L'ANNÉE

le printemps (au printemps) à Lausanne en Suisse : mars, avril, mai

l'été (en été) à Cannes en France : juin, juillet, août

l'automne (en automne) à Dinant en Belgique : septembre, octobre, novembre

l'hiver (en hiver) au Québec : décembre, janvier, février

4-4 Nous sommes en quelle saison ? With your partner, decide which season is being described in each case.

Implementation: 4-4 Ask students to give specific months when appropriate. This exercise introduces cultural information and additional useful vocabulary; explain unfamiliar terms. Remind students that seasons are relative to the hemisphere; southern and northern hemispheres experience seasons at opposite times of the year.

Additional practice: For personalized practice in pairs or small groups, ask students what each season is like in their hometown: *Quel temps fait-il en hiver chez vous (ou chez vos parents) ?* Conclude by having students tell which season they prefer and why: *Quelle saison est-ce que vous préférez ? Pourquoi ?*

MODÈLE En Bretagne, le ciel est souvent couvert, il y a souvent de la pluie, mais il fait bon. On peut jouer au tennis ou au golf.

É1 C'est le printemps ou peut-être l'automne.

É2 Je pense que c'est le printemps parce qu'il y a beaucoup de pluie.

1. En France, on célèbre la fête nationale. Mais c'est la saison des orages : il y a des éclairs et du tonnerre. l'été (*juillet*)
2. Il y a souvent du brouillard en Bourgogne. Il gèle et il y a du verglas. l'hiver
3. À Paris, c'est la rentrée et le temps est variable. Souvent, il y a du vent et le ciel est gris. l'automne (*septembre/octobre*)
4. À la Martinique, il fait très chaud et lourd et il y a des nuages. Il pleut souvent. l'automne
5. On est sûr d'avoir du soleil et un temps chaud en France. Voilà pourquoi les Français partent en vacances. l'été (*juillet/août*)
6. Il y a beaucoup de soleil à Tahiti. On porte un maillot de bain. l'hiver (from the point of view of the northern hemisphere)
7. Partout en France, c'est la belle saison. Le ciel est bleu et il fait très beau. Mais les étudiants sont stressés parce que les examens vont bientôt commencer. le printemps (*mai/juin*)
8. Il fait très beau à la Guadeloupe. Il ne fait pas trop chaud. Il ne pleut pas. C'est le temps idéal pour aller à la plage. l'hiver et le printemps

Sons et lettres

Les voyelles nasales

Both English and French have nasal vowels. In English, any vowel followed by a nasal consonant is automatically nasalized, as in *man*, *pen*, *song*. In French, whether the vowel is nasal or not can make a difference in meaning. For example:

Note: The distinction between /œ̃/ and /ɛ̃/ is not generally made by speakers in the region of Paris, who tend to use /ɛ̃/ only. Because of that, and because /œ̃/ occurs in few words (*un, chacun, quelqu'un, lundi, parfum*), it not useful to insist that students make this distinction.

beau	/bo/	*handsome*	vs.	bon	/bɔ̃/	*good*
ça	/sa/	*that*	vs.	cent	/sɑ̃/	*a hundred*
sec	/sɛk/	*dry*	vs.	cinq	/sɛ̃k/	*five*

There are four nasal vowels in French. Use this phrase to remember them:

un /œ̃/ bon /bɔ̃/ vin /vɛ̃/ blanc /blɑ̃/ *a good white wine*

Nasal vowels are always written with a vowel letter followed by a nasal consonant (**m** or **n**), but that consonant is not usually pronounced: **mon**, **dans**, **cinq**.

- The vowel /ɔ̃/ is usually spelled **on**: l'**on**cle
- The vowel /ɑ̃/ is spelled **an** or **en**: j**an**vier, le v**en**t
- For /ɛ̃/ there are several spellings: mat**in**, le ch**ien**, l'exam**en**, la m**ain**
- The vowel /œ̃/, that many French people pronounce like /ɛ̃/, is spelled **un**: br**un**, l**un**di, quelqu'**un**
- Before **b** and **p**, all nasal vowels are spelled with **m**: c**om**bien, le t**em**ps, **im**possible

Note this exception: le b**on**bon

À vous la parole

04-05 to 04-06

Initial practice: Begin with a discrimination drill. Have students raise their hand when they hear words with a nasal vowel: *bon, l'eau, chanter, Jeanne, beau, mon, cent, sec, ta, vent,* etc. In another discrimination exercise, write the three nasal vowels on the board as: **in an on**, and have students indicate which you have pronounced: *Jean, blond, vingt,* etc.

4-5 Contrastes. Compare the pronunciation of each pair of words. Make sure to pronounce the nasal vowel in the second word.

beau/bon	allô/allons	sec/cinq
fine/fin	Jeanne/Jean	américaine/américain

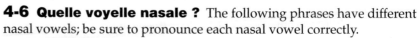

4-6 Quelle voyelle nasale ? The following phrases have different nasal vowels; be sure to pronounce each nasal vowel correctly.

1. le vin/le vent
2. cent pages/cinq pages
3. c'est long/c'est lent
4. il vend/ils vont
5. il est blond/il est blanc

4-7 Phrases. Read each sentence aloud.

1. Allons, allons ! Voyons ! Voyons !
2. En septembre, il y a souvent du vent.
3. Alain et Colin vont à Lyon par le train.
4. On annonce une température de vingt-cinq degrés.

FORMES ET FONCTIONS

1. Les verbes en *-re* comme *attendre*

Presentation: Before presenting this topic, review *-er* and *-ir* verbs to highlight the differences in the number of stems and spoken forms. Stress the importance of a clear articulation of the final consonant in the third person plural for both *-ir* and *-re* verbs; it is this final consonant that distinguishes the singular from the plural in speech.

- Like the **-ir** verbs you have already learned, verbs ending in **-re** have four spoken forms in the present tense; you can always tell whether someone is talking about one person, or more than one, because the **-d**, the consonant heard in the infinitive, is pronounced in the plural forms.

  elles répon**d**ent vs. elle répond

- The written endings for **-re** verbs are the same as for **-ir** verbs like **dormir**, except for the third person singular. Note that the final consonants in the singular forms are never pronounced.

  j'attends (*I wait*) tu entends (*you hear*) il répond (*he answers*)

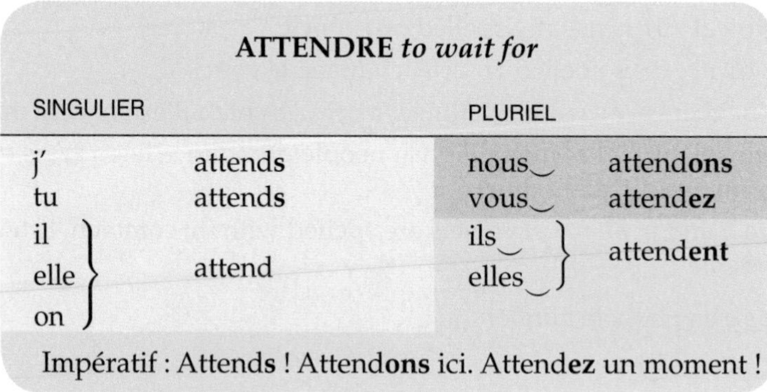

ATTENDRE ***to wait for***

SINGULIER		PLURIEL	
j'	attends	nous	attend**ons**
tu	attends	vous	attend**ez**
il / elle / on	attend	ils / elles	attend**ent**

Impératif : Attends ! Attend**ons** ici. Attend**ez** un moment !

- Here are the most common verbs ending in **-re**.

attendre	*to wait for*	Ils **attendent** le professeur.
descendre	*to go down*	Je **descends.**
de	*to get off*	Elle **descend du** bus.
en ville	*to go downtown*	Vous **descendez en ville** ?
entendre	*to hear*	Tu **entends** cette musique ?
perdre	*to lose*	Il **perd** toujours son portable.
rendre à	*to give back*	Le prof **rend** l'examen à Paul.
rendre visite à	*to visit someone*	Je **rends visite à** ma tante.
répondre à	*to answer*	Vous **répondez à** sa lettre ?
en	*to answer in*	Nous **répondons en** anglais.
vendre	*to sell*	Ils **vendent** des magazines.

Note: Be sure to stress that *rendre visite à* is the equivalent of the English verb "to visit," when a person is involved. Make sure students understand that the cognate *visiter* can only be used with places (e.g., *Je rends visite à mes grands-parents. On visite le musée du Louvre.*).

- English and French often differ in the use of prepositions with verbs:

J'attends le métro. — *I'm waiting* **for** *the subway.*
Il répond **au** professeur. — *He's answering the professor.*
Elle rend visite **à** sa mère. — *She's visiting her mother.*

À vous la parole

4-8 C'est logique. Create logical sentences using the elements given and one of the **-re** verbs.

MODÈLE nous/le métro
- Nous attendons le métro.

1. le professeur/en français en classe — il répond...
2. l'étudiante/ses devoirs au professeur — elle rend...
3. nous/des livres à la bibliothèque — nous rendons...
4. moi/mes parents à Québec — je rends visite à...
5. vous/le train ? — vous attendez...
6. toi/au téléphone ? — tu réponds...
7. elle/son foulard — elle perd...
8. Marc/de la musique — il entend...

Initial practice: Begin with a discrimination drill: one person, or more than one? *Ils attendent le prof. Elle entend le téléphone. Elles vendent la maison. Elle attend le bus. Ils répondent au prof. Elle descend du bus. Elles perdent leurs cahiers. Ils entendent la musique. Il rend visite aux grands-parents,* etc. Follow up with a simple substitution drill. Start first by contrasting third-person plural and third-person singular with visual cuing: *Elles descendent en ville* (next, cue the singular with one finger). *—Elle descend en ville.* Then proceed with the other forms: *Nous descendons en ville; moi. —Je descends en ville.*

4-9 Réponses personnelles. Use the questions to interview your partner. Then share with the class what you have learned.

MODÈLE É1 À qui est-ce que tu rends visite le week-end ?
É2 Je rends visite à mes parents. Et toi ?
É1 Je rends visite à mes amis.

1. À qui est-ce que tu rends visite le week-end ?
2. Est-ce que tu perds souvent tes vêtements ?
3. Est-ce que tu revends tes livres à la fin du semestre ?
4. Est-ce que tu réponds rapidement à tes messages ?
5. Quand est-ce que tu descends en ville, et pourquoi ?

Implementation: 4-9 Have students compare their responses.

Presentation: This topic can be presented inductively in class. Begin by describing your own activities during, for example, the past weekend. Then ask students questions about their own weekend, using yes/no, either/or, and short-answer questions that do not require students to use the new forms. Then ask students to tell you what time frame you are talking about, and whether they can tell how to form the *passé composé*. For students who are visual learners, you could display the text of your weekend activities on a transparency or slide with the forms in the *passé composé* highlighted.

2. Le passé composé avec *avoir*

- To express an action completed in the past, use the **passé composé**. The **passé composé** is a past tense composed of an auxiliary, or helping verb, and the past participle of the verb that expresses the action. Usually, the present tense of **avoir** is the helping verb.

J'**ai travaillé** hier.	*I worked yesterday.*
Tu **as mangé** ?	*Did you eat?*
Il **a fait** bon ce week-end.	*The weather was nice this weekend.*
Nous **avons écouté** la météo à la radio.	*We listened to the weather forecast on the radio.*
Vous **avez regardé** la météo à la télé.	*You watched the weather forecast on TV.*
Ils **ont annoncé** du beau temps à la radio.	*They predicted nice weather on the radio.*

- The specific meaning of the **passé composé** depends on the verb and on the context.

Hier on **a montré** un film à la télé.	*Yesterday they showed a film on TV.*
Est-ce que tu **as préparé** l'examen ?	*Have you studied for the test?*
L'hiver dernier il **a fait** très froid.	*Last winter it was very cold.*
Est-ce qu'elle **a travaillé** hier ?	*Did she work yesterday?*

- To form the past participle:
  - for **-er** verbs, add **-é** to the base (the infinitive form minus the **-er** ending):

quitt**er**	J'ai quitt**é** la maison à huit heures.	*I left home at eight o'clock.*

  - for **-ir** verbs, add **-i** to the base (the infinitive form minus the **-ir** ending):

dorm**ir**	Tu as dorm**i** pendant le concert ?	*You slept during the concert?*

  - for **-re** verbs, add **-u** to the base (the infinitive form minus the **-re** ending):

attend**re**	Ils ont attend**u** devant le café.	*They waited in front of the café.*

Note: The past participle for the irregular verb *aller* is not supplied here since it is conjugated with *être* in the *passé composé*. Verbs conjugated with *être* are presented in L. 2 of this chapter.

- Here are past participles for irregular verbs that you know.

avoir	J'ai **eu** une bonne note.	*I got a good grade.*
être	On a **été** surpris.	*We were surprised.*
faire	Il a **fait** beau.	*It was nice weather.*
mettre	J'ai **mis** un chapeau.	*I put on a hat.*
pleuvoir	Il a **plu** hier.	*It rained yesterday.*

Note: You might point out that short adverbs such as *déjà* and *beaucoup* are placed after the helping verb.

- In negative sentences, place **ne** (**n'**) and **pas** around the conjugated auxiliary verb.

Il **n'**a **pas** fait beau hier.	*The weather wasn't nice yesterday.*
Nos parents **n'**ont **pas** téléphoné.	*Our parents didn't call.*

- The following expressions are useful for referring to the past.

hier	*yesterday*
avant-hier	*the day before yesterday*
samedi dernier	*last Saturday*
l'année dernière	*last year*
il y a longtemps	*a long time ago*
il y a deux jours	*two days ago*
ce jour-là	*that day*
à ce moment-là	*at that moment*

Initial practice: Begin with a discrimination drill: *aujourd'hui ou hier ? Je vais en classe. J'ai fait les devoirs. J'ai regardé la télé. Il neige. Nous avons travaillé. Tu regardes la météo. J'ai bien dormi.* Follow with simple substitution drills a) to practice the forms of the verb *avoir: Nous avons travaillé ; Clarice — Elle a travaillé*, etc.; b) to practice negation: *Elle n'a pas travaillé ; nous ? Nous n'avons pas travaillé*, etc.; c) to practice regular and irregular past participles: *Elle travaille. — Elle a travaillé ; Elle fait la cuisine. — Elle a fait la cuisine.*, etc.

Implementation: 4-10 Students are instructed to use expressions from the word bank to avoid the unnatural use of *avoir* and *être* in the *passé composé;* these weather expressions would more naturally appear in the *imparfait.* Expressions using *faire* and other verbs, however, occur frequently in the *passé composé* when used to tell what the weather was like at a particular point in time.

À vous la parole

11
14 **4-10 La météo d'hier.** Look at the weather map and tell what the weather was like yesterday in Canada and in New England using words and expressions from the list.

faire beau	neiger
faire du vent	ne pas faire très beau
geler	pleuvoir

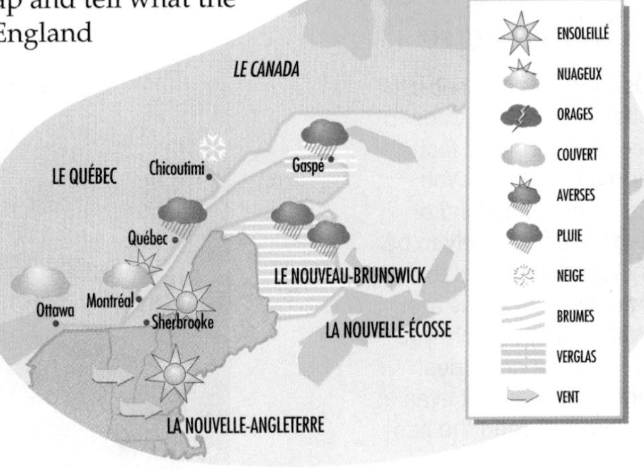

MODÈLE Au Nouveau-Brunswick ?
- Au Nouveau-Brunswick, il a gelé et il a plu.

1. À Chicoutimi ? Il a neigé.
2. En Nouvelle-Angleterre ? Il a fait beau; il a fait du vent.
3. À Montréal ? Il n'a pas fait très beau.
4. À Gaspé ? Il a plu. Il a gelé.
5. À Sherbrooke ? Il a fait beau.
6. À Ottawa ? Il n'a pas fait beau.

4-11 Mais c'est logique ! With your partner, imagine what different people did yesterday. Try to think of as many possibilities as you can.

MODÈLE Qu'est-ce que Julie a fait dans le magasin hier ?
- Elle a acheté une jolie robe.
- Elle a travaillé.

1. Qu'est-ce que vous avez fait au parc ce matin ?
2. Qu'est-ce que les Brunet ont fait à la piscine l'été dernier ?
3. Qu'est-ce que tu as fait à la bibliothèque hier ?
4. Qu'est-ce que nous avons fait en classe hier ?
5. Qu'est-ce que tu as fait chez toi hier soir ?
6. Qu'est-ce que David a fait au stade avant-hier ?
7. Qu'est-ce que vos camarades ont fait chez eux le week-end dernier ?
8. Qu'est-ce que le prof a fait dans son bureau ce matin ?

Implementation: 4-11 Point out to students at the beginning that asking *Qu'est-ce que vous avez fait hier soir ?* does not necessarily require that the answer begin with the verb *faire.* It is simply a general question. It might help students to show the similarity with English, where the question "What did you do yesterday?" would not normally be answered by saying something like "I *did* watch television." Follow up by having students compare their answers.

Additional practice: Put students into small groups to describe their activities of the previous day. The group must then decide whether each student was *très active/actif, assez active/actif*, or *(assez) sédentaire* (put these categories on the board). Follow up by having each group tell what they decided, and have them justify their response.

Note: You might point out to students that the *DOM* are a favored destination for the French during their winter and spring vacations; these locales are sure to have warm weather at those times. Vacation times and activities are treated in more depth in Ch. 4, L. 2.

4-12 Normalement, mais... What do you normally do? Tell your partner about your habits and the occasional exceptions.

MODÈLE dormir

• Normalement, je dors jusqu'à sept heures, mais samedi dernier, j'ai dormi jusqu'à dix heures.

1. dormir
2. manger
3. quitter la maison
4. travailler à la bibliothèque
5. jouer
6. regarder la télé
7. passer l'été

Lisons

4-13 Martinique : Guide pratique.

Stratégie

Use the title and subtitles of a text as clues to understanding its focus and organization. You can learn what kind of information is likely to be included and what the major subdivisions are. With this approach, you will know a great deal about the content even before you read the passage as a whole.

La baie de St-Pierre à la Martinique

Key: Avant de lire 1) the intended audience is those who are planning to travel there; brainstorm a list with students; this might include: information about visas, climate, what to visit and so forth 2) general information and practical concerns 3) Students' answers will vary, but should include the main topics listed in the subheads.

A. Avant de lire. The following passage is excerpted from a travel guide written by **le Comité Martiniquais du Tourisme**. Martinique is a frequent travel destination for the French, since it is a **département d'outre-mer** and because of its mild climate during winter months. Before reading, look at the title and the various subtitles to get a sense of the focus and organization of this passage.

1. The title of the booklet is *Martinique : Guide pratique*. Who do you think is the intended audience for a *Guide pratique*? What kind of information would you expect to be included in a "practical guide"?
2. Now look at the two major subtitles that appear in red type. They set up the two major divisions of this text. What is the focus of each?
3. Finally, look at the eight subheads in black type. These indicate the topic of each paragraph. Considering these subheads together with what you have determined about the focus and organization of the text, summarize what you know already about its content.

B. En lisant. As you read each section, look for the following information.

1. What is the capital of Martinique?
2. How far is Martinique from France?

3. What is the climate like?
4. Name three natural resources of Martinique.
5. Which languages are spoken and understood in Martinique?
6. As a North American, do you need a visa to enter Martinique? What is required?
7. What type of clothes would you need to bring to visit Martinique?

Key: *En lisant* 1) Fort-de-France 2) 7,000 kilometers 3) warm comfortable climate, not too hot, around 27°C (or about 80°F) 4) rum, sugar, bananas 5) French, Creole, English in tourist regions 6) No visa is required for a stay of under three months; proof of identity is required 7) casual summer clothes, sweaters for evening, sunglasses

Martinique : Guide pratique

Informations générales

Histoire et administration

Christophe Colomb débarque à la Martinique en 1502 et depuis 1635, excepté de courtes périodes d'occupation anglaise, elle partage[1] les destinées de la France. Département français depuis 1946 et région depuis 1982, sa structure administrative et politique est identique à celle des départements de la métropole. Siège[2] de la préfecture, Fort-de-France est la capitale administrative, commerciale et culturelle de la Martinique.

Géographie

La Martinique fait partie du groupe des petites Antilles ou « Îles au vent ». Elle est baignée à l'Ouest par la Mer des Antilles et à l'Est par l'Océan Atlantique. Elle se trouve à environ 7.000 km de la France et 440 km du continent américain.

Climat

Le climat est relativement doux à la Martinique et la chaleur n'y est jamais insupportable. La température moyenne se situe aux environs de 27°C, mais sur les hauteurs, il fait plus frais. De l'Est et du Nord-est, des brises régulières, les alizés, rafraîchissent l'atmosphère en permanence.

Ressources économiques

Principales ressources naturelles de l'île : le rhum, le sucre, l'ananas, la banane. La Martinique produit également des conserves de fruits, des confitures et des jus de fruits locaux. Le tourisme connaît un essor[3] remarquable et tend à devenir le secteur économique de pointe.

Langue

Le français est parlé et compris par toute la population mais on entend beaucoup le créole. Bien entendu, l'anglais est également parlé surtout dans les lieux touristiques.

Informations pratiques

Formalités d'entrée

Les Français peuvent entrer en Martinique avec leur carte nationale d'identité ou leur passeport. Les ressortissants des États-Unis et du Canada sont admis sans visa pour un séjour inférieur à trois mois. Une pièce d'identité est toutefois requise.

Conseils vestimentaires

Au pays de l'éternel été, vous porterez des vêtements légers et décontractés pour vos excursions : maillot de bain, short et sandales pour la plage. Les femmes s'habillent généralement le soir davantage[4] que les messieurs pour lesquels veste et cravate ne sont exigés que[5] très rarement. Toutefois, n'oubliez pas un lainage et vos lunettes de soleil.

Monnaie

La monnaie légale est l'Euro. Le dollar américain est accepté ainsi que tout autre paiement par chèque de voyage ou carte de crédit.

[1]*shares* [2]*Seat* [3]*development* [4]*more* [5]*are only required*

C. En regardant de plus près. Now that you understand the focus and general content of this text, examine the following elements closely.

1. Look at the noun **les ressortissants** in the section **Formalités d'entrée**. Can you see an **-ir** verb in the noun? Which one? Given the meaning of that verb and the context, what does the word **ressortissants** mean?
2. The word **vestimentaires** in the section **Conseils vestimentaires** is related to another French word you know. Given the context, what do you think this adjective means?
3. In the same section, you see the noun **un lainage**. Can you see a noun in this word that describes a type of material? Given its meaning and the context, what do you think **un lainage** is?

Key: *En regardant de plus près* 1) the verb is *sortir*; students could guess someone going out of, or someone leaving a place; in this context it refers to people who are coming from the U.S. or Canada 2) this is related to *vêtements* and refers to advice about clothing 3) the word is *laine*; so *un lainage* is clothing made of wool, or in this context, a sweater or wrap for the evening

D. Après avoir lu. Discuss the following questions with your classmates.

1. How well did your initial summary of the content of this guide correspond with the specific information that actually was provided?
2. What information, if any, do you think is missing for potential visitors to Martinique?
3. Based on the information provided, would you be interested in visiting Martinique? Why or why not?

Leçon 2 On part en vacances !

POINTS DE DÉPART

Des activités par tous les temps

Preparation: You might show the video montage *Vive les vacances !* at the beginning of L. 2, as it provides examples of vacation activities at different times of the year. Ask students to identify locations (*la plage, la montagne, la ville*), seasons, weather, and activities that they see. The video clip *La Côte d'Azur: destination de rêve* can also be used in L. 2. In this clip, a young woman describes attractions of the *Côte d'Azur*. See MFL/SAM for a complete treatment.

Presentation: Show the vacation activities (MFL/Instructor's Resources) to present the new vocabulary. Describe each scene briefly; display each image without labels (MFL/Instructor's Resources), and test comprehension by having students point to the activity you name. As a prelude to Ex. 4-14, have students associate each activity with a place, a season, and weather conditions. Have students repeat the new vocabulary, using either/or questions: *on fait du ski nautique ou de la voile ?*, etc. Complete Ex. 4-14 before presenting the dialogue.

À la plage, au bord de la mer ou au lac, on fait...
du ski nautique
du surf
de la voile
de la planche à voile
et on bronze.

À la campagne, on fait...
des pique-niques
du cheval
du vélo
et de la moto.

À la montagne, on fait...
du camping
de l'alpinisme
des randonnées
du ski
du surf des neiges
et de la motoneige.

En ville, on fait...
du tourisme
un tour au parc
des courses
du shopping
et on visite des musées
et des monuments.

Projets de vacances

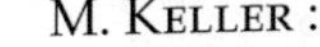

M. KELLER : Cette année, on va pas aux sports d'hiver.
MAX : Ah, non, c'est pas vrai ! Zut alors !
M. KELLER : Si, cette année, vous n'allez pas faire du ski en février, mais du ski nautique.
CARLINE : Chouette ! Alors on va aux Antilles ? À Tahiti ?
M. KELLER : Pas tout à fait, ma grande. J'ai des billets d'avion pour aller à la Réunion, dans l'océan Indien.
MAX : Bravo ! Vive la Réunion !
CARLINE : Et la voile, la planche à voile !
M. KELLER : Et vive la pêche et le repos !

Note: The locations mentioned in the dialogue—*les Antilles, Tahiti, la Réunion*—are either *départements* or *collectivités d'outre-mer*, so all are logical choices for a French family. Locate each place on a map.

Note: This dialogue introduces some typical exclamations used in French. In normal conversational style, negative *ne/n'* is usually dropped by native speakers of French. However, point out that it is better for students learning French to pronounce the *ne/n'*, as its loss by non-native speakers is perceived negatively by many French speakers. Thus, students should say *Ce n'est pas vrai !* Have students listen to the dialogue. Check comprehension by having students pick out the preferred activities of each person. You can use this exchange as a point of departure for discussing *Les vacances des Français*. Follow up with Ex. 4-15 and 4-16.

04-18 to 04-21

À vous la parole

Key: 4-14 *Answers may vary.* 1) On fait du ski nautique/de la natation/du surf/de la voile. On bronze. 2) On fait des pique-niques/du cheval/du vélo/de la moto. 3) On bronze. 4) On fait du camping/des randonnées/des pique-niques. 5) On fait de la voile/de la planche à voile. 6) On visite des musées. On fait des courses/du shopping. 7) On fait du tourisme/un tour au parc. On visite des monuments. 8) On visite des musées. On fait du shopping.

4-14 Qu'est-ce qu'on fait ? Answer each question by suggesting logical activities.

MODÈLE Qu'est-ce qu'on fait à la montagne, quand il y a de la neige ?
- On fait du ski.

OU On fait du surf des neiges.

1. Qu'est-ce qu'on fait à la plage, en été ?
2. Qu'est-ce qu'on fait à la campagne, quand il fait beau ?
3. Qu'est-ce qu'on fait au bord de la mer, quand il y a un beau soleil ?
4. Qu'est-ce qu'on fait à la montagne, au printemps ?
5. Qu'est-ce qu'on fait au lac, quand il y a du vent ?
6. Qu'est-ce qu'on fait en ville, quand il fait très chaud ?
7. Qu'est-ce qu'on fait en ville, quand il fait beau ?
8. Qu'est-ce qu'on fait en ville, quand il fait mauvais ?

Implementation: 4-15 Let students take turns suggesting an activity. Note that the reactions come from the dialogue *Projets de vacances*. Encourage students to be dramatic as they react with an appropriate expression to suggestions from their partner.

4-15 Suggestions. Suggest a suitable activity for each location to your partner and see what his or her reaction is!

MODÈLE Vous êtes à la montagne.

É1 On va faire une randonnée.

É2 Super ! J'adore la nature !

OU Zut alors ! Je n'ai pas de bonnes chaussures !

1. Vous êtes à la montagne.
2. Vous êtes à la plage.
3. Vous êtes à la campagne.
4. Vous êtes en ville.

Implementation: 4-16 Follow up by having students report back on their ideal vacation.

4-16 Les vacances idéales. Discuss your ideal vacation with a classmate.

Additional practice: Have students complete the following activity. They may need additional vocabulary depending on what city or region they describe.

À l'Office du Tourisme. Explain to your partner what tourists typically do in your region.

MODÈLE É1 J'habite à Asheville, en Caroline du Nord. Nous sommes à la montagne. Il fait beau en été et les gens font du camping et des randonnées. En hiver, il neige et les gens font du ski. Et toi ?

É2 Moi, j'habite à Baltimore, dans le Maryland. C'est près de l'océan. Il y a un port et un grand aquarium, ...

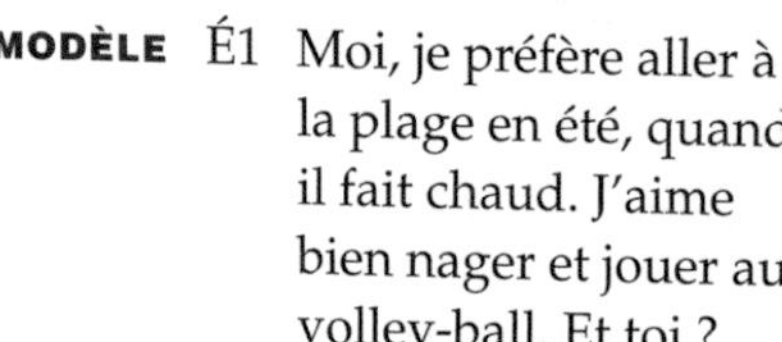

MODÈLE É1 Moi, je préfère aller à la plage en été, quand il fait chaud. J'aime bien nager et jouer au volley-ball. Et toi ?

É2 Pour moi, les vacances idéales, c'est la montagne en hiver. J'adore faire du ski et du surf des neiges…

Mes vacances idéales, c'est l'été dans les Alpes. Me voici près de Pralognon la Vanoise, une petite station de ski en Savoie. J'adore faire des randonnées.

Presentation: Use the school calendar to review important cultural concepts such as *la rentrée*—going back to school in September—and holiday periods in France. Establishing zones makes it possible to avoid major traffic difficulties when everyone leaves on vacation and cuts down on overcrowding at the most popular destinations. Guadeloupe, Martinique, Guyane, etc., are included since their status as *DOM* make them a part of France just like the metropolitan departments, even though the vacation periods are determined locally. Note that these are all popular vacation destinations for the French.

Vie et culture

Les vacances des Français

Look at the calendar to identify the various holiday periods for French school children. Notice that France is divided into three zones for two of the vacation periods; the map shows the location of each zone. Can you explain this division into zones? Think about when these vacation periods take place, what French people might do, and where they would most likely go during these times. What other places, besides metropolitan France, figure into the map? Why would these places be included?

Since 1982, all salaried workers in France have had the right to five weeks of paid vacation each year. With the advent of the 35-hour workweek in 2000, the French began to take more frequent, and shorter, vacations, often opting for long weekend trips. Throughout France, however, it is still not unusual to see many small businesses (restaurants, hairdressers, shops, bakeries, etc.) closed for several weeks in the months of July or August.

ZONE A
Caen, Clermont-Ferrand, Grenoble, Lyon, Montpellier, Nancy-Metz, Nantes, Rennes, Toulouse

Rentrée scolaire des élèves	Toussaint	Noël	Hiver	Printemps	Début des vacances d'été
le mardi 04-09-12	du samedi 27-10-12 au jeudi 08-11-12	du samedi 22-12-12 au lundi 07-01-13	du samedi 23-02-13 au lundi 11-03-13	du samedi 20-04-13 au lundi 06-05-13	le jeudi 04-07-13

ZONE B
Aix-Marseille, Amiens, Besançon, Dijon, Lille, Limoges, Nice, Orléans-Tours, Poitiers, Reims, Rouen, Strasbourg

Rentrée scolaire des élèves	Toussaint	Noël	Hiver	Printemps	Début des vacances d'été
le mardi 04-09-12	du samedi 27-10-12 au jeudi 08-11-12	du samedi 22-12-12 au lundi 07-01-13	du samedi 16-02-13 au lundi 04-03-13	du samedi 13-04-13 au lundi 29-04-13	le jeudi 04-07-13

ZONE C
Bordeaux, Créteil, Paris, Versailles

Rentrée scolaire des élèves	Toussaint	Noël	Hiver	Printemps	Début des vacances d'été
le mardi 04-09-12	du samedi 27-10-12 au jeudi 08-11-12	du samedi 22-12-12 au lundi 07-01-13	du samedi 02-03-13 au lundi 18-03-10	du samedi 27-04-10 au lundi 13-05-10	le jeudi 04-07-13

Le départ en vacances a lieu après la classe, la reprise des cours le matin des jours indiqués.

ET VOUS ?

1. How many weeks of paid vacation are typical in the United States? How does this situation compare with that of France? What factors might account for any differences?
2. The right to longer paid vacations has often been a factor in labor negotiations in France. Knowing this, and that many businesses shut down for weeks at a time for vacation, what conclusions can you draw about the value the French place on vacations? Do North Americans place a similar value on vacations?

Sons et lettres

Les voyelles nasales et les voyelles orales plus consonne nasale

Presentation: Demonstrate for students a careful articulation of the final /n/ for words in the left-hand column. To practice other pairs of female-male names (like *Simone/Simon*), use *Jeanne/Jean, Adrienne/Adrien, Yvonne/Yvon.*

Compare the following pairs of words; the first ends with a final pronounced consonant (**-n** or **-m**) and the second ends in a nasal vowel. Only the second word contains a nasal vowel; notice the difference as you repeat these words.

bonne /bɔn/	bon /bɔ̃/
Simone /simɔn/	Simon /simɔ̃/
ma cousine /kuzin/	mon cousin /kuzɛ̃/
l'année /lane/	l'an /lɑ̃/

Initial practice: Begin with an exercise that requires a change from masculine to feminine, and vice versa : *Il est bon. —Elle est bonne ; Il est brun ; Ils sont canadiens ; Il est américain ; C'est Jean ; mon cousin ; mes voisins ; Voilà Simon ; Ils sont bons.*

For words containing a nasal vowel, pronounce each syllable slowly, and do not pronounce **-m** or **-n** when it follows the nasal vowel:

le camp	le cam-ping	la cam-pagne
mon	mon-ter	la mon-tagne

04-22 to 04-23

À vous la parole

Implementation: 4-17 Have students pronounce the second word syllable-by-syllable several times, and then as a word: *mon, mon tagne, montagne.* Additional words with nasal vowels include: *rentrer, penser, chanter, combien, la campagne, impossible.*

4-17 Les groupes de mots. As you pronounce these words, pay close attention to the pronunciation of the nasal vowel.

1. mon — mon-tagne
2. sans — san-té (*health*)
3. camp — cam-ping
4. franc — fran-çaise
5. l'un — lun-di

4-18 Les phrases. Read each sentence out loud.

1. Il fait bon en automne.
2. Mettons notre blouson et nos gants.
3. Jean et Jeanne vont en Bourgogne en juin.
4. Au printemps, Marianne va en Louisiane chez son oncle.
5. Lundi, nous faisons une randonnée à la montagne avec nos parents.

Implementation: 4-19 Students should recognize that the repetition of nasal vowels in the Verlaine poem helps produce a melancholic mood. Verlaine was 18 years old when he wrote this poem; you might read it in its entirety for students. The complete text of the poem can be found in the collection *Poèmes saturniens* or on the Web. See MFL/SAM for a treatment of another Verlaine poem, *Il pleure dans mon cœur.*

4-19 Poème. Repeat these two lines from a poem by Verlaine.

> Les sanglots° longs des violons de l'automne
> Blessent° mon cœur d'une langueur monotone.
>
> —Extrait de Paul Verlaine, « *Chanson d'automne* »

sobbing
strike

FORMES ET FONCTIONS

1. Le passé composé avec *être*

Presentation: Have students pick out the complete paradigm of the *passé composé* with *être* through the examples provided. You might show contrasts like *Je suis allé/e à la bibliothèque* vs. *J'ai trouvé le livre de Simenon* and ask students what type of expression follows the verb. Point out that verbs that form the *passé composé* with *être* do not take a direct object, only adverbial complements. In fact, if a direct object does follow, the verb *avoir* must be used: *Je suis sorti ce matin* vs. *J'ai sorti le chien; Il est monté au bureau* vs. *Il a monté les ordinateurs au bureau*. Also, not all verbs of motion form the *passé composé* with *être: Nous avons traversé la rue ; tu as quitté l'université ?* Note that these verbs take a direct object. Verbs conjugated like *venir* are presented in Ch. 8, L. 2. Refer students to Appendix 2 for conjugations of *naître* and *mourir*.

- To tell what you did in the past, you have already learned that most French verbs form the **passé composé** with the present tense of **avoir**. However, some verbs use the present tense forms of **être** as an auxiliary. These are usually verbs of motion:

descendre	*to go down*	Nous **sommes descendues** en ville pour dîner.
rentrer	*to go/come back home*	Nous **sommes rentrés** tard après une journée de ski.
monter	*to go up*	Lucie **est montée** dans sa chambre.
rester	*to stay*	Ils **sont restés** au lac tout l'après-midi.
sortir	*to go out*	Rémy **est sorti** en ville avec Juliette pour faire du tourisme.
partir	*to leave*	Vous **êtes parties** ensemble à la montagne ?
venir	*to come*	Il **est venu** à la campagne avec nous pour un pique-nique.
aller	*to go*	Tu **es allé** à la plage ce week-end ?
naître	*to be born*	Elle **est née** en 1992.
devenir	*to become*	Elle **est devenue** professeur.
entrer	*to go/come in*	Anne **est entrée** dans le magasin.
retourner	*to return*	Elles **sont retournées** en France.
tomber	*to fall*	Elle **est tombée** dans la rue (*street*).
revenir	*to come back*	Elle **est revenue** à l'Office du Tourisme hier matin.
arriver	*to arrive*	Je **suis arrivé** en ville vers dix heures du matin.
mourir	*to die*	Il **est mort** l'été dernier.
passer	*to go/come by*	On **est passés** chez toi hier.

- For verbs that form the **passé composé** with **être**, the past participle agrees in gender and number with the subject.

Mon frère est arrivé hier.	*My brother arrived yesterday.*
Ma sœur est arrivé**e** ce matin.	*My sister arrived this morning.*
Ses cousins sont allé**s** au musée.	*Her cousins went to the museum.*
Ses cousines sont descendu**es** en ville aussi.	*Her cousins went downtown too.*

- Pronominal verbs also use **être** in the **passé composé**. Note, however, that when a noun follows the verb, no past participle agreement is made.

Il s'est endormi.	*He fell asleep.*
Ils se sont couché**s**.	*They went to bed.*
Elle s'est lavé**e**.	*She washed up.*
Elle s'est lavé les cheveux.	*She washed her hair.*

- To narrate a series of events or actions, use the following expressions:

D'abord elle s'est lavée, **ensuite** elle s'est habillée et **puis** elle a mangé.	*First she washed up, next she got dressed, and then she ate.*
Après, elle s'est brossé les dents et **enfin** elle est partie au travail.	*Afterwards, she brushed her teeth and finally, she left for work.*

Fiche pratique

You have learned that you can use a mnemonic device to recall facts that must be memorized. The list of verbs conjugated with **être** in the **passé composé** is easy to remember if you use a mnemonic device such as the acronym "Dr. & Mrs. P. Vandertramp" (each letter stands for a verb conjugated with **être**).

Presentation: The learning strategy focuses on mnemonic devices: display, explain, and distribute the illustration of the "house of *être*," (MFL/Instructor's Resoures); Point out that the list of verbs is organized according to the "Dr. & Mrs. P. Vandertramp" mnemonic. Remind students that they used this strategy in Ch. 3, L. 3 for the prenominal adjectives, where they learned the BRAGS mnemonic.

Note: Agreement of the past participle with the subject pronoun *on* is variable. Agreement can be made where *on* replaces *nous*; thus, in this example, the past participle *passés* indicates that the understood subject is masculine plural. On a strictly grammatical basis there is no agreement, since *on* is a third-person indefinite singular pronoun.

Initial practice: Begin with this comprehension-based activity. To practice forms orally, begin with a discrimination drill: tell a story in the past and have students raise their hands when they hear a verb conjugated with *être: Nous avons décidé de préparer une fête. J'ai téléphoné à Alain. Il est venu chez moi. On a téléphoné à nos amis. Patricia et Francine sont arrivées tout de suite. Aurélie est arrivée un peu plus tard. Nous avons écouté de la musique. Alain est allé au supermarché pour chercher du coca-cola. Nous avons dansé. Nos amis sont partis vers minuit*, etc. Review the forms of *être* with simple substitution drills: *Je suis parti ; nous ; eux*, etc. ; *Je me suis réveillé/e ; toi ; vous*, etc. Follow with a transformation drill, present to past: *Je voyage. —J'ai voyagé ; Je pars. —Je suis parti/e.*

04-24 to 04-27

4-20 La vie des serveurs. Working as a server is difficult. Read each sentence carefully in order to determine if it refers to servers nowadays (**maintenant**) or in the past (**au passé**).

Les serveurs…

	maintenant	au passé
MODÈLE … sont stressés.	✓	
1. … sont arrivés à l'heure.		✓
2. … sont énergiques.	✓	
3. … sont entrés dans le bar.		✓
4. … sont assez jeunes.	✓	
5. … sont devenus des amis.		✓
6. … sont fatigués.	✓	
7. … sont sortis ensemble.		✓
8. … sont réservés.	✓	
9. … sont allés au cinéma.		✓

Based on the information above, is it easier to be a server now or was it easier in the past? Why?

4-21 L'après-midi de M. Dumont. Tell what M. Dumont did yesterday afternoon using the **passé composé**. *Answers may vary.*

Cet après-midi, M. Dumont va sortir faire une promenade. Sa femme [est restée] va rester à la maison pour préparer le dîner. Alors, M. Dumont [est sorti] va sortir avec son chien, Castor. Ils [sont partis] vont partir vers trois heures, et ils [sont passés] vont passer chez un ami de M. Dumont. Ensuite, ils [sont allés] vont aller au parc, et ils [sont entrés] vont entrer au zoo. Finalement, ils [sont descendus] vont descendre par l'avenue principale, et ils [sont rentrés] vont rentrer à la maison vers cinq heures.

MODÈLE • Hier après-midi, M. Dumont est sorti faire une promenade.

Implementation: 4-22 To prepare for the narrative, review the useful adverbs *d'abord, ensuite, après, puis, enfin*, and have students first narrate in the present tense. You might have students work in pairs. You may also ask them to go beyond the pictures and imagine other logical activities. As a follow-up, have several pairs present their narratives and have the class vote on the best one.

4-22 Le samedi de Maxime. Tell how Maxime spent last Saturday. Don't forget to use the expressions you have learned to sequence events in a narrative: **d'abord, ensuite, après, puis, enfin.**

MODÈLE • D'abord, Maxime a quitté sa chambre à huit heures. Ensuite, il…
OU • D'abord, Maxime est sorti à huit heures. Après, il…

Ensuite, il est allé au restaurant et il a mangé.

Après, il est parti pour le stade; il est arrivé à 10 h.

À 11 h, il a joué au rugby.

Il est retourné à sa chambre et il a fait ses devoirs.

Maxime et sa copine Julie sont allés au cinéma à 20 h 20.

Il est rentré chez lui à 1 h du matin et il s'est couché.

4-23 Et vous ? What did you do yesterday? Where did you go? With whom? Discuss your day with your partner.

MODÈLE • Hier, dimanche, je ne suis pas allé/e à la fac. J'ai quitté mon appartement vers neuf heures, et ensuite…

Variation: 4-23 Have students tell about last weekend, last summer, etc.

2. Les questions avec *quel*

- The interrogative adjective **quel** is used to ask *which?* or *what?* Although **quel** agrees in number and gender with the noun it modifies, it is always pronounced the same, unless a plural form, **quels** or **quelles**, modifies a noun beginning with a vowel and liaison occurs.

Quel écrivain est-ce que tu préfères ?	*Which writer do you prefer?*
Quelle musique est-ce qu'il préfère ?	*What type of music does he prefer?*
Quels musées est-ce que tu aimes ?	*Which museums do you like?*
Quelles‿affiches est-ce que tu vas acheter ?	*Which posters are you going to buy?*

Presentation: To present *quel*, display the sentence examples and ask students to explain the differences in spelling; point out *enchaînement* and *liaison* before nouns beginning with a vowel, in the singular and plural, respectively. Additional practice is provided in the SAM/MFL.

- **Quel** is used in a number of fixed interrogative expressions:

Quel temps fait-il ?	*What's the weather like?*
Quelle heure est-il ?	*What time is it?*
Quelle est la date aujourd'hui ?	*What's today's date?*
Quel âge as-tu ?	*How old are you?*

Note: Since many of these examples involve inversion, focus on having students learn them as fixed phrases; do not teach or stress inversion here.

- **Quel** can also be used before a form of the verb **être**, followed by the noun it modifies:

Quelle est ta saison préférée ?	*What's your favorite season?*
Quelles sont les meilleures résidences ?	*Which are the best residence halls?*

04-28 to 04-31

À vous la parole

Initial practice: Begin with a quick drill: *Tu vois la plage ? — Quelle plage ? ; Tu vois le monsieur ? les enfants ? le cheval ? les vélos ? la montagne ? les skis ? les billets ?*

4-24 Petite épreuve. Ask your partner for the following information.

les jours de la semaine

É1 Quels sont les jours de la semaine ?
É2 Lundi, mardi, …

1. les jours de la semaine
2. les mois de l'année
3. les saisons de l'année
4. la date de la fête nationale française
5. la date de son anniversaire
6. sa saison préférée

Note: 4-25 If you want students to have written practice, you might ask them to write out their questions. Additional written practice is provided in the SAM/MFL.

4-25 Une interview. Interview your partner to discover his or her preferences.

MODÈLE la saison

É1 Quelle saison est-ce que tu préfères ?
É2 Je préfère l'automne. Et toi, quelle est ta saison préférée ?
É1 Moi, j'adore le printemps.

1. la saison
2. la ville
3. l'artiste
4. les acteurs
5. le sport
6. les activités culturelles

Observons

04-55 to 04-57

Presentation: *Avant de regarder.* Encourage students to use these phrases and the photos as clues to where the two people went and what they did; have students anticipate other information and specific vocabulary they might hear in the clip. Additional activities for a third speaker who describes vacation possibilities in her homeland of Quebec are in the SAM/MFL.

4-26 Des superbes vacances.

A. Avant de regarder. In this video clip, Corinne and Édouard describe memorable vacations. Look at the photos and the expressions below and decide where you think they each went. What do you think they did while they were there?

Corinne :
J'ai pu voir des crocodiles…
…ils ont un beau hamac.
… j'en ai profité pour faire des photos avec Mickey, Daisy, Donald…

Édouard :
… je suis parti en croisière en bateau à voile.
… on a découvert… toutes les îles italiennes.

B. En regardant. As you watch, answer the following questions.

1. Check all the places that each person mentions:

Corinne:

____ la Californie	✓ les États-Unis	✓ les Everglades	✓ la Floride
____ Miami	____ New York	✓ Orlando	____ Paris

Édouard:

✓ Antibes	✓ la Corse	✓ la France	____ la Grèce
____ l'île Maurice	✓ Naples	____ Nice	____ Rome

2. Corinne and Édouard did not spend their vacations alone. Who was with them? Corinne: with family at her cousin's home; Édouard: with three friends
3. What did Corinne and Édouard do during their vacations? Corinne: saw crocodiles, beautiful gardens, Mickey Mouse, Daisy and Donald Duck at Disney World in Orlando; Édouard: sailed to Corsica, the Italian islands, and Naples

C. Après avoir regardé. Now discuss the following questions with your classmates.

1. Why do you think that both Corinne and Édouard thought their vacations were particularly memorable?
2. Have you visited any of the places mentioned by Corinne or Édouard? If so, what did you see and what did you do there?
3. What would you consider to be a fabulous vacation? Do your ideas correspond to the vacations described by Corinne and Édouard or shown in the photos? Why, or why not?

On fait du bateau à l'Île Curieuse aux Seychelles.

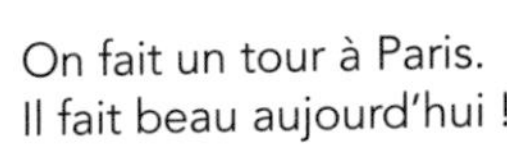

On fait un tour à Paris. Il fait beau aujourd'hui !

Script: *Observons.*

CORINNE : En septembre 2001, j'étais aux États-Unis en Floride chez ma famille. Et ils m'ont fait un petit peu visiter euh le la la région. Donc, ils m'ont amenée aux Everglades. J'ai pu voir des crocodiles et euh... cette photo me plaît beaucoup parce que... la première fois que je tenais un petit crocodile qui a failli me manger les doigts d'ailleurs.

Et sinon, les familles ont des belles villas avec des très beaux jardins ce que je n'ai pas la chance d'avoir ici. Et ils ont un beau hamac. J'étais très contente de pouvoir... poser dedans avec mes petites cousines et mes petits cousins.

Évidemment j'ai pas... je suis allée à Orlando je pouvais pas éviter. J'adore Disney donc vu que je connaissais celui en France je voulais absolument voir le Walt Disney américain et donc j'en ai profité pour faire des photos avec Mickey, Daisy, Donald et visiter tout le parc.

ÉDOUARD : Donc cet été j'ai eu un été très sympathique puisque je suis parti en croisière euh en bateau euh... à voile. Je suis parti de... Antibes euh jusqu'à Naples durant trois semaines avec trois autres amis euh et on a découvert euh la Corse, euh euh toutes les îles italiennes jusqu'à arriver à Naples euh où je suis resté trois jours et je suis revenu en train en France. Et c'est vraiment des vraiment des vacances très très bonnes.

Leçon 3 Je vous invite

Presentation: Display the cultural activities (MFL/Instructor's Resoures) and describe them; ask for examples of ballets, plays, concerts, and exhibitions; use the mini-dialogues to introduce formulas for inviting, accepting, and refusing. Treat *tu veux m'accompagner/Vous voulez nous accompagner ?* as lexical chunks. The verb *vouloir* is presented in Ch. 8, L 3. Test students' comprehension of these items by asking them to point to the activity you describe, using the unlabeled illustrations (MFL/Instructor's Resoures). Find out which of these cultural activities your students prefer, using either/or questions, so that students repeat key vocabulary.

POINTS DE DÉPART

Qu'est-ce qu'on propose ?

—On organise une petite fête samedi soir ; tu es libre ?
—Non, désolée, je suis prise.

—On ne joue pas au tennis à cause de la pluie, alors, je t'accompagne à l'exposition ?
—Oui, c'est super ; on se retrouve devant le musée ?

—Vous êtes libres samedi ? J'ai des places pour un spectacle de danse.
—Ah oui, c'est très gentil à vous !

—Alors, rendez-vous au Palais des Congrès pour voir le concert de rock ?
—Oui, à 19h30.

—Tu veux nous accompagner au théâtre ? On va voir une pièce de Molière.
—Volontiers ! J'adore le théâtre.

—Il pleut, donc qu'est-ce qu'on fait cet après-midi ?
—Il y a un bon film à la Cinémathèque.
—Super ! On y va ensemble ?

—On va passer une soirée tranquille chez nous.
—Je regrette, je ne suis pas libre. Je travaille demain soir.

POUR INVITER QUELQU'UN

Tu es/Vous êtes libre/s ?
On y va ensemble ?
Tu veux m'accompagner ?/Vous voulez nous accompagner ?

POUR ACCEPTER UNE INVITATION

Oui, je suis libre.
(J'accepte) Avec plaisir.
C'est gentil à toi/vous.
Je suis ravi/e.
Volontiers.

POUR REFUSER UNE INVITATION

Je suis désolé/e... | je ne suis pas libre.
Je regrette... | je suis pris/e.
C'est dommage, ... | j'ai déjà un rendez-vous.

Presentation: Students may be surprised to learn that a Ministry of Culture exists in France. To test comprehension, ask the class to rank these activities in popularity on a scale from 1 to 10. Students can work in pairs or small groups to answer the questions; follow up with the class as a whole.

Vie et culture

Les pratiques culturelles

This document shows the results of a recent survey by the French Ministry of Culture. What does the heading tell you about the information summarized here and how it is organized? Consider the following questions with your classmates:

1. According to these statistics, what are the most popular cultural activities for the French?
2. If you were to construct a similar list for your friends and family, how might it resemble or differ from what you see here?

It is common for the French to go with friends and family to concerts, movies, and museums. Often such activities are included in a family's vacation plans.

PRATIQUES CULTURELLES

Sur 100 Français de 15 ans et plus, au cours des douze derniers mois :

Sont allés :

au Musée	30
au Monument historique	30
à une Exposition de peinture ou de sculpture	24
à une Exposition de photographie	15
à une Galerie d'art	15
au Cinéma	57
au Théâtre	19
au Concert de rock	10
au Spectacle de danse	8
au Concert de musique classique	7
au Concert de jazz	6
au Concert d'un autre genre de musique	13

Source : Ministère de la Culture, *Mini-chiffres clés 2011*

Implementation: 4-27 Treat the schedule first as a short reading; have students identify the main categories of activities taking place, then describe some of the specific events. Once students are familiar with the schedule, go on to complete the exercise. If you teach in a smart classroom, you may also have students visit the Centre Pompidou web site to see what the most current events are.

04-35 to 04-38

À vous la parole

4-27 Qu'est-ce qu'on peut faire ? Le Centre Pompidou is a museum in Paris that also has movie theaters, conference rooms, and performance halls. With a partner, look over the program and describe the various activities.

AGENDA

TOUTES LES MANIFESTATIONS

CENTRE POMPIDOU – Art, culture, musée, expositions, cinémas, conférences, débats, spectacles, concerts.

EXPOSITIONS AU CENTRE

elles@centrepompidou, artistes femmes dans les collections du Musée national d'art moderne
Plus de cent-vingt œuvres et trente-cinq artistes renouvellent cette exposition consacrée aux artistes femmes.

27 mai – 21 février
11h00 – 21h00
Musée

Arman
Le Centre Pompidou consacre une exposition rétrospective à Arman, l'une des figures magistrales de l'art de l'après-guerre.

22 septembre – 10 janvier
11h00 – 21h00
Galerie 2

CINÉMAS

Film

15 septembre – 29 juin
Cycle
Autour des collections cinématographiques, entre cinéma expérimental, documentaire, film d'artiste et vidéo, le rendez-vous régulier intitulé "Film", proposé par le Musée national d'art moderne, présente des séances thématiques et des cartes blanches.

19:00 – ***Autour d'Eugène Freyssinet,*** Cinéma 2

Prospectif cinéma

30 septembre – 25 novembre

10 – 12 avril
Cycle
Le service Création contemporaine et prospective du Musée national d'art moderne, en collaboration avec les Cinémas du Centre Pompidou, dévoile un nouveau cinéma prospectif d'artistes plasticiens de la jeune génération française et étrangère et vous donne rendez-vous tous les derniers jeudis du mois.

Cinéma 2, Cinéma 1

SPECTACLES–CONCERTS

CO-ME-DI-A
musique et danse
Deux scènes séparées mais synchronisées, l'une à Graz en Autriche, l'autre à Paris, provoque l'illusion d'une proximité entre les solistes grâce à la technologie du streaming.

25 novembre
20h00
Ircam - Espace de projection

These New Puritans
Musique
Le rock anguleux de These New Puritans est insoumis et inclassable.

18 décembre
20h30
Grande salle

MODÈLE É1 Le dernier jeudi du mois, il y a un film dans la série Prospectif cinéma.

É2 Et regarde, il y a un spectacle de musique et danse le 25 novembre à 20 h.

Note: 4-28 These brief exchanges prepare students for the more extended and open-ended activity in Ex. 4-29.

4-28 Oui ou non ? With a classmate, imagine that you find yourselves in the following situations. What will you say?

MODÈLE On vous invite à aller au musée demain. Vous refusez.

É1 Tu veux m'accompanger au musée demain ? Il y a une bonne exposition.

É2 Je regrette (ou Désolé/e), je ne suis pas libre.

1. On vous invite à un concert. Vous êtes ravi/e d'y aller.
2. On vous invite à aller au théâtre. Vous demandez quelle pièce on joue.
3. On vous invite à faire une randonnée, mais vous n'aimez pas les promenades.
4. On cherche quelqu'un pour jouer au bridge. Vous aimez ce jeu.
5. On a des places pour un concert de rock. Vous aimez ce type de musique, mais vous avez un rendez-vous ce jour-là.
6. On a deux places pour un spectacle de danse. Vous demandez, « C'est pour quel soir ? », et puis vous acceptez.

4-29 Des invitations. Issue invitations to three people in your class, who will accept or refuse, based on their preferences.

1. First, make a list of the activities you will suggest and the people you will invite. Don't forget your instructor!
2. Next, issue your invitations and see what the responses are. Respond as well to your classmates' invitations.
3. Finally, compare notes: Whom did you invite? For what activity? How did each person respond?

Implementation: 4-29 Have students work individually to prepare their lists of people to invite and activities to suggest. Once students have their lists prepared, they should circulate and everyone should invite three people in the class. You can follow up by asking students who they invited and if anyone accepted.

FORMES ET FONCTIONS

1. Les verbes comme *préférer* et l'emploi de l'infinitif

- For verbs conjugated like **préférer**, the singular forms and the third person plural form of the present tense show a change from **é** /e/ to **è** /ɛ/. In all of these forms the endings are silent.

—Quel genre de musique est-ce que vous préférez ?
—Nous préférons la musique classique.
—Vous préférez le rap ?

—Nous, on préfère le jazz.
—Eux, ils préfèrent le rock.
—Non, moi, je préfère le RnB.

PRÉFÉRER *to prefer*

SINGULIER		PLURIEL	
je	préfère	nous	préfér**ons**
tu	préfèr**es**	vous	préfér**ez**
il / elle / on	préfère	ils / elles	préfèr**ent**

PASSÉ COMPOSÉ : J'**ai préféré** le spectacle de danse.

Presentation: To present inductively, discuss students' preferences for cultural activities e.g., *Jessica adore le cinéma ; elle préfère les films de George Clooney. Steve aime les concerts ; il préfère les concerts de jazz. Et vous, vous préférez les concerts de jazz ou de musique classique ?* Then display the verb chart and ask how this verb is similar to other *-er* verbs students have learned; you might draw a "boot" to illustrate the fact that all the singular forms and the third person plural are pronounced alike. Be sure that students notice accent changes, and point out that these reflect the pronunciation: /e/ in open syllables: *préférons* /pre fe rɔ̃/; /ɛ/ in closed syllables: *préfère* /pre fɛr/.

Expansion: In addition to *répéter* (introduced in L. prélim.) and *suggérer*, you might provide other verbs conjugated like *préférer : espérer, compléter ;* only *préférer* is practiced in this lesson. To practice *suggérer*, you might use:

SUGGESTION: Qu'est-ce que tu suggères ?
—On va au musée voir l'exposition ?
—Non, moi, je suggère aller au ciné. Ou Marie et moi, on suggère aller au ciné.

- Other verbs that show the same type of change are **répéter** (*to repeat*) and **suggérer** (*to suggest*):

Rép**é**tons après le professeur.
Qu'est-ce que vous sugg**é**rez ?

Rép**è**te après moi !
Qu'est-ce que tu sugg**è**res ?

- **Préférer** may be followed by a noun or by an infinitive:

Je préfère **le cinéma**.	*I prefer movies.*
Il préfère **aller** au cinéma.	*He prefers to go to the movies.*

Presentation: Remind students of the placement of the negative in infinitive constructions.

- Use the following verbs to talk about likes and dislikes; all, like **préférer**, can be followed by a noun or an infinitive:

détester	*to detest*
aimer bien	*to like fairly well*
aimer	*to like or to love*
aimer beaucoup	*to like or love a lot*
préférer	*to prefer*
adorer	*to adore*

Initial practice: Begin with a discrimination drill: have students write the letter è or é based on the form they hear: *je préfère, nous préférons*, etc. Follow with a substitution drill: *Je préfère le jazz ; vous ? — Vous préférez le jazz*, etc.

04-39 to 04-42

À vous la parole

4-30 Activités préférées. These students are supposed to be studying, but they can't stop thinking about the weekend and what they would prefer to be doing. Tell what each person prefers.

Expansion: 4-30 Ask students what they like to do on the weekend.

MODÈLE Pauline préfère organiser une fête.

Exposition
Pauline
Nicole préfère voir un film
Grégory préfère regarder la télé
Christine préfère aller au spectacle de danse
Nicolas préfère aller au concert de rock
Thomas préfère aller au musée

4-31 Samedi soir. Decide with your partner what each of these people prefers to do on Saturday evening.

MODÈLE Marie-Laure est très sociable.

É1 Elle préfère organiser des fêtes.
OU É2 Elle préfère dîner avec ses amies.

Expansion: 4-31 Items may have more than one logical response; encourage students to think of several.

1. Fred et ses amis adorent l'art moderne.
2. Mathilde est très réservée.
3. Nous aimons la musique.
4. Le copain de Sabrina aime le théâtre.
5. Vous n'aimez pas le rock.
6. La mère de mon amie aime bien la danse.
7. Je suis assez paresseuse.
8. Tu n'aimes pas beaucoup le cinéma.

Additional practice: Have students discuss in pairs and then share with the class what they love to do, and what they absolutely hate doing. Be sure to provide clear models:

adorer :

É1 Moi, j'adore aller au cinéma le week-end.
É2 Moi non, j'adore surtout écouter de la musique.

détester :

É1 Je déteste faire des courses le week-end.
É2 Moi aussi, je déteste ça.

To share with the class: *Moi, j'adore écouter de la musique, mais elle, elle adore aller au cinéma. On déteste faire des courses le week-end.*

4-32 Vos préférences. Discuss your preferences in the following categories with your partner. Then share your findings with the class.

MODÈLE les films : un DVD chez toi ou un film au cinéma ?

É1 Est-ce que tu préfères regarder un DVD chez toi ou voir un film au cinéma ?
É2 Je préfère aller au cinéma, et toi ?
É1 C'est trop cher. J'aime bien regarder les DVD chez moi.

(*plus tard*) :

É2 Moi, j'aime le cinéma mais Travis préfère les DVD.

1. les films : un DVD chez toi ou un film au cinéma ?
2. les concerts de musique : le rock ou le jazz ?
3. les spectacles : un spectacle de danse ou une pièce de théâtre ?
4. les soirées : une fête chez des amis ou une soirée tranquille chez vous ?
5. les musées : l'art moderne ou la photographie ?
6. les animaux : les chats ou les chiens ?

Les Français préfèrent les chats. Ils ont 10,7 millions de chats et 7,8 millions de chiens.

2. Les verbes comme *acheter* et *appeler*

Presentation: Review regular *-er* verbs and verbs like *préférer* before treating this section: use quick substitution drills and have students summarize the number of spoken forms. Remind them of the alternation /e/ vs./ɛ/, and link this to the nature of the syllable: open syllables end in /e/, closed syllables in /ɛ/ + a consonant sound; this is the same alternation they will observe in the new verbs. Emphasize pattern similarities and the link to what students already know.

- You have learned that for verbs like **préférer** (*to prefer*), the second vowel in the singular forms and the third person plural form of the present tense are spelled and pronounced like the **è** in **mère**:

  Je préf**è**re le cinéma. Ils préf**è**rent le théâtre.

- Verbs like **acheter** (*to buy*) and **appeler** (*to call*) similarly show changes in the singular forms and in the third person plural. The final vowel in these forms is also pronounced like the /ɛ/ in **mère**.
- This pronunciation change is reflected in the spelling by the use of the **accent grave** in verbs like **acheter**.

acheter	*to buy*	Qu'est-ce que tu **achètes** ?
amener	*to bring a person*	Ils **amènent** leurs enfants au théâtre.
lever	*to raise*	Elle ne **lève** jamais le doigt (*finger*).

- Verbs like **appeler** reflect the pronunciation change by doubling the final consonant of the base in the singular and the third person plural forms:

appeler	*to call*	J'**appelle** le théâtre pour avoir des places ?
épeler	*to spell*	Il **épelle** son nom.
jeter	*to throw (out)*	Elle ne **jette** pas les billets des spectacles qu'elle a vus.

- The **nous** and **vous** forms for these verbs are two syllables long:

  nous ach~~e~~tons vous app~~e~~lez

ACHETER *to buy*

SINGULIER		PLURIEL	
j'	achète	nous	achetons
tu	achètes	vous	achetez
il / elle / on	achète	ils / elles	achètent

IMPÉRATIF : **Achète** une affiche ! **Achetez** une jolie carte ! **Achetons** un souvenir.

PASSÉ COMPOSÉ : **J'ai acheté** le programme.

Initial practice: Begin with a discrimination drill; have students choose or write out the verb form they hear in sentences: *Il appelle son chien. Nous jetons les billets. Elles amènent les enfants. Vous appelez le théâtre ? Tu achètes un programme ? Tu jettes le programme ? Nous achetons des places en ligne. Il épelle son nom.* Since pronunciation differences are reflected in the spelling, written practice is appropriate. Follow with simple substitution drills to practice correct pronunciation: *J'appelle le chien ; nous ? — Nous appelons le chien,* etc.

APPELER *to call*

SINGULIER		PLURIEL	
j'	appelle	nous‿	appelons
tu	appelles	vous‿	appelez
il / elle / on	appelle	ils‿ / elles‿	appellent

IMPÉRATIF : **Appelle** le théâtre ! **Appelez** le cinéma ! **Appelons** le musée !

PASSÉ COMPOSÉ : Nous **avons appelé** nos parents.

04-43 to 04-46

À vous la parole

Implementation: 4-33 This exercise recycles clothing vocabulary from Ch. 3, L. 3 and vacation activities from L. 2 of this chapter. You may decide to review clothing vocabulary briefly before beginning the activity.

4-33 Des achats. What clothes should one buy in the following situations ? *Answers may vary.*

MODÈLE Je dois aller à un mariage.
- J'achète un costume bleu marine.

1. Nous allons à la Réunion pour les vacances. Nous achetons…
2. Mes amis vont à un concert de rock. Ils achètent…
3. David va voir un spectacle de danse classique. Il achète…
4. Maryse passe ses vacances au bord de la mer. Elle achète…
5. Vous aimez faire du cheval. Vous achetez…
6. Christiane est très élégante quand elle va au théâtre. Elle achète…
7. Nous aimons les vêtements très décontractés (*relaxed*) pour les vacances. Nous achetons…
8. Je n'ai pas beaucoup d'argent. J'achète…

Expansion: 4-34 Vary the form used by having students imagine they are speaking to more than one co-renter.

4-34 Mais pourquoi ? Imagine that your roommate is driving you crazy. Ask him or her why he/she does the following things.

MODÈLE jeter mon affiche préférée
É1 Pourquoi est-ce que tu jettes mon affiche préférée ?
É2 Je n'aime pas ton affiche. Elle est moche.

1. acheter beaucoup de magazines
2. ne pas appeler tes parents
3. porter mon beau pull rouge
4. ne pas épeler correctement mon nom
5. acheter toujours des chips et du chocolat
6. jeter mon CD préféré
7. appeler tous tes amis

4-35 Une interview. Interview your partner to find out whether or not he or she does the following.

Expansion: 4-35 As a follow-up, have students tell something they learned about their partner. This encourages the use of the third person singular form.

MODÈLE jette ses vieux tickets de concerts

É1 Est-ce que tu jettes tes vieux tickets de concerts ?

É2 Non, je ne jette pas mes vieux tickets ; je garde mes tickets en souvenir.

1. appelle ses parents tous les week-ends
2. achète beaucoup de CD
3. achète des magazines
4. se lève toujours avant huit heures
5. jette ses vieux tickets de concerts
6. jette toujours ses devoirs et examens corrigés
7. amène toujours des amis quand il/elle est invité/e à une fête

Écrivons

Note: 4-36 Many web sites offer suggestions for creating personalized invitations. Encourage students to show their creativity in completing the activity; you might assign this to be completed at home and then follow up in class as indicated in the exercise.

4-36 Une carte invitation

A. Avant d'écrire. On what occasions do you invite people to your home to celebrate? birthdays? holidays? a new job? a new home? Create an invitation for a celebration with friends or family. Decide what information you need to provide and make a list of practical and personal details that you want to include. Be sure to look at the model to confirm that you have not forgotten anything!

B. En écrivant. Now, write your invitation, using your notes. Following the model, begin with the practical information and then add any personal details and creative elements.

C. En révisant. As you re-read your invitation, think about the following questions and make any necessary changes.

1. Analyze the content: did you include all the necessary details?
2. Analyze your invitation for style and form: did you follow the model? Did you add any creative elements?

D. Après avoir écrit. Now give your invitation to a classmate and see how he/she responds.

Ça s'arrose!

Pourquoi : On fête les 22 ans de Julia

Où : chez Christophe et Annie
12, rue de la Harpe

Quand : samedi, le 9 mai à partir de 20h

Précisions : Téléphonez-nous au 01.22.08.87 pour nous dire si vous êtes libres. Apportez un plat à partager et un petit cadeau, SVP. Le thème de la fête, c'est « le cinéma ». C'est une surprise, donc n'en parlez pas à Julia !

Stratégie

Some written forms of communication, such as invitations, require a specific format and careful presentation of the information. Be sure to keep these conventions in mind as you write.

Leçon 

le temps à toutes les saisons (f.)	*the weather in all seasons*
Quel temps fait-il ?	*What's the weather like?*
Il fait beau.	*It's beautiful weather.*
Il fait bon.	*It's warm/perfect (weather).*
Il fait chaud.	*It's hot (weather).*
Il fait frais.	*It's cool (weather).*
Il fait froid.	*It's cold (weather).*
Il fait mauvais.	*The weather's bad.*
Il fait lourd.	*It's humid.*
Il gèle. (geler)	*It's freezing. (to freeze)*
Il neige. (neiger)	*It's snowing. (to snow)*
Il pleut. (pleuvoir) (la pluie)	*It's raining. (to rain) (rain)*
Il y a du brouillard.	*It's foggy.*
Il y a des éclairs (m.).	*It's lightning.*
Il y a des nuages (m.).	*It's cloudy.*
Il y a un orage.	*It's stormy weather.*
Il y a du soleil.	*It's sunny.*
Il y a du tonnerre.	*It's thundering.*
Il y a du vent.	*It's windy.*
Il y a du verglas.	*It's icy, slippery.*
Le ciel est bleu.	*The sky is blue.*
Le ciel est couvert.	*The sky is overcast.*
Le ciel est gris.	*The sky is gray.*

pour parler de la température	*to talk about the temperature*
Il fait 10 degrés (m.) Celsius.	*It's 10 degrees Celsius.*
J'ai chaud/froid.	*I'm hot/cold.*
la météo(rologie)	*weather, weather report*

les saisons (f.)	*the seasons*
au printemps (m.)	*in the spring*
en été (m.)	*in the summer*
en automne (m.)	*in the fall*
en hiver (m.)	*in the winter*

verbes en *-re*	*-re verbs*
attendre	*to wait for*
descendre	*to go down*
entendre	*to hear*
perdre	*to lose*
rendre à	*to give back*
rendre visite à	*to visit someone*
répondre à	*to answer*
vendre	*to sell*

pour parler du passé	*to talk about the past*
hier	*yesterday*
avant-hier	*the day before yesterday*
samedi dernier	*last Saturday*
l'année dernière	*last year*
il y a longtemps	*a long time ago*
il y a deux jours	*two days ago*
ce jour-là	*that day*
à ce moment-là	*at that moment*

Leçon 2

les vacances (f. pl.)	*vacation*
partir en vacances	*to go on vacation*
un billet (d'avion)	*(plane) ticket*
des destinations (f.)	*destinations*
la campagne	*countryside*
le lac	*lake*
la mer	*sea*
au bord de la mer	*at the seashore*
la montagne	*mountains*
la plage	*beach*
la ville	*city*
la pêche (aller à la pêche)	*fishing (to go fishing)*
des projets (m.) de vacances	*vacation plans*
le repos	*rest*
les sports (m.) d'hiver	*winter sports*

des activités (f.)	*activities*
bronzer	*to get a tan*
faire…	
de l'alpinisme (m.)	*to go mountain climbing*
du camping	*to camp, to go camping*
du cheval	*to go horseback riding*
de la moto	*to ride a motorcycle*
de la motoneige	*to go snowmobiling*
un pique-nique	*to picnic*
de la planche à voile	*to windsurf*
une randonnée	*to take a hike*
du shopping	*to shop*
du ski	*to ski*
du ski nautique	*to water ski*
du surf	*to go surfing*
du surf des neiges	*to go snowboarding*
du tourisme	*to go touring, to go sightseeing*
de la voile	*to go sailing*
un tour au parc	*to take a walk in the park*
visiter des musées ou des monuments	*to visit museums or monuments*

quelques expressions utiles	*some useful expressions*
Bravo !	*Great! Well done!*
Ce n'est pas vrai !	*It can't be!*
Chouette !	*Neat!*
Pas tout à fait !	*Not quite!*
Vive… (la Réunion) !	*Hurray for . . . (Reunion Island)!*

quelques verbes conjugués avec *être* au passé composé	*some verbs conjugated with* être *in the* passé composé
aller	*to go*
arriver	*to arrive*
descendre	*to go down*
devenir	*to become*
entrer	*to go/come in*
monter	*to go up*
mourir	*to die*
naître	*to be born*
partir	*to leave*
passer	*to go/come by*
rentrer	*to go/come home*
rester	*to stay*
retourner	*to go back, to return*
revenir	*to come back*
sortir	*to go out*
tomber	*to fall*
venir	*to come*

pour faire un récit	*to construct a narrative*
d'abord	*first*
ensuite	*next*
après	*after, after that*
puis	*then*
enfin	*finally*

pour poser une question	*to ask a question*
quel/s, quelle/s	*which*
Quelle est votre saison préférée ?	*What is your favorite season?*

Leçon 3

pour inviter quelqu'un	*to invite someone*
Tu es/Vous êtes libre(s) ?	*Are you free?*
On y va ensemble ?	*Shall we go (there) together?*
Tu veux/Vous voulez m'accompagner ?	*Would you like to come with me?*

pour accepter une invitation	*to accept an invitation*
Oui, je suis libre.	*Yes, I am free.*
(J'accepte) Avec plaisir.	*(I accept) With pleasure.*
C'est gentil à toi/vous.	*That's kind of you.*
Je suis ravi/e.	*I am delighted.*
Volontiers.	*With pleasure./Gladly.*

pour refuser une invitation	*to refuse an invitation*
Je suis désolé/e…	*I'm sorry . . .*
C'est dommage…	*It's too bad . . .*
Je regrette…	*I'm sorry . . .*
Je ne suis pas libre.	*I'm not free.*
Je suis pris/e.	*I'm busy.*
J'ai déjà un rendez-vous.	*I already have a meeting/date/appointment.*

des distractions (f.)	*fun activities*
aller à un concert	*to go to a concert*
voir une pièce	*to watch a play*
passer une soirée tranquille	*to spend a quiet evening*
une place	*seat, place*
se retrouver	*to meet*
un spectacle	*show*

quelques verbes utiles	*some useful verbs*
acheter	*to buy*
amener	*to bring (a person)*
(s') appeler	*(to be named), to call*
épeler	*to spell*
jeter	*to throw, to throw away*
(se) lever	*(to get up), to raise*
préférer	*to prefer*
suggérer	*to suggest*

une expression utile	*a useful expression*
à cause de	*because of*

Qui va au marché ? Qu'est-ce qu'ils cherchent ? Qu'est-ce que vous aimez trouver au marché ?

5 Du marché à la table

After completing this chapter, you should be able to:

- Order food and drink in a restaurant
- Talk about meals and a wide variety of dishes
- Shop for food
- Specify quantities
- Describe the importance of cuisine and regional dishes in the Francophone world

Leçon 1 Qu'est-ce que vous prenez ?

POINTS DE DÉPART

Au café

Presentation: Examine the photo and treat the dialogue first, letting students listen to the recording. Test students' comprehension: *On va au McDo ou au café ?*, etc. Explain key expressions such as *avoir faim* and *avoir soif* using description, circumlocution, and examples. Remind students that they have learned other expressions with *avoir* : *avoir froid, avoir chaud, avoir envie de.* Treat the expression *je voudrais* as a lexical item; polite requests using the conditional are taught in Ch. 10, L. 1. Point out the popularity of fast-food restaurants in France—see the **Vie et culture** notes for more details. The café continues to play a part in the life of most French people as a place to socialize. Ask students whether they can think of a place that plays a similar role in their life.

ROMAIN : J'ai faim. On va au McDo ?
HÉLÈNE : Des hamburgers, des frites et du coca, quelle horreur ! Allons au café, c'est plus sympa.

(au café)
LE SERVEUR : Qu'est-ce que je vous sers ?
HÉLÈNE : J'ai très soif. Je voudrais seulement quelque chose à boire. Euh, une limonade, s'il vous plaît.
ROMAIN : Moi, j'ai faim. Je prends un croque-monsieur et une bière.

(plus tard)
ROMAIN : Monsieur ! … L'addition, s'il vous plaît.
LE SERVEUR : J'arrive… Voilà.
HÉLÈNE : C'est combien ?
ROMAIN : Dix-huit euros. On partage ?
HÉLÈNE : Sans problème.

Presentation: Present the vocabulary using the visual of café fare (MFL, Instructor's Resources). Highlight the learning strategy and explain that it will be used throughout the chapter as students add to their food-related vocabulary. Encourage them to develop additional groupings that they find meaningful and useful. Describe items in each semantic grouping to make meaning clear, for example: *un citron pressé, c'est du jus de citron avec de l'eau et du sucre.* Point out that gender indications (m./f.) in items using an expression of quantity refer to the food or drink pictured; e.g., *une bouteille de coca* (m.). Test comprehension using the unlabelled art (MFL, Instructor's Resources): *Montrez le thé*, etc., then have students repeat, using either/or questions: *C'est un café ou un chocolat chaud ?*

Des boissons chaudes

une tasse de chocolat chaud

un café crème

un thé nature, un thé au lait

Des boissons rafraîchissantes

une cannette de limonade

un Orangina

une bouteille de coca

une cuillère

un verre de jus d'orange

un citron pressé

du sucre

de l'eau minérale (f.)

des glaçons (m.)

Des boissons alcoolisées

du vin rouge

une bière

Des casse-croûte

Fiche pratique

To learn new vocabulary, such as the food-related vocabulary in this chapter, it is helpful to organize words and expressions into logically related groupings. For example, like the illustrations on this page, you can group together hot drinks, cold drinks, and snacks. Or, you can make lists of foods you typically eat at certain meals; foods you typically eat with certain courses; types of foods (for example, fruits, vegetables, and meats); foods you purchase in a particular type of container or amount (in a box, in a package, by the dozen, etc.).

Note: The French generally drink less coffee than Americans, but prefer a stronger coffee. You might give students some of the more specific terms, *un déca, un crème, un expresso.* A customer may order *de l'eau minérale plate (Vittel, Évian) ou gazeuse (Perrier, Badoit). L'Orangina* and *la limonade* are also carbonated drinks. *Un croque-monsieur* is a grilled ham-and-cheese sandwich made with *pain de mie.* Most other sandwiches are made using *de la baguette.* Canadians refer to *un coca* as *un coke* and *une glace* as *une crème glacée.*

05-01 to 05-04

À vous la parole

5-1 Proposez des boissons. Proposez des boissons…

> Implementation: 5-1 Display the unlabelled café items (MFL, Instructor's Resources) as students complete the exercise. Note that all direction lines for the **À vous la parole** sections are in French beginning in Ch. 5.

MODÈLE chaudes
- un café, un thé, un chocolat chaud *Answers may vary.*

1. rafraîchissantes une limonade, un Orangina, un coca, un jus d'orange, un citron pressé, de l'eau minérale
2. gazeuses (*carbonated*) une limonade, un Orangina, un coca, un Perrier
3. alcoolisées une bière, du vin
4. qui contiennent du jus de fruit un jus d'orange, un citron pressé, une limonade, un Orangina, du vin
5. qui contiennent de la caféine un café, un thé, un chocolat chaud, un coca
6. à prendre avec le dîner de l'eau, du vin, de la bière

5-2 Qu'est-ce que vous désirez ? Vous êtes au café ou au restaurant avec un/e partenaire. Dites ce que vous préférez d'après la situation donnée.

MODÈLE Vous êtes au McDo.
É1 Pour moi, un cheeseburger et un coca.
É2 Un hamburger avec des frites et une limonade.

1. Il fait très chaud.
2. Vous avez très froid.
3. Vous devez travailler très tard.
4. Il est 14h et vous n'avez pas mangé.
5. C'est le matin.
6. Vous mangez une pizza et vous avez envie de boire quelque chose.
7. Vous avez très faim.
8. Vous avez très soif.

5-3 Au café. À tour de rôle, imaginez que vous êtes le serveur ou la serveuse. Vous prenez la commande (*order*) de vos camarades qui sont les clients.

> Implementation: 5-3 Use as a role-play activity. You may choose to act the part of the server. Use the photo of a café as a prompt, or bring in empty cups and bottles as props to enliven the activity.

MODÈLE É1 Madame !
É2 Vous désirez ?
É1 Un café crème.
É2 Oui, et pour vous, mademoiselle ?
É3 Je voudrais un sandwich au jambon.
É2 C'est tout ?
É3 Non, une bière aussi, s'il vous plaît.
É2 Alors, pour monsieur, un café crème, et pour mademoiselle, un sandwich au jambon et une bière.

Vie et culture

La restauration rapide

En France la restauration rapide représente 24 % des dépenses[1] au restaurant, mais ces restaurants comptent pour seulement 2 % du nombre total d'établissements. La chaîne la plus importante[2] est McDonald's, avec 1.134 restaurants en 2008. Mais la part des hamburgers reste limitée : les Français mangent neuf fois plus de sandwichs et six fois plus de pizzas. Ils achètent leurs sandwichs surtout dans des chaînes spécialisées (Paul, Brioche Dorée, Point Chaud), mais il existe d'autres options : en voici quelques-unes. Quelle option est-ce que vous préférez ?

[1]*expenditures* [2]*biggest*

ET VOUS ?

1. Quelles options existent pour les Français quand ils ont envie de manger rapidement ? et pour vous ? Est-ce qu'il y a beaucoup de chaînes de restauration chez vous ?
2. Pourquoi est-ce que les gens fréquentent ces restaurants ?

Une crêperie à St-Malo

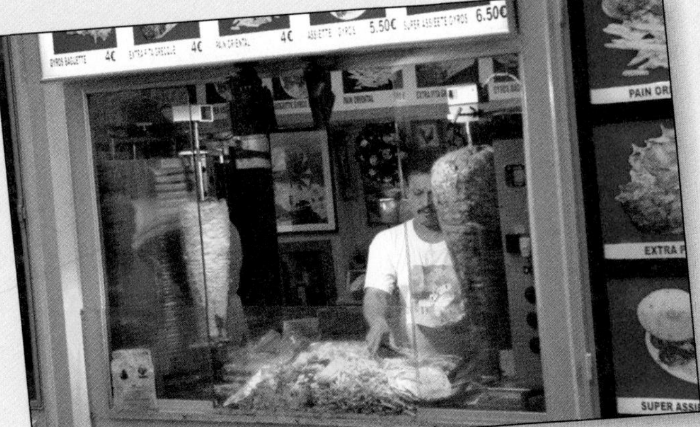
Un fast-food turc à Paris

Des moules frites à Lille

Ce Quick à Roubaix sert des hamburgers halal.

Implementation: Information in the text is adapted from *Francoscopie 2010*, p. 189. Have students describe what they see in the photos; what would they most likely order? In second place for fast-food restaurants is *Quick*, with about 320 restaurants; *Paul* has 281, and *Brioche dorée*, 256. Often the French grab a snack or eat on the run, stopping at vending machines, bakeries, and stands on the street, in airports, and train and subway stations.

Sons et lettres

La voyelle /y/

The vowel /y/, as in **tu**, is generally spelled with the letter **u**. To pronounce /y/, your tongue must be forward and your lips rounded, protruding, and tense. As you pronounce /y/, think of the vowel /i/ of **ici**. It is important to make a distinction between /y/ and the /u/ of **tout**, as many words in French are distinguished by these two vowels.

À vous la parole

5-4 Imitation. Répétez et arrondissez les lèvres pour bien prononcer /y/ !

tu du jus du sucre des crudités Jules Bruno Lucie Suzanne

5-5 Contrastes. Attention de bien distinguer entre /y/ (écrit *u*) et /u/ (écrit *ou*) quand vous répétez les mots suivants.

tu	tout	bouteille	bu
du	doux	rouge	rue
jus	joue	debout	début

5-6 Salutations. Imaginez que vous travaillez au café et dites bonjour à vos amis et à vos clients.

MODÈLES Bruno
- Salut, Bruno.

Madame Dupont
- Bonjour, Madame Dupont.

1. Bruno
2. Lucie
3. Suzanne
4. Madame Dumont
5. Monsieur Dumas
6. Madame Camus

FORMES ET FONCTIONS

1. Les verbes *prendre* et *boire*

The verbs **prendre** and **boire** are irregular.

PRENDRE *to take, to have (food or drink)*

SINGULIER		PLURIEL	
je	prends	nous	prenons
tu	prends	vous	prenez
il / elle / on	prend	ils / elles	prennent

IMPÉRATIF : **Prends** un café ! **Prenez** du vin ! **Prenons** une pizza !
PASSÉ COMPOSÉ : **J'ai pris** un chocolat chaud.

Note: In American English, /uw/ (as in *do, two*) is intermediate phonetically between French /y/ and /u/. It is important to give students a clear acoustic model. Note that /y/ is high pitched and is most easily produced with the consonants /t/, /d/, /s/, /z/, as in *tu, du, su,* and *zut*. Have students think of /i/, the most high pitched vowel of French, as they produce /y/. Before practicing /y/, review /u/ and have students produce a tense and back /u/. That vowel is low pitched and most easily produced with the consonants /p/, /b/, /m/, as in *poux, boue,* and *moue*.

Initial practice: Begin with a discrimination drill; students raise their hand when they hear /y/: *tout, du, rue, qui, vous, Gilles, Camus, Lalou, boulot, Dumont, Manou, debout, douche, Bruno, couche, habille, Julie.*

Implementation: 5-6 Before completing, remind students about the difference in formality when greeting a friend or someone with whom you have a more formal relationship. Point out that *Salut, Mme Dumont* would not be acceptable, although *Bonjour, Suzanne* would be fine.

Presentation: These irregular verbs have three stems. Introduce the verbs inductively using questions and the vocabulary of the lesson; this should follow very naturally from the presentation and practice of the café fare, for example, as you follow up on Ex. 5-2. Ask students to tell how many different spoken forms they hear (four). Show how the vowel changes in the third-person plural: for *prendre*, from the vowel /ø/ in *prenons*, to the vowel /ɛ/ in *prennent;* for *boire*, from the vowel /y/ in *buvons*, to the sound /wa/ in *boivent*. Like other verbs with four spoken forms, the final consonant heard in the third-person plural is dropped in the singular forms. In addition, *prendre* exhibits a vowel change: /ɑ̃/ in the singular forms, /ɛ/ in the third-person plural. Point out to students that when *boire* is used without a complement, it is understood that one is talking about drinking alcohol. *Ils boivent* means "They drink (alcohol)" or "They are drinkers."

BOIRE *to drink*			
SINGULIER		PLURIEL	
je	**bois**	nous	**buvons**
tu	**bois**	vous	**buvez**
il / elle / on	**boit**	ils / elles	**boivent**

IMPÉRATIF : Ne **bois** pas ça ! **Buvez** de l'eau ! Ne **buvons** pas trop !
PASSÉ COMPOSÉ : J'**ai bu** un café.

- The verb **prendre** is used with foods or beverages.

Je **prends** un citron pressé.	*I'm having lemonade.*
—Qu'est-ce que tu **as pris** ?	*—What did you have?*
—Un coca.	*—A Coke.*
On **prend** un sandwich au jambon et des frites.	*We're having a ham sandwich and fries.*

- **Prendre** also means *to take.*

On **prend** le bus ou un taxi ?	*Shall we take the bus or a taxi?*
Tu **prends** ton sac ?	*Are you taking your bag?*

- **Apprendre**, *to learn,* and **comprendre**, *to understand,* are formed like **prendre**.

Tu **apprends** l'italien ?	*You're learning Italian?*
Ils **comprennent** l'arabe.	*They understand Arabic.*

- **Boire** means *to drink.*

Qu'est-ce que tu **bois** ?	*What are you drinking?*
On **boit** du vin rouge.	*We're drinking red wine.*
Je n'**ai** pas **bu** de café aujourd'hui.	*I didn't drink any coffee today.*

Initial practice: Begin with a discrimination drill: one person, or more than one? *Il prend une bière. Elles prennent du café. Prends une pizza ! Elles boivent du coca. Il boit beaucoup. Elle boit une limonade. Ils prennent des frites. Ils boivent le week-end. Il prend de l'eau minérale. Elle boit trop de café. Elles prennent le bus.* Follow with a simple substitution drill: *Je prends du café* (*nous, eux, lui,* etc.) ; *Qu'est-ce que tu bois* (*nous, vous, eux,* etc.) ?

À vous la parole

05-07 to 05-11

5-7 Quelle consommation ? Qu'est-ce que ces personnes prennent ou boivent ?

Answers may vary.

MODÈLE la dame âgée ?
• Elle prend un café crème.
OU • Elle boit un café crème.

1. et le jeune homme ?
Il prend une bière.

2. et son amie ?
Elle prend de l'eau minérale.

3. et les enfants ?
Ils prennent une glace.

4. et le monsieur ?
Il prend un thé.

5. et la petite fille ?
Elle prend un coca.

6. et ces hommes ?
Ils prennent un sandwich et du vin.

5-8 C'est logique. Posez une question logique pour savoir quelles langues ces personnes comprennent ou apprennent. Voici la liste des langues :

Implementation: 5-8 Before completing the exercise, go over the list of languages, perhaps even matching languages to place names in the exercise.

l'allemand, l'espagnol, le français, l'italien, le portugais, le russe

MODÈLE Bruno habite au Portugal.
- Alors il comprend le portugais ?

Je vais en Russie.
- Alors tu apprends le russe ?

1. Isabella habite en Italie. Alors elle comprend l'italien ?
2. J'habite en Russie. Alors tu comprends le russe ?
3. Franz habite en Allemagne. Alors il comprend l'allemand ?
4. Nous habitons en France. Alors vous comprenez le français ?
5. Mes cousins habitent en Espagne. Alors ils comprennent l'espagnol ?
6. Guillaume et Pierre vont à Moscou. Alors ils apprennent le russe ?
7. Nous allons au Mexique. Alors vous apprenez l'espagnol ?
8. Mélanie va en Allemagne. Alors elle apprend l'allemand ?
9. Je vais au Portugal. Alors tu apprends le portugais ?
10. Nous allons au Québec. Alors vous apprenez le français ?

5-9 Vos habitudes. Dites ce que vous prenez dans ces situations. Comparez votre réponse avec la réponse de votre partenaire.

Implementation: 5-9 This can be completed in pairs or small groups; then have students compare answers. You may wish to complete this exercise after introducing the partitive, since students may wish to use this structure (e.g., *je prends du café*).

MODÈLE le matin, avant (*before*) d'aller en classe ?
É1 Moi, je prends un café noir.
É2 Et moi, un jus d'orange.

1. pendant la journée ?
2. quand vous n'avez pas le temps de manger ?
3. le soir, quand vous avez envie de vous endormir ?
4. quand vous regardez la télé ?
5. quand vous êtes au cinéma ?
6. quand vous sortez avec des amis ?
7. quand vous avez très soif ?

2. L'article partitif

Presentation: To present this topic inductively, provide additional examples similar to those found in the text in order to help students discover the differences between a) mass and count nouns; b) use of the indefinite versus the partitive articles with unspecified nouns; c) use of the definite article with presupposed nouns or nouns used in a general sense. Based on the examples, ask students to summarize when the partitive article is used.

- Nouns are of two types in French and in English. *Count nouns* refer to things that can be counted, such as oranges and bananas. *Mass nouns* are things that normally are not counted, like coffee, tea, sugar, and water. Notice that count nouns can be made plural; mass nouns are normally used only in the singular. Look at the following examples:

J'aime **le** café, mais pas **le** thé.	*I like coffee, but not tea.*
J'adore **les** oranges, mais je déteste **les** bananes.	*I love oranges, but I hate bananas.*

- When you refer to a noun not previously specified, use the indefinite article if it is a count noun.

Il a mangé **un** sandwich.	*He ate a sandwich.*
Je prends **une** pizza.	*I'm having a pizza.*
Elle a acheté **des** croissants.	*She bought some croissants.*

Use one of the three forms of the *partitive article* if it is a mass noun.

Tu voudrais **du** coca ?	*Would you like some Coke?*
Tu prends **de la** glace ?	*Do you want some ice cream?*
Je sers **de l'**eau minérale.	*I'm serving mineral water.*

Note: In both French and English we sometimes use the singular indefinite article with mass nouns: *Je voudrais une bière*, "I'd like a beer." *Des* is the plural form of the indefinite article. The partitive article is used with mass nouns and the indefinite article with count nouns. Both of these articles contrast with the definite article. Depending on the verb, the definite article carries the meaning of generic or of previously identified, specified, or presupposed: *J'aime le vin* (generic), *Où est le vin ?* (presupposed), *Tu as acheté la pizza ?* (presupposed). The examples provided here, and the first exercises, emphasize these distinctions. Use the examples to illustrate these points as you explain.

- In the examples below, note the differences in meaning between the definite article, on the one hand, and the indefinite and partitive articles on the other. The definite article denotes a specific or presupposed item. The indefinite or partitive article denotes an unspecified item.

Definite article	**Indefinite or partitive article**
Il a pris **l'**orange. *He took the orange.* *(the specific orange)*	Il a pris **une** orange. *He took an orange.* *(any orange)*
Vous prenez **les** sandwichs ? *Are you taking the sandwiches?* *(these particular sandwiches)*	Vous prenez **des** sandwichs ? *Are you taking sandwiches?* *(any sandwiches)*
Elle mange **le** pain. *She's eating the bread.* *(this specific bread)*	Elle mange **du** pain. *She's eating some bread.* *(any bread)*

- The definite article is also used when nouns are used in a general sense, to express preferences.

J'aime **le** vin mais je n'aime pas **la** bière.	*I like wine but I do not like beer.*

- In negative sentences, both the indefinite and the partitive articles are replaced by **de/d'**:

Il prend **un** Orangina ?	—Non, non, il ne prend pas **d'**Orangina.
Vous avez **des** glaçons ?	—Non, on n'a pas **de** glaçons, mademoiselle.
Vous servez **du** thé ?	—Non, nous ne servons pas **de** thé, monsieur.

À vous la parole

12 15

5-10 Qu'est-ce que Chloé mange ? Regardez bien la liste des aliments suivants. Notez la forme de l'article dans chaque cas pour bien déterminer si Chloé prend les aliments suivants ou pas.

	Elle prend…	Elle ne prend pas…	
MODÈLE	____	✓	… de glace.
1.	✓	____	… du thé nature.
2.	____	✓	… de café crème.
3.	✓	____	… de la salade.
4.	✓	____	… de l'eau minérale.
5.	____	✓	… de frites.
6.	____	✓	… de sucre.
7.	✓	____	… des fruits.

D'après les habitudes de Chloé, est-ce qu'elle va probablement maigrir ou grossir ? Expliquez votre réponse.

Implementation: 5-10 Begin practice with this comprehension-based activity to help students recognize forms of the partitive. Help students figure out the meaning of the verbs *maigrir* and *grossir* based on context and the adjectives *maigre* and *gros/se*. These verbs are presented in the **Formes et fonctions** section of L. 2. For practice in producing forms, use simple substitution drills. Begin by having students manipulate familiar forms: *Vous prenez du café ? — Oui, j'aime le café*, etc. This allows them to hear multiple examples of the partitive used in context. Remind students of the importance of the verb in determining the choice of article. Next have students use the new partitive forms: *Vous aimez le café ? — Oui, donnez-moi du café*, etc. Drill the negative forms as well: *De la glace ? Je ne prends pas de glace ; de l'eau minérale ? du thé ?*, etc.

5-11 Ce n'est pas logique ! Corrigez ces phrases illogiques.

MODÈLE Avec le café, je prends du vin blanc.
- Avec le café, je ne prends pas de vin blanc ; je prends du sucre.

1. Comme dessert, je prends une pizza.
2. Avec une pizza, je prends du café.
3. Quand j'ai très soif, je prends du vin.
4. Généralement, je prends de la bière avec des glaçons.
5. Quand il fait très chaud, on prend du chocolat chaud.
6. Dans un thé au lait, on met des frites.
7. Quand on a faim, on prend de la limonade.
8. Quand on a soif, on prend une pizza.

Additional practice: For another simple exercise, put realia or pictures depicting types of food and drink in a bag. A student holding the bag answers questions from others about the contents: *Il y a du coca dans le sac ? — Oui, voilà le coca. Il y a des sandwichs ? — Non, il n'y a pas de sandwichs*, etc.

5-12 Vos habitudes et préférences. Complétez chaque phrase et comparez votre réponse avec la réponse de votre partenaire.

MODÈLE Le matin, je prends toujours…
É1 Le matin, je prends toujours du café.
É2 Je déteste le café. Moi, je prends toujours du thé.

1. Le matin, je prends toujours…
2. Quand je vais au McDo, je prends toujours…
3. Le week-end, je prends…
4. Quand j'ai très soif, j'aime…
5. Quand je travaille très tard le soir, je prends souvent…
6. Ma boisson préférée, c'est…

Implementation 5-12 This contrasts the use of the non-definite (indefinite and partitive) articles to that of the definite article. As a follow-up, have students report back what their partner said.

Lisons

Stratégie

Read a text such as a recipe intensively. Make sure you understand each step as it is outlined before you proceed.

5-13 Une recette canadienne.

A. Avant de lire. Have you ever purchased any food products from Canada? If so, what? Can you think of some local products that might be characteristic of québécois cuisine? A famous one is **le sirop d'érable**. Late winter and early spring marks **le temps des sucres** in Quebec. This is when maple sap is collected to make syrup and when visitors flock to the **cabanes à sucre** to observe the syrup-making process, enjoy a good meal, and listen to traditional music. Maple syrup is a main ingredient in traditional québécois cooking, used in everything from marinades to vegetable dishes and desserts.

Look at the recipe and the photos that accompany it. What do you think will probably be among the main ingredients? Read the recipe through, line by line, making sure you understand the procedures, the ingredients, and the quantities involved.

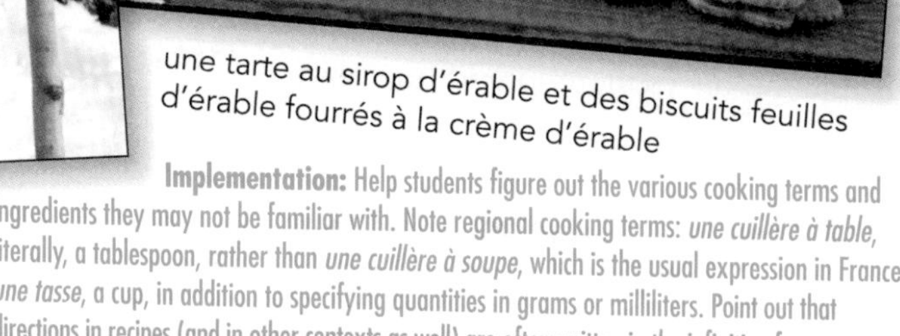

une tarte au sirop d'érable et des biscuits feuilles d'érable fourrés à la crème d'érable

On utilise la sève des érables pour faire du sirop d'érable.

Implementation: Help students figure out the various cooking terms and ingredients they may not be familiar with. Note regional cooking terms: *une cuillère à table*, literally, a tablespoon, rather than *une cuillère à soupe*, which is the usual expression in France; *une tasse*, a cup, in addition to specifying quantities in grams or milliliters. Point out that directions in recipes (and in other contexts as well) are often written in the infinitive form.

Key: *En lisant.* 1) une description avec le temps de préparation et de cuisson et la difficulté de la recette ; une liste des ingrédients ; les instructions pour préparer la recette 2) 2 pâtes à tarte, du sirop d'érable, de la crème 35 %, du beurre, de la farine, des œufs.

B. En lisant. Trouvez les réponses aux questions suivantes.

1. La recette est divisée en trois parties. Quelles sont ces trois parties ?
2. Dressez une liste des ingrédients, par exemple : 2 pâtes à tarte, …

C. En regardant de plus près. Maintenant examinez quelques caractéristiques du texte.

1. Quand on prépare une recette, il est très important de bien mesurer les ingrédients. Quel est le sens exact des mots et des abréviations suivants ? Donnez les équivalents en anglais.
   a. g *gram*
   b. ml *milliliter*
   c. 1 cuillère à table *one tablespoon*
   d. 1 et 1/2 tasses *1 1/2 cups*

Implementation: *En regardant de plus près.* Help students use the context and their knowledge of cooking and baking procedures to answer these questions.

2. Les verbes suivants indiquent les méthodes de préparation. Quel est le sens en anglais de chaque verbe ?
   a. chauffer heat b. faire fondre melt
   c. ajouter add d. mélanger mix
   e. laisser refroidir let cool
   f. garnir line/fill
   g. préchauffer preheat
   h. incorporer add
   i. verser pour
   j. faire cuire cook
3. Donnez le sens en anglais des expressions suivantes qui font partie intégrale de la recette.
   a. deux assiettes à tarte 2 pie pans
   b. la pâte à cuire the crust to bake
   c. les fonds de tarte the bottom of the crusts
   d. le mélange d'érable tiédi the cooled-off maple syrup mixture

D. Après avoir lu. Discutez de ces questions avec vos camarades de classe.

1. Pourquoi, à votre avis, est-ce que c'est un bon exemple d'un plat québécois ?
2. Est-ce que vous connaissez une autre recette qui ressemble à celle-ci ? Quelle est cette recette ?
3. Essayez cette recette, et apportez-la en classe !

Dans une cabane à sucre, on goûte des plats préparés avec du sirop d'érable.

Tarte au sirop d'érable

Temps de préparation : 10 mn
Temps de cuisson : 30 mn
Difficulté : facile

Ingrédients

2 pâtes[1] à tarte
1 et 1/2 tasses (375 ml) de sirop d'érable
1/2 tasse (125 ml) de crème 35 %
1/3 tasse (80 g) de beurre
1 cuillère à table de farine [2]
3 œufs

Préparation

1. Dans une casserole, chauffer le sirop d'érable et la crème 35 % jusqu'à l'ébullition.[3]
2. Retirer du feu[4].
3. Faire fondre le beurre dans le mélange, ajouter la farine et bien mélanger.
4. Laisser refroidir.
5. Garnir deux assiettes à tarte avec la pâte à cuire.
6. Préchauffer le four à 375 F (190 C) et cuire les fonds de tarte 15 mn.
7. Incorporer les œufs dans le mélange d'érable tiédi.
8. Verser la garniture[4] au sirop d'érable dans les deux assiettes à tarte.
9. Faire cuire à 300 F (150 C) pendant 20 mn.

[1] *crusts* [2] *flour* [3] *boiling* [4] *remove from heat* [5] *filling*

Implementation: *Après avoir lu.* C'est un bon exemple d'un plat régional parce qu'il contient un produit local, le sirop d'érable.

Expansion: At some point in the chapter, you may wish to assign groups of students to prepare various *plats régionaux*. This could be in the context of a school wide or national French festival (for example, the AATF's *La semaine du français* in November or the international weeks of *la Francophonie* during the last two weeks in March), or simply as an extracurricular activity for an honors section or motivated group of students. Authentic French and francophone recipes can be found online.

Leçon 2 À table !

Presentation: Present the vocabulary scene by scene, using the visuals for meals (MFL, Instructor's Resources). You may want to treat this vocabulary over two days, for example, treating breakfast vocabulary on day 1 and the other meals on day 2. Show on a map where the various families live. Describe each meal, model pronunciation, then test comprehension by having students point to the item you name. Have students repeat the new words, using either/or questions: *C'est du beurre ou de la confiture ?*, etc. As you move from one group to the next, review the most useful words already presented.

Teach the superordinate terms *une entrée, un plat principal, un dessert*, as well as *une viande* and *un légume*. These words appear in the **Vie et culture** notes and throughout the lesson and are helpful in organizing the various food words into categories for practice and review, as outlined in the learning strategy in L. 1.

Review: To review the food vocabulary, have students compete in teams to see how many items each team can list for a specific category. This allows students to implement the learning strategy presented for vocabulary in L. 1. Send one member of each team to the board for each category and give them a limited amount of time to write their lists. Sample categories: *les boissons rafraîchissantes ; les fruits ; les légumes ; les desserts.*

POINTS DE DÉPART

Les repas

Les Sangala habitent à Bordeaux ; ils prennent le petit-déjeuner vers huit heures.

Les Canadiens prennent souvent un petit-déjeuner copieux.

Les Dupuis habitent une ferme en Touraine ; ils déjeunent chez eux à midi et demi.

Marie-Christelle, Janique et Guillaume habitent en Belgique ; ils prennent le goûter vers quatre heures.

M. et Mme Haddad habitent en Algérie ; ils dînent vers huit heures.

Note: Cultural features include: times for meals, size of meals, choices of snacks. *Une rôtie* (Can.) is a type of toast. *Bacon* is pronounced/bekɔn/. In Canada, the meals are: *le déjeuner, le dîner, le souper.* Small children often have an after-school snack, *le goûter*, or *le quatre heures* (*une collation* in Canada) around four o'clock, since dinner is typically served around eight o'clock. They may have *un pain au chocolat* (a chocolate croissant), or a portion of a *baguette* with a piece of chocolate inside (*du pain avec du chocolat*), *un fruit, un yaourt*, or *des tartines*, with juice or water to drink.

Implementation: Use the restaurant menu to illustrate the categories described in the note and to provide additional examples of *entrées, plats principaux,* and *desserts.* Remind students that *une entrée* is a starter or appetizer and that *le plat principal* refers to the main course. Note the differences between the two menus offered, in terms of price and choice.

Vie et culture

Les repas en France

Regardez ces menus affichés devant un petit restaurant : en quoi consiste un repas typique ? D'abord, il y a une entrée ; indiquez une ou deux des entrées proposées. Ensuite, il y a un plat principal (de la viande ou du poisson) servi avec un légume. Après, on choisit un fromage ou un dessert. À la fin du repas, on prend le café.

Les Français prennent le temps de manger, et ils restent à table en moyenne[1] deux heures par jour. Le dîner est le repas principal, et en général on dîne vers huit heures du soir. Souvent, on regarde le journal télévisé pendant l'heure du dîner.

Si la durée[2] des repas reste stable, le temps de la préparation diminue. Les Français utilisent de plus en plus des produits congelés[3], le four à micro-ondes[4] et des plats préparés. À la maison, le dîner traditionnel avec trois plats successifs n'est plus courant : entrée, plat garni et dessert sont réduits en général à deux plats.

[1]*on average* [2]*length* [3]*frozen* [4]*microwave*

ET VOUS ?

1. Regardez les menus du petit restaurant : quel menu et quels plats est-ce que vous préférez et pourquoi ?
2. Les Français restent assez longtemps à table. Comment est-ce que vous expliquez cela ?
3. Est-ce que vos habitudes sont semblables aux habitudes des Français ou différents ? Expliquez votre réponse.

Note: Data on length of meals is taken from *Francoscopie 2010*, p. 180–181. Breakfast is the shortest meal: on average 18 minutes on weekdays and 34 minutes on weekends. Lunch away from home lasts on average 38 minutes, but only 29 minutes if eaten in the workplace. Dinner lasts on average 35 minutes during the week and 42 minutes on the weekend. Many French people enjoy entertaining in their homes for special occasions such as birthdays, baptisms, confirmations, etc., and the focus of the get-together is frequently an elaborate meal. Saturday dinner and Sunday lunch are the most usual times to invite guests.

Implementation: 5-14 Begin by having students identify the meal depicted in the photo on the next page. Point out that M. Maisonneuve could be having breakfast in the restaurant pictured here and that since he is in Canada, his meal would be referred to as *le déjeuner*.

05-19 to 05-22

À vous la parole

5-14 Quel repas ? Selon la description, identifiez le repas.

MODÈLE M. Maisonneuve prend des œufs sur le plat avec du jambon et des rôties.
- Il prend le petit-déjeuner.

1. Mme Lopez donne des pains au chocolat et du lait à ses enfants. Ils prennent le goûter.
2. Mme Leroux prend seulement du café et un croissant. Elle prend le petit-déjeuner.
3. Nicolas prend un yaourt et une pomme. Il prend le goûter.
4. M. et Mme Poirier prennent des œufs avec des rôties. Ils prennent le petit-déjeuner.
5. Il est une heure ; les Schumann mangent du poisson avec du riz. Ils prennent le déje
6. Nous sommes à Montréal, le soir. Mme Ladouceur sert de la soupe. Elle prend le c

Expansion: 5-14 Personalize by having students describe one of their typical meals and let classmates guess which meal it is.

7. Avant de retourner au bureau, Marion et Gaëlle prennent un hamburger et des frites au McDo. Elles prennent le déjeuner.
8. Il est huit heures du soir, et les Deleuze mangent du rosbif et des pommes de terre. Ils prennent le dîner.

C'est quel repas ? Qu'est-ce qu'on prend ?

5-15 Quels ingrédients ? Avec quoi est-ce qu'on fait les plats suivants ? Avec un/e partenaire, mettez-vous d'accord sur les ingrédients.

MODÈLE une omelette ?

É1 Avec quoi est-ce qu'on fait une omelette ?
É2 On fait une omelette avec des œufs, du lait et du beurre.
É1 Et aussi avec du jambon.

1. un citron pressé ?
2. une omelette ?
3. un sandwich ?
4. une salade de fruits ?
5. une tartine ?
6. un croque-monsieur ?
7. un café au lait ?
8. un pain au chocolat ?

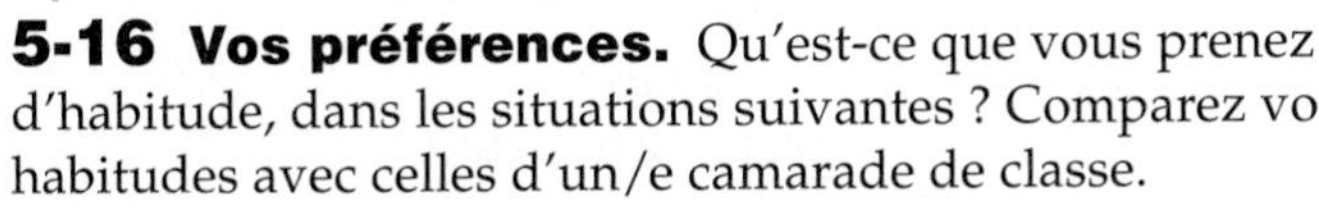

Expansion: 5-16 Follow up by having several students report back some of their partner's preferences.

5-16 Vos préférences. Qu'est-ce que vous prenez d'habitude, dans les situations suivantes ? Comparez vos habitudes avec celles d'un/e camarade de classe.

MODÈLE comme boisson, au petit-déjeuner ?

É1 D'habitude, je prends du café avec du sucre.
É2 Moi, je ne prends pas de café au petit-déjeuner ; je prends du jus d'orange.

1. comme boisson, au petit-déjeuner ?
2. à manger, au petit-déjeuner ?
3. à manger, au déjeuner ?
4. comme goûter, l'après-midi ?
5. quand vous avez envie de prendre une boisson, l'après-midi ?
6. comme boisson, au dîner ?
7. quand vous n'avez pas dîné, tard le soir ?
8. quand vous êtes très stressé/e ?
9. comme boisson, quand vous avez des invités ?

Additional practice: *Les bonnes combinaisons. Qu'est-ce qu'on prend avec la boisson ou l'aliment mentionné ? avec le café ? —du sucre ou du lait ; avec le thé ? avec le pain ? avec les œufs ? avec le poulet ? avec le poisson ? avec le fromage ? avec les hamburgers ?*

Sons et lettres

Les voyelles /ø/ et /œ/

To pronounce the vowel /ø/ of **deux**, start from the position of /e/ as in **des** and round the lips. The lips should also be tense and moved forward. It is important to lengthen the sound while continuing to keep the lips rounded, protruded, and tense. Typically, /ø/ occurs at the end of words and syllables and before the consonant /z/: **deux**, **jeu**, **peu**, **sérieuse**. When it is pronounced, the *mute e* (in words like **le**, **se**, **ne**, and **vendredi**) is usually pronounced with the vowel /ø/ of **deux**.

Presentation: This vowel distinction is often difficult for speakers of English to perceive and produce in isolation. You may wish to use the text audio to practice this distinction with your class. Stress the distribution facts, namely that /œ/ occurs before a consonant and /ø/ in open syllables. To differentiate /ø/ from /œ/, have students place their hand below their chin, pronounce /ø/ first, then drop the chin and pronounce /œ/. The downward hand movement makes the jaw movement more apparent.

To pronounce the vowel /œ/ of **leur**, start from the position of /ø/ and drop your jaw so that your mouth is open wider. Both vowels are usually spelled **eu**. The vowel /œ/ is also spelled as **œu**, as in **sœur**. The vowel /œ/ of **leur** occurs before a pronounced consonant, except for /z/ as mentioned above.

/ø/	**/œ/**
le bl**eu**	le b**eu**rre
l**e** dîner	l**eu**r dîner
des **œu**fs	un **œu**f
vendred**i**	il déj**eu**ne

05-23 to 05-24

Initial practice: Begin with a discrimination drill; have students tell which of the two vowels they hear (the vowel of *deux* or that of *leur*) for words you read aloud such as *œuf, beurre, tailleur, bleu, jeudi, couleur, monsieur, peu, serveur, serveuse, sœur, neuf, hamburger.*

À vous la parole

5-17 Contrastes. Répétez chaque paire de mots et comparez les voyelles.

/y/ vs /ø/	**/ø/ vs /œ/**
du / deux	ne / neuf
lu / le	eux / sœurs
du jus / deux jeux	le bleu / leur beurre

5-18 Au féminin. Donnez la forme correspondante au féminin.

MODÈLE il est sérieux
• elle est sérieuse

1. il est ambitieux
2. il est serveur
3. il est généreux
4. ils sont nombreux
5. il est paresseux

5-19 Phrases. Répétez chaque phrase.

1. Des œufs bleus ? Ce n'est pas sérieux !
2. Le neveu de Monsieur Meunier déjeune à deux heures.
3. La sœur de Madame Francœur porte un tailleur bleu.
4. Je prends un hamburger ; lui, un croque-monsieur.
5. Depardieu est un acteur ; Montesquieu, un auteur ; mon neveu, un serveur.

FORMES ET FONCTIONS

1. Les questions avec les pronoms interrogatifs : *qu'est-ce qui, qu'est-ce que, qui* et *quoi*

Presentation: Review question formation from Ch. 2, L. 1 and Ch. 4, L. 2. Ask questions using the new expressions and have students answer logically. Then present the new information using examples. Show examples of *qui, qui est-ce que,* and *qu'est-ce qui* in minimal pairs: *Qu'est-ce qui est sur la photo ? / Qui est sur la photo ? ; Qu'est-ce que vous attendez ? / Qui est-ce que vous attendez ?*

- To ask *what*, use **qu'est-ce qui** and **qu'est-ce que**:
- **Qu'est-ce qui** is used as the subject of a question and is followed by a verb:

Qu'est-ce qui se passe ?	*What's happening?*
Qu'est-ce qui est sur la photo ?	*What's in the photo?*

- **Qu'est-ce que** is used as the direct object and is followed by the subject of the sentence:

Qu'est-ce que vous prenez ?	*What are you having?*
Qu'est-ce que tu as mis dans la sauce ?	*What did you put in the sauce?*

- To ask *who* or *whom*, use **qui**:
- When **qui** is the subject, it is followed directly by the verb:

Qui prépare le dîner ?	*Who's making dinner?*
Qui n'aime pas le chocolat ?	*Who doesn't like chocolate?*

- When **qui** is the direct object, use **est-ce que** before the subject of the sentence:

Qui est-ce que tu aimes ?	*Whom do you like?*
Qui est-ce qu'ils invitent ?	*Whom are they inviting?*

- When a verb requires a preposition, that preposition precedes **qui**:

À qui est-ce que tu parles ?	*Whom are you talking to?*
Avec qui est-ce que tu dînes ce soir ?	*Whom are you having dinner with tonight?*

- After prepositions, use **quoi** to ask *what*:

Avec quoi est-ce qu'on fait la sauce ?	*What are we making the sauce with?*
De quoi est-ce qu'il va parler ?	*What is he going to speak about?*

Fiche pratique

To help learn whether to use **qu'est-ce qui/qu'est-ce que** or **qui/qui est-ce que** to ask a question, practice repeating simple questions with short answers out loud. For example, Qu'est-ce qui est sur la table ? —une tarte. Qui est sur la table ? —le serveur ! Qu'est-ce que tu regardes ? —le menu. Qui est-ce que tu regardes ? —le serveur.

Note: As the examples illustrate, questions in informal, spoken English often feature preposition stranding, that is, the preposition can fall at the end of the question. The same is not true in French. Point out to students that the preposition must be at the beginning of the question, before the interrogative pronoun.

You can stress the difference between questions using *qui* or *quoi* with the following questions and answers: *Avec **qui** est-ce que tu joues au tennis ? —Avec ma sœur. Avec **quoi** est-ce que tu joues au tennis ? —Avec ma nouvelle raquette.*

À vous la parole

25

28 **5-20 La curieuse.** La petite sœur d'Élodie est très curieuse et lui pose beaucoup de questions. Pour chaque question, indiquez si elle parle d'une chose ou d'une personne.

Initial practice: Begin with this comprehension-based activity that helps students recognize and understand the forms before they are asked to produce questions.

	une chose	une personne
MODÈLE Qu'est-ce que tu prends ?	✓	___
1. Qu'est-ce que tu regardes ?	✓	___
2. Qui est-ce que tu préfères ?	___	✓
3. Qui est-ce que tu attends ?	___	✓
4. Qui est-ce que tu invites ?	___	✓
5. De quoi est-ce que tu parles ?	✓	___
6. Avec qui est-ce que tu vas dîner ?	___	✓
7. Qu'est-ce que tu vas manger ?	✓	___
8. De qui est-ce que tu parles ?	___	✓

À votre avis, est-ce que la sœur d'Élodie s'intéresse plus aux personnes ou aux objets ? Pourquoi ?

Implementation: 5-21 Once students have completed the exercise in pairs, follow up by having different groups tell the questions that were asked.

5-21 Un dîner d'amis. La famille Dupont invite des amis à dîner. Avec un/e partenaire, suivez le modèle et jouez les rôles de Mme Dupont et de son mari.

MODÈLES É1 Dis, chéri, *Damien* a acheté les boissons ?
É2 Mais non.
É1 Alors, *qui* a acheté les boissons ?

É2 Dis, chéri, ta cousine va venir *avec les Berti* ?
É1 Mais non, ma chérie.
É2 Alors, *avec qui est-ce qu'* elle va venir ?

1. On a demandé *à Suzanne* d'apporter le dessert ? … à qui est-ce qu'on a demandé d'apporter le dessert ?
2. *Damien* va chercher le fromage ? … qui va chercher le fromage ?
3. Stéphane va inviter *sa fiancée* ? … qui est-ce qu'il va inviter ?
4. On va acheter *des tomates* pour la salade ? … qu'est-ce qu'on va acheter ?
5. On va faire *une sauce pour la viande* ? … qu'est-ce qu'on va faire ?
6. *Tu* vas téléphoner aux invités ? … qui va téléphoner aux invités ?
7. On va faire la sauce *avec du beurre* ? … avec quoi est-ce qu'on va faire la sauce ?

Implementation: 5-22 Put students on teams to play this popular game. Or, to simplify, have students volunteer responses at random.

5-22 Jéopardy ! Avec deux partenaires, jouez au Jéopardy. La première personne va donner une réponse choisie de la liste. Les deux autres vont consulter la liste des verbes pour pouvoir poser une question logique. La première à poser sa question peut donner la réponse suivante.

MODÈLES É1 de la musique classique
É2 Qu'est-ce que vous écoutez ?
É1 C'est bon. Alors, c'est à toi.

É2 à mes parents
É3 À qui est-ce que tu téléphones ?
É2 Oui, à toi alors !

admirer écouter manger parler regarder réviser téléphoner

Réponses à choisir :

la télévision
Bill et Melinda Gates
de la musique classique
de la pizza
à mon copain
la sociologie
le manuel de français
à mes parents
de politique
Carrie Underwood

Note: 5-22 Bill Gates is the founder of Microsoft and with his wife, of the Bill and Melinda Gates Foundation. According to its web site, the Foundation is dedicated to bringing innovations in health and learning to the global community. Carrie Underwood is a young country music star.

Implementation: 5-23 Model for students how to ask and answer questions before putting them to work in pairs. Follow up by having students report what they learned about their partner.

5-23 On va tout savoir. Interviewez un/e partenaire pour apprendre tous les détails de sa vie universitaire.

MODÈLES habiter
- Où est-ce que tu habites ? Avec qui est-ce que tu habites ?

faire comme études
- Qu'est-ce que tu fais comme études ?

1. habiter
2. faire comme études
3. manger typiquement
4. sortir le soir
5. faire le week-end

2. Les verbes en *-ir* comme *choisir*

- Like other **-ir** verbs you have learned, verbs like **choisir** have four spoken forms. The final /s/ of the plural form is dropped in the singular.

  ils **choisissent** /ʃwazis/ la glace   il **choisit** /ʃwazi/ la tarte

  To form the present indicative of verbs like **choisir**, add **-iss-** to the base for the plural forms: **chois ir → chois -iss-**.

CHOISIR ***to choose***

SINGULIER		PLURIEL	
je	chois**is**	nous	chois**issons**
tu	chois**is**	vous	chois**issez**
il / elle / on	chois**it**	ils / elles	chois**issent**

IMPÉRATIF : Ne **choisis** pas ça ! **Choisissez** le poisson ! **Choisissons** un dessert !

PASSÉ COMPOSÉ : J'ai déjà **choisi**.

Presentation: To present inductively, use pictures of various dishes or menus and discuss your choices and those of the students: *Comme plat principal, moi, je choisis le poisson et vous, quel plat principal est-ce que vous choisissez ?* Then quickly review *-ir* verbs (*les enfants s'endorment après le dîner ; leur père s'endort devant la télé*) and *-re* verbs (*il attend le dessert ; ses parents attendent le café*) and remind students that for all two-stem verbs, the spoken singular forms are derived by dropping the final consonant sound of the third-person plural form. Ask students to derive the forms for *choisir*, then for other verbs in the list.

- Some **-ir/-iss-** verbs are derived from common adjectives. They express the meaning that someone or something is becoming more like the adjective:

rouge	*red*	**rougir**	*to blush*
pâle	*pale*	**pâlir**	*to become pale*
maigre	*thin, skinny*	**maigrir**	*to lose weight*
grosse	*large, fat*	**grossir**	*to gain weight*
grande	*large, tall*	**grandir**	*to grow taller, to grow up (for children)*

Note: You might also wish to teach the verb *mincir* (a near synonym to *maigrir*), which means to get slimmer. Other verbs in *-ir/-iss-* correspond to English verbs in "-ish": *finir, punir, établir, démolir.*

- Some other common verbs conjugated like **choisir** are:

finir	*to finish*	Tu **as fini** la soupe ?
obéir à	*to obey*	**Obéis à** ta mère ! Pas de chocolat dans ta chambre !
désobéir à	*to disobey*	Ces enfants **désobéissent** toujours **à** leur père.
punir	*to punish*	Tu **punis** ton fils parce qu'il n'a pas mangé ses carottes ? C'est ridicule.
réfléchir à	*to think*	Je **réfléchis à** l'entrée que je préfère.
réussir à	*to succeed*	Elle ne **réussit** pas **à** appeler le serveur.
	to pass	Il **a** bien **réussi à** son examen. (ou Il **a réussi** son examen.)

05-29 to 05-32

À vous la parole

Initial practice: Begin with a discrimination drill: one person, or more than one? *Elle grandit. Ils maigrissent. Ils finissent. Elle obéit. Elle choisit bien. Ils rougissent. Il réussit. Elles réfléchissent*, etc. Follow with one or two simple substitution drills: *Je maigris ; nous ; lui*, etc. You might also include a transformation drill, present to past or vice versa: *Nous choisissons un fromage. — Nous avons choisi un fromage*, etc.

5-24 Des enfants modèles ? Est-ce que ces enfants obéissent ou désobéissent à leurs parents ?

MODÈLE Delphine ne s'essuie pas quand elle sort de la douche.
• Elle désobéit à ses parents.

1. Fabien mange du chocolat dans sa chambre. Il désobéit...
2. Laetitia et Fabien font leurs devoirs devant la télé. Ils désobéissent...
3. Tu manges bien tous les matins avant d'aller à l'école. Tu obéis...
4. Fabien et Delphine jouent au basket sur la terrasse. Ils déobéissent...
5. Laetitia ne mange jamais dans sa chambre. Elle obéit...
6. Vous ne sortez pas quand vous avez un examen à préparer. Vous obéissez...
7. Delphine et vous, vous mettez la musique très fort. Vous désobéissez...
8. J'aide mes parents à préparer le dîner. J'obéis...

Expansion: 5-25 After completing the activity, have students report back what they and their partners decided.

5-25 Le choix est à vous ! Qu'est-ce que vous choisissez ? En groupes de trois ou quatre, comparez votre réponse avec la réponse de vos partenaires.

MODÈLE entre un coca et une bière

É1 Entre un coca et une bière, moi, je choisis une bière.

É2 Pas moi ! Je choisis un coca.

É3 Moi aussi, donc toi et moi, on choisit un coca.

1. entre une soupe aux poissons et une soupe aux carottes
2. entre le poulet et le poisson
3. entre les haricots verts et les asperges
4. entre le fromage et le yaourt
5. entre une poire et une banane
6. entre une glace et une tarte
7. entre le thé et le café

Implementation: 5-26 Use as a mixing activity. Have students ask only two questions of each person before moving on to someone else. Give students a limited amount of time to work, then follow up by having them ask questions about the items for which they did not find a response.

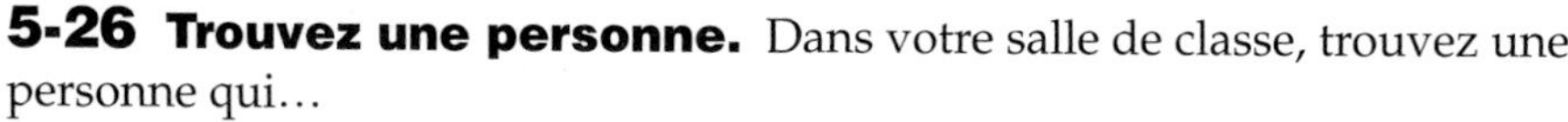

5-26 Trouvez une personne. Dans votre salle de classe, trouvez une personne qui…

MODÈLE finit toujours ses devoirs avant d'arriver en classe

É1 Est-ce que tu finis toujours tes devoirs avant d'arriver en classe ?

É2 Non, je ne finis pas toujours mes devoirs avant d'arriver en classe.

OU Oui, je finis toujours mes devoirs avant d'arriver en classe.

1. rougit toujours quand il/elle parle devant un groupe
2. finit toujours ses devoirs avant d'arriver en classe
3. grossit toujours en hiver
4. grandit toujours (*still*)
5. réfléchit toujours avant de répondre
6. réussit toujours à ses examens
7. maigrit quand il/elle est stressé/e
8. grossit quand il/elle est stressé/e
9. ne désobéit jamais à ses parents

Observons

5-27 Voici des spécialités de chez nous.

A. Avant de regarder. Est-ce que vous avez déjà dîné dans un restaurant marocain ? africain ? Si oui, quelles sont les spécialités que vous avez goûtées ? Regardez la photo du buffet et identifiez ces plats du Bénin. Sur la photo, il y a du poulet, des épinards et des fruits comme des plaintains. Regardez le couscous ; qu'est-ce qu'il faut pour faire un bon couscous ?

Voici un buffet plein de spécialités du Bénin.

Est-ce que vous avez déjà mangé du couscous ? Où ?

Script: ***Observons.*** Note that the elements in brackets reflect standard usage and have been added to the written transcripts. They were not pronounced by the speaker(s) in question. The word *épinard* is usually used in the plural, *les épinards*, contrary to this speaker's usage here.

BIENVENU : Donc, chez nous, au Bénin, voici… euh… quelques-uns des plats que nous mangeons. Vous avez ici de l'épinard préparé avec du poulet, des crevettes. L'épinard est accompagné de, de pâte. Ça peut être de la pâte de maïs, ça peut être aussi de, du plantain pilé. Alors le plantain, c'est une forme de banane euh, que nous avons ici. Ça, c'est la banane plantain. On peut la piler, pour avoir une pâte comme celle-ci.

FADOUA : Alors, mon plat préféré, que l'on mange tous les vendredis au Maroc, c'est le couscous. Alors, le couscous, alors, déjà il faut un couscoussier. Alors un couscoussier, c'est une sorte de marmite avec un… un support au-dessus à trous. Donc en bas, on fait revenir les oignons avec les épices et de la viande, on met de l'eau, et dans l'eau on met euh des tomates, des carottes, des navets, euh [de] la citrouille, tous les légumes de saison. Une fois que la graine est bien cuite, c'est-à-dire qu'on, qu'on sent qu'elle est un peu moelleuse et plus craquante, alors on sert le couscous, c'est-à-dire que… on sert le couscous euh sur un plat, on fait un puits, où l'on met des… des légumes, et les légumes, on les met sur le couscous, et à côté on met deux bols, où on a un bouillon. Ça permet de mouiller le couscous, c'est-à-dire qu'on met le couscous dans l'assiette, et on met un peu plus d'eau selon notre goût.

LA SERVEUSE : À table, mesdames. C'est prêt.

B. En regardant. Deux personnes vont décrire des spécialités de leur région. Trouvez toutes les bonnes réponses à chaque question.

1. Bienvenu décrit des spécialités du…
   a. Mali. b. Bénin. c. Cameroun.
2. D'abord, c'est de l'épinard avec…
   a. du poulet. b. du porc. c. des crevettes.
3. L'épinard est accompagné de pâte faite de…
   a. riz. b. maïs. c. plantain.
4. Le plantain, c'est une forme de…
   a. céréales. b. légume. c. banane.
5. Fadoua décrit une spécialité du…
   a. Maroc. b. Tchad. c. Midi de la France.
6. Pour préparer ce plat, il faut…
   a. un grand four. b. un couscoussier. c. une casserole.
7. Comme ingrédients, on peut mettre…
   a. de la viande. b. du poisson. c. des tomates. d. des carottes. e. des oignons. f. des navets (*turnips*). g. des concombres.
8. Pour servir, on met un bol avec du bouillon pour…
   a. boire. b. mélanger (*mix*) les ingrédients. c. mouiller (*moisten*) le plat.

C. Après avoir regardé. Quel plat est-ce que vous voudriez essayer et pourquoi ?

Leçon 3 Faisons des courses

Presentation: Present the vocabulary using the grocery store image (MFL, Instructor's Resources) and describing what one can find in each of the grocery store sections. Many of the products will be familiar to students, and some new items can be presented first for receptive control only. Note the spelling of *crèmerie* based on the 1990 orthographic reform and the dropping of *ne* in *C'est pas sur la liste*, which is characteristic of spoken French. Test students' comprehension by having them point to an item you name; have them repeat, using either/or questions: *Ce sont des petits pois ou des champignons ?*, etc. Then move on to the dialogue.

POINTS DE DÉPART

Allons au supermarché

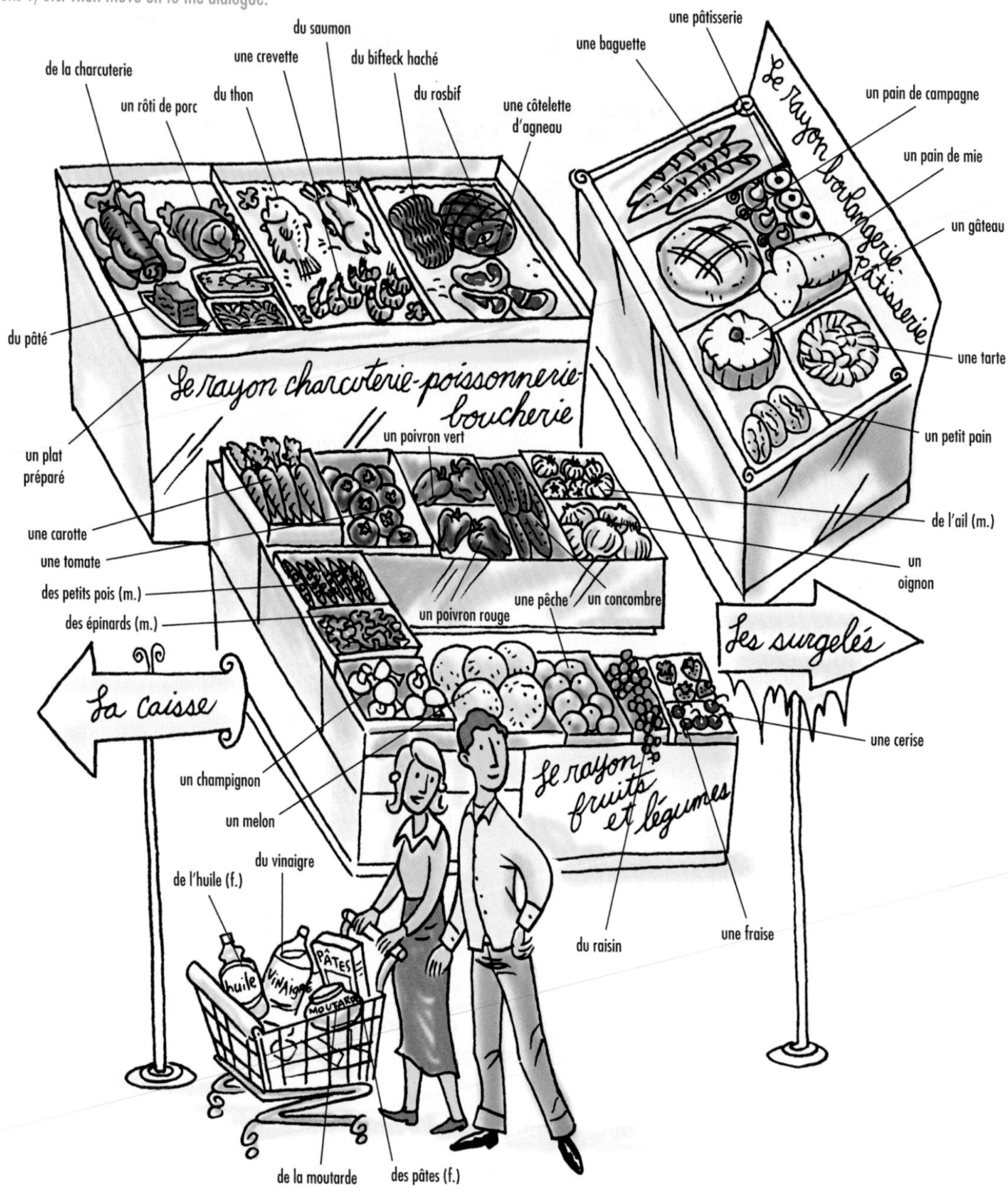

C'est samedi. Les Mathieu font des courses à Super U. Ils se trouvent au rayon fruits et légumes.

M. MATHIEU : Qu'est-ce qu'on prend comme fruits ? Des cerises ? Elles sont belles.
MME MATHIEU : Mais elles sont trop chères. Sept euros le kilo !
M. MATHIEU : Alors, prenons des pêches !
MME MATHIEU : D'accord. Tu veux passer au rayon crèmerie ? On a besoin d'une douzaine d'œufs, d'une bouteille de lait, d'un morceau de cantal et aussi peut-être d'un bon camembert. Moi, je vais au rayon charcuterie pour chercher quelques tranches de jambon et du pâté. On se retrouve à la caisse ?

(quelques minutes plus tard)
M. MATHIEU : Regarde, chérie, j'ai trouvé cette boîte de sardines, un pot de moutarde à l'ancienne et ce paquet de chips bio.
MME MATHIEU : Tu es incorrigible ! C'est pas sur la liste, tout ça !

Presentation: Let students listen to the dialogue, then ask questions to check comprehension. Point out the expression *avoir besoin de* and compare it to *avoir envie de*, taught in Ch. 3, L. 3. Have students role-play, using parts of the dialogue and varying the vocabulary: *Qu'est-ce qu'on prend comme fruits ? —Des cerises ?* Be sure to provide a clear model. Use the **Vie et culture** notes to talk about where people shop for food.

Expansion: In conjunction with this section, you might wish to present the video clip *Pour faire une vinaigrette*, which includes key vocabulary and focuses on the ingredients needed and the process of preparing a simple recipe.

À vous la parole

5-28 Quel rayon ? Nous sommes au supermarché. Où est-ce que vous entendez cela ? Choisissez vos réponses dans cette liste.

au rayon crèmerie	au rayon boulangerie-pâtisserie
au rayon charcuterie	au rayon fruits et légumes
au rayon boucherie	au rayon surgelés
au rayon poissonnerie	à la caisse

MODÈLE Je voudrais une demi-douzaine de petits pains, s'il vous plaît.
• C'est au rayon boulangerie-pâtisserie.

1. Je mets les croissants dans un sac ? C'est au rayon boulangerie-pâtisserie.
2. Qu'est-ce que tu préfères, le pâté de campagne ou le jambon ? C'est au rayon charcuterie.
3. Vous avez des sardines ? C'est au rayon poissonnerie.
4. Comme dessert, on prend de la glace ou un sorbet ? C'est au rayon surgelés.
5. Je vous recommande le brie, madame. C'est au rayon crèmerie.
6. Il y a des côtelettes d'agneau et du poulet. C'est au rayon boucherie.
7. La pâtissière fait des gâteaux délicieux ! C'est au rayon boulangerie-pâtisserie.
8. Les melons sont beaux, mais ils sont chers. C'est au rayon fruits et légumes.
9. Donne-moi mon sac, chéri ; on doit payer maintenant. C'est à la caisse.

Variation: 5-28 Bring in a net bag of food items and have students guess where you would have bought them. For items that you wish to make part of students' productive vocabulary, play "Kim's Game": show students 8–10 articles that you then hide from view; they must write down a list of those articles.

Implementation: Use the photos to help convey the meaning of the text and check for general comprehension: have students identify the various shopping options (neighborhood shops supermarkets, superstores, and fresh markets) and summarize what items are generally purchased at each. Find out wh students shop where they do: is it for convenience's sake, for variety, to save money, to find local and organic products? These considerations also influence the choices of the French about where to shop. Help students see the relationship between words such as *le boulanger* (a person) and *la boulangerie* (a place). Help them derive from context the meaning of the expressions *faire leur marché, fruits et légumes… biologiques.*

Vie et culture

Pour faire des courses

Regardez ces photos. Qu'est-ce qu'on achète dans chaque endroit ? Où est-ce que vous préférez faire des courses et pourquoi ?

Pour faire des courses, les Français ont beaucoup de choix. Ils vont chez les petits commerçants ou ils font leurs courses dans les grandes surfaces. Par exemple, le matin, beaucoup de Français achètent la baguette du petit-déjeuner chez le boulanger. Mais la majorité des Français vont faire des courses une ou deux fois par semaine dans les supermarchés comme Casino ou les hypermarchés comme Intermarché ou Carrefour. Comme les supermarchés, les hypermarchés offrent toutes sortes d'aliments[1]. Mais en plus, on y trouve des vêtements, des livres, des CD, des appareils électroniques (comme des télés, des lecteurs DVD, des ordinateurs, etc.), et différentes choses pour la maison.

Pour acheter des fruits et des légumes frais[2] ou biologiques, les Français aiment faire leur marché, surtout le week-end. Il est vrai que les marchés sont moins pratiques que les supermarchés, en particulier en hiver ou quand il pleut. Alors pourquoi est-ce que les gens préfèrent les marchés ? C'est parce que les produits sont plus frais et les marchés sont plus animés. On y trouve une grande variété de couleurs, d'odeurs et de bruits[3].

[1]*food* [2]*fresh* [3]*noises*

On trouve de tout dans une grande surface.

Dans cette épicerie on vend des produits bio et régionaux.

Un marché en plein air à Nîmes.

 **5-29 Des achats.** Qu'est-ce que ces gens ont acheté ? Avec un/e partenaire, suggérez un ou deux produits.

MODÈLE Pauline se trouve au rayon boucherie.
É1 Elle achète un rôti.
É2 Et aussi un poulet.

1. Nicolas est passé au rayon boulangerie.
2. M. Dumas va faire une salade.
3. Mme Ducastel est allée au rayon fruits et légumes pour acheter des fruits.
4. M. et Mme Camus vont servir du poisson.

5. Matthieu a seulement acheté des surgelés.
6. Gaëlle est allée au rayon crèmerie.
7. Christophe est passé au rayon légumes.
8. Lucie va faire une vinaigrette.

Implementation: 5-30 Before completing this activity, review with students the meaning of *l'entrée* and *le plat principal*, both of which were presented in the **Vie et culture** notes in L. 2. Remind students to use vocabulary they have already learned to complete this exercise. As a follow-up, have each group describe their menu and have the class vote on the best.

5-30 Un grand dîner. Avec un/e partenaire, planifiez un grand dîner avec des amis. Quelle occasion est-ce que vous allez fêter ? Qu'est-ce que vous allez servir comme entrée ? comme plat principal ? comme légume ? comme fromage ? comme boisson ? comme dessert ?

MODÈLE É1 Comme entrée, on va acheter du jambon et des crudités.
É2 Je déteste ça. Je préfère les crevettes.
É1 C'est cher, mais d'accord. Et comme plat principal ? …

Presentation: Review the expressions students already know with a communicative activity, perhaps one taken from Ch. 3, L. 1, before presenting the new material. Use the visual of quantities (MFL, Instructor's Resources) to introduce these expressions; test comprehension by showing the image without labels (MFL, Instructor's Resources) and asking students to point to the item you describe.
Point out that *un bol* is generally reserved for coffee in the morning and/or cereal. Soup would be served in *une assiette creuse*, especially in formal situations; at home, one might serve *un bol de soupe*. Have students tell: a) what items they would buy in the quantities specified: *une boîte ? —une boîte de sardines, une boîte de céréales*, etc. b) how much of a product they would normally buy: *Des carottes ? —un kilo de carottes. Des sardines ? —une boîte de sardines. Des tomates ? du vin ? des œufs ? du riz ? du brie ? des pommes de terre ? des poivrons ? de l'huile ? des crevettes ? des petits pois ?* Next, have students imagine they're making vegetable soup, and tell what they buy/don't buy: *Des pêches ? —Non, je n'achète pas de pêches. Des carottes ? des oignons ? des haricots verts ? des tomates ? des pommes ? des asperges ? de la salade ? de l'ail ? des pommes de terre ?*

FORMES ET FONCTIONS

1. Les expressions de quantité

- In **Chapitre 3, Leçon 1**, you learned that adverbs of quantity are followed by **de/d'** when used with nouns.

trop de	Il y a **trop de** sucre.	*There's too much sugar.*
beaucoup de	Il mange **beaucoup de** riz.	*He eats lots of rice.*
assez de	Vous avez **assez d'**huile ?	*Do you have enough oil?*
peu de	Je mange **peu de** choux.	*I eat very little cabbage.*
ne... pas de	Tu **n'**as **pas de** sel ?	*Don't you have any salt?*

- Nouns of measure are used in the same way.

une tasse de	Prends **une tasse de** café.	*Have a cup of coffee.*
une boîte de	Donne-moi **une boîte de** sardines.	*Give me a can of sardines.*
	On va prendre **une boîte de** céréales ?	*Are we going to get a box of cereal?*
un kilo de	Achète **un kilo de** navets.	*Buy a kilo of turnips.*
un litre de	Il faut **un litre de** lait.	*We need a liter of milk.*

- Here are some useful expressions for specifying quantity.

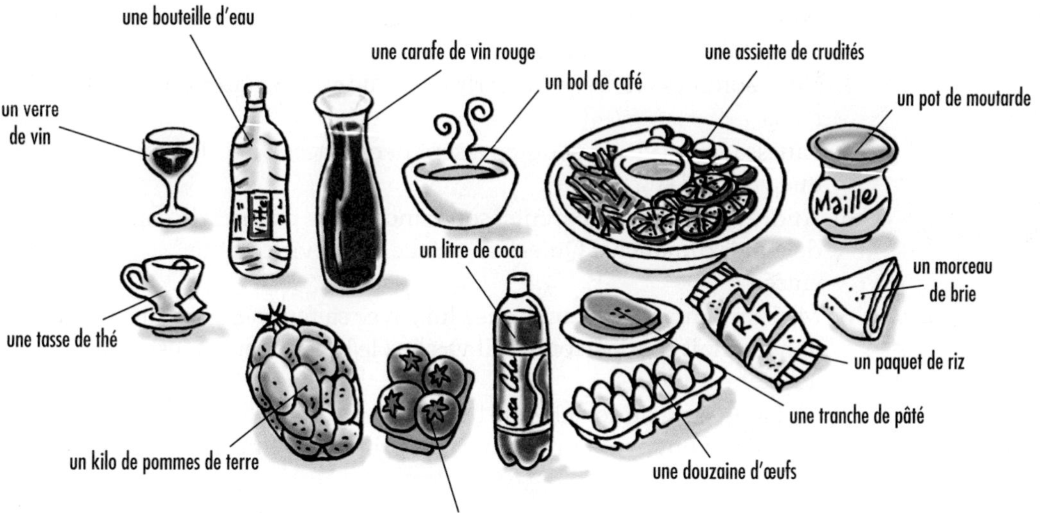

À vous la parole

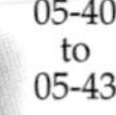

05-40 to 05-43

5-31 À table. Quelle quantité de ces aliments est-ce que vous prenez ?

MODÈLE Vous prenez de l'eau ? *Answers may vary.*
• Oui, donnez-moi un verre d'eau.

1. Vous prenez du jambon ? …une tranche de jambon.
2. Vous prenez du café au lait ? …une tasse de café au lait.
3. Vous prenez du pain ? …une tranche de pain.
4. Vous prenez des crudités ? …une assiette de crudités.
5. Vous prenez du vin ? …un verre de vin.
6. Vous prenez de la viande ? …deux tranches de viande.
7. Vous prenez du fromage ? …un morceau de fromage.
8. Vous prenez du thé ? …une tasse de thé.

5-32 Un pot-au-feu. Qu'est-ce qu'il faut pour faire un pot-au-feu ? Regardez l'image du « pot-au-feu géant » préparé pour un festival d'été en Bretagne. Avec un/e partenaire, décidez de quelle quantité il faudrait pour préparer un pot-au-feu pour votre famille.

MODÈLE É1 Pour un pot-au-feu géant, il faut 260 kg de viande ! Et pour ta famille ?
É2 Pour ma famille, il faut seulement un kilo de viande…

5-33 Préparation pour un repas. Qu'est-ce qu'il faut acheter, et en quelles quantités ? Décidez avec votre partenaire.

MODÈLE Marion va faire une omelette au jambon pour quatre personnes.
É1 Elle doit acheter une douzaine d'œufs.
É2 Et aussi quatre tranches de jambon.
É1 Oui, c'est ça.

1. Cédric va inviter deux amis à prendre le dessert.
2. Mme Salazar va faire un rôti de porc et des petits pois pour elle, son mari et leurs trois enfants.
3. Nous sommes en hiver. M. Bertrand voudrait préparer une salade de fruits.
4. Vanessa va servir du saumon à sept personnes. Quels légumes est-ce que vous lui suggérez ?
5. Audrey a invité ses parents, son fiancé et les parents de son fiancé à déjeuner dimanche. Qu'est-ce qu'elle va servir comme entrée ?
6. M. Charpentier a des amis chez lui ; avec sa femme, ses deux enfants et lui, ça fait sept personnes. Il va chez le boulanger. Qu'est-ce qu'il va acheter ?
7. M. Papin a invité son chef de bureau et sa femme à dîner. Qu'est-ce que les Papin vont préparer comme plat principal ? Et comme dessert ?

Additional practice: For a more personalized activity, put students into groups of three or four to plan a meal. Have them write out their menu and grocery list. Give them five minutes to work, then let each group describe their meal.
Vous préparez un repas. Vous et vos amis, vous avez invité des gens à dîner. D'abord, décidez d'un menu. Ensuite, préparez une liste de choses à acheter. Enfin, distribuez les responsabilités : qui achète quoi, et où ?

MODÈLE É1 Comme entrée, on va servir des crudités.
É2 Oui, c'est bon et ce n'est pas cher. Ensuite, du rosbif ou du poulet ?
É3 Moi, je préfère le poulet avec des haricots verts.
É1 Donc, on va au rayon boucherie pour acheter un gros poulet de quatre kilos.
É2 Je vais au marché samedi matin pour acheter deux kilos de haricots verts et…

Suggestions : un dîner d'anniversaire ; un pique-nique ; un petit-déjeuner copieux ; un repas pas cher

2. Le pronom partitif *en*

- The pronoun **en** replaces nouns used with the partitive article or the plural indefinite article **des**:

Vous avez acheté **de l'ail** ?	*Did you buy garlic?*
—Oui, j'**en** ai acheté.	*—Yes, I bought some.*
Il n'y a pas **de sucre** ?	*There isn't any sugar?*
—Si, il y **en** a.	*—Yes, there is some.*
Qui prend **des fraises à la crème** ?	*Who's having strawberries with cream?*
—Jérémy **en** prend. Il aime bien ça.	*—Jeremy's having some. He likes that.*

Presentation: To present inductively, show examples similar to those found here, and have students analyze the use and placement of *en*. No agreement of the past participle is made with *en*.

Note: The object pronoun *en* is placed after the conjugated verb in affirmative commands and joined to it by a hyphen: *Donnez-en à Suzanne !* *En* is placed before the conjugated verb in negative commands: *N'en donnez pas à Paul !* The use of *en* with the imperative is not practiced here.

- The pronoun **en** can be used to replace nouns modified by an expression of quantity (including numbers). In this case, the expression of quantity is placed at the end of the sentence.

Il faut beaucoup de sucre pour cette recette?	*Do you need a lot of sugar for this recipe?*
—Oui, il **en** faut beaucoup.	*—Yes, you need a lot (of it).*
Tu as pris **du vin rouge** ?	*Did you have some red wine?*
—Oui, j'**en** ai bu un verre.	*—Yes, I drank a glass (of it).*
Combien de poivrons rouges est-ce que vous allez prendre ?	*How many red peppers are you going to get?*
—Nous allons **en** prendre trois.	*—We'll get three (of them).*

Presentation: Point out the useful expression *il faut*, used in the examples here and in the exercises below. Compare to *avoir besoin de*, presented in the opening dialogue. The use of *il faut* with an infinitive is taught in more detail in Ch. 9, L. 2.

- As the examples above show, **en** is placed immediately before the conjugated verb of a sentence, unless there is an infinitive. In that case, it precedes the infinitive.

Additional practice: a) Show a picture of a market (for example, MFL, Instructor's Resources) and ask students whether they can see certain items: *Il y a des carottes ? —Non, il n'y en a pas./—Oui, il y en a.* b) Have students express their preferences as you point out various items: *Voici des poivrons. —J'aime bien les poivrons ; je vais en acheter un kilo./—Je n'aime pas les poivrons ; je ne vais pas en acheter.* See the SAM/MFL for written practice that mixes the use of *en* with the various tenses.

À vous la parole

5-34 Qu'est-ce qu'il a acheté ? David achète des provisions. D'après les indications, qu'est-ce qu'il a acheté ? Avec un/e partenaire, trouvez des possibilités.

Implementation: 5-34 This initial exercise simply helps students make the form-meaning link between the use of the pronoun *en* and the expressions of quantity. Follow up by having students share their responses.

MODÈLE Il en a acheté une douzaine.

É1 Il a acheté une douzaine d'œufs.

É2 Il a acheté une douzaine de citrons.

1. Il en a pris un pot.
2. Il en a acheté un morceau.
3. Il en a pris une douzaine.
4. Il en a acheté une bouteille.
5. Il en a pris deux paquets.
6. Il en a demandé deux.
7. Il en a pris beaucoup.
8. Il en a acheté un kilo.
9. Il en a demandé dix tranches.
10. Il en a acheté une boîte.

5-35 Elle en prend combien ? Voici la liste des provisions que Mme Serre achète pour sa famille. Quelles quantités est-ce qu'il lui faut ?

MODÈLE des carottes

- Elle en achète un kilo.

- carottes
- oignons
- petits pains
- pâtes
- moutarde
- vin
- eau minérale
- lait
- œufs
- saumon

5-36 Vous en avez combien ? Donnez une réponse logique et personnalisée, et comparez-la avec la réponse de votre partenaire. Ensuite, comparez vos réponses avec les autres étudiants dans votre cours.

MODÈLE des sœurs ?

É1 J'en ai une.

É2 Je n'en ai pas.

1. des sœurs ?
2. des frères ?
3. des amis ?
4. des problèmes ?
5. de l'argent ?
6. des devoirs ?
7. des responsabilités ?
8. des vacances ?

Parlons

5-37 Les plats régionaux.

A. Avant de parler. Les Français ont la réputation de bien manger et boire. C'est une réputation bien méritée. La cuisine française est très variée. Chaque région a ses plats particuliers qui dépendent de son climat, de ses produits et de ses traditions culturelles. Voici une liste de quelques spécialités régionales en France :

- la bouillabaisse marseillaise
- la choucroute alsacienne
- la quiche lorraine
- les crêpes bretonnes
- le coq au vin bourguignon
- la fondue savoyarde

Preparation: *Avant de parler.* To begin, show the video montage *Traditions gastronomiques* and ask students whether they recognize specific regional dishes or can identify ingredients.

Est-ce que vous connaissez déjà certains de ces plats ?

B. En parlant. Avec un/e partenaire, regardez ces images de spécialités et de plats régionaux. Décrivez chaque photo et essayez d'identifier le plat.

MODÈLE É1 Regarde cette image. C'est une soupe.

É2 Oui, une soupe de poissons. Il y a des morceaux de poissons.

É1 Oui, et aussi des tomates parce que la soupe est rouge.

É2 C'est la bouillabaisse marseillaise ?

É1 C'est possible. Oui, c'est ça.

C. Après avoir parlé. Est-ce que vous et votre partenaire avez identifié tous les plats ? Comparez vos réponses aux réponses de vos camarades de classe.

Implementation: *Après avoir parlé.* Locate the various regions on a map and discuss why particular specialties might come from each region. For example, Marseille is a seaport city, hence the fish soup.

Leçon 

au café ou au restaurant	*in the cafe or in the restaurant*
l'addition (f.)	*bill*
avoir faim	*to be hungry*
avoir soif	*to be thirsty*
boire	*to drink*
prendre	*to take, to have (food or drink)*
des boissons chaudes	*hot drinks*
un café (crème)	*coffee (with cream)*
un chocolat chaud	*hot chocolate*
un thé (au lait/nature)	*tea (with/without milk)*
des boissons rafraîchissantes	*cold drinks*
un citron pressé	*lemonade*
un coca(-cola)	*cola*
de l'eau (f.) (minérale)	*(mineral) water*
un jus d'orange	*orange juice*
une limonade	*lemon-lime soft drink*
un Orangina	*orange soda*
des boissons alcoolisées	*alcoholic drinks*
une bière	*beer*
du vin (rouge, blanc, rosé)	*(red, white, rosé) wine*
des casse-croûte (m. inv.)	*snacks*
un croque-monsieur	*grilled ham-and-cheese sandwich*
des crudités (f.)	*cut-up raw vegetables*
des frites (f.)	*French fries*
une glace	*ice cream*
un *hamburger	*hamburger*
une pizza	*pizza*
une salade verte	*green salad*
un sandwich (au jambon, au fromage)	*(ham, cheese) sandwich*
quelques expressions utiles	*some useful expressions*
apprendre	*to learn*
une bouteille	*bottle*
une cannette	*(soda) can*
comprendre	*to understand*
une cuillère	*spoon*
des glaçons (m.)	*ice cubes*
je voudrais…	*I would like . . .*
partager	*to share*
quelle horreur !	*how awful!*
quelque chose (à manger, à boire)	*something (to eat, to drink)*
sans problème	*no problem*
un serveur/une serveuse	*server*
seulement	*only*
du sucre	*sugar*
une tasse	*cup*
un verre	*glass*

Leçon 2

les repas	*meals*
le petit-déjeuner	*breakfast*
le déjeuner	*lunch*
le goûter	*afternoon snack*
le dîner	*dinner*
au petit-déjeuner	*at breakfast*
prendre le petit-déjeuner	*to have breakfast*
le bacon	*bacon*
le beurre	*butter*
un café au lait	*coffee with milk*
des céréales (f. pl.)	*cereal*
la confiture	*jam*
un croissant	*croissant*
un œuf (sur le plat/au plat)	*(fried) egg*
du pain	*bread*
un pain au chocolat	*chocolate croissant*
une rôtie	*piece of toast (Can.)*
une tartine	*slice of bread with butter and/or jam*
une tranche de pain grillé	*slice of toast*
au déjeuner	*at lunch*
une entrée	*appetizer or starter*
un plat principal	*main dish*
un dessert	*dessert*
des aliments (m.)	*food*
une asperge	*asparagus*
un biscuit	*cookie*
le fromage	*cheese*
les *haricots verts (m.)	*green beans*
un légume	*vegetable*
le poisson	*fish*
une pomme de terre	*potato*
le poulet	*chicken*
le riz	*rice*
une soupe	*soup*
une tarte aux pommes	*apple pie*
la viande	*meat*
un yaourt	*yogurt*
des fruits (m.)	*fruits*
une banane	*banana*
une poire	*pear*
une pomme	*apple*
des épices (f.)	*spices*
le poivre	*pepper*
le sel	*salt*
autres mots utiles	*other useful words*
un bol (de café au lait)	*bowl (of coffee with hot milk)*
une carafe (d'eau)	*carafe (of water)*

pour décrire	*to describe*
copieux/-euse	*copious, hearty*
grillé/e	*grilled, toasted*
pour poser une question	*to ask a question*
qu'est-ce que/qui… ?	*what . . . ?*
qui ?	*who?*
quoi ?	*what?*
verbes en *-ir* comme *choisir*	*verbs ending in* -ir *like* choisir
choisir	*to choose*
désobéir à	*to disobey*
finir	*to finish*
grandir	*to grow taller, to grow up (for children)*
grossir	*to gain weight*
maigrir	*to lose weight*
obéir à	*to obey*
pâlir	*to become pale*
punir	*to punish*
réfléchir à	*to think*
réussir (à)	*to succeed/to pass*
rougir	*to blush*

Leçon 3

les rayons du supermarché	*supermarket aisles*
le rayon boulangerie-pâtisserie	*bakery/pastry aisle*
une baguette	*long, thin loaf of bread*
un gâteau	*cake*
un pain de campagne	*round loaf of bread*
un pain de mie	*loaf of sliced bread*
une pâtisserie	*pastry*
des petits pains (m.)	*rolls*
une tarte	*pie*
le rayon boucherie	*meat counter*
du bifteck haché	*ground beef*
une côtelette d'agneau	*lamb chop*
du rosbif	*roast beef*
le rayon charcuterie	*deli counter*
du pâté	*pâté*
des plats (m.) préparés	*prepared dishes*
un rôti (de porc)	*(pork) roast*
le rayon crèmerie	*dairy products aisle*
le rayon fruits et légumes	*produce aisle*
une fraise	*strawberry*
un melon	*cantaloupe*
une pêche	*peach*
du raisin	*grapes*
de l'ail (m.)	*garlic*
une carotte	*carrot*
un champignon	*mushroom*
un chou, des choux	*cabbage*
un concombre	*cucumber*
les épinards (m.)	*spinach*
un navet	*turnip*
un oignon	*onion*
les petits pois (m.)	*peas*
un poivron (rouge, vert)	*(red, green) pepper*
une tomate	*tomato*
le rayon poissonnerie	*fish counter*
une crevette	*shrimp*
du saumon	*salmon*
du thon	*tuna*
le rayon surgelés	*frozen foods section*
les surgelés (m.)	*frozen foods*
des condiments	*condiments*
l'huile (f.)	*oil*
la moutarde	*mustard*
le vinaigre	*vinegar*
pour faire les courses	*to shop for food*
un/e commerçant/e	*shopkeeper, merchant*
une épicerie	*small grocery store*
une grande surface	*superstore*
des quantités (f.)	*quantities*
une assiette de (crudités)	*plate of (raw vegetables)*
une boîte de (sardines)	*can of (sardines)*
une boîte de (céréales)	*box of (cereal)*
un demi-kilo de (tomates)	*half-kilo of (tomatoes)*
une douzaine d'(œufs)	*dozen (eggs)*
un kilo de (pommes)	*kilo of (apples)*
un litre de (lait)	*liter of (milk)*
un morceau de (fromage)	*piece of (cheese)*
un paquet de (pâtes)	*package of (pasta)*
un pot de (moutarde)	*jar of (mustard)*
une tranche de (pâté)	*slice of (pâté)*
quelques expressions utiles	*some useful expressions*
avoir besoin de	*to need*
J'ai besoin d'huile.	*I need (some) oil.*
il faut	*to need*
Il faut quatre œufs.	*We need four eggs.*
biologique	*organic*
une tomate bio(logique)	*organic tomato*
la caisse	*cash register*
délicieux/-euse	*delicious*
frais/fraîche	*fresh*
se trouver	*to be located*

Vocabulaire

Est-ce que cette maison est semblable aux maisons dans la région où vous habitez ? Pourquoi ?

6 Nous sommes chez nous

Leçon 1 La vie en ville

Leçon 2 Je suis chez moi

Leçon 3 La vie à la campagne

After completing this chapter, you should be able to:

- Talk about where you live
- Specify dates, distances, and prices
- Identify geographical features
- Make suggestions
- Describe situations and settings in the past
- Understand concepts of home and regionalism in France

Leçon 1 La vie en ville

POINTS DE DÉPART

Chez les Santini

Les Santini habitent à Paris dans le dix-huitième arrondissement, près de Montmartre, un quartier animé de Paris. M. et Mme Santini ont deux enfants, Nicolas et Véronique. Ils habitent un bel immeuble dans une rue tranquille d'un quartier résidentiel.

L'appartement des Santini est au sixième étage — on prend les escaliers ou l'ascenseur pour monter. C'est un cinq-pièces avec une grande salle de séjour, une salle à manger et trois chambres. Chaque enfant a sa propre chambre. Il y a aussi une salle de bains, des toilettes (des W.-C.) et une cuisine. L'appartement a un balcon qui donne sur la rue, et dans la chambre de M. et Mme Santini, il y a même un petit balcon qui donne sur la cour. Au sous-sol, il y a un garage où les Santini garent leur voiture. Ils ont des voisins sympathiques au cinquième étage.

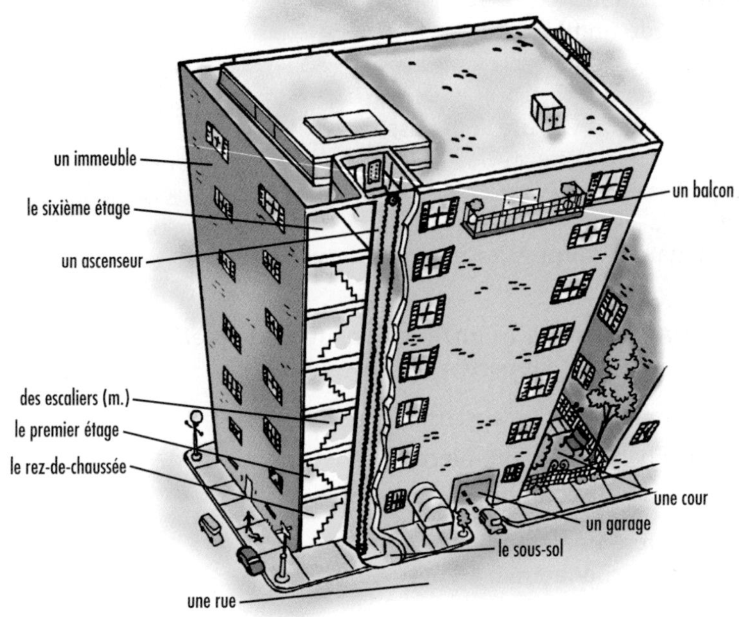

Presentation: Use the photo and line drawings (MFL, Instructor's Resources) to present the vocabulary. Have students listen to the description as you show the visuals, elaborating where appropriate. Explain that Paris is divided into 20 *arrondissements* or neighborhoods. Explain the distinction between *salle de bains/toilettes, W.-C.* (from English *water closet*). In France, the kitchen and bath are not included when counting the number of rooms. Test comprehension by having students point to the feature you name, using the unlabeled art (MFL, Instructor's Resources) or by having them describe activities: *Dans la cuisine ? — On prépare le dîner, on mange*, etc. Next have students repeat key words and phrases: *C'est la cuisine ou le séjour ? — C'est le séjour*, etc.

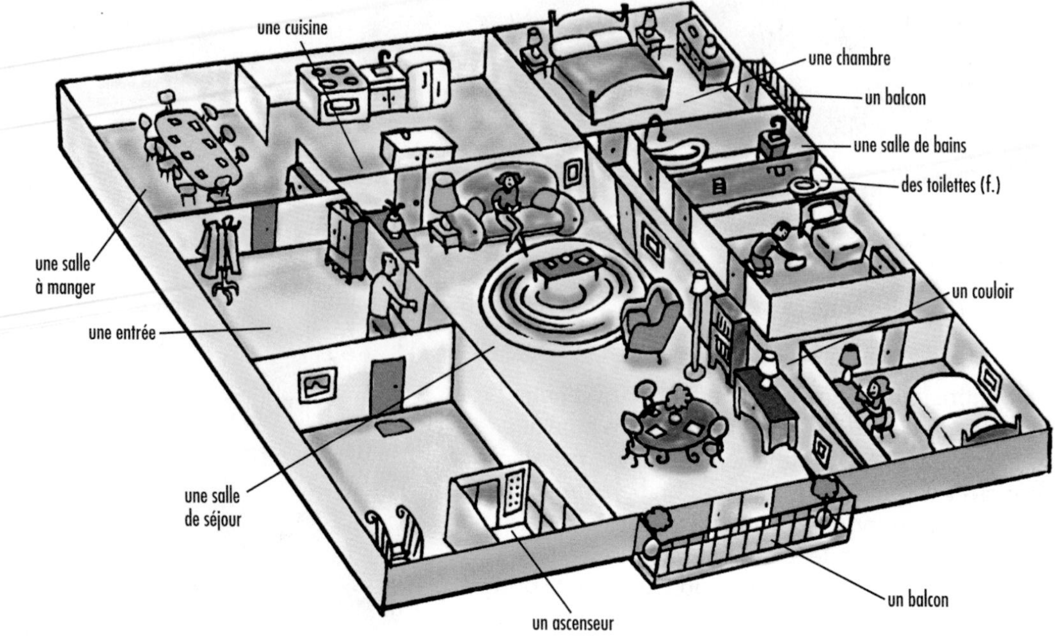

Additional practice: Put students in pairs or small groups and ask them to compare where they prefer to carry out the following activities: *faire la sieste ; regarder un film ; faire les devoirs ; dîner ; écouter de la musique ; parler avec des amis.* Before beginning, model the exercise with one or more students:

T *J'aime aller dans ma chambre pour faire la sieste. Et vous ?*

É1 Moi, je préfère faire la sieste dans la salle de séjour, devant la télé. Et toi ?

É2 Moi, j'aime aller sur le balcon quand il fait beau.

Have students report back to the class on their preferences and the preferences of their classmates. Ask follow-up questions such as *Pourquoi est-ce que vous préférez faire la sieste dans la salle de séjour ?*

06-01 to 06-05

À vous la parole

6-1 Où est-ce qu'ils sont ? Expliquez où sont ces gens. *Answers may vary.*

Implementation: 6-1 This ex cise can be completed with boo closed. Read each description a have students indicate where t person is located. Students do know the expression *frapper à porte* ; as you read this descrip mime the action or knock on t classroom door or a table to he them understand. Remind stud of the meaning of the verb *me* and ask them to guess what th expression *mettre la table* mea

MODÈLE Nicolas fait ses devoirs.
- Il est dans sa chambre.

1. Mme Santini prépare le dîner pour la famille. dans la cuisine
2. Véronique met la table. dans la salle à manger
3. M. Santini regarde un film à la télé. dans la salle de séjour
4. Nicolas prend une douche. dans la salle de bains
5. Les enfants jouent aux cartes. dans la chambre / la salle de séjour
6. M. Santini regarde les voitures qui passent. sur le balcon
7. Le voisin frappe à la porte. dans l'entrée
8. M. Santini prépare le café. dans la cuisine
9. Véronique fait la sieste. dans sa chambre
10. Mme Santini gare la voiture. dans le garage /au sous-sol

6-2 Une comparaison. Avec un/e partenaire, comparez l'endroit (*place*) où vous habitez avec l'appartement des Santini.

Implementation: 6-2 Treat *Où habitent les Français ?* in the **Vie et culture** section before completing this activity to introduce needed vocabulary such as *un/e propriétaire, un deux-pièces,* and *un appartement de cinq pièces.*

MODÈLE Les Santini habitent un appartement de cinq pièces.
É1 Moi, j'habite un deux-pièces.
É2 Moi, j'ai une chambre à la résidence.

1. Les Santini habitent une grande ville.
2. Ils habitent un quartier animé.

3. Ils habitent un bel immeuble.
4. Ils sont propriétaires.
5. Ils habitent au sixième étage.
6. Il y a un ascenseur et aussi des escaliers dans l'immeuble.
7. Les Santini habitent un appartement de cinq pièces.
8. Chez les Santini, il y a une belle cuisine.
9. Il y a trois chambres chez eux.
10. Chez eux, la salle de bains et les toilettes sont séparées.

6-3 Trois appartements. Voici trois appartements. Avec un/e partenaire, décrivez chaque appartement et choisissez l'appartement que vous préférez.

Expansion: 6-3 As a follow-up, have students draw and describe their current home or apartment; their ideal apartment.

Note: 6-3 Point out that *une terrasse* is bigger than *un balcon* and can be used as an additional living space, with a table and chairs for eating outside, for example.

MODÈLE • Le premier appartement est un deux-pièces. Il y a une petite chambre et un séjour. Il y a une terrasse, ... Je préfère... , parce que...

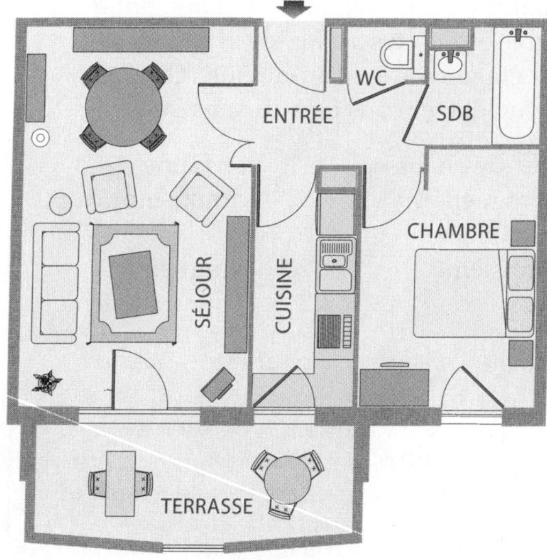

Appartement n° 1

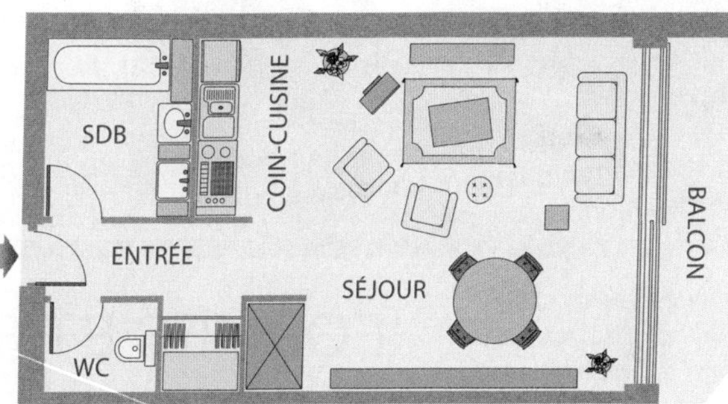

Appartement n° 2

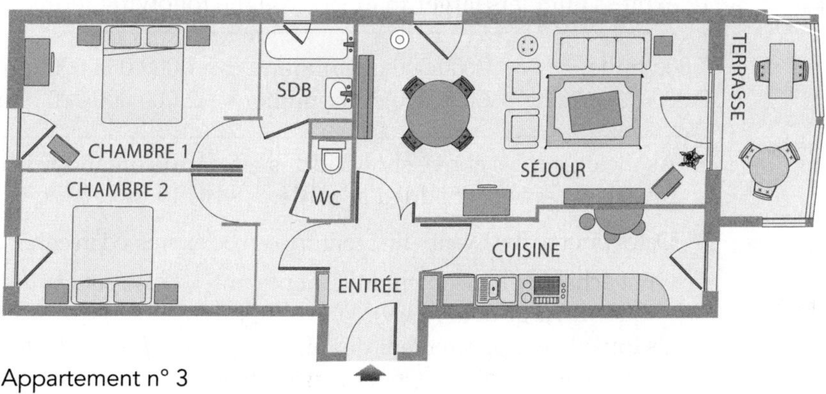

Appartement n° 3

Presentation: Guide students to discover the meaning of key words such as *loyer, charges comprises, propriétaire,* and *locataire,* using cognates and context; these words are used in Ex. 6-2 and should be added to productive vocabulary. Students may be unfamiliar with buying an apartment; this can be compared to condominium or co-op housing. You may wish to introduce the phrase *habiter en banlieue* (to live in the suburbs). Note that the expression *la banlieue* in French can have a rather negative connotation and often refers to poorer neighborhoods filled with subsidized housing, and in *la banlieue parisienne,* with immigrants. Use the photo to describe home construction in France and compare it with construction in North America.

Vie et culture

Où habitent les Français ?

Environ[1] 57 % des familles en France habitent une maison individuelle, mais dans les centres urbains, les appartements sont plus nombreux. Environ 41 % des Français habitent un appartement. La majorité des Français (57.5 %) sont propriétaires de leur maison ou appartement. Les autres sont des locataires, c'est-à-dire qu'ils louent leur appartement ou leur maison et payent un loyer chaque mois. Quelquefois, les charges (l'eau, l'électricité et le gaz) sont comprises[2] dans le loyer et quelquefois c'est en supplément.

Dans les quartiers résidentiels des grandes villes, beaucoup de familles habitent un appartement dans un grand immeuble. En France, le nombre de pièces (sans compter la cuisine, la salle de bains ou les toilettes) détermine la classification des appartements et des maisons. Un studio est un appartement avec une seule pièce (plus, éventuellement[3], cuisine, salle de bains et toilettes). Est-ce que la majorité des Américains habitent des maisons individuelles ou des appartements ?

Voici une maison typiquement française en Côte d'Or, près de Dijon.

À quel étage ?

Regardez l'immeuble à la page 177 et surtout **le rez-de-chaussée** et **le premier étage**. Est-ce que c'est le même système où vous habitez ? En France, quand vous entrez dans un bâtiment ou un immeuble, vous êtes au **rez-de-chaussée** et **le premier étage** se trouve au-dessus[4]. Si vous descendez un étage, vous êtes au **sous-sol**.

RdeCh	rez-de-chaussée	11^{e}	onzième
1er	premier	12^{e}	douzième
2^{e}	deuxième	…	
3^{e}	troisième	20^{e}	vingtième
…		21^{e}	vingt-et-unième

[1]*approximately* [2]*included* [3]peut-être [4]*above*

Presentation: Point out the special forms *premier/première, second/e* (the latter term used when there are only two items in a series). You may wish to provide your students with a full list of ordinals to complement the examples given here. Practice by having students write down the ordinal you say: *treizième, vingt-et-unième,* etc. (Students write: 13e, 21e, etc.) Next have students read the ordinals you write.

Note: Homes in France are generally constructed of stone, brick, or block, considered more durable than wood. The majority of single-family homes in France, especially in towns and cities, are actually connected to one another, either as row houses or as duplexes. Point out the presence of the wall and grill surrounding the house, and the tiled roof. According to the 2010 U.S. Census, the majority of American households owned their homes. In North America, apartments (and homes) are advertised based on the number of bedrooms. A two-bedroom apartment in the U.S. would generally be equivalent to *un appartement trois-pièces* in France.

Note: Following the orthographic reform of 1990, all compound numbers, including dates, are written with hyphens. You may wish to point out that students will likely encounter examples of the traditional system in which numbers under one hundred are written with a hyphen (except for the forms *x et un*) while numbers above one hundred are not. The new system has the merit of reducing the exceptional forms that students (and speakers of French) must learn.

FORMES ET FONCTIONS

Presentation: Review numbers up to 999 before treating this topic. In treating large numbers, we focus here on their use in dates, prices (for housing), and distances.

1. Les nombres à partir de mille

To express numbers larger than 999, use the following terms:

1 000 mille	1 000 000 un-million	1 000 000 000 un-milliard
2 000 deux-mille	2 000 000 deux-millions	2 000 000 000 deux-milliards

- As the examples above show, add **-s** after **million** and **milliard** in the plural. No **-s** is ever added to **mille**. **Note:** The spelling *mil* may also be used in dates.
- Dates prior to the twenty-first century can be expressed in either of two ways:

On a acheté la maison en mille-neuf-cent-quatre-vingt-neuf (1989). — *We bought the house in 1989.*

Ils louent cet appartement depuis dix-neuf-cent-quatre-vingt-dix-neuf (1999). — *They've been renting that apartment since 1999.*

Dates in the twenty-first century and beyond are expressed with **deux-mille**:

Elle habite là depuis deux-mille-neuf (2009). — *She's been living there since 2009.*

- A comma is used in French where we would use a decimal point.

Environ trois virgule trois pour cent (3,3 %) des ménages en France sont logés gratuitement à cause de leur travail. — *About three point three percent (3.3%) of French households live in free housing, due to their work situation.*

- Use a space or a period to separate out thousands and other large numbers.

De Lille à Ajaccio (en Corse), ça fait 1 061 kilomètres. — *From Lille to Ajaccio (in Corsica), it's 1,061 kilometers.*

De Paris à Montréal, ça fait 5.511 kilomètres. — *From Paris to Montreal, it's 5,511 kilometers.*

- Use **de/d'** after **million**:

À Paris, il y a plus de 11 000 000 **d'**habitants. — *The city of Paris has more than 11,000,000 inhabitants.*

À vous la parole

Initial practice: Begin by having students write the number you say; say the number you write. For Ex. 6-4, use a map of France, from the end pages or the map in this chapter, to show the location of the regions and departments. Note that *Normandie* and *Bretagne* refer to regions, whereas the other places listed are all departments.

6-4 Maisons de rêve. Regardez ces annonces pour des belles propriétés à vendre en France. Dites combien coûte chaque maison ou appartement.

MODÈLE Normandie : maison ancienne avec vue sur la mer ; Prix : 775.000 €
- La maison en Normandie coûte sept-cent-soixante-quinze-mille euros.

1. **CÔTE D'OR :** une ferme restaurée ; **Prix : 371.650 €**
2. **BRETAGNE :** propriété de charme près de la mer ; **Prix : 636.000 €**
3. **LOIRE-ATLANTIQUE :** la vue sur l'océan ; **Prix : 768.000 €**
4. **ALPES-MARITIMES :** un charme fou ; **Prix : 1.280.000 €**
5. **CHARENTE-MARITIME :** grand appartement, excellent état ; **Prix : 247.850 €**
6. **TARN-ET-GARONNE :** maison ancienne, à rénover ; **Prix : 110.000 €**

Key: 6-4 1) trois-cent-soixante-et-onze-mille-six-cent-cinquante euros 2) six-cent-trente-six-mille euros 3) sept-cent-soixante-huit-mille euros 4) un-million-deux-cent-quatre-vingt-mille euros 5) deux-cent-quarante-sept-mille-huit-cent-cinquante euros 6) cent-dix-mille euros

Additional practice: To practice distances, ask students to imagine that they are traveling by train between two French cities and to compare the distance one-way and round-trip. Provide a model such as:

MODÈLE Rouen – Toulouse / 650 km
É1 De Rouen à Toulouse, ça fait six-cent-cinquante kilomètres.
É2 Donc, mille-trois-cents kilomètres aller-retour.

1. Caen – Nice / 840 km
2. Rennes – Marseille / 760 km
3. Strasbourg – Bordeaux / 760 km
4. Calais – Cannes / 910 km
5. Metz – Pau / 820 km
6. Paris – Menton / 700 km

6-5 Un peu d'histoire. Est-ce que vous êtes doué/e en histoire ? Avec un/e partenaire, trouvez la bonne date pour chaque évènement.

MODÈLE 1804
- En mille-huit-cent-quatre les Haïtiens déclarent leur indépendance.

1066	Les Haïtiens déclarent leur indépendance. (1804)
1492	La Révolution française commence. (1789)
1776	Les Normands arrivent en Angleterre. (1066)
1789	Le premier président noir est élu aux États-Unis. (2008)
1804	La Première Guerre mondiale commence. (1914)
1860	Les attentats du 11 septembre ont lieu. (2001)
1914	La Seconde Guerre mondiale commence. (1939)
1939	La Guerre de Sécession commence. (1860)
2001	Jefferson écrit la Déclaration d'Indépendance américaine. (1776)
2008	Christophe Colomb découvre l'Amérique. (1492)

Note: 6-6 Point out that the French read phone numbers as a series of two numbers. To say an American phone number, they frequently read the first part as a three-number series followed by two series of two numbers.

6-6 Chiffres importants. Partagez ces renseignements avec un/e partenaire.

MODÈLES date de naissance (*birth*)

É1 C'est le quatorze février, mille-neuf-cent-quatre-vingt-sept. (14/02/1987)

numéro de téléphone

É2 C'est le cinq-cent-cinquante-cinq, zéro huit, trente-sept. (555-0837)

1. date de naissance
2. numéro de téléphone
3. code postal

2. Les pronoms compléments d'objet direct *le, la, l', les*

Presentation: Use classroom objects to present the direct-object pronouns inductively; for example, give a ruler to a student and say: *Donnez la règle à Susan.* After the student does it, you say: *Elle la donne à Susan.* Continue to demonstrate *le, les,* and *l'* and display additional examples. Ask students to summarize rules. Point out to students that use of the pronoun allows the speaker to avoid redundancy and repetition.

- A direct object receives the action of a verb, answering the question *whom* or *what*. For example, **la voiture** is the direct object in the following sentence: **Elle gare la voiture**. A direct-object pronoun can replace a direct-object noun; it agrees in gender and number with the noun it replaces.

Elle gare **la voiture** ?	Oui, elle **la** gare.	*Yes, she is parking it.*
Elle regarde **le voisin** ?	Oui, elle **le** regarde.	*Yes, she is looking at him.*
Elle achète **l'appartement** ?	Oui, elle **l'**achète.	*Yes, she is buying it.*
Elle aime bien **les voisins** ?	Oui, elle **les**‿aime bien. /z/	*Yes, she likes them.*

- Here are the third person forms of the direct-object pronouns. In the plural, liaison /z/ is pronounced before a vowel.

	SINGULIER	PLURIEL
masc.	**le**	**les**
m./f. + voyelle	**l'**	**les**‿ /z/
fém.	**la**	**les**

Note: Dislocation is a frequent and useful conversational feature in spoken French and is practiced in Ex. 6-8.

- Normally, direct-object pronouns precede the conjugated verb.

—Vous aimez l'appartement en centre-ville ?	—*Do you like the downtown apartment?*
—Oui, on **l'**aime bien. Ce n'est pas trop cher.	—*Yes, we like it. It's not too expensive.*
—Où sont les escaliers ?	—*Where are the stairs?*
—Je ne sais pas, je ne **les** ai pas remarqués.	—*I don't know, I didn't notice them.*

Note: Past participle agreement with a preceding direct object pronoun is treated below.

- A direct-object pronoun precedes an infinitive:

—Tu vas payer les charges ?	—*Are you going to pay the utilities?*
—Mais bien sûr, je vais **les** payer ; je **les** paye tous les mois, non ?	—*Well, of course I'm going to pay them; I pay them every month, don't I?*

- The negative **ne** never comes between an object pronoun and verb:

Les voisins, on ne **les** voit jamais.	*. . . we never see them.*
L'appartement, je ne **l'**ai pas acheté.	*. . . I didn't buy it.*
La voiture, je ne vais pas **la** garer.	*. . . I'm not going to park it.*

Fiche pratique

In French you cannot emphasize a word by adding stress to it, as in English: "Did you see *John* or *Bill*?" "I saw *John*." One way to emphasize a word or phrase in French is to place it at the very beginning of the sentence, and put a pronoun equivalent in its place: **Les voisins**, tu **les** aimes ?

- To point out people or objects, the direct-object pronouns precede **voilà**:

  Sylvie ? **La** voilà. — *Sylvie? There she is.*
  Mes CD ? **Les** voilà. — *My CDs? There they are.*

- Note the placement of direct-object pronouns in commands:

  In negative commands, the object pronoun precedes the conjugated verb:

  Cet appartement ? Ne **le** montrez pas ! — *. . . Don't show it!*

  In affirmative commands, an object pronoun is placed after the conjugated verb and is joined to it by a hyphen:

  Le nouveau studio ? Montrez-**le** à Susan ! — *. . . Show it to Susan!*

- In the **passé composé**, the past participle agrees in gender and number with a preceding direct-object pronoun:

  J'ai donné **le CD** à Justine. — Je **l'**ai donné à Justine.
  J'ai donné **la lampe** à Yann. — Je **l'**ai donn**ée** à Yann.
  J'ai donné **les livres** à Coralie. — Je **les** ai donn**és** à Coralie.
  J'ai donné **les affiches** à Thibaut. — Je **les** ai donn**ées** à Thibaut.

À vous la parole

6-7 On joue à cache-cache. Cécile joue à cache-cache (*hide-and-seek*) avec sa sœur, son frère et ses chats. Pour chaque phrase, décidez si elle cherche (ou trouve) sa sœur, son frère ou ses chats.

Elle…	sa sœur	son frère	ses chats
MODÈLE … la cherche dans la cour.	✓		
1. … les cherche dans le séjour.			✓
2. … le cherche dans la cuisine.		✓	
3. … la cherche sur la terrasse.	✓		
4. … le cherche partout (*everywhere*).		✓	
5. … les trouve sur le balcon.			✓
6. … la trouve dans sa chambre.	✓		
7. … le cherche encore.		✓	

Qui a trouvé le meilleur endroit (*place*) pour se cacher ? Pourquoi ?

6-8 Les opinions sont partagées ! Décidez avec un/e partenaire si vous êtes d'accord ou non.

MODÈLE On les aime : les films ? les examens ?
É1 Les films, on les aime.
É2 Les examens, on ne les aime pas.

1. On l'aime beaucoup : la danse ? le théâtre ?
2. On l'aime bien : le golf ? le football ?
3. On les écoute toujours : les parents ? les professeurs ?
4. On les déteste : les jours de pluie ? les jours d'orage ?
5. On les regarde souvent : les films ? les documentaires ?
6. On la visite souvent : la ville de New York ? la France ?
7. On l'adore : le français ? l'histoire ?
8. On les aime : les pique-niques ? les vacances ?

Note: Past participle agreement affects only the pronunciation of participles that end with a consonant. The addition of the feminine marker *-e* causes the consonant to be pronounced. Compare *Le livre, je l'ai pris ; La lettre, je l'ai prise ; Les lettres, je les ai prises* with *Ce livre, je l'ai donné à Paul ; Cette lettre, je l'ai donnée à Karine ; Ces lettres, je les ai données au musée.* For that reason, past participle agreement is presented largely for recognition. You may also provide appropriate written practice. As this agreement is largely a spelling convention, it is no surprise that native speakers often omit it in writing or in casual speech.

Initial practice: Begin with this activity to establish a form-meaning connection between the direct-object pronouns and their referents. Then display sentences such as the following and have students supply possible nouns for the object pronouns: *Je l'ai regardé à la télé. — le film ; Elle l'a acheté en ville. Nous allons le choisir demain. Il l'appelle le soir. Ils la regardent beaucoup. Tu la gares toujours au parking ? Je les trouve très chers. Vous le préparez ? Elles les portent tous les jours.* To simplify, you could provide students with three choices for each sentence : *Je l'ai regardé à la télé. –la pièce de théâtre, le film, les acteurs.* Continue with simple substitution drills to practice forms: *Le crayon ? — Le voilà ; Les devoirs ? — Les voilà ; Le tableau ? La porte ? Les fenêtres ? Le professeur ? Les livres ? Les cahiers ? L'examen ? L'affiche ? Le stylo ?*, etc.

Additional practice: To practice the placement of direct-object pronouns with *voilà*, use an activity like the following.
Où est-ce que c'est rangé ? David s'installe dans un nouvel appartement, mais il ne trouve plus rien ! Jouez les rôles de David et de son copain avec un/e partenaire.

MODÈLE É1 Où sont mes casseroles (*pots*) ?
É2 Les voilà, dans la cuisine.

1. Où est ma télé ?
2. Où sont mes livres ?
3. Où est mon manteau ?
4. Où sont mes CD ?
5. Où est mon mixer ?
6. Où sont mes photos ?
7. Où est mon ordinateur ?
8. Où est mon affiche de Paris ?

Expansion: 6-9 Ask students to state how often they do each activity, using the following model:

MODÈLE É1 *Tu aimes faire la cuisine ?*
É2 *Oui, j'aime la faire ; je la fais souvent. Et toi ?*
É3 *Non, moi, je n'aime pas la faire ; je la fais rarement.*

Provide students with a scale of frequency adverbs: *ne… jamais ; rarement ; quelquefois ; souvent ; toujours.*

6-9 Les occupations et les loisirs. Quels sont les occupations et les loisirs de vos camarades de classe ? Posez des questions à deux camarades, et ensuite comparez les réponses.

MODÈLE faire la cuisine
É1 Tu aimes faire la cuisine ?
É2 Oui, j'aime la faire. Et toi ?
É3 Non, je n'aime pas la faire.

1. faire la cuisine
2. faire les devoirs
3. écouter la radio le matin
4. mettre la table
5. inviter tes amis
6. préparer les repas
7. regarder la télé pendant le dîner

Script: *Observons*

MONSIEUR LE MAIRE DE SEILLANS : Oui, eh bien, nous sommes dans un vieux village provençal. Euh, Seillans fait partie des 148 plus beaux villages de France. Il a été sélectionné parce qu'il a un patrimoine très ancien, qui a gardé tout son caractère, son authenticité et euh beaucoup de charme…

Ce village comprend aussi euh de nombreuses fontaines, des placettes ombragées. Euh, c'est un village typiquement provençal parce qu'il est perché, sur une colline. Et en cette saison, en automne, on a le plaisir de découvrir des paysages magnifiques…

C'est un village provençal aussi qui a son terroir, avec la culture de l'olivier, de la vigne… donc des produits locaux qui sont très appréciés.

GRAND-PÈRE ROUSTAN : C'est… C'est du vin. C'est du vin de Seillans. Château de Selves.

Observons

Presentation: Show Seillans on a map of France. In order to be identified as a *village classé*, a village must be selected by the association *Les plus beaux villages de France* and meet strict criteria.

06-54 to 06-56

6-10 Visitons Seillans.

A. Avant de regarder. Dans cette séquence vidéo, nous allons « visiter Seillans ». Seillans se trouve dans le Midi de la France, pas très loin de la Côte d'Azur. Regardez la photo de Seillans pour répondre à ces questions.

1. Qui est la personne qui va faire le guide dans la séquence vidéo, à votre avis ?
2. Seillans, c'est un centre urbain, une grande ville ou un petit village ?
3. À votre avis, quels aspects de Seillans est-ce que le guide va nous montrer ?

B. En regardant. Maintenant, regardez la séquence vidéo pour trouver la bonne réponse.

1. Seillans se trouve dans quelle région de la France ?
2. Seillans, c'est un village classé : pourquoi ?
3. À Seillans, vous allez remarquer (cochez les bonnes réponses) :

_✓_ des belles fontaines
____ des villas magnifiques
_✓_ des petites places avec des arbres
_✓_ des églises romanes
_✓_ des collines boisées
_✓_ des paysages spectaculaires

4. Quels sont les produits locaux bien appréciés ?

_✓_ le vin ____ la lavande _✓_ les olives ____ le coton

Seillans se trouve dans le Sud, en Provence.

Seillans est classé parmi les 148 plus beaux villages de France à cause de son patrimoine ancien, son caractère, son authenticité et son charme.

C. Après avoir regardé. D'après la description, est-ce que Seillans est un endroit que vous voudriez visiter un jour ? Pourquoi ?

Leçon 2 Je suis chez moi

POINTS DE DÉPART

Chez Christelle

Christelle habite un vieil immeuble rénové dans le centre-ville de Nice. Son studio se trouve sous les toits : il n'est pas très chic, mais il est spacieux et assez agréable. En plus, il n'est pas cher : son loyer est de seulement 460 euros par mois. Le studio est meublé : il y a une belle armoire ancienne pour ranger ses vêtements et une étagère pour ranger ses livres. Les autres meubles sont un peu abîmés, mais ils sont confortables, surtout le lit et le fauteuil. Par terre, il y a un beau tapis, et il y a des rideaux neufs à la fenêtre. Il y a des affiches aux murs et des plantes sur les petites tables. Le coin cuisine est petit mais bien équipé : il y a un petit réfrigérateur à côté de l'évier et une cuisinière avec un four. Il y a aussi des grands placards — c'est très pratique pour mettre ses affaires, comme la vaisselle. Il y a aussi une salle de bains moderne et des W.-C.

Voici l'immeuble où se trouve le studio de Christelle.

Presentation: Have students listen to the description; use the photo and the labeled drawing of Christelle's room (MFL, Instructor's Resources) to present this vocabulary. Test comprehension by having students point to items you name as you show the unlabeled room (MFL, Instructor's Resources), or ask what various items are used for: *Un lit ? — C'est pour dormir*, etc. Next have students repeat key terms (*C'est une armoire ou un bureau ?*) and group descriptive words as opposites: *abîmée/neuve ; ancienne/moderne*, etc. For further practice with key vocabulary linked to housing, investigate sites on the Web with ads for people seeking *des colocataires.* It is increasingly common for students or young professionals in France to share an apartment or a house (*la colocation*) without being in a romantic relationship or having a family connection. It is estimated that up to 50% of young people age 18–24 have practiced *la colocation*, including 62% of students.

Presentation: Display a map of Paris with the *arrondissements* clearly indicated and have students locate Pauline's *quartier* (*le quatorzième arrondissement*) as well as the Santini's *quartier* (*le dix-huitième arrondissement*). Explain that each neighborhood has a particular feel and character, such as the Jewish quarter in le Marais (*le troisième et le quatrième arrondissements*). Show images of *les petits commerçants* from various *quartiers* (*la boulangerie, l'épicerie, la boucherie, la charcuterie, le tabac*) to recycle the vocabulary and cultural ideas from Ch. 5.

Vie et culture

06-52

Le quartier

Dans les grandes villes, c'est le quartier qui donne un aspect plus personnel à la vie urbaine souvent trop impersonnelle. Chaque quartier est comme une petite communauté : il y a le café du coin[1] et les petits commerçants. C'est possible d'y faire ses courses tous les jours. Il y a souvent un marché certains jours de la semaine.

Regardez la séquence vidéo, *Mon quartier*, où une jeune Parisienne décrit son quartier. Quels aspects de son quartier est-ce qu'elle aime en particulier ? Et vous, est-ce que vous habitez aussi dans un quartier ? Est-ce que vous avez aussi le sentiment de faire partie d'une petite communauté ? Pourquoi ?

[1]*corner*

Pauline achète son pain à la boulangerie du coin.

06-17 to 06-20

À vous la parole

6-11 Chez Christelle. Décrivez l'appartement où habite Christelle en choisissant un adjectif approprié.

Variation: 6-11 To provide review of prenominal adjective forms, have students reply with: *C'est un vieil immeuble.* Note that the adjective *neuf/neuve* is irregular in its formation.

MODÈLE L'immeuble est neuf ou vieux ?
• L'immeuble est vieux.

Expansion: 6-11 Have students use the same sentences to describe the place where they live.

1. Le studio est spacieux ou petit ? Le studio est spacieux.
2. Le loyer est cher ou pas cher ? Le loyer n'est pas cher.
3. Le fauteuil est confortable ou pas confortable ? Le fauteuil est confortable.
4. La salle de bains est ancienne ou moderne ? La salle de bains est moderne.
5. L'armoire est neuve ou ancienne ? L'armoire est ancienne.
6. Les rideaux sont neufs ou vieux ? Les rideaux sont neufs.
7. Le tapis est abîmé ou beau ? Le tapis est beau.
8. Le coin cuisine est bien équipé ou mal équipé ? Le coin cuisine est bien équipé.

Vincent Van Gogh, « La chambre de Van Gogh à Arles », 1889. Oil on canvas. 57.5 × 74 cm. Musée d'Orsay, Paris, France. Erich Lessing/Art Resource, NY.

6-12 La chambre de Van Gogh. Van Gogh (1853–1890), un artiste néerlandais bien connu, a habité en France. Voici un de ses tableaux ; c'est sa chambre en Provence. Décrivez cette chambre en cinq ou six phrases.

MODÈLE • Dans cette chambre, il y a un petit lit. À côté du lit, il y a…

Implementation: 6-12 Before completing, go over the prepositions included in the **Points de départ**: *dans, sous, par terre, à la fenêtre, aux murs, sur, à côté de.* Point out that *sur* is used to talk about things placed on horizontal surfaces. Use the preposition *à* for items on vertical surfaces, for example, *L'affiche est au mur.* You might also have students indicate what is *not* in the room, e.g., *Il n'y a pas de tapis*, etc. As a follow-up, use other famous paintings of interiors to practice this vocabulary; allow students to work in pairs or groups.

6-13 Ma chambre. Avec un/e partenaire, décrivez votre chambre à la résidence, dans votre maison ou votre appartement, ou chez vos parents. N'oubliez pas de parler de ce que vous avez fait pour rendre votre environnement plus personnel. Pour commencer, répondez à ces questions :

Quels meubles est-ce qu'il y a ?
Qu'est-ce qu'il y a aux murs ? par terre ?
Quels objets personnels — des photos, des plantes — est-ce qu'il y a ?
Quelles couleurs est-ce qu'il y a dans la chambre ?

MODÈLE É1 J'habite une petite chambre dans la résidence universitaire. Dans ma chambre, il y a deux lits, deux bureaux et des étagères.
É2 Moi aussi, j'habite une chambre dans la résidence. Qu'est-ce que tu as fait pour rendre ta chambre plus personnelle ?
É1 J'ai mis des plantes ; j'adore les plantes. Et toi ?
É2 Moi, j'ai mis un beau tapis par terre et beaucoup d'affiches aux murs. C'est très bien chez moi.

Variation: 6-13 Modify by having one student describe his/her room while the partner tries to draw it.

FORMES ET FONCTIONS

1. Les pronoms compléments d'objet indirect *lui* et *leur*

Presentation: Review the forms of the direct-object pronouns with a transformation drill before introducing the indirect-object pronouns: *Je regarde la télé. —Je la regarde ; les voisins —Je les regarde ; le toit ; les fenêtres ; l'ascenseur ; la cuisinière ; le balcon*, etc. Present the new forms with a narrative: *Aujourd'hui, j'ai rendez-vous avec un collègue ; je lui téléphone pour vérifier. J'ai cours avec mes étudiants à 10h ; je leur rends les devoirs. Je déjeune avec une amie ; c'est son anniversaire et je lui offre un cadeau*, etc. Present these examples both orally and in written form, and ask students to explain usage.

- You have learned that nouns that function as direct objects answer the question *whom?* or *what?*; they follow the verb directly and can be replaced by a direct-object pronoun.

Tu prends **cet appartement** ?	—Oui, je **le** prends.
Elle attend **le propriétaire** ?	—Oui, elle **l'**attend.
Vous aimez **ces appartements** ?	—Non, on ne **les** aime pas.

- In French, nouns that function as indirect objects are generally introduced by the preposition **à**; they often answer the question *to whom?* and they always refer to a person or an animal.

Je donne le loyer **à la propriétaire**.	*I'm giving the rent* ***to the landlady***. (or, *I'm giving* ***the landlady*** *the rent.*)
Tu as répondu **à tes parents** ?	*Did you answer* ***your parents****?*

In the sentences above, the indirect-object pronouns **lui** (*to him, to her*) and **leur** (*to them*) can be substituted for **à la propriétaire** and **à tes parents**.

Je **lui** donne le loyer.	*I'm giving the rent* ***to him/her***.
Tu **leur** as répondu ?	*Did you answer* ***them****?*

- Like other object pronouns, **lui** and **leur** are placed immediately before the conjugated verb, unless there is an infinitive. If there is an infinitive in the sentence, **lui** and **leur** precede the infinitive.

Je **lui** parle du loyer.	*I'm speaking* ***to him/her*** *about the rent.*
Nous **leur** avons téléphoné.	*We called* ***them*** *up.*
Tu vas **lui** donner l'argent pour les charges ?	*Are you going to give* ***him/her*** *the money for utilities?*
Elle va **leur** expliquer combien ça coûte par mois.	*She is going to explain* ***to them*** *how much it costs per month.*

Presentation: Students should be able to summarize placement rules on their own, since the indirect-object pronouns function in the same way as the direct-object pronouns that they have already seen. Point out that in the *passé composé*, the past participle never agrees with a preceding indirect-object pronoun.

- In affirmative commands, **lui** and **leur** are placed immediately after the verb and are joined to it by a hyphen:

Donne-**lui** ta nouvelle adresse.	*Give **her/him** your new address.*
Téléphone-**leur** à propos de l'appartement.	*Call **them** about the apartment.*

In negative commands, **lui** and **leur** are placed immediately before the conjugated verb:

Ne **lui** prête pas l'appartement.	*Don't loan the apartment **to him/her**.*

- Two main groups of verbs take indirect objects.

VERBS OF COMMUNICATION

demander	*to ask*	On va **leur** demander l'adresse.
expliquer	*to explain*	Tu vas **lui** expliquer le problème ?
montrer	*to show*	Qui va **lui** montrer la chambre ?
parler	*to speak*	Je **leur** parle souvent au téléphone.
répondre	*to answer*	Elle ne **leur** a pas répondu.
téléphoner	*to phone*	Nous **leur** avons téléphoné hier.

Note: This construction is ambiguous for the verb *acheter: Je lui achète un livre* (I'm buying a book for/from him). For greater clarity: *J'achète un livre pour mon frère.* Point out to students that *offrir*, like *ouvrir*, takes *-er* verb endings. A full conjugation is in Appendix 2.

VERBS OF TRANSFER

acheter	*to buy*	Je **leur** ai acheté un petit appartement.
apporter	*to bring*	La propriétaire **lui** a apporté la lettre.
donner	*to give*	On va **leur** donner l'adresse.
emprunter	*to borrow*	Je **lui** emprunte la voiture.
offrir	*to give (a gift)*	Elle **lui** offre un cadeau pour son anniversaire.
prêter	*to lend*	Tu **leur** prêtes ton studio ?
remettre	*to hand in/over*	Nous **lui** avons remis le loyer.
rendre	*to give back*	Je **lui** ai rendu le livre.

Initial practice: Begin with this activity to establish a form-meaning connection between the indirect-object pronouns and their referents. For additional discrimination practice, ask students to find two logical possibilities for each of these sentences: *Je lui offre souvent des cadeaux — à mon petit frère ; à mon copain. Je leur téléphone souvent le week-end. Je lui ai rendu visite l'été passé. J'ai envie de lui donner mon adresse. J'aime leur parler. Je lui prête mes affaires. Je leur explique mes problèmes. Quelquefois, je lui demande de l'argent. Je leur offre des cadeaux.* For productive practice, use a simple substitution drill: *Je réponds au prof. — Je lui réponds ; à mes parents ; à Suzanne ; à mes amis ; à mon frère ; à mes colocataires ; au serveur ; à mon meilleur ami ; à mes cousins.*

06-21 to 06-24

À vous la parole

6-14 À qui est-ce qu'on parle ? Romain parle de ses habitudes. Pour chaque phrase, décidez s'il parle à sa copine ou à ses parents.

Normalement, je…

	à ma copine	à mes parents
MODÈLE … lui téléphone une ou deux fois par jour.	✓	
1. … leur téléphone le week-end.		✓
2. … lui parle quand je suis frustré.	✓	
3. … lui parle quand je me lève le matin.	✓	
4. … lui téléphone quand j'ai des problèmes.	✓	
5. … leur parle quand j'ai besoin d'argent.		✓
6. … lui téléphone quand j'ai envie de sortir.	✓	
7. … leur parle quand c'est bientôt les vacances.		✓

D'après ces descriptions, à qui est-ce qu'il parle le plus souvent ?

6-15 Qu'est-ce qu'on offre ? Les personnes suivantes ont acheté un nouvel appartement. D'après les indications, qu'est-ce qu'on leur offre comme cadeau ? *Answers may vary.*

Variation: 6-15 This can be personalized by asking students about the interests of their family and friends and having others suggest suitable gifts.

MODÈLE Ma sœur n'a pas grand-chose aux murs.
• Je lui offre une belle affiche.

1. Mes parents ont un nouveau lecteur DVD. Je leur offre…
2. Mon oncle adore faire la cuisine. Je lui offre…
3. Ma tante adore les plantes et les fleurs (*flowers*). Je lui offre…
4. Ma cousine aime les livres. Je lui offre…
5. Mes grands-parents aiment la musique. Je leur offre…
6. Mon cousin n'a pas de colocataire. Je lui offre…
7. Mes amis ont une belle terrasse. Je leur offre…

6-16 Rarement, souvent ou jamais ? Interviewez un/e camarade de classe pour savoir avec quelle fréquence il/elle fait les choses suivantes : **rarement**, **souvent** ou **jamais** ?

Implementation: 6-16 Follow up by having students report back what they learned.

MODÈLE prêter tes vêtements à ta/ton colocataire
É1 Est-ce que tu prêtes tes vêtements à ta colocataire ?
É2 Non, je ne lui prête jamais mes vêtements.
OU Oui, je lui prête souvent mes pull-overs.

1. rendre les devoirs au professeur
2. expliquer tes problèmes à tes parents
3. parler à tes parents
4. offrir des cadeaux à tes amis
5. demander de l'argent à tes parents
6. emprunter des vêtements à tes amis
7. achèter des bonbons pour tes nièces et tes neveux
8. emprunter de l'argent à tes amis

2. Les pronoms compléments d'objet *me, te, nous, vous*

Presentation: Before treating this topic, use substitution drills to review direct- and indirect-object pronouns in the third person: *le, la, l', les* (Ch. 6, L. 1); *lui, leur* (this lesson). Present the new information using numerous examples and having students summarize rules.

- You have learned that nouns that function as direct objects answer the question *whom?* or *what?*; they follow the verb directly and can be replaced by a direct-object pronoun.

  Tu entends **les voisins** ? — Oui, je **les** entends.

- Nouns that function as indirect objects are generally introduced by the preposition **à**; they often answer the question *to whom?* and they generally refer to a person.

  Tu donnes l'adresse **à ta sœur et son mari** ? — Oui, je **leur** donne l'adresse.

- The pronouns **me/m'**, **te/t'**, **nous**, and **vous** function as direct-object pronouns, corresponding to **le**, **la**, **l'**, and **les**. They also serve as indirect-object pronouns, corresponding to **lui** and **leur**.

Direct-object pronouns

Tu **m'**attends devant l'immeuble ?	*Will you wait for me in front of the building?*
Je vais **vous** inviter à dîner.	*I'm going to invite you to dinner.*

Indirect-object pronouns

Je **te** téléphone tout de suite.	*I'll call you right away.*
Il **nous** a offert un cadeau.	*He gave us a gift.*

- Here is a summary of object pronouns:

	PERSONNE	DIRECT	INDIRECT
SINGULIER	$1^{\text{ère}}$	me/m'	
	2^{e}	te/t'	
	3e *m.*	le/l'	lui
	f.	la/l'	
PLURIEL	$1^{\text{ère}}$	nous	
	2^{e}	vous	
	3^{e}	les	leur

Initial practice: Begin with substitution drills: *Il les regarde ; nous, toi,* etc. *Elle lui parle ; vous, moi,* etc.

Variation: 6-17 Modify to practice plural forms: *Vous allez nous aider ?,* etc.

06-25 to 06-28

À vous la parole

6-17 Esprit de contradiction ou pas ? Vous allez proposer quelque chose. Un/e de vos partenaires va donner son accord, l'autre va refuser.

MODÈLE É1 Tu m'attends ?
É2 Oui, je t'attends.
É3 Non, je ne t'attends pas.

1. Tu m'aides à ranger l'appartement ?
2. Tu me téléphones ?
3. Tu m'invites chez toi ?
4. Tu me prêtes ton studio à Paris ?
5. Tu vas me répondre ?
6. Tu vas me montrer ta chambre ?
7. Tu vas m'accompagner à la piscine ?

Expansion: 6-18 Ask students to come up with other possibilities in pairs. Have students vote on which pair has the best scenario.

6-18 Du chantage. Répondez que vous êtes d'accord.

MODÈLE Je t'invite à dîner si tu me prêtes de l'argent.
- Alors, je te prête de l'argent.

1. Je te réponds si tu me donnes ton adresse.
2. Je te téléphone si tu me donnes ton numéro de téléphone.
3. On t'accompagne au musée si tu nous invites à la fête.
4. On t'offre le dessert si tu nous aides à ranger le garage.
5. Je t'amène au cinéma si tu me prêtes ta voiture demain.
6. Je répare ton vélo si tu m'expliques le problème de maths.
7. On t'offre une glace si tu nous accompagnes à la bibliothèque.

6-19 Qu'est-ce qu'ils font ? Qu'est-ce que ces gens font pour vous ? Parlez-en avec un/e camarade, et ensuite comparez vos réponses avec celles des autres étudiants.

MODÈLE vos parents

É1 Qu'est-ce que tes parents font pour toi ?

É2 Ils me téléphonent le week-end ; ils me prêtent de l'argent pour payer mes études ; ils m'offrent des cadeaux.

1. votre frère ou sœur
2. votre colocataire
3. votre meilleur/e ami/e
4. votre copain/copine ou votre mari/femme
5. vos professeurs
6. vos parents

Implementation: 6-19 Conduct as a paired activity; students will use *te* and *me* with each other. Have them report back, using *me, lui, nous*; then summarize by listing generalities for each category: *Vos parents, ils vous prêtent de l'argent, ils vous écoutent*, etc.

Écrivons

6-20 La ville de...

A. Avant d'écrire. Vous allez préparer une brochure publicitaire — comme la brochure pour Nice à la page suivante — sur une ville de France qui vous intéresse. Pour commencer, identifiez les personnes pour qui vous allez préparer la brochure : est-ce qu'elles sont sportives ? artistiques, gastronomes, adultes, étudiants, enfants... ? Ensuite, en fonction de leurs intérêts, répondez aux questions suivantes en consultant des guides, des vidéos touristiques et des sites Internet.

1. Où se trouve cette ville en France ? (près de la mer ? à côté de Paris ? à la montagne ?)
2. Quels sont les sites touristiques les plus intéressants dans cette ville ? Décrivez-les.
3. Quelles activités est-ce qu'on y pratique ? Est-ce qu'il y a des activités, par exemple, pour les personnes qui aiment le sport, les beaux-arts, l'histoire ? pour les enfants, les jeunes, les personnes âgées ?

Presentation: As an introduction to the writing activity, treat the brochure as a reading. Have students look at the pictures on the cover to get some ideas about where the city is located and popular activities there. Then have them look at the various sub-sections of the brochure and summarize the information that can be gleaned from each part. Ask them what type of additional information they would want to include about the city they will be presenting. Students can find information about cities and regions in France online.

B. En écrivant. Maintenant, utilisez vos informations pour préparer une brochure. Regardez comme modèle la brochure pour Nice.

1. D'abord, rédigez un texte de quatre petits paragraphes qui décrit la ville : un paragraphe pour l'introduction et trois paragraphes qui présentent trois aspects différents (sites touristiques, sports, évènements culturels, ...) de la ville. N'oubliez pas les personnes pour qui vous préparez la brochure.
2. Ajoutez des images (photos, dessins, tableaux) de la ville.
3. Donnez un titre à votre brochure.

Stratégie

When preparing a promotional brochure, think about who your readers will be and how best to reach them with well-chosen content and an enticing presentation.

C. En révisant. Relisez votre brochure et réfléchissez aux questions suivantes. Faites tous les changements nécessaires.

1. Analysez le contenu : est-ce que vous avez décrit des sites et des activités qui vont probablement intéresser votre public ?
2. Analysez le style et la forme : est-ce que vous avez bien organisé votre brochure pour intéresser le public visé ? Est-ce que vous donnez une description vive et colorée de la région pour attirer l'attention de vos lecteurs ? Est-ce que vous avez inclus des photos, des tableaux ou des dessins ?

Expansion: As an alternative follow-up, divide the class into two groups: one group staffs "tourist booths" to promote its city; the other group circulates to gain information about each city. Then switch roles.

D. Après avoir écrit. Présentez votre ville à vos camarades de classe et essayez de les persuader de la visiter.

NICE
Ville d'histoire
Ville d'art
Ville où il fait bon vivre

NICE

Il y a 400 000 ans, les hommes vivent déjà à Nice. Vers 400 ans av. J–C, les Grecs viennent par la mer pour établir Nikai « la victorieuse ». En 14 av. J.C., les Romains fondent Cemenelum (Cimiez) sur une colline. Actuellement, on peut y visiter les arènes, un bel amphithéâtre et les thermes publics. Pas loin, on peut apprécier l'art contemporain avec le Musée Matisse. Nice est devenue une grande ville touristique, appréciée autant pour ses sites historiques et son art que pour son port et ses belles plages.

À Découvrir, à Visiter

Les Monuments

La colline du château Bus Ligne (32), Tramway Ligne (T1)

Site choisi par les Grecs il y a quelques millénaires et la fondation de la ville de Nice.

La Cathédrale Sainte-Reparate Tramway Ligne (T1)

Le plus vaste sanctuaire dans le Vieux-Nice, son bel et somptueux intérieur est inspiré de la Basilique St Pierre à Rome.

Le Cours Saleya Tramway Ligne (T1)

Zone piétonne au cours du Vieux-Nice avec des terrasses de restaurants, le marché aux fleurs et aux légumes, le marché aux antiquaires.

Les Musées

Musée Matisse Bus Ligne (17), Ligne (22), Ligne (15)

Dans une belle villa de XVIIIe, la collection personnelle de l'artiste qui a séjourné à Nice de 1917 jusqu'à sa mort en 1954.

Musée national Marc Chagall Bus Ligne (22), Ligne (15)

Musée créé et construit à la demande de l'artiste pour exposer les 17 grands tableaux présentant son Message Biblique.

Musée et site Archéologique de Nice-Cemenelum Bus Ligne (17), Ligne (22), Ligne (15)

Visiter les arènes, l'amphithéâtre, les thermes publics et un musée qui expose les objets datant de l'âge des métaux jusqu'au Moyen Âge.

Musée de Paléontologie humaine de Terra Amata Bus Ligne (T32), Ligne (81)

Musée installé sur un campement préhistorique qui date de 400 000 ans, près du port.

Leçon 3 La vie à la campagne

Presentation: Using the photo that opens the lesson, describe the house, related activities, and surroundings. Have students listen to the dialogue, and test comprehension using simple questions: *La villa des Santini est située en ville ?*, etc. Point out the location of Haute-Normandie on a map of France, and ask students to speculate about why it might be an ideal location for a vacation home for Parisians (e.g., its location not too far from Paris and also not far from the sea, in this case the English Channel).

POINTS DE DÉPART

Tout près de la nature

Les Santini possèdent une petite villa qui se trouve en Haute-Normandie. Ce n'est pas très loin de Paris et à une heure de la mer. Ils ont passé le week-end dernier là-bas. M. Santini en parle avec son collègue M. Deleuze.

M. DELEUZE : Qu'est-ce que vous avez fait le week-end dernier ?
M. SANTINI : On est allés à la campagne où nous avons une petite maison.
M. DELEUZE : C'était bien ?
M. SANTINI : Formidable ! C'était calme, j'ai bricolé, je suis allé à la pêche et avec les enfants, on s'est promenés dans les bois. Dimanche, on est allé à Honfleur et on a fait un pique-nique au bord de la mer.
M. DELEUZE : Vous avez un jardin aussi ?
M. SANTINI : Oh, on a un petit potager et quelques arbres fruitiers, c'est tout. C'est ma femme qui s'occupe de tout cela.
M. DELEUZE : Alors, il me semble que vous avez passé un week-end agréable.
M. SANTINI : En effet, on se détend toujours quand on est à la campagne. C'est un endroit très calme.

La résidence secondaire des Santini en Haute-Normandie ; ils peuvent bricoler et faire du jardinage le week-end et pendant les vacances.

Presentation: Present the vocabulary by describing the drawing of natural sites (MFL, Instructor's Resources); you might use additional photos or slides to enrich the presentation. Test comprehension of key words by having students point to (using the unlabeled art, MFL, Instructor's Resources), or draw, the geographical features you name. Have them suggest activities appropriate for the places pictured. Repeat key words and phrases: *C'est un lac ou une rivière ?*, then continue with the cultural notes and exercises. For honors or other advanced classes, there is a story from *Le Petit Nicolas et les copains* which would work quite well here: *Le chouette bol d'air*. Illustrations of a small country house with a vegetable garden and fruit trees accompany the story.

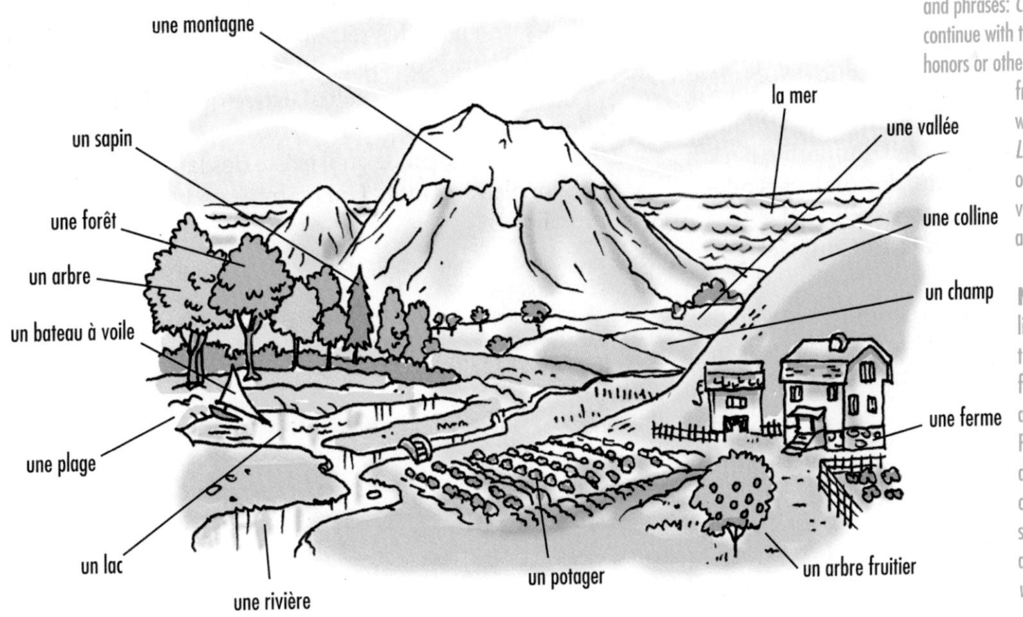

Note: About 10% of French families own a *résidence secondaire*; this statistic is down a bit from a few years ago, for both economic and sociological reasons: the French like to vary their vacation destinations. A house in a town or a village is *une maison* ; in the suburbs, *un pavillon* ; in a resort area or away from the city, *une villa*.

Presentation: As you read this passage, have students look at the map in their textbook or display the map of France (MFL, Instructor's Resources). Have them identify the water borders and the borders with neighboring countries. Ask students to point out on the map the various regions mentioned. The 22 *régions administratives* (27 with the *régions d'outre-mer*, including Mayotte, which became a *département* and *région d'outre-mer* in 2011) were established by *la loi de décentralisation* in 1982 to provide a context and means for economic development and to recognize the particular cultural history of the regions. That is why many (but not all) have retained the traditional names of the old provinces.

Vie et culture

Les régions de France

06-53

Pour les Français, la France a la forme d'une figure géométrique. Regardez la carte et essayez de voir quelle figure. Oui, c'est un hexagone. C'est un hexagone équilibré, avec trois côtés bordés par des mers et trois côtés limités par d'autres pays[1]. Comment s'appellent les mers et les pays qui bordent la France ?

Les frontières[2] de la France d'aujourd'hui ne sont pas des frontières naturelles. En fait, l'Hexagone est le résultat d'évènements politiques qui ont réuni[3] peu à peu des peuples de langues et de cultures différentes. Par exemple, la Bretagne a été ajoutée[4] en 1532 ; le Pays Basque en 1620 ; le Roussillon (la région autour de Perpignan) en 1659 ; l'Alsace en 1681 ; la Corse en 1768 ; la Savoie et la région de Nice en 1860.

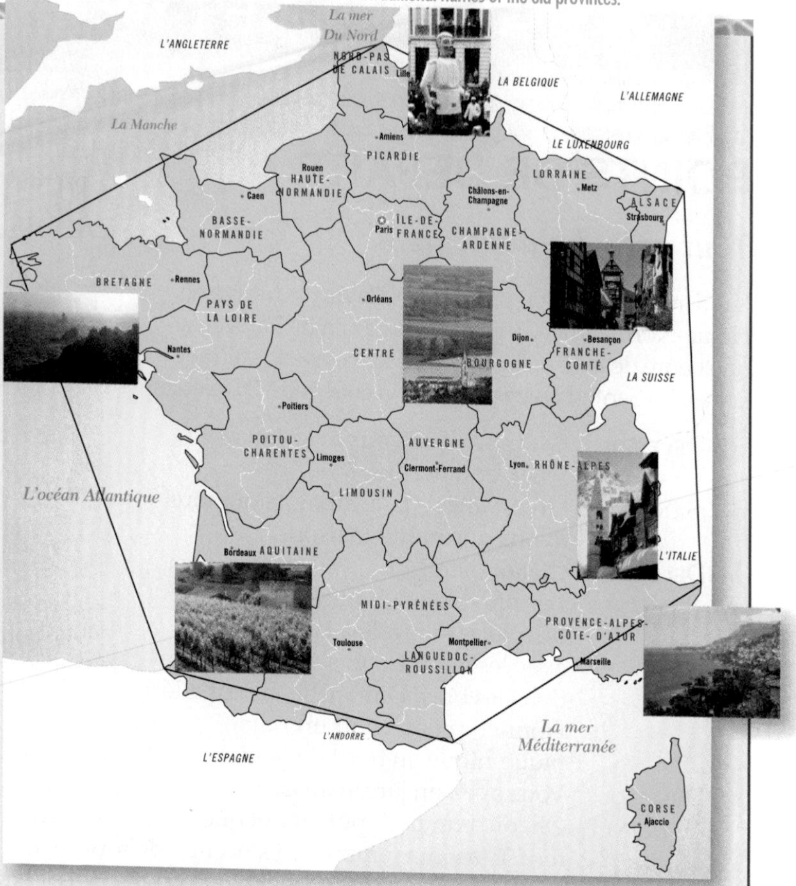

La mer Du Nord
L'ANGLETERRE
NORD-PAS-DE CALAIS
Lille
LA BELGIQUE
L'ALLEMAGNE
La Manche
Amiens
PICARDIE
LE LUXEMBOURG
Rouen
HAUTE-NORMANDIE
Caen
LORRAINE
Metz
Châlons-en-Champagne
ALSACE
Strasbourg
BASSE-NORMANDIE
ÎLE-DE-FRANCE
Paris
CHAMPAGNE-ARDENNE
BRETAGNE
Rennes
PAYS DE LA LOIRE
Orléans
Nantes
CENTRE
Dijon
Besançon
BOURGOGNE
FRANCHE-COMTÉ
LA SUISSE
Poitiers
POITOU-CHARENTES
Limoges
AUVERGNE
Clermont-Ferrand
Lyon
RHÔNE-ALPES
L'océan Atlantique
LIMOUSIN
Bordeaux
AQUITAINE
L'ITALIE
MIDI-PYRÉNÉES
PROVENCE-ALPES-CÔTE-D'AZUR
Toulouse
Montpellier
LANGUEDOC-ROUSSILLON
Marseille
L'ANDORRE
La mer Méditerranée
L'ESPAGNE
CORSE
Ajaccio

Les langues de France

Les habitants des régions françaises ont conservé une partie de leur culture à travers la musique, les fêtes, la cuisine et les langues régionales. Les communautés locales font un effort pour préserver ces langues, et on commence à enseigner les langues régionales à l'école. Voici quelques exemples de la langue de ces régions qui, tous, veulent dire : « Venez chez nous en... ! »

- En Bretagne, le breton : **Deit genomb é Breizh !**
- En Alsace et en Lorraine, des dialectes allemands : **Komme zü uns ens Elsass !**
- En Corse, le corse : **Venite in Corsica !**

Regardez la séquence vidéo *À la découverte de la France : les provinces*. Combien de régions différentes est-ce que vous identifiez ?

Note: The U.S. Census identifies four regions: Midwest, South, Northeast, and West; students may identify others as well.

ET VOUS ?

1. Faites une liste des régions des États-Unis. Quelles sortes de spécialités (la musique, les plats régionaux, les fêtes) est-ce qu'on trouve dans ces régions?
2. D'après vous, est-ce qu'il existe des langues régionales aux États-Unis comme en France ? Expliquez.

Note: The French government formerly recognized seven regional languages: three Romance — *l'occitan, le catalan, le corse* ; two Germanic — *le flamand, l'alsacien* ; one Celtic — *le breton* ; and *le basque*, of unknown origin. In the 1990s, *le créole* was added to this list of languages, although in each of the DOM a different Creole language is spoken. In 1999, a total of seventy-five regional languages were recognized, including the languages of *la Nouvelle Calédonie* and *la Polynésie française* (Tahiti). Refer students to online search engines to learn more about *les langues de France*.

[1]*other countries* [2]*borders* [3]*united* [4]*added*

Have students compare the development of modern France with the development of the U.S., from the thirteen original colonies to the addition of the Louisiana Purchase, Florida, Texas, California, Alaska, etc. Point out the vast geographic and cultural diversity of France. For example, houses in the north of France are built differently than those in the south, people cook with butter in the north and with olive oil in the south, certain regions are well known for their products such as *camembert, champagne, cidre, foie gras, nougat, olives*. Have students look at the photos and comment on the regional variety that is displayed in each: going clockwise from the top: one of the many "*Fêtes des Géants*" celebrations that occur annually throughout *le Nord*, this one in Lille; the medieval town of Riquewihr in Alsace; the town of Val d'Isère in Savoie; la Côte d'Azur; a vineyard and *château de vin* in Bordeaux in Aquitaine; the Pointe du Raz in Bretagne; the village of Saint Père in Bourgogne.

À vous la parole

6-21 Où aller ? Suggérez le meilleur endroit pour chaque activité mentionnée.

MODÈLE pour faire de la pêche
- Allons au bord d'une rivière.

OU Allons au bord de la mer.

OU Allons au lac.

1. pour faire du ski
2. pour faire un pique-nique
3. pour nager
4. pour faire une promenade dans la nature
5. pour faire du cheval
6. pour faire de la voile
7. pour faire du camping

Additional practice: Put students into small groups to plan an outing. Direct them as follows: *Faites des projets pour une sortie. Imaginez qu'il fait beau et que vous avez une journée de libre. Choisissez une destination et des activités.* You might choose to impose certain constraints—time of year, distance they may travel, amount of money they may spend, etc. Be sure to provide a model, such as:

É1 On va à la montagne ?

É2 Je préfère aller au bord d'un lac.

É3 Moi aussi. J'adore nager et…

6-22 Plaisirs de la ville, plaisirs de la campagne. Vous préférez habiter la ville ou la campagne ? Pourquoi ? Discutez de votre préférence avec un/e partenaire et dressez une liste des avantages et des inconvénients.

MODÈLE É1 Moi, je préfère habiter la ville ; il y a beaucoup de bons restaurants et de cinémas.

É2 Il y a trop d'activité et trop de voitures en ville ; je préfère le calme à la campagne…

la ville : avantages = les restaurants, les cinémas, …
inconvénients = les voitures, …

la campagne : avantages = le calme, …

Implementation: 6-22 This can also be carried out as a whole-class activity, or students can be put into small groups as follows: advantages of the city, advantages of the country, disadvantages of the city, disadvantages of the country. Circulate as groups prepare their lists and help out with ideas and vocabulary. Have groups report back, and summarize information orally and visually before students are polled to express their personal preference. As an additional follow-up, students can write about their personal preference.

6-23 La maison de vos rêves. Imaginez que vous pouvez acheter une résidence secondaire. Décrivez-la d'après vos préférences, et comparez vos idées avec celles d'un/e partenaire.

1. Elle se trouve au bord de la mer ? à la montagne ? à la campagne ?
2. C'est une grande ou une petite maison ? simple ou élégante ?
3. Qu'est-ce que vous faites quand vous allez dans votre résidence secondaire ?

MODÈLE • Ma résidence secondaire se trouve à la montagne. C'est un petit chalet, très simple mais confortable. Là-bas, il ne fait pas trop chaud en été, et il y a toujours de la neige en hiver. En été, j'aime faire des randonnées, et en hiver, j'adore faire du ski.

Variation: 6-23 Ask students to make a sketch of their dream house to share with the class. As students share their visions of their dream houses, have the class decide whose house is the most luxurious, the most practical, the most realistic, etc.

Presentation: It would be best to present this material after presenting the forms of the imperfect in the first **Formes et fonctions** of this lesson, since the pronunciation of the semi-vowel [j] is a crucial element in the pronunciation of the first- and second-person plural forms.

Note: In *étudie*, the final *-e* is not pronounced. Note the intervocalic glide that occurs before the vowel-initial syllable in the words: *client* /klijɑ̃/, *oublier* /ublije/.

Note: To help students remember some frequent words where **-ill-** is pronounced as / il /, introduce this sentence as a mnemonic device: *Mille personnes habitent ce village tranquille ; dans la ville c'est un-million.*

06-36 to 06-37

Initial practice: Begin with a discrimination drill contrasting the first- and second-person plural of the present versus the corresponding forms of the imperfect. Have students raise their hand when they hear the imperfect (and therefore the glide /j/): *nous lisons, nous lisions, vous écrivez, vous écriviez, nous disions, nous disons, vous fêtez, vous fêtiez, nous célébrons, nous célébrions, nous jouions, nous jouons, vous chantez, vous chantiez.*

You may also wish to add a drill in which students transform from the present to the imperfect: *vous écrivez* → *vous écriviez ; nous dansons, vous mangez, vous passez, nous faisons, nous allons, vous achetez, vous finissez, nous préférons.*

Note: Remind students that the sequence *-ill* in words like *ville, tranquille*, and *mille* and its derivatives: *un-million, des milliards, des milliers*, is pronounced as / il /.

Sons et lettres

La semi-voyelle /j/

When the letter **i** immediately precedes a vowel sound, it is pronounced /j/, as in the English word *yes*. It forms a single syllable with the following vowel. Compare:

étudie / étudiez — fruit / fruitier — mari / marié

Note that when **i** is preceded by a group of consonants and followed by a vowel sound, it is pronounced /i/ and forms a separate syllable. Compare:

le lien / le cli-ent — bien / ou-bli-er — Pierre / pro-pri-é-taire

The letter **y** is often pronounced /j/:

loyer — s'essuyer — yaourt — il **y** a / il n'**y** a pas

La prononciation de *-ill-*

The combination of letters **-ill-** has two pronunciations: with the /l/ sound of **il** or the /j/ sound at the end of **travail**. It is difficult to predict how that combination is to be pronounced in a given word; the pronunciation of individual words must be memorized. Compare:

/l/		/j/	
mille	un million	la fille	la famille
la ville	le village	se maquiller	elle se maquille
tranquille		s'habiller	gentille

À vous la parole

6-24 Imitation. Répétez ces mots ou expressions qui contiennent la semi-voyelle /j/ devant une voyelle orale.

mieux	le premier	officiel	un cinq-pièces
les escaliers	le quartier	la rivière	monsieur
la société	l'évier	vous chantiez	nous voulions

6-25 Contrastes. Prononcez ces paires de mots ou d'expressions en faisant bien la différence de prononciation de la lettre *i*.

1. la vie / les vieux
2. l'ami / le mieux
3. le cri / crier
4. le mari / le mariage
5. elle étudie / elle va étudier
6. il est parti / nous partions

6-26 Phrases. Maintenant lisez ces phrases.

1. Le loyer du studio au quatrième étage n'est pas cher, mais il faut prendre les escaliers ; il n'**y** a pas d'ascenseur.
2. Mille famil**les** habitent ce village tranquille ; dans la ville c'est un-million d'après les statistiques officielles.
3. Dans ce quartier résidentiel et tranquille, il y a des studios et des beaux deux-pièces avec un loyer peu cher.

FORMES ET FONCTIONS

1. Faire des suggestions avec l'imparfait

Note: This section focuses on the formation of the *imparfait*. For that reason, we use a function of the *imparfait* unrelated to the expression of past events. You might point out that the main use of the *imparfait* is to express certain types of past events and that this function is taught in the next section, which you will want to treat on a subsequent day.

- The imperfect (**l'imparfait**) is a tense that is used in a variety of ways. For example, it is used with **si** to make suggestions and to soften commands.

Si on **faisait** une promenade ?	*Shall we take a walk?*
Si tu **allais** à la pêche ?	*Why don't you go fishing?*
Si on **allait** à la montagne ?	*How about going to the mountains?*

- To form the **imparfait**, drop the **-ons** ending of the **nous** form of the present tense and add the **imparfait** endings. The only exception to this rule is the verb **être**, which has an irregular stem, **ét-**, as shown below.

Presentation: Show students how the rule for formation of the *imparfait* works for irregular verbs they have learned: *faire* → *nous faisons* → *il faisait, nous faisions*, etc. Point out that the singular and third-person plural forms are pronounced alike. In pronouncing these endings, French speakers vary between /e/, as in *thé*, and /ɛ/, as in *cette*.

L'IMPARFAIT

INFINITIVE	jouer	partir	finir	descendre	**être**
NOUS FORM	jouons	partons	finissons	descendons	
IMPARFAIT STEM	**jou-**	**part-**	**finiss-**	**descend-**	**ét-**
je	jou**ais**	part**ais**	finiss**ais**	descend**ais**	ét**ais**
tu	jou**ais**	part**ais**	finiss**ais**	descend**ais**	ét**ais**
il / elle / on	jou**ait**	part**ait**	finiss**ait**	descend**ait**	ét**ait**
nous	jou**ions**	part**ions**	finiss**ions**	descend**ions**	ét**ions**
vous	jou**iez**	part**iez**	finiss**iez**	descend**iez**	ét**iez**
ils / elles	jou**aient**	part**aient**	finiss**aient**	descend**aient**	ét**aient**

À vous la parole

38

41 **6-27 Un week-end à la campagne.** Transformez ces ordres en suggestions.

MODÈLES Jouons au golf !
- Si on jouait au golf ?

Mets la table !
- Si tu mettais la table ?

1. Faisons une randonnée ! Si on faisait…
2. Travaille dans le jardin ! Si tu travaillais…
3. Descendez au bord du lac ! Si vous descendiez…
4. Organisons un pique-nique ! Si on organisait…
5. Faites une promenade dans la forêt ! Si vous faisiez…
6. Cherchons des tomates ! Si on cherchait…
7. Fais du bricolage ! Si tu faisais…
8. Allons à la pêche ! Si on allait…
9. Faisons de la voile ! Si on faisait…

Note: You might remind students to picture the "boot" shape (as discussed in the **Fiche pratique** in Ch. 1, L. 3 for regular *-er* verbs) as they imagine themselves writing out the various endings for the imperfect. The imperfect also displays the boot shape and has three spoken forms.

Initial practice: Begin with a substitution drill: *Si on allait à la piscine ? nous, toi, vous*, etc.

Follow with a transformation drill that allows students to practice multiple verbs: *On va au lac ? —Si on allait au lac ? On fait une promenade ? —Si on faisait une promenade ? On part à la campagne ? On attend les amis ? On finit les devoirs ?*, etc.

Fiche pratique

As you encounter a new verb tense, use several of your senses to help you learn the new forms. For example, practice repeating the **imparfait** forms of the verb **finir** out loud: **je finissais, tu finissais, elle finissait,** etc., while forming a picture in your mind of your hand writing out the endings **-ais, -ais, -ait,** etc., for each form.

6-28 Pour une sortie. En groupes de trois personnes, organisez une petite sortie. Mettez-vous d'accord sur l'endroit et les distractions. Utilisez les verbes indiqués.

MODÈLE aller ; apporter ; faire
É1 Si on allait à la plage ? (ou chez Tracy ?, etc.)
É2 Si tu apportais ta guitare ?
É3 Si on faisait un pique-nique ?

1. aller
2. apporter
3. acheter
4. jouer
5. faire
6. inviter

2. L'imparfait : la description au passé

Presentation: Treat this topic on day 2 of the lesson; first review forms using a substitution drill: *Si tu jouais au tennis ; nous, lui*, etc.

- You have just learned to use the **imparfait** to make suggestions. You can also use this tense to describe situations and settings in the past.
  - To indicate the time:

    Il **était** une heure du matin. — *It was one o'clock in the morning.*
    C'**était** en hiver. — *It was during the winter.*
  - To describe the weather:

    Il **pleuvait** et il **faisait** froid. — *It was raining and it was cold.*
    Le ciel **était** gris. — *The sky was gray.*
  - To describe people and places:

    C'**était** une belle maison. — *It was a nice house.*
    La dame **avait** les cheveux roux. — *The woman had red hair.*
    Elle **portait** un manteau noir. — *She was wearing a black coat.*
  - To express feelings or describe emotions:

    Nous **avions** froid. — *We were cold.*
    Ils **étaient** contents. — *They were happy.*
- Use the **imparfait** to express habitual actions in the past:

  Tous les week-ends, on **faisait** une randonnée dans les bois. — *Every weekend we would take (we took) a hike in the woods.*
  Quand j'étais petit, on **passait** les vacances chez mes grands-parents. — *When I was little, we used to spend vacations at my grandparents'.*

Here are some expressions often used with the **imparfait** to describe things that were done on a routine basis:

Presentation: Remind students that *le* used before a day of the week or a word like *week-end* changes the meaning to "every Monday" or "every weekend," for example.

quelquefois	*sometimes*
souvent	*often*
d'habitude	*usually*
toujours	*always*
le lundi, le week-end	*every Monday, every weekend*
tous les jours, tous les soirs	*every day, every evening*
toutes les semaines	*every week*

À vous la parole

6-29 Un après-midi en famille. Regardez l'image de cette famille à Biarritz et complétez les phrases pour décrire leur après-midi.

MODÈLE Ce / être le mois de juin
- C'était le mois de juin.

1. les enfants / jouer dans le jardin Les enfants jouaient…
2. le grand-père / parle avec sa petite-fille Le grand-père parlait…
3. le fils / jouer au foot Le fils jouait…
4. leur mère et leur tante / boire un jus d'orange Leur mère et leur tante buvaient…
5. les femmes / regarder les enfants et leur père Les femmes regardaient…
6. leur frère / préparer le repas Leur frère préparait…
7. le chien et les chats / dormir Le chien et les chats dormaient…

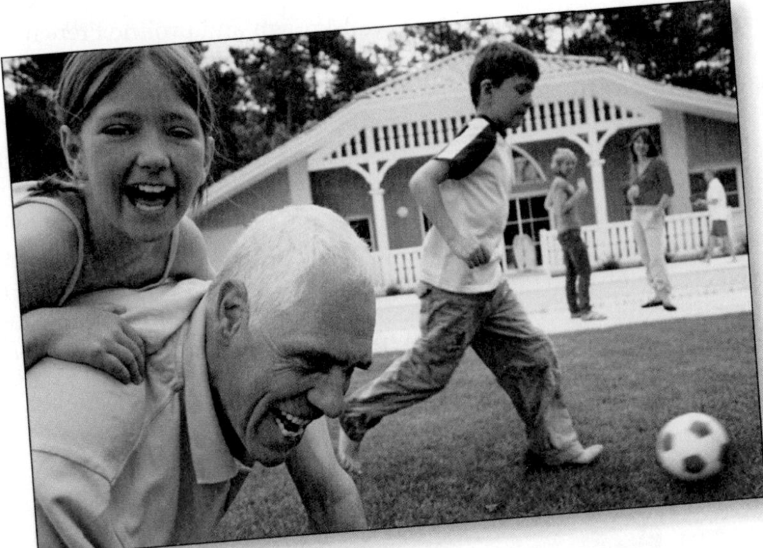

6-30 Votre premier cours de langue. Avec un/e partenaire, parlez de votre premier cours de langue. Est-ce que vous aviez des expériences semblables ou pas ?

MODÈLE le prof

É1 Mon premier prof de français s'appelait M. Dell. Il était grand et assez mince. Il était très dynamique et assez drôle. Et toi ?

É2 Mon premier prof d'espagnol s'appelait Señora Glatis. Elle était très sympa et très énergique. Je l'adorais !

1. l'heure du cours
2. l'endroit (le bâtiment, la salle de classe ou le campus…)
3. le prof
4. les autres étudiants ou élèves
5. vos émotions/sentiments
6. le travail
7. les activités habituelles

Implementation: 6-30 If this is the first language course for some students, suggest that they focus on the first few weeks of the semester and describe what things were like and how they felt at that point. It may be helpful to brainstorm a list of questions and possible reponses with students before completing the activity. For example, *À quelle heure était votre cours ? Où était le cours ? Combien d'étudiants/élèves est-ce qu'il y avait dans le cours ? Comment était le professeur ?*

Implementation: 6-32 Have students work in pairs; as they report back what they have learned, ask follow-up questions. This exercise can lead into the reading in **Lisons**.

6-31 Votre enfance. Posez des questions à un/e camarade de classe pour savoir ce qu'il/elle faisait pendant son enfance.

MODÈLE habiter ici

É1 Est-ce que tu habitais ici ?

É2 Non, j'habitais à Chicago avec mes parents.

1. habiter ici
2. avoir des animaux
3. aimer aller à l'école
4. faire du sport
5. jouer d'un instrument
6. aller souvent chez des amis
7. partir souvent en vacances
8. avoir une résidence secondaire

Stratégie

To understand a narrative, it is often helpful to identify the main characters and the nature of their relationships with each other. Then as you read and reread the passage, focus on defining the significance of each character and how he or she figures in the story.

Presentation: Link this reading to the notion of place developed in the chapter by having students make the connection that Morocco is a place where French is spoken and that Zinna's description of her home and neighborhood are very specific to a particular place. Ask students to describe the photo that accompanies the reading and to discuss the feelings/associations that it may evoke. As you work with the text, you might ask students what they know about Morocco and how it compares with the photo. You might have them do some Internet research on *le Mellah*.

Key: *Avant de lire.* Characters mentioned include: *Gazelle/Tomi ; Zinna ; le père de Zinna et son oncle Moché ; Khadija ; la (vieille) tante Rahel (une voisine)*. Help students see that *Gazelle* is a nickname for *Tomi* and ask them why Tomi might be referred to as a "gazelle." The opening lines of the story explain: « *Il s'appelait Tomi, mais Zinna l'appelait Gazelle, à cause de son autre nom, Arzel, parce qu'elle disait que c'était ce que ça voulait dire, en arabe. C'était peut-être pour ça qu'il savait courir si vite.* »

Key: *En lisant.* 1) Zinna parle à Gazelle/Tomi ; le matin ; à la plage 2) la maison de Zinna : vieille, petite, une pièce en bas, une chambre en haut, une échelle pour aller sur le toit (pour laver les vêtements) ; la maison de Rahel, la maison bleue : grande, il y a une grande porte bleue et des fenêtres bleues à l'étage ; il y a un balcon rond 3) Rahel habite la deuxième maison. Elle est riche et vieille ; on l'appelle « tante ». Elle est célibataire ; elle a toujours refusé le mariage. Une femme riche et indépendante qui habite seule n'est pas habituelle dans cette société.

Lisons

6-32 Quand j'étais toute petite.

A. Avant de lire. J.M.G. Le Clézio, a well-known and prolific French author, was awarded the Nobel Prize for literature in 2008. The excerpt you are about to read is from *Printemps et autres saisons*, a collection of short stories. Each one is set in a different season and tells the story of a particular woman. In this excerpt, Zinna, a young woman who has left her home in Morocco for the South of France, describes her childhood home in the **Mellah** (the Jewish quarter). Before you begin reading, skim the text and make a list of all the characters mentioned; take note especially of an essential character who figures prominently in the story: Zinna's elderly neighbor, **la tante Rahel**. Consider as you read why Rahel, whom Zinna never actually encounters in person, is very important to her narrative.

B. En lisant. Répondez aux questions suivantes.

1. Ce texte est principalement une conversation. À qui est-ce que Zinna parle ? Quand est-ce qu'elle raconte son histoire ? Où ?
2. Zinna décrit deux maisons ; ce sont les maisons de qui ? Décrivez chaque maison : elles sont grandes ou petites ? Elles ont combien de pièces ? Combien d'étages ? Est-ce qu'il y a d'autres détails intéressants ?
3. Qui habite la deuxième maison ? Cette personne est comment ? Pourquoi est-ce que Zinna la trouve fascinante ?

« Tu sais, Gazelle, quand j'étais toute petite, il n'y avait pas de plus beau quartier que le Mellah. »

Zinna commençait toujours ainsi. Elle s'asseyait sur la plage, et Tomi se mettait à côté d'elle. C'était généralement le matin…

« Alors, nous habitions une maison très vieille, étroite, juste une pièce en bas où couchait mon père avec mon oncle Moché, et moi j'étais dans la chambre du haut. Il y avait une échelle[1] pour grimper[2] sur le toit[3], là où était le lavoir[4]. C'était moi qui lavais le linge, quelquefois Khadija venait m'aider, elle était grosse, elle n'arrivait pas à grimper l'échelle, il fallait[5] la pousser. À côté de chez nous, il y avait la maison bleue. Elle n'était pas bleue, mais on l'appelait comme ça parce qu'elle avait une grande porte peinte en bleu, et les fenêtres à l'étage aussi étaient peintes en bleu. Il y avait surtout une fenêtre très haute, au premier, qui donnait sur un balcon rond. C'était la maison d'une vieille femme qu'on appelait la tante Rahel, mais elle n'était pas vraiment notre tante. On disait qu'elle était très riche, qu'elle n'avait jamais voulu se marier. Elle vivait[6] toute seule dans cette grande maison, avec ce balcon où les pigeons venaient se percher. Tous les jours, j'allais voir sa maison. De son balcon, je rêvais[7] qu'on pouvait voir tout le paysage, la ville, la rivière avec les barques qui traversaient, jusqu'à la mer. La vieille Rahel n'ouvrait jamais sa fenêtre, elle ne se mettait jamais au balcon pour regarder… »

[1]*ladder* [2]*climb* [3]*roof* [4]*washtub* [5]*it was necessary* [6]*lived* [7]*imagined*

C. En regardant de plus près. Maintenant, considérez la structure et la signification de ce texte.

1. Au début, comment est-ce que nous savons que Tomi (Gazelle) a l'habitude d'entendre des histoires de la vie de Zinna dans le Mellah ?
2. Zinna a un souvenir très précis du toit de sa maison d'enfance : décrivez les activités et les personnes qui font partie de cette mémoire.
3. Zinna compare le toit de sa maison avec le balcon de sa voisine, Rahel. Qu'est-ce que nous apprenons de la vie de Rahel ? Zinna n'a pas visité le balcon de la maison de Rahel. Quelles sortes de choses est-ce qu'elle imagine être possible du balcon de Rahel ?

D. Après avoir lu. Discutez de ces questions avec vos camarades de classe.

1. Quelles sont les différences entre Zinna et Rahel ? Pourquoi est-ce que ces différences sont importantes ?
2. Est-ce que vous avez le souvenir d'un endroit lié avec une personne qui a marqué votre imagination ? Quelle idée est-ce que vous associez à cet endroit ?

Key: *En regardant de plus près.* 1) l'emploi de l'imparfait et des adverbes comme *toujours, généralement* 2) Il y avait une échelle pour aller sur le toit. Zinna lavait les vêtements là. Khadija l'aidait quelquefois. Elle était grosse et Zinna devait la pousser parce qu'elle avait des difficultés pour monter. 3) Rahel n'ouvrait jamais sa fenêtre ; elle ne regardait jamais la vue de son balcon. Zinna imagine qu'on peut voir la campagne, la ville, la rivière, des bateaux et même la mer de ce balcon.

Key: *Après avoir lu.* Zinna est jeune et sa famille n'a pas beaucoup d'argent. Ses activités sont routines (par exemple, laver les vêtements) et assez limitées. Rahel est vieille et riche, et Zinna imagine qu'elle a beaucoup de possibilités (par exemple qu'elle peut voir beaucoup de choses de son balcon). Ces possibilités évoquent la curiosité de la jeune Zinna et lui donne envie de découvrir d'autres choses que sa maison et son quartier.

Leçon 

pour décrire un immeuble	*to describe a building*
un ascenseur	*elevator*
un bâtiment	*building*
une cour	*courtyard*
des escaliers (m.)	*staircase, stairs*
un étage	*floor (of a building)*
un garage	*garage*
garer la voiture	*to park the car*
le rez-de-chaussée	*ground floor*
le sous-sol	*basement*
un/e voisin/e	*neighbor*

pour situer un immeuble	*to situate a building*
animé/e	*lively, animated*
un arrondissement	*Parisian city district*
un quartier (résidentiel)	*(residential) neighborhood*
une rue	*street*
tranquille	*quiet, tranquil*

pour parler d'un appartement	*to talk about an apartment*
un balcon	*balcony*
une chambre	*bedroom*
les charges (f. pl.) (sont comprises)	*utilities (are included)*
un cinq-pièces	*3-bedroom apartment with living room and dining room*
un couloir	*hallway*
une cuisine	*kitchen*
donner sur	*to look out onto or lead out to*
une entrée	*entrance, foyer*
un/e locataire	*renter*
louer	*to rent*
le loyer	*the rent*
un/e propriétaire	*homeowner; landlord/landlady*
une salle à manger	*dining room*
une salle de bains	*bathroom*
un séjour, une salle de séjour	*living room*
un studio	*studio apartment*
une terrasse	*terrace*
des toilettes (f. pl.), des W.-C. (m. pl.)	*toilet, water closet*
les nombres à partir de 1 000	**numbers from 1,000**
mille	*thousand*
un-million	*a million*
un-milliard	*a billion*

autres mots utiles	*other useful words*
chaque	*each*
même	*even*
propre	*own*

à quel étage ?	*on what floor?*
rez-de-chaussée (RdeCh)	*ground floor*
1er premier	*first*
2e deuxième	*second*
3e troisième	*third*
10e dixième	*tenth*
11e onzième	*eleventh*
12e douzième	*twelfth*
13e treizième	*thirteenth*
19e dix-neuvième	*nineteenth*
20e vingtième	*twentieth*
21e vingt-et-unième	*twenty-first*

Leçon 

le mobilier	*home furnishings*
une armoire	*armoire, wardrobe*
un canapé	*couch*
une cuisinière	*stove*
une étagère	*bookcase, (book) shelf*
un évier	*kitchen sink*
un fauteuil	*armchair*
un four	*oven*
une lampe	*lamp*
un lit	*bed*
un meuble	*piece of furniture*
des placards (m.)	*cupboards, kitchen cabinets*
une plante	*plant*
un réfrigérateur, un frigo	*refrigerator, fridge*
des rideaux (m.)	*curtains*
une table basse	*coffee table*
un tapis	*rug*
la vaisselle	*tableware, dishes*

pour décrire un appartement ou un meuble	*to describe an apartment or a piece of furniture*
à côté de	*next to, beside*
abîmé/e	*worn, worn out*
agréable	*pleasant*
ancien/ne	*old, antique*
le centre-ville	*downtown*
chic (inv.)	*stylish*
avec coin cuisine	*with a kitchenette*

confortable	*comfortable (said of objects or places)*
équipé/e	*equipped*
meublé/e	*furnished*
moderne	*modern*
un mur	*wall*
neuf/neuve	*brand new*
par terre	*on the floor*
pratique	*practical*
rénové/e	*renovated*
sous les toits	*in the attic*
sous	*under*
spacieux/-euse	*spacious*
sur	*on top of*
le toit	*roof*

autres mots utiles	*other useful words*
des affaires (f.)	*belongings, things*
coûter	*to cost*
ranger	*to put up, to put away*
seulement	*only*
surtout	*above all*

quelques verbes de communication et de transfert	*some verbs of communication and transfer*
apporter	*to bring*
demander	*to ask*
emprunter	*to borrow*
expliquer	*to explain*
offrir (un cadeau)	*to give (a gift)*
prêter	*to lend*
remettre	*to hand in/over*

Leçon 3

la vie à la campagne	*life in the country*
se détendre	*to relax*
une ferme	*farm*
un jardin	*garden, yard*
un potager	*vegetable garden*
une villa	*detached house (not in the city); villa*

dans la nature	*in nature*
un arbre (fruitier)	*(fruit) tree*
un bateau (à voile)	*(sail)boat*
les bois (m. pl.)	*woods*
un champ	*field*
une colline	*hill*
une forêt	*forest*
un lac	*lake*
une rivière	*large stream or river (tributary)*
un sapin	*evergreen tree*
une vallée	*valley*

autres mots utiles	*other useful words*
au bord (du lac, de la mer)	*on the shore (of the lake, sea)*
un endroit	*place*
en effet	*yes, indeed*
formidable	*great*
il me semble	*it seems to me*
là(-bas)	*there*
s'occuper de	*to take care of*
posséder	*to own*

pour parler des activités habituelles dans le passé	*to talk about habitual activities in the past*
d'habitude	*usually*
le lundi	*every Monday, on Mondays*
le week-end	*every weekend, on weekends*
quelquefois	*sometimes*
souvent	*often*
toujours	*always*
tous les jours, tous les soirs	*every day, every evening*
toutes les semaines	*every week*

Vocabulaire

Qu'est-ce que cette femme fait ? Pourquoi ?

7 La santé et le bien-être

After completing this chapter, you should be able to:

- Discuss health and well-being
- Give advice
- Describe and narrate past events
- Express emotions
- Discuss rites and rituals in the Francophone world

Leçon 1 La santé

POINTS DE DÉPART

Presentation: Present the parts of the body using the visual (MFL, Instructor's Resources), naming and describing the body parts: *Voici les yeux ; vous avez deux yeux ; c'est pour regarder. Au singulier, c'est un œil*, etc. Or you might present this vocabulary using TPR: *Touchez le bras, la main, la jambe, les yeux*, etc. Test student comprehension by playing "Simon says" (*Jacques a dit…*). Using the unlabeled art (MFL, Instructor's Resources), have students repeat the new vocabulary by identifying parts of the body: *C'est une oreille ou un œil ?*, then have them name parts of the body that come in twos — *les oreilles, les yeux, les bras, les jambes, les mains* ; then those for which they have only one: *un cœur, une tête, un estomac*. Students may also see the verb *essayer* conjugated as *ils essaient*.

To present this vocabulary over two days, begin with parts of the body, the expression *avoir mal*, and Ex. 7-1. On day two, present *Êtes-vous en forme ?*, the **Vie et culture**, and Ex. 7-2 and 7-3.

Santé physique et morale

Baptiste et Charlotte font très attention à leur santé. Ils n'ont pas beaucoup de temps libre parce qu'ils travaillent beaucoup, mais ils essayent de bien manger et de faire régulièrement de l'exercice. Charlotte aime bien les cours de fitness. Son mari est handicapé ; il doit se servir d'un fauteuil roulant, mais il est très sportif. Il fait souvent de la musculation, et il joue au basket-fauteuil avec des copains.

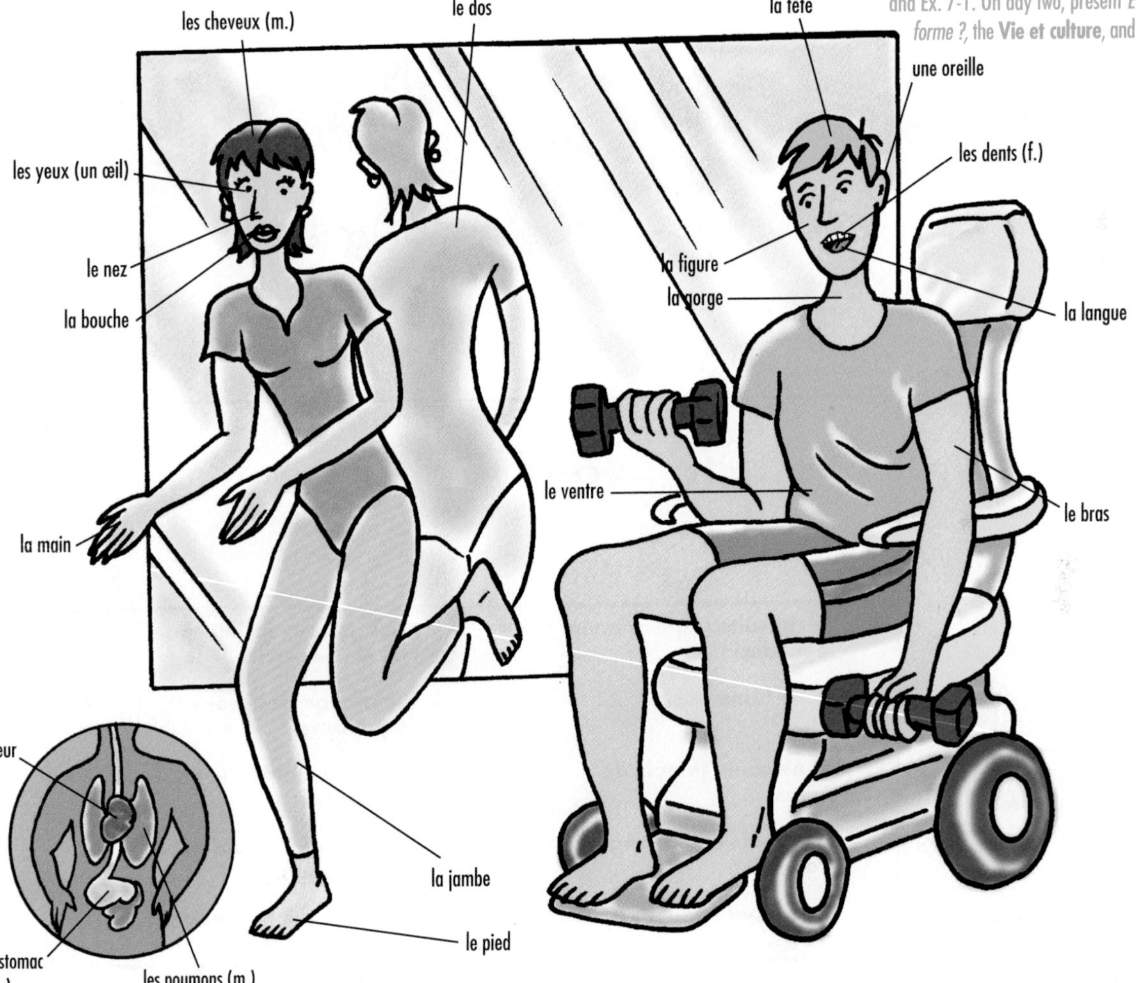

Note: A limited number of terms relating to physical disabilities are presented in this lesson. You may wish to present more specific terms relating to disabilities: *quelqu'un qui ne voit pas est aveugle ou non-voyant ; si on ne peut pas entendre, on est sourd ou malentendant ; si on a des problèmes à marcher, on peut utiliser une canne ou un déambulateur ; des gens qui ont perdu une jambe ou un bras sont des amputés et ils peuvent se servir des prothèses ou des béquilles. Les aveugles peuvent se servir des chiens guides et d'autres personnes handicapées peuvent être aidées par des chiens d'assistance.*

VOUS AVEZ MAL ?

To indicate the location of body pains in French, use the expression **avoir mal à** plus the definite article and the body part. Remember that the preposition **à** contracts with the definite articles **le** and **les**:

J'**ai mal à la** tête.	*I have a headache.*
Il **a mal au** cœur.	*He's nauseated.*
Elle **a mal aux** pieds.	*Her feet hurt.*
Tu **as mal au** ventre ?	*Do you have a stomach ache?*
J'**ai mal partout.**	*I hurt everywhere.*

Presentation: Choose a "victim" from among the students, and use a toy hammer or bat to pretend you are inflicting pain on that person. Have students answer the question, *Où est-ce qu'il/elle a mal ?* You might focus on body parts not mentioned in Ex. 7-1.

07-01 to 07-04

Implementation: 7-1 Use the image of the hikers (MFL, Instructor's Resources) to complete the exercise.

Key: 7-1 Thérèse a mal au pied ; Denis a mal au ventre ; Mme Parizeau a mal à la main ; M. Dubosc a mal à la tête ; Paul a mal à la jambe.

À vous la parole

7-1 J'ai mal ! Dites où ces personnes ont mal.

MODÈLE Christiane
• Christiane, elle a mal au dos.

Presentation: Present this vocabulary by having students take the quiz individually or in pairs. First provide a model: *Est-ce que vous consultez le médecin et le dentiste régulièrement ? Moi, par exemple, je vais chez le médecin une fois par an et chez le dentiste deux fois par an.* As you work through the list of good and bad health practices, provide examples: *un repas équilibré, c'est des chips et un coca ? Non, c'est des protéines, des légumes comme des carottes et des concombres, des fruits et des céréales.* Use cognates (*découvrir, c'est déterminer*) and paraphrase (*grignoter, c'est manger un peu entre les repas*) to help make meaning clear. For the expression *suivre un régime*, point out that students may also hear *être au régime* and *faire un régime.* Follow up by asking students whether they are (or their partner is) in good or bad health, and have them explain why.

Êtes-vous en forme ?
Faites le test pour le savoir.

1. **Je consulte régulièrement le médecin.** ☐ vrai ☐ faux
2. **Je fais souvent du sport ou de l'exercice.** ☐ vrai ☐ faux
3. **Je ne fume pas.** ☐ vrai ☐ faux
4. **Je mange des repas équilibrés.** ☐ vrai ☐ faux
5. **Je ne saute jamais de repas.** ☐ vrai ☐ faux
6. **Je me détends de temps en temps.** ☐ vrai ☐ faux
7. **Je ne suis pas de régimes trop stricts.** ☐ vrai ☐ faux
8. **Je bois de l'alcool avec modération.** ☐ vrai ☐ faux
9. **Je grignote peu entre les repas.** ☐ vrai ☐ faux
10. **Je dors huit heures par nuit.** ☐ vrai ☐ faux

Pour découvrir votre profil, comptez un point pour chaque « vrai ».
8 à 10 points : Bravo ! Vous êtes en super bonne forme.
5 à 7 points : Ça va, mais vous pouvez mieux faire !
3 à 4 points : Franchement, vous avez du travail pour retrouver la forme !
0 à 2 points : Oh là là, la crise ! Il faut passer à l'action.

Vie et culture

Presentation: As students watch the video clip, have them make two lists: one for the sources of stress presented and one for the ways in which people try to counteract these stresses. Ask them if what they see and hear is comparable to the situation in their own living environment.

La médecine en France

Quels aspects de la vie contribuent à notre sens du bien-être ? Un facteur important, c'est l'accès aux soins médicaux[1]. Les Français ont un excellent système médical. Ils sont tous assurés[2] par un système de Sécurité sociale qui couvre les dépenses[3] médicales de presque toute la population. Les malades doivent payer le médecin et le pharmacien, mais la majorité des frais[4] médicaux sont remboursés. La vaste majorité (89 %) des Français se disent en bonne santé, mais paradoxalement, les Français sont les plus gros consommateurs de médicaments en Europe. Comment est-ce que le système médical chez vous diffère du système français ?

Le stress

07-51

Regardez la séquence vidéo *On se stresse et on se détend.*

1. Quelles sont les sources de stress mentionnées ? Quelles sont les méthodes employées par les gens que vous observez pour réduire le stress ?
2. Est-ce que vous pensez que le stress se manifeste en Amérique du Nord de la même façon qu'en France ? Pourquoi ?

[1]*medical care* [2]*insured* [3]*expenses* [4]*fees*

Note: Medical care in France is ranked first worldwide. Life expectancy for the French continues to rise: in 2008, it reached 84.3 years for women and 77.5 years for men, among the highest averages in the world. Together cardiovascular disease and cancer cause more than one in two deaths (cardiovascular disease is the number one killer for women, cancer number two; the reverse is true for men). Mental illness is on the rise, and the French are the world's number one consumers of psychotropic, or mood-altering, drugs (*Francoscopie 2010*). One reason for the high consumption of medications may be the relatively low cost of prescription drugs, which are subsidized by *la Sécu*. Point out that whereas Social Security in the U.S. concerns primarily pensions, and Medicaid/Medicare provide medical benefits to the poor and elderly, *la Sécu* in France is a more comprehensive and universal system including medical and disability benefits, family allocations, and pensions.

7-2 Des bons conseils. Avec un/e partenaire, offrez des conseils à chaque personne.

Implementation: 7-2 Point out the use of *il faut/il ne faut pas* plus infinitive as you model this exercise.

MODÈLE J'ai grossi de cinq kilos.

É1 Il faut suivre un régime.

É2 Et il ne faut pas grignoter entre les repas !

1. Je suis toujours fatigué.
2. J'ai très mal au dos.
3. Je voudrais maigrir un peu.
4. Je suis très stressé.
5. J'adore les chips et le coca, mais j'ai tendance à grossir.
6. J'ai très mal aux dents.
7. Je fume un paquet de cigarettes par jour.
8. Je n'ai pas le temps de manger le matin.

7-3 Pour combattre le stress. Avec un/e partenaire, dressez une liste de choses qui sont des sources de stress pour vous. Ensuite, établissez une autre liste de solutions pour combattre le stress. Comparez vos listes avec celles de vos camarades de classe. Qu'est-ce qui cause le stress chez les étudiants en général ? Quelles sont les solutions les plus efficaces pour combattre le stress, selon vous ?

MODÈLE les causes du stress

É1 Pour moi, ce sont les examens qui causent du stress.

É2 Et pour moi, c'est ma colocataire et…

les solutions

É1 Moi, pour réduire le stress, je fais du sport.

É2 Et moi, j'écoute de la musique et…

Qu'est-ce qu'elles font pour combattre le stress ?

Sons et lettres

Les consonnes *s* et *z*

The letter **s** may represent either the sound /s/ or the sound /z/. A number of word pairs are distinguished by these two consonant sounds. Between two vowels, **-ss-** is pronounced as /s/ and **-s-** as /z/:

le de**ss**ert	*dessert*	le dé**s**ert	*desert*
le cou**ss**in	*cushion*	le cou**s**in	*cousin*
le poi**ss**on	*fish*	le poi**s**on	*poison*

Note: This rule covers most of the vocabulary presented in **Points de départ.** The pronunciation of **-s** after a nasal vowel is somewhat more complex. For example, in the prefix *trans-*, *-s* is pronounced /z/ before a vowel. Compare: *transporter* vs. *transiter.*

At the beginning of words, the letter **s** is pronounced /s/; in liaison it is pronounced /z/. Compare:

ils **s**ont/il**s**‿ont   vous **s**avez/vou**s**‿avez

After a nasal vowel written with **n**, the letter **s** is pronounced /s/:

con**s**ervation   pen**s**er   en**s**emble

Next to a consonant, **s** is pronounced /s/:

rembour**s**er   re**s**ter   l'e**s**tomac   re**s**pirer

But note the exception **Alsace**, where **s** is pronounced /z/.

The letter **c** is also pronounced /s/ before the letters **e** and **i** or when spelled with a cedilla.

cent   **c**igarette   **ç**a   gar**ç**on

The letter **x** is pronounced:

• /s/ in:	si**x**	soi**x**ante	Bru**x**elles
• liaison /z/ in:	si**x**‿hommes	di**x**‿aspirines	
• /gz/ in:	l'e**x**amen	e**x**agérer	e**x**actement
• /ks/ in:	le ta**x**i	l'e**x**périence	e**x**cellent

Note: In France the *-x* of *Bruxelles* is usually pronounced /ks/. Make sure students understand that the *-x* of *six* is only pronounced /s/ when the word is pronounced alone or at the end of a phrase: *— Tu as combien de frères et de sœurs ? — J'en ai six [sis] ; — On est le combien aujourd'hui ? — Le six [sis].* In liaison, the *-x* is pronounced /z/: *six‿hommes.*

Initial practice: Begin with a discrimination drill: are the two words or expressions the same or different? *le poisson/le poison ; le coussin/le coussin ; le dessert/le désert ; ils ont/ils sont ; le poison/le poison ; le cousin/le coussin ; ils ont/ils ont.* Students might also be amused by the following tongue twister: *Un chasseur sachant chasser sait chasser sans son chien.*

07-05 to 07-06

Expansion: 7-5 Have students work in pairs to come up with English equivalents for these proverbs. They might suggest some variants on the following: Fish without drink is not fit to eat; It's better to be healthy than rich; Youth is wasted on the young.

À vous la parole

7-4 Contrastes. Prononcez chaque groupe de mots.

passé / basé
les Écossaises / les Anglaises
soixante / exacte
ils passent / ils se taisent
Alceste / l'Alsace
exotique / dix

7-5 Proverbes. Répétez ces proverbes.

1. Poisson sans boisson, c'est poison.
2. Santé passe richesse.
3. Si jeunesse savait, si vieillesse pouvait.

FORMES ET FONCTIONS

1. Les verbes *devoir, pouvoir* et *vouloir*

The verbs **devoir**, **pouvoir**, and **vouloir** are irregular.

DEVOIR *must, to have to, to be supposed to*

SINGULIER		PLURIEL	
je	dois	nous	devo**ns**
tu	dois	vous	deve**z**
il / elle / on	doit	ils / elles	doi**vent**

POUVOIR *can, to be able*

SINGULIER		PLURIEL	
je	peux	nous	pouvo**ns**
tu	peux	vous	pouve**z**
il / elle / on	peut	ils / elles	peu**vent**

VOULOIR *to want*

SINGULIER		PLURIEL	
je	veux	nous	voulo**ns**
tu	veux	vous	voule**z**
il / elle / on	veut	ils / elles	veu**lent**

Presentation: Present these verbs inductively by telling things you want to do, cannot do, and must do. For example, *Ce soir, je veux aller au ciné pour voir un film. Mais, je ne peux pas. Je dois préparer mon cours pour demain, et je dois corriger les essais. Et vous, qu'est-ce que vous voulez faire ce soir ? Vous voulez regarder la télé ? aller au match de basket ? Est-ce que vous pouvez ? Oui, c'est possible. Ou non, ce n'est pas possible. Qu'est-ce que vous devez faire : travailler ? préparer un examen ? faire les devoirs ?* Display similar examples and have students provide quasi-synonyms for each: *vouloir* = *désirer, pouvoir* = *c'est possible, devoir* = *c'est nécessaire.* Finish by displaying verb charts and asking students to find similarities among these verbs and with other verbs they know (i.e., for all three verbs, singular forms are pronounced alike, although the spelling is different; like the *-re* verbs, there is a pronounced final consonant in the third-person plural form that is lost in the singular; plural endings are the same as for all regular verbs).

These verbs are often used:

- With an infinitive:

Tu **dois** travailler ?	*Do you have to work?*
Tu ne **peux** pas arriver ce soir ?	*Can't you arrive this evening?*
Non, je **veux** arriver demain matin.	*No, I want to arrive tomorrow morning.*

Presentation: Remind students of similar constructions they have learned: *aller* plus the infinitive in the *futur proche,* and verbs of preference plus the infinitive; remind them also of the placement of the negative in infinitive constructions.

- To soften commands and make suggestions. Compare:

Faites plus d'exercice !	*Do more exercise!*
Vous **devez** faire plus d'exercice.	*You must exercise more.*
Appelez le médecin !	*Call the doctor!*
Vous **voulez** bien appeler le médecin ?	*Will you call the doctor?*
Vous **pouvez** appeler le médecin ?	*Can you call the doctor?*

- The verb **devoir** also has the meaning *to owe*:

Mon frère **doit** 50 € à ma sœur.	*My brother owes my sister 50 euros.*
Combien est-ce que je vous **dois** ?	*How much do I owe you?*

- **Vouloir** is used in a number of useful expressions:

On va au gymnase ?	*How about going to the gym?*
—Je **veux** bien.	*—OK.*
Qu'est-ce que vous **voulez** (tu **veux**) dire ?	*What do you mean?*
Qu'est-ce que ça **veut** dire ?	*What does that mean?*

À vous la parole

07-07 to 07-10

Initial practice: **7-6** Begin with this comprehension-based exercise. To practice forms, first use a discrimination drill: one person, or more than one? *Ils peuvent faire du sport. Elle veut grignoter. Ils doivent travailler. Il peut suivre un régime. Elles peuvent se détendre. Ils veulent aller à une fête. Il veut danser. Elles peuvent jouer au foot. Il doit aider sa mère. Ils veulent faire du vélo. Elle veut faire de la natation*, etc. Follow up with substitution drills for *vouloir* and *pouvoir*: *Je veux nager ; nous. — Nous voulons nager*, etc.
Next complete Ex. 7-7 and 7-8, which integrate practice of *vouloir* and *pouvoir*. To practice *devoir* as well, use Ex. 7-9.

7-6 Poli ou impoli ? Jean-Marc travaille dans un gymnase. Regardez ses instructions aux employés : est-ce qu'il est poli ou impoli ?

	poli	impoli
MODÈLE • Vous pouvez aider ces messieurs ?	✓	
1. Apportez-moi des serviettes !		✓
2. Vous voulez bien nettoyer ces vélos ?	✓	
3. Vous pouvez attendre un instant ?	✓	
4. Vous voulez bien rester près de la piscine ?	✓	
5. Téléphonez à ces clients !		✓
6. Vous pouvez m'aider un instant ?	✓	
7. Vous voulez téléphoner au directeur ?	✓	
8. Fermez la porte du bureau !		✓

Quand on est stressé, on n'est pas toujours très poli. Est-ce que Jean-Marc est très stressé aujourd'hui, à votre avis ? Expliquez votre réponse.

Expansion: **7-7** Have students describe their own health issues, and let classmates suggest a suitable remedy.

7-7 Pour une meilleure santé Qu'est-ce que ces personnes peuvent faire pour avoir une meilleure santé ? Avec un/e partenaire, offrez des suggestions.

MODÈLE Sarah veut faire de l'exercice, mais elle n'est pas douée pour le sport.
É1 Elle peut faire de la marche, par exemple.
É2 Elle peut faire du vélo aussi.

1. Adrien veut maigir de dix kilos.
2. Gaëlle et Alexandra veulent se détendre.
3. Je veux dormir mieux la nuit.
4. Nous voulons manger mieux.
5. Jean-Baptiste veut arrêter de fumer.
6. Audrey est très douée pour le sport.
7. Simon et David veulent boire moins d'alcool.

Implementation: **7-8** First brainstorm with the whole class some appropriate questions for each item. Examples:
1. Où est-ce que tu veux voyager ?
2. Est-ce que tu veux te marier ?
3. Est-ce que tu veux avoir des enfants ? Combien ?
4. Est-ce que tu veux gagner beaucoup d'argent ?

Then put students in pairs to compare answers.

7-8 Vouloir, c'est pouvoir. Qu'est-ce que vous voulez faire après l'université ? Comparez vos idées avec celles d'un/e partenaire.

MODÈLE habiter
É1 Où est-ce que tu veux habiter ?
É2 Moi, je veux habiter une grande ville, comme New York. Et toi ?
É1 Moi, je ne veux pas habiter une grande ville ; je veux habiter à la campagne.

1. habiter
2. voyager
3. se marier
4. avoir des enfants
5. gagner de l'argent

Expansion: **7-9** As a follow-up, have each student share his / her excuse, then vote on who has the most original / the most plausible / the most far-fetched excuse.

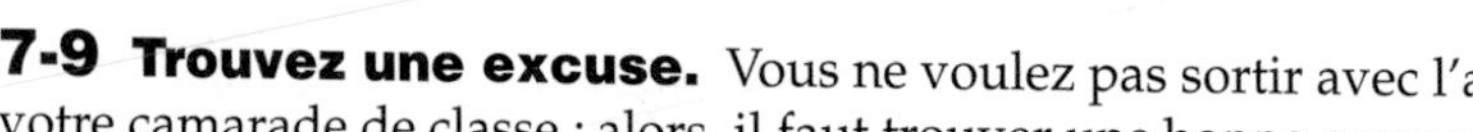

7-9 Trouvez une excuse. Vous ne voulez pas sortir avec l'ami/e de votre camarade de classe ; alors, il faut trouver une bonne excuse !

MODÈLE • Je ne peux pas sortir ce soir avec ton ami/e ; je dois préparer un examen et téléphoner à mes parents.

2. L'imparfait et le passé composé : description et narration

As you know, both the **passé composé** and the **imparfait** express past actions and states. They serve different functions in a narrative, however.

- The **passé composé** indicates that an event in the past has been completed. In a story or narrative, the **passé composé** is used to recount actions or events that move the story forward. In other words, the **passé composé** advances the plot; it answers the question, *What happened?* Consider the opening sentences of the following narrative.

Bruno **a terminé** son match de raquetball à 16h. Il **a quitté** le gymnase.	*Bruno finished his racquetball game at 4 pm. He left the gym.*

- In contrast, the **imparfait** provides background information. It describes the setting or situation and answers the questions: *What were the circumstances? What was going on?* Compare the use of the **passé composé** and the **imparfait** as the narrative about Bruno's experience continues:

Bruno **était** fatigué. Il **voulait** manger. Mais il **devait** rentrer pour se doucher d'abord. Donc il **a pris** le bus pour aller chez lui. Et il **s'est lavé**. Finalement, il **a téléphoné** à Diane pour aller dîner. Il **se sentait** beaucoup mieux déjà !	*Bruno was tired. He wanted to eat. But he had to go home to take a shower first. So he took the bus home. And he got cleaned up. Finally, he called Diane to go have dinner. He felt much better already!*

- Use the **imparfait** to describe time, weather, ongoing actions, physical characteristics, psychological states and feelings, intentions, and thoughts. The following verbs, when used in the past, usually appear in the **imparfait**.

avoir	Elle **avait** vingt ans en 2012.
devoir	Elle **devait** consulter son médecin.
être	Ils **étaient** contents de maigrir un peu.
faire	Il **faisait** froid. (*in weather expressions*)
penser	Je **pensais** qu'elle avait mal partout après notre randonnée.
pouvoir	Il ne **pouvait** pas suivre de régime.
vouloir	Ils ne **voulaient** pas grignoter entre les repas.

Presentation: Review the forms of the *passé composé* and the *imparfait* before introducing this topic. This section contrasting the two tenses focuses on the functions of description and narration; the terms "background" and "foreground" can also be used. Have students study the examples in the second bullet point to decide whether they involve description or narration; for visual impact, you might divide these examples into two columns.

Presentation: Provide additional examples related to the **Fiche pratique**: *Ils ont été à Paris* (They went to Paris); *Elle n'a pas voulu le faire* (She refused to do it); *Elle a pu ouvrir la porte* (She managed to open the door).

Fiche pratique

Certain verbs, when used in the past, generally occur in the **imparfait**. When these verbs are used in the **passé composé**, they have a specific meaning. Compare, for example: **elle avait dix ans** (*she was ten years old*) and **elle a eu dix ans** (*she turned ten / celebrated her tenth birthday*).

À vous la parole

11 • 14

7-10 Des excuses. Pourquoi est-ce que ces gens ne sont pas venus en classe ? Expliquez la situation ou l'évènement, selon le cas.

MODÈLE Vanessa : elle / être malade
• Vanessa n'est pas venue parce qu'elle était malade.

David : il / tomber dans les escaliers
• David n'est pas venu parce qu'il est tombé dans les escaliers.

1. Ben : sa mère / téléphoner lui a téléphoné
2. Adrien : il / rater l'autobus a raté
3. Marie : elle / avoir mal à la tête avait
4. Guillaume : son chien / manger ses devoirs a mangé
5. Annick : elle / préparer un examen préparait
6. Grégory : il / travailler à la bibliothèque travaillait
7. Claire : elle / avoir un accident a eu
8. Koffi : il / devoir terminer un rapport devait terminer

Note: 7-10 Students saw the past participle of *venir* in Ch. 4, L. 2. The full conjugation is presented in Ch. 8, L. 2.

Expansion: 7-10 After completing the exercise, have students give you their own excuses for not coming to class, not doing their homework, etc.

Note: 7-11 Since choice of the *passé composé* vs. *imparfait* often depends on the speaker's perspective, in some cases either tense can be correct.

Key: 7-11 1) faisait 2) avait 3) allais 4) est passée 5) ai essayé, ne pouvais pas/n'ai pas pu 6) ai heurté 7) sont sortis 8) n'étaient pas 9) étais, n'a été blessé/n'était blessé 10) ai téléphoné 11) sont arrivés

Implementation: 7-12 To simplify, lead students through the story by asking questions as you display the drawings (MFL, Instructor's Resources). Then have students use the key expressions provided (plus others, if you like) to describe their day yesterday. Use your own day as a model. Let students work in pairs and report back what they learned about their partner's day.

Key: 7-12 *Hier, c'était samedi. Adrien s'est réveillé à huit heures. Il faisait beau. Il n'avait pas de cours. Adrien était à table. Le téléphone a sonné. C'était Julie. Elle voulait jouer au tennis. Adrien a dit « oui ». L'après-midi, il faisait chaud et ils ont joué au tennis. Adrien est tombé. Julie était anxieuse. Ils sont allés à l'hôpital. Le médecin a dit que ce n'était pas sérieux.*

7-11 Un accident de voiture. Racontez cette histoire au passé ; employez le passé composé ou l'imparfait, selon le cas.

MODÈLE Il est huit heures du soir.
- Il était huit heures du soir.

1. Il fait très froid.
2. Il y a du verglas sur la route.
3. Je vais un peu vite (*fast*).
4. Soudain, une autre voiture passe devant moi.
5. J'essaye de m'arrêter, mais je ne peux pas.
6. Je heurte (*hit*) l'autre voiture.
7. Deux hommes sortent de cette voiture.
8. Ils ne sont pas contents.
9. Mais moi, je suis content parce que personne n'est blessé (*injured*).
10. Je téléphone à la police.
11. Ils arrivent tout de suite après.

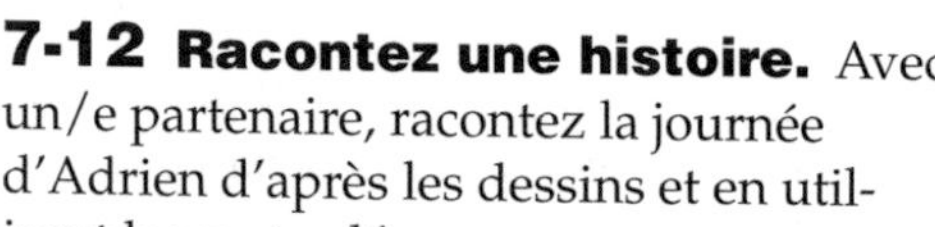

7-12 Racontez une histoire. Avec un/e partenaire, racontez la journée d'Adrien d'après les dessins et en utilisant les mots-clés.

MODÈLE • Hier, c'était samedi. Adrien s'est réveillé à huit heures, …

A. **être samedi, se réveiller, faire beau, ne pas avoir cours**

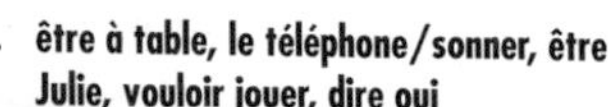

B. **être à table, le téléphone/sonner, être Julie, vouloir jouer, dire oui**

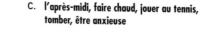

C. **l'après-midi, faire chaud, jouer au tennis, tomber, être anxieuse**

D. **aller à l'hôpital, le médecin / dire / ne pas être sérieux**

Maintenant, racontez votre journée d'hier à un/e partenaire.

Stratégie

When you need to give advice in writing, remember that there are different ways to go about it. You can be direct and use the imperative, or you can use expressions such as **il faut** and **il est important de.** Also, you can use forms of the verbs **devoir** or **pouvoir** to lay out alternatives.

Écrivons

Implementation: *Avant d'écrire.* Begin by treating the text as a reading. Help students understand the meaning of unfamiliar words using cognates and context; find a synonym for *supprimer* and *sauter* (*éliminer*). Walk them through the analysis of the question and response, which serves as a model for their own writing.

7-13 Les conseils du docteur.

A. Avant d'écrire. Dans le journal *La Gazette du Matin*, le docteur Kabango répond aux lecteurs qui demandent des conseils pour se remettre en bonne forme.

Analysez une lettre et sa réponse :

1. Quel est le problème posé par le lecteur ? Qu'est-ce que le lecteur propose de faire ?
2. Est-ce que le docteur Kabango trouve que ce sont des bonnes solutions ? Quels sont ses conseils ? Comment est-ce qu'il les exprime ?

POUR GARDER LA FORME

LES CONSEILS DU DOCTEUR KABANGO

J'ai tendance à grossir et je voudrais commencer un régime pour maigrir. Est-ce que je devrais éliminer toutes les graisses[1] de mon régime ? Est-ce que je pourrais supprimer complètement certains repas ?

Dr Kabango : *Il est important de faire attention de ne pas trop grossir. Mais il faut surtout éviter de sauter des repas. Vous devez faire des repas équilibrés, donc, manger des graisses en quantité raisonnable. Consommez beaucoup de fruits et de légumes avec des protéines équilibrées comme le yaourt et le fromage. Surtout ne grignotez pas entre les repas ou quand vous regardez la télévision. N'oubliez pas le rôle de l'exercice physique pour maintenir votre poids[2] idéal.*

[1]*fat* [2]*weight*

B. En écrivant. Le docteur Kabango part en vacances et c'est maintenant à vous de répondre aux lecteurs ! Examinez les lettres suivantes et choisissez une lettre à laquelle vous voudriez répondre.

Implementation: *En écrivant.* You might go over both letters before having students write. Writing can be completed as a whole-class, small group, pair, or individual activity. Follow up as indicated in **En révisant** and **Après avoir écrit**.

J'ai 28 ans. Depuis cinq ans, je ne fais plus de sport et j'ai grossi de dix kilos — surtout au ventre. Je voudrais recommencer à faire du sport. Qu'est-ce que vous me conseillez ?

J'ai beaucoup de responsabilités au travail et je ne trouve pas le temps pour me détendre. En plus, je ne dors pas bien et je commence à faire des migraines. Je me sens[1] de plus en plus stressé. Qu'est-ce que vous me conseillez pour retrouver mon équilibre ?

[1]*feel*

1. D'abord analysez la lettre. Quel est le problème posé ?
2. Faites une liste des stratégies spécifiques que vous voulez proposer pour solutionner le problème. Décidez comment vous pouvez exprimer ces stratégies de façon concise et variée.
3. Ensuite, écrivez votre réponse.

C. En révisant. Maintenant relisez votre réponse et réfléchissez aux questions suivantes. Faites tous les changements nécessaires.

1. Analysez le contenu : est-ce que vous avez bien identifié le problème ? Est-ce que vous proposez des solutions pratiques ?
2. Examinez le style et la forme : est-ce que vous avez utilisé des formes appropriées et variées pour offrir des conseils ?

D. Après avoir écrit. Échangez votre lettre avec celle d'un/e camarade de classe. Qui a écrit les conseils les plus pratiques et efficaces (*effective*) ? Partagez vos idées avec tous vos camarades.

Leçon 2 Les grands évènements de la vie

Presentation: Use the photographs (MFL, Instructor's Resources) to tell the story of important events in Sophie's life. Point out cultural information conveyed by the photos and captions: Catholic customs and holidays, the civil and religious wedding ceremonies. Include information contained in the **Vie et culture** notes. Encourage cross-cultural comparison by asking what major childhood events students' own family albums contain that are not pictured here. Some examples might include: first day of school, rituals related to other faith traditions, prom, graduation. Test comprehension by having students point to the event you describe; tell the date of Sophie's birthday and of their own birthday. Have students repeat key words. Adapt by creating your own slide show of noteworthy events in your own family.

POINTS DE DÉPART

Les grands évènements

La mère de Sophie regarde son album de photos.

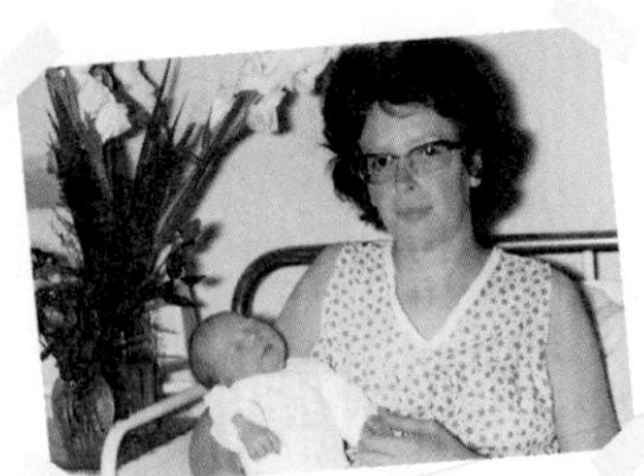

Le 9 mai 1985, Sophie est née ; elle était adorable !

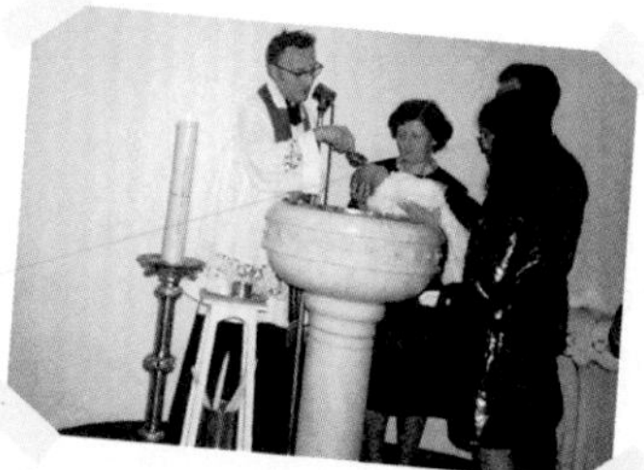

Voilà Sophie à son baptême, avec sa marraine et son parrain.

Le jour de Noël 1987 ; Sophie avait 2 ans. Que de cadeaux !

C'était l'anniversaire de Sophie : elle a fait un vœu et elle a soufflé les bougies!

L'été 2000, Sophie a passé les grandes vacances à la plage avec son amie Virginie.

Le mariage de Sophie et Arnaud. La cérémonie civile a eu lieu à la mairie et ensuite la cérémonie religieuse, à l'église ; la mariée était en blanc, le marié en smoking ! Les voilà avec le prêtre et leurs témoins.

Implementation: Create a chart to summarize, with columns for students to fill in: *Nom de la fête ; Date ; Activités spécifiques.* Let students add in American holidays (Halloween, Thanksgiving, and 4th of July, for example), to discuss similarities and differences. Show the video montage *Les rites et les rituels*, which features various national and religious holidays and rituals. See if students can match the events they see in the clip to holidays and events mentioned here. Point out the following vocabulary: *jour férié, galette, cacher, œuf en chocolat, muguet, défilé, bal populaire, feu d'artifice, fleur.* Students will need these words to complete the exercises and will find them useful to talk about holidays in general. Captions have not been provided for the photos; encourage students to identify the holiday illustrated in each: *Pâques, le premier mai/la fête du Travail, la Chandeleur.*

Vie et culture

Les fêtes religieuses et officielles

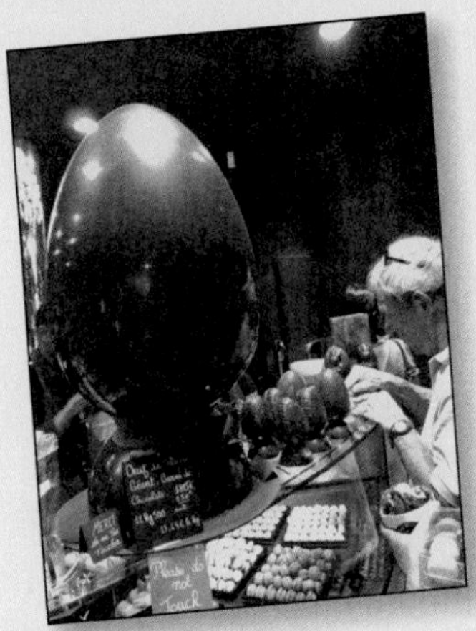

Certains jours fériés en France sont des fêtes traditionnelles catholiques et d'autres sont des fêtes nationales.

Noël est la plus grande fête de l'année. On décore le sapin et l'on échange des cadeaux. Le soir du 24 décembre, on prépare un grand dîner, le réveillon.

Le jour de l'An est précédé par le réveillon de la Saint-Sylvestre, la nuit du 31 décembre.

Le jour des Rois (l'Épiphanie) a lieu le 6 janvier. On partage un gâteau, la galette des rois, dans lequel on a caché la fève — un petit personnage en plastique ou en céramique. La personne qui trouve la fève dans sa part de galette est nommée le roi ou la reine[1] et porte une couronne en papier.

La Chandeleur, c'est le 2 février. Traditionnellement, on mange des crêpes. Si vous faites sauter[2] une crêpe et elle retombe dans la poêle[3], vous allez avoir de la chance toute l'année.

Pâques. Pour Pâques, en France on peut voir des œufs et des poules[4] en chocolat dans les vitrines de toutes les pâtisseries et les confiseries. Le lundi de Pâques est un jour férié.

La fête du Travail. Le premier mai, on organise des défilés et l'on offre du muguet[5] aux membres de sa famille. C'est aussi un jour férié.

La fête nationale. Cette grande fête célèbre le début de la Révolution le 14 juillet 1789. Le matin, les Parisiens assistent au grand défilé militaire sur les Champs-Élysées, retransmis en direct à la télévision. Le soir, toutes les villes organisent des bals populaires et l'on tire un feu d'artifice.

Expansion: Suggest that students get more information about unfamiliar holidays that interest them by looking them up on the Internet and reporting to the class. Or, put students into small groups to discuss a) their favorite holiday and how they celebrate it, or b) the most significant holiday for North Americans, and why.

La Toussaint. Le 1er novembre, on honore les morts de la famille en mettant des fleurs, surtout des chrysanthèmes, sur leur tombe.

Le Ramadan. Le ramadan est un rituel pratiqué par les musulmans. On compte entre cinq et six millions de musulmans en France, où l'islam est la deuxième religion après le catholicisme. Le ramadan est une période de jeûne[6]. Pendant cette période, les musulmans ne peuvent ni manger, ni[7] boire pendant la journée. Mais au coucher du soleil, les familles et les amis partagent des grands repas.

ET VOUS ?

07-52

1. Regardez la séquence vidéo, *Les rites et les rituels*. Quelles occasions est-ce qu'on fête ?
2. Est-ce que vous célébrez certaines de ces fêtes dans votre région ? Est-ce que vos traditions sont différentes des traditions des Français ? Expliquez pourquoi.
3. À votre avis, est-ce que les fêtes nationales sont plus importantes chez vous que chez les Français ? Et les fêtes religieuses ?

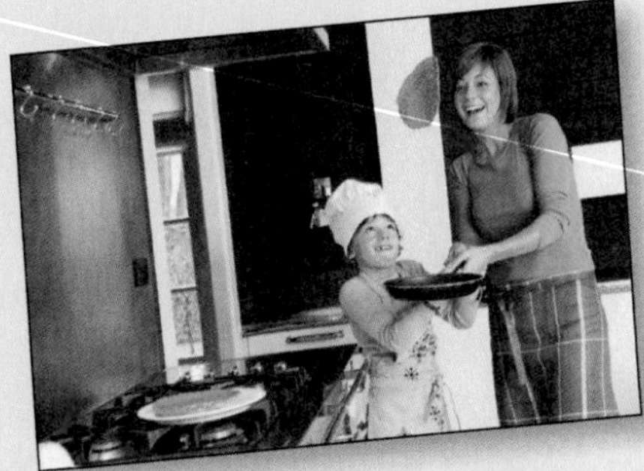

[1] *king or queen* [2] *flip* [3] *frying pan* [4] *hens*
[5] *lily of the valley* [6] *fasting* [7] *neither, nor*

Implementation: Read the expressions aloud and model pronunciation. Point out the liaison with *Bon anniversaire !* and *Joyeux anniversaire !* Go back to the events in Sophie's life and have students decide which would be the most appropriate greeting/s in each case; follow up with Ex. 7-14.

LES VŒUX

Meilleurs vœux !	*Best wishes!*
Félicitations !	*Congratulations!*
Bon/Joyeux anniversaire !	*Happy Birthday!*
Joyeux anniversaire de mariage !	*Happy Anniversary!*
Joyeux Noël !	*Merry Christmas!*
Bonne année !	*Happy New Year!*
Bon voyage !	*Have a good trip!*
Bonnes vacances !	*Have a good vacation!*

À vous la parole

07-18 to 07-21

7-14 Qu'est-ce qu'on dit ? Qu'est-ce que vous dites dans les situations suivantes ? *Answers may vary.*

MODÈLE C'est l'anniversaire de votre mère.
- Je dis, « Bon anniversaire, maman ! »

1. Vos amis ont eu un enfant. Félicitations !
2. C'est le 25 décembre. Joyeux Noël !
3. C'est la Saint-Sylvestre. Bonne année !
4. Vous assistez à un mariage. Meilleurs vœux ! / Félicitations !
5. Votre ami fête ses 20 ans. Bon/Joyeux anniversaire !
6. Vos parents fêtent leurs 25 ans de mariage. Joyeux anniversaire de mariage !
7. C'est le jour de l'An. Bonne année !
8. Vos cousins partent en voyage. Bon voyage !

Implementation: **7-15** Since multiple responses are possible, you might have each group make a list and compare answers at the end. The video montage (*Les rites et les rituels*) could accompany Ex. 7-15, since many of the items listed can be seen in the clip.

7-15 Jeu d'association. À quelle occasion est-ce que vous associez ces choses ou ces personnes ? Parlez-en avec un/e partenaire.

MODÈLE un voyage

É1 Ce sont les grandes vacances.

É2 C'est un mariage.

1. un gâteau
2. des cadeaux
3. un document officiel
4. un grand dîner
5. un défilé militaire
6. des fleurs
7. la marraine
8. le maire (*mayor*)
9. le prêtre (*priest*), le pasteur, le rabbin, l'imam
10. un bébé

7-16 Tous les éléments. Quels sont les éléments importants pour une fête ? Avec un/e partenaire, décrivez une fête d'après les éléments suivants : **l'endroit, les gens importants, les vêtements/les accessoires, les activités.**

MODÈLE un anniversaire

É1 On peut fêter un anniversaire à la maison ou dans un restaurant, par exemple.

É2 Normalement, la famille et les amis sont présents. Il y a souvent un gâteau avec des bougies.

É1 Oui, on chante et on offre des cadeaux.

1. Noël
2. un mariage
3. un baptême
4. la fête nationale
5. les grandes vacances

FORMES ET FONCTIONS

1. L'imparfait et le passé composé : d'autres contrastes

As you have seen, the choice of the **imparfait** or the **passé composé** to express past events or circumstances often depends on the context and the speaker's view of the action or situation.

- Use the **passé composé** to express:
  - an action or state that occurred at a specific point in time:

Elle est née **le jeudi 9 mai 1991**.	*She was born on Thursday, May 9, 1991.*

  - an action or state that occurred a specified number of times:

Elle a visité le Canada **deux fois**.	*She visited Canada twice.*

- Use the **imparfait** to express:
  - enduring states in the past:

Cécile était une enfant très sérieuse.	*Cécile was a very studious child.*

  - habitual actions in the past:

D'habitude, sa famille allait au parc **le dimanche**.	*Usually his family would go to the park on Sundays.*

- Use the **imparfait** to express an ongoing action or state interrupted by another action, which is expressed by the **passé composé**.

Sophie **regardait** la télé quand sa marraine **a téléphoné**.	*Sophie was watching TV when her godmother called.*
Ils **quittaient** l'église quand il **a commencé** à pleuvoir.	*They were leaving the church when it started to rain.*

- Finally, some actions or states can be expressed either in the **passé composé** or the **imparfait**, depending on what the speaker means to say.

Elle **était** malade pendant les vacances.	*She was sick during the vacation.* (emphasis on her state of being sick)
Elle **a été** malade pendant les vacances.	*She got sick during the vacation.* (emphasis on the act of getting sick)
Il **avait** peur.	*He was afraid.*
Il **a eu** peur.	*He got scared/Something scared him.*

Presentation: Review uses of the *passé composé* and *imparfait* as presented in Ch. 6, L. 3 and Ch. 7, L. 1. First, have students brainstorm to list uses of each tense; use this summary as a point of departure for review practice before presenting the new information. A narrative such as that provided in Ex. 7-11 or 7-12, or in the corresponding section of the SAM/MFL, would offer a good basis for review. This section focuses on adverbial cues to one-time versus habitual actions in the past and the use of the *imparfait* for ongoing actions as opposed to punctual actions. Review the various adverbial cues to repeated/habitual action, including use of the definite article with days of the week: *dimanche* (on Sunday) vs. *le dimanche* (on Sundays).

Fiche pratique

The **imparfait** can often be translated as "used to . . . ," "would . . . ," "was [doing something]," or "was feeling . . ." When in doubt about whether to use the **imparfait** or the **passé composé**, try substituting these expressions in the sentence to see whether one of them fits the context.

Initial practice: Begin with a discrimination drill: have students decide whether you are describing a one-time or habitual action. *J'allais souvent au cinéma. Un jour, j'ai vu un film extraordinaire. Je partais souvent en vacances avec ma famille. On est allés au Canada deux fois. L'été dernier, on a visité le Rocher percé et l'île Bonaventure.*

07-22 to 07-25

À vous la parole

7-17 L'exception confirme la règle ! Le semestre passé, Chloé avait des habitudes très précises. Mais le jour de son examen final, elle a eu des problèmes. Expliquez !

Note: 7-17 This exercise contrasts one-time events with habitual actions in the past.

MODÈLE arriver en avance
- D'habitude, elle arrivait en avance.
- Mais ce jour-là, elle n'est pas arrivée en avance.

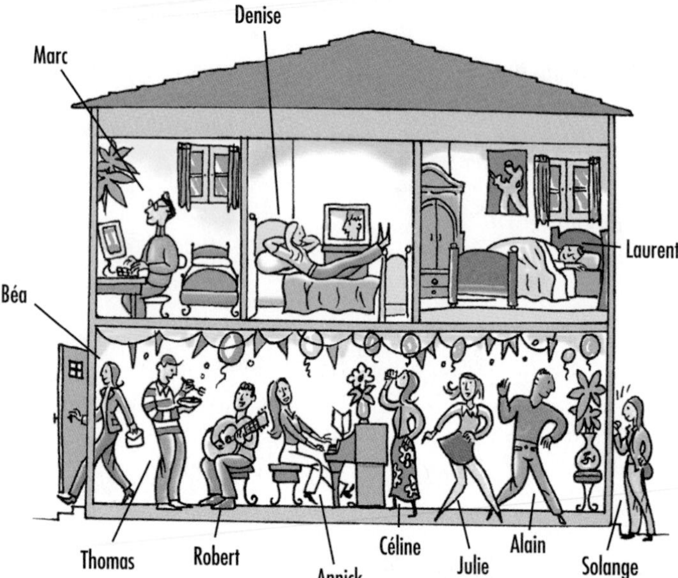

1. quitter la maison à huit heures quittait, n'a pas quitté
2. arriver la première arrivait, n'est pas arrivée
3. apporter son cahier apportait, n'a pas apporté
4. réviser sa leçon révisait, n'a pas révisé
5. finir ses devoirs finissait, n'a pas fini
6. ne pas oublier ses livres n'oubliait pas, a oublié
7. travailler à la bibliothèque travaillait, n'a pas travaillé
8. appeler ses amis appelait, n'a pas appelé

7-18 Qu'est-ce qu'ils faisaient ? Décrivez ce que ces gens faisaient quand Solange est arrivée à la fête.

MODÈLE • Quand Solange est arrivée, Marc travaillait dans sa chambre.

Note: 7-18 This exercise contrasts ongoing actions interrupted by punctual specific actions in the past. Use the house visual (MFL, Instructor's Resources) to cue.

Key: 7-18 Denise regardait la télé ; Laurent dormait ; Alain et Julie dansaient ; Céline buvait ; Annick jouait du piano ; Robert jouait de la guitare ; Thomas mangeait ; Béa partait

Implementation: 7-19 This exercise mixes ongoing states, habitual actions, and one-time events in the past. To simplify and allow students to focus on the verb forms, brainstorm with students or supply a list of adjectives and verb infinitives for them to choose from. Point out that #8 refers to the plans students had for the future when they were 15; for example, *Je voulais être médecin.*

7-19 Mes quinze ans. Avec un/e partenaire, parlez de vos quinze ans. Comment est-ce que vous étiez ? Qu'est-ce que vous faisiez ? Qu'est-ce que vous avez fait ?

MODÈLES le caractère

É1 Moi, à quinze ans, j'étais très timide.

É2 Moi, à quinze ans, j'étais très indépendant et individualiste.

les voyages

É1 À quinze ans, je suis allée à Washington, D.C. pour visiter les monuments et les musées.

É2 Et moi, je suis allé en Floride avec ma famille.

1. le caractère
2. le physique
3. les amis
4. le sport
5. les voyages
6. les études
7. la musique
8. les projets d'avenir

Presentation: This treatment allows for recycling of adjective placement and prenominal adjective forms, taught in Ch. 3, L. 3. Review those before presenting this new material. Point out to students that adjectives like *belle* follow the same pattern as the demonstrative, with two spoken and three written forms in the singular: *belle/bel/beau ; cette/cet/ce.*

2. L'adjectif démonstratif

- The demonstrative adjective is used to point out specific people or things that are close at hand. The singular form corresponds to *this* or *that* in English, the plural, to *these* or *those.*

Tu aimes **les** fêtes ?	*Do you like holidays (in general)?*
Tu aimes **cette** fête ?	*Do you like this holiday?*

- Note the masculine singular form used before a noun beginning with a vowel sound. It is pronounced like the feminine form but has a different spelling.

Regarde **ce** gros gâteau !	*Look at this big cake!*
Regarde **cet** œuf en chocolat !	*Look at that chocolate egg!*
Regarde **cette** belle mariée !	*Look at that beautiful bride!*

- Here are the forms of the demonstrative adjective.

	FÉMININ	MASCULIN	
		devant voyelle	*devant consonne*
SINGULIER	**cette** fête	**cet**‿anniversaire	**ce** gâteau
PLURIEL	**ces**‿affiches	**ces**‿anniversaires	**ces** cadeaux

À vous la parole

26

29 **7-20 Un mariage à la mosquée.** Voici des commentaires sur un mariage musulman à la mosquée de Paris. Pour chaque commentaire, décidez si l'on parle d'un homme ou d'une femme.

	homme	femme
MODÈLE • Cet iman fait une prière.	✓	
1. Cette mariée est habillée en blanc.		✓
2. Ce marié lui offre le cadeau traditionnel, le mahr.	✓	
3. Cet invité accompagne le marié.	✓	
4. Cet iman lit un texte du Koran.	✓	
5. Cette enfant est adorable.		✓
6. Ce témoin observe quand on signe le contrat de mariage.	✓	
7. Cette invitée va à la réception pour les femmes.		✓
8. Cet invité va au dîner, le Walima.	✓	

Est-ce qu'il y a plus d'hommes ou de femmes à la cérémonie ?

Implementation: 7-20 Begin with this comprehension-based activity that focuses students' attention on written cues to gender. Following Ex. 7-20, you might provide listening practice with a simple discrimination drill: *masculin, féminin ou impossible à dire ? Regarde ce gâteau ; cette poule en chocolat ; ce muguet ; ces bougies ; cet œuf ; ce sapin ; cette fleur ; ce cadeau*, etc. Follow with a substitution drill: *Tu aimes cette fête ? gâteau. — Tu aimes ce gâteau ? ; bougies ; cadeau ; sapin ; vacances ; cérémonie ; église*, etc.

7-21 Regarde ça ! Imaginez que vous regardez des photos dans un album. Montrez les choses que vous remarquez à votre ami/e.

MODÈLE un gros gâteau
• Regarde ce gros gâteau !

1. une belle église cette belle église
2. des beaux feux d'artifice ces beaux feux d'artifice
3. des bougies ces bougies
4. des œufs en chocolat ces œufs en chocolat
5. un pot de chrysanthèmes ce pot de chrysanthèmes
6. des cadeaux magnifiques ces cadeaux magnifiques
7. un grand sapin ce grand sapin
8. du muguet ce muguet

Implementation: 7-21 This exercise can be cued with visuals if you have them available.

Implementation: 7-22 This exercise allows students to practice dislocation, a very common and useful structure in spoken French. It recycles information from the **Vie et culture** notes of this lesson and can be used in conjunction with that topic if you wish. Answers will vary, but culturally appropriate responses have been included for some items.

Additional practice: You might have students work in pairs to create definitions with which to test their classmates. This could be structured as a game with two teams.

Qu'est-ce que c'est ?
Proposez une définition ; vos camarades de classe doivent trouver la réponse.

MODÈLES É1 Ces fleurs sont pour les tombes le premier novembre.
É2 Ce sont des chrysanthèmes.
É3 Cette cérémonie a lieu dans une église, souvent avec un bébé.
É4 C'est un baptême.

Implementation: *Avant de regarder.* You might work with students to develop this list and put the expressions on the board. See the SAM/MFL for activities that accompany the third speaker, a young woman who discusses her experiences with the rites of baptism and communion in the Catholic Church.

Script: *Observons*

MARIE-JULIE : Je m'appelle Marie-Julie Kerharo, mais à toutes les fois où* je rentre au Québec, c'est Marie-Julie Lavoie parce qu'au Québec, les femmes doivent préserver leur nom de jeune fille tout le reste de leur vie. C'est une loi qui date des années 80, si je ne m'abuse pas, c'est 1986. Et depuis lors, les femmes n'ont pas le choix, elles doivent garder leur nom de jeune fille, même si elles sont mariées.

*In Standard French, *mais toutes les fois que...*

MONSIEUR LE MAIRE DE SEILLANS : Bonjour, j'ai le plaisir de vous accueillir dans la salle des mariages de la commune de Seillans. Je suis le maire et en cette qualité, je célèbre les mariages des habitants de la commune. C'est une cérémonie officielle, qui consiste à recueillir le consentement des mariés, en présence de deux ou quatre témoins.

BARBARA : Bonjour, bonjour Monsieur le maire.

M. LE MAIRE : Bonjour, Barbara.

BARBARA : Voilà, je m'appelle Barbara Roustan, je suis, euh, j'habite à Seillans. Il ne faut pas oublier aussi, je me suis mariée en 1988 dans cette salle de mariage. Et c'était un petit peu original parce que ma future belle-mère à l'époque était le maire de Seillans en 1988 et donc, elle était très émue à l'issue de ce mariage, de nous marier, et c'était magnifique, parce que c'était très familial et en même temps, c'était un mariage, voilà, un petit peu spécial.

7-22 Qu'est-ce que vous offrez ? Imaginez que vous offrez un cadeau et identifiez l'occasion. *Answers will vary.*

MODÈLE du muguet
• Ce muguet, c'est pour le premier mai.

1. des chrysanthèmes *Ces chrysanthèmes, c'est pour la Toussaint.*
2. une poule en chocolat *Cette poule en chocolat, c'est pour Pâques.*
3. des roses rouges *Ces roses rouges, ...*
4. une carte de vœux *Cette carte de vœux, c'est pour le Nouvel An (par exemple).*
5. un gâteau au chocolat *Ce gâteau au chocolat, ...*
6. une galette *Cette galette, c'est pour la fête des Rois.*
7. des crêpes *Ces crêpes, c'est pour la Chandeleur.*
8. un gros bouquet de fleurs *Ce gros bouquet de fleurs, ...*

Observons

07-53 to 07-55

7-23 Rites et traditions.

A. Avant de regarder. Vous allez écouter des personnes qui parlent d'évènements importants dans leur vie. Quels sont les évènements les plus importants dans la vie d'une personne ? Préparez une liste avec vos camarades de classe.

MODÈLE • la naissance (*birth*) d'un enfant, le baptême, la bar et la bat mitsva...

B. En regardant. Pour chaque personne, répondez aux questions.

Marie-Julie

1. Marie-Julie explique qu'au Québec, lorsqu'elles se marient, les femmes doivent garder...
   a. leur nom de jeune fille (circled) b. le nom de leur mari c. les deux noms
2. C'est...
   a. une vieille coutume b. une loi récente (circled)
   c. une tradition dans certaines familles

Monsieur le Maire de Seillans et Barbara

3. Pour lui, le mariage est un acte...
   a. de foi (*faith*) b. familial c. officiel (circled)
4. Les participants à la cérémonie sont : le maire, les mariés, et...
   a. leurs parents b. leurs amis c. leurs témoins (circled)
5. Pour Barbara, son mariage était un peu spécial parce que... était le maire.
   a. sa mère b. sa future belle-mère (circled) c. son futur mari

C. Après avoir regardé. Maintenant discutez des questions suivantes avec vos camarades de classe.

1. Est-ce que les femmes qui se marient chez vous peuvent choisir leur nom ? Quelles sont les traditions dans votre communauté ?
2. En quoi est-ce que les mariages chez vous sont semblables aux mariages en France et au Québec ? En quoi est-ce qu'ils sont différents ?

Leçon 3 Les émotions

POINTS DE DÉPART

Pour exprimer les sentiments et les émotions

MÉLANIE : Tu as l'air content, toi !
ANTOINE : En effet, je suis ravi. Écoute la bonne nouvelle : mon frère s'est fiancé. Il va se marier au mois de juin.
MÉLANIE : C'est super. Elle est comment, sa fiancée ?
ANTOINE : Elle est très sympa ; on s'entend bien. Mais dis-moi, qu'est-ce que tu as, toi ? Tu n'as pas l'air heureuse. Tu te fais du souci ?
MÉLANIE : Eh bien, je suis assez inquiète ; je n'ai pas de nouvelles de ma sœur. Elle a eu un bébé le mois dernier et elle se dispute beaucoup avec son mari. Elle doit se reposer, mais c'est elle qui fait tout le travail.
ANTOINE : Calme-toi. Elle est probablement trop occupée pour t'appeler. Téléphone-lui.

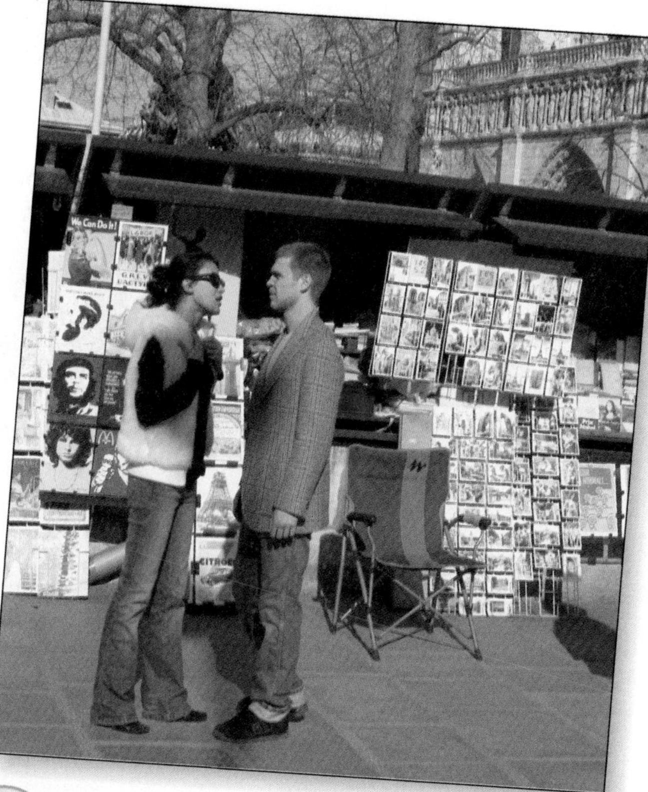

LES SENTIMENTS

être heureux / -euse, content / e, ravi / e
être inquiet / inquiète, anxieux / -euse
être furieux / -euse, fâché / e, en colère
être amoureux / -euse ; tomber amoureux / -euse
être triste, malheureux / -euse
être surpris / e
être embarrassé / e, gêné / e
être jaloux / -ouse

Presentation: Begin by having students listen to the dialogue as they look at the photo and text. Then use mime and description to present the vocabulary list in the shaded box. Finally, use the illustrations of emotions (MFL, Instructor's Resources) to model typical phrases; describe the situations by re-using the key vocabulary. Test comprehension by having students point to a picture of the attitude you describe or mime the emotion. Have students repeat key words and phrases: *Elle est heureuse ou elle est furieuse ?*, etc.

QU'EST-CE QU'ON DIT QUAND ON PERD SON SANG-FROID ?

Presentation: Point out that *sois* and *soyez* are irregular imperative forms for the verb *être*.

Vie et culture

Les Français s'expriment

Il y a beaucoup d'expressions fixes que les Français utilisent pour exprimer les émotions. (L'accent et l'intonation sont très importants aussi !) Est-ce que vous pouvez marier les expressions de la colonne de gauche aux émotions de la colonne de droite ?

1. Mon Dieu ! Oh, là, là ! b
2. Super ! Sensationnel ! Formidable ! a
3. Oh, pardon ! Je suis désolé/e ! e
4. Oh, zut ! Mince ! g
5. Bof ! Ça m'est égal. c
6. Ma chérie/mon chéri, mon cœur, ma puce d
7. C'est pas vrai ! Pas possible ! Incroyable ! f
8. Espèce d'imbécile ! Crétin ! Quel idiot ! h

a. la joie
b. l'inquiétude
c. l'indifférence
d. la tendresse
e. l'embarras
f. la surprise
g. la frustration
h. la colère

Presentation: Relate the exclamations in the **Vie et culture** to the emotions presented earlier. Provide formal and familiar forms where appropriate. Have students listen to the recording and repeat the phrases. Demonstrate the proper intonation patterns, including the *accent d'insistance émotionnelle : **F**ormidable ! **Cr**étin !*, etc. Many terms of endearment are based on names for animals: *ma puce, ma biche*, etc.

ET VOUS ?

Le mot juste. Qu'est-ce que vous dites dans les situations suivantes ? Choisissez votre réponse dans la liste ci-dessus (*above*).

1. Vous avez perdu vos devoirs. 4
2. Vous avez eu une bonne note à un examen difficile. 2
3. Vos amis hésitent entre le cinéma ou un DVD ; vous n'avez pas d'opinion. 5
4. Vous regardez un enfant adorable, votre nièce ou votre neveu. 6
5. Votre colocataire a emprunté votre livre de français et l'a perdu. 4, 7, 8
6. Vous avez fait tomber un vase chez la grand-mère de votre ami. 3
7. Vous apprenez que votre ami/e a eu un accident de voiture. 1, 7

À vous la parole

7-24 Lire les expressions de la figure. Est-ce que vous et votre partenaire savez lire les émotions peintes sur le visage d'une personne ?

MODÈLE É1 Cette dame a l'air malheureuse ; peut-être qu'elle a entendu des mauvaises nouvelles.
É2 Je pense qu'elle est anxieuse parce qu'elle n'a pas de nouvelles de son ami.

Implementation: 7-24, 7-25 Students may work in pairs or groups. Have them come up with as many alternatives as possible, then compare notes with the class as a whole.

Expansion: 7-24, 7-25 For each item, have students choose an appropriate expression from the list in **Vie et culture**.

1. 
2. 
3. 
4. 

7-25 Des conseils. Quels conseils est-ce que vous et votre partenaire pouvez donner aux personnes suivantes ?

MODÈLE Votre colocataire a des soucis.
- Ne t'en fais pas ! Ça va s'arranger.

1. Une amie est très anxieuse avant un examen.
2. Votre ami est furieux parce qu'il pense qu'on l'a insulté.
3. Un monsieur se fâche parce qu'il n'y a pas de place dans l'autobus.
4. Votre amie a tendance à être un peu jalouse.
5. Votre petit frère pleure parce qu'il ne trouve pas son DVD préféré.
6. Une femme est furieuse et elle crie très fort parce qu'on a pris son sac.
7. Vos copains sont anxieux avant un match de tennis.
8. Vos camarades s'inquiètent de leurs notes d'examens ce semestre.

Expansion: 7-25 Have students work in pairs to make up their own situations and reactions. They might create a short scene based on their scenario and then act it out in front of the class.

Additional practice: Conduct a mixing activity where students interact with three other people. Provide a model: *Ça va aujourd'hui ? — Pas vraiment. J'ai un examen important et je suis un peu anxieux. — Ne t'en fais pas ! Tu vas réussir à cet examen.* Follow up by having students tell what they learned about the people they spoke to. As a variation, perhaps on another class day, have students tell each other what's new and react to the news: *Quoi de neuf ? — Eh bien, je vais bientôt me marier. Ah bon ? C'est formidable !* You might have students act out their conversations for the class.

7-26 Les sentiments. Expliquez à votre partenaire dans quelle/s situation/s vous ressentez les sentiments suivants.

MODÈLE la tristesse
- Je suis triste quand mes amis se disputent.

1. le bonheur
2. la jalousie
3. l'inquiétude
4. l'anxiété
5. la colère
6. la surprise
7. la frustration

Implementation: 7-26 Nouns are for recognition only. Help students discover their meanings by associating them with the adjectives they know. For example, knowing *heureux* and *malheureux* helps them understand *le bonheur*.

Presentation: Before treating this topic, review reflexive pronominal verbs presented in Ch. 3, L. 1. Treat the verbs in this **Formes et fonctions** as new vocabulary. Remind students that several of these were presented in the **Points de départ** for L. 2 and L. 3. Review stem and spelling changes for *s'appeler/se rappeler, s'ennuyer, s'inquiéter, se promener.* Conjugations are provided in Appendix 2.

FORMES ET FONCTIONS

1. Les verbes pronominaux idiomatiques

- Certain verbs change meaning when combined with a reflexive pronoun:

appeler	J'appelle mon chien.	*I'm calling my dog.*
s'appeler	Je **m'appelle** David.	*My name is David.*
entendre	J'entends un bruit.	*I hear a noise.*
s'entendre avec	Je **m'entends** bien avec eux.	*I get along well with them.*

- Here are some additional idiomatic pronominal verbs:

s'amuser	Ils **se sont** bien **amusés**.	*They had a lot of fun.*
s'arranger	Ça va **s'arranger** !	*It will be all right!*
se calmer	**Calmez-vous** !	*Calm down!*
se dépêcher	Il **se dépêche** toujours.	*He always hurries.*
se détendre	Tu dois **te détendre**.	*You must relax.*
se disputer	Ils **se disputent** souvent.	*They often argue.*
s'ennuyer	Je **m'ennuie** !	*I'm bored!*
se fâcher	Elle **se fâche** contre lui.	*She's getting angry at him.*
s'inquiéter	Ne **t'inquiète** pas !	*Don't worry!*
s'intéresser à	Tu **t'intéresses à** la musique ?	*Are you interested in music?*
s'occuper de	Tu **t'occupes de** lui ?	*Are you taking care of him?*
se passer	Qu'est-ce qui **se passe** ?	*What's happening?*
se promener	Elle **se promène** souvent.	*She often takes walks.*
se rappeler	Je ne **me rappelle** pas.	*I don't remember.*
se reposer	On **se repose**.	*We're resting.*
se retrouver	On **se retrouve** ici ?	*Shall we meet here?*

Presentation: Point out that there is no agreement of the past participle of *se téléphoner* because this verb takes an indirect object.

- Many verbs can be used with a reflexive pronoun to show that the action is mutual, or reciprocal. In English we sometimes use the phrase *each other* to express this idea.

se téléphoner	Nous **nous** sommes téléphoné.	*We phoned each other.*
se rencontrer	On **s'**est déjà rencontrés.	*We've already met.*
s'embrasser	Ils **se** sont embrassés.	*They kissed.*
se fiancer	Ils **se** sont fiancés.	*They got engaged.*
se marier	Ils **se** sont mariés.	*They got married.*
se séparer	Ils **se** sont séparés.	*They separated.*

À vous la parole

7-27 À la maternelle. Christophe se rappelle sa classe à l'école maternelle. Pour compléter ses descriptions, choisissez un verbe qui convient dans la liste ci-dessous.

MODÈLE La maîtresse était toujours calme.
• Elle ne se fâchait jamais.

s'amuser	se dépêcher	s'ennuyer	s'entendre
se fâcher	s'occuper de	se rappeler	se reposer

1. Pendant la récréation, les enfants jouaient ensemble.
2. À midi, on avait beaucoup de temps pour aller à la cantine.
3. Une vieille femme préparait le déjeuner.
4. Après le déjeuner, tout le monde faisait la sieste.
5. Jacques et moi, nous étions des bons amis.
6. Je trouvais nos activités en classe très intéressantes.
7. Jacques n'oubliait jamais ses leçons.

Initial practice: Begin with a discrimination drill: have students raise their hand when they hear a verb used pronominally: *Ils se reposent. Il essuie la table. Elle s'appelle Stéphanie. J'entends un bruit. Ils s'entendent bien. Elle embrasse son fiancé. Je m'ennuie. On va se promener. Vous passez chez moi demain ? Ils se séparent ?*, etc. Follow up with a substitution drill to review forms: *Je m'amuse ; toi. —Tu t'amuses*, etc.

Key: 7-27 1) Ils s'amusaient. 2) On ne se dépêchait pas. 3) Elle s'occupait du déjeuner. 4) On se reposait. 5) Nous nous entendions bien. 6) Je m'intéressais à nos activités. / Je ne m'ennuyais jamais/pas. 7) Il se rappelait toujours ses leçons.

7-28 Histoire d'amour. Racontez cette histoire d'amour en vous servant des verbes indiqués.

MODÈLE se rencontrer
• Ils se sont rencontrés au cinéma.

1. se parler
2. tomber amoureux
3. se fiancer
4. se marier
5. s'entendre bien
6. se disputer
7. se séparer
8. divorcer

Variation: 7-28 Vary by suggesting that students present the love stories of famous couples of their choosing (e.g., Marc Antony and Cleopatra, Romeo and Juliet, Barak and Michelle Obama, Angelina Jolie and Brad Pitt) or even of friends and/or family members. Point out that not all verbs are used pronominally (*tomber, divorcer*). Students may work in pairs or groups to complete this adaptation.

7-29 Trouvez une personne. Trouvez une personne qui...

MODÈLE s'entend bien avec ses parents
É1 Est-ce que tu t'entends bien avec tes parents ?
É2 Non, je ne m'entends pas bien avec eux.
OU Oui, je m'entends bien avec eux.

1. s'entend bien avec ses parents
2. se rappelle son premier jour à l'école
3. s'amuse quelquefois pendant le cours de français
4. s'occupe toujours du dîner le soir
5. ne se fâche jamais
6. s'est dépêchée ce matin
7. va se détendre ce week-end
8. se rappelle les heures de bureau du professeur

Expansion: 7-29 Use as a mixing exercise; let students ask each other a maximum of two questions before moving on to someone else. After a few minutes, have students compare notes, asking questions about items they did not find. Take the opportunity to ask follow-up questions.

Additional practice: Have students explain to a partner under what circumstances they do the following: *se fâcher, s'inquiéter, s'amuser, se dépêcher, se reposer, s'ennuyer, se détendre*. Provide a model: *Quand est-ce que tu te fâches ? —Je me fâche quand ma sœur emprunte mes vêtements.*

2. Les verbes *connaître* et *savoir*

The verbs **connaître** and **savoir** both mean *to know*, but they are used in different ways.

Note: Except for the use of the circumflex accent in the third-person singular (which is optional since the orthographic reform of 1990), the present-tense forms of *connaître* are predictable, like regular *-ir/-iss-* verbs: beginning with the base *connaiss-*, the final consonant is lost in the singular forms. You might want to call attention to the use of the past participle as an adjective—*connu/e, inconnu/e*—because of its frequent use.

- **Connaître** means *to be acquainted with* or *to be familiar with* and usually refers to places and persons; **connaître** is always followed by a noun:

Je **connais** bien sa famille.	*I know his/her family well.*
Il ne **connaît** pas Abidjan.	*He is not familiar with Abidjan.*
Vous **connaissez** cette chanson ?	*Are you familiar with this song?*

- When used in the **passé composé** with persons, **connaître** means *to have met.*

J'**ai connu** mon copain l'été dernier.	*I met my boyfriend last summer.*

CONNAÎTRE ***to know, to be familiar with***

SINGULIER		PLURIEL	
je	connai**s**	nous	connaiss**ons**
tu	connai**s**	vous	connaiss**ez**
il / elle / on	connaî**t**	ils / elles	connaiss**ent**

PASSÉ COMPOSÉ : J'**ai connu** Jamila l'été dernier.

- **Savoir** generally means *to know facts, information*, or *how to do something.* It can be used in five types of constructions:
  - Followed by an infinitive:

Tu **sais** faire du yoga ?	*Do you know how to do yoga?*
Ma mère ne **sait** pas se détendre.	*My mother doesn't know how to relax.*

Note: In cases where the complement is a noun, native speaker usage is nuanced: one can say *Je connais le code de la route ; son adresse ; ses opinions.* But for things that are learned by rote memory, native speakers use *savoir : il sait mon numéro de téléphone ; elle sait sa leçon.*

  - Followed by a noun:

Il **sait** sa leçon par cœur.	*He knows his lesson by heart.*
Je ne **sais** pas tout.	*I don't know everything.*
Nous **savons** la réponse.	*We know the answer.*

  - Followed by a sentence introduced by **que**:

Je **sais qu**'ils sont séparés.	*I know that they are separated.*
Elle **sait que** nous nous sommes fiancés.	*She knows that we got engaged.*

- Followed by a sentence introduced by a question word or **si** (*whether*).

Je ne **sais** pas **comment** sa copine s'appelle.	*I don't know his girlfriend's name.*
Tu **sais si** elle va venir pour Noël ?	*Do you know if she's coming for Christmas?*

- Used alone:

Qu'est-ce qu'elles **savent** ?	*What do they know?*
Je **sais**.	*I know.*

- When used to talk about the past, **savoir** in the **imparfait** means *knew*.

Elle **savait** que nous étions fatigués.	*She knew that we were tired.*

- When used in the **passé composé**, **savoir** means *to have learned* or *found out*.

J'**ai su** qu'elle était malade hier.	*I found out that she was sick yesterday.*

SAVOIR ***to know***

SINGULIER		PLURIEL	
je	sais	nous	sav**ons**
tu	sais	vous	sav**ez**
il / elle / on	sait	ils / elles	sav**ent**

PASSÉ COMPOSÉ : J'**ai su** où il habitait.

Note: In the present tense of *savoir*, the irregularity consists of the change of the vowel /sa/ in the infinitive and plural forms to /se/ (or for some speakers, /sɛ/) in the singular forms; there is a corresponding spelling change. As the final consonant of the stem, the loss of /v/ in the singular forms is predictable.

À vous la parole

7-30 Les connaissances de famille. Avec un/e partenaire, dites qui vous connaissez et qui vous ne connaissez pas dans la famille des personnes indiquées.

MODÈLE votre beau-frère/belle-sœur
- Je connais la sœur de mon beau-frère, mais je ne connais pas sa mère.

1. votre beau-frère/belle-sœur
2. votre colocataire
3. vos voisins
4. votre prof de français
5. votre meilleur/e ami/e
6. votre ami/e
7. votre femme/mari/fiancé/e

Initial practice: Begin with a discrimination drill: one person, or more than one? *Ils savent nager. Elle sait danser. Il connaît mon frère. Elles connaissent bien Paris. Elles savent parler français. Il sait bien parler. Il connaît ses voisins. Ils connaissent cette ville. Elle sait tout*, etc. Follow with simple substitution drills for each verb: *Je sais nager ; vous ; lui*, etc.; and *Je connais Paris ; toi ; nous*, etc.

Implementation: 7-31 Help students discover the meaning of *espion* through context and perhaps an example: *James Bond, c'est un espion.* Students may play the role of an Interpol inspector and question their classmates: *Est-ce que vous savez où il travaille ?* Students answer appropriately.

Additional practice: Ask students what the following people know how to do. Be sure to provide a model: *les membres de l'équipe « Les Canadiens » de Montréal ? — Ils savent bien jouer au hockey sur glace. Fred Astaire et Ginger Rogers ; Placido Domingo ; Serena Williams ; J.K. Rowling ; votre prof de français ; votre frère ou sœur ; votre meilleur/e ami/e ; vous.* Have students suggest other famous people and expand on the second half of the exercise by having several students provide their own personalized responses.

7-31 L'espion international. L'Interpol recherche Claude Martin, un grand espion. Est-ce que vous le connaissez ? Qu'est-ce que vous savez à son sujet ? Faites des phrases en employant **connaître** ou **savoir**.

MODÈLES où il travaille
- Je sais où il travaille.

Lyons, la ville où il est né
- Je connais la ville où il est né.

1. M. Martin Je connais…
2. qu'il parle portugais Je sais…
3. les noms de ses camarades Je sais…
4. sa femme Je connais…
5. quand il est parti d'Italie Je sais…
6. qu'il parle allemand Je sais…
7. où M. Martin habite Je sais…
8. pourquoi il est allé en Belgique Je sais…
9. ses amis à Liège Je connais…
10. quand il va repartir Je sais…

Implementation: 7-32 Use as a mixing activity. Give students a limited amount of time to circulate, asking a maximum of two questions of each person before moving on to someone else. Follow up by having students ask about the items they did not find: *Qui sait jouer de la guitare ?* Ask additional questions to find out more information as appropriate.

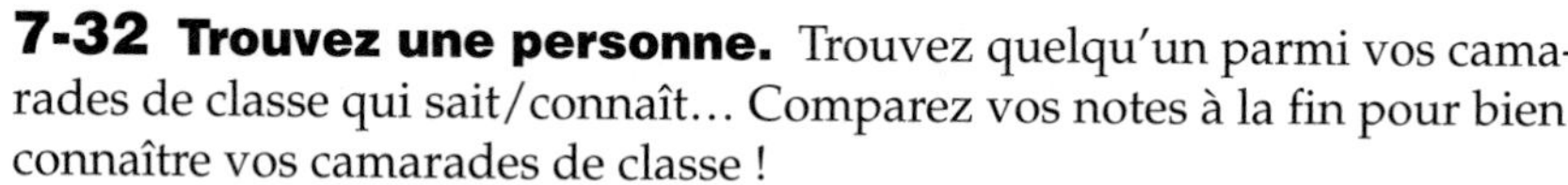

7-32 Trouvez une personne. Trouvez quelqu'un parmi vos camarades de classe qui sait/connaît… Comparez vos notes à la fin pour bien connaître vos camarades de classe !

MODÈLE jouer de la guitare
- Est-ce que tu sais jouer de la guitare ?

1. parler italien tu sais…
2. une personne célèbre tu connais…
3. le président de l'université tu connais…
4. faire du ski tu sais…
5. la ville de Washington, D.C. tu connais…
6. la Belgique tu connais…
7. jouer d'un instrument tu sais…
8. le prénom du professeur tu sais…
9. combien d'étudiants il y a à l'université tu sais…

Preparation: *Avant de lire.* Ask students what they know about the history of Louisiana and the French heritage there. Ancelet is wearing a costume for *Mardi gras.* A professor at the University of Louisiana at Lafayette, Ancelet is one of the leading activists for the maintenance of Cajun (Louisiana) French.

Lisons

7-33 Je suis cadien.

Stratégie

Put yourself in the writer's place to better understand his/her point of view. Consider whether there may be aspects of the writer's background or experience that have shaped his or her perspective, reactions, and focus.

A. Avant de lire. The title of this poem, *Je suis cadien*, gives you essential information about the identity of the poet, Barry Ancelet (who takes the pen name Jean Arceneaux). He speaks **le français cadien**, and he is a descendent of French speakers who fled to Louisiana in the eighteenth century from the former French colony of **Acadie** (the present-day Canadian provinces of Nova Scotia and New Brunswick). After **Acadie** was ceded to England, the Acadians refused allegiance to the British crown. In the early 20th century, compulsory schooling in English was introduced in the regions of Louisiana where Cajuns

Voici le poète, Barry Ancelet. Pourquoi, à votre avis, est-ce qu'il est habillé ainsi ?

had lived in relative isolation. They were forbidden to speak their heritage language, Cajun French (also called Louisiana French), and were punished if they did.

Since the title of the poem announces the poet's Cajun French identity, are you surprised to see that the first lines are in English? Why do you think the poem is written in two languages, Cajun French and English? Can you put yourself in the narrator's place, identifying with his feelings as a Louisiana schoolboy? What message do you think he will attempt to convey?

B. En lisant. Le poète exprime les pensées et les émotions d'un enfant cadien qui allait à l'école publique en Louisiane. En lisant un extrait de ce poème, répondez aux questions suivantes.

1. Pourquoi est-ce que le poète répète la première phrase plusieurs fois ? À quelle punition pendant « leur temps de recess » est-ce qu'il fait référence ?
2. Le poète écrit au vers (*line*) 9, « Ça fait mal ; ça fait honte ». Quelle situation est-ce qu'il décrit ?
3. Dans les vers 25 à 42, on explique à l'enfant pourquoi il doit parler anglais. Est-ce que vous pouvez résumer les arguments ?
4. L'enfant n'est pas convaincu. Comment est-ce que les derniers vers (52 à 57) montrent cela ?

Key: ***En lisant.*** 1) Les enfants devaient écrire la phrase au tableau pendant leur temps de recess (en français standard, pendant la récréation). C'était pour punir les enfants parce qu'ils parlaient français à l'école. 2) Il exprime l'attitude des enfants quand ils étaient punis. 3) C'est plus facile, on n'a pas besoin du français, et on est vraiment américain si on parle anglais. 4) L'enfant demande, quelle langue est-ce qu'il faut utiliser pour rire, pour pleurer, pour crier, pour chanter, pour aimer, pour vivre ?

Note: The poem is written in *le français cadien* and departs from Standard French in the following ways: 1) general deletion of *ne* in the negative, *On sait jamais* 2) no elision in *que eux* 3) deletion of *il* before *faut*. Most of these features are also found in the variety of everyday spoken French called *le français familier.*

Implementation: You might discuss with students the issue of voice in the poem: go through the text and help them determine at what points the poet is speaking, at what points it is the child, and at what points others are speaking to the child.

JE SUIS CADIEN (*suite poètique*)

I will not speak French on the school grounds.
I will not speak French on the school grounds.
I will not speak French...
I will not speak French...
I will not speak French...
Hé ! Ils sont pas bêtes, ces salauds°.
Après mille fois, ça commence à pénétrer
Dans n'importe quel esprit°.
Ça fait mal ; ça fait honte°.
Et on ne speak pas French on the school grounds
Et ni anywhere else non plus.
Jamais avec des étrangers.
On sait jamais qui a l'autorité
De faire écrire ces sacrées° lignes
À n'importe quel âge.
Surtout pas avec les enfants.
Faut jamais que eux, ils passent leur temps de recess
À écrire ces sacrées lignes.

I will not speak French on the school grounds.
I will not speak French on the school grounds.

Faut pas qu'ils aient besoin° d'écrire ça
Parce qu'il faut pas qu'ils parlent français du tout.
Ça laisse voir° qu'on est rien que° des Cadiens.
Don't mind us, we're just poor coonasses,
Basse classe, faut cacher ça°.
Faut dépasser ça.
Faut parler en anglais.
Faut regarder la télévision en anglais.
Faut écouter la radio en anglais
Comme de bons Américains.
Why not just go ahead and learn English,

Don't fight it, it's much easier anyway,
No bilingual bills, no bilingual publicity.
No danger of internal frontiers.
Enseignez l'anglais aux enfants.
Rendez-les tout le long°,
Tout le long jusqu'aux discos,
Jusqu'au Million Dollar Man.
On a pas réellement besoin de parler français quand même°.

salauds° *bastards*
esprit° *anybody's head*
ça fait honte° *makes you ashamed*
sacrées° *damned*
Faut pas qu'ils aient besoin° *They shouldn't have to*
Ça laisse voir°; rien que° *It shows; nothing but*
faut cacher ça° *gotta hide it*
Rendez-les tout le long° *Take them all the way*
quand même° *anyway*

C'est les États-Unis ici.
Land of the Free.
On restera toujours° rien que des poor coonasses.

I will not speak French on the school grounds.
I will not speak French on the school grounds.

Coonass, non, non, ça gêne pas°.
C'est juste un petit nom.
Ça veut rien dire.
C'est pour s'amuser, ça gêne pas.
On aime ça, c'est cute.
Ça nous fait pas fâchés°.
Ça nous fait rire°.
Mais quand on doit rire, c'est en quelle langue qu'on rit ?
Et pour pleurer, c'est en quelle langue qu'on pleure ?
Et pour crier ?
Et chanter ?
Et aimer ?
Et vivre ?

will always be

that doesn't bother us

That doesn't make us mad.

laugh

cry

C. En regardant de plus près. Le poète permet au lecteur (*reader*) de s'identifier avec l'enfant cadien.

1. Pourquoi est-ce que le poème mélange (*mix*) l'anglais et le français ?
2. Dans le texte, on utilise un nom péjoratif : quelle est la réaction de l'enfant quand il entend ce nom ? Quelle est votre réaction quand vous le lisez ? Quelle réaction est-ce que le poète cherche, à votre avis ?
3. Le poème finit par une série de questions ; quel est l'effet de ces questions sur le lecteur ?

Key: ***En regardant de plus près.*** 1) Pour montrer les différents points de vue et la tension entre les anglophones et les francophones. 2) Il dit, « c'est cute, ça nous gêne pas, c'est juste un petit nom » ; mais pour le lecteur, c'est choquant et très péjoratif. Voici le commentaire d'Ancelet à ce propos : « L'auteur essaie de montrer que ce terme, qui a été en effet adopté par un certain segment de la population cadienne comme "terme valorisant", est en fait un terme qui reflète l'internalisation de l'américanisation brutale qu'on a subie. Mais le narrateur ne l'utilise pas pour adresser quelqu'un d'autre ; il l'utilise malheureusement pour s'adresser lui-même. Le poème finit par mettre en question la valeur du terme dans une sorte de catharsis ». 3) Le poète montre que la langue française, c'est très important pour sa vie, c'est son identité.

D. Après avoir lu. Discutez de ces questions avec vos camarades de classe.

1. Est-ce que vous pouvez vous identifier avec le point de vue et les émotions exprimés dans ce poème ? Pourquoi ?
2. Est-ce que vous connaissez un peu l'histoire des immigrés qui sont arrivés aux États-Unis à la fin du XIXe et au début du XXe siècles ? Est-ce que l'expérience de l'enfant cadien décrite dans ce poème ressemble à l'expérience des enfants de ces immigrés, ou non ?

Expansion: ***Après avoir lu.*** You might share your own cultural heritage with students, and ask: Est-ce qu'il y a un héritage culturel particulier qui est reconnu dans votre famille ou votre communauté ? Est-ce que les gens font un effort d'apprendre plus sur cet héritage ou de l'honorer ? De quelle(s) façon(s) ?

Leçon 1

le corps humain	the human body
la bouche	*mouth*
le bras	*arm*
les cheveux (m.)	*hair*
le cœur	*heart*
le dos	*back*
les dents (f.)	*teeth*
l'estomac (m.)	*stomach*
la figure	*face*
la gorge	*throat*
la jambe	*leg*
la langue	*tongue*
la main	*hand*
le nez	*nose*
l'œil (m.) (les yeux)	*eye (eyes)*
l'oreille (f.)	*ear*
le pied	*foot*
les poumons (m.)	*lungs*
la tête	*head*
le ventre	*belly, abdomen*

des maux, un mal	aches and pains
avoir mal à (la tête)	*to hurt (to have a headache)*
avoir mal partout	*to hurt everywhere*
avoir mal au cœur	*to be nauseated*
avoir mal au ventre	*to have a stomach ache*

pour parler des *handicaps	to talk about handicaps
le basket-fauteuil	*wheelchair basketball*
être *handicapé/e	*to be handicapped*
un fauteuil roulant	*a wheelchair*

pour rester en forme	to stay in shape
combattre/réduire le stress	*fight/reduce stress*
consulter le médecin	*to see the doctor*
essayer (de bien manger)	*to try (to eat well)*
faire de l'exercice (m.)	*to exercise*
faire de la musculation	*to do strength/resistance training/lift weights*
faire/suivre un régime	*to (be on a) diet*
un repas équilibré	*balanced meal*
la santé	*health*

choses à éviter pour rester en forme	things to avoid to stay in shape
l'alcool (m.)	*alcohol*
fumer	*to smoke*
grignoter	*to snack*
sauter (un repas)	*to skip (a meal)*

quelques verbes	some verbs
devoir	*to have to, must, to owe*
pouvoir	*to be able to, can*
vouloir	*to want (to)*

Leçon 

les grands évènements de la vie	major life events
un anniversaire	*birthday, anniversary*
un baptême	*baptism*
une bougie	*candle*
un cadeau	*gift*
une cérémonie civile	*civil ceremony*
une fête religieuse	*religious holiday*
les grandes vacances	*summer vacation*
un mariage	*wedding*
un/e marié/e	*groom/bride*
une marraine	*godmother*
un parrain	*godfather*
un témoin	*witness*

des vœux	wishes
un vœu	*wish*
Meilleurs vœux !	*Best wishes!*
Félicitations !	*Congratulations!*
Bon/Joyeux anniversaire !	*Happy Birthday!*
Joyeux anniversaire de mariage !	*Happy Anniversary!*
Joyeux Noël !	*Merry Christmas!*
Bonne année !	*Happy New Year!*
Bon voyage !	*Have a good trip!*
Bonnes vacances !	*Have a good vacation!*

pour parler des fêtes	to talk about holidays
avoir lieu	*to take place*
un bal populaire	*a street dance*
cacher	*to hide*
un défilé	*parade*
fêter	*to celebrate*
un feu d'artifice	*fireworks*
une fève	*token hidden in a king cake*
une fleur	*flower*
une galette	*type of cake*
un jour férié	*legal holiday*
le muguet	*lily of the valley*
un œuf en chocolat	*chocolate egg*
le réveillon (de Noël, du Jour de l'An)	*dinner or party (for Christmas Eve, for New Year's Eve)*
un sapin	*evergreen tree, Christmas tree*
souffler (les bougies)	*to blow (out candles)*

Leçon 3

les sentiments	*feelings*
avoir l'air (d'être) + adj.	*to seem, to appear (to be) + adj.*
Qu'est-ce que tu as ?	*What's wrong?*
amoureux/-euse	*in love*
tomber amoureux/-euse	*to fall in love*
anxieux/-euse	*anxious*
content/e	*happy*
embarrassé/e	*embarrassed*
en colère	*angry*
fâché/e	*angry*
furieux/-euse	*furious*
gêné/e	*bothered, embarrassed*
heureux/-euse	*happy*
inquiet/inquiète	*uneasy, anxious, worried*
jaloux/-ouse	*jealous*
malheureux/-euse	*unhappy*
ravi/e	*delighted*
surpris/e	*surprised*
triste	*sad*

pour exprimer les sentiments	*to express feelings*
Crétin !	*Moron!*
crier	*to yell*
perdre son sang-froid	*to lose one's composure*
pleurer	*to cry*

quelques verbes pronominaux	*some pronominal verbs*
s'amuser	*to have fun*
s'appeler	*to be named, called*
s'arranger	*to work out, to be all right*
se calmer	*to calm down*
se disputer	*to argue*
s'ennuyer	*to become bored*
s'entendre (avec)	*to get along (with)*
se fâcher (contre)	*to get angry (at, with)*
se faire du souci	*to worry*
Ne t'en fais pas ! / Ne vous en faites pas !	*Don't worry!*
s'inquiéter	*to worry*
s'intéresser à	*to be interested in*
se passer	*to happen*
se rappeler	*to remember*
se reposer	*to rest*
se retrouver	*to meet up*
se téléphoner	*to phone each another*

dans la vie sentimentale	*in one's emotional life*
divorcer	*to get divorced*
s'embrasser	*to kiss*
se fiancer	*to get engaged*
se marier	*to get married*
se rencontrer	*to meet (for the first time)*
se séparer	*to separate*

quelques verbes utiles	*some useful verbs*
connaître	*to know, to be familiar with*
savoir	*to know*

quelques expressions utiles	*some useful expressions*
Ce n'est pas grave.	*It's not serious.*
fort (adv.)	*loudly*
Je vous/t'en prie	*Please*
Ne sois pas…	*Don't be . . .*
une nouvelle	*piece of news*
si	*so; whether, if*
Soyez calme !	*Be calm!*
Ne sois pas furieuse !	*Don't be angry!*

Vocabulaire

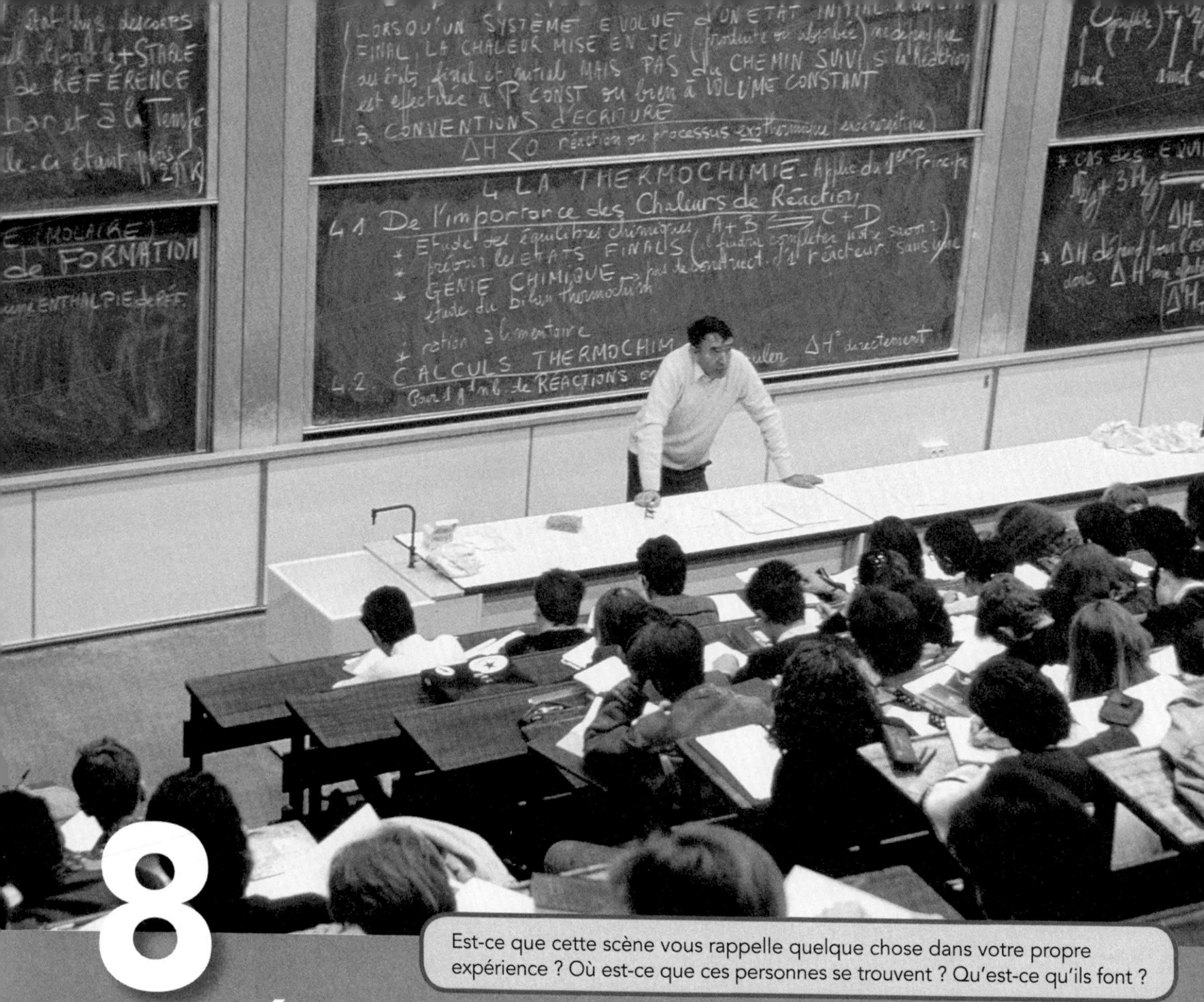

8

Est-ce que cette scène vous rappelle quelque chose dans votre propre expérience ? Où est-ce que ces personnes se trouvent ? Qu'est-ce qu'ils font ?

Études et professions

After completing this chapter, you should be able to:

- Talk about a university and courses of study
- Talk about jobs and the workplace
- Make comparisons
- Compare education and the workplace in the United States, France, and Quebec

Leçon 1 Nous allons à la fac

Presentation: You may wish to present this vocabulary over two days. Present campus vocabulary on day 1 with Ex. 8-1 and 8-2; review the campus and present prepositions on day 2, compeleting Ex. 8-3. Present campus vocabulary using the labeled campus map (MFL, Instructor's Resources). Identify each location pictured, then have students describe related activities: *Dans le Centre étudiant ? — On regarde la télé, on mange, on parle avec des copains.* Check comprehension by having students point to the places you name or describe. Reinforce the distinction between *la librairie* and *la bibliothèque*, which students first learned in Ch. 2, L. 3. Note the abbreviated expressions *la bibli* and *la B.U.*, which are frequently used in France, as are *le resto U* and *la cafétéria*. Point out that in *le resto U*, students can have a full meal (*une entrée, un plat principal, un dessert*) whereas in *une cafétéria*, they can purchase lighter fare (*des pizzas, des salades, des sandwichs,...*). A dining hall on a North American campus is more similar to *un restaurant universitaire*. Demonstrate each preposition using the map. Have students name the places you describe: *Qu'est-ce qui est derrière le Centre des sports ? — Ce sont les terrains de sport.* Then practice prepositions using a map of another university campus; have students correct statements you make: *Est-ce que la bibliothèque est loin du stationnement ? — Non, elle est près du stationnement.*

POINTS DE DÉPART

À la fac

Je m'appelle Julie et je suis en deuxième année d'études à l'Université de Montréal. Je vais à l'université du lundi au vendredi ; j'ai tous mes cours ici. Après les cours, je retrouve mes amis au café dans le centre étudiant. En fin de semaine, je travaille à la bibliothèque. J'habite un appartement, mais j'ai des amis qui habitent en résidence. On mange ensemble quelquefois à la cafétéria ou au restaurant si on a plus de temps et si on veut bien manger. Trois ou quatre fois par semaine, on fait du sport au centre sportif.

Voici un plan du campus. Si vous arrivez à UdeM en voiture, le stationnement se trouve à droite du pavillon principal. Il faut avoir un permis pour stationner sur le campus. Si vous arrivez en métro, il y a une station juste en face du pavillon principal. Pour circuler sur le campus, il y a la navette. Dans le pavillon principal, il y a une librairie et des bureaux administratifs. Les résidences se trouvent à gauche et le centre étudiant est juste à côté. On y trouve un cinéma, un café, le bureau des inscriptions et des bureaux d'associations étudiantes. Le centre sportif est tout près des résidences, et les terrains de sport sont juste derrière.

Presentation: Lead into the cultural content of Ch. 8 by discussing reasons for the presence of French in Quebec. You might discuss how the universities in Quebec reflect its special situation as a French-speaking province in Canada. Ask students if there are examples of American universities that reflect divergent cultural identities; they may mention historically black colleges or schools in Louisiana that have departments devoted to the study of local culture. Be sure to point out the various regionalisms in the text and introduce their standard French equivalents. For example, *aller à l'université = aller à la fac ; la fin de semaine = le week-end ; le stationnement = le parc de stationnement, le garage ou le parking.*

PRÉPOSITIONS DE LIEU

à droite de	à gauche de
en face de	à côté de
dans	
(tout) près de	loin de
devant	derrière

Note: In keeping with the cultural content of Ch. 8 and our attention to regional differences in French, we focus on Quebec in the chapter on university studies, since the North American educational systems are more similar to each other than they are to the French system. The **Lisons** in L.1 presents issues related to **la Loi 101** and the use of French as the only official language of Quebec; the **Écoutons** in L. 2 features a dialogue between Canadian speakers, using a regional accent.

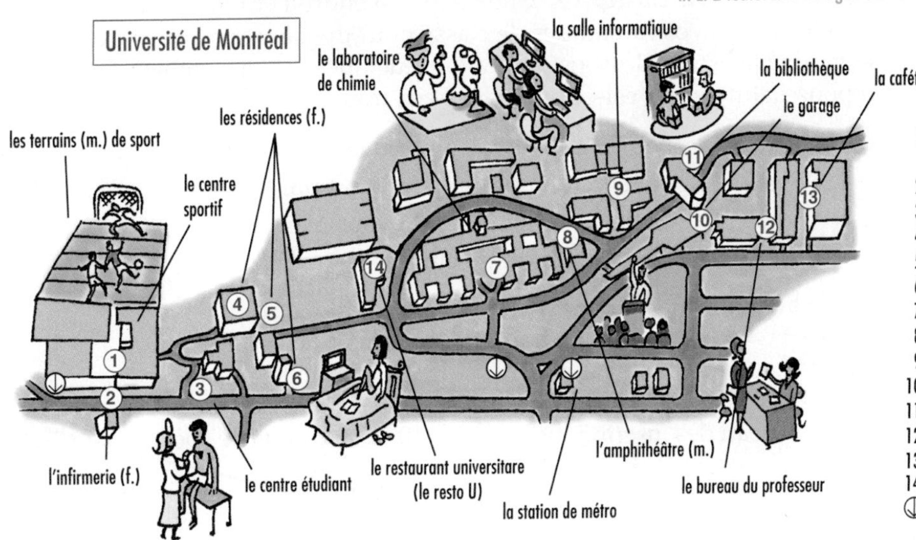

1. Centre d'éducation physique et des sports (CEPSUM)
2. Pavillon 2101, boul. Édouard-Montpetit
3. Pavillon J.-A.-DeSève (centre étudiant)
4. Résidence C
5. Résidence A
6. Résidence Thérèse-Casgrain
7. Pavillon principal
8. Pavillon Claire-McNicoll
9. Pavillon André-Aisenstadt
10. Stationnement Louis-Colin
11. Pavillon Samuel-Bronfman
12. Pavillon Lionel-Groulx
13. Pavillon 3200, rue Jean-Brillant
14. le restaurant universitare (le resto U)

Ⓣ Station de métro

08-01 to 08-04

À vous la parole

Implementation: 8-1: You may complete this activity orally without having students look at their books.

8-1 Dans quel endroit ? Indiquez où on entend typiquement ces questions ou ces commentaires. *Answers may vary.*

MODÈLE Vous avez un permis pour votre voiture ?
• au parc de stationnement ou au garage

1. Voilà le bureau de l'association des étudiants étrangers (*foreign*). au centre étudiant
2. Le match commence dans dix minutes. aux terrains de sport/au centre sportif
3. Aujourd'hui, nous allons parler des évènements qui précédaient la Révolution française. à l'amphithéâtre/en salle de classe
4. Écoute ! C'est une explosion ! au labo de chimie
5. Où se trouvent les dictionnaires du français, s'il vous plaît ? à la bibliothèque/à la librairie
6. On regarde la télé ce soir ou on joue au Scrabble ? à la résidence/au centre étudiant
7. Je me suis fait très mal au genou. à l'infirmerie/chez le médecin
8. Désolé, monsieur, je ne peux pas venir en classe demain. au bureau du prof(esseur)/en classe/à l'amphithéâtre
9. Cet ordinateur ne marche pas bien. Vous pouvez m'aider ? à la salle informatique
10. Je dois acheter tous ces livres pour mes cours ? C'est cher ! à la librairie

Additional practice: As a brief personalized activity between Ex. 8-1 and 8-2, have students tell a partner where they are going after French class and have them report back what they have learned.

8-2 Vos endroits préférés. Avec un/e partenaire, parlez de vos endroits préférés sur le campus pour chaque activité. Ensuite, parlez de vos préférences avec vos camarades de classe.

MODÈLE pour dîner ?

É1 Moi, je préfère la cafétéria ; c'est rapide et très pratique. Et toi ?

É2 Moi, je préfère le resto U au centre étudiant ; il y a beaucoup plus de choix.

É1 (*aux autres étudiants*) Pour dîner, je préfère la cafétéria parce que c'est rapide et pratique, mais Anne préfère le resto U au centre étudiant…

1. pour dîner ?
2. pour travailler ?
3. pour voir un film ?
4. pour parler avec des amis ?
5. pour pratiquer un sport ?
6. pour préparer un examen ?

Implementation: 8-3 Follow up by having students compare answers and choose the best response.

Additional practice: Show the image of the UdeM campus map (MFL, Instructor's Resources) and ask students to imagine that they are in the courtyard of the *Pavillon principal.* Have them take turns asking and indicating where the following places are located: *la station de métro ; le terrain de foot ; le parc de stationnement ; la Résidence A ; un café ; la piscine ; une librairie ; le centre étudiant.*

MODÈLE É1 *La station de métro, s'il vous plaît ?*
É2 *Ce n'est pas loin ; c'est juste en face d'ici.*

Remind students of other ways to ask for directions: *Où se trouve… ? C'est loin/près d'ici… ? Je cherche…, C'est où… ?* As a follow-up, provide students with a map of your campus and have them work in pairs to label the map in French.

8-3 Sur votre campus. Choisissez un endroit sur votre campus et circulez parmi vos camarades de classe pour demander où ça se trouve. Regardez la liste ci-dessous pour avoir quelques idées. Combien de réponses différentes est-ce que vous avez trouvé ?

MODÈLE É1 C'est où, la résidence Cambridge ?

É2 La résidence Cambridge, c'est tout près des terrains de sport.

É1 La résidence Cambridge, s'il vous plaît ?

É3 C'est en face du centre étudiant.

1. la bibliothèque
2. les bureaux de l'administration
3. le centre étudiant
4. la piscine
5. le bureau des inscriptions
6. le théâtre
7. la librairie
8. le resto U
9. l'infirmerie
10. les terrains de sport

Implementation: Point out that, whereas the *Québécois baccalauréat* is equivalent to the American B.A. or B.S., the French *baccalauréat (le bac)* is an examination that must be passed before a student can finish the *lycée* and is a condition for admission to a university. The French *bac* is discussed further in the **Vie et culture** section of L. 2. Help students understand that the *CÉGEP* prepares Canadian students for university work and may account for a shorter time spent at a university; recently, however, many Québécois universities have moved to a four-year *baccalauréat*.

Vie et culture

La Sorbonne a été fondée à Paris en 1253. Elle se trouve au cœur du Quartier latin, un quartier animé avec beaucoup de cafés et de librairies.

L'Université de Montréal est la plus grande université au Canada. Son campus se trouve juste à l'extérieur de la ville. Cette université offre une grande variété de majeurs et de diplômes professionnels.

Note: In Montreal there are four universities: two are French-speaking, *l'Université de Montréal (l'UdeM)* and *l'Université du Québec à Montréal (l'UQAM)*; and two are English-speaking, *McGill University* and *Concordia University*.

Le système éducatif au Québec

Le système éducatif au Québec est organisé différemment du système américain. Les études secondaires durent cinq ans ; normalement les élèves terminent le secondaire à l'âge de 17 ans et passent les deux années suivantes dans un **CÉGEP (Collège d'enseignement général et professionnel)**. Ensuite, ils peuvent poursuivre[1] leurs études à l'université où ils peuvent préparer **un baccalauréat**, **une maîtrise** ou **un doctorat**. Comme dans les universités américaines, les étudiants canadiens peuvent choisir de préparer un diplôme spécialisé dans un seul champ[2] d'études, **une majeure**, ou alors de choisir une majeure dans un champ et **une mineure** dans un autre.

Le campus dans l'université française

En France, la plupart des universités n'ont pas de campus centralisé comme c'est généralement le cas en Amérique du Nord. Dans les grands centres urbains comme Paris, Strasbourg ou Nice, les différentes facultés se trouvent séparées dans des bâtiments éparpillés.[3]

Les étudiants français parlent de **la fac** ; ils disent, par exemple, **Je vais à la fac ce matin.** Pour se réunir avec leurs amis et pour travailler, les étudiants se retrouvent souvent dans un café près de la fac. Normalement, les activités sociales et sportives que nous connaissons en Amérique du Nord ne font pas partie de la vie universitaire en France. Quelques universités françaises ont des résidences qui se trouvent près des facultés. À Paris, il existe quelques résidences mais elles sont situées loin du Quartier latin où se trouvent la Sorbonne et quelques autres universités. Souvent, les étudiants logés dans les résidences sont des étudiants étrangers[4] ; la plupart des étudiants français à Paris et ailleurs en France vivent chez leurs parents ou louent une chambre en ville.

ET VOUS ?

1. Est-ce qu'il y a des établissements dans votre région qui sont comparables au **CÉGEP** au Québec ? Lesquels ?
2. Comparez votre campus à un campus français typique. Pensez à son emplacement, sa grandeur, les bâtiments qui s'y trouvent et la disposition des bâtiments et des services.
3. Où est-ce que la plupart des étudiants de votre université sont logés ? Est-ce que c'est comme la situation en France ? Pourquoi ?

[1]*continuer* [2]*field* [3]*spread out* [4]*foreign*

Note: In early stages of acquisition, it is important to focus on the avoidance of glided vowels because Americans tend to produce these in final position. For that reason, it is unwise to insist that students contrast /e/ and /ɛ/ in open syllables. Although that contrast is typical of Standard French (SF) and Canadian French speakers who differentiate between, for example, *le pré* (meadow) and *le prêt* (loan), it is not made by the majority of people in France. They follow what is called *la loi de position:* /e/ at the end of a word or syllable (open syllable); /ɛ/ before a consonant (closed syllable). You might want to follow this rule and use /e/ in *anglais, français, des, est,* and inside words in open syllables, for example, *intelligente.*

When /e/ and /ɛ/ occur in non-final syllables, many speakers replace them by a vowel intermediate in pronunciation between the two. This is the case in *derrière,* even though the vowel occurs before the consonant /r/ in the same syllable, or in *déteste,* even if it is written with *é.* Most French speakers pronounce the letter sequences *-ai-* and *-ei-* at the end of words and syllables as /e/, for example, in the imperfect tense endings (*j'allais, ils étaient*) and in forms like *se peigner,* as well as the verb form *est,* although the pronunciation with /ɛ/ is considered more standard in each case.

08-05 to 08-06

Sons et lettres

Les voyelles / e / et / ɛ /

The vowels of the words **et** and **mère** differ by the degree of tension with which they are pronounced and where they occur in words. The vowel of **et**, /e/, must be pronounced with a lot of tension and without any glide; otherwise the vowel of the English word *day* is produced. To avoid producing a glide, keep the vowel short and hold your hand under your chin to make sure it does not drop as you say /e/; your lips should stay tense, in a smiling position. The vowel /e/ occurs generally only at the end of words or syllables, and it is often written with **é**, or **e** followed by a silent consonant letter. It also occurs in the endings **-ez**, **-er**, and **-ier**.

la t**é**l**é** | **e**t | ass**ez** | **é**cout**ez** | r**é**p**é**t**er** | janv**ier**

The vowel of **mère**, /ɛ/, is pronounced with less tension than /e/, but still without any glide. It usually occurs before a pronounced consonant at the end of words or syllables and is spelled with **è**, **ê**, or **e** followed by a pronounced consonant. It is also spelled **ei** or **ai** in **seize** or **j'aime**, for example.

derri**è**re | le coll**è**ge | la f**ê**te | la nav**e**tte | **e**lle | il dét**e**ste

À vous la parole

8-4 Contrastes. Comparez la prononciation de chaque paire de mots : le premier mot contient /e/ et le second /ɛ/. Écoutez d'abord et ensuite répétez chaque mot.

et/être | André/Daniel | assez/seize
préférer/je préfère | répéter/je répète | la cafétéria/la bibliothèque

Initial practice: Begin with a discrimination drill; have students indicate whether they hear the vowel /e/ or /ɛ/: *belle, les, mère, résidence, navette, cahier, et, elle, deuxième, métro, année, derrière,* etc.

8-5 Des phrases. Répétez chaque phrase.

1. Hervé attend la prochaine navette à la station de métro.
2. Elle s'appelle Danielle ; elle est en troisième année d'études.
3. Son père, André, appelle l'université pour avoir de ses nouvelles.
4. Son prof d'anglais est assez âgé, mais il est très énergique.
5. La bibliothèque est derrière la résidence pour les étudiants de première année.

FORMES ET FONCTIONS

Note: Adverbs were presented in Ch. 3, L. 1. The comparative and superlative of adjectives are treated in Ch. 8, L. 2.

1. Le comparatif et le superlatif des adverbes

- You have been using adverbs to make your descriptions more precise.

Elle s'endort. — *She's falling asleep.*
Elle s'endort **souvent** en classe. — *She often falls sleeps in class.*
Elle s'endort **facilement** devant la télé. — *She falls asleep easily in front of the TV.*
Elle s'endort **rarement** avant minuit. — *She rarely falls asleep before midnight.*

- The expressions **plus… que** (*more than*), **moins… que** (*less than*) and **aussi… que** (*as much as*) can be used with adverbs to make comparisons.

plus… que	Il travaille **plus** souvent **que** moi.	*He studies more often than I do.*
aussi… que	Tu parles français **aussi** bien **que** lui.	*You speak French as well as he does.*
moins… que	En semaine, il sort **moins** souvent **que** moi.	*During the week, he goes out less often than I do.*

When a pronoun follows **que** in a comparison, it must be a stressed pronoun. A complete list of stressed pronouns in French are shown below with their corresponding subject pronouns:

moi	je	**nous**	on/nous
toi	tu	**vous**	vous
lui	il	**eux**	ils
elle	elle	**elles**	elles

- The adverb **bien** has an irregular comparative form **mieux**, as shown below:

Je chante bien.	*I sing well.*
Je chante aussi bien que toi.	*I sing as well as you do.*
Je chante moins bien que lui.	*I don't sing as well as he does.*
Tu chantes **mieux** que nous.	*You sing* **better** *than we do.*

- When comparing amounts, **plus, moins**, and **autant** are followed by **de/d'** and a noun:

plus de… que	Elle a **plus de** travail **que** nous.	*She has more work than we do.*
moins de… que	Il a **moins de** devoirs **que** vous.	*He has less homework than you.*
autant de… que	J'ai **autant d'**examens **que** vous.	*I have as many exams as you.*

- To express a superlative, use the definite article **le** and **plus, moins**, or **mieux**:

Elle sort **le moins souvent**.	*She goes out the least often.*
Tu chantes **le mieux**.	*You sing the best.*
Il a **le plus de** travail.	*He has the most work.*

Presentation: Briefly review the use and placement of adverbs before introducing this topic. To present inductively, show examples of comparisons between yourself and members of your family and/or between students in the class (e.g., *Ben et Dana mangent à la cafétéria trois fois par jour, mais Suzanne mange à la cafétéria seulement deux fois par jour ; elle va à la cafétéria moins souvent que Ben et Dana. Dana mange à la cafétéria aussi souvent que Ben.*). Ask students to identify the terms used to make comparisons and to equate simple symbols such as +, –, = with the words *plus, moins, aussi/autant.*

Presentation: Students have seen and used stressed pronouns in earlier chapters. The forms are summarized here because of their use with the comparative. You may wish to remind students that stressed pronouns are also used in short questions without a verb, *Ça va bien, et toi ?*; as the second subject in a sentence, *Damien et moi…*; for emphasis, *Lui, il exagère tout le temps*; and after *c'est* and *ce sont, C'est lui. Ce sont eux.*

Note: The irregular form, *mieux*, is the most frequent comparative adverb. Make sure that students see many examples with this form, as it is the focus of Ex. 8-6.

À vous la parole

8-6 Comparaisons. Qui fait le mieux ? Comparez vos réponses avec les réponses de votre partenaire.

MODÈLE Qui chante mieux, vous ou votre mère ?
É1 Ma mère chante mieux que moi.
É2 Moi aussi, je chante moins bien que ma mère.

1. Qui chante mieux, vous ou votre mère ?
2. Qui travaille mieux, vous ou votre meilleur/e ami/e ?

3. Qui écrit mieux, vous ou votre ami/e ?
4. Qui parle mieux le français, vous ou votre professeur ?
5. Qui mange mieux, vous ou votre père ?
6. Qui réussit mieux aux examens, vous ou votre colocataire ?
7. Qui s'habillent mieux, les étudiants ou les professeurs ?

Implementation: 8-7 If students do not have a roommate, encourage them to compare their routine with that of a brother, sister, spouse, parent, or friend.

8-7 Vos habitudes. Est-ce que ces comparaisons sont vraies ou fausses pour vous ? Discutez de vos réponses avec un/e partenaire.

MODÈLE Je me lève plus tôt que mon/ma colocataire.

É1 C'est vrai : moi, je me lève à 7h, et mon colocataire se lève à 8h. Donc, je me lève plus tôt que lui.

É2 Pour moi, c'est faux : mon colocataire se lève plus tôt que moi. Je me lève rarement avant 10h du matin.

1. Je me lève plus tôt que mon/ma colocataire.
2. Mon/Ma colocataire travaille plus que moi.
3. Je sors plus souvent que mon/ma colocataire.
4. Je mange moins souvent au resto U que mon/ma colocataire.
5. Mon/Ma colocataire réussit mieux que moi aux examens.
6. Mon/Ma colocataire parle moins fréquemment avec ses profs que moi.
7. Je travaille plus tard la nuit que mon/ma colocataire.
8. Mon/Ma colocataire écrit mieux que moi.

Additional practice: To practice comparatives with quantities, use this simple exercise. To increase difficulty, replace classroom objects with abstract nouns such as *stress, problèmes, difficultés, joie de vivre, succès, courage, patience*, etc.
Plus ou moins ? Comparez ce que vous avez dans votre sac à dos avec ce que votre partenaire a dans le sien.

MODÈLE Qui a le plus de stylos ?
- Moi, j'ai le plus de stylos ; j'ai trois stylos, et toi, tu as deux stylos.

OU • Tu as moins de stylos que moi.

OU • J'ai plus de stylos que toi.

1. stylos 2. livres 3. cahiers 4. crayons 5. devoirs 6. argent 7. photos

8-8 Championnat de famille. Qui sont les champions dans votre famille et dans les familles de vos camarades de classe ? Posez des questions pour le savoir.

MODÈLE chanter

É1 Qui chante le mieux dans votre famille ?

É2 Ma grande sœur Stéphanie chante le mieux.

É3 Dans ma famille, c'est moi. Je chante le mieux !

1. chanter
2. danser
3. s'habiller
4. cuisiner
5. jouer au tennis/au golf/au foot/au basket
6. écrire
7. parler français

2. Les expressions indéfinies et négatives

Presentation: The expressions *quelquefois* and *ne... jamais* were presented in Ch. 3, L. 1; here they are treated more systematically along with other indefinite and negative expressions. Present using these examples and others, which provide a context for understanding meaning and usage.

- Look at the following exchanges:

—Tu fais **quelque chose** maintenant ? —Non, je **ne** fais **rien** de spécial.	*—Are you doing something now?* *—No, I'm not doing anything special.*
—Il y a **quelqu'un** à la porte ? —Non, il **n'**y a **personne**.	*—Is there someone at the door?* *—No, there's no one there.*
—Tu prends **quelquefois** la navette ? —Non, je **ne** prends **jamais** la navette.	*—Do you take the shuttle sometimes?* *—No, I never take the shuttle.*

As you can see in the exchanges above, the negative expressions are composed of two parts: **ne…** plus another element carrying the specific meaning.

- These negative expressions may also be used alone:

  —Qu'est-ce que tu as ? —**Rien.**
  —Qui va t'aider avec cet examen ? —**Personne.**
  —Tu as mangé dans ce restaurant ? —**Jamais.**

- **Rien** and **personne** may be used as the subject of a sentence; **ne** still precedes the verb:

  Rien ne s'est passé hier. *Nothing happened yesterday.*
  Personne n'est venu au bureau du prof. *No one came to the prof's office.*

Presentation: Show example sentences and have students describe placement for *rien* and *personne* when they function as the subject.

The following chart summarizes indefinite and negative expressions referring to time, things, and persons:

INDÉFINI	NÉGATIF
quelquefois	ne … jamais
quelque chose	ne … rien
quelqu'un	ne … personne

- Note the placement of negative and indefinite expressions in the **passé composé** and **futur proche**:

  —Tu **n'**as **rien** appris ? —Si, j'ai appris **quelque chose.**
  —Tu **n'**a **jamais** travaillé ici ? —Si, j'ai travaillé ici **quelquefois.**
  —Tu **n'**as vu **personne** ? —Si, j'ai vu **quelqu'un.**
  —Il **ne** va **rien** faire ? —Si, il va faire **quelque chose.**
  —Il **ne** va **jamais** nous aider ? —Si, il va nous aider **quelquefois.**
  —Il **ne** va inviter **personne** ? —Si, il va inviter **quelqu'un.**

Presentation: Make sure students notice the difference in placement for *personne* in compound tenses.

À vous la parole

8-9 Au négatif. Répondez avec une expression négative.

Implementation: 8-9 First complete the exercise by having students respond only with the negative expression. Then repeat the exercise, having students respond with a full sentence.

MODÈLE Qu'est-ce que tu regardes ?
• Rien. Je ne regarde rien.

1. Qu'est-ce que tu écoutes ? Rien. Je n'écoute rien.
2. Qui nous a invité à dîner ? Personne. Personne ne nous a invité à dîner.
3. Quand est-ce qu'ils vont arriver ? Jamais. Ils ne vont jamais arriver.
4. Qu'est-ce qu'il y a dans ton sac ? Rien. Il n'y a rien dans mon sac.
5. Qui est-ce que tu écoutes ? Personne. Je n'écoute personne.
6. Qu'est-ce que tu prends ? Rien. Je ne prends rien.
7. Quand est-ce que tu vas à la bibliothèque ? Jamais. Je ne vais jamais à la bibliothèque.
8. Qui est-ce que tu aimes ? Personne. Je n'aime personne.

8-10 Une petite contradiction. Dites le contraire dans vos réponses !

MODÈLES Est-ce qu'il y a quelqu'un dans l'amphithéâtre ?
- Non, il n'y a personne.

Vous ne travaillez jamais à la bibliothèque ?
- Si, je travaille quelquefois à la bibli.

1. Il y a quelque chose écrit au tableau ? Non, il n'y a rien écrit…
2. Est-ce que quelqu'un l'a invitée à la fête ? Non, personne ne l'a invitée…
3. Vous achetez quelque chose à la librairie ? Non, je n'achète rien…
4. Vous ne prenez rien à la cafétéria ? Si je prends quelque chose…
5. Personne n'a appelé pendant le cours ? Si, quelqu'un a appelé…
6. Il ne mange jamais au restaurant universitaire ? Si, il mange quelquefois…
7. Vous préparez quelquefois le dîner ? Non, je ne prépare jamais…
8. Il y a quelqu'un à la porte de la salle informatique ? Non, il n'y a personne…

Implementation: 8-11 Follow up by having students report something they learned about their partner, or solicit multiple answers for each item.

8-11 Des situations. Pour chaque situation, discutez avec un/e partenaire de ce que vous faites. Utilisez **ne… jamais, ne… personne, ne… rien** et leurs contraires **quelquefois, quelqu'un** et **quelque chose.**

MODÈLE quand vous travaillez dans la salle informatique

É1 Qu'est-ce que tu fais quand tu travailles dans la salle informatique ?

É2 Je ne prends jamais de boisson et je ne mange rien parce que c'est interdit. Quelquefois, je mange du chewing-gum. Et toi ?

É1 Moi, je ne travaille jamais dans la salle informatique parce que les moniteurs sont assez désagréables. Je travaille quelquefois au café avec mon ordinateur portable.

1. quand vous travaillez dans la salle informatique
2. quand vous allez au café après les cours
3. quand vous sortez avec des amis le week-end
4. quand vous partez en vacances en famille
5. quand vous avez beaucoup de travail à la fac
6. quand vous organisez une fête pour des amis
7. quand vous êtes en cours de français
8. quand vous avez un week-end de libre sur le campus

Lisons

8-12 Le français au Québec.

Note: Statistics about the population and number of French speakers are based on the official census data from 2006.

Stratégie

It is often useful to skim a text quickly to get the gist. This will orient you to the topic and help you understand the content more readily as you read again.

A. Avant de lire. Canada is officially bilingual, and more than seven million of the country's 31 million citizens speak French as their native language. Most French Canadians live in the province of Quebec, where native French speakers comprise approximately 80 percent of the population. Montreal is the second largest Francophone city in the world, after Paris.

This excerpt provides more information about the use of French in Québec. It is from a publication entitled **Emménager à Montréal** (*Moving to Montreal*), a guide for people relocating to Montreal. Skim the three paragraphs of the text to answer these questions:

1. What is the general topic of the excerpt?
2. Each paragraph addresses a specific aspect of the general topic; explain what that is in each case.

Key: ***Avant de lire.*** *Answers will vary, but may include:* 1) education, the school system (point out the words *éducation* and *école*, but also *enseignement*) 2) laws or government regulations related to education; the existence of French- and English-speaking schools; resources for learning French.

L'enseignement[1] au Québec

Au Québec, le ministère de l'Éducation est l'organisme gouvernemental responsable de la supervision de tous les niveaux[2] d'enseignement de la province. En 1977, la Loi 101 – ou la Charte de la langue française — a été adoptée par le gouvernement du Québec. Selon la Loi 101, tous les enfants doivent obtenir[3] leur éducation en français jusqu'au niveau post-secondaire. Il existe cependant des exceptions à cette règle. Par exemple, les résidents temporaires du Québec peuvent fréquenter une école anglophone.

Le système scolaire, de la prématernelle et jusqu'à la cinquième année du secondaire, a deux branches parallèles, l'une anglophone et l'autre francophone. Les étudiants qui vont dans une école post-secondaire peuvent décider de la langue qu'ils désirent apprendre, et il n'est pas rare que des étudiants francophones choisissent de fréquenter une université de langue anglaise et vice versa.

Bien s'exprimer en français

La vie de tous les jours peut s'avérer[4] compliquée si on ne possède pas au moins une connaissance de base du français. Des cours sont offerts gratuitement aux nouveaux venus en provenance d'un pays non francophone par le ministère des Relations avec les Citoyens et de l'Immigration. Pour de plus amples renseignements téléphonez au 514-864-9191 ou visitez www.immq.gouv.qc.ca.

[1] *education* [2] *levels* [3] *obtain* [4] *être*

Source : *Emménager à Montréal*, 2006–2007, www.movingto.com

B. En lisant. Maintenant relisez le texte attentivement et trouvez les réponses aux questions suivantes.

1. Le premier paragraphe mentionne la Loi 101. Quand est-ce que cette Loi a été adoptée ? Par qui ? Quel aspect de la Loi est traité dans ce texte ?
2. Le texte parle d'une exception à cette Loi. C'est pour qui ? Quelle est cette exception ?
3. Le deuxième paragraphe décrit deux « branches parallèles » ou deux systèmes. De quoi est-ce qu'on parle ?
4. D'après ce texte, les étudiants universitaires à Montréal ont un certain avantage. Quel est cet avantage ?
5. Quels sont les moyens d'apprendre le français pour ceux qui ne le parlent pas et qui vont s'installer à Montréal ?

Key: *En lisant.* 1) La Loi 101 a été adoptée en 1977 par le gouvernement du Québec. D'après cette loi, les enfants doivent aller à l'école en français jusqu'au niveau post-secondaire. 2) Il y a une exception pour les résidents temporaires. Ils peuvent aller à une école anglophone. 3) Les deux branches sont les deux systèmes scolaires — un système anglophone et un système francophone. 4) Les étudiants peuvent choisir de faire les études universitaires dans une université de langue française ou de langue anglaise. 5) Des cours gratuits sont offerts par le ministère des Relations avec les Citoyens et de l'Immigration.

Le vieux Montréal

Key: ***En regardant de plus près.*** 1) *rule* 2) *newcomers* 3) *free of charge* 4) *knowledge*

Implementation: ***Après avoir lu.*** This legislative text is easy to understand because of the large number of cognates and students' background knowledge based on the reading in this section. The Preamble specifically grants the right to develop and maintain their native language and culture to the Inuit and the Amerindian peoples of Quebec and places this legislation in the wider global context of a revalorization of ethnic heritage. Have students compare this attitude with the prevailing thoughts in the United States regarding the establishment of an English-only law. Point out that there is currently no national law specifying English as the official language although some groups have expressed support for such a law. Pressure from these groups has led about half of the states to declare English as an official language. Ask students if they feel a national English-only law is necessary and if it would be beneficial and in what ways.

C. En regardant de plus près. Examinez le texte plus en détail.

1. Dans le premier paragraphe, vous voyez le mot **règle**. Vous connaissez déjà une signification pour le mot **règle.** D'après le contexte, quelle est une autre signification ?
2. Dans le dernier paragraphe on parle des **nouveaux venus**. Vous connaissez le mot **venu** comme le participe passé du verbe **venir.** Quelle est sa signification ici quand c'est utilisé comme un substantif (*noun*) ?
3. Dans le dernier paragraphe, quelle est la signification de **gratuitement** dans la phrase « … **des cours sont offerts gratuitement** » ?
4. Dans le dernier paragraphe, vous voyez le mot **connaissance**. Vous connaissez déjà le verbe **connaître**. Quelle est la signification de ce substantif ?

D. Après avoir lu. Discutez de ces questions avec vos camarades de classe.

1. Voici un extrait du préambule de la Loi 101. Lisez-le et identifiez les cinq domaines où le français est défini comme « **la langue normale et habituelle** ».
2. Malgré le fait que la Loi 101 déclare le français comme la seule langue officielle du Québec, les droits linguistiques des gens qui ont d'autres langues maternelles sont protégés. Trouvez le passage de la Loi 101 qui exprime cette idée. Est-ce que vous êtes d'accord avec cette proposition ? Pourquoi ?
3. Pensez à la situation linguistique de votre communauté ou de votre état. Est-ce que les enfants ont la possibilité d'assister à l'école dans la langue de leur choix ? Est-ce que vous pensez que les parents doivent pouvoir choisir la langue d'enseignement de leurs enfants ? Pourquoi ?

CHARTE DE LA LANGUE FRANÇAISE
PRÉAMBULE

Langue distinctive d'un peuple majoritairement francophone, la langue française permet au peuple québécois d'exprimer son identité.

L'Assemblée nationale reconnaît la volonté des Québécois d'assurer la qualité et le rayonnement de la langue française. Elle est donc résolue à faire du français la langue de l'État et de la Loi aussi bien que la langue normale et habituelle du travail, de l'enseignement, des communications, du commerce et des affaires.

L'Assemblée nationale entend poursuivre cet objectif dans un esprit de justice et d'ouverture, dans le respect des institutions de la communauté québécoise d'expression anglaise et celui des minorités ethniques, dont elle reconnaît l'apport précieux au développement du Québec.

L'Assemblée nationale reconnaît aux Amérindiens et aux Inuit du Québec, descendants des premiers habitants du pays, le droit qu'ils ont de maintenir et de développer leur langue et culture d'origine.

Ces principes s'inscrivent dans le mouvement universel de revalorisation des cultures nationales qui confère à chaque peuple l'obligation d'apporter une contribution particulière à la communauté internationale.

Leçon 2 Une formation professionnelle

POINTS DE DÉPART

Des programmes d'études et des cours

MAT 16392 Mathématiques pour scientifiques
CHM 10124 Chimie physique II
CHM 10101 Laboratoire de chimie physique
FRN 21036 Communications pour scientifiques
BIO 22049 Écologie et environnement
STT 10400 Probabilités et statistique
ECN 11487 Théorie macroéconomique I
ECN 11498 Relations économiques internationales
ANL 14960 Advanced English I
POL 19606 Politique économique du Canada et du Québec

Claire Paradis

Gilles Robillard

Claire et Gilles sont étudiants à l'Université Laval. Claire prépare un diplôme en chimie avec une concentration en chimie de l'environnement ; Gilles prépare un diplôme en économique. Ils parlent de leurs cours :

GILLES : Qu'est-ce que tu as comme cours ce semestre ?
CLAIRE : Un cours de chimie en labo, un cours de maths, un cours d'écologie et un cours de français.
GILLES : C'est intéressant, ton cours d'écologie ?
CLAIRE : C'est assez ennuyeux, mais c'est un cours obligatoire. En fait, je n'ai pas de cours facultatif ce semestre. Et ton cours de sciences po, ça va ?
GILLES : Ben, il est intéressant, ce cours, mais difficile.
CLAIRE : Il y a beaucoup d'examens ?
GILLES : Non, il y a seulement un examen final, mais il y a deux devoirs à faire. Le prof m'a mis une note assez médiocre au premier devoir.

Presentation: Have students examine the boxed course listings and use cognates to determine what courses each student is taking and what each is likely to be majoring in. Have students pay attention to the course prefixes as well as the titles. These are actual courses found in the University of Laval catalogue. Listen to the dialogue, then check comprehension: pose questions that can be answered with the appropriate student's name: *Qui suit un cours de chimie ? Qui a un cours de sciences politiques ?* Continue with more specific questions, such as the following:
Claire prépare un diplôme en sciences économiques ou en chimie ? Elle a une concentration en chimie physique ou en écologie ? Et Gilles, quel diplôme est-ce qu'il prépare ? Combien de cours est-ce qu'il suit ? Ce trimestre, Claire suit un cours d'écologie ? Pour quel cours est-ce qu'elle travaille au laboratoire ? Elle suit un cours de maths ?

Presentation: Show the course listings as you model pronunciation for the disciplines and courses, and provide explanations where necessary. Ask: *Qui suit un cours de littérature ? C'est un cours de littérature américaine ou anglaise ?*, etc., to provide additional contextualization of the new words. As an early productive exercise, have students classify specific courses according to area of study: *La sociologie ? — C'est un cours de sciences humaines.* Depending on the interests of your students or the focus of your school, you may wish to introduce other disciplines such as *la criminologie, la nutrition, la kinésiologie, la médecine du sport, l'astronomie.*

QU'EST-CE QUE VOUS ÉTUDIEZ ?

les lettres :	l'histoire, une langue étrangère (l'allemand, l'espagnol), la communication, la littérature, la philosophie
les sciences humaines :	l'anthropologie, la psychologie, les sciences politiques, la sociologie
les sciences naturelles :	la biologie, l'écologie, la botanique, la zoologie
les sciences physiques :	la chimie, la physique
les sciences économiques :	la comptabilité, l'économie, la gestion
les arts du spectacle :	le théâtre, la danse, le cinéma
les beaux-arts :	le dessin, la musique, la peinture

l'informatique	le droit	le génie	les relations internationales
les mathématiques	le journalisme	la médecine	les sciences de l'éducation

Fiche pratique

The verb **suivre** "to follow" is used idiomatically in French to indicate what courses one is taking. Every language uses idioms; for example, in English, we "take" a course. What other idioms have you learned in French? Be on the lookout for such expressions, and be careful not to translate them literally.

POUR PARLER DES COURS :

Je suis un cours d'histoire.	*I'm taking a history course.*
J'ai des bonnes notes en maths. C'est assez facile.	*I have good grades in math. It's quite easy.*
Je fais un devoir pour mon cours de sciences po.	*I'm working on an assignment for my poly sci class.*
Je lis un roman pour mon cours d'allemand.	*I'm reading a novel for my German class.*
Je passe un examen en cours de chimie lundi.	*I'm taking an exam in my chemistry class Monday.*
Je vais réussir mon examen d'espagnol, je travaille beaucoup.	*I'm going to pass my Spanish exam, I'm studying hard.*
Je prépare un exposé pour le cours d'histoire.	*I'm preparing an oral presentation for history class.*
Je prépare un diplôme en biologie.	*I'm majoring in biology.*
Je me spécialise en biologie.	*I'm majoring in biology.*
La fac offre une spécialisation en écologie.	*The university has an ecology major.*

Presentation: Remind students of other idioms they have learned, such as: *s'appeler, avoir + âge, avoir faim/soif/froid/chaud, avoir envie de, faire de + sport.*

Note: This vocabulary is provided to help students talk about their experiences as students and should be presented conversationally as you discuss courses and activities. The verbs *suivre* and *lire* are treated here as lexical items. Students already know the forms *écrivez* and *lisez*; complete paradigms for *écrire* and *lire* are presented in the **Formes et fonctions** of this lesson. The full conjugation of *suivre* is provided in Appendix 2. You may wish to teach students to understand the question *"Quel cours est-ce que vous suivez ?"* and to produce questions such as *"Tu suis un cours de maths ?"*

08-18 to 08-21

À vous la parole

8-13 La majeure. D'après les cours qu'ils suivent, quels diplômes est-ce que vous pensez que ces étudiants québécois préparent ?

MODÈLE Guillaume : Principes de chimie analytique ; Chimie physique moléculaire ; Mathématiques pour chimistes

- Il prépare sans doute un diplôme en chimie.

Implementation: 8-13 The terms *une majeure, une mineure* are used in Canada. Point out to students that the concept of a minor does not exist in France, and that the term *une spécialisation* is used there to indicate one's major.

1. Cécile : L'Europe moderne ; Introduction à l'étude des États-Unis ; Histoire générale des sciences Elle… en histoire.
2. Arnaud : Civilisation allemande ; Allemand écrit 1 ; Cours pratique d'allemand parlé Il… en allemand (une langue étrangère)
3. Romain : Introduction aux concepts sociologiques ; Communication et organisation ; Psychologie sociale Il… en sociologie.
4. Jennifer : Théorie macroéconomique ; Éléments de microéconomique ; Statistique pour économistes Elle… en économie.
5. Ben : Histoire politique du Québec ; Éléments de politique ; Géographie du développement Il… en sciences politiques.
6. Anne-Marie : Biologie expérimentale ; Principes d'écologie ; Introduction à la génétique Elle… en biologie.
7. Aurélie : Systèmes éducatifs du Québec ; Philosophie de l'éducation ; Sociologie de l'école Elle… en sciences de l'éducation.

Note: 8-13 The courses listed are actual course titles from the UdeM catalogue.

8-14 Votre diplôme et vos cours. Comparez votre majeur et votre mineur avec un/e partenaire et parlez des cours que vous suivez ce semestre.

MODÈLE É1 Je prépare un B.A. en sciences politiques. J'ai une mineure en français. Et toi ?

É2 Moi, je me spécialise en mathématiques, mais je n'ai pas de mineure.

É1 Ce semestre je suis deux cours d'histoire, un cours obligatoire de sociologie et ce cours de français.

É2 Bien sûr, je suis un cours de français et j'ai aussi trois cours de maths ! Je n'ai pas pu choisir un cours facultatif ce semestre.

Implementation: 8-14 We are using the term B.A. to reflect the experience of American students. Canadian students would prepare *un baccalauréat* and French students *une licence* ou *un master*. You may wish to have students make a chart with their partner's schedule. Create a sample schedule using the list of courses for Claire or Gilles. Provide blank schedule forms and have students report back to the class.

8-15 Le travail à faire. Qu'est-ce que vous avez à faire ce week-end pour vos cours ? Comparez vos responsabilités avec celles de votre partenaire.

MODÈLE É1 J'ai beaucoup de travail en ce moment : je prépare un exposé pour mon cours de sociologie et j'ai deux examens vendredi.

É2 Moi aussi, j'ai beaucoup de travail : je prépare un essai pour mon cours d'histoire et j'ai un gros projet pour mon cours de gestion.

Cette étudiante à l'Université Laval prépare un exposé en plein air.

Implementation: Ask students to compare requirements for entrance into American universities with those for French universities. What are the advantages and disadvantages of each? Unlike admission to the universities, admission to the *Grandes Écoles* is highly competitive and selective.

Vie et culture

Help students understand that the recent reforms are designed to allow students to move easily from one European country to another to study, complete an internship, or work. Compare the North American system: Is it standardized? Is it easy to move from one place to another? What are the advantages of a standardized and a non standardized system?

L'université française et la réforme européenne

En France, les systèmes scolaire et universitaire ne sont pas organisés de la même façon que les systèmes américains ou canadiens correspondants. Avant de quitter le lycée, les élèves passent un examen national rigoureux, **le baccalauréat (le bac)**. Les élèves qui réussissent ont le droit[1] d'entrer dans le système universitaire. Les études universitaires ne coûtent pas cher en France. Il y a seulement des frais d'inscription[2] à régler (en 2010, c'était seulement 174 € pour l'année).

Les étudiants peuvent aussi continuer leurs études dans des institutions universitaires plus spécialisées : les Grandes Écoles. Les plus prestigieuses des Grandes Écoles sont l'École des Mines, qui prépare des ingénieurs, l'Institut des Sciences Politiques (Sciences Po), l'École Normale Supérieure (l'ENS), l'École Polytechnique (l'X) et l'École des Hautes Études Commerciales (HEC). L'entrée dans les Grandes Écoles est très compétitive. Les étudiants qui veulent entrer dans une Grande École particulière doivent passer un concours d'entrée[3]. Après le bac, ils s'inscrivent dans les classes préparatoires (ou prépas) organisées dans certains lycées. Ces classes durent deux ans. Un grand nombre d'hommes politiques, de leaders dans le monde du commerce et de l'industrie et de professeurs d'université ont été formés dans les Grandes Écoles.

Récemment, la France a participé à un projet de réforme de son système universitaire en accord avec 32 autres pays[4] européens. Selon cette réforme, l'année universitaire est maintenant divisée en deux semestres, un système commun de crédits a été établi et les diplômes sont standardisés : on obtient la licence après trois ans d'études, le master après cinq ans et le doctorat après huit ans.

Ces élèves vérifient leurs résultats au baccalauréat. Est-ce que vous prenez connaissance de vos résultats d'examen de la même manière ? Pourquoi ?

  Je suis étudiant

08-53

Regardez la séquence vidéo *Je suis étudiant*, filmée à l'Université de Nice. Identifiez les endroits sur le campus que vous reconnaissez et les disciplines que chaque personne étudie (ou bien enseigne !)

ET VOUS ?

1. Est-ce que vous aimeriez devoir réussir à un examen national très rigoureux, comme le bac, avant de terminer le lycée et pour pouvoir entrer à l'université ?
2. Qu'est-ce que vous pensez des préparatifs que les étudiants qui veulent entrer dans les Grandes Écoles sont obligés de faire ? Est-ce qu'il y a des équivalents en Amérique du Nord ?

[1]peuvent [2]*registration fees* [3]*competitive entrance exam* [4]*countries*

Note: The French government has set as an educational goal to have 80% of all high school students obtain the *bac*. In 2008, the national statistic reached 64% (compared to 30% in the early seventies), with 88.8% of those who actually took the *bac général* in 2009 passing. (*Francoscopie* 2010, p. 81). Compare this to 1982, when only 64.8% of candidates who took the test passed (*Francoscopie* 2007, p. 76).

Sons et lettres

Les voyelles / o / et / ɔ /

The vowel of **beau**, /o/, is short and tense, in contrast to the longer, glided vowel of English *bow*. Hold your hand under your chin to make sure it does not drop as you say **beau**; your lips should stay rounded and tense. The vowel /o/generally occurs at the end of words or syllables, and it is written with **o, ô, au/x, eau/x**, or combinations of **o** and silent consonants:

au resto U   il est t**ô**t   **aux** bur**eaux**   le m**o**t   il est gr**o**s

The vowel of **sport**, / ɔ /, is pronounced with less tension than /o/, but still without any glide. It usually occurs before a pronounced consonant and is spelled **o**:

le pr**o**f   il est f**o**rt   Yv**o**nne   il ad**o**re

In a few words, / o / occurs before a pronounced consonant.

le dipl**ô**me   les **au**tres   à g**au**che   elle est gr**o**sse

Note: As was the case for the mid-vowel pair / e / and / ɛ /, the most important goal for American speakers is to avoid the production of a glide. The pronunciation we present here reflects Standard French usage and does not strictly follow the *loi de position* mentioned in the annotation for the treatment of the other pair of mid-vowels. Speakers in the south of France routinely produce the vowel / ɔ / in closed syllables, in words such as gauche [gɔʃ] and rose [rɔz] that are pronounced [goʃ] and [roz] by SF speakers.

À vous la parole

8-16 Contrastes. Écoutez bien pour faire la distinction entre chaque paire de mots. Le premier mot a le son / o / et le deuxième le son / ɔ /. Ensuite, répétez.

le stylo/la gomme   Bruno/Yvonne   la radio/la porte
le piano/la note   Mme Lebeau/M. Lefort   il est beau/elle est bonne

Initial practice: Begin with a discrimination drill, asking students to tell whether they hear the vowel of *beau* or that of *fort : gros, bureau, bonne, prof, mot, diplôme, fort, trop, golf.*

8-17 Les abréviations. Les étudiants français utilisent beaucoup d'abréviations pour parler de leurs cours et d'autres aspects de la vie universitaire. Un grand nombre de ces abréviations terminent avec le son / o / comme dans la liste ci-dessous. Avec un/e partenaire, prononcez chaque abréviation et mariez-la au mot d'origine.

1. le labo b → b
2. le resto U f
3. la compo g
4. les sciences po d
5. la psycho h
6. la philo c
7. la socio e
8. le dico a

a. le dictionnaire
b. le laboratoire
c. la philosophie
d. les sciences politiques
e. la sociologie
f. le restaurant universitaire
g. la composition
h. la psychologie

Presentation: To present the verb *dire*, demonstrate how one says *Bonjour !* in various countries: En Allemagne, ils disent *Guten Tag !* En Italie, on dit *Buon giorno !* et vous, vous dites *Hello !*, etc. Ask students to summarize the forms of this irregular verb, then compare the verb charts for all three verbs. Stress the importance of a clear release of the final consonant in the third-person plural: *écrit* vs. *écrivent ; lit* vs. *lisent ; dit* vs. *disent ;* point out the irregular form *dites*, and ask students what other verbs they know show this irregularity (*être/êtes ; faire/faites*).

FORMES ET FONCTIONS

1. Les verbes de communication *écrire, lire* et *dire*

- Here are three useful verbs of communication: **écrire**, *to write*; **lire**, *to read*; **dire**, *to say, to tell*.

ÉCRIRE *to write;* **LIRE** *to read;* **DIRE** *to say, to tell*

SINGULIER		PLURIEL	
je/j'	écris	nous	écriv**ons**
	lis		lis**ons**
	dis		dis**ons**
tu	écris	vous	écriv**ez**
	lis		lis**ez**
	dis		**dites**
il / elle / on	écri**t**	ils / elles	écriv**ent**
	li**t**		lis**ent**
	di**t**		dis**ent**
IMPÉRATIF :	Écris !	Écrivons !	Écrivez !
	Lis !	Lisons !	Lisez !
	Dis !	Disons !	Dites !
PASSÉ COMPOSÉ :	il a **écrit**, il a **lu**, il a **dit**		

- **Décrire**, *to describe*, is conjugated like **écrire**.
- All these verbs can take direct and indirect objects.

J'écris **un mail à mon prof**. — *I'm writing an email to my professor.*
Tu **leur** dis **bonjour** de ma part ? — *Will you say hello to them for me?*
Elles ne mentent jamais ; elles disent toujours **la vérité**. — *They never lie; they always tell the truth.*
Elle lit **ses poèmes à ses amis**, mais elle ne **les** lit pas **à ses parents**. — *She reads her poems to her friends, but she doesn't read them to her parents.*

08-24 to 08-27

À vous la parole

Initial practice: Begin with a discrimination drill, singular vs. plural, for all three verbs. One person, or more than one? *Ils disent bonjour. Elle lit le journal. Il écrit une lettre. Ils lisent beaucoup. Elle ne dit pas grand-chose. Elles écrivent bien. Ils disent toujours « oui ». Il lit des articles. Elles lisent un magazine*, etc. Follow with substitution drills: *Elle écrit une lettre ; nous. —Nous écrivons une lettre*, etc.

8-18 Étudiants étrangers. Tout le monde est d'accord ! Comment est-ce que ces étudiants disent « oui » ? Choisissez un mot de la liste : **oui, da, ja, sì, sí, yes.** *Answers may vary.*

MODÈLE Maria est italienne.
- Elle dit *sì*.

1. Peter et Helmut sont allemands. Ils disent *ja*.
2. Louis-Jean est haïtien. Il dit *oui*.
3. Moi, je suis russe. Je dis *da*.
4. Isabel est mexicaine. Elle dit *sí*.
5. Michèle et moi, nous sommes belges. Nous disons *oui* ou *ja*.
6. Toi, tu es américaine. Tu dis *yes*.
7. Georges et toi, vous êtes suisses. Vous dites *ja, oui* ou *sì*.
8. Alan, il est anglais. Il dit *yes*.

8-19 Qu'est-ce qu'ils écrivent ? Choisissez dans la liste ce que ces étudiants écrivent.

MODÈLE Marc travaille pour le journal de l'université.
- Il écrit des articles.

des articles	des critiques	des essais	des lettres
des pièces	des poèmes	des programmes	des recettes

1. Amélie et moi, nous étudions l'informatique. Nous écrivons des programmes.
2. Maxime et toi, vous êtes des bons correspondants. Vous écrivez des lettres.
3. Je suis étudiant en littérature. J'écris des essais.
4. Laetitia est étudiante en nutrition ; elle adore utiliser des produits bio. Elle écrit des recettes.
5. Jessica et Florian sont poètes. Ils écrivent des poèmes.
6. Tu travailles pour un magazine pour étudiants. Tu écris des articles.
7. Élodie va toujours au cinéma pour voir les nouveaux films. Elle écrit des critiques.
8. Adrien est dans le département de théâtre. Il écrit des pièces.

Expansion: 8-19: The verb *lire* does not have its own exercise, but you could expand on Ex. 8-19 by asking students what these people read (e.g., #1, *Nous écrivons des programmes et nous lisons des livres d'informatique*). You could also ask students what they are currently reading for their coursework or what they have read in French so far. The verb *lire* is recycled in Ch. 10, L. 3 with the presentation of various reading materials.

8-20 Sondage. Trouvez une personne qui…

MODÈLE lit le journal tous les jours
É1 Est-ce que tu lis le journal tous les jours ?
É2 Oui, je lis le *New York Times*.
OU Non, je ne lis pas le journal.

1. lit le journal tous les jours
2. écrit souvent à ses grands-parents
3. dit toujours la vérité
4. écrit pour le journal de l'université
5. a lu une biographie récemment
6. va écrire des mails ce soir
7. lit son horoscope tous les jours
8. a écrit un poème

Implementation: 8-20 Use as a mixing activity. Tell students to ask no more than two questions per person before moving on to another student. Limit time, and follow up by having students ask questions about the items they did not find. Synthesize the information gathered: How many people read a newspaper every day? How often do students write to their grandparents? What was the hardest category to get a positive response for?, etc.

2. Le comparatif et le superlatif des adjectifs

- In the previous lesson, you learned to use the expressions **plus… que**, **moins… que**, and **aussi… que** with adverbs to make comparisons.

Je lis **plus** souvent **que** lui.	*I read more often than he does.*
Tu écris **aussi** bien **que** moi.	*You write as well as I do.*
Il sort **moins** souvent **que** toi.	*He goes out less often than you do.*

- To compare the qualities of two people or things, use these same expressions with an adjective. The adjective you use agrees with the first noun.

Son deuxième roman est **plus** connu **que** son premier.	*Her second novel is more well known than her first.*
La librairie en ville est **moins** chère **que** la librairie de la fac.	*The bookstore in town is less expensive than the university bookstore.*
Mes cours ce semestre sont **aussi** intéressants **que** ses cours.	*My classes this semester are as interesting as her courses.*

Preparation: Before presenting this material, briefly review the comparative of adverbs and nouns, treated in Ch. 8, L. 1, with examples that include questions and answers such as *Qui lit le plus souvent ? Qui doit écrire le plus d'essais ? Qui lit le moins ?* Have students summarize rules and identify the words used to make comparisons: *plus, moins, aussi*, and the conjunction *que*.

Presentation: Comparatives and superlatives can be presented inductively in class using appropriate visuals, or by having various students stand up, and then comparing them: *Sarah est plus grande que Julie*, etc. Be attentive, however, to students' sensitivity about their looks, especially with regard to their weight.

- When comparing people, remember to use stressed pronouns after **que**:

Christiane est plus sérieuse que **moi**.	*Christiane is more serious than I am.*
Vous êtes moins travailleur qu'**eux**.	*You are not as hardworking as they are.*
Je suis aussi motivée que **lui**.	*I'm as motivated as he is.*

- The adjective **bon** has an irregular comparative form **meilleur/e**, as shown below:

Ce livre est bon.	*This book is good.*
En fait, ce livre est **meilleur** que le dernier livre que j'ai lu.	*In fact, this book is better than the last book I read.*
Le dernier livre était moins bon.	*The last book was less good.*

- To express the superlative, use the definite article **le**, **la**, or **les** with **plus**, **moins**, or **meilleur/e**:

La nouvelle librairie est **la moins** chère.	*The new bookstore is the least expensive.*
Les profs de langues sont **les plus** énergiques.	*Language teachers are the most energetic.*
Le dictionnaire en ligne est **le meilleur**.	*The online dictionary is the best.*

08-28 to 08-29

À vous la parole

Initial practice: First test comprehension using a visual (a photo, image, or actual students) and questions to which students respond with a name: *Qui est moins grande, Brigitte ou Pauline ? —Brigitte. Qui est plus âgé, le prof ou Tom ?*, etc. Using names of famous people, you can also have students make simple comparisons using *plus* and *moins;* you might also suggest possible adjectives.

8-21 Comparez la vie universitaire. Répondez aux questions suivantes. Si vous avez besoin d'aide pour certaines questions, relisez les sections **Vie et culture** dans ce chapitre. Answers may vary.

MODÈLE Quel examen est le plus rigoureux : le bac français ou le SAT américain ?
- Le bac français est plus rigoreux que le SAT.

1. Qu'est-ce qui est plus prestigieux en France : une Grande École ou une université ? Une Grande École est plus prestigieuse qu'une université.
2. Quel prof est le plus interéssant : un prof répétitif ou un prof dynamique ? Un prof dynamique est plus intéressant qu'un prof répétitif.
3. Quelles études secondaires sont les plus longues : les études secondaires aux États-Unis ou au Québec ? Les études secondaires c sont plus longues que les études secondaires aux Ét
4. Quelles études universitaires sont les moins chères : les études universitaires en France ou les études universitaires aux États-Unis ? Les études universitaires en France sont moins chères que les études universitaires aux États-Unis.
5. Quel cours est le plus compliqué : un cours de français débutant ou un cours de neurobiologie cellulaire ? Un cours de neurobiologie cellulaire est plus compliqué qu'un cours de français.
6. Quel ouvrage de référence est le plus long : un dictionnaire ou une encyclopédie ? Une encyclopédie est plus longue qu'un dictionnaire.

Implementation: 8-21 Refer students back to the cultural information presented in the **Vie et culture** sections of this chapter or review that information before beginning. For some questions, not all students may be in agreement. Encourage students to argue for their point of view by providing more details or supporting facts.

Expansion: 8-21 Ask students to justify their answers to all the questions. Model this by explaining that *le bac français* is more rigorous than the SAT because it covers most of the material covered in the secondary school curriculum and because it features open-ended questions, problems, and essays as well as individual oral examinations. In addition, *le bac* is an exam that can be failed, in contrast to the SAT, which simply measures students against one another.

8-22 Comparisons. Regardez bien ces gens qui attendent le métro pour aller à l'Université de Montréal. Avec un/e partenaire décrivez-les en utilisant le comparatif et le superlatif.

MODÈLE É1 Sabrina est plus petite que Marie-Ange.

É2 Oui, mais Marie-Ange est plus chic.

É1 D'accord, mais Sabrina est la plus mignonne (*cute*).

Implementation: 8-22 Begin by having the class look at the picture and brainstorm as many adjectives as possible to describe the people in the picture. Ask them to speculate on the relationships among them, their likely courses of study, and the activities they like. You could impose a time limit and see which pair of students can come up with the most (properly formed) comparisons in the time given.

Additional practice: This can be used for an additional group activity, perhaps for review. Consider providing a measuring tape in centimeters or a conversion chart to enable students to complete this exercise using the metric system. **Les stars.** En groupes de 3 ou 4, comparez-vous ! Qui est…

MODÈLE le plus grand ?

É1 Qui est le plus grand de nous quatre ?

É2 Moi, je fais 1 m 75.

É3 Et moi, 1 m 80.

É1 Moi, je suis assez petite.

É4 Alors, Max est le plus grand.

1. le plus grand ? **2.** le plus jeune ? **3.** le plus sociable ? **4.** le plus travailleur ? **5.** le moins doué pour le sport ? **6.** le plus doué pour les langues étrangères ? **7.** le meilleur musicien ? **8.** le meilleur étudiant en français ?

8-23 Comparez-vous ! Dites à votre partenaire comment vous vous comparez avec vos amis et les membres de votre famille.

MODÈLE votre mère et vous

É1 Ma mère est plus petite que moi, je suis plus grand qu'elle. Elle est plus patiente et plus généreuse que moi.

É2 Ma mère est beaucoup plus grande que moi, mais elle est plus forte. Elle est plus amusante, mais moins sportive que moi.

1. votre mère et vous
2. votre père et vous
3. votre frère ou votre sœur et vous
4. votre ami/e et vous
5. votre colocataire et vous
6. votre professeur et vous

Implementation: 8-24 This activity reinforces the idea that living languages evolve over time and vary from region to region. Our view is that no particular variety of French is superior to others, but rather that each regional variety functions in its own context. Students should be able to recognize and respect regional linguistic differences, even if they don't produce them in their own speech and writing. Explain to students that the Standard French they are learning (sometimes called International French) is based on the French spoken by educated persons in Paris. You might suggest that the differences between the regional French spoken in Canada and that of France are similar to differences in American and British English: primarily differences of pronunciation, vocabulary, and fixed expressions.

Écoutons

8-24 La fin de semaine : au parfum québécois.

A. Avant d'écouter. Comme vous l'avez appris, il y a des différences entre le français parlé au Québec et en France. Est-ce que vous pouvez signaler quelques différences de vocabulaire que vous vous rappelez (par exemple, **une majeure** vs. **une spécialisation** ou **des rôties** vs. **du pain grillé**) ? Il y a aussi des différences grammaticales et des différences de prononciation. Voici une liste de quelques expressions fréquentes en français québécois.

Implementation: ***En écoutant.*** Students may need to listen to the dialogue several times to note all of the Quebec expressions used. You may wish to ask them to "translate" the messages into Standard French. Note also that there are several instances of *ne* deletion in the following messages; this feature is typical of spoken French in all regional varieties.

Script: Écoutons

ALEX : Allô, c'est moi, Alex. Je t'appelle pour t'inviter à dîner dimanche à midi et demi à la maison. Tu te souviens de Sabrina, la blonde de mon frère ? Et bien, elle va être là avec ses parents. Je veux te les introduire. Si tu veux, amène ton chum, Olivier. Appelle-moi pour me dire si tu peux venir. À prochaine.

ZOÉ : Allô, c'est Zoé. Qu'est-ce qu'on fait cette fin de semaine ? Tu as planifié quelqu'chose ? J'ai envie d'aller au ciné. J'ai checké et il y a un bon film samedi vers trois heures. Écoute, on peut magasiner au centre d'achats, voir le film et ensuite prendre une crème glacée. Si tu veux, on prend mon char. Je passe te chercher vers une heure. C'est beau ?

EMMA : Salut, C'est Emma. Écoute, tu vas pas me croire, mais je tombe en amour. Il s'appelle Samuel et je l'ai connu à ma job. Il est très beau et intelligent. C'est un étudiant en génie qui adore faire la cuisine. Je suis tellement contente. On arrête pas de jaser de tout et d'avoir du fun. Je suis désolée mais je peux pas passer chez toi vendredi soir ; avec Samuel, on va voir une pièce de théâtre. Je t'appelle bientôt. Bonjour, là.

au Québec	**en France**
avoir du fun	s'amuser
checker	vérifier
dîner	déjeuner
introduire	présenter
jaser	discuter
magasiner	faire du shopping
planifier	faire des projets
tomber en amour	tomber amoureux/-euse de
une char	une voiture
ma blonde	ma petite amie
mon chum	mon petit ami
le centre d'achats	le centre commercial
la crème glacée	la glace
la fin de semaine	le week-end
une job	un job
allô	bonjour
O.K., c'est beau	d'accord, c'est bon
bienvenue	il n'y a pas de quoi
à prochaine	à la prochaine
bonjour	au revoir

Expansion: ***Après avoir écouté.*** Have students use the Quebec words and expressions listed to create a dialogue with one or two classmates. Possible scenarios might include: running into a friend on campus and introducing him/her to your boyfriend/girlfriend; calling a friend to invite him/her to do something fun – he/she would like to come but there is a problem; running into an ex-boyfriend/girlfriend on campus and trying to impress him or her. Encourage students to develop their conversations orally, without writing down a script. Then have each group perform their dialogue for the rest of the class—and let the class decide who did the best job!

B. En écoutant. Imaginez que vous êtes étudiant/e étranger/-ère à l'Université de Montréal et que le week-end approche. Écoutez ces messages que quelques amis québécois ont laissés dans votre boîte vocale (*voice mail*) et complétez le tableau avec les détails importants.

1. La première fois que vous écoutez ces messages, notez qui a appelé et pourquoi.
2. Écoutez une deuxième fois et ajoutez quelques détails importants pour chaque message.
3. Écoutez de nouveau et notez les expressions québécoises que vous remarquez. Connaissez-vous les équivalents en français international ?

Qui	**Pourquoi**	**Détails**	**Expressions québécoises**
1. *Alex*			*Allô,*
2.	*pour sortir samedi après-midi*		*fin de semaine,*
3.		*Il s'appelle Samuel*	

Note: ***Après avoir écouté.*** Some typical regional differences in English include: 1) pronunciation of merry/marry/Mary 2) usage of the words soda/pop/soft drink; students can probably add many more examples.

C. Après avoir écouté. Est-ce que vous avez eu du mal à comprendre les messages de ces jeunes Québécois ? Pourquoi ? Est-ce que vous avez les mêmes difficultés à comprendre les personnes qui parlent anglais comme langue maternelle mais qui viennent d'un autre pays (*country*) ou région anglophone ? Expliquez.

Presentation: Use the opening questions and other similar ones to introduce the topic. Present the names of places, job types, and occupations using the labeled groupings (MFL, Instructor's Resources). Describe what each person does. Test comprehension by changing to the images without labels (MFL, Instructor's Resources) and having students point out the person you name; then elicit repetitions with either/or questions: *C'est une pharmacienne ou une infirmière ?*

Leçon 3 Choix de carrière

Presentation: Point out that *la clinique* is a false cognate, referring to a private hospital. *Un/e fonctionnaire* is any government employee, including postal workers, *SNCF* employees, and teachers. Depending on the interests of your class, you may want to introduce additional professional vocabulary such as *un chef d'entreprise, un banquier, un cadre, un/e gérant/e, un directeur/une directrice, un/e psychologue, travailler dans la publicité*, etc.

POINTS DE DÉPART

Qu'est-ce que vous voulez faire comme travail ?

Dans quel domaine est-ce que vous voulez travailler ? Est-ce que vous voulez aider les gens, comme les médecins, par exemple ? Est-ce que vous voulez voyager, comme certains journalistes ? Est-ce que vous êtes doué pour les mathématiques, comme les comptables ?

À l'hôpital ou à la clinique

Au bureau

Les artistes

Les services

Les fonctionnaires

Initial practice: For each place named, tell which person would not work there: *un bureau : un avocat, un secrétaire, un serveur.* Recycle vocabulary dealing with college coursework: *Pour être médecin ? — On étudie la biologie, la chimie, la médecine*, etc. Ask students what profession they associate with famous names: Pablo Picasso, Marie Curie, Whoopi Goldberg, Albert Einstein, Diane Sawyer, etc. Once they have been given a few examples, have students suggest others.

Presentation: Once students are familiar with the names of professions, introduce the chart of job characteristics. Have students provide an example for each job characteristic: *Dans quelle profession est-ce qu'on a beaucoup de prestige ? — Un médecin a beaucoup de prestige*, etc. For now, treat the relative pronoun *où* as a fixed expression; it is presented in Ch. 10, L. 3.

Initial practice: You might include drills that focus on form as a clue to gender. Begin with a discrimination drill: *un homme, une femme ou impossible à dire ? Michèle est informaticienne. Pascal/e est dentiste. René est avocat. Pascale est serveuse. Claude est infirmière. Pascal est infirmier. Michèle est vendeuse. André est représentant de commerce. Dominique est fonctionnaire*, etc. Remind students of the rule that derives masculine variable adjectives from the feminine by loss of the final pronounced consonant. The same rule applies to some professions: *Elle est avocate → Il est avocat*, etc. Review the importance of a strong release of the final consonant for the feminine. Be sure to treat the **Vie et culture** section related to the feminization of names of professions.

08-35 to 08-38

Expansion: 8-25 Expand on this exercise by including the opposites, for example, *on ne gagne pas beaucoup d'argent* or *un diplôme universitaire est nécessaire.*

QU'EST-CE QUI VOUS INTÉRESSE ?

Je veux avoir…	Je cherche un travail où…
un bon salaire	on peut voyager
beaucoup de prestige	on peut aider les gens
beaucoup de responsabilités	on n'est pas trop stressé
un contact avec le public	on est très autonome
un travail en plein air	on gagne beaucoup d'argent

Implemenation: 8-25 You may choose to do a modified oral version of this exercise in conjunction with your presentation of the job characteristics.

À vous la parole

8-25 Classez les métiers. Pour chaque description, identifiez quelques métiers ou professions qui y correspondent. *Answers may vary.*

MODÈLE On gagne beaucoup d'argent.
- Un avocat gagne beaucoup d'argent.
- Un acteur connu gagne beaucoup d'argent.

1. On est très autonome. un écrivain, un/e musicien/ne
2. On travaille en plein air. un agent de police, un facteur
3. Un diplôme universitaire n'est pas nécessaire. un/e technicien/ne, un vendeur
4. On n'est pas très stressé. un écrivain, un facteur
5. On a un contact avec le public. un professeur, un/e avocat/e
6. On a beaucoup de prestige. un/e avocat/e, un médecin
7. On peut travailler avec les enfants. un médecin, un/e infirmier/ière
8. On peut voyager. une femme d'affaires, un/e journaliste

8-26 Aptitudes et goûts. D'après leur description, quel est le métier probable des gens suivants ? *Answers may vary.*

MODÈLE Rémi est sociable. Il aime aider les gens avec leurs problèmes.
- Il va être assistant social.

1. Lucie s'intéresse au théâtre. Elle danse et elle chante très bien. actrice
2. Kévin aime le travail précis. Il est très bon en maths. comptable, ingénieur
3. Stéphanie est énergique et sociable. Elle aime voyager, et elle aime le contact avec le public. femme d'affaires, journaliste, représentante de commerce
4. Camille s'intéresse à l'informatique et elle aime écrire des programmes. informaticienne
5. Nicolas est très doué pour les sciences ; mais il préfère un travail solitaire. technicien
6. Nathalie adore écrire et elle a fait des études de sciences politiques ; elle veut vivre à Washington ou à New York un jour. journaliste, professeur d'université, a
7. Charline s'intéresse à l'architecture ; elle aime dessiner des maisons mais surtout des immeubles. architecte
8. Grégorie aime travailler avec les enfants ; il est calme et patient. professeur, infirmier, assistant social

ote: Canadians and the Swiss have used the form *la professeure* for some time, whereas in France this form is frowned on. The French have no difficulty, however, using *la prof* and *une prof* in casual conversation. Additional feminine forms for professions include *une écrivaine, une ingénieure.* In countries like Switzerland and Canada, these terms have been officially accepted and are in fairly widespread use. Even in France, it is becoming increasingly common to hear references to female government officials such as *Madame la Ministre*, on news reports and in the press, for example.

Vie et culture

La féminisation des noms de professions

Partout dans le monde, les femmes font carrière dans les professions qui étaient autrefois réservées aux hommes. La langue doit changer pour refléter ces nouvelles réalités. Par exemple, en anglais, on a tendance à employer des termes neutres, sans marque de genre, par exemple, on dit *server* au lieu de *waiter* ou *waitress* ou bien *firefighter* à la place de *fireman*. Le français procède autrement : la plupart des mots qui désignent des professions ont une forme marquée pour le genre masculin ou le genre féminin, par exemple, **un acteur** et **une actrice**. Cependant, il y a quelques professions qui n'ont pas de forme féminine, comme **professeur** ou **médecin.** Pour désigner une femme qui est médecin, il faut dire, **c'est un médecin femme**. Dans le cas d'une femme qui est professeur, on l'appelle **Madame le Professeur**, et les étudiants diraient **Mon professeur de chimie est Madame Durand**. Par contre, au Canada et en Suisse, les étudiants utilisent le terme **une professeure** et ils disent par exemple, **Ma professeure de psychologie s'appelle Madame Laurent**. C'est vrai aussi que même en France, en français parlé on dit **la prof** ou **une prof**.

Implementation: You might ask students to generate additional examples of this trend in English, such as police officer, mail carrier, and sales associate.

ET VOUS ?

1. D'après ce que vous avez appris, donnez quelques exemples de noms de professions qui ont :
   a. une forme invariable
   b. une forme invariable mais des articles variables
   c. des formes masculines et féminines distinctes
2. D'après vous, pourquoi est-ce que les anglophones préfèrent des termes neutres qui ne précisent pas le genre, tandis que les pays francophones semblent préférer des termes qui sont spécifiés pour le genre ?

Un chef de bureau parle avec ses employés.

Key: ***Et vous ?*** *Answers may vary.* 1) Réponses possibles : a. *un professeur, un écrivain, un médecin, un ingénieur* b. *un/e dentiste, un/e architecte, un/e journaliste, un/e fonctionnaire* c. *une agente, un agent de police ; une avocate, un avocat ; une factrice, un facteur ; une infirmière, un infirmier ; une musicienne, un musicien ; une vendeuse, un vendeur ; une actrice, un acteur ; une technicienne, un technicien ; une pharmacienne, un pharmacien ; une assistante sociale, un assistant social* 2) En anglais, la situation normale c'est de ne pas marquer le genre des noms tandis qu'en français, c'est le contraire. Donc, chaque langue semble changer pour correspondre à sa grammaire et pour préciser que les métiers sont ouverts à tout le monde et pas seulement aux gens d'un sexe particulier.

Implementation: 8-27 You may need to introduce additional vocabulary, based on students' interests and career plans.

8-27 Vos projets de carrière. Parlez de vos projets de carrière en groupes de trois ou quatre. N'oubliez pas de parler de ce que vous ne voulez pas faire également.

MODÈLE É1 Toi, Mike, qu'est-ce que tu voudrais faire comme travail ?
É2 Je veux être assistant social. J'aime beaucoup aider les gens et j'ai un bon contact avec les gens. Je fais des études de psychologie.
É1 Et toi, Margot, qu'est-ce que tu veux faire ?
É3 Je ne sais pas vraiment. Mais, je sais que je ne veux pas être avocate. Ma mère est avocate. J'ai l'impression qu'on travaille trop. C'est trop stressant.

Presentation: You may also wish to present the functional difference between the two patterns, which is related to the notion of topic vs. comment. For example, if Céline Dion has already been mentioned in the conversation, one is more likely to use the first pattern, *elle est chanteuse.* If however she is being introduced into the conversation, one would be more likely to use *Céline Dion, c'est une chanteuse.* Display examples of the two patterns and explain usage, being sure to point out the difference between modified and proper nouns on the one hand versus unmodified nouns on the other. You may also wish to point out that the structure *il(s)/elle(s) + être* is also used with adjectives when referring to a person. Compare *Il est français* with *C'est un Français* or *Il est bizarre* (a person) with *C'est bizarre* (a situation or thing).

FORMES ET FONCTIONS

1. *C'est* et *il est*

- The expressions **c'est** and **il/elle est** in French have similar meanings but are used in different contexts. Consider the following sentences.

C'est Céline Dion. **Elle est** chanteuse.	*This is Céline Dion. She's a singer.*
C'est une chanteuse québécoise.	*She's a singer from Quebec.*
C'est la chanteuse canadienne la plus connue aux États-Unis.	*She's the best known Canadian singer in the United States.*

- Use **c'est/ce sont** + a proper or a modified noun. Modifed nouns are those that are modified by an adjective or preceded by a definite or indefinite article.

C'est Juliette Binoche.	*This is Juliette Binoche.*
Mme Dumont, **c'est** le chef du département.	*Ms. Dumont is the department chair.*
Leurs parents ? **Ce sont** des architectes.	*Their parents? They're architects.*
C'est une excellente musicienne.	*She's an excellent musician.*
Ce sont des avocats ambitieux.	*They are ambitious lawyers.*

- Use **il/elle est** or **ils/elles sont** + an unmodified noun when indicating someone's profession. Note that a person's name can also be used in this construction as the subject of **être**.

Elle est musicienne.	*She is a musician.*
Ils sont fonctionnaires.	*They are civil servants.*
Diane **est** avocate.	*Diane is an attorney.*

Fiche pratique

Some distinctions made in French have no clear English equivalent. For that reason, try to avoid translating directly from English into French, and instead focus on the French structures. For example, when talking about professions in French, learn the differences in usage between the structures **Il est prof** and **C'est un prof**, which both mean *He's a teacher*, without being swayed by English usage.

À vous la parole

Initial practice: Using the unlabeled images of professions from the **Points de départ** (MFL, Instructor's Resources), have students identify the profession of each person shown: *C'est une infirmière*, etc. Draw students' attention to the information presented in the **Fiche pratique** and insist on the fact that *C'est* and *Ce sont* are used with indefinite or definite articles and that the subject pronoun cannot be used in this context, contrary to English usage.

39
)
42 **8-28 Professions et traits de caractère.** Pour chaque profession, suggérez une qualité appropriée. *Answers may vary.*

Implementation: 8-28 To prepare, review adjectives and brainstorm characteristics of people in certain professions: *une infirmière = gentille, généreuse ; un avocat =sérieux, ambitieux ; un écrivain = individualiste*, etc.

MODÈLE Anne est infirmière.
- C'est une infirmière calme.

1. Delphine est avocate. C'est une avocate intelligente.
2. Rémi est assistant social. C'est un assistant social sympa.
3. Virginie est médecin. C'est un médecin gentil.
4. Max est représentant de commerce. C'est un représentant de commerce ambitieux.
5. Coralie est musicienne. C'est une musicienne douée.
6. Florian et Sylvie sont informaticiens. Ce sont des informaticiens individualistes.
7. Hugo et Jessica sont serveurs. Ce sont des serveurs sociables.
8. Sandra et Alex sont professeurs. Ce sont des professeurs dynamiques.

8-29 Identification. Identifiez la nationalité (**américain/e** ou **français/e**) et la profession de ces personnes connues.

Variations: 8-29: Use pictures of these well-known individuals as cues and suggest some local celebrities as well. Have students suggest additional possibilities; this could be structured as a game. Or simplify by having students give the profession only: *Jules Verne ? C'est un écrivain.*

MODÈLE Jules Verne
- C'est un écrivain français.

1. Gustave Eiffel C'est un ingénieur français.
2. Barbra Streisand C'est une chanteuse/une actrice américaine.
3. Gérard Depardieu C'est un acteur français.
4. Louis Pasteur C'est un médecin/chercheur français.
5. Sonia Sotomayor C'est une avocate américaine.
6. Christiane Amanpour C'est une journaliste américaine.
7. Frank Lloyd Wright C'est un architecte américain.
8. Toni Morrison C'est un écrivain américain.

8-30 Quelle est leur profession ? Discutez avec votre partenaire les métiers et professions des gens que vous connaissez.

MODÈLE votre mère

É1 Ma mère travaille au labo dans un hôpital. Elle est technicienne. Elle aime la science, et elle aide les gens.

É2 Ma mère travaille à la maison ; c'est une femme au foyer (*homemaker*). Elle s'occupe de la maison, des repas et des finances.

1. votre mère
2. votre père
3. votre frère ou sœur
4. votre grand-père
5. votre oncle

2. Le verbe *venir*

Presentation: Present this verb inductively by providing many oral examples and asking questions that model the various forms: *Je viens de Chicago ; et vous, vous venez de Chicago aussi ? Et vos parents, ils viennent de…*, etc. Ask students to summarize forms and display the verb chart. The main irregularity of this verb is the change from *ven-* /vən/ to *vienn-* /vjɛn/. The change to a nasal vowel in the singular forms is predictable from the loss of the final /n/ (it is analogous to the alternation *italienne/italien*, for example). The unstable *e* of *venons, venez*, and *venu* is usually dropped.

- The verb **venir** means *to come* or *to come from*:

VENIR *to come, to come from*

SINGULIER		PLURIEL	
je	viens	nous	ven**ons**
tu	viens	vous	ven**ez**
il / elle / on	vient	ils / elles	vienn**ent**

IMPÉRATIF : **Viens** ! **Venez** ici ! **Venons** voir ces cartes !

PASSÉ COMPOSÉ : Elle **est venue** hier.

- **Devenir** (*to become*), **revenir** (*to come back*), **tenir** (*to hold*), **retenir** (*to hold, to book a room/a seat*), **maintenir** (*to affirm, to uphold*), **soutenir** (*to support*), and **obtenir** (*to obtain*) are conjugated like **venir**:

Qu'est-ce que vous **devenez** maintenant ?	*What's new with you these days?*
Quand est-ce que tu **reviens** de la fac ?	*When are you coming back from college?*
Il **tenait** son livre à la main.	*He held his book in his hand.*
Elle essaie de **retenir** toutes ces informations.	*She is trying to retain all that information.*
Il **a retenu** deux places pour la pièce.	*He booked/reserved two seats for the play.*
Je **maintiens** que c'est vrai.	*I maintain that it's true.*
Le Sénat **soutient** le Président.	*The Senate is supporting the President.*
J'ai **obtenu** mon diplôme en mai.	*I got my degree in May.*

- To express an event that has just occurred, use **venir de** plus an infinitive.

Le médecin **vient de terminer** la consultation.	*The physician has just finished the visit.*
Nous **venons de quitter** le bureau.	*We've just left the office.*

08-43 to 08-46

À vous la parole

Initial practice: Begin with a discrimination drill: one person, or more than one? *Il vient demain. Elles viennent de Bruxelles. Viens ici ! Ils retiennent des places. Elle vient de partir. Elles tiennent leurs livres. Ils viennent avec moi. Il obtient un diplôme en sociologie. Elles viennent de Paris. Ils deviennent fatigués. Elle soutient ses employés*, etc. Follow up with a simple substitution drill: *Je viens ce soir ; nous, lui*, etc.

8-31 Du retour au travail. Dites d'où ces employés de bureau reviennent après la pause-déjeuner d'après les descriptions. *Answers may vary.*

MODÈLE Angélique devait commander des nouveaux chèques et retirer de l'argent.
- Elle revient de la banque.

1. Marine et Amélie avaient des courses à faire. Elles reviennent du centre commercial/du marché/du magasin.
2. Cédric a retrouvé sa femme pour prendre un café et discuter un peu. Il revient du café.
3. Nous avons déjeuné avec nos collègues. Nous revenons du restaurant/de la cafétéria.
4. J'ai dû acheter un livre pour offrir à ma mère. Je reviens de la librairie.
5. Sébastien et Sophie ont cherché des places pour le spectacle ce soir. Ils reviennent du théâtre.
6. Karine et Sandra ont acheté des biscuits, du café et du sucre pour la réunion cet après-midi. Elles reviennent du supermarché.
7. Damien a cherché les médicaments pour son fils qui est resté à la maison avec une fièvre. Il revient de la pharmacie.

Expansion: 8-32: Have students discuss with a partner how they have changed from last semester or last year or perhaps from when they were in high school. Share answers with the class.

8-32 L'entretien annuel d'évaluation professionelle. Comment est-ce que ces professionnels ont changé depuis leur dernière évaluation professionnelle ? Choisissez l'adjectif qui convient dans la liste et précisez-le avec **plus** ou **moins**: *Answers may vary.*

ambitieux	calme	discipliné	dynamique
égoïste	paresseux	sociable	stressé

MODÈLE J'ai de plus en plus de travail et de moins en moins de temps.
- Je deviens plus stressée.

1. Tu ne travailles pas beaucoup ces jours-ci. Tu deviens plus paresseux.
2. Roger recherche de plus en plus les conseils de ses supérieurs pour avancer. Il devient plus ambitieux.
3. Nous faisons un cours de yoga après le travail trois fois par semaine. Nous devenons moins stressés.
4. Mes employés arrivent à l'heure plus souvent. Ils deviennent plus disciplinés.
5. C'est fini. Je ne donne rien aux autres secrétaires. Cela suffit ! Je deviens plus égoïste.
6. Vous parlez à plus de collègues maintenant. Vous devenez plus sociable.

8-33 Avant de venir en classe. Qu'est-ce que vous venez de faire, juste avant d'arriver en classe ? Expliquez-le à un/e partenaire.

MODÈLE É1 Moi, je viens de déjeuner au resto U. Et toi ?
É2 Moi, je viens de travailler dans la salle informatique. Je viens de terminer mes devoirs.

Implementation: 8-34 Discuss the questions in **Avant de regarder** with the class as a whole, or let students work in pairs or small groups. Show the location of Seillans on a map, and later, of Marseille, where Barbara completed her studies. Ask students if they remember the village of Seillans from the **Observons** in Ch. 6, L 1. If you have not shown it yet, you may choose to do so now in conjunction with this segment. To expand on Barbara's work, you could ask students to comment on the architecture of Seillans and speculate on what kind of work she might do (i.e., a lot of renovation).

Note: The *École Normale Supérieure d'Architecture Marseille Luminy*, where Barbara studied, is a *Grande École*. Within the School of Architecture, the *Département de préparation à l'administration générale* prepares candidates for national examinations that are part of the professional credentialing process.

Observons

-54
o
-56

8-34 Études et travail.

Barbara au travail

A. Avant de regarder. Qu'est-ce que vous voulez faire après vos études ? Comment est-ce que vous vous préparez à votre future profession ? Dressez une liste des aspects positifs et négatifs de cette profession. Dans cette séquence, Barbara décrit ses études et son travail. Elle vit et travaille à Seillans, un petit village dans le sud de la France. Regardez l'image de Barbara. Quelle est sa profession à votre avis ?

B. En regardant. Entourez toutes les bonnes réponses.

1. Barbara est…
   a. journaliste b. architecte c. avocate d. professeur
2. Elle a fait ses études dans la ville de…
   a. Strasbourg b. Toulon c. Paris d. Marseille
3. Elle a étudié à…
   a. la Faculté de Droit b. l'École d'Architecture et des Beaux-Arts
   c. l'École de Médecine d. l'École d'Ingénieurs
4. Avec sa spécialisation, Barbara a fait… ans d'études et de formation professionnelle.
   a. trois b. cinq c. sept d. dix
5. Est-ce que Barbara aime sa profession ?
   a. oui b. non
6. Quelles sont les raisons qu'elle donne pour aimer son travail ?
   a. Elle est disponible pour ses enfants. b. Elle a beaucoup de responsabilités.
   c. Elle gagne bien sa vie. d. Ses horaires sont souples.
   e. Le travail est intéressant.

C. Après avoir regardé. Est-ce que le travail de Barbara vous intéresse ? Pourquoi ? Qu'est-ce que vous recherchez dans une profession ? Discutez avec vos camarades de classe.

Script: *Observons*

BARBARA : Voilà, mais je suis architecte, je suis diplômée par le gouvernement, DPAG [Département de préparation à l'administration générale]. J'ai fait mon diplôme à Marseille, dans les Bouches-du-Rhône, à l'École d'Architecture et les Beaux-Arts. Et donc, euh, je suis diplômée depuis 1986. J'ai fait sept ans d'études et puis trois ans après de spécialisation pour le, bah, le bâtiment parasismique. J'aime beaucoup mon travail, parce que je suis ici principalement sur les maisons de Seillans, avec des projets de rénovation et un peu de création aussi. Et j'aime beaucoup ce métier parce que, on est disponible pour les horaires, on peut travailler à la maison, pour mes enfants, je peux travailler aussi euh, des rendez-vous de chantier, dehors et donc j'ai des horaires euh, c'est assez souple, voilà, au niveau des horaires. Donc j'aime beaucoup ce travail, et j'aime surtout euh, Seillans, parce que c'est, c'est vraiment typique, les maisons que l'on fait ici en Provence et c'est aussi très intéressant, mais il y a beaucoup aussi de clientèle anglaise, donc étrangère, qui vient de s'installer. Voilà. Mais c'est très intéressant.

Leçon 

à l'université, à la fac(ulté)	*at the university, at college*
un amphithéâtre	*lecture hall*
des associations (f.) étudiantes	*student organizations*
la bibliothèque universitaire (la BU)	*university library*
des bureaux (m.) administratifs	*administrative offices*
le bureau des inscriptions	*registrar's office*
le bureau du professeur	*professor's office*
la cafétéria	*cafeteria*
le centre étudiant	*student union*
le centre sportif	*sports complex*
une infirmerie	*health center*
un labo(ratoire) de chimie	*chemistry lab*
un parc de stationnement	*parking lot (Can.)*
un pavillon (le pavillion principal)	*building (main building)*
un plan du campus	*campus map*
la résidence	*residence hall*
le restaurant universitaire (le resto U)	*dining hall*
une salle informatique	*computer lab*
une station de métro	*subway, metro stop*
un terrain de sport	*playing field, court*

prépositions de lieu	*prepositions*
à côté de	*next to, beside*
à droite de	*to the right of*
à gauche de	*to the left of*
dans	*in, inside*
derrière	*behind*
devant	*in front of*
en face de	*across from*
loin de	*far from*
(tout) près de	*(very) close to, near*

pour comparer	*to compare*
aussi… que	*as . . . as*
autant de… que	*as many . . . as*
moins (de)… que	*less . . . than*
plus (de)… que	*more . . . than*
mieux que	*better than*
le mieux	*the best*

quelques expressions indéfinies et négatives	*some indefinite and negative expressions*
quelque chose	*something*
quelquefois	*sometimes*
quelqu'un	*someone*
ne… jamais	*never*
ne… personne	*no one*
ne… rien	*nothing*

autres mots utiles	*other useful words*
un cours	*course*
une fin de semaine	*weekend (Can.)*
une navette	*shuttle, bus*
un permis	*permit*

Leçon 2

des cours (m.)	*courses*
l'allemand (m.)	*German*
l'espagnol (m.)	*Spanish*
Voir aussi à la page 246	*See also p. 246*

les facultés (f.)	*colleges, schools*
les arts (m.) du spectacle	*performing arts*
les beaux-arts (m.)	*fine arts*
le droit	*law*
le génie	*engineering*
la gestion	*business management*
l'informatique	*computer science*
le journalisme	*journalism*
les lettres (f.)	*humanities*
la médecine	*medicine*
les sciences de l'éducation (f.)	*education*
les sciences économiques	*economics*
les sciences humaines	*social sciences*
les sciences naturelles	*natural sciences*
les sciences physiques	*physical sciences*

pour parler des études (f.)	*to talk about studies*
un baccalauréat (en sciences économiques)	*B.A or B.S. degree (in economics) (Can.)*
une concentration	*concentration, emphasis*
un dictionnaire	*dictionary*
un diplôme (en beaux-arts)	*degree (in fine arts)*
une majeure (en sociologie)	*major (in sociology) (Can.)*
une mineure (en français)	*minor (in French) (Can.)*
une note (avoir une note, mettre une note)	*grade (to have/receive a grade, give a grade)*
préparer un diplôme (en chimie)	*to do a degree (in chemistry)*
un roman	*novel*
un semestre	*semester*
une spécialisation (en génie)	*major (in engineering) (Fr.)*
se spécialiser (en biologie)	*to major (in biology) (Fr.)*
suivre un cours	*to take a course*

des devoirs (m.)	*assignments, homework*
un devoir	*essay, assignment*
un essai	*essay*
un examen	*exam*
passer un examen	*to take an exam*
réussir un examen	*to pass an exam*
un exposé	*oral presentation*
un projet	*project*
pour décrire les cours, les examens, les notes	*to describe courses, tests, grades*
difficile	*difficult*
ennuyeux/ennuyeuse	*boring, tedious*
facile	*easy*
facultatif/-ive	*optional, elective*
final/e	*final*
intéressant/e	*interesting*
médiocre	*mediocre*
(le/la/les) meilleur/e/s	*better (best)*
obligatoire	*mandatory, required*
verbes de communication	*verbs of communication*
décrire	*to describe*
dire	*to say, to tell*
écrire	*to write*
lire	*to read*

Leçon 3

où on travaille	*where people work*
un bureau	*office*
une clinique	*private hospital*
un hôpital	*public hospital*
des métiers (m.) et des professions (f.)	*jobs and professions*
un acteur/une actrice	*actor/actress*
un/e agent/e de police	*police officer*
un/e architecte	*architect*
un/e artiste	*artist*
un/e assistant/e social/e	*social worker*
un/e avocat/e	*lawyer*
un chanteur/une chanteuse	*singer*
un/e comptable	*accountant*
un/e dentiste	*dentist*
un écrivain	*writer*
un facteur/une factrice	*mail carrier*
une femme/un homme d'affaires	*businesswoman/businessman*
un/e fonctionnaire	*government worker*
un infirmier/une infirmière	*nurse*
un/e informaticien/ne	*computer scientist*
un ingénieur	*engineer*
un/e journaliste	*journalist*
un médecin	*physician*
un/e musicien/ne	*musician*
un/e pharmacien/ne	*pharmacist*
un professeur, une professeure	*teacher, professor* (Can.)
un/e représentant/e de commerce	*sales representative*
un/e secrétaire	*secretary*
un serveur/une serveuse	*server*
un/e technicien/ne	*(lab) technician*
un vendeur/une vendeuse	*sales associate*
autres mots utiles	*other useful words*
l'argent (m.)	*money*
autonome	*independent*
une carrière	*career*
être doué/e	*to be talented*
les gens (m.)	*people*
en plein air	*outdoors*
le prestige	*prestige*
le public (un contact avec le public)	*the public (contact with the public)*
la responsabilité	*responsibility*
un salaire	*salary*
les services (m.)	*the service sector*
le travail	*work*
quelques verbes	*some verbs*
aider les gens	*to help people*
chercher	*to look for*
devenir	*to become*
gagner (de l'argent)	*to earn (money), to win*
maintenir	*to affirm, to uphold*
obtenir	*to obtain*
retenir	*to hold, to book*
revenir	*to come back*
soutenir	*to support*
tenir	*to hold*
venir	*to come*
venir de + *inf.*	*to have just done something*
voyager	*to travel*

Vocabulaire

Pourquoi est-ce que ces deux amoureux se quittent sur le quai de la gare de Lyon à Paris ? Partir, c'est mourir un peu !

9 Voyageons !

After completing this chapter, you should be able to:

- Describe future plans
- Make travel plans
- Make arrangements for lodgings
- Describe places and people
- Express obligation and wishes
- Describe some major French cities, especially Paris

Leçon 1 Projets de voyage

POINTS DE DÉPART

Comment y aller ?

M. et Mme Mathieu partent en vacances au Maroc. Ils prennent un taxi pour aller à la gare, puis le train pour aller à l'aéroport prendre leur vol. Ils ont beaucoup de valises.

MME MATHIEU : Tu as tout ? On n'a rien oublié ?
M. MATHIEU : Voyons. On a besoin de nos passeports et de nos billets. Tout est là. Non, je n'ai rien oublié. Et toi, tu n'as rien oublié ?
MME MATHIEU : Mais si ! J'ai laissé mon nouveau appareil photo numérique sur la table dans la cuisine, zut !
M. MATHIEU : Ne t'en fais pas. J'ai mon appareil numérique ; je te le prête si tu veux.
MME MATHIEU : Merci, mon chéri, c'est très gentil.

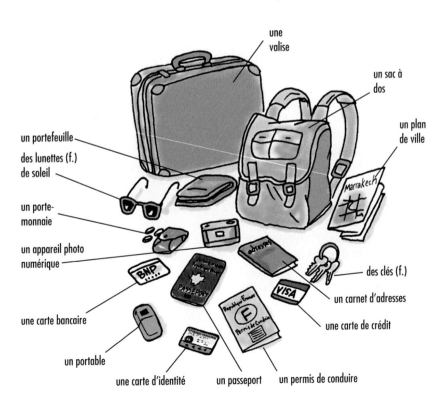

une valise
un sac à dos
un plan de ville
un portefeuille
des lunettes (f.) de soleil
un porte-monnaie
un appareil photo numérique
des clés (f.)
un carnet d'adresses
une carte bancaire
une carte de crédit
un portable
une carte d'identité
un passeport
un permis de conduire

Presentation: Use the drawing of the taxi (MFL, Instructor's Resources) as you describe the Mathieus' trip. Let students listen to the dialogue, then ask simple comprehension questions: *Comment est-ce que les Mathieu voyagent ? Quelle est leur destination ? Qu'est-ce que M. Mathieu emporte ? Qu'est-ce que Mme Mathieu a oublié ? Quelle est la solution proposée par M. Mathieu ?* Point out the expression *avoir besoin de*, taught in Ch. 5, L. 3. Tell students to imagine that the class is taking a trip to Paris and that there are things you must bring because you need them. Start off with *nous avons besoin de nos passeports* and ask students to provide other examples. You may also wish to review the conjugation of the verb *avoir* and remind students of another expression they learned in Ch. 3, L. 3: *avoir envie de.*

Presentation: Use the visual of the hand luggage (MFL, Instructor's Resources) to present the vocabulary of travel items; provide a description for each item. Test comprehension by having students point to the items you name; then have them repeat: *C'est un passeport ou un permis ?* The French refer to their driver's license as *le papier rose.* You might also use objects to enliven this presentation. Then complete Ex. 9-1.

Presentation: Use visuals (for example, magazine ads) or verbal cues (*Air France, c'est des avions,* etc.) to convey the meaning for means of transportation. Explain the difference between *un bus* (operating within a city) and *un car* (operating between cities). Test comprehension, have students repeat, then move on to Ex. 9-2 and 9-3.

LES MOYENS DE TRANSPORT

l'avion (m.)	le car	la moto	le tram(way)
le bateau	le métro	le taxi	le vélo
le bus	la mobylette	le train	la voiture

When specifying a means of transportation, use . . .

- **prendre** plus the means of transportation preceded by an article or possessive:

Je prends **le** métro.	*I'm taking the subway.*
Ils prennent **un** taxi.	*They're taking a taxi.*
Elle prend **son** vélo.	*She's taking her bike.*

- verbs of travel such as **aller**, **partir**, or **voyager** are followed by the preposition **en** or **à**, as specified below. In these cases, no article is used.

en avion, **en** bateau, **en** bus, **en** car, **en** métro, **en** taxi, **en** train, **en** tramway, **en** voiture, **à** mobylette, **à** moto, **à** pied, **à** vélo

Nous partons **en** avion pour le Mali.	*We're leaving by plane for Mali.*
Moi, je vais au travail **en** métro, mais Christine va au travail **à** pied.	*I take the subway to work, but Christine goes to work on foot.*
Ils préfèrent voyager **en** train.	*They prefer to travel by train.*

09-01 to 09-04

À vous la parole

Additional practice: Put students in groups and ask: *Est-ce que vous avez un sac, un sac à dos, un pantalon ou une jupe avec des poches ? Qu'est-ce qu'il y a à l'intérieur ? Comparez ce que vous avez avec un/e partenaire. Qui a les objets les plus intéressants ?* Provide a model: *Voilà mon sac. Voyons, j'ai un portefeuille avec mon permis de conduire et ma carte bancaire, j'ai des lunettes, un carnet d'adresses et un stylo. —Moi, je n'ai pas de sac. Dans mes poches, j'ai mon portefeuille avec un peu d'argent et mon permis et ma carte étudiante, et voilà mes clés.*

9-1 Qu'est-ce qu'il faut ? De quoi est-ce que les touristes ont besoin ?

MODÈLE pour trouver les monuments dans une grande ville ?
- Il faut un plan de la ville. *Answers may vary.*

1. pour payer l'hôtel ? une carte bancaire, une carte de crédit
2. pour louer une voiture ? un permis de conduire, une carte de crédit, une carte d'identité
3. pour ranger leur argent ? un portefeuille, un porte-monnaie
4. pour prendre des photos ? un appareil photo numérique, un portable
5. pour aller dans un pays étranger ? un passeport, une carte d'identité [for Europeans in Europe]
6. pour rentrer dans leur chambre d'hôtel ? une clé
7. pour téléphoner ? un portable
8. pour mettre leurs affaires ? une valise, un sac à dos

Vie et culture

09-52

Voyager en train en France

Regardez la séquence vidéo, *On prend le train*. Comment sont les trains français ? Pourquoi, à votre avis, est-ce que les Français, et les Européens en général, voyagent plus souvent en train que les Nord-Américains ?

En France, le système ferroviaire[1] est nationalisé. Tous les trains sont sous le contrôle de la Société Nationale des Chemins de Fer Français (la SNCF). Le TGV (Train à Grande Vitesse) est un des trains les plus rapides au monde. Par exemple, il parcourt[2] les 400 kilomètres qui séparent Lyon de Paris en seulement deux heures. Regardez la carte du réseau TGV : quelles sont les régions desservies par le train rapide ? Où est-ce que vous voudriez voyager en TGV ?

Depuis 1994, on peut traverser la Manche entre la France et l'Angleterre en train, en passant par le « Chunnel. » Ce tunnel est important, parce qu'il relie l'Angleterre au continent européen. Ainsi, au départ de Lyon, il faut seulement cinq heures pour arriver en Angleterre.

[1]*railway* [2]*covers*

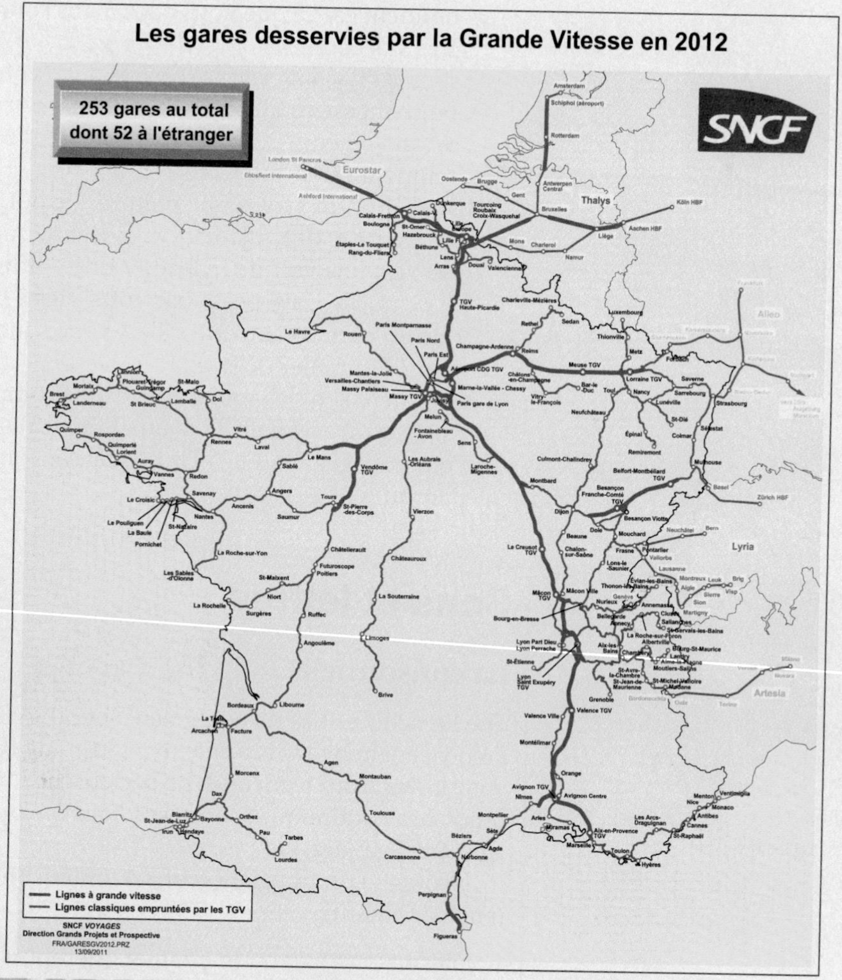

Implementation: Show the brief video clip (*On prend le train*) and help students identify locations and activities pictured and mentioned in the voice-over. Make sure students understand the importance of the TGV and the Chunnel. Some of your students may have traveled by train in Europe and even via the Chunnel; ask them to share their impressions.

Key: 9-2 *Answers may vary.* 1) prendre le train, l'avion, la voiture 2) prendre l'avion 3) aller à pied 4) aller à pied, à vélo, à mobylette, en tram, en bus 5) prendre le métro, le bus, la mobylette, le tram, aller à pied, à vélo 6) prendre la voiture, aller à vélo 7) prendre le train, l'avion 8) prendre l'avion, aller en bateau

9-2 Quel moyen de transport ? D'après les indications, quel/s moyen/s de transport est-ce que les personnes suivantes vont probablement utiliser ?

MODÈLE Adeline habite près de Paris ; elle va faire des courses à Paris.
- Elle va prendre le train pour aller à Paris, et ensuite le métro ou l'autobus pour faire ses courses.

1. Mme Duclair habite à Paris ; elle va rendre visite à sa grand-mère à Lyon.
2. Les Lefranc vont quitter la France pour passer des vacances aux Antilles.
3. La petite Hélène va à l'école primaire près de chez elle.
4. Robert habite une ville moyenne ; il va au centre-ville pour faire ses courses.
5. M. Rolland doit traverser Paris pour aller au travail.
6. Maxime et Amélie vont faire un pique-nique à la campagne.
7. Mme Antonine voyage pour son travail : elle va à Lyon, à Rome et à Berlin.
8. Les Leclair vont visiter les îles grecques pendant les vacances.

Implementation: 9-3 Give students a limited amount of time to work in pairs, then bring the class together to compare responses.

9-3 Comment y aller ? Avec un/e partenaire, discutez de ces questions. Ensuite, comparez vos réponses et vos conclusions avec les conclusions de vos camarades de classe.

1. Comment est-ce que vous allez à vos cours ? Comment est-ce que vous faites vos courses ?
2. Est-ce qu'il y a un service de bus dans votre ville ? Un métro ? Un tram ? Comment est-ce que les habitants de votre ville vont au travail habituellement ?
3. Comment est-ce que vous rentrez chez vous pour les vacances ?
4. Est-ce que vous avez une voiture ? Si oui, quelle sorte de voiture : une voiture française, allemande, coréenne, japonaise, américaine ? Est-ce que c'est une voiture hybride ? une voiture électrique ?
5. Est-ce que le train passe par votre ville ? Où est-ce qu'on peut aller en train en partant de votre ville ? Est-ce que vous avez déjà voyagé en train ? Pour aller où ?
6. Comment sont les trains américains comparés aux trains français ? Est-ce qu'il existe un TGV aux États-Unis ?
7. Pour voyager aux États-Unis, quel est votre moyen de transport préféré ? Pourquoi ?

Sons et lettres

La consonne *r*

Note: The American *r* is a retroflex *r*; the tongue curves back. Tell students not to curl or roll their tongue to produce the French *r*. Before words beginning with a vowel, a word-final *r* (like all final consonants) is pronounced as if it were part of the next word.

The French /r/ has no equivalent sound in English. To pronounce /r/ in French, begin by saying **aga**; then, keeping the tip of your tongue against your lower front teeth and the back of the tongue against the soft palate, produce a continuous sound: **ara**. Practice by alternating the two sounds: **aga**/**ara**, **aga**/**ara**, etc.

Note the pronunciation of /r/ in **liaison** and linking across words (**enchaînement**).

Liaison :	le premier‿aéroport	le dernier‿avion
Enchaînement :	un séjour‿agréable	Il sort‿avec moi.

À vous la parole

9-4 Répétitions. Répétez les mots suivants.

la route	la rose	la rue	le métro	Paris
prendre	première	la gare	le car	la voiture

9-5 La forme correcte. Donnez les formes de la troisième personne (singulier et pluriel) du présent de l'indicatif des verbes suivants.

MODÈLE servir
- elle sert, elles servent

sortir   partir   dormir   maigrir   prendre

9-6 Phrases. Répétez chaque phrase.

1. On prend le car au coin de la rue.
2. Le train s'arrête à la gare du Nord.
3. Marie part pour la **R**ussie en avril.

FORMES ET FONCTIONS

1. Le futur

- One may express future events in French using the **futur proche** or the **futur**. The two grammatical structures do not carry precisely the same meaning for French speakers. Compare:

  a. Ma tante **va avoir** un enfant. — *My aunt's going to have a baby.*
  b. Ils vont se marier et ils **auront** beaucoup d'enfants. — *They're going to get married, and they'll have lots of kids.*

In **a** we assume that the aunt is expecting. In **b** it is not certain that the couple to be married will have *any* children, let alone many.

- The difference between the **futur proche** and the **futur** is not primarily one of nearness or remoteness of the future event, but of its degree of certainty or definiteness. Compare:

Je **vais faire** la cuisine.	*I'm going to cook (right away).*
Je **ferai** la cuisine plus tard.	*I'll do the cooking later (perhaps).*
L'été prochain je **vais aller** en Suisse.	*Next summer I'm going to Switzerland (definite).*
Un jour, j'**irai** en Afrique.	*Someday I'll go to Africa (indefinite).*

- Use the **futur** to soften instructions.

  Vous **traverserez** l'avenue et vous **tournerez** à gauche dans la rue Colbert. — *You cross the avenue and turn left at Colbert Street.*

Note: In view of its link with intentionality, it is also appropriate to refer to *le futur proche* as *le futur défini*, and to the so-called *futur simple* as *le futur indéfini*. The exercises stress the semantic and pragmatic distinctions between the two structures. Students can also express the notion of the future by using the present tense plus an adverbial expression: *Ils partent demain.*

Note: The future stem is the same as the infinitive, except that: a) the final -e of -re verbs is dropped: *apprendre, j'apprendrai*; b) the -e of -er verbs is an unstable e and may or may not be pronounced, depending on the number of consonant sounds that follow or precede: *tu chantéras, tu parleras.*

- To form the future tense, add the future endings to the future stem. The future stem of regular verbs is the infinitive (for verbs ending in **-re**, remove the final **-e** from the infinitive).

LE FUTUR

Infinitive Ending: Future Stem:	-er chanter-	-ir partir-	-re vendr-
je	chant~~e~~**rai**	partir**ai**	vendr**ai**
tu	chant~~e~~**ras**	partir**as**	vendr**as**
il / elle / on	chant~~e~~**ra**	partir**a**	vendr**a**
nous	chant~~e~~**rons**	partir**ons**	vendr**ons**
vous	chant~~e~~**rez**	partir**ez**	vendr**ez**
ils / elles	chant~~e~~**ront**	partir**ont**	vendr**ont**

Note: *Amener, (se) lever,* and *(se) promener* show the same irregular future stem change as *acheter. Épeler* and *jeter* show the same stem change as *appeler.* In both cases, the pronunciation of the vowel [ɛ] is indicated by the *accent grave* or the double consonant. *Préférer*-type verbs (*préférer, espérer, répéter, suggérer*) are included here based on the 1990 Orthographic reform (règle 3a): « *On accentue sur le modèle de **semer** les futurs et conditionnels des verbes du type **céder : je cèderai, je cèderais.*** » As with the *acheter*-type verbs, the *accent grave* here clearly indicates the pronunciation of [ɛ]. For formation of the conditional, see Ch. 10, L. 1.

- The following verbs have irregular future stems:

acheter	j'**achèter**ai	devoir	je **devr**ai	pleuvoir	il **pleuvr**a
aller	j'**ir**ai	être	je **ser**ai	pouvoir	je **pourr**ai
appeler	j'**appeller**ai	faire	je **fer**ai	savoir	je **saur**ai
avoir	j'**aur**ai	préférer	je **préfèrer**ai	vouloir	je **voudr**ai

09-07 to 09-10

À vous la parole

Initial practice: Begin with the comprehension-based activity, Ex. 9-7. Next use discrimination drills to practice other distinctions: have students raise their hand when they hear a future event described: *Ils sont allés en Grèce l'été dernier. Ils iront en Espagne l'été prochain. Je prendrai l'avion pour aller en Belgique. Nous voyageons souvent en train. Elle attend le bus devant chez elle. Tu partiras vraiment toute seule en Europe ? Vous avez oublié les billets ? Je n'oublierai pas mon appareil cette fois-ci. Elles vont en ville en car tous les vendredis. Elle achètera son billet la semaine prochaine.* One person, or more than one ? *Il sera en retard. Ils feront le travail. Elle prendra le bus. Il louera une voiture. Ils voyageront en première classe. Elles feront le tour du monde en avion. Elle prendra beaucoup de photos. Ils rendront visite à des amis. Elles achèteront des souvenirs à Paris.* Practice with transformation drills to emphasize future stems: *je suis (je serai) ; je regarde (je regarderai) ; je dors (je dormirai)*, etc. Continue with substitution drills for each regular verb group: *Je travaillerai beaucoup ; nous. —Nous travaillerons beaucoup*, etc. *Il sortira ce weekend ; nous. —Nous sortirons ce weekend*, etc. *Elle attendra à l'aéroport ; moi. —J'attendrai à l'aéroport.*

9-7 Projets de voyage. Adèle pense faire un voyage au Québec cet hiver. Pour chaque activité décrite, notez si c'est sûr qu'elle va le faire.

Adèle…	sûr	pas sûr
MODÈLES va acheter un guide du Québec.	✓	
fera une excursion en bateau.		✓
1. va obtenir un passeport.	✓	
2. va acheter des tickets de métro sur Internet.	✓	
3. téléphonera à ses amis au Québec.		✓
4. achètera un nouvel appareil numérique.		✓
5. va réserver une chambre d'hôtel.	✓	
6. achètera des nouvelles chaussures.		✓
7. va préparer son itinéraire.	✓	
8. visitera l'île d'Orléans.		✓

Est-ce qu'Adèle a bien planifié les détails de son voyage, à votre avis ? Pourquoi ?

9-8 Prévisions météo. Voici les prévisions météo pour le Canada et pour le monde entier. Quel temps est prévu pour les villes indiquées?

Au Pays		Demain	Le monde		Demain
Calgary	P/Nuageux	19/3	Berlin	Ensoleillé	14/3
Edmonton	P/Nuageux	15/2	Bruxelles	Ensoleillé	16/5
Moncton	Ensoleillé	17/6	Buenos Aires	Nuageux	15/11
Ottawa	Ensoleillé	18/6	Honolulu	P/Nuageux	29/23
Québec	Ensoleillé	18/5	Lisbonne	Ensoleillé	27/14
Régina	P/Nuageux	11/2	Londres	P/Nuageux	19/8
Saskatoon	Ensoleillé	12/1	Los Angeles	Ensoleillé	23/12
Vancouver	Averses	14/8	New Delhi	P/Nuageux	34/23
Victoria	Averses	13/8	New York	P/Nuageux	17/11
Winnipeg	Nuageux	12/5	Paris	Ensoleillé	19/6

MODÈLE à Ottawa

- Demain, il fera beau. La température sera de 18 degrés. Le soir, elle descendra jusqu'à 6 degrés. *Answers may vary.*

1. à Québec Il fera beau… / 18° / 5°
2. à Winnipeg Il y aura des nuages… / 12° / 5°
3. à Calgary Il y aura des nuages et il pleuvra… / 19° / 3°
4. à Vancouver Il y aura de la pluie… / 14° / 8°
5. à Paris Il y aura du soleil… / 19° / 6°
6. à Bruxelles Il fera beau… / 16° / 5°
7. à Londres Le ciel sera couvert et il y aura de la pluie… / 19° / 8°
8. à Honolulu Il y aura des nuages et il pleuvra… / 29° / 23°

Note: Typically the *futur* (*indéfini*) is used in weather forecasts, since weather is anything but fully predictable and certain: *Mardi sera marqué par une crête de haute pression qui apportera du soleil à l'ensemble des régions.*

Implementation: 9-8 First review weather terms: Ask students what the weather is like today and what the forecast is for the coming days or weekend. Have students provide a weather expression for each indication in the chart: *Averses ou Pluie = Il pleuvra. Nuageux = Il y aura des nuages. Ensoleillé = Il fera beau ou Il y aura du soleil.*

9-9 Boule de cristal. Imaginez que vous allez chez une voyante. Voici ses prédictions. Avec un/e partenaire, tirez-en des conclusions. Voyons si vous avez compris la même chose.

Implementation: 9-9 Pretend you are the fortune teller and act out the role! Vary the exercise by having students take either the optimist's or the pessimist's point of view. The verb *voir* is presented in Ch. 10, L. 1. Treat *je vois que* and *je vous vois* here as lexical expressions.

MODÈLE Je vois que beaucoup d'argent passe entre vos mains.
É1 Alors, je serai très riche.
É2 Alors, je travaillerai dans une banque.

1. Je vois que vous voyagez beaucoup à cause du travail.
2. Je vois beaucoup d'enfants dans votre avenir.
3. Je vous vois devant une grande maison.
4. Je vous vois en compagnie d'une belle femme/d'un bel homme.
5. Je vois que vous avez beaucoup d'amis.
6. Je vois que vous êtes très célèbre.

Additonal practice: Use this pair activity for further practice:
L'an 2050. Parlez de vos prédictions pour l'an 2050 avec un/e partenaire.

MODÈLE travailler dans les usines (*factories*)
É1 Personne ne travaillera dans les usines.
É2 Tout le travail sera fait par des robots.

1. utiliser des ordinateurs
2. lire des livres
3. voyager en train
4. parler anglais
5. explorer la planète Mars
6. habiter sur la Lune ou dans l'espace
7. choisir une femme comme présidente

Help students discover the meaning of the words *Lune* and *espace* through the cognates "lunar, space" and the context. See whether they can come up with additional examples of how things might be in 2050 using verbs they know.

2. Le pronom *y*

- The pronoun **y** means *there*. It refers back to the name of a place, which can be introduced by a preposition such as **à**, **en**, **chez**, **devant**, or **à côté de**, for example.

—Tu es allé **en Provence** l'été dernier ?	—*You went to Provence last summer?*
—Oui, j'**y** suis allé avec mes parents.	—*Yes, I went there with my parents.*
—Tes cousins habitent **au Canada** ?	—*Your cousins live in Canada?*
—Non, ils n'**y** habitent plus.	—*No, they don't live there anymore.*
—Qui va aller **chez Cécile** ?	—*Who's going to Cécile's house?*
—Pas moi ; je n'aime pas **y** aller.	—*Not me; I don't like going there.*

Presentation: Start with the examples and ask students to provide the meaning and rules. Or, tell a story about your travels, using *y* and asking students questions about whether they have been to the various places. For example: *L'été dernier, je suis allée en Angleterre avec ma famille. On y est allés en avion. D'abord, on a visité Liverpool. Ma nièce y habite et fait ses études à l'Université de Liverpool. Est-ce que vous avez déjà visité l'Angleterre ? Comment est-ce que vous y êtes allé/e ? En avion ? Et Londres ? Vous y êtes allé/e aussi ? Comment ?*, etc.

- Like the object pronouns, **y** is placed immediately before the conjugated verb, unless there is an infinitive. When there is an infinitive, the pronoun goes immediately in front of it.

Tu **y** vas ?	*Are you going there?*
Paris ? Oui, nous **y** sommes allés l'été dernier.	*Paris? Yes, we went there last summer.*
Cet hôtel est abominable. Je ne peux plus **y** rester.	*This hotel is awful. I can't stay here any longer.*

09-11 to 09-14

À vous la parole

Implementation: 9-10 This tests students' understanding of the use of the pronoun *y*; to simplify, have students answer with the location only.

9-10 C'est logique. De quelle ville francophone est-ce qu'on parle ? Il y a souvent plusieurs possibilités. *Answers may vary.*

> **En Afrique** : Dakar, Abidjan, Bamako
> **En Amérique du Nord** : Québec, Montréal, La Nouvelle-Orléans
> **Les DOM** : Fort-de-France (Martinique), Pointe-à-Pitre (Guadeloupe), Cayenne (Guyane)
> **En Europe** : Paris, Genève, Bruxelles, Nice

MODÈLE On y va pour les sports d'hiver.
- À Genève

OU
- À Montréal

1. On y trouve des belles plages. Nice, Fort-de-France, Pointe-à-Pitre, Cayenne
2. Les gens y parlent créole. Fort-de-France, Pointe-à-Pitre, La Nouvelle-Orléans
3. On y parle anglais et français. Pointe-à-Pitre, Fort-de-France, Montréal, La Nouvelle-Orléans
4. On y parle wolof et français. Dakar
5. On y parle flamand et français. Bruxelles
6. On y va pour le Carnaval. La Nouvelle-Orléans, Nice, Cayenne
7. Les Américains y vont pour parler français sans quitter l'Amérique du Nord. Québec, Montréal, La Nouvelle-Orléans, Fort-de-France, Pointe-à-Pitre

Initial practice: To practice the placement of the pronoun *y*, complete quick substitution drills: *J'y suis allé/e ; nous. —Nous y sommes allés*, etc. ; *Je vais y aller ; toi. —Tu vas y aller*, etc. Then move on to Ex. 9-11.

9-11 Les voyageurs. En choisissant l'expression appropriée dans la colonne B, dites pourquoi les personnes suivantes visitent les endroits indiqués.

MODÈLE Les Kerboul sont allés à La Nouvelle-Orléans.
- Ils y sont allés pour voir le Carnaval.

A	B
1. Les Kerboul sont allés à La Nouvelle-Orléans.	a. acheter du bon vin
2. Les Dupuis vont aller dans les Alpes.	b. voir le Carnaval
3. Raymond veut aller en Guadeloupe.	c. visiter les pyramides
4. Arnaud va aller à Paris.	d. visiter la tour Eiffel
5. Les Brunet sont allés sur la Côte d'Azur.	e. apprendre l'espagnol
6. Christiane voudrait aller au Mexique.	f. apprendre le créole
7. Les Santini vont en Égypte.	g. nager et bronzer
8. M. Lescure va aller dans la région de Bordeaux.	h. faire du ski

Key: 9-11 1) b ; Ils y sont allés pour voir le Carnaval. 2) h ; Ils vont y aller pour faire du ski. 3) f ; Il veut y aller pour apprendre le créole. 4) d ; Il va y aller pour visiter la Tour Eiffel. 5) g ; Ils y sont allés pour nager et bronzer. 6) e, c ; Elle y va pour apprendre l'espagnol/pour visiter les pyramides. 7) c ; Ils y vont pour visiter les pyramides. 8) a ; Il va y aller pour acheter du bon vin.

9-12 Vos habitudes. Demandez à votre partenaire s'il/si elle va aux endroits suivants pendant les vacances. Il/Elle doit vous donner une raison pour justifier sa réponse.

Expansion: 9-12 Have students add other places.

MODÈLE dans des bons restaurants
É1 Tu vas quelquefois dans des bons restaurants ?
É2 Non, je n'y vais jamais.
É1 Pourquoi ?
É2 Parce qu'ils sont très chers et je n'ai pas assez d'argent pour y aller.

1. au théâtre
2. à des concerts de musique classique
3. à Disneyland ou à Disney World
4. au musée
5. en Louisiane
6. en Europe
7. aux Antilles
8. dans un pays francophone

Observons

Note: 9-13 Édouard mentions the **Bibliothèque François-Mitterand**, shown in the photos on the next page. The four towers represent open books and form the corners of an inner courtyard that is planted with trees to resemble a forest.

9-13 Mes impressions de Paris.

A. Avant de regarder. Est-ce que vous avez déjà visité Paris ? Même si vous n'avez jamais visité Paris, quelle idée est-ce que vous avez de cette ville célèbre ? Dans cette séquence, vous allez entendre deux Niçois qui décrivent leurs impressions de Paris.

B. En regardant. Trouvez la réponse (ou les réponses) à chaque question.

1. Fabienne dit qu'il y a toujours un petit conflit entre…
   a. les Français et les Américains.
   b. les Parisiens et les Niçois.
   c. les hommes et les femmes.
2. Pour elle, ce n'est pas un problème parce qu'elle…
   a. est mariée avec un Parisien.
   b. adore les Américains.
   c. est née à Paris.
3. À Paris, elle aime surtout…
   a. la tour Eiffel.
   b. le climat.
   c. le shopping.
4. Édouard est allé à Paris pour…
   a. voir sa famille.
   b. travailler.
   c. passer des vacances.

La place de la Concorde et la Tour Eiffel

Script: *Observons*

FABIENNE : Alors je suis niçoise, mais je vais vous parler un petit peu de Paris. Nous, nous sommes dans le Sud de la France, Paris est beaucoup plus dans le Nord de la France. Nous avons, entre les Niçois et les Parisiens, toujours un petit conflit, qui ne se dit pas toujours, mais je suis mariée avec un Parisien, donc, j'ai dû faire mon deuil de cela. J'ai visité Paris un petit peu contrainte et forcée, et finalement cette ville m'a beaucoup plu, je… je dois le reconnaître. Peut-être pas la tour Eiffel, parce que c'est un monument qui [ne] m'a pas vraiment étonnée, peut-être à force de le voir en photo. Maintenant, j'ai adoré vraiment toutes les activités, le shopping à Paris, chose que nous n'avons pas à Nice, peut-être. Nous avons à Nice le climat, à Paris, ils ont toutes les activités. Et euh… j'aime bien les Parisiens, finalement.

ÉDOUARD : J'aime beaucoup Paris, c'est un lieu où je vais souvent, et où j'ai travaillé notamment. Et j'ai pu découvrir beaucoup d'endroits cet été, notamment la Bibliothèque François-Mitterrand, qui est un endroit très… très intéressant, je trouve. Mais il y a d'autres endroits, comme l'Opéra, qui est… bon, que tout le monde connaît et qui est… que je trouve magnifique. Euh, et sinon, euh bien, évidemment tous les grands monuments, comme la Concorde, la tour Eiffel. Et, euh… c'est un lieu où j'aime bien aller, euh… en vacances,… pour travailler…

5. Il a découvert beaucoup de monuments, par exemple :
__✓__ l'Opéra de Paris _____ l'Arc de Triomphe __✓__ la place de la Concorde
_____ le Louvre __✓__ la tour Eiffel __✓__ la bibliothèque François-Mitterrand

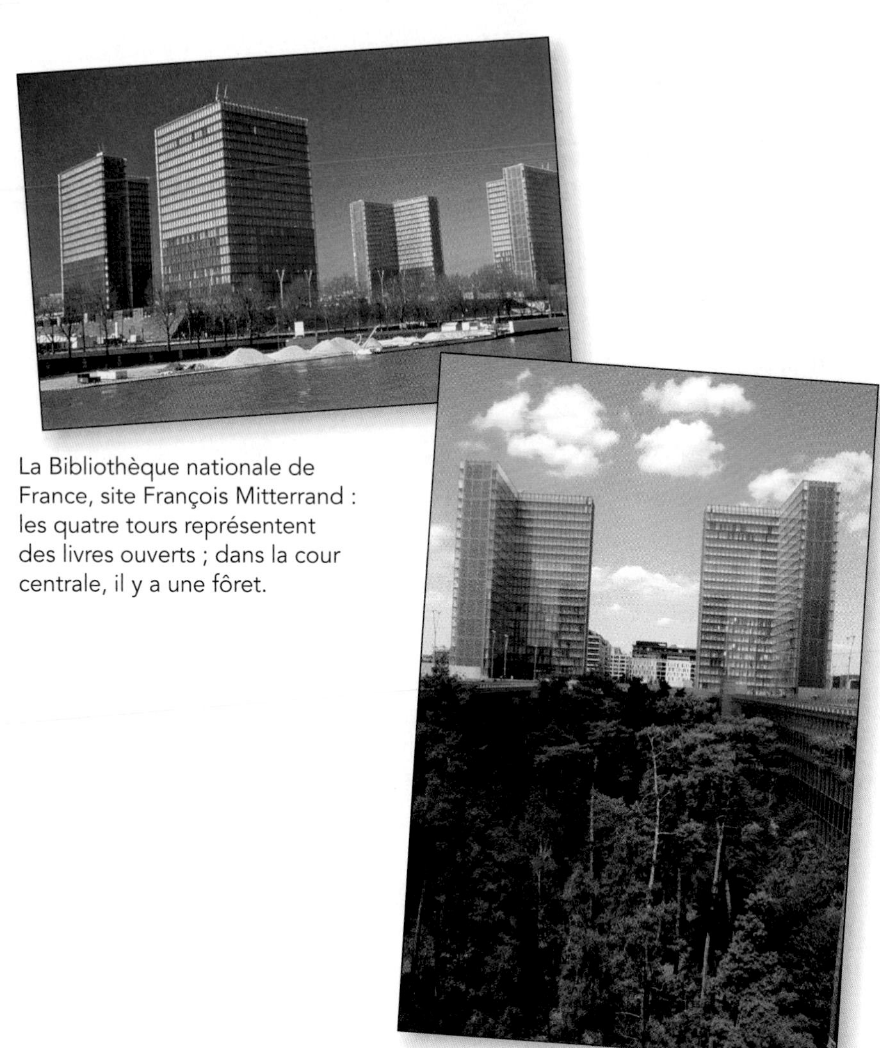

La Bibliothèque nationale de France, site François Mitterrand : les quatre tours représentent des livres ouverts ; dans la cour centrale, il y a une fôret.

C. Après avoir regardé. Maintenant discutez de ces questions avec vos camarades de classe.

1. Fabienne remarque qu'il y a un petit conflit entre les gens du Nord (les Parisiens) et les gens du Sud (les Niçois). Comment pourriez-vous expliquer ce conflit ? Est-ce qu'il existe des tensions ou de la concurrence (*competition*) entre les gens de régions différentes chez vous ? Si oui, pourquoi ?
2. Fabienne n'est pas très impressionnée quand elle voit la tour Eiffel pour la première fois. Pourquoi ? Est-ce que vous avez déjà eu cette expérience, de voir un monument ou une œuvre d'art célèbre pour la première fois et d'être déçu/e (*disappointed*) ?
3. Est-ce que les impressions de Fabienne et Édouard vous étonnent (*surprise*) ? Pourquoi ? Est-ce qu'elles diffèrent de vos propres impressions de Paris ?

Leçon 2 Destinations

POINTS DE DÉPART

Où est-ce qu'on va ?

Presentation: Use the photos and introductions to provide an overview of countries and nationalities. Find the places mentioned on a world map (MFL, Instructor's Resources), or ask students to use the world map in the end pages. You might ask students to use these brief introductions as a model for introducing themselves.

Je m'appelle David Diouf. Je suis du Sénégal et j'étudie à Paris. Ma langue maternelle, c'est le wolof, mais je parle aussi français. Je vais bientôt prendre l'avion pour aller à Dakar. Je vais passer les vacances chez moi, au Sénégal, cet été.

Je suis Jérémie Duclos. Je suis suisse et j'habite à Lausanne. Je parle allemand aussi bien que français. Je suis venu à Bruxelles pour une réunion de travail. Demain je vais rentrer en Suisse.

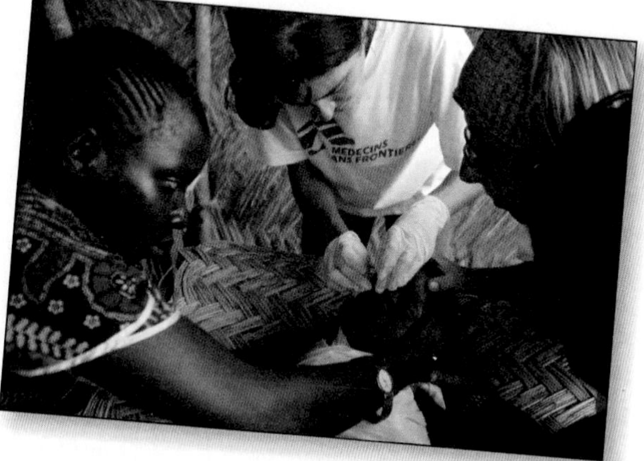

Mon nom, c'est Brigitte Piron. Je suis belge et j'habite à Bruxelles. Je retourne au Mali, où je vais reprendre mon travail pour Médecins sans Frontières.

Note: Whereas North Americans think of seven continents: *L'Afrique, l'Asie, l'Australie, l'Amérique du Nord, l'Amérique du Sud, l'Europe,* and *l'Antarctique*, the French divide the world into five continents: *l'Afrique, l'Asie, l'Amérique, l'Europe,* and *l'Océanie.*

Note: The name of the inhabitants of a country is usually derived from the adjective of nationality, but it is written with a capital letter when used as a noun: *un Chinois, une Anglaise, les Ivoiriens.* The name of the language is often derived from the masculine form of the adjective of nationality: *les Portugais parlent portugais.* There are many exceptions, however: *en Algérie, on parle arabe, berbère et français ; en Suisse, on parle allemand, français, italien et romanche.*

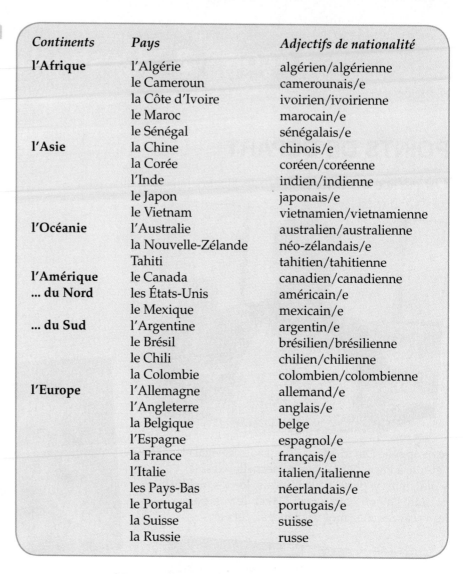

Continents	*Pays*	*Adjectifs de nationalité*
l'Afrique	l'Algérie	algérien/algérienne
	le Cameroun	camerounais/e
	la Côte d'Ivoire	ivoirien/ivoirienne
	le Maroc	marocain/e
	le Sénégal	sénégalais/e
l'Asie	la Chine	chinois/e
	la Corée	coréen/coréenne
	l'Inde	indien/indienne
	le Japon	japonais/e
	le Vietnam	vietnamien/vietnamienne
l'Océanie	l'Australie	australien/australienne
	la Nouvelle-Zélande	néo-zélandais/e
	Tahiti	tahitien/tahitienne
l'Amérique	le Canada	canadien/canadienne
... du Nord	les États-Unis	américain/e
	le Mexique	mexicain/e
... du Sud	l'Argentine	argentin/e
	le Brésil	brésilien/brésilienne
	le Chili	chilien/chilienne
	la Colombie	colombien/colombienne
l'Europe	l'Allemagne	allemand/e
	l'Angleterre	anglais/e
	la Belgique	belge
	l'Espagne	espagnol/e
	la France	français/e
	l'Italie	italien/italienne
	les Pays-Bas	néerlandais/e
	le Portugal	portugais/e
	la Suisse	suisse
	la Russie	russe

Presentation: Remind students that they learned in Ch. 2, L. 2 to use the prepositions *à/de* with cities: *Elle arrive à Paris, Ils sont de Dijon/d'Angers.* Use the sample introductions to further illustrate the use of prepositions with names of countries.

- To express *to, at, in,* or *from* with the name of countries and continents, use the following prepositions in French:

	feminine	**masculine + vowel**	**masculine + consonant**	**plural**
to, at, in	**en** Suisse	**en** Irak	**au** Maroc	**aux** Pays-Bas
from	**de** Belgique **d'**Afrique	**d'**Iran	**du** Canada	**des** États-Unis

Note: All continents are feminine. As a general rule, country names that end in *-e* are feminine (exceptions are *le Mexique, le Mozambique, le Zimbabwe, le Belize*). In general, names of countries that end in any letter other than *-e* are masculine (such as le *Canada, le Brésil, les États-Unis, l'Iran*). However, the preposition *en* is used for masculine countries when they begin with a vowel (*en Irak, en Iran, en Israël*).

Presentation: Begin discussion of this cultural note with a think-pair-share brainstorm activity. Ask each student to take out a piece of paper and write down the first three things that come to mind when you say "Paris." Then have students compare their list with that of a partner. Finally, make a list on the board with input from the whole class. As you write their responses on the board, group the answers together into categories (e.g., *les monuments, les musées, la cuisine, le shopping, l'histoire*, etc.), but without writing the names of these categories. After you've finished, ask students to identify and label each group. You could also ask if any students have visited Paris and have them share their experiences and/or bring in any souvenirs they collected.

Vie et culture

Paris, Ville Lumière

09-53

Regardez la séquence vidéo, *Paris, Ville Lumière*. Paris, comme vous le savez, est la capitale de la France. C'est aussi la ville la plus visitée du monde. C'est une belle ville remplie[1] d'histoire, de monuments intéressants, d'églises, de bons restaurants, de grands magasins et de petites boutiques de spécialités.

La ville de Paris est connue sous le nom de *Ville Lumière*. D'où cette désignation vient-elle ? C'est parce qu'à la fin du XIXe siècle et au début du XXe, Paris était le centre artistique et culturel du monde et la capitale de l'élégance, du luxe et des plaisirs. Beaucoup d'écrivains, de musiciens et d'artistes passaient au moins un an dans la *Ville Lumière* pour apprendre leur métier ou trouver de l'inspiration. Voilà pourquoi on appelle la fin du XIXe siècle en France *la Belle Époque*.

Connaissez-vous des Américains célèbres qui ont visité Paris ou qui ont vécu[2] à Paris ? Quelle est l'importance de leur séjour[3] en France ?

[1]*full of* [2]*lived* [3]*stay*

Implementation: Treat the note by having students look for main ideas: what will they find in Paris ? Why is Paris known as the "City of Light ?" Students may also have heard of the "Gay Nineties," an expression used in the United States for this same period.

Josephine Baker a été une vedette des Folies Bergères pendant les années vingt et trente. Cette Américaine est devenue citoyenne française. Elle a reçu la médaille de la Légion d'honneur et à sa mort a été enterrée à Paris.

La Place du Tertre à Montmartre

Expansion: Assign a writing activity giving students the opportunity to practice presentational writing skills, consistent with Standard 1.3 in the *National Standards for Foreign Language Learning*. Students may work individually or with a partner to write brief biographies of a famous American who stayed in Paris. Examples include: diplomats Benjamin Franklin, Thomas Jefferson, and Woodrow Wilson; writers Gertrude Stein, Ernest Hemingway, and F. Scott Fitzgerald; musicians Louis Armstrong, Aaron Copland, and George Gershwin; entertainers Josephine Baker and Isadora Duncan; and artists Mary Cassatt and Man Ray. Allow students a few days to prepare their biographies, and ask them to include photos of the person (students may wish to use presentational software as they report). In addition to encyclopedias and the Internet, other useful resources include: Gopnik, Adam, ed., *Americans in Paris: a literary anthology*. New York: Library of America, 2004. Kennedy, J. Gerald. *Imagining Paris: exile, writing, and American identity*. New Haven: Yale University Press, 1993. Morton, Brian. *Americans in Paris: An Anecdotal Street Guide*. Ann Arbor: The Olivia and Hill Press, 1984. Stovall, Tyler Edward. *Paris noir : African Americans in the City of Light*. Boston: Houghton Mifflin, 1996. Have students exchange descriptions for the purposes of peer editing. Then have them compare the experiences of their historical figures. Which people had similar experiences ? Speculate on why this might be so.

09-18
to
09-22

À vous la parole

Initial practice: To practice continents, name a country and have students tell on which continent the country is found: *le Vietnam ? — Le Vietnam est en Asie. le Sénégal ? — Le Sénégal est en Afrique. le Mexique ; les Pays-Bas ; le Brésil ; le Maroc ; la Chine ; l'Italie ; le Canada ; le Cameroun ; la Suisse ; l'Australie ; la Côte d'Ivoire*, etc. Here country names can be for recognition only. Continue with simple substitution drills: *Je vais en France ; Canada ; Belgique ; Mexique ; Brésil ; Inde ; Suisse ; Pays-Bas ; Japon ; Côte d'Ivoire ; Italie ; Chine ; Portugal*, etc. *Je suis des États-Unis ; Pays-Bas ; France ; Portugal ; Sénégal ; Angleterre ; Colombie ; Maroc ; Espagne ; Australie ; Brésil ; Algérie ; Canada*, etc. Follow with an exercise where students match capitals and countries: *Dakar ? — Dakar est au Sénégal ; Tokyo ? (au Japon) ; Paris ? (en France) ; Lisbonne ? (au Portugal) ; Bruxelles ? (en Belgique) ; Ottawa ? (au Canada) ; Rabat ? (au Maroc) ; Yaoundé ? (au Cameroun) ; Hanoï ? (au Vietnam) ; Amsterdam ? (aux Pays-Bas) ; Canberra ? (en Australie) ; Madrid ? (en Espagne) ; Alger ? (en Algérie) ; Beijing ? (en Chine) ; Delhi ? (en Inde) ; Bogota ? (en Colombie) ; Buenos Aires ? (en Argentine) ; Berne ? (en Suisse) ; Brasilia ? (au Brésil).*

9-14 On va où ? Décidez dans quel pays on ira, d'après la description.

MODÈLE On visitera le palais de Buckingham et le *British Museum*.
- On ira en Angleterre.

1. On s'installera à la terrasse d'un café pour admirer la tour Eiffel. en France
2. On boira un cappuccino et on regardera les gondoles qui passent. en Italie
3. Nous verrons des pyramides aztèques. au Mexique
4. On pourra visiter les souks (*les marchés*) de Marrakech. au Maroc
5. On visitera le château Frontenac à Québec. au Canada
6. Là-bas, on verra l'administration centrale de la Communauté Européenne. en Belgique
7. C'est le seul pays d'Europe où l'on aura l'occasion de parler espagnol. en Espagne

9-15 Présentations. Selon l'endroit où chaque personne habite, indiquez sa nationalité et des langues possibles. *Answers may vary.*

MODÈLE Luc Auger habite à Québec.
- Il est canadien. Il parle français et probablement un peu anglais.

1. María Garcia est de Buenos Aires. argentine ; espagnol
2. Sylvie Gerniers habite à Bruxelles. belge ; français, flamand, allemand
3. Chantal Dupuis est de Genève. suisse ; français, allemand, italien
4. Paolo Dos Santos habite à Rio de Janeiro. brésilien ; portugais
5. Helmut Müller est de Berlin. allemand ; allemand
6. María Verdi habite à Milan. italienne ; italien
7. Jin Lu ? Elle est de Beijing. chinoise ; chinois

Implementation: 9-16 Ask students if they have relatives or friends in other countries. Follow up by asking about trips students may have already made overseas.

Additional practice: As a culminating activity, have students assume a new identity (with a name indicative of the target language they choose) and introduce themselves. Classmates can take notes and then be asked to recall the new identity of each student. This can become a fun game; you may want to give students a day to prepare.

9-16 Un voyage. Avec un/e partenaire, imaginez que vous partez visiter un pays lointain. Quel pays est-ce que vous choisirez ? Qu'est-ce que vous y ferez ?

MODÈLE É1 J'irai en Suisse, parce que j'ai des cousins là-bas. Je ferai du ski dans les Alpes.

É2 Et moi, je visiterai l'Égypte. J'irai à Gizeh pour voir les pyramides.

FORMES ET FONCTIONS

1. Les expressions de nécessité

Note: This section allows students to gain familiarity with impersonal expressions before using them in complex sentences with the subjunctive, taught in the next **Formes et fonctions** section; teach the two sections on different days. Using the infinitive with these expressions is a good strategy for avoiding the more complex constructions with the subjunctive and is a tactic often employed by native speakers.

- You learned in **Chapitre 7, Leçon 1** to use the impersonal expression **il faut** with an infinitive to describe what one *must* or *has to* do.

Il ne faut pas oublier ton passeport.	*You mustn't forget your passport.*
Cet été, **il faut rentrer** au Sénégal.	*This summer, we have to go home to Senegal.*

- You can also use the following expressions that include the impersonal subject **il** with an infinitive to express obligation.

il vaut mieux	*it is better to*
il est nécessaire de	*it is necessary to*
il est important de	*it is important to*
il est utile de	*it is useful to*

Il vaut mieux louer une voiture pour se déplacer.	*It's better to rent a car in order to get around.*
Il est utile de consulter une carte quand on voyage.	*It's useful to refer to a map when you travel.*
Il est nécessaire d'avoir un passeport pour voyager à l'étranger.	*You must have a passport to travel abroad.*
En été, **il est important de porter** des lunettes de soleil.	*In summer, it's important to wear sunglasses.*

Initial practice: Begin with a quick exercise: *En classe, il faut ou il ne faut pas ? Parler français ? — Il faut parler français. Parler anglais? — Il ne faut pas parler anglais. Manger? Écouter le prof ? Regarder son portable ? Écouter son iPod ? Arriver à l'heure ? Oublier son livre ? Travailler ? Vérifier son mail ?*, etc.

À vous la parole

23–26

9-17 Oui ou non ? Quand on passe ses vacances à la plage, est-ce qu'il faut faire les choses suivantes ? *Answers may vary.*

Variation: 9-17 Vary the destination: *à la montagne ?*

MODÈLE apporter des bottes ?
- Non, il ne faut pas apporter de bottes. Il vaut mieux apporter des sandales.

1. prendre des lunettes de soleil ? Oui, il faut prendre des lunettes de soleil.
2. se mettre de la crème solaire (*sunscreen*) ? Oui, il faut se mettre de la crème solaire.
3. porter un manteau ? Non, il ne faut pas porter un manteau. Il vaut mieux porter un short et un tee-shirt.
4. amener le chien ? Non, il ne faut pas amener son chien. Il vaut mieux laisser le chien à la maison.
5. apporter un appareil numérique ? Oui, il faut apporter un appareil numérique.
6. faire du ski ? Non, il ne faut pas faire du ski. Il faut faire du ski nautique.
7. se promener en bateau ? Oui, il faut se promener en bateau.

9-18 Préparons le voyage. Qu'est-ce qu'il est nécessaire de faire avant de voyager ? Discutez de cela avec un/e partenaire.

MODÈLE Nous allons partir à l'étranger.
É1 Il est important d'avoir un passeport.
É2 Il est peut-être nécessaire d'avoir un visa aussi.

1. On voudrait prendre des belles photos.
2. Nous allons voyager en train.
3. On va rester dans un hôtel.
4. Je ne connais pas très bien la ville.
5. Je ne veux pas payer en liquide (*with cash*).
6. C'est un climat tropical là où nous allons.

9-19 S.O.S. Voyages ! Avec un groupe de camarades de classe, proposez un voyage et offrez, à tour de rôle, des conseils pour bien réussir la visite.

MODÈLE É1 Je voudrais visiter la ville de New York.
É2 Je connais New York ; il faut absolument voir la statue de la Liberté.
É3 Il est important de visiter les beaux musées aussi.
É4 Et il ne faut pas prendre un taxi en ville ; c'est trop cher. Il vaut mieux prendre le métro ou le bus.

Presentation: Point out that complex sentences contain two clauses, each with its own inflected verb, connected, in the case of the subjunctive, by the conjunction *que*. Make it clear that the verb in the main clause is in the indicative; it is only the verb in the subordinate clause that may be in the subjunctive. You may wish to remind students that not every subordinate clause introduced by *que/qu'* takes a verb in the subjunctive. The use of the subjunctive is determined by the verb in the main clause; constructions such as *Je sais que..., Il dit que...*, do not take the subjunctive in the second clause. This point is elaborated in Ch. 10, L. 1.

2. Le subjonctif des verbes réguliers : le subjonctif avec les expressions de nécessité

You have learned to use the indicative mood to state facts and ask questions, and the imperative to express commands and give directions. When you wish to express a subjective point of view—obligation or necessity, for example—it is often necessary to use the subjunctive. The subjunctive usually occurs in the second clause of a complex sentence—a sentence that has two parts, or clauses, each with a different subject. The second clause is always introduced by **que/qu'**. Compare the use of the present indicative and the present subjunctive in the sentences below.

Nous **partons** de bonne heure.	*We're leaving early.*
Il est important que nous **partions** de bonne heure.	*It is important that we leave early.*
Vous **écoutez** le guide.	*You're listening to the guide.*
Il vaut mieux que vous **écoutiez** le guide.	*It's best that you listen to the guide.*

- Note that the impersonal expressions of obligation that you have learned require the subjunctive when they are followed by a second clause with its own subject and verb, rather than an infinitive.

Il faut réserver l'hôtel.	Il faut **que nous réservions** l'hôtel.
Il ne faut pas oublier les billets.	Il ne faut pas **que vous oubliiez** les billets.
Il est nécessaire de partir tôt le matin.	Il est nécessaire **que tu partes** tôt le matin.
Il est important d'attendre le bus.	Il est important **qu'il attende** le bus.
Il est utile d'acheter des tickets de métro.	Il est utile **que tu achètes** des tickets de métro.
Il vaut mieux écouter le guide.	Il vaut mieux **que vous écoutiez** le guide.

Presentation: Point out that the endings for singular and third-person plural forms of the present subjunctive are the same as the endings for the present indicative of *-er* verbs and that, for the *nous* and *vous* forms, the present subjunctive endings are the same as those of the imperfect.
For two-stem verbs, contrast corresponding forms of the present indicative and the present subjunctive of the singular forms so that students clearly hear the final consonant present in the present subjunctive forms: *je dors/il faut que je dorme, tu sors/il vaut mieux que tu sortes.* Point out that the present subjunctive of all regular verbs follows the 'boot' pattern presented in Ch. 1 for -er verbs.

- All regular verbs take the same set of present subjunctive endings. These endings are added to the present stem, which is found by dropping the present indicative ending **-ent** from the **ils/elles** form.

LE SUBJONCTIF

INFINITIVE ENDING:	-er	-ir	-ir/-iss-	-re
ils/elles forms	**donn**ent	**dorm**ent	**grossiss**ent	**descend**ent
Il faut que...				
je	donne	dorme	grossisse	descende
tu	donnes	dormes	grossisses	descendes
il / elle / on	donne	dorme	grossisse	descende
nous	donn**ions**	dorm**ions**	grossiss**ions**	descend**ions**
vous	donn**iez**	dorm**iez**	grossiss**iez**	descend**iez**
ils / elles	donn**ent**	dorm**ent**	grossiss**ent**	descend**ent**

27

⋊ À vous la parole ⋊

30 **9-20 Préparatifs de voyage.** Les Meunier préparent un voyage aux Seychelles et ils en discutent avec leur oncle Henri. Voici les commentaires et les conseils d'Oncle Henri : dans chaque cas, cochez le commentaire (**je sais que**) ou le conseil (**il faut que**).

	Je sais que vous…	Il faut que vous…	
MODÈLES	____	✓	… achetiez des billets d'avion bien en avance.
	✓	____	… consultez des guides touristiques.
1.	____	✓	… trouviez un bon hôtel.
2.	____	✓	… louiez une voiture.
3.	____	✓	… achetiez un appareil numérique.
4.	✓	____	… apportez des vêtements légers.
5.	____	✓	… prépariez un itinéraire.
6.	____	✓	… écriviez à l'Office de Tourisme.
7.	✓	____	… allez sur des sites web pour chercher des renseignements.

Est-ce que les Meunier ont déjà fait beaucoup de préparations ou est-ce qu'ils ont toujours beaucoup de choses à faire ?

9-21 Oui ou non ? On voyage en région francophone ; est-ce qu'il est important de faire les choses suivantes ou non ?

MODÈLES Mes amis veulent dormir toute la journée.
- Il ne faut pas qu'ils dorment toute la journée.

Nous ne voulons pas attendre le guide.
- Il faut que vous attendiez le guide.

1. Nous ne voulons pas visiter des musées. Il faut que vous visitiez des musées.
2. Mes amis veulent parler anglais tout le temps. Il ne faut pas qu'ils parlent anglais.
3. J'oublie tout le temps mon passeport. Il ne faut pas que tu oublies ton passeport.
4. Je n'aime pas suivre le guide. Il faut que tu suives le guide.
5. Nous ne voulons pas descendre dans des caves. Il faut que vous descendiez dans des caves.
6. Elles n'aiment pas acheter des souvenirs. Il faut qu'elles achètent des souvenirs.
7. Nous ne voulons pas sortir au restaurant. Il faut que vous sortiez au restaurant.

À Nice, quand il fait beau, il faut que vous mangiez sur la terrasse. C'est très agréable.

Initial practice: Begin with Ex. 9-20, a comprehension-based activity that requires students to distinguish between the indicative and the subjunctive in complex sentences. Follow with a discrimination drill that focuses on the use of the impersonal expressions of necessity: subjunctive or infinitive? *Il faut acheter les billets. Il faut que vous achetiez les billets. Il faut qu'on parte. Il faut partir. Il est nécessaire de continuer. Il est nécessaire que vous continuiez. Il vaut mieux appeler l'hôtel. Il vaut mieux que tu appelles l'hôtel. Il est urgent que tu finisses ce travail. Il est urgent de finir ce travail. Il est important de bien manger. Il est important que vous mangiez bien,* etc. Continue with substitution drills for all regular verb conjugations: *Il est important que je dorme ; vous. — Il est important que vous dormiez,* etc.

9-22 C'est logique. Qu'est-ce qu'on dit dans chaque cas ? Travaillez avec un/e partenaire, et choisissez des verbes dans la liste suivante.

MODÈLE une mère à son enfant
É1 Il faut que tu manges tes légumes !
É2 Il ne faut pas que tu joues dans la rue !

arrêter	finir	jouer	manger	parler
payer	rendre	réserver	téléphoner	travailler

Implementation: 9-22 As a follow-up, have students compare their answers. To simplify, we are treating the verb *payer* as a regular *-er* verb (*je paye, nous payons*, etc.). Verbs in *-ayer* can also be conjugated with *ai* (*je paie, tu paies, il paie*, but *nous payons*).

1. un professeur à ses élèves
2. une étudiante à sa colocataire
3. un agent de police à un automobiliste
4. une sœur à son petit frère
5. un médecin à un patient
6. un agent de voyage à son client
7. une jeune femme à son mari
8. une patronne (*boss*) à son employée

9-23 Obligations. Qu'est-ce que vous avez à faire ? Pour chaque verbe de la liste, précisez vos obligations en discutant avec un/e partenaire. Ensuite, comparez vos responsabilités avec celles de vos camarades de classe.

MODÈLE écrire
É1 Il faut que j'écrive un essai pour mon cours de composition.
É2 Et moi, il faut que j'écrive un mail à ma mère.

1. écrire
2. travailler
3. rendre
4. finir
5. téléphoner
6. sortir

Parlons

Expansion: 9-24 If you have a collection of maps (e.g., from the department stores in Paris), you could bring them to class and have students work in groups to find the monuments on the *bateau-mouche* map and label them. You might also assign this as homework and have students use the Internet to find maps of Paris as well as tourist guides.

Note: *Plle* is the abbreviation for *passerelle*, a footbridge. The footbridge, *la passerelle Léopold-Sédar-Senghor*, was formerly known as *la passerelle Solférino*.

Implementation: 9-24 Treat the **Vie et culture** before completing Ex. 9-24.

9-24 La visite d'un monument.

Une façon agréable de voir les monuments de Paris est de prendre un bateau-mouche. Ces bateaux font des circuits touristiques avec des commentaires sur tous les monuments qui se trouvent au bord de la Seine. Regardez ce détail d'un plan de Paris et identifiez les monuments que vous reconnaissez.

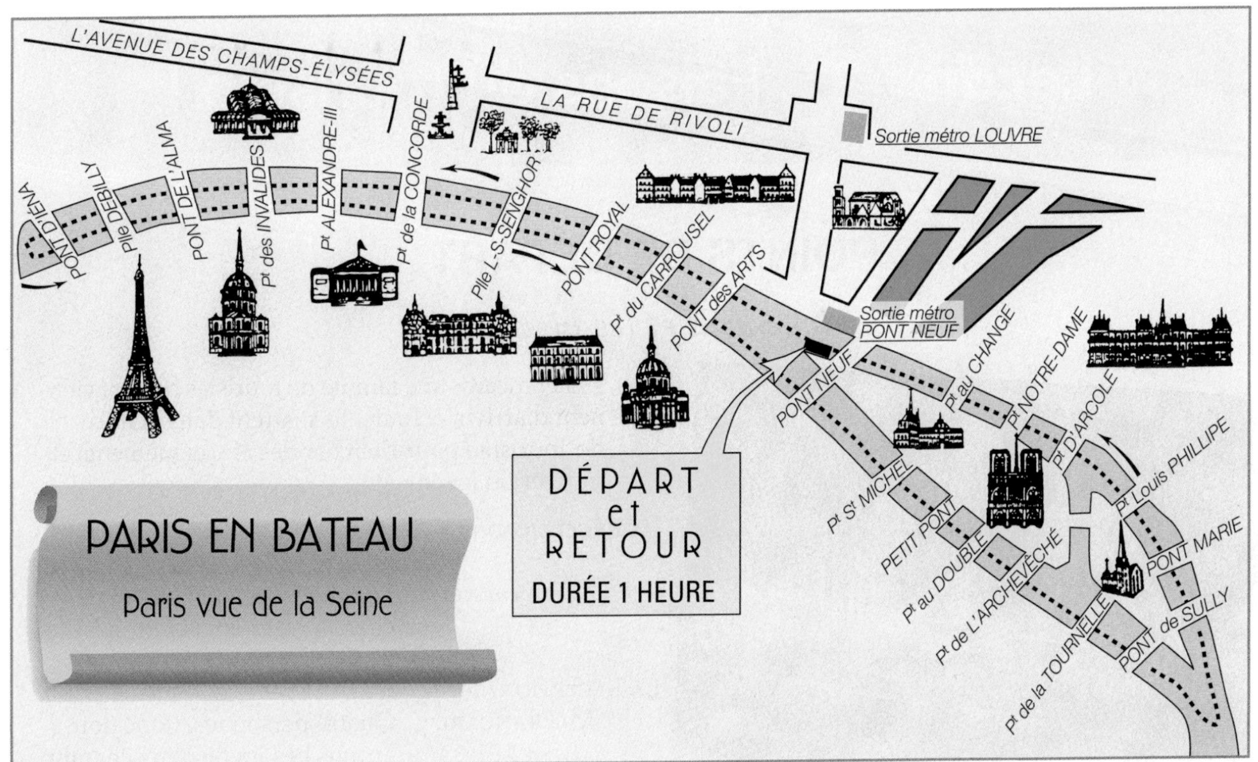

A. Avant de parler. Maintenant, c'est à vous de jouer le rôle d'un/e guide à bord d'un bateau-mouche à Paris. D'abord, choisissez un monument. Voici quelques possibilités :

1. l'Hôtel de Ville
2. la Conciergerie
3. les jardins des Tuileries
4. le musée d'Orsay
5. l'obélisque de la Concorde
6. le Pont Neuf
7. la tour Eiffel
8. Notre-Dame de Paris
9. les Invalides
10. le Louvre
11. le Grand Palais
12. l'Institut de France

Ensuite, préparez une description de votre monument ; considérez les questions suivantes :

1. Où se trouve ce monument ? Dans quel arrondissement ? Dans quelle rue ? À côté de quels autres sites importants ? Est-ce qu'il y a une station de métro à proximité ?
2. Quand est-ce que ce monument a été construit ? Par qui ? Pourquoi est-ce que ce monument est important aujourd'hui ?

Pour trouver des renseignements, consultez Internet et des guides touristiques.

B. En parlant. Présentez votre monument à vos camarades de classe. N'oubliez pas de montrer des images de votre monument !

C. Après avoir parlé. Quelles sont les présentations les plus intéressantes ? Quels monuments est-ce que vous voudriez visiter maintenant ? Pourquoi ?

Implementation: *Avant de parler.* This speaking activity gives students the opportunity to practice presentational speaking skills, consistent with Standard 1.3 in the *National Standards for Foreign Language Learning.* If you wish, you may expand the activity to include monuments not visible from *les bateaux-mouches* such as: *l'arc de Triomphe, les Champs-Élysées, Montmartre et le Sacré-Cœur, la Sorbonne, le Centre Pompidou (Beaubourg), le cimetière du Père-Lachaise, le Moulin Rouge, le Panthéon, la Bibliothèque nationale site François-Mitterrand, les Catacombes.* Students may work independently or with a partner for this activity. Allow students a few days to prepare their presentations. Consider giving a model presentation so students know what you expect of them. Following the presentations, discuss and summarize the information conveyed. As a follow-up, you might have students work with a partner to plan an itinerary for the monuments they would most like to visit in one day. In addition to guide books and the Internet, useful resources for this activity include: Applefield, David. *Paris Inside Out: The Insider's Handbook to Life in Paris.* Guilford, CT: Insiders' Guides, 2005; Mroue, Haas. *Frommer's Memorable Walks in Paris.* Hoboken, NJ: Frommer's. 2006; Tillier, Alan. *Paris, DK Eyewitness Travel Guides.* New York: DK Publications, 2010 (ebook version available).

Leçon 3 Faisons du tourisme !

POINTS DE DÉPART

Le logement et les visites

La place Plumereau à Tours

Les Francard, une famille de touristes belges, viennent d'arriver à Tours. Ils rentrent dans l'Office de Tourisme pour chercher des renseignements et trouver un logement.

LA RÉCEPTIONNISTE : Bonjour, monsieur. Bonjour, madame.

M. FRANCARD : Bonjour, madame. Nous cherchons un logement pas trop cher pour trois nuits.

LA RÉCEPTIONNISTE : Oui, vous êtes combien ?

M. FRANCARD : Quatre personnes, donc nous aurons besoin de deux chambres.

LA RÉCEPTIONNISTE : Je peux vous proposer un petit hôtel deux étoiles en centre-ville. C'est 75 euros par chambre.

M. FRANCARD : Ça nous convient très bien.

LA RÉCEPTIONNISTE : Bon, alors, je vais faire une réservation sur Internet pour les deux chambres pour trois nuits.

...

LA RÉCEPTIONNISTE : Bon, vous serez à l'Hôtel Château Fleuri ; ce n'est pas très loin d'ici.

M. FRANCARD : L'hôtel se trouve où exactement ?

LA RÉCEPTIONNISTE : Tenez, voici un plan du centre-ville. En sortant d'ici, vous allez prendre le boulevard. Ensuite vous tournez à droite dans la rue de Buffon. Continuez tout droit ; vous allez traverser la rue Émile Zola et ensuite prendre la rue de la Scellerie à gauche. L'hôtel se trouve au 7, rue de la Scellerie.

M. FRANCARD : Alors, à droite dans la rue de Buffon et à gauche dans la rue de la Scellerie. Merci, madame, et au revoir.

LA RÉCEPTIONNISTE : Je vous en prie, monsieur, au revoir.

Presentation: You may wish to present this material over two days. If so, then treat the dialogue, directions, and the **Vie et culture** note on lodgings on day 1, completing Ex. 9-25 and 9-26; treat historical and cultural sites on day 2, and complete Ex. 9-27.
To present, have students listen to the opening dialogue. Ask simple questions to test comprehension. *Qui cherche un logement ? Pour combien de personnes ? Combien de temps est-ce que les Francard vont passer en Touraine ? Quel type de logement est-ce qu'on leur propose ? Où se trouve l'hôtel ?* The *Office de Tourisme* for the city of Tours has its own web site, which includes a page for making hotel reservations. Using the detail map of *Tours* (MFL, Instructor's Resources), have students trace the route the Francard family will take to their hotel; have them find the *place Plumereau*, shown in the photo. Illustrate the meaning of each of the expressions in the shaded box, using the detail map.

POUR INDIQUER LE CHEMIN

prendre la rue, l'avenue, le boulevard, la première/la deuxième à droite...
traverser la place...
tourner à droite/à gauche dans le boulevard...
continuer tout droit jusqu'à la rue...

Tours, le centre-ville

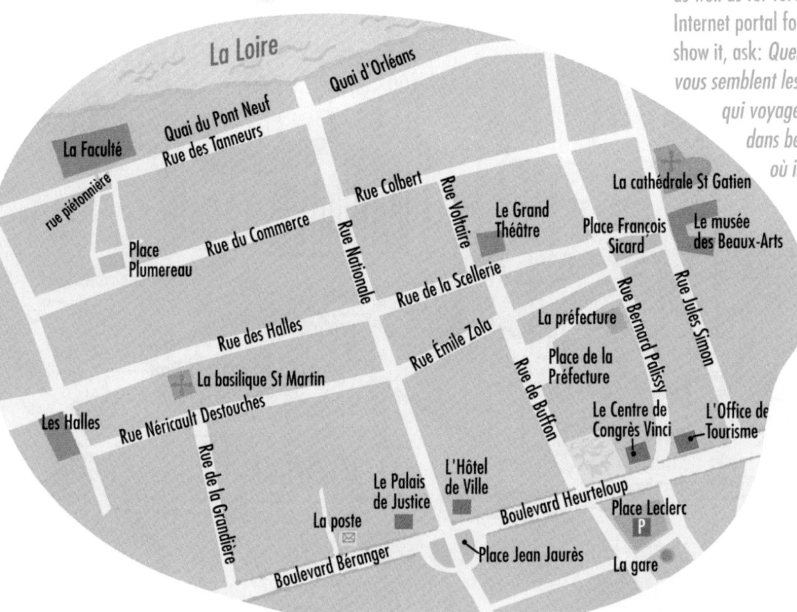

Expansion: To expand the cultural content of the lesson, point out to students that the *Office de Tourisme* is an important resource for the French as well as for foreign travelers in France. You may want to display the Internet portal for *les Offices de Tourisme et Syndicats d'Initiative.* As you show it, ask: *Quels services sont proposés aux voyageurs ? Quels services vous semblent les plus importants pour un Français ? pour un Américain qui voyage en France ?* and explain: *Un Office de Tourisme existe dans beaucoup de lieux touristiques en France, donc c'est l'endroit où il faut aller pour commencer à planifier un séjour.*

Presentation: As you discuss the map of Tours, point out streets and squares named for well-known writers (Voltaire, Émile Zola, (Philippe) Néricault Destouches); artists/composers (François Sicard, Bernard Palissy, (Pierre-Jean de) Béranger); statesmen (Jules Simon, (Jean-Baptiste) Colbert, Jean Jaurès); scientists (le Baron Heurteloup, le Comte de Buffon).

Vie et culture

Le logement

Si vous cherchez un logement pas cher en France, vous avez différents choix selon vos désirs et votre budget. Regardez les images : quels sont les avantages et les inconvénients de chaque option ? Quel type de logement est-ce que vous préférez et pourquoi ? Est-ce que vous avez les mêmes possibilités de logement dans votre pays ?

Si on est jeune, on peut rester dans une auberge de jeunesse.

Pendant l'été en France, les campings sont pleins de gens qui voyagent avec des caravanes, des camping-cars ou simplement une tente.

Une autre possibilité est de rester chez l'habitant, dans un gîte rural à la campagne. C'est surtout une bonne option si on veut établir un contact avec les gens du pays.

Des sites historiques et culturels

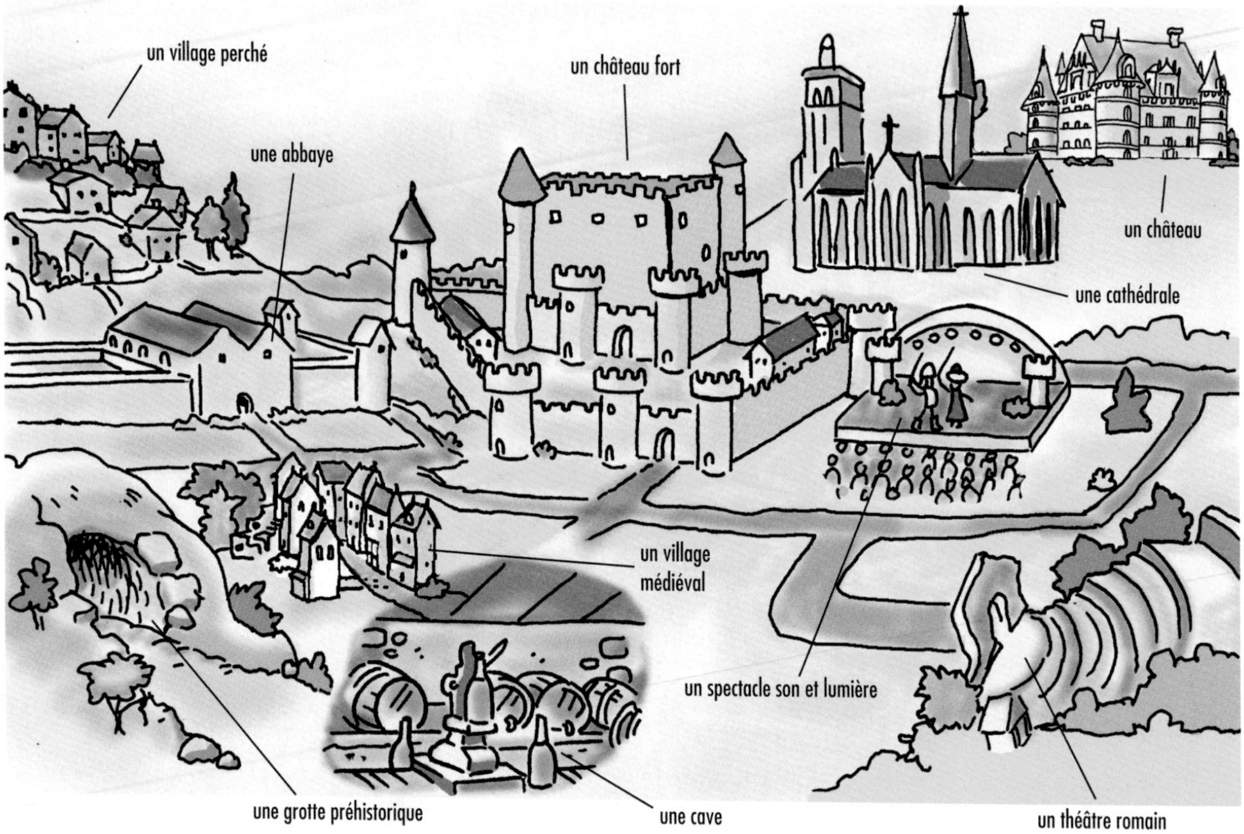

un village perché
un château fort
une abbaye
un château
une cathédrale
un village médiéval
un spectacle son et lumière
une grotte préhistorique
une cave
un théâtre romain

Implementation: You may wish to present historical and cultural sites on day 2 of the lesson. If so, this presentation can be enriched with slides, photos, or postcards of various locations in France. Use the drawing (MFL, Instructor's Resources) to introduce the basic vocabulary: model pronunciation and describe each location. Test comprehension by having students point to the place you name. Have them repeat key terms by identifying: *C'est une cave ou une abbaye ?*, etc. Follow up with Ex. 9-27.

09-34 to 09-37

À vous la parole

9-25 Où est-ce qu'ils vont loger ? D'après la description des touristes suivants, dites où ils vont probablement loger.

Key: 9-25 *Answers may vary.* 1) un hôtel 2) une auberge de jeunesse/un camping 3) un camping 4) une auberge de jeunesse/un camping 5) un camping 6) un gîte rural 7) un hôtel

MODÈLE Les Merten voudraient établir un contact avec les gens de la région.
• Ils vont loger dans un gîte rural.

1. Les Martini voudraient une chambre avec mini-bar, télévision et téléphone.
2. Christelle va passer trois jours à Bordeaux, mais c'est une étudiante et elle a un budget modeste.
3. Les Garcia voyagent avec leur caravane.
4. Max et ses copains veulent passer plusieurs semaines en Suisse sans dépenser (*spending*) trop d'argent.
5. Sébastien aime la nature ; il voyage à vélo et avec sa tente.
6. Les Smith aiment la campagne et ils voudraient pratiquer leur français.
7. Les Bénini voyagent en train et voudraient rester en ville.

9-26 Les bonnes indications. Imaginez que vous êtes devant la gare de Tours. Regardez le plan et suivez les indications données pour dire où vous arrivez. Choisissez votre destination dans la liste suivante.

MODÈLE É1 Vous tournez à gauche dans le boulevard Heurteloup, ensuite à droite dans la rue Nationale et à droite dans la rue de la Scellerie. Vous arrivez au coin (*corner*) de cette rue et de la rue Voltaire.

É2 À gauche dans le boulevard Heurteloup ? et ensuite à droite dans la rue Nationale ?

É1 Oui. Et après, à droite dans la rue de la Scellerie jusqu'à la rue Voltaire.

É2 C'est le Grand Théâtre ?

É1 Oui, c'est ça.

la Cathédrale Saint-Gatien	la Basilique Saint-Martin
le Grand Théâtre	les Halles
le Musée des Beaux-Arts	la Place Plumereau
la Préfecture de police	la Poste

1. Vous traversez le boulevard Heurteloup. Vous prenez la rue Bernard Palissy et vous continuez tout droit. À la place François Sicard, vous tournez à droite. le Musée des Beaux-Arts
2. Vous tournez à gauche dans le boulevard Heurteloup et vous traversez la place Jean Jaurès. C'est sur votre droite à côté du Palais de Justice, un peu plus loin. la Poste
3. Vous tournez à gauche dans le boulevard Heurteloup, vous traversez la rue Nationale et vous continuez tout droit. Vous prenez la deuxième rue à droite. Vous arrivez dans la rue Néricault Destouches. C'est là, en face de vous. la Basilique Saint-Martin
4. Le plus facile, c'est de suivre la rue Nationale jusqu'à la Loire et de prendre la rue des Tanneurs juste avant le quai du Pont-Neuf. Ensuite, vous tournez à gauche en face de la fac dans une petite rue piétonnière (*pedestrian street*). la Place Plumereau
5. Traversez le boulevard Heurteloup et prenez la rue de Buffon. Tournez à droite à la place de la Préfecture et continuez tout droit. C'est au coin de la rue Bernard Palissy sur votre droite. la Préfecture de police
6. Traversez le boulevard Heurteloup, prenez la rue de Buffon, tournez à gauche dans la rue de la Scellerie et continuez tout droit. Traversez la rue Nationale. Suivez la rue des Halles. C'est au bout (*at the end*) de la rue sur votre gauche. les Halles

Implementation: 9-26 Display the detail map of Tours (MFL, Instructor's Resources) and have students take turns giving directions to their partner. Treat the **Fiche Pratique** as you model the activity, and show how the dialogue at the beginning of the lesson illustrates this strategy.

Fiche pratique

When someone gives you directions, it is helpful to confirm that you have understood by repeating or summarizing briefly what you have been told.

Additional practice: To practice giving directions, put students in pairs and give each pair a slip of paper with a starting point and a destination. Using the detail map of Tours, they can develop a set of directions, providing only the starting point and not the destination. Have each group exchange papers with another pair, who then try to follow the directions. See how many groups are successful. Suggested departure points/destinations: *de la gare à la Cathédrale St Gatien ; de la gare à l'Hôtel de Ville ; de l'Hôtel de Ville à la Faculté des lettres ; de la Cathédrale St Gatien à la Poste ; de la Place Plumereau à l'Hôtel de Ville ; du Musée des Beaux-Arts à la Place Plumereau.* As an alternative, use the map of the town of Richelieu found in Ch. 2, L. 3 to practice giving and following directions.

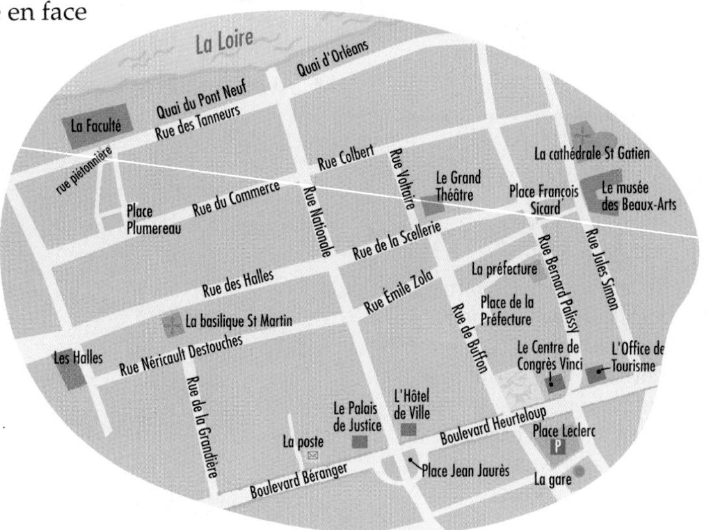

Implementation: 9-27 Have the class compare answers to see which pair came up with the most exciting things to do.

Additional practice: The following activity provides a review of the future tense. You might assign as homework and have students consult web sites and report back the next day. **Rêvons aux vacances.** Avec un/e partenaire, imaginez un voyage dans la ville ou l'endroit indiqué. Qu'est-ce que vous ferez ?

MODÈLE à Strasbourg
É1 Nous nous promènerons dans la vieille ville. Nous visiterons la cathédrale.
É2 Nous mangerons également une bonne choucroute.

1. en Touraine
2. à la Martinique
3. à La Nouvelle-Orléans
4. au Maroc
5. à Tahiti
6. au Québec
7. en Suisse
8. à Paris

Note: In her 1997 book, *Patterns Across Spoken and Written French : Empirical Research on the Interaction Among Forms, Functions, and Genres*, O'Connor Di Vito reports that 78% of occurring subjunctives consist of regular *-er* verbs and the irregular verbs *avoir, être, faire,* and *pouvoir*. The percentage rises to 94% if the verbs *attendre, dire, finir, prendre,* and *venir* are added to the list. The most frequent irregulars are presented here; the full conjugations of all irregular verbs are in Appendix 2. Point out that two-stem irregular verbs in the subjunctive follow the boot pattern. The subjunctive forms of *avoir* and *être* are used in commands: *Soyez raisonnable ! Aie de la patience !*, as taught in Ch. 7, L. 3.

Fiche pratique

To learn irregular verb forms, try writing them down or repeating them out loud. Whichever technique works best for you, focus both on exceptional forms and on any patterns that you see.

9-27 À l'Office de Tourisme. Avec un/e partenaire, quelles visites est-ce que vous recommandez à ces touristes ?

MODÈLE Jérôme et Camille sont très sportifs et ils aiment les beaux paysages.
É1 Ils peuvent faire du cyclotourisme.
É2 Oui. Comme ça, ils se promèneront dans la nature et ils visiteront tous les petits villages.

1. Les Martin sont fascinés par la préhistoire.
2. Sophie aime tout ce qui est spectacle.
3. Mme Francard s'intéresse à l'architecture de la Renaissance.
4. M. Francard aime surtout l'architecture militaire.
5. Pierre a étudié l'histoire des religions.
6. M. Dupin voudrait goûter les meilleurs vins de la région.
7. Audrey se passionne pour les antiquités romaines.
8. Vincent voudrait découvrir des petits villages médiévaux.

FORMES ET FONCTIONS

1. Le subjonctif de quelques verbes irréguliers

- A small number of verbs, including **faire** and **pouvoir**, have a special stem for the subjunctive.

faire	**fass-**	Il vaut mieux qu'elle **fass**e un tour du quartier.
pouvoir	**puiss-**	Il faut qu'ils **puiss**ent dormir à l'hôtel.

- Some irregular verbs have two stems in the subjunctive: one for the singular forms and the third person plural, the other for the **nous** and **vous** forms. The second stem is based on the **nous** form of the present indicative.

venir	**vienn-**	Il faut que tu **vienn**es avec nous.
	ven-	Il vaut mieux que vous **ven**iez en taxi.
prendre	**prenn-**	Il ne faut pas que tu **prenn**es le bus.
	pren-	Il est important que nous **pren**ions beaucoup de photos.

- **Avoir** and **être** show many irregularities:

	AVOIR	ÊTRE
j'/je	**aie**	**sois**
tu	**aies**	**sois**
il / elle / on	**ait**	**soit**
nous	**ayons**	**soyons**
vous	**ayez**	**soyez**
ils / elles	**aient**	**soient**

À vous la parole

9-28 Les Francard en voyage. Mme Francard précise ce qu'il faut que chaque personne fasse/prenne/apporte pour le voyage.

MODÈLE les enfants/faire leur valise
- Il faut que les enfants fassent leur valise.

1. moi/avoir suffisamment d'argent que j'aie...
2. mon mari/pouvoir réserver des chambres d'hôtel qu'il puisse...
3. notre fils/avoir son iPod qu'il ait...
4. mon mari et moi/être patients avec les enfants que nous soyons...
5. mon mari/faire des courses avant de partir qu'il fasse...
6. notre fille/pouvoir apporter son ordinateur qu'elle puisse...
7. nous/faire des achats que nous fassions...
8. nous/retenir des places dans le train que nous retenions...

Initial practice: Begin by having students identify the irregular verb used in the examples you provide: *Il est important que je puisse consulter le guide (pouvoir). Il est essentiel que tu sois raisonnable (être). Il faut que tu fasses un tour (faire). Il vaut mieux que tu viennes avec nous (venir). Il est utile que tu aies un plan de la ville (avoir)*, etc. Continue with transformation drills, indicative to subjunctive: *Il fait beau. —Il faut qu'il fasse beau ; Il peut voir le musée ; Il est raisonnable ; Il fait des achats ; Il peut rester en ville*, etc.

9-29 Conseils pour un voyage à Dakar. Un de vos amis va se rendre à Dakar. Vous allez lui donner des conseils utiles.

MODÈLE faire une liste de vêtements à emporter
- Il faut que tu fasses une liste de vêtements à emporter.

1. obtenir un visa que tu obtiennes...
2. avoir une carte de crédit que tu aies...
3. prendre l'avion à Paris que tu prennes...
4. être prudent quand tu sors le soir que tu sois...
5. faire attention aux voitures dans la rue que tu fasses...
6. prendre un dictionnaire bilingue que tu prennes...
7. faire un tour dans le quartier tout de suite pour te familiariser que tu fasses...
8. pouvoir dire « merci » dans la langue du pays que tu puisses...

Expansion: 9-29 Complete the exercise a second time, using the formal form. Indicate that students are to give advice to a group of friends who are traveling.

Implementation: 9-30 To ensure a successful activity, you might assign regions a day in advance so that students have time to search the Internet for information to share. Alternatively, allow students to choose a region with which they are familiar.

9-30 Voyages de rêve. Avec des camarades, offrez des conseils pour bien profiter des voyages en régions francophones.

MODÈLE en Bourgogne

É1 Il est important que vous visitiez Dijon.

É2 Il faut que vous goûtiez des bons vins de Bourgogne.

É3 Il faut que vous fassiez un tour à Beaune.

É4 Il est important aussi que vous mangiez du pain d'épices.

1. au Québec
2. en Suisse romande
3. en Louisiane
4. au Maroc
5. à la Martinique

On trouve souvent en Bourgogne les tuiles colorées comme celles des toits de l'Hôtel-Dieu des Hospices de Beaune.

2. Le subjonctif avec les expressions de volonté

Implementation: Review the forms of the subjunctive and its use with expressions of necessity before presenting this topic.

- When the main verb of a sentence expresses a desire or wish, the verb of the following subordinate clause is usually in the subjunctive.

Elles souhaitent qu'il **vienne** aussi.	*They wish that he would come, too.*
Il exige qu'on **attende** jusqu'à demain.	*He demands that we wait until tomorrow.*

Note: *Espérer* is an exception and is followed by the future tense: *J'espère qu'il viendra demain.*

Here are some verbs used to express desires or wishes that are followed by the subjunctive:

aimer	demander	exiger	souhaiter
aimer mieux	désirer	préférer	vouloir

- When the subject is the same for both parts of the sentence, use an infinitive construction instead of the subjunctive. Compare the following examples.

Il voudrait **rester** ici.	*He'd like to stay here.*
Il voudrait **que ses enfants restent** ici.	*He'd like his children to stay here.*
Moi, je voudrais **dormir** et je veux **que** toi, **tu te couches** bientôt aussi.	*As for me, I'd like to sleep, and I'd like for you to go to bed soon as well.*

09-42 to 09-45

À vous la parole

Note: 9-31 This exercise contrasts use of the infinitive when the subject is the same in both clauses, with use of the subjunctive when the two subjects are different. Make sure that students are clear about this distinction.

9-31 Pas si vite ! Julien part en vacances et il exprime des idées un peu extravagantes. Son père n'est pas d'accord et il veut que Julien soit plus raisonnable ; expliquez les vœux de son père. *Answers may vary.*

MODÈLE Je veux dormir dans un hôtel trois étoiles.
- Moi, je ne veux pas que tu dormes dans un hôtel trois étoiles.

OU • Je veux que tu dormes dans une auberge de jeunesse.

1. Je préfère sortir tout seul le soir. … que tu sortes avec un groupe.
2. Je désire prendre un taxi pour visiter la ville. … que tu prennes le bus.
3. Je souhaite faire des promenades en bateau. … que tu fasses des promenades à pied.
4. J'aime mieux voyager en première classe. … que tu voyages en deuxième classe.
5. Je ne veux pas visiter les petits villages. … que tu visites les petits villages.
6. Je demande de partir pour un mois. … que tu partes pour quinze jours.
7. Je voudrais dîner dans des restaurants deux étoiles. … que tu dînes dans des cafés.

9-32 À l'Office de Tourisme. Nicolas cherche des nouveaux employés et il décrit ses préférences aux candidats.

MODÈLE aider ces touristes
- Je demande que vous aidiez ces touristes.

OU • Je souhaite que vous aidiez ces touristes.

1. pouvoir décrire toutes les attractions touristiques … que vous puissiez…
2. connaître bien la ville … que vous connaissiez…

3. pouvoir parler trois langues … que vous puissiez…
4. être toujours à l'heure … que vous soyez…
5. avoir de la patience avec les clients difficiles … que vous ayez…
6. être disponibles (*available*) aux visiteurs … que vous soyez…
7. devenir experts dans l'histoire de la région … que vous deveniez…

9-33 Harmonie ou conflit. Discuter de ces sujets avec un/e partenaire : pour chaque catégorie, dites si vous et vos parents partagez les mêmes souhaits, désirs, etc.

Implementation: 9-33 Follow up by comparing answers for the class as a whole.

MODÈLE votre future profession : votre souhait

É1 Je souhaite être actrice. Mes parents veulent que je sois médecin.

É2 Mes parents veulent que je sois architecte et moi aussi. J'adore dessiner et je veux travailler comme architecte.

1. vos études : votre souhait
2. vos projets pour l'été prochain : votre préférence
3. votre prochain voyage : votre désir
4. votre future profession : votre souhait
5. votre futur/e mari ou femme : votre préférence
6. vos futurs enfants : votre souhait
7. votre lieu de résidence éventuel : votre désir

Lisons

Implementation: *Avant de lire.* Put students in small groups to discuss these questions, along with the reading strategy.

9-34 Le Tour du monde en quatre-vingts jours.

A. Avant de lire. Connaissez-vous ce roman très connu, écrit au XIXe siècle par l'écrivain français Jules Verne ? Le personnage principal, Phileas Fogg, est un Anglais flegmatique et excentrique qui mène une vie réglée comme une montre. Le mercredi 2 octobre 1872, dans son Reform-Club, il soutient qu'avec les moyens de transport modernes, on peut maintenant parcourir la Terre en quatre-vingts jours seulement. Il lance un pari (*makes a wager*) : s'il n'est pas de retour le samedi 21 décembre à huit heures quarante-cinq du soir, il perd tout. Avant de lire le passage que nous reproduisons ici, réfléchissez aux questions suivantes :

Phileas Fogg, dessiné par Alphonse de Neuville pour l'édition de 1873 du *Tour du monde en quatre-vingts jours*

1. Cette histoire se passe en 1872. Quels moyens de transport est-ce que Phileas Fogg va probablement utiliser pendant son voyage ? Faites-en une liste.
2. À votre avis, comment est-ce que Phileas Fogg pourra prouver à ses amis qu'il aura fait le tour du monde ?
3. Est-ce que Phileas Fogg est une personne à prendre des risques ? Comment va-t-il probablement organiser son voyage autour du monde ?

Stratégie

Use your knowledge of the historical context to better understand a narrative that takes place in another era. What characteristics of the period and what events might color or shape the story? What historical realities might distinguish the various places described?

4. Dans l'extrait que vous allez lire, vous verrez quelques verbes au **passé simple**, un temps littéraire. Le **passé simple** exprime une action au passé, comme le **passé composé**. Pour chaque verbe indiqué au **passé simple**, trouvez son équivalent au **passé composé** :

Note: The goal in introducing the *passé simple* is for students to recognize the meaning of the verbs and understand that the *passé simple* expresses events in the past; there is no need to present the verb paradigm or to drill forms.

Verbes au passé simple		Verbes au passé composé
répondit		**s'est arrêté**
répondirent	ont répondu	**a demandé**
demanda	a demandé	**sont entrés**
montèrent	sont montés	**a fait**
s'arrêta	s'est arrêté	**s'est mis**
entrèrent	sont entrés	**sont montés**
fit	a fait	**ont pris**
prirent	ont pris	**ont répondu**
se mit	s'est mis	**a répondu**

Key: ***En lisant.*** 1) 1920 heures, 115.200 minutes 2) le mercredi 2 octobre à huit heures quarante-cinq du soir 3) un cab et puis le train 4) le samedi 21 décembre 1872 à huit heures du soir, dans le salon du Reform-Club 5) son domestique, Jean Passepartout 6) à Paris 7) en montrant les visas apposés sur son passeport 8) à huit heures quarante-cinq du soir.

B. En lisant. Trouvez les réponses aux questions suivantes.

1. Phileas Fogg parie qu'il fera le tour du monde en quatre-vingts jours, c'est-à-dire, en combien d'heures ? combien de minutes ?
2. Quand est-ce qu'il partira ?
3. Quel moyen de transport est-ce qu'il prendra au départ ?
4. Quand est-ce qu'il sera de retour et où ?
5. Qui l'accompagnera ?
6. Où est-ce qu'ils s'arrêteront d'abord ?
7. Comment est-ce que Phileas Fogg propose de prouver qu'il a bien fait le tour du monde ?
8. À quelle heure est-ce que les voyageurs quittent la gare de Charing-Cross ?

LE TOUR DU MONDE EN QUATRE-VINGTS JOURS

—Un bon Anglais ne plaisante[1] jamais, quand il s'agit d'une chose aussi sérieuse qu'un pari[2], répondit Phileas Fogg. Je parie vingt-mille livres contre qui voudra que je ferai le tour de la terre en quatre-vingts jours ou moins, soit[3] dix-neuf-cent-vingt heures ou cent-quinze-mille-deux-cents minutes. Acceptez-vous ?

—Nous acceptons, répondirent MM. Stuart, Fallentin, Sullivan, Flanagan et Ralph, après s'être entendus.

—Bien, dit Mr. Fogg. Le train de Douvres part à huit heures quarante-cinq. Je le prendrai.

—Ce soir même ? demanda Stuart.

—Ce soir même, répondit Phileas Fogg. Donc, ajouta-t-il en consultant un calendrier de poche, puisque c'est aujourd'hui mercredi 2 octobre, je devrai être de retour à Londres, dans ce salon même du Reform-Club, le samedi 21 décembre, à huit heures quarante-cinq du soir... [Phileas Fogg retourne à la maison pour se préparer et chercher son domestique Jean Passepartout.]

Une station de voitures se trouvait à l'extrémité de Saville-row. Phileas Fogg et son domestique montèrent dans un cab, qui se dirigea rapidement vers la gare de Charing-Cross... À huit heures vingt, le cab s'arrêta devant... la gare. Passepartout sauta à terre[4]...

Mr. Fogg et lui entrèrent aussitôt dans la grande salle de la gare. Là, Phileas Fogg donna à Passepartout l'ordre de prendre deux billets de première classe pour Paris. Puis, se retournant, il aperçut[5] ses cinq collègues du Reform-Club.

« Messieurs, je pars, dit-il, et les divers visas apposés sur un passeport que j'emporte à cet effet vous permettront, au retour, de contrôler mon itinéraire...

—Vous n'oubliez pas que vous devez être revenu ? ... fit observer Andrew Stuart.

—Dans quatre-vingts jours, répondit Mr. Fogg, le samedi 21 décembre 1872, à huit heures du soir. Au revoir, messieurs. »

À huit heures quarante, Phileas Fogg et son domestique prirent place dans le même compartiment. À huit heures quarante-cinq... le train se mit en marche.

Source : Jules Verne, *Le tour du monde en quatre-vingts jours*

[1]raconte des histoires drôles [2]*a bet, a wager* [3]*in other words* [4]est descendu [5]a vu

C. En regardant de plus près. Examinez le texte plus en détail.

1. Phileas Fogg est accompagné de son domestique, Jean « Passepartout ». Pourquoi est-ce que c'est un nom amusant ?
2. Le texte nous indique quelle sorte de personne est Phileas Fogg ; dans chaque cas, trouvez un exemple qui illustre la description.

MODÈLE Phileas Fogg est un homme riche.
- Il prend des billets de train de première classe.

ou • Il a un domestique.

a. Il habite un beau quartier de Londres.
b. Il est très ponctuel.
c. Il aime la précision.
d. Il prend rapidement des décisions.

Key: *En regardant de plus près.* 1) « Passepartout » veut dire, « aller partout » et le domestique va accompagner Fogg partout où il va 2) a. Il habite Saville Row b. Il arrive dans son compartiment à 8h40 et le train part à 8h45 c. Il précise le nombre de jours, le nombre d'heures et le nombre de minutes de son voyage d. Il décide de partir le jour même.

D. Après avoir lu. Discutez des questions suivantes avec vos camarades de classe.

1. Voici l'itinéraire de Phileas Fogg publié dans le journal britannique *The Morning Chronicle*. Est-ce que vous pensez qu'il est vraiment possible pour Fogg d'accomplir son voyage en l'espace de quatre-vingts jours ? Pourquoi ?

LE TOUR DU MONDE EN QUATRE-VINGTS JOURS

De Londres à Suez par le Mont-Cenis et Brindisi, railways et paquebots	7 jours
De Suez à Bombay, paquebot	13 jours
De Bombay à Calcutta, railway	3 jours
De Calcutta à Hong-Kong (Chine), paquebot	13 jours
De Hong-Kong à Yokohama (Japon), paquebot	6 jours
De Yokohama à San Francisco, paquebot	22 jours
De San Francisco à New York, railroad	7 jours
De New York à Londres, paquebot et railway	9 jours
Total	80 jours

Expansion: *Après avoir lu.* In 1988 Michael Palin attempted to duplicate Fogg's journey in a BBC documentary miniseries called *Michael Palin: Around the World in 80 Days*, returning to London with mere hours to spare. The best-known film version is the 1956 film starring David Niven and Cantinflas; the movie earned five Oscars. A 1989 TV miniseries starred Pierce Brosnan as Fogg, Eric Idle as Passepartout, and Peter Ustinov as Detective Fix.

2. Est-ce que vous avez lu en traduction anglaise un roman de Jules Verne ou vu un film basé sur un de ses romans ? Parmi ses romans on trouve : *Vingt mille lieues sous les mers, L'île mystérieuse, Voyage au centre de la Terre* et *De la Terre à la Lune*. Si vous en connaissez un, discutez-en avec vos camarades de classe.
3. Si vous aimez la science-fiction, cherchez un de ces romans à la bibliothèque ou louez un DVD—peut-être même une adaptation du *Tour du monde en quatre-vingts jours* !

Note: These titles are given in their original spelling and do not follow the orthographic reform of 1990. Point out to students that they will see compound numbers such as *vingt-mille* with and without the hyphen.

Leçon 

moyens (m.) de transport	*means of transportation*
à pied	*on foot*
un avion	*plane*
un bus	*city bus*
un car	*excursion bus, intercity bus*
un métro	*subway*
une mobylette	*moped, motor scooter*
une moto	*motorcycle*
un taxi	*taxi*
un train	*train*
un tram(way)	*light rail*

pour faire un voyage	*to take a trip*
un aéroport	*airport*
un appareil (photo) numérique	*digital camera*
un carnet d'adresses	*address book*
une carte bancaire	*debit card*
une carte de crédit	*credit card*
une carte d'identité	*French national ID card*
une clé	*key*
un passeport	*passport*
un permis de conduire	*driver's licence*
un plan de ville	*city map*
un portable	*cell phone*
un portefeuille	*wallet*
un porte-monnaie (inv.)	*change purse*
un sac à dos	*backpack*
une valise	*suitcase*
un vol	*flight*

quelques expressions utiles	*some useful expressions*
avoir besoin de	*to need*
un billet	*(train, plane) ticket*
un ticket	*(subway) ticket*
oublier	*to forget*
tout	*everything*
Voyons…	*Let's see . . .*

Leçon 

les continents (m.)	*continents*
Voir à la page 276	*See page 276*

des pays (m.)	*countries*
Voir à la page 276	*See page 276*

des adjectifs de nationalité	*nationalities*
Voir à la page 276	*See page 276*

expressions de nécessité	*expressions of obligation*
Il est important de/que	*It is important (that)*
Il est nécessaire de/que	*It is necessary (that)*
Il est utile de/que	*It is useful (that)*
Il faut (que)/Il ne faut pas (que)	*You must/must not*
Il vaut mieux (que)	*It is better (best) (that)*

autres mots utiles	*other useful words*
aussi bien que	*as well as*
une frontière	*border*
une langue maternelle	*native language*
une réunion	*meeting*

Leçon 

le logement	*lodgings*
une auberge (de jeunesse)	*inn, (youth) hostel*
un camping	*campground*
un camping-car	*recreational vehicle*
une caravane	*trailer*
faire une réservation sur Internet	*to make a reservation online*
un gîte (rural)	*(rural) bed and breakfast*
loger (dans un hôtel une étoile)	*to stay (in a one-star hotel)*
une tente	*tent*

pour se renseigner	*to get information*
un guide	*guide (tour guide or guide book)*
Je vous en prie.	*You're welcome.*
un Office de Tourisme	*tourism office*
des renseignements (m.)	*information*

pour indiquer le chemin	*to give directions*
une avenue	*avenue*
un boulevard	*boulevard*
le chemin	*way*
continuer (tout droit)	*to keep going (straight ahead)*
tourner (à droite/à gauche)	*to turn (right/left)*
traverser	*to cross*

des sites (m.) historiques et culturels	*historical and cultural sites*
une abbaye	*abbey*
une cathédrale	*cathedral*
une cave	*wine cellar*
un château	*chateau*
un château fort	*fortress*
une grotte préhistorique	*prehistoric cave*
un spectacle son et lumière	*sound and light historical production*
un théâtre romain	*Roman theater*
un village médiéval	*medieval village*
un village perché	*village perched on a hillside*

quelques verbes de volonté qui exigent le subjonctif	*some verbs of volition that require the subjunctive*
aimer mieux	*to prefer*
désirer	*to desire, to want*
exiger	*to require, to demand*
souhaiter	*to hope, to wish*
demander	*to ask*
préférer	*to prefer*
vouloir	*to want*

Vocabulaire

10

Steve Martin joue le rôle de l'Inspecteur Clouseau dans le film *La Panthère rose*, tourné à Paris.

Quoi de neuf ? cinéma et médias

After completing this chapter, you should be able to:

- Express opinions about the media
- Express hypothetical situations and possible results
- Discuss cinema, television, reading habits, and computer use in the French-speaking world

Leçon 1 Le grand et le petit écran

POINTS DE DÉPART

Qu'est-ce qu'il y a à la télé ?

Presentation: As you begin this lesson, ask students what they know about Francophone TV, film, and the press. Encourage them to search the Internet for the many links to French periodicals, news media, and television channels and programs online. Students can also watch French news clips with apps for smartphones and i-devices.

Presentation: You may wish to teach this vocabulary over two days; if so, then present television vocabulary and complete Ex. 10-1 and 10-2 on day 1; continue with the **Vie et culture**, film vocabulary, and Ex. 10-3 on day 2.

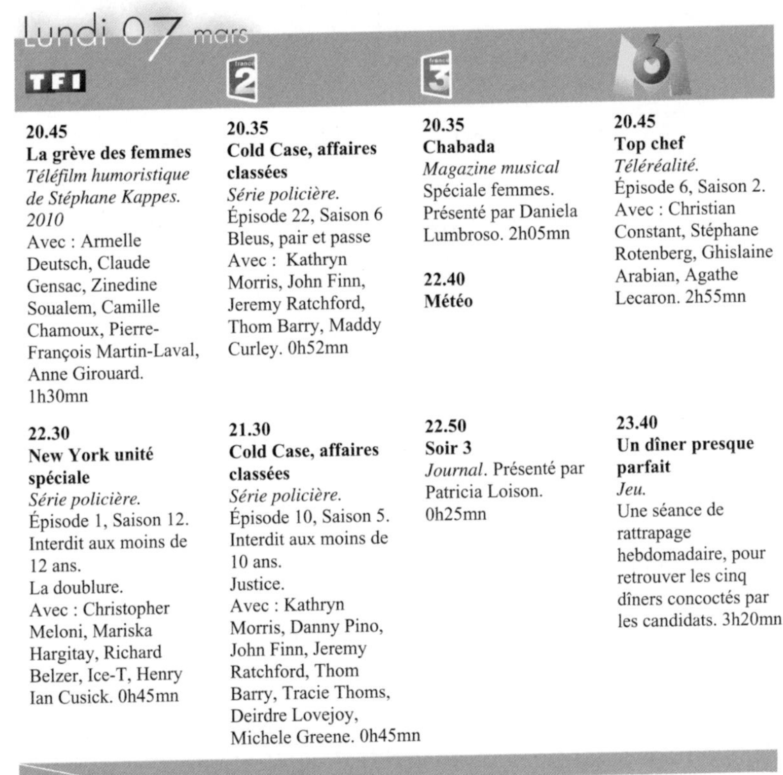

Lundi 07 mars

TF1	France 2	France 3	M6
20.45 **La grève des femmes** *Téléfilm humoristique de Stéphane Kappes. 2010* Avec : Armelle Deutsch, Claude Gensac, Zinedine Soualem, Camille Chamoux, Pierre-François Martin-Laval, Anne Girouard. 1h30mn	**20.35** **Cold Case, affaires classées** *Série policière.* Épisode 22, Saison 6 Bleus, pair et passe Avec : Kathryn Morris, John Finn, Jeremy Ratchford, Thom Barry, Maddy Curley. 0h52mn	**20.35** **Chabada** *Magazine musical* Spéciale femmes. Présenté par Daniela Lumbroso. 2h05mn **22.40** **Météo**	**20.45** **Top chef** *Téléréalité.* Épisode 6, Saison 2. Avec : Christian Constant, Stéphane Rotenberg, Ghislaine Arabian, Agathe Lecaron. 2h55mn
22.30 **New York unité spéciale** *Série policière.* Épisode 1, Saison 12. Interdit aux moins de 12 ans. La doublure. Avec : Christopher Meloni, Mariska Hargitay, Richard Belzer, Ice-T, Henry Ian Cusick. 0h45mn	**21.30** **Cold Case, affaires classées** *Série policière.* Épisode 10, Saison 5. Interdit aux moins de 10 ans. Justice. Avec : Kathryn Morris, Danny Pino, John Finn, Jeremy Ratchford, Thom Barry, Tracie Thoms, Deirdre Lovejoy, Michele Greene. 0h45mn	**22.50** **Soir 3** *Journal*. Présenté par Patricia Loison. 0h25mn	**23.40** **Un dîner presque parfait** *Jeu.* Une séance de rattrapage hebdomadaire, pour retrouver les cinq dîners concoctés par les candidats. 3h20mn

CHRISTELLE : Qu'est-ce qu'il y a à la télé ce soir ?

THOMAS : Attends, je vais regarder le programme… Bon, sur TF1, il y a un téléfilm français à 8 h 45 et une série policière à 10 h 30. Sur France 2, il y a deux épisodes d'une autre série policière que j'aime bien. Sur France 3, il y a un magazine musical qui a l'air intéressant.

CHRISTELLE : Bof ! Je n'ai pas tellement envie de voir une série policière ce soir.

THOMAS : Pourquoi ?

CHRISTELLE : Je n'aime pas toutes ces séries américaines qui passent à la télé et qui sont doublées ; je préfère les regarder en VO pour pratiquer mon anglais.

THOMAS : Tu rigoles ? Les films ont quelquefois des sous-titres, mais jamais les séries. Regarde, sur M6, il y a une émission de téléréalité bien française, *Top chef*. Tu veux la regarder ?

CHRISTELLE : Pourquoi pas ? Tu peux allumer la télé ?

THOMAS : Mais, c'est toi qui as la télécommande !

Presentation: Treat the TV listings first as a reading. As an overview, have students describe TV listings and programming in general: typical format, types of programs shown at particular times of the day, etc. Note: the use of the 24-hour clock; that programs do not always begin on the hour or half-hour; general programming tendencies. Show the dialogue as students listen. Have students match information in the dialogue to information in the listings provided. Use the dialogue as a model for the role-play activity in Ex. 10-2. Point out the colloquial expressions *Bof !* and *Tu rigoles ?* and help students figure out their meaning. A less familiar way of saying *Tu rigoles ?* would be *Tu plaisantes ?* You can obtain current TV listings on the Internet; you may want to display a current listing as you present the vocabulary list, *Des genres d'émissions*.

Presentation: The vocabulary allows students to name and describe types of programs, make choices or suggestions, and express an opinion about a program or programming in general. Describe the types of programs. To test comprehension, have students give examples of program types; these may be taken from the listings or given in English. Follow with simple repetition drills, using a specific example: *« Bones » c'est un documentaire ou une série ?* Let students make logical groupings of the programs: *pour s'informer, pour s'amuser*, etc.

DES GENRES D'ÉMISSIONS

un dessin animé
un divertissement
un documentaire
une émission de musique
une émission sportive
une émission de téléachat
une émission de téléréalité
un feuilleton
un film, un téléfilm
un film étranger en version originale (VO), en version française (VF)
un jeu télévisé
le journal télévisé (le JT), les informations (les infos)
un magazine
un reportage
une série

10-01 to 10-04

À vous la parole

Implementation: 10-1 This exercise requires students to use contextual clues to identify program types. As an alternative, check online listings for French or French Canadian television programming and, based on the titles, have students identify the program types. Or have students tell what kind of program they associate with specific people : *Michael Moore ? — un documentaire ; Diane Sawyer ?*, etc. Ask students to generate examples on their own.

10-1 Quel genre d'émission ? Imaginez que vous lisez le programme télé. Selon ces descriptions partielles, déterminez avec un/e partenaire le genre de chaque émission. *Answers may vary.*

MODÈLE dernier épisode
É1 C'est peut-être une série.
É2 S'il y a des épisodes, c'est probablement un feuilleton.

1. avec notre invitée, la chanteuse… une émission de musique
2. l'astrologie face à la science un documentaire
3. le journal de la semaine le journal télévisé
4. à gagner cette semaine : un voyage à Tahiti un jeu télévisé
5. série américaine une série/un feuilleton
6. Coupe de France de football. Quart de finale. une émission sportive
7. les dernières aventures de Babar, le roi éléphant un dessin animé

Implementation: 10-2 Display the listings (MFL, Instructor's Resources) or provide a set of current listings from the Web. As an alternative, give students a specific time and have them choose a program from the listings.

10-2 Les émissions d'aujourd'hui. Qu'est-ce qu'on peut regarder aujourd'hui ? Avec un/e partenaire, jouez les rôles de deux amis. Consultez le programme télé au début de cette leçon et discutez de vos choix.

MODÈLE É1 J'ai envie de regarder un match.
É2 Il n'y a pas de match ce soir. Si on regardait un film ?

1. J'aime bien les films.
2. J'adore les séries américaines.
3. Il n'y a pas de magazine sur France 3 ce soir ?
4. Est-ce qu'il y a une émission de téléréalité ce soir ?
5. J'ai envie de regarder quelque chose de différent.
6. J'ai mal à la tête, alors rien de sérieux pour moi ce soir !
7. Il y a un documentaire ce soir ?

Presentation: Present the various types of films using the descriptions and, if you wish, photos from magazines, newspapers, or web sites for films. Have students help you elaborate on the descriptions provided. Point out to students that *comédie* often means "drama" in French (for example, *La comédie française*) and that *une comédie musicale* therefore refers to any kind of musical, not just musical comedy.

Find out whether students know famous actors, actresses, and directors: *Nicole Kidman ? — C'est une actrice australienne. Elle est très belle et elle joue souvent dans des drames psychologiques.* Other possibilities: Halle Berry, Audrey Tautou, Orlando Bloom, Isabelle Adjani, Jennifer Hudson, Colin Firth, Gérard Depardieu, Jean Reno, Scarlett Johansson, les frères Cohen, Peter Jackson, Ron Howard, Ang Lee.

Initial practice: Begin with a recognition exercise: *Donnez-moi un exemple d'un film d'aventures.* Begin student production with a simple repetition drill: *« James Bond » est-ce que c'est le personnage principal dans un film d'aventures ou un film d'espionnage ?* Then have students identify the genre of various films: *Agents secrets* [film d'espionnage] ; *La petite souris* [dessin animé] ; *Burlesque* [comédie musicale] ; *Des hommes et des dieux* [drame psychologique] ;

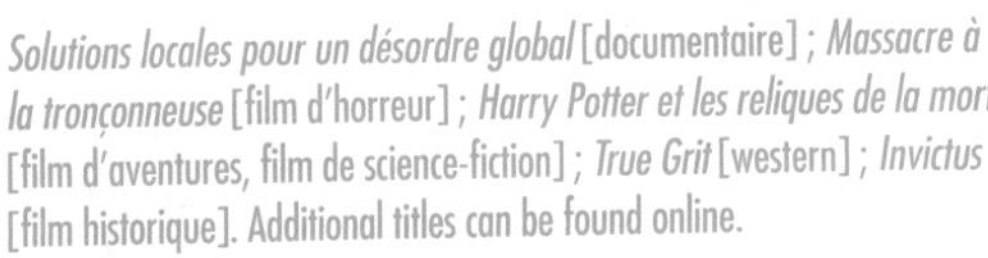

Solutions locales pour un désordre global [documentaire] ; *Massacre à la tronçonneuse* [film d'horreur] ; *Harry Potter et les reliques de la mort* [film d'aventures, film de science-fiction] ; *True Grit* [western] ; *Invictus* [film historique]. Additional titles can be found online.

DES GENRES DE FILMS

une comédie	raconte les mésaventures amusantes des gens
une comédie dramatique	raconte une histoire pleine de drames mais avec des moments assez drôles
une comédie musicale	raconte une histoire dansée et chantée
une comédie romantique	raconte les histoires d'amour des personnages, souvent avec des grandes vedettes dans le rôle des personnages principaux
un dessin animé	est fait surtout pour les enfants à partir d'images dessinées et puis filmées ; il y a souvent, par exemple, des animaux qui parlent
un documentaire	est un reportage sur la société, l'histoire, la nature, la science, la religion, etc.
un drame	raconte un évènement sérieux
un drame psychologique	examine les relations entre les gens
un film d'action	raconte une histoire avec beaucoup de scènes d'action, quelquefois avec de la violence
un film d'animation	n'est pas fait avec des acteurs mais avec des effets spéciaux, des images dessinées, des images faites sur ordinateur, etc.
un film d'aventures	raconte les aventures d'un personnage courageux
un film d'espionnage	est plein de suspense, avec des agents secrets qui partent en mission
un film historique	raconte des évènements historiques ou la vie d'un personnage historique
un film d'horreur	doit faire peur aux gens ; il y a des monstres, des fantômes, des vampires ou bien des psychopathes
un film policier	raconte un crime et l'enquête (*investigation*) pour retrouver le criminel
un film de science-fiction	raconte des évènements futuristes et imaginaires
un western	est un film d'aventures avec des cow-boys dans le Far West

À la mort de leur mère, les jumeaux Jeanne (Mélissa Désormeaux-Poulinet) et Simon (Maxim Gaudette) Marwan apprennent l'existence d'un père et d'un demi-frère jusqu'à là inconnus. Ils partent à la recherche de leur famille et de son histoire dans un pays du Moyen-Orient. Ce drame québécois, *Incendies*, tourné par le réalisateur Denis Villeneuve, est sorti en septembre 2010 et il a remporté plusieurs prix internationaux.

Note: The film *Incendies* was nominated for an Oscar as Best Foreign Language Film of the Year in 2011 and won several major international awards, including nine Jutras and eight Genie awards from the Academy of Canadian Cinema and Television. Its awards include best film, best screenplay, best director, and best actress. *Incendies* also won *le prix du public* at the *Festival international du film francophone de Namur* in October 2010. Ask if any students have seen this critically acclaimed film, which is based on a play by Wajdi Mouwad, a Lebanese-born Canadian writer, actor, and director. You may wish to show excerpts of the film in class or ask students to watch it outside of class.

Implementation: 10-3 Time permitting, have each group compare their results with those of the other groups and summarize results for the class as a whole.

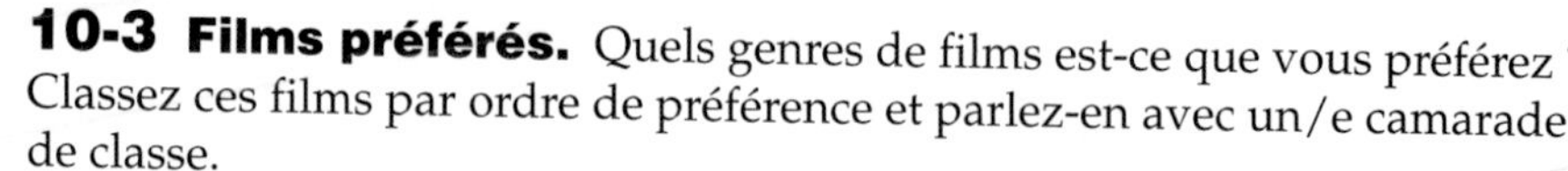

10-3 Films préférés. Quels genres de films est-ce que vous préférez ? Classez ces films par ordre de préférence et parlez-en avec un/e camarade de classe.

Presentation: Show the video montage *Le cinéma* to provide a visual overview of the Cannes film festival. Ask students if they recognize any actors, actresses, producers, and directors. Once students have read the text and shared their answers to the questions, see whether they can narrate the various events shown in the montage. Ask students if they enjoy watching the Oscars and if so, why, and whether they are familiar with any other film festivals. Ask them to identify any similarities (the red carpet for the Oscars and *la montée des marches* for Cannes) and differences (the *Palme* as opposed to the Oscar, *faire la bise* as opposed to a hug) between American events such as the Oscars, the Emmys, or the Grammys and *le festival de Cannes. La soirée des Jutra* is similar to the Oscars in that it is a single night award show. FESPACO and FIFF are more like Cannes in that they are festivals that take place over several days. The African film festival FESPACO takes place in odd-numbered years beginning in late February; the *Festival International du Film Francophone de Namur* takes place in Belgium every year in October. Encourage students to discover more information about these festivals and film events online.

MODÈLE

moi	mon partenaire
1. comédies romantiques	1. films d'aventure
2. films historiques	2. westerns
3. drames psychologiques	3. films policiers

É1 J'aime surtout les comédies romantiques, parce que ce n'est pas trop sérieux. Mais je regarde aussi des films historiques et des drames psychologiques. Et toi ?

É2 J'aime les films d'aventure, surtout les westerns. J'aime aussi les films policiers. Je regarde des séries policières toutes les semaines. Donc j'ai une préférence pour les films pleins d'action.

Vie et culture

Les festivals internationaux de films

10-52

Est-ce que vous savez qu'il y a de nombreux festivals francophones de films chaque année ? Pouvez-vous en nommer quelques-uns ? Sans doute, vous avez entendu parler du Festival International du Film à Cannes. Regardez la séquence vidéo, *Le cinéma*. Est-ce que ce festival ressemble à un festival que vous avez déjà vu (à la télévision peut-être) ? Comment ? Est-ce qu'il y a des éléments qui sont typiquement français ou internationaux ?

Pour savoir quels sont les meilleurs films francophones, vous avez plusieurs choix. Pour les meilleurs films canadiens, vous pouvez regarder Le Gala des Jutra. C'est le festival cinématographique qui a lieu chaque année au mois de mars au Québec. Pour le cinéma africain, le FESPACO (le Festival Panafricain du Cinéma et de la Télévision de Ouagadougou) a lieu tous les deux ans à Ouagadougou, au Burkina Faso. Ce grand festival a pour objectif de favoriser la diffusion de toutes les œuvres du cinéma africain. Par contre, le Festival International du Film Francophone de Namur qui a lieu chaque octobre en Belgique met en honneur plus de cent films venus de partout dans le monde francophone. Ce festival est soutenu par l'Organisation internationale de la Francophonie et il est jumelé avec le FESPACO. Il joue un rôle important dans la diffusion du film francophone. Est-ce que vous connaissez des films francophones ? Lesquels ?

Un jeune homme à vélo sous une affiche qui annonce le Festival Panafricain du Cinéma et de la Télévision de Ouagadougou

Sons et lettres

Les semi-voyelles /w/ et /ɥ/

The semivowel /w/ is always followed by a vowel, and that vowel is very often /a/. To pronounce /w/, start from the word "tweet" in English: *tweet*/**toi**.

When followed by the sound /a/, this semivowel is usually spelled **oi**, as in **moi** or **trois**. It can also be spelled **ou**, as in **oui** or **jouer**. The spelling **oy** represents the sound /waj/, as in **employé** or **royal**. The semivowel /w/ also occurs in combination with the nasal vowel /ɛ̃/. In this case, it is spelled **oin**: **loin** or **moins**.

To pronounce the semivowel /ɥ/, as in **lui**, start from the /y/ of **lu** but pronounce it together with the following vowel: **lu**/**lui**.

The sound /ɥ/ is frequently followed by the vowel /i/: **huit**, **je suis**, **la nuit**, **bruit**, but not exclusively: **nuage**, **ennuyeux**, **s'essuyer**. It is always spelled with the letter **u** followed by another vowel.

Note: When the combination *ou* occurs before a vowel, it may be pronounced as the semivowel /w/ or the corresponding vowel /u/: *louer* /lwe/ (one syllable) or /lue/ (two syllables). Most of these cases involve verb forms (stem plus ending): *jouer, nous jouons, vous jouez*. However, it is preferable for students to pronounce forms like *un souhait* or *un jouet* with /w/. But note, as was the case for *i*, when *ou* occurs after consonant groups, the pronunciation of /u/ is obligatory. Compare: *louer* /lwe/ or /lue/ versus *trouer* /true/. However, the combination *oi* is pronounced /wa/ in this context: *trois*. The same principle applies to *u* before vowels: *nuage, tuer*.

Note: The distinction between /w/ and /ɥ/ is a difficult one for American speakers to perceive and to articulate, partly due to the difficulty with the pairs /u/ and /y/. You may wish to use the audio program to present this exercise in class (MFL, Chapter Resources) and/or to assign it as homework in addition to the activities in the SAM/MFL. Note that Belgian speakers do not differentiate between the semi-vowels /w/ and /ɥ/. For these speakers, the sequence "ui" is always pronounced as /w/. Thus, both *lui* and *Louis* are pronounced /lwi/.

À vous la parole

-05 to -06

10-4 Contrastes. Prononcez et comparez les paires de mots suivantes.

la j**oi**e	j**oy**eux	un m**oi**s	m**oin**s
le r**oi**	r**oy**al	la l**oi**	**loin**
l'empl**oi**	empl**oy**er		

Maintenant, prononcez et comparez les mots avec /w/ et /ɥ/.

oui	h**ui**t	L**ou**is	l**ui**
j**oin**t	j**uin**	le s**oi**r	ess**ui**e

10-5 Comptine. Écoutez cette comptine et ensuite lisez-la à haute voix.

Tr**oi**s petits princes
Sortant du Paradis, bisc**uit**
Clarinette, clarinette
Nos souliers° ont des lunettes

Un, deux tr**oi**s, Vive la reine°
Un deux tr**oi**s, Vive le r**oi**°

souliers: *chaussures*
reine: *queen*
roi: *king*

Presentation: Point out that these verbs have three spoken forms and follow the "boot" pattern. The third-person singular and plural forms sound alike: *il croit/ils croient; elle voit/elles voient*. The *nous* and *vous* forms contain the sound /j/, as in English "yes." The sound /j/ is reflected by the letter *y*: *croyons, voyez*.

FORMES ET FONCTIONS

1. Les verbes *croire* et *voir* ; la conjonction *que*

- Here are the forms of the irregular verbs **croire** and **voir**.

CROIRE ***to believe*** **VOIR** ***to see***

SINGULIER			PLURIEL		
je	crois	vois	nous	croy**ons**	voy**ons**
tu	crois	vois	vous	croy**ez**	voy**ez**
il / elle / on	croi**t**	voi**t**	ils / elles	croi**ent**	voi**ent**

IMPÉRATIF : **Crois**-moi ! **Croyez**-nous ! **Croyons** aux jeunes !
Vois ta mère pour l'argent ! **Voyez** mes belles tomates !
Voyons !

PASSÉ COMPOSÉ : J'ai **cru** qu'il partait. J'ai **vu** ce film.

FUTUR : Je le **croir**ai quand je le **verr**ai.

- Use the verb **croire**:
  - to indicate that you believe someone or something:

Je **crois** Thomas.	*I believe Thomas.*
L'histoire de cette actrice ? Nous la **croyons**.	*This actress's story? We believe it.*

  - to indicate that you believe in something or someone. In this case, use **croire** along with the preposition **à**.

Nous **croyons à** l'avenir du cinéma.	*We believe in the future of film.*
Ils **croient au** Père Noël.	*They believe in Santa Claus.*

  - Note, however, the following special expression.

Nous **croyons en** Dieu.	*We believe in God.*

- Here are some common expressions using **croire**:

Je crois./Je crois que oui.	*I think so.*
Je ne crois pas./Je crois que non.	*I don't think so.*

Note: Use these expressions to remind students that a complex sentence with the conjunction *que* is not always followed by the subjunctive. You may wish to explain that these expressions take the subjunctive when used in the negative: *Je crois que c'est un bon acteur./Je ne crois pas que ce soit un bon acteur.* However, this is not obligatory in spoken French.

- To express an opinion, use a verb such as **croire** or **penser** plus the conjunction **que**. Notice that the conjunction is not always expressed in English but must be present in French. The verb **trouver** can also be used in this way with the conjunction **que**.

Je **crois que** ce film va gagner un prix.	*I think* (*that*) *this film will win an award.*
Ils **pensent que** Tim Burton est un grand réalisateur.	*They think* (*that*) *Tim Burton is a great director.*
Elles **trouvent que** ce film est trop long.	*They think* (*that*) *this movie is too long.*

- To report what someone says or knows, use the verb **dire** or **savoir** plus the conjunction **que**.

Elle dit **qu'**elle ne se sent pas bien.	*She says (that) she's not feeling well.*
Il dit **que** son frère viendra avec nous au ciné.	*He says (that) his brother will come with us to the movies.*
Ils savent **que** je n'aime pas les films en VO.	*They know that I do not like movies with subtitles.*

- To state an observed fact, use the verb **voir** plus the conjunction **que**:

Je vois **que** tu as un nouvel écran plat.	*I see that you have a new flat screen TV.*

Note: We avoid the use of past tense with *dire que* in order to avoid agreement of tenses. If you wish to present this feature, provide multiple examples: *Elle a dit que ce film était excellent*, etc.

À vous la parole

Initial practice: Begin with a substitution drill for *croire*: *Je crois au Père Noël ; vous. — Vous croyez au Père Noël*, etc.

Implementation: 10-6 Make sure students understand all the possible responses before beginning. Help them figure out the meaning of *avenir* from *à* plus *venir*.

10-6 Les croyances. À quoi croient ces personnes ? Pour chaque phrase, choisissez dans la liste suivante la réponse qui convient.

MODÈLE Mme Martin achète des billets de LOTO chaque semaine.
- Elle croit à la chance.

Réponses possibles :

l'amour	la chance	la médecine
l'argent	Dieu	le Père Noël
l'avenir	la discipline	le plaisir

1. M. Gervais a trois enfants et il est très autoritaire. Il croit à la discipline.
2. Anne a six ans, son frère a quatre ans. Ils croient au Père Noël.
3. Geoffrey est un jeune homme sentimental. Il croit à l'amour.
4. Vous travaillez vingt-quatre heures sur vingt-quatre. Vous croyez à l'argent.
5. M. Leblanc va à l'église tous les dimanches. Il croit en Dieu.
6. Nous sortons jusqu'à trois heures du matin tous les soirs. Nous croyons au plaisir.
7. Je voudrais avoir beaucoup d'enfants. Je crois à l'avenir.
8. Quand ça ne va pas bien, Alex va tout de suite voir le médecin. Il croit à la médecine.

Initial practice: Begin with a substitution drill for *voir*: *Je vois un éléphant ; toi. –Tu vois un éléphant*, etc.

Implementation: 10-7 Be sure to present the information in the **Vie et culture** before completing this activity. Encourage students to be creative in their responses and to come up with more than one possibility for each situation.

10-7 Que de choses à voir ! Expliquez ce que chaque personne voit — attention au temps du verbe ! *Answers may vary.*

MODÈLE Nous avons regardé un documentaire sur Paris.
- Nous avons vu la tour Eiffel.

Les Davy sont au ciné avec leurs petits-enfants.
- Ils voient des dessins animés et des films d'animation.

1. J'irai à Cannes pour le festival de films. Je verrai des stars.
2. Vous êtes allés à Montréal pour la soirée des Jutra ? Vous avez vu des réalisateurs québécois ?
3. Ils vont visiter Hollywood. Ils verront les maisons des stars.
4. Tu visites la ville de Park City pour le festival Sundance au mois de janvier ? Tu vois beaucoup de neige ?

5. Elles sont allées à Ougadougou au mois de février. Elles ont vu des films africains.
6. Nous sommes à New York. Nous voyons des comédies musicales sur Broadway.
7. Cet hiver, ma copine ira au cinéma. Elle verra beaucoup de comédies romantiques.

Implementation: 10-8 Go over the model with students before putting them in pairs to consider the topics. To help frame the discussion, you might have students express each item as a question: *Est-ce que la télé peut informer les gens ? Comment ?*

10-8 Les opinions sur les médias. Quelle est votre opinion et l'opinion de votre partenaire ? Comparez vos idées avec les idées de vos camarades de classe.

MODÈLE La télé peut informer les gens.

É1 Oui, je crois que la télé peut informer les gens.

É2 Je suis tout à fait d'accord, je crois qu'il est utile de regarder le journal télévisé, par exemple.

(*aux autres*) Nous croyons que la télé peut informer les gens. Par exemple, ...

1. La télé peut informer les gens.
2. Les acteurs ont une responsabilité par rapport à la société.
3. Les séries américaines donnent une fausse (*false*) image de la vie aux États-Unis.
4. Les films et la télé banalisent la violence.
5. Regarder la télé peut être très instructif pour les enfants.
6. Avoir la télévision haute définition compatible 3D est absolument nécessaire.

Presentation: Many of these expressions were introduced in Ch. 7, L. 3. You may wish to review them with an activity from that lesson before presenting their use in the subjunctive. Provide examples as in the text and have students analyze. Let students create additional examples using the expressions in the list. Make sure to point out that contrary to the expressions just learned above (*croire que, voir que, trouver que, dire que*, etc.), these expressions are always followed by the subjunctive in the clause introduced by *que*.

2. Le subjonctif avec les expressions d'émotion

- When the main clause of a sentence expresses an emotion, such as anger, fear, joy, or sadness, the verb of the subordinate clause is always in the subjunctive.

Je regrette que vous **partiez** si tôt.	*I'm sorry (that) you're leaving so soon.*
Elle est contente que tu **viennes** avec nous.	*She's happy (that) you're coming with us.*

Here are some verbs and expressions that convey emotion and are followed by the subjunctive:

avoir peur	être fâché/e	être triste
être content/e	être furieux/-euse	Il est/C'est dommage que
être déçu/e	être heureux/-euse	Il est/C'est étonnant que
être désolé/e	être inquiet/inquiète	Il est/C'est malheureux que
être enchanté/e	être ravi/e	regretter
être étonné/e	être surpris/e	

It is important to remember that not every clause introduced by **que/qu'** includes a verb in the subjunctive. The use of the indicative or subjunctive in the subordinate clause is determined by the verb in the main clause. Compare the following examples:

Je **suis contente** qu'elle **vienne** demain.	*I am happy (that) she is coming tomorrow.*
Je **sais** qu'elle **vient** demain.	*I know (that) she is coming tomorrow.*
Il **veut** que nous **partions** de bonne heure.	*He wants us to leave early.*
Il **dit** qu'on **part** de bonne heure.	*He says that we are leaving early.*
Il **faut** que tu **dises** la vérité.	*It is necessary that you tell the truth.*
Je **crois** que tu **dis** la vérité.	*I believe (that) you are telling the truth.*

Note: After learning to use the subjunctive in subordinate clauses with expressions of obligation, desire, and emotion, many students have a tendency to overgeneralize and use the subjunctive after each instance of the conjunction *que.* Point out that the subjunctive is only used in a limited number of cases, depending on the verb or expression in the main clause. Draw their attention to the verbs presented in this lesson and in previous lessons that do not take the subjunctive: *croire, voir, penser, trouver, dire, savoir.* Ex. 10-11 provides practice with this distinction.

- When the subject is the same for both parts of a sentence, use an infinitive construction preceded by **de** instead of a clause introduced by **que** + the subjunctive. Compare the following examples:

Elle est contente **de regarder** cette émission.	*She's happy to watch this show.*
Elle est contente **que vous regardiez** cette émission avec elle.	*She's happy (that) you are watching this show with her.*
Je regrette **de ne pas pouvoir** venir.	*I'm sorry not to be able to come.*
Je regrette **que tu ne puisses pas** venir.	*I'm sorry (that) you will not be able to come.*

À vous la parole

10-9 Soirée gala pour les Césars. Morgane organise une soirée gala pour ses amis chez elle. Ils vont regarder la Cérémonie des Césars à la manière des grandes vedettes de cinéma. Morgane est très contente à l'approche de cette grande soirée pour beaucoup de raisons. Pour chaque raison donnée, décidez si elle est contente pour elle-même ou pour les autres.

Elle est contente…	**pour elle-même**	**pour les autres**
MODÈLE … de faire la fête avec ses amis.	✓	
… que sa sœur puisse venir.		✓
1. … de voir toutes ces vedettes à la télé.	✓	
2. … d'avoir un grand téléviseur haute-définition pour la soirée.	✓	
3. … que ses parents soient d'accord pour servir du champagne.		✓
4. … de s'habiller en robe de soirée élégante.	✓	
5. … que ses amis se maquillent et se coiffent comme des stars.		✓
6. … qu'ils aient un tapis rouge pour la soirée.		✓
7. … que le jour arrive bientôt.		✓
8. … que vous soyez là aussi.		✓

Est-ce que vous pensez que Morgane est plus contente pour elle-même ou pour les autres ? Pourquoi ?

Implementation: 10-9 This comprehension based activity draws students' attention to the fact that expressions of emotion are only followed by the subjunctive when there are two different subjects. Point out that *un téléviseur* is used to refer to a television set, especially in a formal or sales context. Informally, French speakers refer to their television set as *la télé.* The *Césars* are awards given annually to French films.

Implementation: 10-10 For the model sentences, have students identify which was spoken by a man and which by a woman. Display the list of expressions of emotion requiring the subjunctive to provide students with ideas for the exercise. To expand, elicit multiple reactions to each statement. Follow up by calling on groups at random to give their reactions.

10-10 Que d'émotions ! Avec un/e partenaire, réagissez à ces annonces de votre professeur. Comparez vos réactions avec les réactions de vos camarades de classe.

MODÈLE Il n'y a pas de devoirs ce soir.

É1 Je suis surpris qu'il n'y ait pas de devoirs.

É2 Je suis contente qu'il n'y ait pas de devoirs.

Vous aurez un examen vendredi.

É1 C'est dommage qu'on ait un examen vendredi.

É2 Oui, je suis étonnée d'avoir un autre examen.

1. Il n'y aura pas cours demain.
2. Tout le monde ira au restaurant ensemble ce week-end.
3. Je vous achèterai un souvenir en France cet été.
4. Vous n'aurez pas d'examen final.
5. Les résultats du dernier examen sont excellents.
6. Vous faites beaucoup de progrès en français.

Implementation: 10-11 Model a few items with the class as a whole before having students work in groups. Remind students of the distinction between expressions that take the subjunctive in the subordinate clause and those that do not. Also point out that when there is only one subject, they need to use *de* plus an infinitive. You may wish to begin by reviewing each expression and deciding if the subjunctive or the indicative should be used in the subordinate clause.

10-11 On va tout savoir. Complétez chaque phrase et comparez vos réponses avec celles de vos camarades de classe.

MODÈLES À propos de cette semaine, je suis heureux/-euse que…

É1 Je suis heureuse que ma petite sœur vienne me voir ce week-end. Et toi ?

É2 Je suis heureux que mon cours de biologie finisse cette semaine. Et toi ?

É3 Je suis heureux d'avoir une bonne note pour l'examen de français !

À propos des films étrangers, je trouve que…

É1 Je trouve que les films en VO sont meilleurs que les films doublés.

É2 Je n'aime pas les sous-titres. Je trouve que les films doublés sont meilleurs.

É3 Moi, je trouve que les films américains sont les meilleurs. Je n'aime pas les films étrangers.

1. À propos de ce semestre, je suis heureux/-euse que…
2. À propos de mes amis, je pense que…
3. À propos de mes profs, je suis surpris/e que…
4. À propos des acteurs, je crois que…
5. À propos des regrets, je regrette que…
6. À propos de l'avenir, j'ai peur que…
7. À propos de ma famille, je sais que…

Observons

10-12 Réflexions sur le cinéma.

Implementation: *Avant de regarder.* Have students describe what they see in the picture of the *Festival de Cannes* and help them generate a list of things they could see and do during the festival. Refer back to the **Vie et culture** section for more information.

A. Avant de regarder. Imaginez que vous habitez les environs de Cannes : qu'est-ce que vous pouvez faire au moment du Festival International du Film ? Faites une liste d'activités possibles. Vous allez entendre une Niçoise qui décrit sa propre expérience, puis un étudiant à l'Université de Nice qui décrit ses préférences cinématographiques.

Le Palais des Festivals à Cannes

B. En regardant. Trouvez toutes les bonnes réponses à chaque question.

1. Selon Fabienne, des célébrités viennent à Cannes…
   (a. de tous les pays.)
   b. à tous moments.
   c. pour les vacances.
   (d. pour la promotion de leurs films.)
2. Fabienne… à Cannes au moment du festival.
   a. ne va jamais (b. est souvent) c. va tous les ans
3. Elle a eu l'occasion… quelques célébrités.
   (a. de voir) b. de dîner avec c. d'interviewer
4. Édouard va au cinéma…
   (a. aussi souvent que possible.) b. très souvent. c. tous les soirs.
5. Le dernier film qu'il a vu, c'était un film…
   a. américain. b. espagnol. (c. français.)
6. Pour lui, un grand classique du cinéma, c'est…
   a. *Harry, un ami qui vous veut du bien.*
   b. *L'auberge espagnole.*
   (c. *Le Seigneur des anneaux.*)
   (d. *Matrix.*)

C. Après avoir regardé. Maintenant discutez des questions suivantes avec vos camarades de classe.

1. Est-ce qu'il est possible pour les gens chez vous de côtoyer (*to get close to*) des célébrités comme le fait Fabienne à Cannes ? Pourquoi est-ce que les gens aiment cela, à votre avis ?
2. Est-ce que vous êtes d'accord avec Édouard quand il nomme des « grands classiques » ? Quels sont les grands films classiques pour vous ?

Implementation: *Après avoir regardé.* As a follow-up, have the class create a list of classic films, then develop a description in French for each of them.

Script: *Observons*

FABIENNE : Vous savez que sur la Côte d'Azur nous avons Cannes, qui est pas très loin de Nice. Vous avez un tas de célébrités, de toutes nationalités qui euh viennent pour la promotion de leurs films. Je suis um très souvent aussi sur la ville de Cannes, donc j'aperçois souvent le Festival de Cannes et j'ai eu l'occasion de côtoyer quelques petites célébrités — un petit coucou, comme ça de… de quelques minutes. Voilà.

ÉDOUARD : Donc j'aime beaucoup le cinéma. Euh, j'y vais autant que je peux, ce qui est pas beaucoup, en tant que… parce que je suis étudiant. Euh mais dès que je peux, par contre, je loue un… un DVD et je regarde ça avec des amis. Les derniers films que j'ai vus, c'est *Harry, un ami qui vous veut du bien*, euh un film français. Ou sinon, *L'auberge espagnole*. Je vous conseille de le voir, d'ailleurs. Euh sinon, ben, les grands classiques, comme euh *Le Seigneur des anneaux*, ou *Matrix*. Et euh, j'espère bientôt en voir un autre, ce soir peut-être.

Leçon 2 Êtes-vous branché informatique ?

Presentation: Have students take the quiz individually, with a partner, or as a whole class. Go over any difficult words or expressions. Students will most likely be familiar with most of this vocabulary since it is heavily based on cognates. Go over the pronunciation and point out, for example, that *MP3* is pronounced as / ɛmpetrwa / whereas most i-devices are pronounced as if they were English for example, iPod is pronounced as /aɪpad/. We are using the term *un mail*, pronounced / mel / and also spelled *mél* to refer to an e-mail message and *e-mail* /imel/ to refer to the medium: *je t'envoie un mail ; Nous vous confirmerons la réservation par e-mail.* In 2003 the Académie française recommended the Québécois term *courriel* (*courrier électronique*) and it was declared the official term by the French Minister of Culture. But *un mail (mél)* and *e-mail* are the most widely used terms.

POINTS DE DÉPART

Êtes-vous technophile ou technophobe ?

Voulez-vous savoir où vous en êtes dans la révolution informatique ? Alors, répondez aux questions suivantes pour découvrir si vous êtes technophile ou technophobe.

Première partie :

1. Qu'est-ce que vous faites pour acheter vos livres au début du semestre ?

a. Je les cherche et je les commande avec mon smartphone.
b. Je fais de la recherche en ligne (avec un navigateur web bien sûr) pour voir où je peux trouver les livres les moins chers et je les commande avec une carte bancaire sur un site web.
c. Je vais à la librairie et je demande de l'aide au libraire.

2. Qu'est-ce que vous faites quand vous devez faire un exposé devant la classe ?

a. Je surfe sur Internet pour trouver des informations et je prépare une présentation multimédia avec de la musique, du texte et des clips vidéo. Bien sûr, je sauvegarde le fichier sur ma clé USB et je m'envoie une copie par e-mail en pièce jointe avant l'exposé.
b. Je prépare un beau poster avec des jolies images que j'ai scannées et imprimées à la maison avec mon imprimante multifonction. J'ajoute aussi quelques photos numériques que j'ai retouchées avec un logiciel sur ordinateur.
c. J'écris mon plan et les idées importantes dans mon cahier. Je fais ma présentation à l'oral devant la classe.

3. Comment est-ce que vous communiquez avec vos amis et vos parents ?

a. Je me sers d'un ordinateur portable et d'une webcam. C'est génial. On peut se voir en même temps qu'on se parle et ça ne coûte pas cher.
b. On s'échange souvent des textos, des photos et des vidéos avec nos portables. Et on s'envoie des liens pour des sites web intéressants.
c. Je leur téléphone de temps en temps et j'écris des cartes postales une fois par mois.

4. Qu'est-ce que vous faites pour vous détendre ?

a. Je télécharge des clips vidéo et des émissions de télé ou je surfe sur Internet avec mon iPad en écoutant de la musique bien sûr.
b. J'écoute de la musique avec le lecteur CD de mon ordi portable et je mets à jour mon compte Facebook.
c. Je lis un roman ou des bandes dessinées et quelquefois je me promène s'il fait beau.

Comptez vos points pour la première partie : Les réponses a= 2 points ; b= 1 point ; c=0

Implementation: If you are teaching in a smart classroom or can bring a portable computer and some computer peripherals with you to class, you may wish to begin by pointing out the various parts of the computer and peripherals to further contextualize the presentation.

Deuxième partie :
Maintenant, ajoutez un point pour chaque item de la liste ci-dessous que vous possédez.

- ❑ un baladeur MP3 ou un iPod
- ❑ un clavier sans fil
- ❑ une clé USB
- ❑ un disque dur externe
- ❑ une imprimante
- ❑ une tablette tactile comme le iPad
- ❑ un lecteur/graveur CD/DVD
- ❑ un moniteur avec un écran plat
- ❑ un ordinateur
- ❑ un ordinateur portable
- ❑ un smartphone
- ❑ un réseau sans fil (le wi-fi)
- ❑ une souris optique sans fil
- ❑ un téléphone portable
- ❑ une webcam

Maintenant, additionnez les points pour la première et la deuxième partie.

Quel est votre score ?

20–23 *Vous êtes vraiment technophile. Vous adorez les nouveaux gadgets et vous êtes parmi les premiers à essayer chaque nouvelle technologie. Mais vous passez peut-être un peu trop de temps devant l'écran. Pensez à sortir un peu respirer l'air frais.*

15–19 *Vous aimez bien la technologie et vous savez vous en servir pour faciliter la vie. Attention de ne pas devenir trop dépendante de ces nouvelles technologies.*

6–14 *Vous semblez avoir trouvé le bon équilibre entre le virtuel et le réel. Vous vous servez de la technologie mais vous n'oubliez pas non plus qu'il y a plus que la technologie et la nouveauté dans la vie.*

0–5 *Oh là là, vous n'êtes vraiment pas dans la révolution technologique. Vous ne comprenez pas pourquoi tout le monde semble adorer ces ordinateurs et cet Internet auxquels vous résistez toujours. Mais attention ! Il y a des bons éléments de la technologie qui pourraient vous simplifier la vie. À vous de les trouver.*

Note: Depending on the interests and level of your class, you may wish to introduce additional vocabulary such as, for the computer: *le traitement de texte* (word processor), *le tableur* (spreadsheet), *le tableau de bord* (desktop); for a cell phone: *une batterie, un chargeur;* for a smart phone: *un câble de recharge, une application, la synchronisation, les icônes.* Note that the English borrowing *un smartphone* is currently the preferred word for a smart phone, but the French also refer to *les téléphones intelligents.* In December 2009, *la Commission générale de terminologie et de néologie* proposed the terms *un ordiphone* or *un terminal de poche (TP).* Neither term seems to have caught on in popular usage.

À vous la parole

10-13 Définitions. Trouvez le mot qui correspond à chaque définition.

Variation: 10-13 Have students work in pairs to create their own definitions with which to test classmates.

MODÈLE C'est un appareil qu'on utilise pour imprimer un texte.
- C'est une imprimante. *Answers may vary.*

1. C'est très pratique pour sauvegarder votre travail et le transporter. une clé USB
2. C'est un ordinateur qu'on peut facilement transporter. un ordinateur portable
3. C'est sur cette partie de l'ordinateur qu'on tape (*types*). un clavier
4. C'est un téléphone mobile qu'on peut utiliser pour se connecter à Internet. un smartphone
5. C'est pratique si on veut consulter ses mails, lire le journal ou voir une vidéo en se déplaçant. une tablette/un iPad
6. C'est nécessaire pour se connecter à Internet à partir d'un ordinateur portable. un reseau sans fil/le wi-fi
7. C'est ce que vous faites quand vous sauvegardez la musique d'un site Internet. télécharger
8. Si vous voulez utiliser un ordinateur pour téléphoner à quelqu'un, c'est plus agréable d'en avoir une. une webcam

Note: Contrary to English usage, the proper noun *Internet* does not take an article in French.

10-14 La technologie et vous. Combien de ces appareils est-ce que vous savez utiliser ? Comment est-ce que vous les utilisez ? Comparez vos réponses avec les réponses d'un/e partenaire.

Implementation: 10-14 This allows recycling of vocabulary for other technological devices. Have students work in pairs, then compare responses for the class as a whole. Have students suggest other devices that they use or would like to learn more about.

MODÈLE un lecteur DVD

É1 Mon ordinateur portable a un lecteur DVD. Je regarde beaucoup de DVD, et quelquefois je télécharge des films.

É2 Moi aussi, j'aime les DVD. Je les regarde avec mon lecteur DVD et souvent je regarde des émissions de télévision sur Internet.

1. une clé USB
2. une souris sans fil
3. une webcam
4. un lecteur DVD
5. une tablette
6. un iPod ou un baladeur MP3
7. un clavier sans fil
8. un appareil numérique

Note: In 2009, 65% of French households had a personal computer, and nearly 60% of the French had an Internet connection at home, with 96% of those homes enjoying a high speed connection. Almost half (45%) of the French connect to the Internet at least once a day, and according to a 2008 survey, French Internet users spend more time online than those in any other European country: 67% report being online seven days a week. These and many other interesting facts about computer usage in France can be found in *Francoscopie 2010*, pp. 453–466. The number of computer owners and users has been rising rapidly (increasing from 60% at the end of 2007 to 65% at the end of 2009). The most recent statistics can be found online.

Vie et culture

Les Français et Internet

Combien d'heures par jour est-ce que vous passez devant un ordinateur ou connecté à Internet avec un ordinateur, une tablette ou un smartphone ? Quand vous avez du temps libre, est-ce que vous aimez surfer sur le Web, télécharger de la musique ou communiquer avec vos amis avec la messagerie instantanée, votre compte Facebook ou des mails ? Est-ce que vous pensez que les Français passent autant de temps que vous sur Internet ? D'après un sondage récent (Ipsos MediaCT Profiling 2011), 72 % des Français (soit 36,6 millions) sont des **internautes** (c'est-à-dire des usagers d'Internet). En plus, 1 sur 3 de ces internautes sont également des **mobinautes** (c'est-à-dire qu'ils connectent à Internet de leurs gadgets mobiles (téléphone, tablette,…). Est-ce que vous êtes mobinaute ? Et vos amis et les membres de votre famille ? Pourquoi ?

Le sondage fait par Ipsos a également demandé à un certain nombre d'internautes âgés de 15 ans ou plus d'indiquer les opérations qu'ils ont effectuées sur Internet dans les trente derniers jours. Ce tableau montre une partie des résultats. Comment est-ce que ces usages diffèrent de vos usages ou des usages de vos proches ?

Avec un ordi portable et une connexion wi-fi, on peut se connecter n'importe où.

Note: The chart here presents only some of the Internet practices reported in the results of the IpsosMedia CT Profiling survey of 2011. The complete results are easily found online. Recently, Ipsos has reported on computer, Internet, and mobile device usage on a yearly basis. You might encourage students to find the most recent information online to compare with the information here.

Opérations effectuées via Internet dans les 30 derniers jours (en % des 13 488 internautes sondés, résidants en France et âgés de 15 ans ou plus)

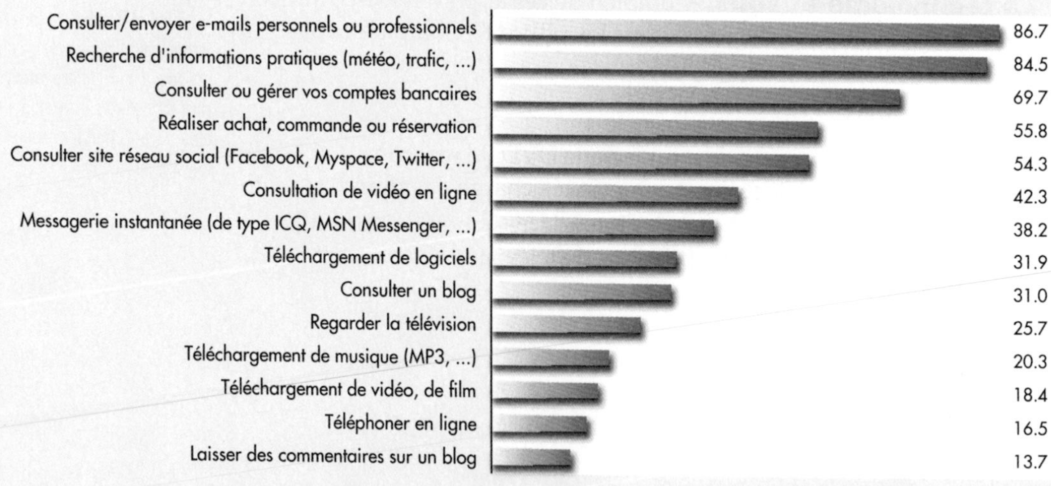

10-15 Internet et vous. Faites un sondage dans votre classe pour déterminer les pourcentages de gens qui utilisent Internet pour les activités suivantes.

Implementation: 10-15 To complete the survey, divide the class into four or five groups; each group should select a leader, a recorder, and a spokesperson. The leader begins by asking the first question. The recorder counts the number of students who respond "yes" to each question. You may wish to prepare a simple worksheet as a handout on which students can record the answers for their group. The spokesperson for each group will provide the figures for how many participate in each activity. Sum up the figures on the board or on a slide. Finish by comparing the class responses with those from the Ipsos survey presented in the **Vie et culture.**

MODÈLES pour envoyer et recevoir des mails

É1 Qui utilise Internet pour envoyer des mails ?

É2 Un, deux, trois, quatre, cinq. Cinq personnes dans notre groupe envoient et reçoivent des mails.

(*plus tard*)

É3 Cinq personnes ou 100 % des membres de notre groupe envoient des mails. Quatre personnes ou 80 % utilisent les réseaux sociaux.

1. pour envoyer et recevoir des mails
2. pour participer à des réseaux sociaux (comme Facebook)
3. pour obtenir des informations pratiques
4. pour accéder à un compte bancaire
5. pour faire des achats ou réserver des places
6. pour lire ou écrire un blog ou faire des commentaires sur un blog
7. pour téléphoner
8. pour voir des films
9. pour regarder des émissions de télé

FORMES ET FONCTIONS

1. Le conditionnel

- You have learned to use the indicative and the subjunctive moods in French as well as the imperative to give commands. To express events or situations that are hypothetical or conjectural, you need to use the conditional mood:

Presentation: Students have seen the use of the conditional with *vouloir*, i.e., *je voudrais* as a lexical item (Ch. 5, L. 1). Remind them of this and provide examples as in the text to introduce the additional uses of the conditional.

J'**aimerais** acheter un ordinateur portable, mais c'est cher.	*I'd like to buy a laptop, but it's expensive.*
Tu **vendrais** vraiment ton iPad ?	*Would you really sell your iPad?*
Nous **voudrions** être riches !	*We would like to be rich!*

- The conditional is formed by adding the imperfect endings to the future stem.

Note: The endings of the singular and third-person plural forms are pronounced the same, with /ɛ/in standard French. However, there is wide variation, and many speakers pronounce these endings with /e/. In Standard French, the first-person singular forms of the future and the conditional differ: *je donnerai* /e/ vs. *je donnerais* /ɛ/. Because of the variation among native speakers, this distinction should not be emphasized at the beginning level.

LE CONDITIONNEL

SINGULIER		PLURIEL	
je	donner**ais**	nous	donner**ions**
tu	donner**ais**	vous	donner**iez**
il / elle / on	donner**ait**	ils / elles	donner**aient**

Note: Refer to the list of irregular future stem changes in Ch. 9, L. 1. *Préférer*-type verbs (*préférer, espérer, répéter, suggérer*) are included here based on the 1990 Orthographic reform. Similar to the *acheter*-type verbs, the accent grave here clearly indicates the pronunciation of /ε/.

Here are the conditional forms of the main verb groups.

VERB GROUP	INFINITIVE	CONDITIONAL
-er	parler	je **parlerais**
-ir	partir	je **partirais**
-re	vendre	je **vendrais**

Verbs that have an irregular future stem use that same stem in the conditional: **j'irais, j'aurais, je serais, je me lèverais, je jetterais, je préfèrerais**, etc.

- The conditional forms of the verbs **devoir**, **pouvoir**, and **vouloir** are also often used to express obligation, to soften commands, and to make suggestions.

Vous **pourriez** lui envoyer un mail.	*You could send him an e-mail.*
On **devrait** acheter une webcam.	*We should buy a webcam.*
Tu **voudrais** m'aider avec cet ordi ?	*Would you like to help me with this computer?*

10-22 to 10-25

À vous la parole

Initial practice: 10-16 This comprehension-based activity focuses students' attention on differences in verb endings between the conditional and the future. Continue with a simple substitution drill to practice these endings: *Je parlerais français ; vous. — Vous parleriez français*, etc. Review irregular stems: *Je suis riche. — Je serais riche ; J'ai une grande maison. — J'aurais une grande maison*, etc.

10-16 Projet ou rêve ? Julien a beaucoup de projets pour l'avenir et beaucoup de rêves (*dreams*). Pour chacune de ses idées, indiquez si c'est un rêve ou un projet d'avenir.

	rêve	projet d'avenir
MODÈLE J'irais en Suisse.	✓	___
1. J'achèterais une tablette tactile.	✓	___
2. Je retrouverai ma clé USB perdue.	___	✓
3. J'irai au Festival de Cannes.	___	✓
4. Je ferais le tour du monde.	✓	___
5. Je travaillerai beaucoup.	___	✓
6. Je travaillerais pour Google.	✓	___
7. J'achèterais une imprimante laser couleur.	✓	___

Est-ce que Julien est plus rêveur ou plus réaliste ? Pourquoi ?

Implementation: 10-17 Follow up by comparing responses for each item and encouraging students to come up with as many suggestions as possible.

10-17 Des bons conseils. Quel conseil est-ce que vous et votre partenaire donneriez à ces personnes ?

MODÈLE Je ne suis pas très bien informé.

É1 À ta place, je regarderais les infos en ligne tous les jours.

É2 Tu devrais surfer sur Internet plus souvent.

Additional practice: Have several students reply for each item, elaborate on their answers, or suggest other possibilities.

Vous aussi ? Avec plus d'argent, qu'est-ce que vous feriez ? Est-ce que vous êtes d'accord avec ces gens ?

1. Ma fille passe trop de temps devant l'ordinateur.
2. J'ai envie de me détendre ce soir.
3. Nous partons bientôt en vacances.

4. Dans ma famille, on se dispute toujours pour se servir de notre nouvelle tablette.
5. J'ai envie de voir un bon film ce week-end mais je n'ai pas beaucoup d'argent.
6. J'ai du mal à choisir mon nouveau téléphone mobile.

MODÈLE Je m'achèterais une nouvelle voiture.
• Moi aussi, je m'achèterais une nouvelle voiture.
OU Moi non, je m'achèterais un grand bateau.

1. Je voyagerais tout le temps.
2. Je ne travaillerais plus.
3. Je partagerais l'argent avec ma famille.
4. Je prêterais de l'argent à mes amis.
5. Je m'achèterais un château en France.
6. J'irais dîner dans les meilleurs restaurants.
7. Je donnerais de l'argent aux personnes en difficulté.

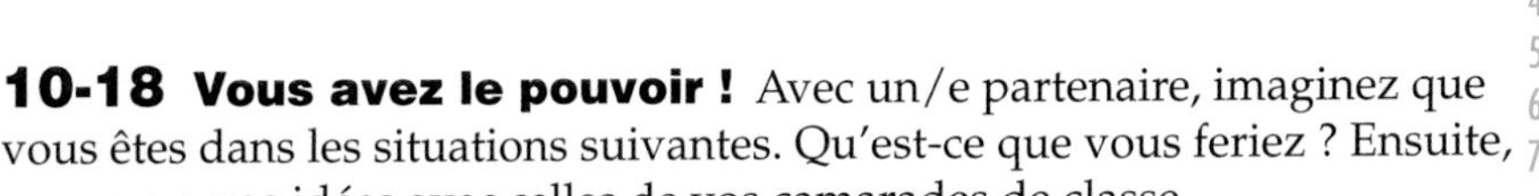

10-18 Vous avez le pouvoir ! Avec un/e partenaire, imaginez que vous êtes dans les situations suivantes. Qu'est-ce que vous feriez ? Ensuite, comparez vos idées avec celles de vos camarades de classe.

MODÈLE Vous êtes le professeur de votre cours de français.
É1 Je donnerais moins de devoirs.
É2 Je ne permettrais pas aux étudiants de parler anglais.

Implementation: 10-18 Have students name other important positions and ask their classmates to say what they would do if they occupied those positions.

1. Vous êtes le professeur de votre cours de français.
2. Vous êtes le président/la présidente de votre université.
3. Vous êtes un acteur/une actrice célèbre.
4. Vous êtes le directeur/la directrice d'une grande chaîne de télévision.
5. Vous êtes le maire de votre ville.
6. Vous êtes le président/la présidente des États-Unis.

2. Les phrases avec *si*

The conjunction **si** is used in a clause that expresses a condition. It is often accompanied by another clause that expresses the result.

- Use **si** plus the present tense to express a condition that, if fulfilled, will result in a certain action (stated in the present or future).

Note: Point out that the clauses may be ordered in either way, as in the examples provided.

Si je **trouve** ce film en ligne, je le **télécharge**/je le **téléchargerai.**	*If I find this movie online, I'm downloading it/I will downlaod it.*
Elle nous **accompagne**/**accompagnera** au cinéma **si** elle **a** le temps.	*She is going/will go with us to the movies if she has the time.*

- Use **si** plus the imperfect if the situation is hypothetical; the result clause will then be in the conditional.

Si j'**avais** assez d'argent, je m'**achèterais** un nouveau smartphone.	*If I had enough money, I would buy myself a new smart phone.*
Ils **pourraient** répondre plus rapidement **s'**il leur **envoyait** un texto.	*They could respond more quickly if he sent them a text message.*

À vous la parole

10-26 to 10-29

Variation: 10-19 and 10-20 To vary or provide review, change the tense/mode: *Si tu achetais un smartphone, ... ; Si tu deviens journaliste, tu écriras..., etc.*

Additional practice: Recycle food vocabulary with the following exercise:
Quels plats ?

MODÈLE des œufs et des champignons
• Si j'avais des œufs et des champignons, je ferais une omelette.

1. des carottes, des tomates et de la salade
2. des fruits de saison
3. du poulet, des carottes et du céléri
4. du lait, des œufs et du sucre
5. du pain, du beurre et du chocolat
6. du jus de citron, du sucre et de l'eau

Key: 10-20 *Answers may vary:* 1) Si vous étiez..., vous gagneriez beaucoup d'argent. 2) Si vous étiez..., vous voyageriez beaucoup. 3) Si vous étiez..., vous connaîtriez des stars. 4) Si vous étiez..., vous feriez beaucoup de concerts. 5) Si vous étiez..., vous auriez un bel appareil numérique. 6) Si vous étiez..., vous pourriez travailler pour Microsoft ou Google ou Facebook. 7) Si vous étiez..., vous vous habilleriez de façon individualiste. 8) Si vous étiez..., vous travailleriez souvent seul/e.

10-19 Pour devenir mobinaute. David explique à son amie Céline comment devenir mobinaute. Terminez chaque phrase d'une façon logique.

MODÈLE Si tu achètes un smartphone, ...
• Si tu achètes un smartphone, tu pourras te connecter à Internet n'importe où (*anywhere*). *Answers may vary.*

1. Si tu as besoin de lire un article en ligne, ... tu téléchargeras l'article
2. Si tu veux rester en contact avec tes amis, ... tu mettras à jour ton profil sur Facebook
3. Si tu veux écouter de la musique, ... tu téléchargeras une chanson
4. Si tu cherches une adresse, ... tu chercheras en ligne
5. Si tu veux avoir les dernières nouvelles, ... tu regarderas des journaux ou des blogs
6. Si tu as le temps de jouer, ... tu joueras avec des amis en ligne
7. Si tu veux regarder un film, ... tu peux commander un film en ligne

10-20 Choix de profession. Certains jeunes ne peuvent pas décider quelle profession choisir. Qu'est-ce qu'ils feraient s'ils choisissaient une profession dans les arts ou dans les médias ?

Implementation: 10-20 Have students suggest other professions and answers.

MODÈLE journaliste
• Si vous étiez journaliste, vous écririez des articles pour un journal, un magazine ou un blog.

1. présentateur/présentatrice à la télé
2. acteur/actrice
3. réalisateur/réalisatrice
4. chanteur/chanteuse
5. photographe
6. informaticien/ne
7. musicien/ne
8. écrivain

Implementation: 10-21 Follow up by having classmates compare answers. Who has the most interesting plans and/or dreams?

10-21 Des rêves et des projets. Qu'est-ce que vous feriez dans les situations suivantes ? Avec un/e partenaire, parlez de vos rêves (*dreams*).

MODÈLE être une actrice/un acteur célèbre
É1 Si tu étais une actrice célèbre, qu'est-ce que tu ferais ?
É2 Je serais très riche et j'habiterais à Beverly Hills.

1. avoir ton diplôme demain
2. être millionnaire
3. trouver un emploi aujourd'hui
4. partir en vacances
5. être en France
6. être le président/la présidente des États-Unis
7. avoir 50 ans

Écrivons

Implementation: 10-22 Before beginning this activity, you might have students visit Francophone web sites where they can see film reviews written and posted by regular viewers; be aware, however, that you may find many slang expressions and grammatical errors typical of spontaneous speech and writing. You may also want to arrange to show a Francophone movie in class or have students borrow one from the library for the purposes of this assignment. This helps curb the need, or desire, for unnecessary translation from English to French.

10-22 Poster la critique d'un film sur un blog

A. Avant d'écrire. Comme vous le savez, il y a plusieurs sites sur le Web où les gens peuvent rédiger et afficher leurs propres critiques sur un film. Choisissez un film que vous avez vu récemment et écrivez une petite critique pour un blog. D'abord, pensez aux éléments importants d'une bonne critique en répondant aux questions suivantes :

1. Notez le nom du réalisateur et des acteurs principaux. Quels rôles est-ce qu'ils jouent ?
2. Faites un résumé assez bref de l'intrigue (*plot*). Pour vous guider, pensez aux critiques de films que vous avez déjà lues.
3. Enfin, quelle est votre opinion de ce film ?

Stratégie

To write a review of a film or a book, be sure to include the expected factual information as well as your personal assessment.

B. En écrivant. Écrivez votre critique avec les détails que vous avez notés dans l'exercice A, et n'oubliez pas de donner votre opinion du film. Utilisez le vocabulaire que vous connaissez.

C. En révisant. Relisez votre critique et réfléchissez aux questions suivantes. Faites tous les changements nécessaires.

1. Analysez le contenu : est-ce que vous avez inclus tous les éléments nécessaires : le titre du film, le nom du réalisateur et des acteurs principaux, un résumé de l'intrigue avec quelques précisions sur l'histoire et votre opinion ?
2. Analysez le style et la forme : est-ce que vous avez utilisé les expressions appropriées pour donner votre opinion du film ? Est-ce que votre résumé du film est bref mais suffisamment clair ? Est-ce que le lecteur aura une bonne idée s'il faut aller voir ce film ou pas après avoir lu votre critique ?

D. Après avoir écrit. Échangez votre critique avec un/e camarade de classe ou lisez votre critique pour vos camarades de classe. Ne donnez pas le titre du film. Les autres vont essayer de deviner de quel film il s'agit (*it's about*).

Implementation: ***Après avoir écrit.*** You might also use the technological resources available on your campus to post the reviews written and ask students to read and react to one or more reviews.

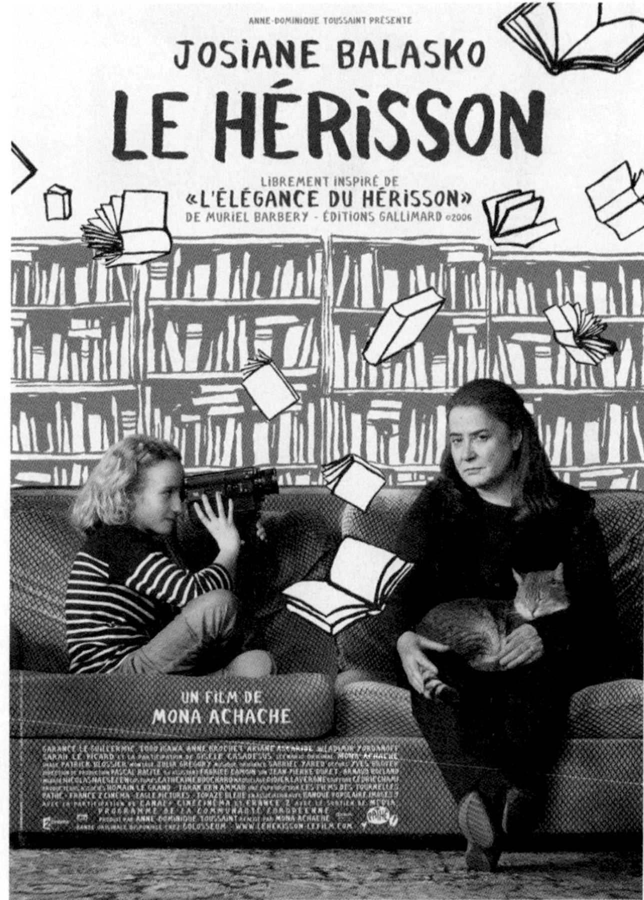

Le Hérisson, un film de Mona Achache, raconte l'histoire d'une petite fille de 11 ans, Paloma, d'une concièrge, Renée Michel, et d'un monsieur japonais, Kakuro Ozu. Ils habitent tous un immeuble à Paris. C'est un très beau film.

Leçon 3 On s'informe

Presentation: To introduce the new vocabulary, have students complete the questionnaire. To check comprehension, total the responses for the group. Have students repeat key words and phrases.

POINTS DE DÉPART

La lecture et vous

Qu'est-ce qu'elle lit ?

Quelles sont vos habitudes de lecture ? Complétez le questionnaire pour en savoir plus ! D'après vos résultats, est-ce que vous êtes un lecteur sérieux, un lecteur occasionnel ou un lecteur pragmatique ? Comparez vos réponses aux réponses de vos camarades de classe.

Indiquez vos trois types de lecture préférés :

- les journaux (nationaux, régionaux, spécialisés — sport, économie)
- les magazines (d'information, de télévision, féminins ou familiaux)
- les romans (d'amour, historiques, policiers, de science-fiction)
- les livres de loisirs (de cuisine, de sport, de bricolage, de jardinage)
- les livres d'art (sur la peinture, l'architecture, le cinéma)
- les livres d'histoire ou les biographies
- les blogs, les forums de discussion et les journaux en ligne
- les poésies
- les bandes dessinées (les BD)
- les ouvrages de référence (le dictionnaire, l'atlas, l'encyclopédie)

Comment choisissez-vous un livre ?

- les recommendations des critiques dans la presse ou en ligne
- les recommendations d'amis
- la réputation de l'auteur
- la publicité

Comment obtenez-vous les livres ?

- vous les empruntez à une bibliothèque
- vous les empruntez à des amis
- vous les achetez dans une librairie
- vous êtes abonné/e à un club lecture
- vous les téléchargez sur votre ordinateur
- vous les téléchargez sur votre lecteur ebook

Pourquoi lisez-vous ?

- pour vous détendre
- pour vous instruire
- pour vous distraire

Où lisez-vous ?

- en vacances
- en voyage
- dans les transports en commun
- à la bibliothèque
- chez vous
- en écoutant de la musique
- au lit pour vous endormir
- devant l'ordinateur

Fiche pratique

To remember new words or expressions that may overlap, associate a meaningful example with each one. For example: **une bande dessinée** : ***Astérix*** ; **un dessin animé** ***: Le Livre de la jungle ;*** **un film d'animation :** ***Toy Story 3.***

Note: Prompt students to find other word pairs that might also cause confusion, such as *une bibliothèque et une librairie, un magazine et un magasin, un chemisier et une chemise,* and to think about how they could apply this same technique.

À vous la parole

10-23 De la lecture pour tout le monde. Quel type de livre, de magazine ou de site web est-ce qu'on pourrait conseiller à chaque personne décrite ici ? *Answers may vary.*

Variation: 10-23 Have students suggest various web sites and/or blogs that correspond to the interests of the people listed.

MODÈLE un enfant

- On pourrait lui suggérer un livre d'enfants ou une bande dessinée.

1. quelqu'un qui prépare son diplôme en journalisme un magazine d'information/un journal national
2. quelqu'un qui adore l'art mais qui n'a pas souvent l'occasion d'aller au musée un livre d'art
3. quelqu'un qui aime bricoler un livre de loisirs sur le bricolage
4. quelqu'un qui apprend l'anglais un dictionnaire français-anglais
5. quelqu'un qui regarde souvent la télévision un magazine de télévision
6. quelqu'un qui s'intéresse à l'histoire un livre d'histoire/une biographie
7. quelqu'un qui adore la science-fiction un roman de science-fiction
8. quelqu'un qui fait beaucoup de sport un journal ou un magazine de sport/une biographie d'un/e athlète

Presentation: To check students' comprehension of the cultural notes, use a recognition exercise: *Donnez-moi un exemple de magazine américain à caractère familial. —Better Homes and Gardens, Family Circle.* Point out that the French tend to buy newspapers and magazines at *un tabac* or *un kiosque*. In contrast, Americans tend to receive home delivery of newspapers and to subscribe to magazines or buy them at the supermarket. The chart indicates the number of readers in thousands (as indicated in the legend) as determined by a survey carried out by AEPM (*Audiences, études sur la presse magazine*). More information can be obtained from their web site. See *Francoscopie 2010*, pp. 439–445 for interesting information on the French press. The French spend half their leisure time in front of the TV, hence the large number of TV magazines. The magazine *Closer* is a *People*-type magazine originating in Great Britain and aimed at a female audience; the French version was launched in 2005. Ask students to identify the most popular magazines in the U.S. According to the Audit Bureau of Circulation, the top ten U.S. periodicals for the period from July to December 2010 are: 1 *AARP The Magazine*, 2 *AARP Bulletin*, 3 *The Costco Connection*, 4 *Better Homes and Gardens*, 5 *Reader's Digest*, 6 *Game Informer*, 7 *National Geographic*, 8 *Good Housekeeping*, 9 *Woman's Day*, 10 *Family Circle*. Note that in contrast to the French figures, which only pertain to weekly and bimonthly magazines, the U.S. figures include weekly, bimonthly, and monthly periodicals.

Vie et culture

La presse française

10-51

Regardez la séquence vidéo, *Je lis la presse*, où Pauline montre et décrit ses journaux et magazines préférés. D'après sa description, qu'est-ce qu'un quotidien ? un hebdomadaire ? un mensuel ?

Pauline achète *Le Monde*, mais elle est abonnée[1] au quotidien *Libération*. Comment est-ce qu'elle décrit son magazine préféré, *Le Nouvel Observateur* ? Quel autre hebdomadaire est-ce qu'elle achète, et pourquoi ? Pauline a acheté un mensuel, *Géo* au kiosque ; pourquoi ?

Voici la liste des dix hebdomadaires et bimensuels les plus lus en France pour la période de juillet 2009 à juin 2010. Pour chaque magazine, identifiez son genre : par exemple, est-ce que c'est un magazine féminin ? un magazine de télévision ? Qu'est-ce que vous pouvez déduire des priorités ou des goûts des gens qui les achètent ?

Le Top Ten des hebdomadaires les plus lus

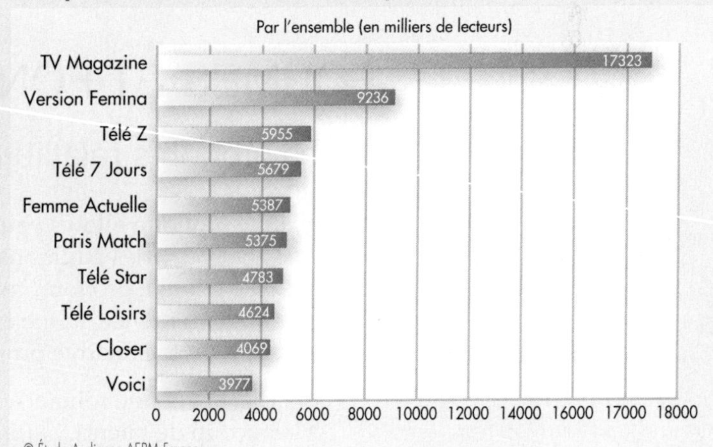

© Étude Audience AEPM France.

[1] *subscribes*

Implementation: 10-24 As a follow-up to this exercise, ask students 1) which of the books and magazines listed they would choose for themselves and why 2) what type of book or magazine they would buy for a friend or family member. Have students role-play a situation in which they ask a bookseller's advice.

Note: *Télérama* includes a guide to TV programming, reviews of current films, and book reviews. It is popular with well-educated readers and is purchased even by people who have no television.

10-24 D'après le titre. D'après le titre, c'est quel genre de livre, de journal ou de magazine ? *Answers may vary.*

MODÈLE *Marie Claire Maison*

- C'est probablement un magazine féminin.

1. *Télérama* un magazine de télévision
2. *Info-Matin* un journal ou un magazine d'information
3. *Elle* un magazine féminin
4. *France Football* un magazine de sport
5. *Bien-Être & Santé* un magazine de santé/familial
6. *Lucky Luke dans le Far West* une bande dessinée
7. *Le Guide Pratique du Droit* un livre de référence
8. *Cuisine Minceur* un livre/un magazine de cuisine

Implementation: 10-25 This activity can be carried out in pairs, in small groups, or as a whole-class exercise; summarize results at the end of group discussion. If you have a wide age range of students in your class, it might be interesting to compare reading practices of the various age groups (for example, the use of e-books either on line or via a dedicated e-book reader or tablet/mobile device; the practice of reading online articles by printing out a paper version versus reading them directly on screen; and so forth).

10-25 Et vous ? Quelles sont vos habitudes ? Comparez-les avec les habitudes d'un/e camarade de classe.

1. Qu'est-ce que vous lisez tous les jours ? — le journal, des magazines ? quel journal et quels magazines ? les infos en ligne ? les profils de vos amis sur Facebook ? les tweets de vos amis ou de quelques célébrités ?
2. Quels ouvrages de référence est-ce que vous consultez chez vous ? à la bibliothèque ? en ligne ? sur votre tablette ou smartphone ?
3. Qu'est-ce que vous lisez pour vos cours ? Est-ce que vous avez beaucoup de lectures en ligne à faire ? Est-ce que vous avez accès à des ebooks pour quelques cours ? Comment est-ce que vous les lisez : en ligne, sur une tablette, avec un lecteur ebook comme Kindle ou Fnacbook ?
4. Qu'est-ce que vous lisez pour vous informer ? pour vous détendre ?
5. Qu'est-ce que vous lisez quand vous êtes en vacances ?
6. Quel est le dernier livre que vous avez lu ? Est-ce que vous êtes en train de lire un livre maintenant ? Lequel ?
7. Quel est votre auteur préféré ? Est-ce que vous avez un journaliste ou un blogueur préféré ? Qui ?
8. Comment est-ce que vous préférez lire pour vous détendre, avec un livre classique, en ligne ou avec un lecteur ebook ?

Presentation: Introduce the relatives through examples. Meaning is fairly straightforward; however, students need to pay particular attention to the use of *où* with expressions of time, since English uses the relative "when." Ex. 10-26 treats this feature. Analyzing complex sentences as two independent clauses helps students understand the fact that relatives have a double function: 1) linking two clauses; 2) replacing a co-referential noun.

Note: Assia Djebar is a well-known Algerian novelist, poet, and film director. She has frequently been mentioned as a candidate for the Nobel Prize.

FORMES ET FONCTIONS

1. Les pronoms relatifs *où* et *qui*

- A relative pronoun allows you to introduce a clause, called a subordinate clause, that provides additional information about a person, place, or thing. The relative pronoun connects the subordinate clause to the main clause of the sentence. In the example below, the subordinate clause, introduced by the relative pronoun **qui**, is set off by brackets.

Assia Djebar est une romancière [**qui** a beaucoup de talent].	*Assia Djebar is a novelist [who is very talented].*
La FNAC est un magasin [**qui** est connu pour la qualité de ses livres].	*FNAC is a store [that is known for the quality of its books].*

In these examples the relative pronoun **qui**, which refers to an author or a store, respectively, is the subject of the subordinate clause. **Qui**, the equivalent of *who*, *which*, or *that* in English, always functions as the subject of the clause it introduces and is always followed by a verb.

- **Où** is used to introduce a place or a time; it is equivalent to the English *where* or *when*.

C'est une librairie [**où** il y a beaucoup de livres d'occasion].	*It's a bookstore [where there are many used books].*
L'automne en France, c'est la saison [**où** le Prix Renaudot est annoncé].	*Autumn in France is the season [when the Renaudot Literary Prize is awarded].*

À vous la parole

10-26 En quelles saisons ? En quelles saisons est-ce qu'on peut faire les activités suivantes ? *Answers may vary.*

Implementation: 10-26 To begin, review the four seasons quickly. As a variation, ask students to describe typical activities during each season, or typical activities on a particular holiday: *Noël ? — C'est un jour où on offre des cadeaux*, etc. Note that more formal usage would prefer *C'est un jour où l'on offre des cadeaux*, or for the model in the textbook, *L'automne est la saison où l'on va à la campagne chercher des pommes*, but this is not necessary in conversational style.

MODÈLE On va à la campagne chercher des pommes.
- L'automne est la saison où on va à la campagne chercher des pommes.

1. On peut faire un pique-nique à la montagne. L'été/le printemps est la saison où…
2. On peut faire du ski. L'hiver est la saison où…
3. On va souvent au bord de la mer. L'été est la saison où…
4. On fait des randonnées dans la forêt. L'automne/le printemps est la saison où…
5. On commence à acheter des livres pour l'année scolaire. L'automne est la saison où…
6. On admire les fleurs à la campagne. Le printemps est la saison où…
7. On va voir les matchs de football américain. L'automne est la saison où…
8. On a envie de voyager dans des pays tropicaux. L'hiver est la saison où…

10-27 Lectures. Voici les lectures récentes de Caroline et de sa famille. Reliez les phrases suivantes avec le pronom relatif **qui**.

Implementation: 10-27 This exercise is rich in cultural information. Follow up with students to find out if they are familiar with the names and works mentioned. Ask them to describe other literary works or authors they admire using the relative pronoun, for example, *J'aime bien John Grisham, qui écrit des romans policiers.*

Additional practice: Other simple exercises to practice use of relative pronouns include: a) recycling professions: *Un acteur ? — C'est un homme qui joue dans des pièces de théatre ou des films. Une serveuse ? — C'est une femme qui travaille dans un restaurant/sert des boissons. Un médecin ? Un professeur ? Un avocat ? Une comptable ? Un guide touristique ? Un fonctionnaire ? Une libraire ? Un agent de voyage ?*, etc.; b) a guessing game: students describe a classmate and let others guess who they're describing: *C'est un étudiant qui joue de la guitare ; C'est une étudiante qui porte des bottes roses*, etc.

MODÈLE Caroline est en train de lire un roman. Il s'appelle *l'Étranger*.
- Caroline est en train de lire un roman qui s'appelle *l'Étranger*.

1. *L'Étranger*, c'est le premier roman d'Albert Camus. ~~Il~~ qui a gagné le prix Nobel en 1957.
2. Sa sœur adore *Le Petit Prince*. ~~Il~~ qui a été écrit par Antoine de Saint-Exupéry.
3. C'est l'histoire d'un petit bonhomme. ~~Il~~ qui vient d'une planète aussi grande qu'une maison.
4. Ses cousins aiment beaucoup les romans *Harry Potter*. ~~Ils~~ qui ont eu un énorme succès partout dans le monde.
5. Harry Potter et ses amis sont des sorciers. ~~Ils~~ qui vont à l'école Hogwarts et apprennent beaucoup de choses.
6. Les parents de Caroline viennent de voir une pièce de théâtre de Molière. ~~Il~~ qui a écrit *Le Malade imaginaire, Tartuffe* et *l'École des femmes*.
7. Ils aiment beaucoup ses pièces. ~~Elles~~ qui sont souvent très drôles.
8. L'oncle de Caroline préfère les œuvres de Victor Hugo. ~~Il~~ qui a écrit au dix-neuvième siècle.
9. Hugo était un auteur prolifique. ~~Il~~ qui a écrit des poèmes, des romans, des pièces de théâtre et des essais.

Implementation: 10-28 At the end, bring the class together as a group to compare responses.

10-28 Quelles sont vos préférences ? Discutez de vos préférences avec un/e partenaire.

MODÈLE J'aime les librairies…

É1 J'aime les librairies qui vendent des livres pas chers.

É2 Moi, j'aime surtout les librairies où il y a un café et des fauteuils pour s'asseoir et lire.

1. J'aime les librairies…
2. Je préfère les bibliothèques…
3. Je n'aime pas les auteurs…
4. J'aime les livres…
5. J'aime surtout lire les les magazines…
6. J'aime les gens…
7. Je n'aime pas beaucoup les gens…

2. Le pronom relatif *que*

- As you have just learned, a relative pronoun enables you to introduce a clause, called a subordinate clause, that provides additional information about a person, place, or thing. The relative pronoun **qui** functions as the subject of the clause it introduces and is followed by the verb of the subordinate clause.

Cet auteur, [**qui** a écrit trois romans,] est très apprécié.	*This author, [who has written three novels,] is much loved.*

Note: With stylistic inversion, the subject may not follow directly: *La FNAC est une librairie qu'apprécient beaucoup les Parisiens.*

- **Que** is used when the relative pronoun functions as the direct object of the subordinate clause. Use **qu'** before words beginning with a vowel sound. The subject of the subordinate clause usually follows **que/qu'**.

C'est un bon dictionnaire. J'aime beaucoup utiliser ce dictionnaire.

C'est un bon dictionnaire [**que** j'aime beaucoup utiliser].	*It's a good dictionary [that I like to use a lot].*

Like **qui**, the relative pronoun **que/qu'** can refer either to a person or a thing.

Le libraire **que** je connais est très aimable.	*The bookseller whom/that I know is very friendly.*
Nous sommes allés à la librairie **que** Mme Lerond a recommandée.	*We went to the bookstore (that) Mrs. Lerond recommended.*

Note: Remind students that this is the case for any direct object that precedes the verb in the *passé composé*. This point was also addressed in Ch. 6, L. 1. In practice, however, most French speakers do not make the oral agreement, and many do not make the orthographic one in informal texts that they write, so we consider this a minor point. The SAM/MFL includes writing activities that focus on placement with the various tenses and rules of agreement.

> Be careful! In English the words *whom* or *that* may be left out, but in French **que** must always be used.

- When you use the **passé composé**, the past participle agrees in number and gender with a preceding direct object. In the examples below, **que/qu'** refers to a feminine and a masculine plural noun respectively, and the feminine and masculine plural forms of the past participle are used.

Voilà les pièces **que** j'ai écrit**es**.	*Here are the plays* (that) *I wrote.*
Vous connaissez les auteurs **qu'**ils ont invit**és** à cette soirée ?	*Do you know the authors* (that) *they invited to this reception?*

À vous la parole

Implementation: 10-29 This exercise features the titles of actual French magazines. To enliven the presentation, display the home page (easily found online) of each magazine. As a variation, have students complete the activity in pairs or encourage them to come up with more than one category of reader for each magazine; for example, *Le Monde : Éducation, c'est un magazine que les étudiants lisent. C'est un magazine que les professeurs d'université lisent.*

10-29 Qui lit ces magazines ? Suggérez qui lit chacun de ces magazines français. Les lecteurs possibles sont : **les jeunes, les enfants, les parents, les étudiants, les femmes, les hommes, les sportifs, les musiciens.** *Answers may vary.*

MODÈLE *Tennis Magazine*
- C'est un magazine que les sportifs lisent.

1. *Neuf mois* ... que les femmes lisent
2. *Auto Moto* ... que les hommes lisent
3. *Science et Vie Junior* ... que les enfants lisent
4. *Le Monde : Éducation* ... que les étudiants lisent
5. *Cuisine Actuelle* ... que les femmes lisent
6. *Sport* ... que les sportifs lisent
7. *J'aime lire* ... que les enfants lisent
8. *La Pêche et les Poissons* ... que les hommes/les sportifs lisent
9. *Parents* ... que les femmes/les parents lisent
10. *Rock & Folk* ... que les musiciens lisent

Avec un iPad, on peut facilement lire *Le Monde* au café

10-30 Pour trouver des livres. Complétez ces phrases avec le pronom relatif qui convient : **qui**, **que** ou **où**.

MODÈLE La Maison de la Presse _______ je connais le mieux se trouve boulevard Auguste Blanqui à Paris et ouvre à 6 h 30 du matin.
- La Maison de la Presse que je connais le mieux se trouve boulevard Auguste Blanqui à Paris et ouvre à 6 h 30 du matin.

1. Quand je visite Paris, je vais toujours à la FNAC, ___où___ on peut trouver beaucoup de livres et de CD pas chers.
2. Pour acheter des journaux, les Français ___qui___ habitent une grande ville peuvent aller à un kiosque.
3. Gibert Jeune est une librairie ___que___ les étudiants visitent régulièrement pour trouver des livres pour leurs cours à la fac.
4. Chez Gibert Jeune, on peut également trouver beaucoup de livres d'occasion ___que___ les étudiants aiment acheter parce qu'ils sont moins chers.
5. À Paris, Rue de Rivoli, il y a une librairie anglophone ___qui___ s'appelle WHSmith.
6. Les touristes aiment regarder des vieux livres et des posters chez les bouquinistes ___qui___ se trouvent au bord de la Seine près de Notre-Dame.
7. La bibliothèque municipale, ___qui___ est ouverte de mardi à samedi, est un bon endroit pour emprunter des bandes dessinées et même des DVD.
8. À la bibliothèque universitaire, vous trouverez beaucoup d'ouvrages de référence ___qu'___ on peut consulter sur place.

Note: 10-30 This activity presents a wealth of cultural information; you may want to include material from this section in your testing of the cultural content of the chapter. If so, be sure to inform students. You may also wish to show pictures of the various places mentioned to make the exercise more meaningful to students.

Implementation: 10-31 This exercise includes all the relative pronouns introduced thus far. The model contains examples of **qui** and **que**; remind students that **où** is also a possibility and model with the sentence: *La rubrique cinéma, c'est la partie du journal où vous trouvez les critiques.* Extend practice by asking students to provide additional examples of vocabulary to be defined. Remind students of the **Fiche pratique** and suggest that using sentences with relatives may be a good strategy for avoiding confusion between similar words. Point out that *un critique* and *une critique* are another such pair.

10-31 Le mot juste. Dans les définitions, on emploie souvent des propositions relatives. Est-ce que vous et votre partenaire pouvez définir les choses suivantes ?

MODÈLE un critique et une critique

É1 Un critique, c'est une personne qui critique des œuvres d'art, comme des livres, des films ou des émissions de télé.

É2 Une critique, c'est l'article qu'un critique écrit dans un journal.

É1 Oui, c'est bizarre. Un critique écrit une critique !

1. une bibliothèque et une librairie
2. un dessin animé et une bande dessinée
3. un dictionnaire et une encyclopédie
4. un magazine et un magasin
5. un prix littéraire et un prix d'achat

Lisons

10-32 La Leçon.

Stratégie

When reading dialogue from a play, be alert to changes in pace and tone that signal development in the characters and the plot. When such changes occur, ask yourself what they mean and how they reinforce the buildup of dramatic tension.

L'intérieur du Théâtre de la Huchette. Est-ce que vous aimeriez voir une pièce dans cette salle ?

Presentation: *Avant de lire.* Have students examine the photo of the interior of the theater in order to visualize the context for the play. The photo shows the three characters in the play: the professor, his housekeeper, and the student.

A. Avant de lire. Depuis plus de cinquante ans, dans une petite rue du Quartier latin à Paris, **le Théâtre de la Huchette** présente les deux pièces les plus connues d'Eugène Ionesco (1909–1994) : ***La cantatrice chauve*** (*The Bald Soprano*) et ***La Leçon*** (tous deux publiés en 1953). Dans ce petit théâtre de quatre-vingt-dix places, des millions de spectateurs ont vu ces deux œuvres modèles du théâtre de l'absurde, un genre littéraire qui a fleuri après la Seconde Guerre mondiale. Le théâtre de l'absurde rejette la structure, les personnages et la logique du théâtre conventionnel dans l'objectif d'exposer un monde à l'envers (*upside down*).

Vous allez lire un extrait de ***La Leçon***. Cet échange entre un professeur et son élève semble bizarre, mais il y a une progression dans le ton et le style qui prédit l'évènement violent, un meurtre, qui sera la fin dramatique de la pièce. Pour bien saisir la tension qui monte, remarquez le changement dans les répliques du professeur et de son élève du début à la fin de cette scène.

B. En lisant. Lisez le texte et ensuite répondez aux questions suivantes.

1. Identifiez quelques aspects comiques de cet extrait.
   MODÈLE Le professeur est très surpris parce que l'élève sait combien font un et un ; …
2. Quelle est l'attitude de l'élève au début : est-ce qu'elle est timide ou est-ce qu'elle est sûre d'elle ? Comment est-ce que ses réponses évoluent pendant la leçon ? Pourquoi ?
3. Comment est le professeur au début : est-ce qu'il est poli et patient, par exemple ? Comment est-ce qu'il change d'attitude au cours de la leçon ? Pourquoi ?
4. Comment est-ce que la relation entre le professeur et son élève a changé à la fin ?

Key: *En lisant.* 1) le professeur pense que l'élève est brillante parce qu'elle sait combien font un et un ; il dit qu'elle est très avancée et qu'elle va obtenir facilement son doctorat ; la nature rapide des questions et des réponses est drôle ; il y a aussi le commentaire du professeur que l'élève est magnifique (simplement à cause de l'addition simple) 2) Au début, l'élève a beaucoup de confiance et elle est très sûre d'elle. Elle devient de moins en moins sûre d'elle. Quand le professeur continue à poser des questions « difficiles », elle ne sait pas comment répondre. Elle commence à paniquer et elle donne des réponses sans réfléchir. 3) Au début, le professeur est poli, il a beaucoup de patience et il encourage l'élève. Ensuite, il devient de plus en plus agressif. Il devient impatient et on a l'impression qu'il veut dominer l'élève. Il essaie de montrer que c'est lui le maître et le plus intelligent. 4) À la fin, le professeur a complètement dominé l'élève. Elle se questionne et elle hésite avant chaque réponse. Il y a un rapport de maître-élève.

LE PROFESSEUR : Bon. Arithmétisons donc un peu.
L'ÉLÈVE : Oui, très volontiers, Monsieur.
LE PROFESSEUR : Cela ne vous ennuierait pas de me dire...
L'ÉLÈVE : Du tout[1], Monsieur, allez-y.
LE PROFESSEUR : Combien font un et un ?
L'ÉLÈVE : Un et un font deux.
LE PROFESSEUR : *émerveillé[2] par le savoir de l'Élève :* Oh, mais c'est très bien. Vous me paraissez[3] très avancée dans vos études. Vous aurez facilement votre doctorat total, Mademoiselle.
L'ÉLÈVE : Je suis bien contente. D'autant plus que[4] c'est vous qui le dites.
LE PROFESSEUR : Poussons plus loin : combien font deux et un ?
L'ÉLÈVE : Trois.
LE PROFESSEUR : Trois et un ?
L'ÉLÈVE : Quatre.
LE PROFESSEUR : Quatre et un ?
L'ÉLÈVE : Cinq.
LE PROFESSEUR : Cinq et un ?
L'ÉLÈVE : Six.
LE PROFESSEUR : Six et un ?
L'ÉLÈVE : Sept.
LE PROFESSEUR : Sept et un ?
L'ÉLÈVE : Huit.
LE PROFESSEUR : Sept et un ?
L'ÉLÈVE : Huit... *bis.*[5]
LE PROFESSEUR : Très bonne réponse. Sept et un ?
L'ÉLÈVE : Huit *ter.*[6]
LE PROFESSEUR : Parfait. Excellent. Sept et un ?
L'ÉLÈVE : Huit *quater.*[7] Et parfois neuf.

[1]*Not at all* [2]*amazed* [3]*seem, appear* [4]*All the more so because* [5]*again* [6]*for a third time* [7]*for a fourth time*

LE PROFESSEUR : Magnifique. Vous êtes magnifique. Vous êtes exquise. Je vous félicite chaleureusement[8], Mademoiselle. Ce n'est pas la peine[9] de continuer. Pour l'addition, vous êtes magistrale. Voyons la soustraction. Dites-moi, seulement, si vous n'êtes pas épuisée[10], combien font quatre moins trois ?

L'ÉLÈVE : Quatre moins trois ?... Quatre moins trois ?

LE PROFESSEUR : Oui. Je veux dire : retirez[11] trois de quatre.

L'ÉLÈVE : Ça fait... sept ?

LE PROFESSEUR : Je m'excuse[12] d'être obligé de vous contredire[13]. Quatre moins trois ne font pas sept. Vous confondez[14] : quatre plus trois font sept, quatre moins trois ne font pas sept... Il ne s'agit plus[15] d'additionner, il faut soustraire maintenant.

L'ÉLÈVE : *s'efforce de comprendre :* Oui... oui...

LE PROFESSEUR : Quatre moins trois font... Combien ?... Combien ?

L'ÉLÈVE : Quatre ?

LE PROFESSEUR : Non, Mademoiselle, ce n'est pas ça.

L'ÉLÈVE : Trois, alors.

LE PROFESSEUR : Non plus, Mademoiselle... Pardon, je dois le dire... Ça ne fait pas ça... mes excuses.

L'ÉLÈVE : Quatre moins trois... Quatre moins trois... Quatre moins trois ?... Ça ne fait tout de même pas dix ?

LE PROFESSEUR : Oh, certainement pas, Mademoiselle. Mais il ne s'agit pas de deviner[16], il faut raisonner. Tâchons[17] de le déduire ensemble. Voulez-vous compter ?

L'ÉLÈVE : Oui, Monsieur. Un... , deux... , euh...

LE PROFESSEUR : Vous savez bien compter ? Jusqu'à combien savez-vous compter ?

L'ÉLÈVE : Je puis[18] compter... à l'infini.

LE PROFESSEUR : Cela n'est pas possible, Mademoiselle.

L'ÉLÈVE : Alors, mettons[19] jusqu'à seize.

LE PROFESSEUR : Cela suffit[20]. Il faut savoir se limiter[21]. Comptez donc, s'il vous plaît, je vous en prie.

L'ÉLÈVE : Un... , deux... , et puis après deux, il y a trois... quatre...

LE PROFESSEUR : Arrêtez-vous, Mademoiselle. Quel nombre est plus grand ? Trois ou quatre ?

L'ÉLÈVE : Euh... trois ou quatre ? Quel est le plus grand ? Le plus grand de trois ou quatre ? Dans quel sens le plus grand ?

LE PROFESSEUR : Il y a des nombres plus petits et d'autres plus grands. Dans les nombres plus grands il y a plus d'unités que dans les petits...

L'ÉLÈVE : ... Que dans les petits nombres ?

LE PROFESSEUR : À moins que[22] les petits aient des unités plus petites. Si elles sont toutes petites, il se peut qu'il[23] y ait plus d'unités dans les petits nombres que dans les grands... s'il s'agit d'autres unités...

L'ÉLÈVE : Dans ce cas, les petits nombres peuvent être plus grands que les grands nombres ?

LE PROFESSEUR : Laissons cela[24]. Ça nous mènerait beaucoup trop loin...

[8] *warmly* [9] *There's no point* [10] *exhausted* [11] *take away* [12] *I am sorry* [13] *to contradict* [14] *confuse* [15] *It's no longer a question* [16] *to guess* [17] Essayons [18] peux [19] Disons [20] *That's enough* [21] *We have to know our limits* [22] *Unless* [23] *it may be that* [24] *Let's drop it*

Key: ***En regardant de plus près.*** 1) Le dialogue est le plus rapide avec les problèmes d'addition. Il ralentit avec la soustraction. Cela signifie un changement dans les attitudes des personnages. C'est peut-être aussi un commentaire sur la nature du système éducatif et l'importance de la mémorisation par cœur. 2) Pour l'élève, on voit qu'elle devient de plus en plus confuse et de moins en moins sûre d'elle et qu'elle pose plus de questions. Pour le professeur, on voit qu'il devient de plus en plus impatient et qu'il commence à donner des explications plus complexes (même si elles ne sont pas toujours logiques).

C. En regardant de plus près. Maintenant examinez quelques caractéristiques du texte.

1. Observez la rapidité du dialogue : à quel moment est-ce que les questions et les réponses se suivent très rapidement ? À quel moment est-ce que les réponses ralentissent (*slow down*) ? Qu'est-ce que cela signale ?
2. Examinez les répliques (*lines*) du professeur et de l'élève séparément : qu'est-ce que cela révèle sur le développement de chaque personnage ?

D. Après avoir lu. Discutez des questions suivantes avec vos camarades de classe.

1. Dans cet extrait, il s'agit d'un dialogue absurde entre le professeur et l'élève. Est-ce que c'est, à votre avis, une critique du système éducatif ? Dans quel sens ?
2. Comment sont les relations entre les professeurs et les élèves, d'après Ionesco ?
3. À la fin de la pièce, il y a un meurtre ; qui va tuer qui, à votre avis ? Expliquez votre réponse.

Key: *Après avoir lu.* 1) Une interprétation possible, c'est que le système éducatif encourage la mémorisation par cœur à un tel point que les élèves ne peuvent pas raisonner et ne sont pas créatifs. 2) Ionesco essaie de démontrer que les professeurs ont trop de pouvoir par rapport aux élèves, même le pouvoir de la vie et la mort. 3) Dans cette pièce, c'est le professeur qui tue l'élève comme il l'a fait avec les quarante élèves précédents. À la fin de la pièce, la sonnette annonce l'arrivée d'un autre élève…

Le Théâtre de la Huchette à Paris. À quelle date est-ce que la première représentation de *La Leçon* a eu lieu ?

Le Théâtre de la Huchette se trouve dans le Quartier Latin près de la place St. Michel. Qu'est-ce qu'on peut visiter aussi dans ce quartier ?

Leçon 1

des genres d'émissions	*kinds of programs*
un dessin animé	*cartoon*
un divertissement	*variety show*
un documentaire	*documentary*
une émission de musique	*music program*
une émission sportive	*sports event*
une émission de téléachat	*infomercial*
une émission de téléréalité	*reality show*
un feuilleton	*soap opera*
un jeu télévisé	*game show*
le journal télévisé (le JT)	*news broadcast*
les informations (f.) (les infos)	*news*
un magazine	*TV magazine*
un reportage	*special report*
une série	*series*
un téléfilm	*made-for-TV movie*

pour regarder la télévision	*to watch TV*
allumer	*to turn on (an appliance)*
une chaîne	*TV station*
un écran	*screen*
un épisode	*episode*
le programme télé	*tv schedule*
une télécommande	*remote control*

des genres de films	*types of films*
une comédie	*comedy*
une comédie dramatique	*dark comedy*
une comédie musicale	*musical*
une comédie romantique	*romantic comedy*
un drame (psychologique)	*(psychological)drama*
un film d'action	*action film*
un film d'animation	*animated film*
un film d'aventures	*adventure film*
un film d'espionnage	*spy film*
un film historique	*historical movie*
un film d'horreur	*horror movie*
un film policier	*detective/police movie*
un film de science-fiction	*science fiction movie*
un western	*western*

pour parler des films	*to talk about films*
célèbre	*famous*
doubler	*to dub*
doublé/e	*dubbed*
le personnage (principal)	*(main) character*
plein de	*full of*
un réalisateur/une réalisatrice	*film director*
des sous-titres (m.)	*subtitles*
tourner (un film)	*to shoot (a film)*
une vedette	*a movie star*
en version française (en VF)	*dubbed in French*
en version originale (en VO)	*in the original language*

quelques verbes	*some verbs*
croire	*to believe*
Je crois que…	*I think that . . .*
Je crois/Je crois que oui	*I think so*
Je ne crois pas/Je crois que non	*I don't think so*
penser	*to think*
raconter	*to tell*
rigoler	*to joke*
Tu rigoles ?	*Are you kidding?*
voir	*to see*

quelques expressions d'émotion qui exigent le subjonctif (voir aussi à la page 304)	*some expressions of emotion that require the subjunctive (see also p. 304)*
avoir peur que	*to be afraid*
être déçu/e que	*to be disappointed*
être désolé/e que	*to be sorry*
Il est/C'est dommage que	*It's too bad, a shame*
être étonné/e que	*to be surprised*
Il est/C'est étonnant que	*It's surprising*

Leçon 2

la technologie	*technology*
un baladeur MP3	*MP3 player*
un clavier (sans fil)	*(wireless) keyboard*
une clé USB	*USB key drive, flash drive*
un disque dur (externe)	*(external) hard drive*
un graveur CD/DVD	*CD/DVD burner*
une imprimante (multifonction)	*(multi-function) printer*
un moniteur (avec un écran plat)	*(flat screen) monitor*
un (ordinateur) portable	*laptop (computer)*
un smartphone	*smart phone*

une souris (sans fil)	*(wireless) mouse*
une tablette tactile	*touch screen tablet*
une webcam	*webcam*

pour se servir de la technologie	*to use technology*
un clip (vidéo)	*(video) clip*
une connexion sans fil	*wireless connection/card*
en ligne	*online*
un fichier	*computer file*
un/e internaute	*Internet user*
un lien	*(web) link*
un logiciel	*software program*
un mail	*e-mail message*
la messagerie instantanée	*instant messaging*
un/e mobinaute	*one who accesses the Internet via a mobile device*
multimédia	*multimedia*
un navigateur (web)	*(web) browser*
par e-mail	*by e-mail (as medium)*
une pièce jointe	*attachment*
la recherche	*research*
un réseau (sans fil), le wi-fi	*(wireless) network, wifi*
un réseau social	*social network*
un site web	*web site*
un texto	*text message*

quelques verbes utiles	*useful verbs*
connecter	*to connect*
échanger	*to exchange*
envoyer	*to send*
essayer	*to try*
imprimer	*to print*
retoucher	*to edit a picture, to touch up*
sauvegarder (un fichier)	*to save (a file)*
se servir de (quelque chose)	*to use (something)*
surfer sur Internet	*to surf the Internet*
télécharger	*to download, to upload, to stream*

autres mots utiles	*other useful words*
C'est génial !	*It's great!*
tout le monde	*everyone*

Leçon 3

On peut lire	*One can read*
un atlas	*atlas*
une bande dessinée (une BD)	*comics, comic book, graphic novel*
une biographie	*biography*
une encyclopédie	*encyclopedia*
un hebdomadaire	*weekly (publication)*
un journal (des journaux)	*newspaper(s)*
un livre d'art	*art book*
un livre de cuisine	*cookbook*
un livre d'histoire	*history book*
un livre de loisirs	*book on leisure time or hobbies*
un magazine	*magazine*
un magazine de télévision	*published TV listings*
un mensuel	*monthly (publication)*
un ouvrage de référence	*reference book*
la poésie	*poetry*
la presse	*the press*
une publicité (une pub)	*advertisement*
un quotidien	*daily (publication)*
un roman	*novel*

pour choisir un livre	*to choose a book*
un auteur	*author*
un critique	*(film, literary) critic*
une critique	*(critical) review*
une recommandation	*recommendation*

où obtenir un livre/magazine	*where to get a book/magazine*
s'abonner (à)	*to subscribe (to)*
être abonné/e	*to be subscribed (to)*
un kiosque	*newsstand*
un lecteur ebook	*e-book reader/device*

autres mots utiles	*other useful words*
se distraire	*to amuse oneself*
s'informer	*to get information*
s'instruire	*to educate oneself, to improve one's mind*

Vocabulaire

Appendices

Appendice 1

L'ALPHABET PHONÉTIQUE INTERNATIONAL

a	**à**, l**a**
e	**é**cout**ez,** r**é**p**é**t**er**
ɛ	**e**lle
i	**i**l, le st**y**lo, G**uy**
o	le styl**o**, bient**ô**t, le tabl**eau**
ɔ	la g**o**mme
u	n**ou**s
y	d**u**
ø	d**eu**x
œ	l**eu**r, la s**œu**r
ɑ̃	l'**en**f**an**t, le j**am**bon
ɛ̃	le cous**in**, l'exam**en**, **im**possible, s**ym**pa
ɔ̃	b**on**jour, c**om**bien
œ̃	**un**, l'alb**um**
j	la n**i**èce, la fi**ll**e, le cra**y**on
ɥ	l**ui**
w	m**oi**, **jou**er, le **w**eek-end
b	le **b**ureau
k	le **c**ahier, **q**ui, le **k**ilo
ʃ	la **ch**aise
d	**d**ans
f	la **f**emme
g	le **g**arçon
ɲ	l'espa**gn**ol
ʒ	le **j**our, **g**entil
l	**l**a, **l**e vi**ll**age
m	**m**ada**m**e
n	**n**euf
ŋ	le campi**ng**
p	le **p**ère
r	la **r**ègle
s	**s**alut, **c**inq, le fran**ç**ai**s**, la bro**ss**e
t	la **t**an**t**e
v	**v**oici
z	**z**éro, la cou**s**ine

Appendice 2 VERBES RÉGULIERS

INFINITIF	PRÉSENT DE L'INDICATIF	PRÉSENT DU SUBJONCTIF	IMPARFAIT	PASSÉ COMPOSÉ	FUTUR	CONDITIONNEL	IMPÉRATIF
verbes **-er**							
regarder *to look at*	*je regarde* *tu regardes* *il* regarde* *nous regardons* *vous regardez* *ils regardent*	*que je regarde* *que tu regardes* *qu'il regarde* *que nous regardions* *que vous regardiez* *qu'ils regardent*	*je regardais* *tu regardais* *il regardait* *nous regardions* *vous regardiez* *ils regardaient*	*j'ai regardé* *tu as regardé* *il a regardé* *nous avons regardé* *vous avez regardé* *ils ont regardé*	*je regarderai* *tu regarderas* *il regardera* *nous regarderons* *vous regarderez* *ils regarderont*	*je regarderais* *tu regarderais* *il regarderait* *nous regarderions* *vous regarderiez* *ils regarderaient*	*regarde* *regardons* *regardez*
verbes **-ir**							
dormir *to sleep*	*je dors* *tu dors* *il dort* *nous dormons* *vous dormez* *ils dorment*	*que je dorme* *que tu dormes* *qu'il dorme* *que nous dormions* *que vous dormiez* *qu'ils dorment*	*je dormais* *tu dormais* *il dormait* *nous dormions* *vous dormiez* *ils dormaient*	*j'ai dormi* *tu as dormi* *il a dormi* *nous avons dormi* *vous avez dormi* *ils ont dormi*	*je dormirai* *tu dormiras* *il dormira* *nous dormirons* *vous dormirez* *ils dormiront*	*je dormirais* *tu dormirais* *il dormirait* *nous dormirions* *vous dormiriez* *ils dormiraient*	*dors* *dormons* *dormez*
verbes **-ir/-iss**							
choisir *to choose*	*je choisis* *tu choisis* *il choisit* *nous choisissons* *vous choisissez* *ils choisissent*	*que je choisisse* *que tu choisisses* *qu'il choisisse* *que nous choisissions* *que vous choisissiez* *qu'ils choisissent*	*je choisissais* *tu choisissais* *il choisissait* *nous choisissions* *vous choisissiez* *ils choisissaient*	*j'ai choisi* *tu as choisi* *il a choisi* *nous avons choisi* *vous avez choisi* *ils ont choisi*	*je choisirai* *tu choisiras* *il choisira* *nous choisirons* *vous choisirez* *ils choisiront*	*je choisirais* *tu choisirais* *il choisirait* *nous choisirions* *vous choisiriez* *ils choisiraient*	*choisis* *choisissons* *choisissez*
verbes **-re**							
vendre *to sell*	*je vends* *tu vends* *il vend* *nous vendons* *vous vendez* *ils vendent*	*que je vende* *que tu vendes* *qu'il vende* *que nous vendions* *que vous vendiez* *qu'ils vendent*	*je vendais* *tu vendais* *il vendait* *nous vendions* *vous vendiez* *ils vendaient*	*j'ai vendu* *tu as vendu* *il a vendu* *nous avons vendu* *vous avez vendu* *ils ont vendu*	*je vendrai* *tu vendras* *il vendra* *nous vendrons* *vous vendrez* *ils vendront*	*je vendrais* *tu vendrais* *il vendrait* *nous vendrions* *vous vendriez* *ils vendraient*	*vends* *vendons* *vendez*
verbes pronominaux							
se laver *to wash oneself*	*je me lave* *tu te laves* *il se lave* *nous nous lavons* *vous vous lavez* *ils se lavent*	*que je me lave* *que tu te laves* *qu'il se lave* *que nous nous lavions* *que vous vous laviez* *qu'ils se lavent*	*je me lavais* *tu te lavais* *il se lavait* *nous nous lavions* *vous vous laviez* *ils se lavaient*	*je me suis lavé/e*** *tu t'es lavé/e* *il/elle s'est lavé/lavée* *nous nous sommes lavé/e/s* *vous vous êtes lavé/e/s* *ils/elles se sont lavés/lavées*	*je me laverai* *tu te laveras* *il se lavera* *nous nous laverons* *vous vous laverez* *ils se laveront*	*je me laverais* *tu te laverais* *il se laverait* *nous nous laverions* *vous vous laveriez* *ils se laveraient*	*lave-toi* *lavons-nous* *lavez-vous*

Comme **dormir** *: s'endormir, mentir, partir, ressentir, se sentir, servir, sortir.*
Comme **choisir** *: désobéir (à), finir, grandir, grossir, maigrir, obéir (à), pâlir, punir, réfléchir (à), réussir (à), rougir.*
Comme **vendre** *: attendre, descendre, se détendre, (s')entendre, perdre, rendre (à), rendre visite (à), répondre (à).*

**For reasons of space, we show only the* il *form for third person singular and plural forms. Recall that the pronouns* elle *and* on *have the same conjugation as* il *in the singular and that* elles *is conjugated the same as* ils *in the plural.*

VERBES IRRÉGULIERS EN -ER

INFINITIF	PRÉSENT DE L'INDICATIF	PRÉSENT DU SUBJONCTIF	IMPARFAIT	PASSÉ COMPOSÉ	FUTUR	CONDITIONNEL	IMPÉRATIF
verbes **-er**							
acheter to buy	j'ach**è**te tu ach**è**tes il* ach**è**te nous achetons vous achetez ils ach**è**tent	que j'ach**è**te que tu ach**è**tes qu'il ach**è**te que nous achetions que vous achetiez qu'ils ach**è**tent	j'achetais	j'ai acheté	j'ach**è**terai	j'ach**è**terais	ach**è**te achetons achetez
appeler to call	j'appe**ll**e tu appe**ll**es il appe**ll**e nous appelons vous appelez ils appe**ll**ent	que j'appe**ll**e que tu appe**ll**es qu'il appe**ll**e que nous appelions que vous appeliez qu'ils appe**ll**ent	j'appelais	j'ai appelé	j'appe**ll**erai	j'appe**ll**erais	appe**ll**e appelons appelez
commencer to begin	je commence tu commences il commence nous commen**ç**ons vous commencez ils commencent	que je commence	je commen**ç**ais nous commencions	j'ai commencé	je commencerai	je commencerais	commence commen**ç**ons commencez
s'essuyer to dry oneself off, to wipe off	je m'ess**ui**e tu t'ess**ui**es il s'ess**ui**e nous nous essuyons vous vous essuyez ils s'ess**ui**ent	que je m'ess**ui**e que tu t'ess**ui**es qu'il s'ess**ui**e que nous nous essuyions que vous vous essuyiez qu'ils s'ess**ui**ent	je m'essuyais	je me suis essuyé/e**	je m'ess**ui**erai	je m'ess**ui**erais	ess**ui**e-toi essuyons-nous essuyez-vous
manger to eat	je mange tu manges il mange nous mang**e**ons vous mangez ils mangent	que je mange	je mang**e**ais nous mangions	j'ai mangé	je mangerai	je mangerais	mange mang**e**ons mangez
préférer to prefer	je préf**è**re tu préf**è**res il préf**è**re nous préférons vous préférez ils préf**è**rent	que je préf**è**re que tu préf**è**res qu'il préf**è**re que nous préférions que vous préfériez qu'ils préf**è**rent	je préférais	j'ai préféré	je préf**è**rerai***	je préf**è**rerais***	

Comme **acheter** *: amener, geler, (se) lever, mener, (se) promener.*
Comme **appeler** *: s'appeler, épeler, jeter, (se) rappeler, rejetter.*
Comme **commencer** *: divorcer, effacer, exercer, se fiancer, lancer, recommencer, remplacer.*
Comme **s'essuyer** *: (s')ennuyer, essuyer. Note that verbs ending in -ayer like essayer and payer can also be conjugated like s'essuyer : j'essaie, je paie.*
Comme **manger** *: (s')arranger, changer, corriger, échanger, exiger, juger, loger, nager, negliger, obliger, partager, protéger, ranger, rédiger, voyager.*
Comme **préférer** *: céder, célébrer, compléter, espérer, exagérer, s'inquiéter, intégrer, interpréter, posséder, procéder, protéger, refléter, régler, répéter, révéler, suggérer.*

**For reasons of space, we show only the il form for third person singular and plural forms. Recall that the pronouns elle and on have the same conjugation as il in the singular and that elles is conjugated the same as ils in the plural.*
***Although agreement of the past participle is shown with reflexive verbs like s'essuyer, recall that when a noun follows the verb, no past participle agreement is made. For example, Elle s'est essuyé les cheveux.*
****Note that the future and conditional forms of the préférer-type verbs (préférer, espérer, répéter, suggérer) are spelled here with an accent grave, based on the 1990 Orthographic reform. The accent grave clearly indicates the pronunciation of [ɛ].*

D'AUTRES VERBES IRRÉGULIERS

INFINITIF	PRÉSENT DE L'INDICATIF		PRÉSENT DU SUBJONCTIF		IMPARFAIT	PASSÉ COMPOSÉ	FUTUR	CONDITIONNEL	IMPÉRATIF
aller *to go*	*je vais* *tu vas* *il* va*	*nous allons* *vous allez* *ils vont*	*que j'aille* *que tu ailles* *qu'il aille*	*que nous allions* *que vous alliez* *qu'ils aillent*	*j'allais*	*je suis allé/e*	*j'irai*	*j'irais*	*va ; vas-y* *allons ; allons-y* *allez ; allez-y*
avoir *to have*	*j'ai* *tu as* *il a*	*nous avons* *vous avez* *ils ont*	*que j'aie* *que tu aies* *qu'il ait*	*que nous ayons* *que vous ayez* *qu'ils aient*	*j'avais*	*j'ai eu*	*j'aurai*	*j'aurais*	*aie* *ayons* *ayez*
boire *to drink*	*je bois* *tu bois* *il boit*	*nous buvons* *vous buvez* *ils boivent*	*que je boive* *que tu boives* *qu'il boive*	*que nous buvions* *que vous buviez* *qu'ils boivent*	*je buvais*	*j'ai bu*	*je boirai*	*je boirais*	*bois* *buvons* *buvez*
combattre *to combat, to fight*	*je combats* *tu combats* *il combat*	*nous combattons* *vous combattez* *ils combattent*	*que je combatte*		*je combattais*	*j'ai combattu*	*je combattrai*	*je combattrais*	*combats* *combattons* *combattez*
connaître *to know, to be acquainted with*	*je connais* *tu connais* *il connaît*	*nous connaissons* *vous connaissez* *ils connaissent*	*que je connaisse*		*je connaissais*	*j'ai connu*	*je connaîtrai*	*je connaîtrais*	
courir *to run*	*je cours* *tu cours* *il court*	*nous courons* *vous courez* *ils courent*	*que je coure*		*je courais*	*j'ai couru*	*je courrai*	*je courrais*	*cours* *courons* *courez*
croire *to believe*	*je crois* *tu crois* *il croit*	*nous croyons* *vous croyez* *ils croient*	*que je croie* *que tu croies* *qu'il croie*	*que nous croyions* *que vous croyiez* *qu'ils croient*	*je croyais*	*j'ai cru*	*je croirai*	*je croirais*	*crois* *croyons* *croyez*
devoir *must, to have to; to owe*	*je dois* *tu dois* *il doit*	*nous devons* *vous devez* *ils doivent*	*que je doive* *que tu doives* *qu'il doive*	*que nous devions* *que vous deviez* *qu'ils doivent*	*je devais*	*j'ai dû*	*je devrai*	*je devrais*	
dire *to say, to tell*	*je dis* *tu dis* *il dit*	*nous disons* *vous dites* *ils disent*	*que je dise*		*je disais*	*j'ai dit*	*je dirai*	*je dirais*	*dis* *disons* *dites*
se distraire *to amuse oneself*	*je me distrais* *tu te distrais* *il se distrait*	*nous nous distrayons* *vous vous distrayez* *ils se distraient*	*que je me distraie* *que tu te distraies* *qu'il se distraie*	*que nous nous distrayions* *que vous vous distrayiez* *qu'ils se distraient*	*je me distrayais*	*je me suis distrait/e*	*je me distrairai*	*je me distrairais*	*distrais-toi* *distrayons-nous* *distrayez-vous*
écrire *to write*	*j'écris* *tu écris* *il écrit*	*nous écrivons* *vous écrivez* *ils écrivent*	*que j'écrive*		*j'écrivais*	*j'ai écrit*	*j'écrirai*	*j'écrirais*	*écris* *écrivons* *écrivez*
envoyer *to send*	*j'envoie* *tu envoies* *il envoie*	*nous envoyons* *vous envoyez* *ils envoient*	*que j'envoie* *que tu envoies* *qu'il envoie*	*que nous envoyions* *que vous envoyiez* *qu'ils envoient*	*j'envoyais*	*j'ai envoyé*	*j'enverrai*	*j'enverrais*	*envoie* *envoyons* *envoyez*

Comme **combattre** *: battre.*
Comme **courir** *: parcourir.*
Comme **devoir** *: recevoir (passé composé : j'ai reçu).*
Comme **dire** *: interdire, prédire.*
Comme **écrire** *: décrire.*
Comme **envoyer** *: employer (futur : j'emploierai), nettoyer (futur : je nettoierai).*
[illegible] singular and plural forms. Recall that the pronouns elle and on have the same conjugation as il in the singular and that elles is conjugated the same as ils in the plural.

INFINITIF	PRÉSENT DE L'INDICATIF	PRÉSENT DU SUBJONCTIF	IMPARFAIT	PASSÉ COMPOSÉ	FUTUR	CONDITIONNEL	IMPÉRATIF
être *to be*	*je suis tu es il* est nous sommes vous êtes ils sont*	*que je sois que tu sois qu'il soit que nous soyons que vous soyez qu'ils soient*	*j'étais*	*j'ai été*	*je serai*	*je serais*	*sois soyons soyez*
faire *to do, to make*	*je fais tu fais il fait nous faisons vous faites ils font*	*que je fasse*	*je faisais*	*j'ai fait*	*je ferai*	*je ferais*	*fais faisons faites*
falloir *to be necessary*	*il faut*	*qu'il faille*	*il fallait*	*il a fallu*	*il faudra*	*il faudrait*	
s'instruire *to educate oneself*	*je m'instruis tu t'instruis il s'instruit nous nous instruisons vous vous instruisez ils s'instruisent*	*que je m'instruise*	*je m'instruisais*	*je me suis instruit/e*	*je m'instruirai*	*je m'instruirais*	*instruis-toi instruisons-nous instruisez-vous*
lire *to read*	*je lis tu lis il lit nous lisons vous lisez ils lisent*	*que je lise*	*je lisais*	*j'ai lu*	*je lirai*	*je lirais*	*lis lisons lisez*
mettre *to put, to put on*	*je mets tu mets il met nous mettons vous mettez ils mettent*	*que je mette*	*je mettais*	*j'ai mis*	*je mettrai*	*je mettrais*	*mets mettons mettez*
mourir *to die*	*je meurs tu meurs il meurt nous mourons vous mourez ils meurent*	*que je meure que tu meures qu'il meure que nous mourions que vous mouriez qu'ils meurent*	*je mourais*	*je suis mort/e*	*je mourrai*	*je mourrais*	
naître *to be born*	*je nais tu nais il naît nous naissons vous naissez ils naissent*	*que je naisse*	*je naissais*	*je suis né/e*	*je naîtrai*	*je naîtrais*	
offrir *to give, to offer*	*j'offre tu offres il offre nous offrons vous offrez ils offrent*	*que j'offre*	*j'offrais*	*j'ai offert*	*j'offrirai*	*j'offrirais*	*offre offrons offrez*
pleuvoir *to rain*	*il pleut*	*qu'il pleuve*	*il pleuvait*	*il a plu*	*il pleuvra*	*il pleuvrait*	
pouvoir *to be able to, can*	*je peux tu peux il peut nous pouvons vous pouvez ils peuvent*	*que je puisse*	*je pouvais*	*j'ai pu*	*je pourrai*	*je pourrais*	
prendre *to take, to have (to eat or drink)*	*je prends tu prends il prend nous prenons vous prenez ils prennent*	*que je prenne que tu prennes qu'il prenne que nous prenions que vous preniez qu'ils prennent*	*je prenais*	*j'ai pris*	*je prendrai*	*je prendrais*	*prends prenons prenez*

Comme **lire** : *relire.*

Comme **mettre** : *permettre, promettre, remettre.*

Comme **offrir** : *couvrir, découvrir, ouvrir.*

Comme **prendre** : *apprendre, comprendre, surprendre.*

**For reasons of space, we show only the* il *form for third person singular and plural forms. Recall that the pronouns* elle *and* on *have the same conjugation as* il *in the singular and that* elles *is conjugated the same as* ils *in the plural.*

INFINITIF	PRÉSENT DE L'INDICATIF		PRÉSENT DU SUBJONCTIF		IMPARFAIT	PASSÉ COMPOSÉ	FUTUR	CONDITIONNEL	IMPÉRATIF
réduire *to reduce*	*je réduis* *tu réduis* *il* réduit*	*nous réduisons* *vous réduisez* *ils réduisent*	*que je réduise*		*je réduisais*	*j'ai réduit*	*je réduirai*	*je réduirais*	*réduis* *réduisons* *réduisez*
rompre *to break,* *to break up*	*je romps* *tu romps* *il rompt*	*nous rompons* *vous rompez* *ils rompent*	*que je rompe*		*je rompais*	*j'ai rompu*	*je romprai*	*je romprais*	*romps* *rompons* *rompez*
savoir *to know,* *to know how*	*je sais* *tu sais* *il sait*	*nous savons* *vous savez* *ils savent*	*que je sache*		*je savais*	*j'ai su*	*je saurai*	*je saurais*	*sache* *sachons* *sachez*
suivre *to follow,* *to take (a course)*	*je suis* *tu suis* *il suit*	*nous suivons* *vous suivez* *ils suivent*	*que je suive*		*je suivais*	*j'ai suivi*	*je suivrai*	*je suivrais*	*suis* *suivons* *suivez*
valoir *to be worth*	*il vaut*		*qu'il vaille*		*il valait*	*il a valu*	*il vaudra*	*il vaudrait*	
venir *to come*	*je viens* *tu viens* *il vient*	*nous venons* *vous venez* *ils viennent*	*que je vienne* *que tu viennes* *qu'il vienne*	*que nous venions* *que vous veniez* *qu'ils viennent*	*je venais*	*je suis venu/e*	*je viendrai*	*je viendrais*	*viens* *venons* *venez*
vivre *to live*	*je vis* *tu vis* *il vit*	*nous vivons* *vous vivez* *ils vivent*	*que je vive*		*je vivais*	*j'ai vécu*	*je vivrai*	*je vivrais*	*vis* *vivons* *vivez*
voir *to see*	*je vois* *tu vois* *il voit*	*nous voyons* *vous voyez* *ils voient*	*que je voie* *que tu voies* *qu'il voie*	*que nous voyions* *que vous voyiez* *qu'ils voient*	*je voyais*	*j'ai vu*	*je verrai*	*je verrais*	*vois* *voyons* *voyez*
vouloir *to want*	*je veux* *tu veux* *il veut*	*nous voulons* *vous voulez* *ils veulent*	*que je veuille* *que tu veuilles* *qu'il veuille*	*que nous voulions* *que vous vouliez* *qu'ils veuillent*	*je voulais*	*j'ai voulu*	*je voudrai*	*je voudrais*	*veuillez*

Comme **réduire** *: conduire, construire, déduire, produire, reproduire.*

Comme **suivre** *: poursuivre.*

Comme **venir** *: appartenir, devenir, maintenir, obtenir, prévenir, retenir, revenir, soutenir, se souvenir, tenir.*

Comme **voir** *: revoir.*

**For reasons of space, we show only the* il *form for third person singular and plural forms. Recall that the pronouns* elle *and* on *have the same conjugation as* il *in the singular and that* elles *is conjugated the same as* ils *in the plural.*

Appendice 3

LEXIQUE FRANÇAIS-ANGLAIS

This glossary lists most French words found in the text and provides the meanings of those words as they are used here. The vocabulary can be divided into two types: productive vocabulary and receptive vocabulary. Productive vocabulary words appear in the **Points de départ** and **Formes et fonctions** sections and occasionally in the **Vie et culture** sections; these words reappear periodically. You are expected to recognize these words when you read and hear them and to use them yourself in exercises and conversational activities. All other words, including those presented in readings and realia, are receptive vocabulary; you are expected only to recognize them and to know their meanings when you see them in written form or hear them in context.

- For all productive vocabulary items, the numbers following an entry indicate the chapter and lesson in which that vocabulary item is first introduced. Since verbs in their infinitive form are occasionally introduced as vocabulary items before their conjugation is presented, refer to the Index to locate where the conjugation is introduced. You will also find the complete conjugation for each verb (or type of verb) in Appendix 2.
- To find the meaning of an expression, try to locate the main word in the expression and look that up. For example, the expression **Je vous en prie** is with the entry for the verb **prier**; the expression **faire du sport** is under the entry for the noun **sport**.
- The gender of nouns is indicated by the abbreviations *m.* for masculine and *f.* for feminine. Feminine and masculine nouns that are closely related in meaning and identical or similar in pronunciation are listed under a single entry: **architecte** *m./f.*; **étudiant** *m.*, **étudiante** *f.* Nouns that occur only in the plural form are followed by the gender indication and *pl.*: **beaux-arts** *m. pl.*, **vacances** *f. pl.* Nouns and adjectives that show no agreement and do not change in the plural or feminine are indicated by the abbreviation *inv.*: **CD** *m. inv.*
- Adjectives with differing masculine and feminine written forms are shown in the masculine form followed by the feminine ending: **allemand/e, ambitieux/-euse, canadien/ne**. For adjectives whose masculine and feminine forms vary considerably, both forms are listed: **cher/chère**. Special prenominal forms of adjectives are given in parentheses: **beau** (**bel**)/**belle**. When necessary for clarity, adjectives and adverbs are indicated by *adj.* and *adv.*, respectively.
- An asterisk (*) before a word indicates that the initial **h** is aspirate: this means that **liaison** and **élision** do not apply.
- The hashmark (†) appears after productive verbs showing some irregularity in conjugation; these verbs appear in their full conjugation in the verb charts, Appendix 2. Verbs showing irregularities in conjugation that are considered part of receptive vocabulary are not always indicated in the glossary, since you are only expected to recognize and not produce these verbs. The conjugations of many of these verbs are similar to conjugations you will find in Appendix 2. For example, the verb **admettre** is conjugated just like the verb **mettre**. For verbs that require a preposition under certain conditions, the latter appears in parentheses: **commencer** (**à** + *inf.*), (**il commence son travail, il commence à travailler**); for verbs that always require a preposition, the preposition is indicated without parentheses: **s'occuper de** (**il s'occupe de moi**).

- Here is a complete list of the abbreviations used in the glossaries:

adj. adjectif/adjective
adv. adverbe/adverb
Can. canadien/Canadian usage
conj. conjonction/conjunction
fam./colloq. familier/colloquial usage
f. féminin/feminine
inf. infinitif/infinitive
inv. invariable
m. masculin/masculine
n. nom/noun
part. passé participe passé/past participle
pl. pluriel/plural
pron. pronom/pronoun
qqch./st. quelque chose/ something
qqn/so. quelqu'un/ someone
reg. régional/regional usage
rel. pron. pronom relatif/relative pronoun
sg. singulier/singular

A

à to, at, in, on, P-1
abbaye *f.* abbey, 9-3
abîmé/e worn, worn out, 6-2
abominable abominable, terrible
abonné/e subscribed, 10-3
  être abonné/e à to be subscribed to, 10-3
abonnement *m.* subscription
s'abonner (à) to subscribe (to), 10-3
d'abord first (of all), 4-2
abréviation *f.* abbreviation
absence *f.* absence
absent/e absent, missing
absolument absolutely
absurde *adj.* absurd, ridiculous, preposterous
accent *m.* accent
accepter (de) to accept
  (J'accepte) avec plaisir, (I accept) with pleasure, 4-3
accès *m.* access
accessoire *m.* accessory
accident *m.* accident
accompagner to accompany, 4-3
  Tu veux/Vous voulez m'accompagner ? Would you like to come with me?, 4-3
accomplir to accomplish
accord : d'accord agreed, OK, all right
  être d'accord to agree
  Je ne suis pas d'accord... I disagree . . .
  Je suis d'accord... I agree . . .
accueillir to welcome
achat *m.* purchase, 4-2
  faire † des achats to shop, 4-2
acheter † to buy, 4-3
acteur *m.*, **actrice** *f.* actor/actress, 8-3
action *f.* action
actif/-ive active
activités *f.* activities, 1-3
actuel/le current
actuellement currently, nowadays
adaptation *f.* adaptation, adapted version
addition *f.* bill, 5-1
additionner to add
adjectif *m.* adjective
admettre † to admit
administratif/-ive administrative, 8-1
administration *f.* administration
admirer to admire
adolescent/e adolescent
adopter to adopt; to pass (a law)
adorable adorable
adorer to adore, to love, 2-1
adresse *f.* address
adulte *m.* adult
adulte *adj.* adult
adverbe *m.* adverb
aérobic *f.* aerobics
aéroport *m.* airport, 9-1
aérosol *m.* aerosol
affaires *f. pl.* belongings, things, 6-2; business, 8-3
  faire † des affaires to be in business
  femme *f.* **d'affaires** businesswoman, 8-3
  homme *m.* **d'affaires** businessman, 8-3
affectueux/-euse affectionate, warm-hearted
affiche *f.* poster, P-2
afficher to post, to post to a web site
affirmatif/-ive affirmative
afin de (+ *inf.*) in order to (+ *verb*)
africain/e African
Afrique *f.* Africa, 9-2
âge *m.* age, 1-2
  d'un certain âge middle-aged, 2-1
  Quel âge as-tu/avez-vous ? How old are you?, 1-2
  Quel est ton/votre âge ? What is your age?, 1-2
âgé/e aged, old, elderly, 2-1
agence *f.* agency
  agence de voyage travel agency
  agence immobilière real estate agency
agenda *m.* datebook, personal calendar
agent de police *m.*, **agente de police** *f.* police officer
s'agir de to be about
  il s'agit de... it's about . . . [+ *n.*, + *inf.*]
agneau *m.* lamb, 5-3
agréable pleasant, 6-2
agricole agricultural
agriculteur *m.*, **agricultrice** *f.* farmer
aider to help, 8-3; **aider** (*qqn* à + *inf.*) to help (*so.* do *st.*)
ail *m.* garlic, 5-3
ailleurs *adv.* somewhere else, elsewhere
aimable lovable
aimer to like, to love, 1-3
  aimer beaucoup to like or love a lot, 8-2
  aimer bien to like fairly well, 8-2
  aimer mieux to prefer, 9-3
aîné/e older (brother/sister)
ainsi (que) thus, in such a way
air *m.* air
  air frais fresh air
  avoir † l'air (bon/mauvais) to appear/ to seem (good/bad), 5-3
  avoir † l'air (d'être) + *adj.* to seem/ to appear (to be) + *adj.*
  en plein air outdoors, 8-3
aisance *f.* ease
aisé/e easy, well off
ajouter to add
alarme *f.* alarm
album *m.* album
alcool *m.* alcohol, 7-1
alcoolisé/e *adj.* containing alcohol, 5-1
alerte *f.* alert
  fausse alerte false alarm
alerte *adj.* alert
Algérie *f.* Algeria, 9-2
algérien/ne Algerian, 9-2
alimentaire *adj.* relating to food
aliments *m. pl.* food, 5-2
Allemagne *f.* Germany, 9-2
allemand *m.* German (language), 8-2
allemand/e *adj.* German, 9-2
aller † to go, 2-3
  Allez au tableau ! Go to the board!, P-2
  Ça ne va pas. Things aren't going well., P-1
  Ça va, et toi ? Fine, and you?, P-1
  Comment allez-vous ? How are you?, P-1
  On y va ensemble? Shall we go (there) together?, 4-3
allô hello (telephone only)
allumer to turn on (an appliance), 10-1
alors so, 2-3; then
alphabet *m.* alphabet
alpinisme *m.* mountain climbing, 4-2
  faire † de l'alpinisme to go mountain climbing, 4-2
alsacien/ne from the region of Alsace
ambassadeur *m.*, **ambassadrice** *f.* ambassador
ambiant/e : à la température ambiante at room temperature

ambitieux/-euse ambitious, 2-1
améliorer to improve
amener † to bring (along) a person, 4-3
américain/e American, 9-2
Amérique *f.* **du Nord** North America, 9-2
Amérique *f.* **du Sud** South America, 9-2
ami *m.*, **amie** *f.* friend, P-1
amoureux/-euse in love, 7-3
  tomber amoureux/-euse (de) to fall in love (with), 7-3
amphithéâtre *m.* amphitheater, lecture hall, 8-1
amusant/e funny, 2-1
s'amuser to have fun, 7-3
an *m.* year, 1-2
  J'ai 19 ans. I am 19 years old., 1-2
analyse *f.* analysis
analyser to analyze
analytique analytical
anchois *m.* anchovy
ancien/ne old, antique, 6-2; former
anglais *m.* English (language), P-2
anglais/e *adj.* English, 9-2
Angleterre *f.* England, 9-2
angoisse *f.* anguish
angoissé/e anguished
animal *m.* animal, 1-1
  animal familier pet, 1-1
animateur *m.*, **animatrice** *f.* organizer
animation *f.* animation, excitement
animé/e lively, animated, 6-1
anneau *m.* wedding ring
année *f.* year, 1-2
  l'année dernière last year, 4-1
  l'année prochaine next year, 2-3
  Bonne année ! Happy New Year!, 7-2
anniversaire *m.* birthday, 1-2
  anniversaire de mariage (wedding) anniversary, 7-2
  Bon anniversaire ! Happy Birthday!, 7-2
  Joyeux anniversaire ! Happy Birthday!, 7-2
  Joyeux anniversaire de mariage ! Happy Anniversary!, 7-2
annonce *f.* advertisement
annoncer to announce
anorak *m.* ski jacket, parka, 3-3
anthropologie *f.* anthropology, 8-2
anxiété *f.* anxiety
anxieux/-euse anxious, 7-3
août August, 1-2
apéritif *m.* **(un apéro)** before-meal drink, 5-2
appareil *m.* appliance, device
  appareil électronique electronic device, appliance
  appareil (photo) numérique digital camera, 9-1
  appareil photo (still) camera, 9-1
appartement *m.* apartment, 3-1
  appartement sous les toits attic apartment, 6-2
appartenir à † to belong to
appel *m.* call
appeler † to call, 4-3
s'appeler † to be named, 7-3
  Je m'appelle... My name is . . . , P-1
apporter to bring (an object), 6-2
apprécier to appreciate
apprendre † (à + *inf.*) to learn (to do *st.*), 5-1
apprentissage *m.* apprenticeship, learning
approcher to approach
approprié/e appropriate
après after, after that, 4-2
  après-midi *m.* afternoon, 1-3
  d'après vous/lui according to you/him, in your/his opinion
  de l'après-midi in the afternoon, P.M., 3-2
aquarium *m.* aquarium
arabe *m.* Arabic (language)
arabe *adj.* Arab, Arabian
arbre *m.* tree, 6-3
archéologie *f.* archaeology
archipel *m.* archipelago
architecte *m./f.* architect, 8-3
architecture *f.* architecture
argent *m.* money, 3-1
argentin/e Argentinian, 9-2
Argentine *f.* Argentina, 9-2
argument *m.* argument
armoire *f.* armoire, wardrobe, 6-2
s'arranger † to be all right, to work out, 7-3
arrêt *m.* stop
arrêter (de + *inf.*) to stop (doing *st.*)
  Arrête ! Stop it!, 2-1
  s'arrêter (de + *inf.*) to stop oneself (from doing *st.*)
arrière back, rear
  arrière-grand-parent *m.* great-grandparent
arriver to arrive, 1-3
arrondissement *m.* Parisian city district, 6-1
arroser to water; to celebrate with wine or champagne
art *m.* art, 10-2
  arts *m. pl.* **du spectacle** performing arts, 8-2
  beaux-arts *m. pl.* fine arts
  livre *m.* **d'art** art book, 10-3
article *m.* article
  articles de toilette *m. pl.* toiletries, 3-1
articulatoire *adj.* articulatory
artifice : feu *m.* **d'artifice** fireworks, 7-2
artificiel/le artificial
artiste *m./f.* artist, 8-3
artistique artistic
ascenseur *m.* elevator, 6-1
asiatique Asiatic
Asie *f.* Asia, 9-2
aspect *m.* aspect
asperge *f.* asparagus, 5-2
aspiré/e aspirated
s'asseoir to sit down
  Asseyez-vous ! Sit down!, P-2
assez rather, 1-1; enough, 3-1
assiette *f.* plate, 5-3
assistant *m.* **social, assistante** *f.* **sociale** social worker, 8-3
assister à to attend, 2-3
association *f.* **(étudiante)** (student) association, 8-1
associé/e associated
associer to associate, to match
astrologie *f.* astrology
astrologue *m./f.* astrologer
astronomie *f.* astronomy, 8-2
athlète *m./f.* athlete
atlas *m.* atlas, 10-3
attendre to wait (for), to expect, 4-1
attention *f.* attention
  faire † attention (à) to pay attention (to); to be careful
attentivement attentively
attitude *f.* attitude, demeanor
attraper to catch
au (à + le) to (the) 2-2
  au-dessous *adv.* below
  au-dessus *adv.* above
  au revoir good-bye, P-1
auberge *f.* inn, 9-3
  auberge de jeunesse youth hostel, 9-3
augmenter to increase
aujourd'hui today, 1-3
auprès de next to, close to
aussi also, P-1
  aussi bien que as well as, 9-2
  aussi... que as . . . as, 8-1
  moi aussi me too
aussitôt que as soon as
Australie *f.* Australia, 9-2
australien/ne Australian, 9-2
autant (de)... que as many/much . . . as, 8-1
auteur *m.* author, 10-3
auto(mobile) *f.* car
automatique automatic
automne *m.* fall, 4-1
autonome independent, 8-3
autonomie *f.* autonomy
autoritaire authoritarian, 7-1
autorité *f.* authority
autoroute *f.* highway
autour around
autre other, another, 2-1
autrefois in the past
autrement otherwise
aux (à + les) to (the) 2-2
avance : (être) en avance (to be) early, 3-2
avant before
avantage *m.* advantage
avant-hier the day before yesterday, 4-1
avec with, 1-3
avenir *m.* future
aventure *f.* adventure, 10-1
  film *m.* **d'aventures** adventure film, 10-1
aventurier *m.*, **aventurière** *f.* adventurer
avenue *f.* avenue, 9-3
avion *m.* plane, 9-1
avis *m.* opinion, 10-3
  à mon avis in my opinion 10-3
avocat *m.*, **avocate** *f.* lawyer, 8-3
avoir † to have, 1-2
avril April, 1-2

B

bac(calauréat) *m.* high-school exit exam (France), 8-2
baccalauréat (en) *m.* B.A. or B.S. degree (in) (*Can.*), 8-2
bacon *m.* bacon, 5-2
bagage *m.* luggage
baguette *f.* French bread (long, thin loaf), 5-3
baignoire *f.* bathtub

bain *m.* bath
maillot *m.* **de bain** bathing suit, 3-3
prendre † un bain to take a bath, 3-1
salle *f.* **de bains** bathroom, 6-1
baisser to lower
bal *m.* ball, dance
bal populaire street dance, 7-2
balade *f.* walk, stroll (*colloq.*)
baladeur *m.* **MP3** MP3 player, 10-2
balcon *m.* balcony, 6-1
ballet *m.* ballet, 2-3
banaliser to make commonplace
banane *f.* banana, 5-2
bande dessinée *f.* **(une BD)** comic, comic strip, 10-3
banlieue *f.* suburb
banque *f.* bank
baptême *m.* baptism, 7-2
bar *m.* bar
bas/se low
en bas downstairs
basilic *m.* basil
basket(-ball) *m.* basketball, 2-2
basket-fauteuil *m.* wheelchair basketball, 7-1
baskets *f. pl.* athletic shoes, 3-3
bateau *m.* **(à voile)** (sail)boat, 6-3
bateau-mouche Paris sight-seeing boat for tourists
bâtiment *m.* building, 6-1
batterie *f.* percussion, drum set, 2-2
battu/e beaten
beau (bel)/belle beautiful, handsome, 2-1
Il fait beau. It's beautiful weather., 4-1
beaucoup a lot, 1-1
beau-frère *m.* brother-in-law
beau-père *m.* stepfather, father-in-law, 1-1
beaux-arts *m. pl.* fine arts, 8-2
beige beige, 3-3
belge Belgian, 9-2
Belgique *f.* Belgium, 9-2
belle-mère *f.* stepmother, mother-in-law, 1-1
belle-sœur *f.* sister-in-law
besoin *m.* need, 5-3
avoir † besoin de to need, 5-3
bête stupid, 2-1
beurre *m.* butter, 5-2
bibliothèque *f.* library, 2-3
bibli *f.* (*Can.*) library, 8-1
bibliothèque municipale (la BM) municipal library, 2-3
bibliothèque universitaire (la BU) university library, 8-1
bien well, fine, P-1
faire † du bien to do (*so.*) good
bien sûr of course, 2-1
bien-être *m.* well-being, 7-1
bientôt soon, 2-3
à bientôt see you soon, P-1
bienvenu/e *adj.* welcome
bienvenue *f.* welcome; you're welcome (*Can.*)
bière *f.* beer, 5-1
bifteck *m.* steak
bifteck haché ground beef, 5-3
bijou *m.* (*pl.* **bijoux**) piece of jewelry
bilingue bilingual
billet *m.* ticket
billet aller-retour round-trip ticket
billet d'avion airplane ticket, 4-2
billet d'entrée ticket (for concert/play), 4-2
billet simple one-way ticket
bimensuel *m.* bimonthly
bio(logique) organic, 5-3
biographie *f.* biography, 10-3
biologie *f.* biology, 8-2
biscuit *m.* cookie, 5-2
bise *f.* kiss
faire † une/la bise to kiss hello/good-bye on the cheeks
bizarre *adj.* odd, strange, peculiar
blanc/blanche white, 3-3
bleu/e blue, 3-3
blog *m.* blog
blond/e blond, 2-1
bloquer to block
blouson *m.* heavy jacket, 3-3
boire † to drink, 5-1
boire † de l'alcool to drink alcohol, 7-1
bois *m.* woods, 6-3; wood
boisson *f.* drink, 5-1
boisson alcoolisée alcoholic beverage, 5-1
boisson chaude hot drink, 5-1
boisson rafraîchissante cold drink, 5-1
boîte *f.* can; box 5-3
boîte postale post office box
boîte vocale voicemail
bol *m.* bowl, 5-2
bon/ne good, 3-3
bonbon *m.* piece of candy
bonheur *m.* happiness, luck
Bon anniversaire ! Happy Birthday!, 7-2
bon marché *adj. inv.* cheap, inexpensive 3-3
Bonne année ! Happy New Year!, 7-2
Bonnes vacances ! Have a good vacation!, 7-2
Bon voyage ! Have a good trip!, 7-2
Il fait bon. It's nice and warm., 4-1
bonjour hello, P-1
bonnet *m.* hat, cap, 3-3
bonnet de laine knitted wool hat, 3-3
bonsoir good evening, P-1
bord *m.* edge, shore, 6-3
au bord (du lac) at the (lake)shore, 6-3
au bord de la mer at the seashore, 6-3
bordé/e bordered, lined
border to border, to line
botanique *f.* botany, 8-2
botte *f.* boot, 3-3
boubou *m.* African robe, dress
bouche *f.* mouth, 7-1
boucher *m.*, **bouchère** *f.* butcher
boucherie *f.* butcher shop, 5-3
bougie *f.* candle, 7-2
bouillabaisse *f.* seafood stew
bouillant/e boiling, boiling hot
bouillir to boil
bouillon *m.* broth, stock
boulanger *m.*, **boulangère** *f.* baker
boulangerie *f.* bakery, 5-3
boulevard *m.* boulevard, 9-3
boulot *m.* work (*colloq.*)
bourguingon/ne from the region of Bourgogne
bout *m.* tip, end
bouteille *f.* bottle, 5-1
boutique *f.* boutique, shop
branché/e plugged in, connected
bras *m.* arm, 7-1
bravo ! great! well done!, 4-2
bref/brève brief
Brésil *m.* Brazil, 9-2
brésilien/ne Brazilian, 9-2
Bretagne *f.* Brittany
breton/ne Breton; from the region of Britanny
bricolage *m.* do-it-yourself projects, odd jobs, 2-2
faire † du bricolage to carry out do-it-yourself projects, 2-2
bricoler to carry out do-it-yourself projects, 2-2
bricoleur *m.*, **bricoleuse** *f.* do-it-yourselfer
brin *m.* sprig, strand
brin de muguet sprig of lily of the valley
brochure *f.* brochure, pamphlet
bronzer to tan, 4-2
brosse *f.* chalkboard eraser, P-2; brush, 3-1
brosse à cheveux hairbrush, 3-1
brosse à dents toothbrush, 3-1
brosser to brush
se brosser to brush one's —, 3-1
se brosser les cheveux to brush one's hair, 3-1
se brosser les dents to brush one's teeth, 3-1
brouillard *m.* fog, 4-1
Il y a du brouillard. It's foggy., 4-1
brouillon *m.* rough draft
bruit *m.* sound, noise
brun/e dark-haired, brunette, 2-1
budget *m.* budget
buffet *m.* buffet
bureau *m.* desk, P-2; office, 1-3
bus *m.* (city) bus, 9-1

C

ça that
Ça dépend. That depends.
Ça ne va pas. Things aren't going well., P-1
Ça va. It's going fine., P-1
Ça va ? How are things?, P-1
C'est ça. That's right.
Comment ça va ? How's it going?, P-1
cabinet *m.* office (doctor's)
câble *m.* cable (television)
caché/e hidden
cacher to hide, 7-2
cadeau *m.* present, gift, 6-2
cadien/ne Cajun
cadre *m.* business executive; frame (for a picture)
café *m.* café, 2-3; coffee, 5-1
café au lait coffee with milk, 5-2
café crème coffee with cream, 5-1
caféine *f.* caffeine
cafétéria *f.* cafeteria, eatery serving snacks and light meals, 8-1
cahier *m.* notebook, P-2

caisse *f.* cash register, 5-3
caissier *m.*, **caissière** *f.* cashier
calcul *m.* calculus, 8-2
calculatrice *f.* calculator, P-2
calendrier *m.* calendar
calme calm, 1-1
se calmer to calm down, 7-3
camarade *m./f.* friend, buddy
  camarade de classe classmate, P-1
Cameroun *m.* Cameroon, 9-2
camerounais/e Cameroonian, 9-2
campagne *f.* countryside, 4-2
  à la campagne in the country, 4-2
camping *m.* campground, 9-3
  faire † du camping to camp, to go camping, 4-2
camping-car *m.* RV, mobile home, 9-3
campus *m.* campus
Canada *m.* Canada, 9-2
canadien/ne Canadian, 9-2
canapé *m.* couch, 6-2
candidat/e *m./f.* candidate
cannette *f.* (soda, beer) can, 5-1
canoë *m.* canoe
capacité *f.* ability
capitale *f.* capital city
car *m.* excursion bus, intercity bus, 9-1
caractère *m.* nature, disposition, character, 1-1
carafe *f.* **(d'eau)** carafe (of water), 5-2
caravane *f.* trailer, 9-3
cardinal/e cardinal
carnet *m.* small notebook
  carnet d'adresses address book, 9-1
carotte *f.* carrot, 5-3
carrière *f.* career, 8-3
  faire † carrière dans to pursue a career in
carte *f.* map, P-2; playing card, 2-2
  à la carte from the menu; cafeteria-style
  carte bancaire debit card, 9-1
  carte de crédit credit card, 9-1
  carte d'identité French national ID card, 9-1
  carte météorologique weather map
  carte postale postcard, 4-2
  jouer aux cartes to play cards, 2-2
cas *m.* case
casquette *f.* baseball cap, 3-3
casse-croûte *m. inv.* snack, 5-1
casserole *f.* saucepan
catégorie *f.* category
cathédrale *f.* cathedral, 9-3
catholicisme *m.* Catholicism
catholique Catholic
cause *f.* cause
  à cause de due to, because of, 4-3
causer to cause; to chat (*colloq.*)
causerie *f.* informal chat (in front of an audience)
cave *f.* wine cellar, 9-3
CD *m. inv.* CD, compact disk, P-2
ce (c') (*pron.*) it, that
  ce sont... these/they are . . . , P-1
  c'est... this/it is . . . , P-1
  c'est-à-dire that is to say
ce (cet), cette, ces (*adj.*) this, that, these, those, 7-2
céder † to relinquish
ceinture *f.* belt
cela that
célèbre famous, 10-1
célébrer † to celebrate
célébrité *f.* celebrity
célibataire single, 1-1
celle *f.* the one
celui *m.* the one
cendre *f.* ash
cendrier *m.* ashtray
cent one hundred, 1-2
centralisé/e centralized
centre *m.* center
  centre étudiant student center, 8-1
  centre sportif sports complex, 8-1
  centre-ville *m.* downtown, 6-2
cependant however
céramique *f.* ceramics, pottery
céramique *adj.* ceramic
céréales *f. pl.* cereal, 5-2
cérémonie *f.* ceremony, 7-2
  cérémonie civile civil wedding service, 7-2
certain/e certain
certainement certainly
ces these, those 7-2
chacun/e each one
chaîne *f.* chain; TV channel, 10-1
chaise *f.* chair, P-2
chambre *f.* bedroom, 3-1
champ *m.* field, 6-3
champignon *m.* mushroom, 5-3
champion *m.*, **championne** *f.* champion
championnat *m.* championship
chance *f.* luck
  avoir † de la chance to be lucky
changement *m.* change
changer † to change
chanson *f.* song
chant *m.* singing
chanter to sing, 3-2
chanteur *m.*, **chanteuse** *f.* singer, 8-3
chapeau *m.* hat, 2-1
chapelle *f.* chapel
chaque each, 6-1
charcuterie *f.* pork butcher shop; cooked pork meats, 5-3
charges *f. pl.* utilities, 6-1
  les charges sont comprises utilities are included, 6-1
chariot *m.* shopping cart
charmant/e charming
chasse *f.* hunting
chat *m.*, **chatte** *f.* cat, 1-1
châtain *adj. inv.* chestnut-colored hair, 2-1
château *m.* castle, 9-3
  château fort fortress, 9-3
chaud hot, 4-1
  Il fait chaud. It's hot (weather)., 4-1
  J'ai chaud. I'm hot., 4-1
chauffeur *m.* driver
chausser to put shoes on
chaussette *f.* sock, 3-3
chausson *m.* slipper
  chausson de danse ballet slipper
chaussure *f.* shoe, 3-3
  chaussures à talons high-heeled shoes, 3-3
chef *m.* boss; chef; chief
chemin *m.* way, 9-3; path
  indiquer le chemin to give directions, 9-3
cheminée *f.* chimney
chemise *f.* man's shirt, 3-3
chemisier *m.* blouse, 3-3
cher/chère expensive, 3-3
chercher to look for, 2-3
chéri/e *m./f.* sweetheart, darling
cheval *m.* horse, 4-2
  faire † du cheval to go horseback riding, 4-2
cheveu *m.* hair, 3-1
  se brosser/laver les cheveux to brush/wash one's hair, 3-1
chez at the home of, at the place of, 1-1
  chez nous at our place, our home, 1-1
chic *adj. inv.* chic, stylish, 6-2
chien *m.*, **chienne** *f.* dog, 1-1
chiffre *m.* numeral, digit
Chili *m.* Chile, 9-2
chilien/ne Chilean, 9-2
chimie *f.* chemistry, 8-2
Chine *f.* China, 9-2
chinois *m.* Chinese (language)
chinois/e *adj.* Chinese, 9-2
chocolat *m.* chocolate, 5-1
  chocolat chaud hot chocolate, 5-1
choisir to choose, 5-2
choix *m.* choice
choquant/e shocking
chorale *f.* choir
chose *f.* thing, 2-2
chou *m.* (*pl.***choux**) cabbage, 5-3
choucroute *f.* sauerkraut
  choucroute garnie sauerkraut with meat
chouette ! neat!, 4-2
chrysanthème *m.* chrysanthemum
ci-dessous below
ci-dessus above
cidre *m.* cider
ciel *m.* sky, 4-1
  Le ciel est couvert. The sky is overcast., 4-1
cigarette *f.* cigarette
cimetière *m.* cemetery
cinéaste *m.* filmmaker
cinéma *m.* cinema, the movies, 2-3; film studies, 8-2
cinématographe *m.* cinematographer
cinématographique *adj.* movie, cinematic
cinq five, 1-2
cinq-pièces *m.* apartment/house with five rooms, plus kitchen and bathroom(s), 6-1
cinquante fifty, 1-2
cinquième fifth, 6-1
citer to cite
citoyen *m.*, **citoyenne** *f.* citizen
citron *m.* lemon, 5-1
  citron pressé (hand-squeezed) lemonade, 5-1
civil/e civil
clair/e clear, light-colored
clarinette *f.* clarinet
classique *m.* classic
classique *adj.* classical (music)

clavier *m.* keyboard, 10-2
clavier sans fil wireless keyboard, 10-2
clé *f.* key, 9-1
clé USB USB key, flash drive, 10-2
climat *m.* climate
clinique *f.* private hospital, 2-1
clip *m.* **(vidéo)** (video) clip, 10-2
coca(-cola) *m.* coke, (coca cola), 5-1
cocher to check off
code *m.* code
code postal postal code, zip code
cœur *m.* heart, 7-1
avoir † mal au cœur to be nauseated, 7-1
se coiffer to fix one's hair, 3-1
coin *m.* corner
au coin de at the corner (of)
avec coin cuisine with a kitchenette, 6-2
colère *f.* anger, 7-3
(être †) en colère (to be) angry, 7-3
collant *m.* pantyhose, 3-3
collège *m.* middle school, 1-3
collier *m.* necklace
colline *f.* hill, 6-3
coloc(ataire) *m./f.* roommate, housemate, 2-1
colocation *f.* renting a house or an apartment together
Colombie *f.* Colombia, 9-2
colombien/ne Colombian, 9-2
colonie *f.* colony
colonne *f.* column
combattre † to combat, to fight
combattre † le stress to fight stress, 7-1
combien how much, 2-1
combien de how many, 2-1
combinaison *f.* combination
combiner to combine
comédie *f.* comedy, drama, 10-1
comédie musicale musical, 10-1
comique *m./f.* comedian
comique *adj.* comical, funny
comique *m.* comedy (genre)
commander to order
comme like, as, 2-1
Comme ci, comme ça. So-so., P-1
commencer † to begin, to start, 3-2
comment how, 2-1
Comment ça va ? How's it going?, P-1
Comment dit-on… ? How do you say . . .?, P-2
Comment tu t'appelles ? What is your name?, P-1
Comment vous appelez-vous ? What is your name?, P-1
commentaire *m.* comment
commerçant *m.*, **commerçante** *f.* merchant, 5-3
petits commerçants *m. pl.* small shop owners, merchants
commerce *m.* business, trade
commun/e common
communauté *f.* community
communément communally, in common
communication *f.* communication, 8-2
communiquer to communicate
compagnie *f.* company
comparaison *f.* comparison
comparatif/-ive comparative
comparer to compare, 3-2
compléter † to complete
compliment *m.* compliment
compliqué/e complicated
comportement *m.* behavior
composé/e composite
composition *f.* in-class essay exam, 8-2
compréhension *f.* comprehension
comprendre † to understand, 5-1
Je ne comprends pas. I don't understand., P-2
compris/e *adj.* included, 6-1
comptabilité *f.* accounting, 8-2
comptable *m./f.* accountant, 8-3
compte *m.* account
compter to count
comptine *f.* nursery rhyme
concentration *f.* concentration, emphasis, 8-2
concept *m.* concept
concerner to concern
concert *m.* concert, 2-2
concierge *m./f.* caretaker, manager
concis/e concise
concombre *m.* cucumber, 5-3
concours *m.* competitive entrance exam
concurrence *f.* competition
condamner to condemn
condiment *m.* condiment, 5-3
conditionnel *m.* conditional tense
conduire † to drive
confiserie *f.* candy store
confiture *f.* jam, 5-2
conflit *m.* conflict
conformiste conformist, 1-1
confort *m.* comfort
confortable comfortable (material objects), 6-2
congé *m.* leave
prendre † congé to take leave, say good-bye
congelé/e frozen
congélateur *m.* freezer
conjonction *f.* conjunction
conjugaison *f.* conjugation
conjugué/e conjugated
connaissance *f.* knowledge, understanding; acquaintance
connaître † to know, to be familiar with, 7-3
connecté/e connected
connecter to connect, 10-2
connexion *f.* **sans fil** wireless connection, 10-2
connu/e known
conquête *f.* conquest
consacrer to devote
conseil *m.* piece of advice
demander un conseil to ask for advice
conseiller to advise
conseiller *m.*, **conseillière** *f.* advisor
conséquence *f.* consequence
conservateur/-trice conservative
conserver to preserve, to keep, to retain
considérer to consider
consister de to consist of
consommateur *m.*, **consommatrice** *f.* consumer
consommation *f.* drink
consonne *f.* consonant
construire † to construct, to build
consultation *f.* visit with a health professional
consulter to consult
consulter le médecin to see a doctor, 7-1
contempler to contemplate
contenir † to contain
content/e happy, 7-3
contenu *m.* content; contents
continent *m.* continent, 9-2
continuer to go on/keep going, 9-3
continuer tout droit to keep going straight ahead, 9-3
continuer (à + *inf.*) to continue (to do *st.*)
contraire *m.* opposite
au contraire on the contrary
contraste *m.* contrast
contribuer to contribute
contrôle *m.* inspection, control, test
convaincre to convince
convaincu/e convinced
conventionnel/le *adj.* conventional, conformist
copain *m.*, **copine** *f.* friend, 1-3
copieux/-euse copious, hearty, 5-2
coq *m.* rooster
coq au vin coq au vin, stewed chicken with wine and mushrooms
Corée *f.* Korea, 9-2
coréen/ne Korean, 9-2
corps *m.* body, 7-1
correspondance *f.* correspondance
correspondant/e *m./f.* penpal
correspondre to correspond
corriger † to correct
costume *m.* man's suit, 3-3
côte *f.* coast
côté *m.* side
à côté de next to, 6-2
de l'autre côté on the other hand
Côte d'Ivoire *f.* Ivory Coast, 9-2
côtelette *f.* **(d'agneau)** (lamb) chop, 5-3
coton *m.* cotton, 3-3
côtoyer to rub elbows with
coucher *m.* **du soleil** sunset
se coucher to go to bed, 3-1
couleur *f.* color, 3-3
couloir *m.* hallway, 6-1
coup *m.* blow, strike, punch
couper to cut
couple *m.* couple
couplet *m.* verse of a poem
cour *f.* courtyard, 6-1
courant/e current, common, ordinary
au courant up-to-date (for a person)
courant *m.* **d'air** draft, breeze
courir † to run, 3-2
couronne *f.* crown
courriel *m.* e-mail message (*Can.*)
courrier électronique *m.* e-mail
cours *m.* course, class, 3-2
au cours de during the course of

course *f.* errand, 2-2
faire † des courses to run errands, 2-2; to go shopping for occasional items
faire † les courses to do the weekly/usual grocery/food shopping, 5-3
court/e short, 3-3
couscous *m.* couscous
couscoussier *m.* couscous steamer
cousin *m.*, **cousine** *f.* cousin, 1-1
coussin *m.* cushion
coussinet *m.* small cushion
coûter to cost, 6-2
coutume *f.* custom
couture *f.* sewing, dressmaking
haute couture designer fashion
couturier *m.* fashion designer
couturière *f.* dressmaker, seamstress
couvert/e covered, overcast
Le ciel est couvert. The sky is overcast., 4-1
couvrir † to cover
craie *f.* stick of chalk, P-2
cravate *f.* tie, 3-3
crayon *m.* pencil, P-2
créer to create
crème *f.* cream, 5-1
crème solaire suntan lotion, sunscreen
crèmerie *f.* dairy store, 5-3
crêpe *f.* crêpe, pancake
Crétin ! Moron!, 7-3
crevette *f.* shrimp, 5-3
crier to yell, 7-3
crime *m.* crime
crise *f.* crisis
cristal *m.* crystal
critère *m.* criterion
critique *f.* critique, criticism, 10-3
critique *m.* critic (person), 10-3
croire † (à, en) to believe (in), 10-1
Je crois/Je crois que oui. I think so., 10-1
Je crois que... I believe that . . ., 10-1
Je ne crois pas/Je crois que non. I don't think so., 10-1
croissant *m.* croissant, 5-2
croque-monsieur *m.* grilled ham-and-cheese sandwich, 5-1
croustillant/e crusty
crudités *f. pl.* cut-up raw vegetables, 5-1
cuiller, cuillère *f.* spoon, 5-1
cuillerée *f.* spoonful
cuir *m.* leather, 3-3
cuisine *f.* kitchen, 6-1
avec coin cuisine with a kitchenette, 6-2
faire † la cuisine to cook, 2-2
livre *m.* **de cuisine** cookbook, 10-3
cuisinière *f.* stove, 6-2
culturel/le cultural

D

d'accord agreed, OK, all right
être d'accord to agree
Je suis d'accord... I agree . . .
Je ne suis pas d'accord... I disagree . . .
dame *f.* lady, P-2
danger *m.* danger
dans in, into, inside, P-2
danse *f.* dance, 2-2
faire † de la danse to dance, to study dance, 2-2
danser to dance
d'après according to
date *f.* date, 1-2
Quelle est la date ? What is the date?, 1-2
davantage more
de (d') from, of, about, P-1
debout standing, on one's feet
être debout to be up, 3-1
début *m.* beginning
décédé/e deceased, 1-1
décembre December, 1-2
déception *f.* disappointment
décider (de + *inf.*) to decide
se décider to make up one's mind
déclaration *f.* declaration
décontracté/e relaxed
décorer to decorate
découverte *f.* discovery
découvrir † to discover
décrire † to describe, 8-2
déçu/e disappointed
être déçu/e (que) to be disappointed (that) 10-1
déduire † to deduce
défaire † to undo
défaite *f.* defeat, loss
défilé *m.* parade, 7-2
définir to define
degré *m.* degree
Il fait vingt degrés. It's 20 degrees (Celsius)., 4-1
dehors outside
en dehors de outside of
déjà already, 3-1
déjeuner *m.* lunch, 5-2
déjeuner to have breakfast/lunch, 1-3
délicieux/-euse delicious, 5-3
demain tomorrow, 2-3
à demain see you tomorrow, P-1
demander to ask, request, 6-2
démarrer to begin, to start
demi/e half
demi-frère *m.* half-brother, stepbrother, 1-1
demi-kilo *m.* half-kilo, 5-3
demi-sœur *f.* half-sister, stepsister, 1-1
faire † demi-tour to make a U-turn
(trois heures) et demi/e (three) thirty (3:30), 3-2
démodé/e old-fashioned, out-of-date, 3-3
démonstratif/-ive demonstrative
dent *f.* tooth, 3-1
se brosser les dents to brush one's teeth, 3-1
se laver les dents to brush one's teeth, 3-1
dentifrice *m.* toothpaste, 3-1
dentiste *m./f.* dentist, 8-3
départ *m.* departure
département *m.* department, regional administrative unit in France
dépasser to exceed
se dépêcher to hurry, 3-1
dépense *f.* expenditure
dépendant/e *adj.* dependent, 10-3
dépendre (de) to depend (upon)
ça dépend it depends
dépenser to spend
depuis since, when, 10-3
depuis combien de temps... ? for how long . . .?, 10-3
depuis quand... ? since when . . .?, 10-3
dernier/-ière last, 3-3
derrière behind, 8-1
des *pl.* some, P-2
des (de + les) from/of (the)
dès que as soon as
désagréable disagreeable, 1-1
désastre *m.* disaster
descendant (de) *m.* descendant (of)
descendre to go down, 4-1
descente *f.* descent
désert *m.* desert
se déshabiller to undress, 3-1
désignation *f.* name, designation
désigner to indicate, to show, to point out
désir *m.* want, wish, desire
désirer to desire, to want, 9-3
désobéir à to disobey, 5-2
désolé/e sorry, 4-3
être désolé/e (que) to be sorry (that) 10-1
Je suis désolé/e I am sorry 4-3
dessert *m.* dessert, 5-2
desservir to serve, to stop at
dessin *m.* drawing, 8-2
dessin animé cartoon, 10-1
dessiner to draw
destination *f.* destination, 4-2
détail *m.* detail
se détendre to relax, 6-3
détente *f.* relaxation; release (of a consonant)
déterminer to determine
détester to detest, 8-2
deux two, 1-2
deux fois par jour twice a day, 3-1
deuxième *m.* second, 6-1
devant in front of, 8-1
développement *m.* development
développer to develop
devenir † to become, 4-2
deviner to guess
devoir *m.* essay, assignment, 8-2
devoir † must, to have to, should, 7-3; to owe
devoirs *m. pl.* homework, P-2
faire † des devoirs to do homework
d'habitude usually, 6-3
dialecte *m.* dialect
dialogue *m.* dialogue
dictionnaire *m.* **(un dico)** dictionary, 8-2
différemment *adv.* differently
différent/e different
différer to differ
difficile difficult, 8-2
diffusion *f.* distribution, broadcasting, circulation
dimanche Sunday, 1-3

diminuer to shorten, to reduce
dîner *m.* dinner, 5-2
dîner to have dinner, 1-3
diplomate *m./f.* diplomat
diplôme *m.* degree, 8-2
  avoir † un diplôme to have a degree
  préparer un diplôme en... to do a degree in . . ., 8-2
dire † to say, to tell, 8-2
  Dites-moi ! Tell me!, 2-3
direct/e direct, straight
  en direct live
discipliné/e disciplined, 1-1
discuter (de) to have a discussion, to talk about
disjoint/e disjointed, stressed (pronouns)
disparaître to disappear
disparition *f.* disappearance
disponible available
disposition *f.* arrangement, layout
se disputer to argue, 7-3
disque *m.* **dur** hard drive, 10-2
  disque dur externe external hard drive, 10-2
distinct/e *adj.* distinct, different
distraction *f.* source of entertainement, diversion, 4-3
se distraire † to amuse oneself, 10-3
divers/e various
diversité *f.* diversity
divertissement *m.* variety show, 10-1
divisé/e divided, split
divorcé/e divorced, 1-1
divorcer † to divorce, 7-3
dix ten, 1-2
dix-huit eighteen, 1-2
dix-huitième eighteenth, 6-1
dixième tenth, 6-1
dix-neuf nineteen, 1-2
dix-neuvième nineteenth, 6-1
dix-sept seventeen, 1-2
dix-septième seventeenth, 6-1
doctorat *m.* doctorate, Ph.D.
documentaire *m.* documentary, 10-1
dodo *m.* (*colloq.*) sleep, 3-1
  faire † dodo (*colloq.*) to go to sleep, 3-1
doigt *m.* finger
domaine *m.* area, field
domestique *m./f.* servant
dommage *m.* harm, injury
  C'est dommage. It's too bad. It's a pity., 4-3
  Il est/C'est dommage que It's too bad that; it's a shame that, 10-1
donc then, therefore, 2-1
donner to give, P-2
  donner sur to look out onto, to lead out to, 6-1
dormir to sleep, 3-2
dos *m.* back, 7-1
dossier *m.* file, case, folder
double *adj.* double
doublé/e dubbed, 10-1
doubler to dub, 10-1
doucement gently, softly
douche *f.* shower, 3-1
  prendre † une douche to take a shower, 3-1
se doucher to shower, 3-1
doué/e talented, 8-3
douleur *f.* pain
doute *m.* doubt
  sans aucun doute without a doubt
  sans doute probably
douter que to doubt that
doux/douce gentle
douzaine *f.* dozen, 5-3
douze twelve, 1-2
douzième twelfth, 6-1
dramatique dramatic
drame psychologique *m.* psychological drama, 10-1
dresser (une liste) to make (a list)
drogue *f. sg.* (illegal) drugs
se droguer to take (illegal) drugs, to be on drugs
droit *m.* law, 8-2; straight, 9-3; right
  avoir † le droit to have the right
  droits de l'homme human rights
  droits linguistiques linguistic rights
  tout droit straight ahead, 9-3
droite *f.* right, 8-1
  à droite (de) to the right (of), 8-1
  tourner à droite turn right, 9-3
drôle amusing, funny, strange, 2-1
du (de + le) from, of (the) 2-2
dur/e hard
durée *f.* length, duration
durer to endure, last
DVD *m. inv.* DVD, P-2
dynamique dynamic, 1-1

E

eau *f.* water, 5-1
  eau de Cologne cologne
  eau minérale mineral water, 5-1
échange *m.* exchange
échanger † to exchange, 10-2
échapper to escape
écharpe *f.* scarf, 3-3
échecs *m. pl.* chess, 2-2
échelle *f.* ladder
éclair *m.* lightning, 4-1
  Il y a des éclairs. It's lightning., 4-1
école *f.* school, 1-3
  école maternelle preschool
  école primaire elementary school
  école secondaire secondary school
écologie *f.* ecology, 8-2
écologique ecological
économie *f.* economics, 8-2
  faire † des économies to save money, 3-3
économique economical
  sciences *f. pl.* **économiques** economics, 8-2
économiser to save
écouter to listen (to), P-2
  Écoutez bien ! Listen carefully!, P-2
  écouter de la musique to listen to music, 1-3
écran *m.* screen, 10-1
  écran plat flat screen, 10-3
écrire † to write, 8-2
  Écrivez votre nom ! Write (down) your name!, P-2
écrivain *m.* writer, 8-3
écureuil *m.* squirrel
éducatif/-ive educational
éducation *f.* education, 8-2; upbringing
  sciences *f. pl.* **de l'éducation**, education 8-2
effacer † to erase, P-2
effectuer to carry out, to perform
effet *m.* effect
  en effet yes, indeed, 6-3
efficace efficient, effective
effort *m.* effort
égal/e equal
également *adv.* also, too, as well
église *f.* Catholic church, 2-3
égoïste selfish, 2-1
élaborer to elaborate
électricité *f.* electricity
électrique electric
électronique electronic
élégance *f.* elegance
élégant/e elegant, 2-1
élément *m.* element
éliminer to eliminate
elle *f.* she, her, it, P-1
  elle-même *f.* herself
elles *f. pl.* they, them, P-1
  elles-mêmes *f. pl.* themselves
e-mail *m.* e-mail (as a medium)
embarras *m.* trouble
embarrassé/e embarrassed, 7-3
s'embrasser to kiss, 7-3
émission *f.* program, 10-1
  émission de musique music program, 10-1
  émission de téléachat infomercial, 10-1
  émission de téléréalité reality show, 10-1
  émission sportive sports event on television, 10-1
emmener † to bring someone along
émotion *f.* emotion
empêcher to prevent
emplacement *m.* location, site
emploi *m.* use; job
employer † to use
emporter to bring *st.*, to take *st.* with
emprunter to borrow, 6-2
en *prep.* to, at, P-1; *pron.* some, any, 5-3
enchaînement *m.* linking
enchanté/e delighted (to meet you), P-1
encore still, yet, again, another, 3-2
  encore un quart d'heure another fifteen minutes, 3-2
encyclopédie *f.* encyclopedia, 10-3
s'endormir to fall asleep, 3-1
endroit *m.* place, 6-3
énergique energetic, 2-1

énervé/e irritable
s'énerver to become irritated/ worked up
enfance *f.* childhood
enfant *m./f.* child, 1-1
enfin finally, 4-2
s'ennuyer † to become bored, 7-3
ennuyeux/-euse boring, tedious, 8-2
enquête *f.* poll
enseignant/e *m./f.* teacher, instructor
enseignement *m.* teaching
enseigner to teach
ensemble together, 1-3
  On y va ensemble ? Shall we go (there) together?, 4-3
ensemble *m.* outfit, 3-3
ensuite next, then, 4-2
entendre to hear, 4-1
  s'entendre (avec) to get along (with), 7-3
  entendre parler de to hear about
enthousiaste enthusiastic
entourer to surround; to circle
entraîneur *m.* trainer, coach
entre between, 3-2
entrée *f.* appetizer or starter, 5-2; entrance, foyer, 6-1
entreprise *f.* firm, place of business
entrer to go/come in, 4-2
entretien *m.* interview
énumérer to enumerate, to list
envers : à l'envers upside down, inside out, backward
envie *f.* desire
  avoir † envie de (+ *n.*, + *inf.*) to want/to desire (*st.*, to do *st.*), 3-3
environ about, approximately
environnement *m.* environment
environs *m. pl.* surroundings
envoyer † to send, 10-2
épais/se *adj.* thick
épaissir to thicken
éparpillé/e scattered, dispersed, spread out
épeler † to spell, 4-3
épice *f.* spice, 5-2
épicerie *f.* grocer's shop, 5-3
épinards *m. pl.* spinach, 5-3
épisode *m.* episode, 10-1
époque *f.* era, time
époux *m.*, **épouse** *f.* spouse
épreuve *f.* test
éprouver to feel, to experience
équilibré/e balanced, 7-1
équipe *f.* team
équipé/e equipped, 6-2
équivalent *m.* equivalent
érable *m.* maple
erreur *f.* mistake, error
escalier *m.* staircase, stairs, 6-1
espace *m.* place, space
Espagne *f.* Spain, 9-2
espagnol *m.* Spanish (language), 8-2
espagnol/e *adj.* Spanish, 9-2
espèces : en espèces in cash
espérer † to hope
espion *m.* spy
espionnage *m.* spying, 10-1
  film *m.* **d'espionnage** spy film, 10-1
essai *m.* essay, 8-2
essayer † (de + ***inf.*****)** to try (to do *st.*), 7-1
essuyer † to dry
  s'essuyer † to dry oneself off, wipe off, 3-1
est *m.* east
estomac *m.* stomach, 7-1
et *conj.* and, P-1
établir to establish
établissement *m.* establishment
étage *m.* floor, 6-1
  premier étage second floor
étagère *f.* bookcase, (book)shelf, 6-2
étape *f.* stage, step (in a process)
état *m.* state
état civil marital status, 1-1
États-Unis *m. pl.* the United States, 9-2
été *m.* summer, 2-3
  l'été prochain next summer, 2-3
étoile *f.* star, 9-3
étonnant/e surprising
  Il est/C'est étonnant que It's surprising (that), 10-1
étonné/e surprised
  être étonné/e (que) to be surprised (that), 10-1
étranger/-ère foreign, 8-2
être † to be, P-1
  être † d'accord to agree
  être † en train de (+ *inf.*) to be busy (doing st.), 3-1
  Ne sois/soyez pas... Don't be . . .,7-3
  Soyez/Sois calme ! Be calm!, 7-3
être *m.* **humain** human being
étude *f.* study, 8-2
  faire † des études to study
étudiant *m.*, **étudiante** *f.* student, P-2
étudier to study
Europe *f.* Europe, 9-2
européen/ne European
eux *m. pl.* they, them, P-1
  eux-mêmes *m. pl.* themselves
évènement *m.* event, 7-2
éventuel/le probable
éventuellement probably, perhaps
évident/e obvious
évier *m.* kitchen sink, 6-2
éviter to avoid, 7-1
évoluer to develop, to change
exact/e exact
exactement exactly
exagérer † to exaggerate
examen *m.* exam, 8-2
  passer un examen to take an exam, 8-2
  préparer un examen to study for an exam
  réussir un examen to pass an exam, 8-2
examiner to examine, to study
excentrique *adj.* eccentric, bizarre
excès *m.* excess
exercice *m.* exercise
  faire † de l'exercice to exercise, 7-1
exiger † to require, to demand, 9-3
exister to exist
exotique exotic
expérience *f.* experience; experiment
expliquer to explain, 6-2
exposé *m.* oral presentation, talk, 8-2
exposer to show, to exhibit, to display
exposition *f.* exhibition, 2-3
expression *f.* expression
exprimer to express
s'exprimer to express oneself
extérieur/e outside, outer
externe external
extrait *m.* exerpt, extract
extrême extreme
extrêmement extremely

F

fabriquer to make, to produce
fac *f. see* **faculté**
face *f.* face, head, side
  en face (de) facing, across (from), 8-1
fâché/e angry, upset, 7-3
se fâcher (contre) to get angry (at, with), 7-3
facile easy, 8-2
facilement easily
faciliter to facilitate, to make easier
façon *f.* way
  de toute façon in any case
facteur *m.*, **factrice** *f.* mail carrier, 8-3
facture *f.* bill
facultatif/-ive optional, elective, 8-2
faculté *f.* college, university, 2-1; school within a college/university, 8-2
faible weak
faim *f.* hunger, 5-1
  avoir † faim to be hungry, 5-1
faire † to do, to make, 2-2
  Ça (ne) fait rien. That doesn't matter.
  deux et deux font quatre 2 + 2 = (equals) 4
  faire † partie de to belong to
  Il fait beau. It's beautiful weather., 4-1
  Ne t'en fais pas /Ne vous en faites pas ! Don't worry!, 7-3
  se faire † du souci to worry, 7-3
faire-part *m. inv.* (birth, wedding) announcement
falloir † to be necessary, to need 7-1
  il faut it's necessary, 3-3; one/you need + *n.*, *inf.*, 5-3
  Il faut... /Il ne faut pas... One must . . . /One must not . . ., 7-1
  Il faut quatre œufs. We need four eggs., 5-3
  Il faut que... It is necessary that/You must . . ., 9-2
  Il ne faut pas que... You must not . . ., 9-2
fameux/-euse famous
familial/e familial, related to family
familier/-ière familiar
famille *f.* family, 1-1
  famille étendue extended family
  famille nombreuse big family, 1-1
  famille recomposée blended family
fanatique *m.* fan, fanatic
fantaisiste fantastic (not based in reality)

fantastique fantastic (great, wonderful); fantasy
fantôme *m.* phantom, ghost
farine *f.* flour
fariné/e floured
fasciné/e fascinated
fatigué/e tired, P-1
faut *see* **falloir**
faute *f.* mistake
  faire † une faute to make a mistake
fauteuil *m.* armchair, 6-2
  basket-fauteuil *m.* wheelchair basketball, 7-1
  fauteuil roulant wheelchair, 7-1
faux/fausse false
favoriser to favor
Félicitations ! Congratulations!, 7-2
féminin/e feminine
féminisation *f.* to make feminine (e.g., names of professions)
femme *f.* wife, woman, 1-1
  femme au foyer housewife
  femme d'affaires businesswoman, 8-3
fenêtre *f.* window, P-2
férié : jour *m.* **férié** legal holiday, 7-2
ferme *f.* farm, 6-3
fermer to close, P-2
festival *m.* festival
fête *f.* party, 2-2; holiday, 7-2
  fête religieuse religious holiday, 7-2
fêter to celebrate, 7-2
feu *m.* fire
  feu d'artifice fireworks, 7-2
  feu rouge stoplight
feuille *f.* sheet of paper; leaf
feuilleton *m.* soap opera, 10-1
feutre *m.* felt-tipped marker, pen, P-2
fève *f.* broad bean; token hidden in a king cake, 7-2
février February, 1-2
fiançailles *f. pl.* engagement
fiancé/e engaged, 1-1
se fiancer † to get engaged, 7-3
fichier *m.* computer file, 10-2
fidèle faithful
fièvre *f.* fever
  avoir † de la fièvre to have a temperature, to run a fever
figure *f.* face, 3-1
  figure géométrique geometric figure
fil *m.* wire; thread; string
  sans fil wireless, 10-2
fille *f.* daughter, girl, 1-1
film *m.* film, 1-3
fils *m.* son, 1-1
fin *f.* end
  fin de semaine week-end (*Can.*), 8-1
fin/e thin, elegant, delicate, 3-3
final/e final, 8-2
finalement finally
finir to finish, 5-2
flamand *m.* Flemish (language)
flegmatique *adj.* phlegmatic, of an unemotional and stolidly calm disposition
fleur *f.* flower, 7-2
fleuri/e flourished, thrived
fleuve *m.* river
flûte *f.* flute
  flûte à bec recorder
  flûte traversière flute
foie *m.* liver
fois *f.* time, 3-1
  deux fois par jour twice a day, 3-1
  x fois par semaine x times a week
  une fois once, one time, 3-1
folklorique folkloric, folk
foncé/e dark colored
fonction *m.* function
fonctionnaire *m./f.* government worker, 8-3
fonctionner to function
fond *m.* bottom, end
  à fond deeply; loudly
fondre to melt
fondu/e melted
fondue *f.* fondue
  fondue bourguignonne meat fondue
  fondue savoyarde cheese fondue
fontaine *f.* fountain
foot(ball) *m.* soccer, 1-3
  football américain *m.* (American) football, 2-2
  jouer au foot 1-3
foraine : fête foraine *f.* fair
forcément inevitably, necessarily
forêt *f.* forest, 6-3
formation *f.* formation; training
  avoir † une formation to have training
forme *f.* shape, form
  être † en forme to be fine, P-1
  être † en pleine forme to be in good shape
  rester en forme to stay in shape, 7-1
former to form
formidable great, 6-3
fort *adv.* loudly, 7-3
fort/e *adj.* strong, stout, 2-1
  château *m.* **fort** fortress, 9-3
forum *m.* forum
  forum de discussion discussion forum, newsgroup
foulard *m.* silk scarf, 3-3
foule *f.* crowd
four *m.* oven, 6-2
  four à micro-ondes microwave oven
fourchette *f.* fork
frais/fraîche fresh, 5-3
  Il fait frais. It's cool (weather)., 4-1
fraise *f.* strawberry, 5-3
français *m.* French (language), 2-2
  en français in French, P-2
  faire † du français to study French, 2-2
français/e *adj.* French, 9-2
France *f.* France, 9-2
francophone French-speaking
francophonie *f.* French-speaking world
fréquence *f.* frequency
fréquent/e frequent
fréquenter to frequent, to patronize
frère *m.* brother, 1-1
frigo *m.* (*colloq.*) fridge, 6-2
frite *f.* French fry, 5-1
froid *m.* (*température*) cold 4-1
  Il fait froid. It's cold (weather)., 4-1
  J'ai froid. I'm cold., 4-1
fromage *m.* cheese, 5-2
frontière *f.* border, 9-2
fruit *m.* fruit, 5-2
  fruits *m. pl.* **de mer** seafood
fruitier/fruitière *adj.* fruit, 6-3
fumé/e *adj.* smoked
fumée *f.* smoke
fumer to smoke, 7-1
fumet *m.* aroma
furieux/-euse furious, 7-3
futur *m.* future tense
  futur proche immediate future

G

gadget *m.* gadget
gagner to win
  gagner de l'argent to earn money, 8-3
galérie *f.* (art) gallery
galette *f.* cake for Epiphany, 7-2; savory dinner crepe made with buckwheat flour
gant *m.* glove, 3-3
  gant de toilette wash mitt, 3-1
garage *m.* garage, 6-1
garantir to guarantee
garçon *m.* boy, 1-1
gare *f.* train station, 2-3
garer to park, 6-1
garni/e : plat *m.* **garni** main dish served with vegetables
garnir to line, to fill; to garnish
gâteau *m.* cake, 5-3
gauche *f.* left, 8-1
  à gauche (de) to the left (of), 8-1
  tourner à gauche to turn left, 9-3
gazeux/-euse carbonated
geler † to freeze, 4-1
  Il gèle. It's freezing (weather)., 4-1
gêné/e bothered, embarrassed, 7-3
gêner to bother, to inconvenience; to embarrass
général/e general
généralement generally
généreux/-euse generous, warm-hearted, 2-1
générique *m.* screen credits
génial : C'est génial. It's great/ awesome., 10-2
génie *m.* engineering, 8-2
genou *m.* (*pl.* **genoux**) knee
genre *m.* (grammatical) gender; kind, type
gens *m. pl.* people, 8-3
gentil/le kind, nice, 2-1
  C'est gentil (à toi/vous). That's kind (of you)., 4-3
géographie *f.* geography
géologie *f.* geology
gestion *f.* management, 8-2
gilet *m.* cardigan sweater, 3-3
gîte *m.* **(rural)** (rural) bed and breakfast, 9-3
glace *f.* ice cream, 5-1
  glace au chocolat chocolate ice cream, 5-1
glaçon *m.* ice cube, 5-1
golf *m.* golf, 1-3
gomme *f.* eraser, P-2
gorge *f.* throat, 7-1
  avoir † mal à la gorge to have a sore throat

goût *m.* taste, liking
goûter *m.* afternoon snack, 5-2
goûter to have a snack, to taste
goutte *f.* drop
gouvernement *m.* government
grâce à thanks to
graisse *f.* fat, grease, 7-1
graissé/e greased
gramme *m.* (*abbr.* gr.) gram
grand-chose *m. inv.* : **pas grand-chose** not very much, not a great deal, 2-2
  ne pas faire † grand-chose to not do much, 2-2
grand/e tall, 2-1
grande surface *f.* superstore, 5-3
grandeur *f.* size
grandir to grow taller, to grow up (for children), 5-2
grand magasin *m.* department store, 3-3
grand-mère *f.* grandmother, 1-1
grand-parent *m.*, (**grands-parents** *pl.*) grandparent, 1-1
grand-père *m.* grandfather, 1-1
gratuit/e free
gratuitement *adv.* for free
grave serious, 7-3
  Ce n'est pas grave. It's not serious., 7-3
graveur *m.* **CD/DVD** CD/DVD burner, 10-2
gravité *f.* gravity, seriousness
grignoter to snack, 7-1
grillé/e grilled, toasted, 5-2
grimper to climb up
grippe *f.* flu
gris/e gray, 3-3
gros/se fat, 2-1
grossir to gain weight, 5-2
grotte *f.* **(préhistorique)** (prehistoric) cave, 9-3
groupe *m.* group
  groupe de consonnes consonant cluster
guerre *f.* war
  Première Guerre mondiale First World War
  Seconde Guerre mondiale Second World War
guide *m.* guide (person or book), 9-3
guidé/e guided
guider to guide
guitare *f.* guitar, 1-3
  guitare basse bass guitar
  guitare électrique electric guitar
gymnase *m.* gym, 2-3
gymnastique *f.* exercises, gymastics
  faire † de la gym to work out, 2-2

H

s'habiller to get dressed, 3-1
habitant *m.* inhabitant
habitation *f.* dwelling, housing
habiter to live (+ location), 1-1
d'habitude usually, 6-3
habituel/le habitual
s'habituer à to get used to
***haché/e** chopped, ground, 5-3
Haïti *m.* Haiti, 9-2
***hamburger** *m.* hamburger, 5-1
***handicap** *m.* handicap, disability, 7-1
***handicapé/e** handicapped, 7-1
  être † *handicapé/e to be handicapped, disabled, 7-1
***haricot** *m.* bean
  ***haricot vert** *m.* green bean, 5-2
harmonica *m.* harmonica, 2-2
harmonie *f.* harmony
***haut/e** high
hebdomadaire *m.* weekly publication, 10-3
hebdomadaire *adj.* weekly, 10-3
***hein !** huh? understood? right?
heure *f.* hour, 3-2
  être † à l'heure to be on time, 3-2
  Il est une heure. It's one o'clock., 3-2
  Quelle heure est-il ? What time is it?
  Vous avez l'heure ? What time is it?, 3-2
heureusement luckily
heureux/-euse happy, 7-3
***heurter** to strike
hexagone *m.* hexagon
hier yesterday, 4-1
histoire *f.* history, 8-2; story
  histoire drôle joke, 2-1
  livre *m.* **d'histoire** history book, 10-3
historique historical, 9-3
  film *m.* **historique** historical film, 10-1
hiver *m.* winter, 4-1
***hockey** *m.* hockey, 2-2
***hollandais/e** Dutch; hollandaise (sauce)
***Hollande** *f.* Holland
***homard** *m.* lobster
homme *m.* man, 1-1
  homme d'affaires businessman, 8-3
honneur *m.* honor
honorer to honor
hôpital *m.* public hospital, 8-3
horloge *f.* clock, 3-2
horreur *f.* horror, 10-1
  film *m.* **d'horreur** horror movie, 10-1
  Quelle horreur ! How awful!, 5-1
***hors** except; outside
***hors d'œuvre** *m. inv.* hors d'oeuvre, appetizer
hôte *m.* guest or host
hôtel *m.* hotel, 2-3
  hôtel une étoile one-star hotel, 9-3
huile *f.* oil, 5-3
  huile d'olive olive oil
***huit** eight, 1-2
huitante eighty (*reg.*)
***huitième** eighth, 6-1
huître *f.* oyster
humain/e human, 7-1
hypermarché *m.* superstore, 5-3

I

ici here, 8-1
idéal/e ideal
idéaliste idealistic, 1-1
idée *f.* idea
identifier to identify
identité *f.* identity
idiomatique idiomatic
il *m.* he, it, P-1
île *f.* island
illustrer to illustrate
ils *m. pl.* they, P-1
il y a there is/are, P-2; ago, 4-1
  il y a deux jours two days ago, 4-1
  il n'y a pas de... there isn't/aren't . . ., P-2
  Il n'y a pas de quoi. You're welcome., P-2
  il y a... que it's been . . ., for . . ., 10-3
illogique illogical
illustre illustrious, famous
imaginaire imaginary
imaginer to imagine
imbécile *m./f.* idiot
immense huge, immense
immeuble *m.* building, 6-1
immigré/e immigrant
immobilier *m.* real estate
immunodéficitaire immunodeficient
imparfait *m.* imperfect tense
impatience *f.* impatience
impératif *m.* imperative
imper(méable) *m.* raincoat, 3-3
impersonnel/le impersonal, cold
importance *f.* importance
important/e important, 9-2; significant, large
  Il est important de/que It is important (that), 9-2
impression *f.* impression
impressionné/e impressed
impressionnisme *m.* Impressionism
impressionniste Impressionist
imprimante *f.* printer, 10-2
  imprimante multifonction multifunction printer, 10-2
imprimer to print, 10-2
inclure to include
inclus/e included
inconvénient *m.* disadvantage, drawback, inconvenience
incorporer to add (in a recipe)
Inde *f.* India, 9-2
indéfini/e indefinite
indication *f.* sign, indication
  indications *f.pl.* directions
indien/ne Indian, 9-2
indifférence *f.* indifference
indigestion *f.* indigestion
indiquer to indicate, 9-3
indiscipliné/e undisciplined, 1-1
indiscret/-ète indiscreet
indispensable necessary
individualiste individualistic, 1-1
individu *m.* individual
individuel/le individual
infection *f.* infection
infinitif *m.* infinitive
infirmerie *f.* health center/clinic, 8-1
infirmier *m.*, **infirmière** *f.* nurse, 8-3
informaticien *m.*, **informaticienne** *f.* computer scientist, 8-3
information *f.* information
informations *f. pl.* **(les infos)** news, 10-1
informatique *f.* computer science, 8-2
s'informer to get information, 10-3
ingénieur *m.* engineer, 8-3
ingrédient *m.* ingredient
innovateur/-trice innovative

innovation *f.* innovation
inquiet/-ète worried, uneasy, anxious, 7-3
s'inquiéter † to worry, 7-3
inscription *f.* registration, enrollment
  bureau *m.* **des inscriptions** registrar's office, 8-1
insensible insensitive
instable unstable
installer to put in, to install
instant *m.* moment, instant
s'instruire † to educate oneself, to improve one's mind, 10-3
instrument *m.* instrument
insulter to insult
insupportable unbearable
intégrer † to incorporate, to integrate
intelligent/e intelligent, smart, 2-1
intensité *f.* intensity
interactif/-ive interactive
interdiction *f.* ban
interdire † to ban, to forbid
interdit/e *adj.* forbidden
intéressant/e interesting, 8-2
s'intéresser (à) to be interested (in), 7-3
intérieur *m.* inside, interior
interlocuteur *m.*, **interlocutrice** *f.* conversational partner, interlocutor
international/e international
internaute *m./f.* Internet user, 10-2
Internet *m.* Internet, 9-3
  surfer sur Internet to surf the Internet, 10-2
interpréter † to interpret
interrogatif/-ive interrogative
interrogation *f.* quiz
interview *f.* interview
interviewer to interview
intime intimate
s'intituler to be titled
intonation *f.* intonation
intrigue *f.* plot, scheme
invariable invariable
invitation *f.* invitation, 4-3
invité *m.*, **invitée** *f.* guest
inviter to invite, 1-3
Irak *m.* Iraq, 9-2
Iran *m.* Iran, 9-2
irrégularité *f.* irregularity
irrégulier/-ière irregular
Islam *m.* Islam
Italie *f.* Italy, 9-2
italien *m.* Italian (language)
italien/ne *adj.* Italian, 9-2
item *m.* item
itinéraire *m.* itinerary, route
ivoirien/ne Ivorian, 9-2

J

jalousie *f.* jealousy
jaloux/-ouse jealous, 7-3
jamais ever
  ne… jamais never, 3-1
jambe *f.* leg, 7-1
jambon *m.* ham, 5-1
janvier January, 1-2
Japon *m.* Japan, 9-2
japonais *m.* Japanese (language)
japonais/e *adj.* Japanese, 9-2
jardin *m.* garden, yard, 1-3
jardinage *m.* gardening, 2-2
  faire † du jardinage to garden, to do some gardening, 2-2
jaser to chatter, prattle (*Can.*)
jaune yellow, 3-3
jazz *m.* jazz, 2-2
je (j') I, P-1
jean *m. sg.* jeans, 3-3
jet *m.* spurt, spray; jet
jeter † to throw/throw out, 4-3
jeu *m.* game, 2-2
  jeu de société board game, 2-2
  jeu électronique video game
  jeu télévisé game show, 10-1
jeudi Thursday, 1-3
jeune *m./f.* young person
jeune *adj.* young, 2-1
jeûne *m.* fast
jeûner to fast
jeunesse *f.* youth, young people
job *m.* **(d'été)** (summer) job
jogging *m.* jogging, 2-2
  faire † du jogging to go jogging, to jog, 2-22
joie *f.* joy
joli/e pretty, 2-1
jouer to play, 1-3
  jouer à to play (a sport), 1-3
  jouer de to play (an instrument), 1-3
  jouer une pièce to perform a play
jour *m.* day, 1-3
  ce jour-là that day, 4-1
  jour férié legal holiday, 7-2
journal *m.* newspaper, 10-3
  journal télévisé (le JT) news broadcast, 10-1
journalisme *m.* journalism, 8-2
journaliste *m./f.* journalist, 8-3
journée *f.* day, 3-1
Joyeux Noël ! Merry Christmas!, 7-2
juger † to judge
juif *m.*, **juive** *f.* Jewish
juillet July, 1-2
juin June, 1-2
jumeau *m.*, **jumelle** *f.* twin
jumelé/e twinned
  ville *f.* **jumelée** sister city
jupe *f.* skirt, 3-3
jus *m.* juice, 5-1
  jus d'orange orange juice, 5-1
jusqu'à until, 3-2
juteux/-euse juicy

K

kayak *m.* kayak
kilo *m.* kilo, 5-3
kiosque *m.* newsstand, 10-3

L

la (l') *f.* the, P-1; *pron.* her, it, 6-1
là there, 6-3
là-bas there, over there, 6-3
labo(ratoire) *m.* laboratory, 8-1
  labo(ratoire) de chimie chemistry lab, 8-1
lac *m.* lake, 4-2
laid/e ugly
laine *f.* wool, 3-3
laïque secular
laisser to leave (alone)
  laisser refroidir to let cool
lait *m.* milk, 5-2
lampe *f.* lamp, 6-2
lancer † to throw
  lancer un pari to make a wager
langage *m.* language
langagier/-ière linguistic, of language
langue *f.* tongue, 7-1; language, 8-2
  langue étrangère foreign language, 8-2
  langue maternelle native language, mother tongue, 9-2
laquelle *f.* which one
large big, large, loose-fitting, roomy, 3-3
lavabo *m.* bathroom sink, 3-1
laver to wash
se laver to wash oneself, 3-1
  se laver la figure to wash one's face, 3-1
  se laver les cheveux to wash one's hair, 3-1
  se laver les dents to brush one's teeth
  se laver les mains to wash one's hands, 3-1
le (l') *m.* the, P-1; *pron.* him, it, 6-1
leader *m.* leader
leçon *f.* lesson, 1-3
  leçon de chant singing lesson, 1-3
lecteur *m.*, **lectrice** *f.* reader
lecteur CD *m.* CD player, P-2
lecteur DVD *m.* DVD player, P-2
lecteur ebook *m.* e-book reader/device, 10-3
lecture *f.* reading
légende *f.* caption; legend; key
leger/-ère lightweight
légume *m.* vegetable, 5-2
lequel *m.* which one
les *pl.* the, P-2; *pron.* them, 6-1
lesquels *m. pl.*, **lesquelles** *f. pl.* which ones
lettre *f.* letter
lettres *f. pl.* humanities, 8-2
leur their, 1-2; *pron.* to them, 6-2
leurs *pl.* their, 1-2
lever † to raise, 4-3
  lever le doigt to raise one's hand
se lever † to get up, 3-1
  Levez-vous ! Get up/Stand up!, P-2
lèvre *f.* lip
liaison *f.* link, liaison
librairie *f.* bookstore, 2-3
libre free (a person), available, 4-3
  Je ne suis pas libre. I'm not free., 4-3
  Tu es/Vous êtes libre(s) ? Are you free?, 4-3
lien *m.* (Web) link, 10-2
lieu *m.* place
  au lieu de instead of
  avoir † lieu to take place, 7-2
  lieu de travail workplace
lieue *f.* league (unit of measurement)
ligne *f.* line
  en ligne online, 10-2
limite *f.* limit, border, edge

limité/e bordered, limited
limonade *f.* lemon-lime carbonated soft drink, 5-1
linguistique *f. sg.* linguistics
lire † to read, 8-2
Lisez les mots… ! Read the words . . .!, P-2
liste *f.* list
lit *m.* bed, 6-2
litre *m.* liter, 5-3
littérature *f.* literature, 8-2
livre *m.* book, P-2
local/e local
locataire *m./f.* tenant, renter, 6-1
location *f.* rental
logé/e housed
logement *m.* lodgings, accommodations, 9-3
loger † to stay (in a hotel), 9-3
logiciel *m.* software program, 10-2
logique logical
loi *f.* law
loin (de) far (from), 8-1
lointain *adj.* distant, faraway
loisir *m.* leisure time, 2-2
livre *m.* **de loisirs** book on leisure time or hobbies, 10-3
loisirs *m. pl.* leisure-time activities, 2-2
long/longue long, 3-3
longtemps a long time, 10-1
il y a longtemps a long time ago, 4-1
lorrain/ne from the region of Lorraine
lorsque when
loto *m.* lottery, 2-2
louer to rent, 6-1
louisianais/e from Louisiana
lourd/e heavy, 4-1
Il fait lourd. It's humid., 4-1
loyer *m.* rent, 6-1
lui *m.* him, P-1; *pron.* to him, to her, 6-2
lui-même *m.* himself
lumière *f.* light
éteindre les lumières to turn off the lights
lundi Monday, 1-3
le lundi every Monday, on Mondays, 6-3
lune (Lune) *f.* moon (the Moon)
être † dans la lune to have one's head in the clouds
lune de miel honeymoon
lunettes *f. pl.* eyeglasses, 3-3
lunettes de soleil sunglasses, 3-3
lutte *f.* struggle; wrestling
lutter to struggle, fight
luxe *m.* luxury
luxueux/-euse luxurious
lycée *m.* high school, 1-3

M

ma *f. sg.* my, 1-1
machine *f.* machine
macroéconomique *f.* macroeconomics
madame (Mme) Mrs., Ms., P-1
mademoiselle (Mlle) Miss, P-1
magasin *m.* store, 3-3
grand magasin department store, 3-3
magazine *m.* TV magazine, 10-1; magazine, 10-3
magazine de télévision published TV listings, 10-3
maghrébin/e North African
magnifique magnificent
mai May, 1-2
maigre skinny, thin, 1-3
maigrir to lose weight, 5-2
mail *m.* e-mail message, 10-2
maillot *m.* **(de bain)** swimsuit, 3-3
main *f.* hand, 3-1
maintenant now, 1-3
maintenir † to maintain, 8-3
maire *m.* mayor
mairie *f.* town hall, 2-3
mais *conj.* but, P-2
maïs *m.* corn
épi *m.* **de maïs** corn on the cob
maison *f.* house, home, 1-3
rester à la maison to stay home, 1-3
maître *m.* master
maîtrise *f.* mastery; M.A. or M.S. degree in former French academic system
majeure *f.* **(en)** academic major (in) (*Can.*), 8-2
majeur/e *adj.* principal, major
majoritairement predominantly
majorité *f.* majority
mal *adv.* badly, P-1
Pas mal. Not bad. P-1
mal *m.* (**maux** *pl.*) pain, ache, 7-1
avoir † du mal (**à** + *inf.*) to have trouble/difficulty (doing *st.*)
avoir † mal to hurt, 7-1
avoir † mal à la tête to have a headache, 7-1
avoir † mal au cœur to be nauseated, 7-1
avoir † mal au ventre to have a stomach ache, 7-1
avoir † mal partout to hurt all over, 7-1
malade *m./f.* sick person
malade *adj.* sick, P-1
maladie *f.* sickness, disease
malgré in spite of
malheureux/-euse unhappy, unfortunate, 7-3
la Manche *f.* English Channel
manière *f.* **de vivre** way of life
manifestation *f.* protest, demonstration
manger † to eat, 2-3
manque *m.* lack
manquer to miss, to be lacking
manteau *m.* overcoat, 3-3
manuel *m.* manual, handbook, textbook
maquillage *m.* makeup, 3-1
se maquiller to put on makeup, 3-1
marche *f.* walking, pace; step
faire † de la marche to walk for exercise, 2-2
marché *m.* market, 2-3
bon marché *adj. inv.* cheap, inexpensive 3-3
marché en plein air open-air market
mardi Tuesday, 1-3
mari *m.* husband, 1-1
mariage *m.* wedding, 7-2; marriage
marié *m.*, **mariée** *f.* bridegroom/bride, 7-2
marié/e married, 1-1
marier to match; to marry (*so.*)
se marier to get married, 7-3
marin/e related to the sea
maritime coastal, seaside, maritime
Maroc *m.* Morocco, 9-2
marocain/e Moroccan, 9-2
marque *f.* mark, sign, label
marquer to mark, to signal
marraine *f.* godmother, 7-2
marron *adj. inv.* brown, 3-3
marquant/e *adj.* outstanding, memorable, prominent
mars March, 1-2
masse *f.* group, mass
master : diplôme de master *m.* M.A. or M.S. degree in current French academic system
match *m.* (**matchs** *pl.*) game (sports), 2-2
mathématiques *f. pl.* **(les maths)** mathematics, 8-2
matière *f.* matter, material, subject
matin *m.* morning, 1-3
du matin in the morning; A.M., 3-2
mauvais/e bad, 3-3
Il fait mauvais. The weather's bad., 4-1
maux *see* **mal**
McDo *m.* McDonald's restaurant
me (m') *pron.* me, to me, 6-2
mécanicien *m.*, **mécanicienne** *f.* mechanic, 8-3
méchant/e mean, naughty, 2-1
médecin *m.* doctor (M.D.), 7-1
médecine *f.* medicine, 8-2
médias *m. pl.* media, 10-1
médical/e medical
médicament *m.* medicine, drug
médiocre mediocre, 8-2
se méfier to be suspicious
meilleur/e *adj.* better, best, 8-2
le/la/les meilleur/e/s the best, 8-2
meilleur/e ami/e *m./f.* best friend
Meilleurs vœux ! Best wishes!, 7-2
mél *m.* e-mail address (France)
mélanger to mix
melon *m.* cantaloupe, 5-3
membre *m.* member
même same, 3-3; even, 6-1
mémoire *f.* memory
mémoire *m.* long essay, M.A. thesis
ménage *m.* household
mener † to lead, to live (a life)
mensuel *m.* monthly publication, 10-3
mensuel/le monthly, 10-3
mental/e mental
menthe *f.* mint
thé *m.* **à la menthe** mint tea
mentionner to mention
mentir to lie, 3-2
mer *f.* sea, 4-2
au bord de la mer at the seashore, 4-2
merci thank you, P-2
mercredi Wednesday, 1-2
mère *f.* mother, 1-1
mériter to earn, to merit

merveilleux/-euse marvelous, wonderful
mes *pl.* my, 1-1
mésaventure *f.* misfortune
message *m.* message
messagerie *f.* voice mail
messagerie instantanée *f.* instant messaging, 10-2
messe *f.* Catholic mass
mesure *f.* measurement
mesurer to measure
métaphore *f.* metaphor
météo(rologie) *f.* weather forecast, 4-1
méthode *f.* method, technique
métier *m.* occupation, job, 8-3
métro *m.* subway, 9-1
metteur en scène *m.* film or stage director
mettre † to put/place, to put on (clothing), to take (time), 3-3
mettre † à jour to update, 10-3
mettre † la table to set the table
meuble *m.* piece of furniture, 6-2
meublé/e furnished, 6-2
meurtre *m.* murder
mexicain/e Mexican, 9-2
Mexique *m.* Mexico, 9-2
micro-ondes *m. inv.* microwave (oven)
midi noon, 3-2
mieux better, 3-2
le mieux the best, 8-1
mieux… que better . . . than, 8-1
militaire military
mille one thousand, 6-1
milliard *m.* billion, 6-1
million *m.* million, 6-1
mince *adj.* thin, slender, 2-1
Mince ! Shoot!, 3-2
mincir to lose weight
mineure *f.* **(en)** (academic) minor (in) (*Can.*), 8-2
mini-jupe *f.* miniskirt, 3-3
ministre *m.* minister, secretary
minorité *f.* minority
minuit midnight, 3-2
minute *f.* minute, 3-1
mobile *adj.* mobile
mobilier *m. sg.* home furnishings, 6-2
mobinaute *m./f.* someone who accesses the Internet via a mobile device, 10-2
mobylette *f.* moped, motor scooter, 9-1
mocassin *m.* loafer, 3-3
moche ugly, 2-1
modalité *f.* mode, modality
mode *f.* fashion, 3-3
à la mode fashionable, 3-3
mode *m.* form, mode
mode articulatoire articulatory mode
mode d'emploi directions
modèle *m.* style, 3-3; model
moderne modern, 6-2
modeste modest
modifier to modify
moi me, P-1
moi-même myself
moins less, 3-2, minus
au moins at least
(deux heures) moins le quart a quarter to (two), 3-2
(deux heures) moins vingt twenty to (two), 3-2
moins (de)… que less . . . than, 8-1
quatre moins deux font deux (4−2=2)
mois *m.* month, 1-2
le mois prochain next month, 2-3
moitié *f.* half
moment *m.* moment, 4-1
à ce moment-là at that moment, 4-1
mon *m. sg.* my, 1-1
monde *m.* world
tout le monde everyone, everybody, 10-2
mondial/e worldwide
moniteur *m.* monitor, 10-2
moniteur avec un écran plat flat-screen monitor, 10-2
monnaie *f.* currency; change
monotone monotonous
monsieur (M.) Mr., P-1; *m.* man, P-2
monstre *m.* monster
montagne *f.* mountain, 4-2
montée *f.* climbing
monter to go up, 4-2; to increase
montre *f.* watch, 3-2
montrer to show, P-2
monument *m.* monument, 2-3
monument aux morts veterans' memorial, 2-3
se moquer de to tease, to mock
morceau *m.* piece, 5-3
mort *f.* death
morts *m. pl.* the dead
mortel/le mortal
mot *m.* word, P-2
mot apparenté cognate
mot-clé keyword
mot juste right word
moto *f.* motorcycle, 4-2
faire † de la moto to ride a motorcyle, 4-2
motoneige *f.* snowmobile, 4-2
faire † de la motoneige to go snowmobiling, 4-2
mouche *f.* fly (insect)
bateau-mouche *m.* Paris sightseeing boat
mouiller to moisten, to wet
se mouiller to get wet
mourir † to die, 4-2
moutarde *f.* mustard, 5-3
moyen *m.* means, way
moyen de transport means of transportation, 9-1
moyenne *f.* average, mean
en moyenne on average
muet/te silent, mute
muguet *m.* lily of the valley, 7-2
brin *m.* **de muguet** sprig of lily of the valley, 7-2
multifonction multifunction, 10-2
multimédia multimedia, 10-2
multiple multiple
municipal/e municipal, 2-3
mur *m.* wall, 6-2
mûr/e ripe, 5-3
musculation *f.* weight lifting, strength training, 7-1
faire † de la musculation to do strength/resistance training; to lift weights, 7-1
musée *m.* museum, 2-3
musical/e *adj.* musical, 10-1
musicien *m.*, **musicienne** *f.* musician, 8-3
musique *f.* music, 1-3
faire † de la musique to play (make) music, 2-2
musulman/e Muslim
mystérieux/-euse mysterious
mythe *m.* myth

N

nager † to swim, 2-3
naissance *f.* birth
naître † to be born, 4-2
narratif/-ive narrative
narration *f.* narrative, account
nasal/e nasal
natation *f.* swimming, 2-2
faire † de la natation to swim, 2-2
nationalisé/e nationalized
nationalité *f.* nationality, 9-2
nature *f.* nature, 6-3
nature *adj. inv.* plain
thé nature tea without milk or lemon, 5-1
navet *m.* turnip, 5-3
navette *f.* shuttle, bus, 8-1
navigateur *m.* **(Web)** (web) browser, 10-2
ne… jamais never, 3-1
ne… pas not, 1-3
ne… personne no one, 8-1
ne… rien nothing, 8-1
nécessaire necessary, 9-2
Il est nécessaire de/que It is necessary (that), 9-2
nécessité *f.* need, necessity
néerlandais *m.* Dutch (language)
néerlandais/e *adj.* Dutch, 9-2
négatif/-ive negative
négliger † to neglect
neige *f.* snow, 4-1
neiger to snow, 4-1
Il neige. It's snowing, 4-1
néo-zélandais/e from New Zealand, 9-2
neuf nine, 1-2
neuf/neuve *adj.* brand-new, 6-2
neutre *adj.* neutral
neuvième ninth, 6-1
neveu *m.* nephew, 1-1
nez *m.* nose, 7-1
nièce *f.* niece, 1-1
Noël *m.* Christmas, 7-2
noir/e black, 3-3
noix *f.* walnut; nut (generic term)
nom *m.* last name, P-2
nombre *m.* number, 1-2
nombreux/-euse numerous, 1-1
nommer to name

non no, P-1
non plus neither
moi non plus me neither
nonante ninety (*reg.*)
nord *m.* north
normalement normally, 1-3
nos *pl.* our, 1-2
note *f.* grade, 8-2
avoir † une note to have/receive a grade, 8-2
mettre † une note to give a grade, 8-2
notre *m./f. sg.* our, 1-2
nourrir to nourish
nourriture *f.* food, nourishment
nous we, P-1; *pron.* us, to us, 6-2
nous-mêmes ourselves
nouveau (nouvel)/nouvelle new, 3-3
de nouveau again, 3-1
nouveauté *f.* novelty, 10-3
nouvelle *f.* piece of news, 7-3
nouvelles *f. pl.* news
Nouvelle-Zélande *f.* New Zealand, 9-2
novembre November, 1-2
nuage *m.* cloud, 4-1
Il y a des nuages. It's cloudy., 4-1
nuit *f.* night, 3-1
numéro *m.* number

O

obéir à to obey, 5-2
objectif *m.* objective, goal, target
obligatoire required, 8-2
obliger † to oblige, to force
observer to observe
obtenir † to obtain, 8-3
occasion *f.* chance, opportunity, occasion
avoir † l'occasion de to have the opportunity to
Occident *m.* the West
occupé/e busy, P-1
s'occuper de to take care of, 6-3
Océanie *f.* Pacific, 9-2
octante eighty (*reg.*)
octobre October, 1-2
odeur *f.* odor
œil *m.* (**yeux** *pl.*) eye, 7-1
œuf *m.* egg, 5-2
œuf en chocolat chocolate egg, 7-2
œufs sur le plat/au plat fried eggs, 5-2
œuvre *f.* work (esp. literary or artistic)
œuvre d'art work of art
Office *m.* **du tourisme** tourism office, 9-3
officiel/le official
offrir † to give (a gift), 6-2
oignon *m.* onion, 5-3
oiseau *m.* bird, 1-1
olive *f.* olive
omelette *f.* omelet
omniprésent/e omnipresent
on one, people in general, we, 1-3
oncle *m.* uncle, 1-1
***onze** eleven, 1-2
***onzième** eleventh, 6-1
opéra *m.* opera
opération *m.* transaction, operation
opinion *f.* opinion
optimiste optimistic, 1-1
option *f.* option, choice
orage *m.* (thunder) storm, 4-1
Il y a un orage. There is a (thunder) storm., 4-1
oral/e oral
orange *f.* orange (fruit), 5-1
orange *adj. inv.* orange, 3-3
Orangina *m.* Orangina orange soda, 5-1
orchestre *m.* orchestra
ordinaire ordinary
ordi(nateur) *m.* computer, P-2
ordinateur portable laptop computer, 10-2
ordre *m.* order
oreille *f.* ear, 7-1
organiser to plan, to organize, 2-2
origine *f.* origin
orphelin/e orphaned
ou or, P-1
où *adv./ rel. pron.* where, 2-1; *rel. pron.* when, 10-3
oublier (de + *inf.***)** to forget (to do *st.*), 2-3
ouest *m.* west
Ouf ! Whew!, 3-2
oui yes, P-1
ouvrage *m.* **de référence** reference book, 10-3
ouverture *f.* opening
ouvrir † to open, P-2

P

pagne *m.* wrap, piece of (African) cloth
pain *m.* bread, 5-2
du pain avec du chocolat bread with chocolate, 5-2
pain au chocolat chocolate croissant, 5-2
pain de campagne round loaf of bread, 5-3
pain de mie loaf of sliced bread, 5-3
pain grillé toast, 5-2
petit pain roll, 5-3
paire *f.* pair, 3-3
paire de chaussures pair of shoes, 3-3
paix *f.* peace
pâle pale
pâlir to become pale, 5-2
panier *m.* basket
pantalon *m. sg.* slacks, 3-3
pantouflard/e homebody, stay-at-home, 2-1
papier *m.* paper
paquet *m.* package, 5-3
par by, through
par e-mail by e-mail (as medium), 10-2
(deux fois) par jour/semaine (twice) a day/week, 3-1
par terre on the floor, 6-2
paragraphe *m.* paragraph
parapluie *m.* umbrella, 3-3
parc *m.* park, 2-3
parc *m.* **de stationnement** parking lot (*Can.*), 8-1
parce que because, 2-1
parcourir † to cover
pardon excuse me, P-2
parent *m.* parent, relative, 1-1
paresseux/-euse lazy, 2-1
parfaitement perfectly, completely
parfois sometimes
parfum *m.* perfume
pari *m.* bet, wager
lancer † un pari to make a bet, to wager
parier to bet
parler to speak, P-2
parler au téléphone to talk on the phone, 1-3
Parlez plus fort ! Speak louder!, P-2
parmi among
paroisse *f.* parish; administrative unit in Louisiana
parrain *m.* godfather, 7-2
part *f.* piece, portion, share
partager † to share, 5-1
partenaire *m./f.* partner
participe *m.* participle
participe passé past participle
participer à to participate in
particulier/-ière particular, specific, exceptional, special
en particulier especially, in particular
partie *f.* part
faire † partie de to belong to
partir to leave, 3-2
à partir de from
partir en vacances to go on vacation, 4-2
partitif/-ive partitive
partout everywhere, all over, 7-1
pas not, P-1
ne... pas not, 1-3
pas du tout not at all
pas mal not bad, P-1
pas tout à fait not quite, 4-2
passage *m.* passage
passager *m.*, **passagère** *f.* passenger
passé *m.* past
passé composé compound past tense
passé simple literary past tense
passeport *m.* passport, 9-1
passer to go/come by, 4-2; to spend (time), 4-3
passer une soirée tranquille to spend a quiet evening, 4-3
se passer to happen, 7-3
passion *f.* passion
passionné/e passionate
patate *f.* potato (*Can.*)
pâte *f.* pasta, 5-3; dough
pâté *m.* pâté, 5-3
patience *f.* patience
patient/e *adj.* patient
patin *m.* **à glace** ice skate; ice-skating
patin *m.* **à roulettes** roller skate; roller-skating
patinage *m.* skating
pâtissier *m.*, **pâtissière** *f.* pastry chef
pâtisserie *f.* pastry, 5-3; pastry shop
patron *m.*, **patronne** *f.* boss
pauvre poor
pavillon *m.* building, 8-1
le pavillon principal main building, 8-1
payer to pay
pays *m.* country, 9-2
Pays-Bas *m. pl.* the Netherlands, 9-2
peau *f.* skin
pêche *f.* peach, 5-3

pêche *f.* fishing, 4-2
aller à la pêche to go fishing, 4-2
peigne *m.* comb, 3-1
peint/e *adj.* painted, depicted
peinture *f.* painting, 8-2
pendant during, for, 3-2
pendant que while
pensée *f.* thought
penser (à/de) to think (of *so.*/about *so.* or *st.*), 10-1
Je pense que… I think that . . .
Je pense que non. I don't think so.
Je pense que oui. I think so.
perdre to lose, to waste, 4-1
perdre son sang-froid to lose one's composure, self-control, 7-3
père *m.* father, 1-1
période *f.* period
permettre † (à, de) to permit (*so.* to do *st.*)
permis *m.* permit, 8-1
permis de conduire driver's license, 9-1
persil *m.* parsley
personnage *m.* character
personnage principal main character, 10-1
personnalisé/e personalized
personne *f.* person, P-1
personne : ne… personne no one, nobody, 5-2
personnel/le personal
perspective *f.* perspective
persuader to persuade
perte *f.* loss
pessimiste pessimistic, 1-1
petit/e short, small, little, 2-1
petit-déjeuner *m.* breakfast, 5-2
petite annonce *f.* classified ad
petite-fille *f.*, **(petites-filles** *pl.*) granddaughter, 1-1
petit-fils *m.*, **(petits-fils** *pl.*) grandson, 1-1
petit pois *m.* pea, 5-3
petits-enfants *m. pl.* grandchildren, 1-1
peu *m.* a little, 1-1
peu à peu little by little, gradually
peuple *m.* people
peur *f.* fear
avoir † peur (de/que)… to be afraid (of/that) . . ., 10-1
faire † peur to frighten, scare
peut-être maybe, 2-1
pharmacie *f.* pharmacy
pharmacien *m.*, **pharmacienne** *f.* pharmacist, 8-3
phénomène *m.* phenomenon
philosophie *f.* philosophy, 8-2
photographe *m./f.* photographer
photo(graphie) *f.* photograph, photography, 2-1
phrase *f.* sentence
physiologie *f.* physiology, 8-2
physique *f. sg.* physics, 8-2
physique *m. sg.* physical traits, 2-1
physique *adj.* physical
piano *m.* piano, 1-3
jouer du piano to play the piano, 1-3
pièce *f.* play, 2-3; room 6-1
un cinq-pièces *m.* apartment with five rooms, plus kitchen and bathroom(s), 6-1
pièce de monnaie coin
pièce jointe (e-mail) attachment, 10-2
pied *m.* foot, 7-1
à pied on foot, 9-1
pierre *f.* stone
piétonnier/-ière for pedestrians
piquant/e spicy, hot
pique-nique *m.* picnic, 4-2
faire † un pique-nique to have a picnic, 4-2
piquer to sting
pire worse
piscine *f.* swimming pool, 2-3
pizza *f.* pizza, 5-1
placard *m.* cupboard, kitchen cabinet, 6-2
place *f.* (city) square, 2-3; seat, place, 4-3
plage *f.* beach, 4-2
se plaindre to complain
plaisanter to joke
Tu plaisantes ! You're joking!
plaisir *m.* pleasure, 4-3
avec plaisir with pleasure, 4-3
plan *m.* map, 8-1, blueprint
plan de ville city map, 9-1
plan du campus map of campus, 8-1
planche *f.* board
planche à voile *f.* windsurfing, windsurfing board, 4-2
faire † de la planche à voile to windsurf, 4-2
planète *f.* planet
planifier to plan
plantain *m.* plantain
plante *f.* plant, 6-2
plat *m.* dish or course, 5-2
plat garni main dish served with vegetables
plat préparé prepared dish, 5-3
plat principal main dish, 5-2
plein/e (de) full (of), 10-1
plein air open air, outdoor, 8-3
pleurer to cry, 7-3
pleuvoir † to rain, 4-1
Il pleut. It's raining., 4-1
pluie *f.* rain, 4-1
plupart : la plupart des *f.* the majority, most
plus *adv.* more; plus
deux plus deux font quatre (2+2=4)
moi non plus me neither
non plus neither
plus (de)… que more . . . than, 8-1
plusieurs several
plutôt more, rather, 10-1
poche *f.* pocket
poêle *f.* frying pan
poème *m.* poem
poésie *f.* poetry, 10-3
poète *m./f.* poet
poignée *f.* handful
point *m.* point, period
poire *f.* pear, 5-2
poirier *m.* pear tree
poison *m.* poison
poisson *m.* fish, 5-2
poissonnerie *f.* seafood shop, 5-3
poitrine *f.* chest
poivre *m.* pepper, 5-2
poivron *m.* (bell) pepper, 5-3
poivron rouge red (bell) pepper, 5-3
poivron vert green (bell) pepper, 5-3
policier : film *m.* **policier** detective/police film, 10-1
polo *m.* polo shirt, 3-3
pomme *f.* apple, 5-2
pomme de terre *f.* potato, 5-2
ponctuel/le punctual
populaire popular
popularité *f.* popularity
porc *m.* pork, 5-3
portable *m.* cell phone, 9-2; laptop computer 10-2
porte *f.* door, P-2
portée *f.* reach
portefeuille *m.* wallet, 9-1
porte-monnaie *m. inv.* change purse, 9-1
porter to wear, 3-3; to carry
portrait *m.* portrait
portugais *m.* Portuguese (language)
portugais/e *adj.* Portuguese, 9-2
Portugal *m.* Portugal, 9-2
posé/e stated, asked; put down
poser to place, to put
poser une question to ask a question, 2-1
positif/-ive positive
posséder † to possess, 6-3
posséssif/-ive possessive
possibilité *f.* possibility
possible possible
postal/e postal
poste *f.* post office
poste *m.* job, position
poster *m.* poster
pot *m.* jar, 5-3
potager *m.* vegetable garden, 6-3
poudre *f.* powder
poudre à pâte baking powder (*Louisiana*)
poule *f.* hen
poulet *m.* chicken, 5-2
pouls *m.* pulse
poumon *m.* lung, 7-1
pour for, 2-1
pour (+ *inf.*) in order to (do *st.*)
pourcentage *m.* percentage
pourquoi why, 2-1
pourquoi pas ? why not?
poursuivre † to pursue, to continue
pousser to push, to encourage
pouvoir *m.* power
pouvoir † can, to be able to, 7-3
poux *m. pl.* lice
pratique *f.* practice
pratique *adj.* practical, 6-2
pratiquer to do, to engage in
pré *m.* meadow
préambule *m.* preamble, prelude
précédé/e preceding
précis/e precise
précision *f.* precision, preciseness
prédécesseur *m.* predecessor
prédiction *f.* prediction
prédire † to predict, to foretell
préfecture *f.* **de police** police headquarters
préférence *f.* preference

préférer † to prefer, 4-3
préhistorique prehistoric, 9-3
premier/-ière first, 1-1
 C'est le premier mai. It's May first., 1-2
 en premier *adv.* first
prendre † to have (to eat or drink); to have a meal, 5-1; to take
 prendre † congé to take leave, say good-bye
 prendre † le petit-déjeuner to have breakfast, 5-2
 prendre † un bain to take a bath, 3-1
 prendre † une douche to take a shower, 3-1
 Prenez un stylo ! Take a pen!, P-2
prénom *m.* first name, P-2
prénominal/e prenominal, before the noun
préparatifs *m. pl.* preparations
préparer to prepare, 1-3
 préparer le dîner to fix dinner, 1-3
 préparer un diplôme (en) to do a degree (in), 8-2
 préparer un examen to study for an exam
 préparer une leçon to prepare for a lesson/class
préposition *f.* preposition
près (de) near (to), 8-1
 tout près (de) very near, 8-1
présent *m.* present, present tense
présentateur *m.*, **présentatrice** *f.* presenter; newscaster
présenter to introduce, present, P-1
 Je te/vous présente Jean-Louis. Let me introduce Jean-Louis to you., P-1
 se présenter to introduce oneself
préserver to preserve, to keep
président/e *m./f.* president
presque almost
presse *f.* press, 10-3
pressé/e squeezed; in a hurry
 citron *m.* **pressé** lemonade, 5-1
prestige *m.* prestige, 8-3
prestigieux/-euse prestigious
prêt/e ready
prêter to lend, 6-2
prétexte *m.* excuse
prêtre *m.* priest
prévenir † to prevent, to avoid; to warn someone
prier to beg, to pray
 Je vous en prie/Je t'en prie. You're welcome., P-2; please, 7-3
prière *f.* prayer
primaire primary
principal/e main, principal, 8-1
printemps *m.* spring, 4-1
 au printemps in the spring
priorité *f.* priority
pris/e : Je suis pris/e. I'm busy. I have a previous engagement., 4-3
privé/e private
privilégier to favor
prix *m.* price, 3-3; prize
probable probable
probablement probably
problème *m.* problem
 sans problème no problem, 5-1
procéder † to procede, to behave
prochain/e next, 2-3
proche *m.* close relative, relation
proche *adj.* close, nearby
producteur *m.*, **productrice** *f.* producer
produit *m.* product
prof *m./f.* (*fam.*) prof, professor
professeur *m.* professor, P-2; teacher, 7-3
professeure *f.* professor, teacher (*Can.*)
profession *f.* profession, 8-3
profond/e deep
programme *m.* program, schedule, platform
 programme d'études course of study
 programme télé TV schedule, listing, 10-1
progression *f.* progression, development
projet *m.* project, 8-2; (future) plan
 projets de vacances *m. pl.* vacation plans, 4-2
promenade *f.* walk, stroll, 2-2
 faire † une promenade to take a walk, 2-2
se promener † to take a walk, 7-3
promettre † (à *qqn* **de** *inf.***)** to promise (*so.* to do *st.*)
pronom *m.* pronoun
 pronom complément d'objet direct direct-object pronoun
 pronom complément d'objet indirect indirect-object pronoun
 pronom disjoint stressed pronoun
 pronom réfléchi reflexive pronoun
 pronom relatif relative pronoun
 pronom sujet subject pronoun
pronominal/e pronominal
prononcer to pronounce
prononciation *f.* pronunciation
propos *m.* remark
 à propos de on the subject of, about
proposer to propose, to suggest
proposition *f.* suggestion, proposal, proposition
 proposition de loi (legislative) bill
propre (one's) own, 6-1; clean
propriétaire *m./f.* landlord/landlady; homeowner, 6-1
prouver to prove
proverbe *m.* proverb
province *f.* province
provisions *f. pl.* food supplies
provoquer to provoke
proximité *f.* nearness, closeness, proximity
prune *f.* plum
psychologie *f.* psychology, 8-2
psychologique psychological
public *m.* public, 8-3
 avoir † un contact avec le public to have contact with the public, 8-3
public/publique *adj.* public
publicitaire *adj.* promotional, advertising
publicité *f.* **(une pub)** advertisement, 10-3
publier to publish
puce *f.* flea
 marché *m.* **aux puces** flea market
puis then, 4-2
pull(-over) *m.* pullover sweater, 3-3
punir to punish, 5-2
punition *f.* punishment

Q

qualification *f.* label, description, qualification
quand when, 2-1
 quand même anyway, just the same
quantité *f.* quantity, 5-3
quarante forty, 1-2
quart *m.* quarter, 3-2
 (deux heures) et quart a quarter after (two), 3-2
 (deux heures) moins le quart a quarter to (two), 3-2
quartier *m.* neighborhood, 6-1
quatorze fourteen, 1-2
quatorzième fourteenth, 6-1
quatre four, 1-2
quatrième fourth, 6-1
quatre-vingts eighty, 1-2
quatre-vingt-dix ninety, 1-2
quatre-vingt-onze ninety-one, 1-2
que (qu') *conj.* that, 8-1
que (qu') *rel. pron.* what, whom, which, that, 10-3
 qu'est-ce que/qui... ? what . . .?, 5-2
 Qu'est-ce que tu as ? What's wrong?, 7-3
quel/le which, 4-2
 Quel âge as-tu/avez-vous ? How old are you?, 1-2
 Quel est ton/votre âge ? What's your age?, 1-2
 Quelle est la date ? What's the date?, 1-2
 Quelle est votre saison préférée ? What's your favorite season?, 4-2
 Quelle heure est-il ? What time is it?, 3-2
 Quel temps fait-il ? What's the weather like?, 4-1
quelque some
quelque chose something, 5-2
 quelque chose à boire something to drink, 5-1
 quelque chose à manger something to eat, 5-1
quelquefois sometimes, 3-1
quelqu'un someone, 8-1
 quelqu'un d'autre someone else
question *f.* question, 2-1
 poser une question to ask a question, 2-1
questionnaire *m.* questionnaire, survey
qui who, whom, 2-1; which, that, 10-3
quiche *f.* quiche
 quiche lorraine quiche with bacon and Swiss cheese
quinze fifteen, 1-2
quinzième fifteenth, 6-1
quitter to leave, 3-2
quoi what, 5-2
 n'importe quoi anything, no matter what
 Quoi de neuf ? What's new?
quotidien *m.* daily publication, 10-3
quotidien/ne *adj.* daily

R

raconter to tell (a story), 10-1
radio *f.* radio, 1-3
 écouter la radio to listen to the radio, 1-3
radio-réveil *m.* clock radio, 3-2
rafraîchissant/e refreshing, cold 5-1
raisin *m.* grape, 5-3
 raisin sec raisin
raison *f.* reason
 avoir † raison to be right
raisonnable reasonable, 1-1
rajouter to add (some) more
ralentir to slow down
randonnée *f.* hike, 4-2
 faire † une randonnée to take a hike, 4-2
ranger † to tidy up, to put away, 6-2; to arrange
rap *m.* rap music
rapide quick, rapid
rapidement quickly, rapidly
rapidité *f.* speed, quickness
rappel *m.* reminder
se rappeler † to remember, 7-3
rapport *m.* relationship; report
rare rare
rarement rarely, 3-1
se raser to shave, 3-1
rasoir *m.* razor, 3-1
rater to miss
ravi/e delighted, 4-3
rayon *m.* supermarket section, aisle, 5-3
 rayon boucherie meat counter, 5-3
 rayon boulangerie-pâtisserie bakery/pastry aisle, 5-3
 rayon charcuterie deli counter, 5-3
 rayon crèmerie dairy aisle, 5-3
 rayon fruits et légumes produce aisle, 5-3
 rayon poissonnerie fish counter, 5-3
 rayon surgelés frozen foods, 5-3
réagir to react
réalisateur *m.*, **réalisatrice** *f.* film director, 10-1
réaliste realistic, 1-1
réalité *f.* reality
récemment recently
recensement *m.* census
récent/e recent
réception *f.* welcome; reception (room)
réceptionniste *m./f.* receptionist
recette *f.* recipe
recevoir † to receive
réchauffer to reheat
recherche *f.* research, 10-2
 à la recherche de in search of
 faire † de la recherche to do research
récipient *m.* container
réciprocité *f.* reciprocity
récit *m.* narrative, 4-2
réciter to recite
recommandation *f.* recommendation, 10-3
recommander to recommend
recommencer (à + *inf.*) † to begin again (to do *st.*)
récompense *f.* reward, award
rédaction *f.* composition, short essay
rédiger † to compose, write

réduire † to reduce, 7-1
réel *m.* what is real, reality
réfléchi/e reflexive; thoughtful
réfléchir à ***qqch.*** to think of/about *st.*, 5-2
refléter † to reflect
réflexion *f.* reflection
réforme *f.* reform
refrain *m.* chorus, refrain
réfrigérateur *m.* (**un frigo,** *colloq.*) refrigerator, 6-2
refuser (de + *inf.*) to refuse (to do *st.*), 4-3
regarder to look at, to watch, 1-3
 regarder la télé to watch TV, 1-3
 regarder un film to watch a film on TV, 1-3
 Regardez le tableau ! Look at the board!, P-2
régime *m.* diet, 7-1
 être † au régime to be on a diet
 faire † /suivre † un régime to diet, 7-1
région *f.* area, region
régional/e regional
règle *f.* ruler, P-2; rule
régler † to settle, to pay for
regret *m.* regret
regretter to be sorry, to regret, 4-3
régulier/-ière regular
régulièrement regularly, 7-1
reine *f.* queen
rejeter † to reject
relation *f.* relation, relationship
 relation familiale *f.* family relation, 1-1
 relations internationales *f.pl.* international relations, 8-2
relier to join, to link together
religieux/-euse religious
religion *f.* religion
relire † to reread
remarié/e remarried, 1-1
rembourser to reimburse
remercier to thank, P-2
remettre † to hand in/over, 6-2
remplacer † to replace
remplir to fill
remue-méninges *m. inv.* brainstorming
rencontrer to meet
 se rencontrer to meet (each other), 7-3
rendez-vous *m.* meeting, date, appointment, 4-3
rendre (à + *qqn*) to hand in (to *so.*), P-2; to give back (to *so.*), 4-1
 rendre visite à *qqn* to visit *so.*, 4-1
rénové/e renovated, 6-2
renseignement *m.* information, 9-3
renseigner to inform
 se renseigner to get information, 9-3
rentrée *f.* back-to-school
rentrer to return home, 3-1; to go/come home, 4-2
répandu/e widespread
réparer to repair
repartir to leave again
repas *m.* meal, 5-2
 repas équilibré balanced meal, 7-1
répéter † to repeat, P-2; to rehearse
replanter to replant
réplique *f.* line, reply, retort

répondre to answer, 4-1
 Répondez en français ! Answer in French!, P-2
reportage *m.* special report (esp. news), 10-1
repos *m.* rest, 4-2
se reposer to rest, 7-3
reprendre † to take back
représentant *m.*, **représentante** *f.* **de commerce** sales representative, 8-3
représentation *f.* (theatrical) production; representation
représenter to represent, to account for
reproduire † to reproduce
réputation *f.* reputation
réseau *m.* network, 10-2
 réseau sans fil wireless network, 10-2
 réseau social social network, 10-2
réservation *f.* reservation, 9-3
 faire une réservation sur Internet to make a reservation online, 9-3
réservé/e reserved, 1-1
réserver to reserve
résidence *f.* residence hall, 2-2
résidentiel/le residential, 6-1
résister to resist
résoudre to resolve, to solve
responsabilité *f.* responsibility, 8-3
restaurant *m.* restaurant, 1-3
 restaurant universitaire (resto U) dining hall, 8-1
restauration *f.* restaurant business; restoration
 restauration rapide fast-food business
rester to stay, 1-3
 rester à la maison to stay home, 1-3
 rester à la résidence to stay in the dorm, 2-2
 rester en forme to stay in shape, 7-1
résultat *m.* result
résumé *m.* summary
résumer to summarize
résurrection *f.* resurrection
retard : être en retard to be late, 3-2
retenir † to retain, 8-3
retomber to fall again
retoucher to edit, to touch up, 10-2
retour *m.* return
 de retour *adv.* back
retourner to go back, to return 4-2
retraite *f.* retirement
 prendre † la retraite to retire
retransmis/e broadcast
retrouver (*qqn*) to meet up with (*so.*), 8-1
se retrouver to meet, 4-3; to meet up with, 7-3
réunion *f.* meeting, 9-2
se réunir to get together
réussir (à) to succeed/pass, 5-2
rêve *m.* dream
 faire † un rêve to have a dream
réveil *m.* alarm clock, 3-2
réveillé/e awake
(se) réveiller to wake up, 3-1
réveillon *m.*
 réveillon de Noël Christmas Eve dinner or party, 7-2

réveillon du Jour de l'An New Year's Eve dinner or party, 7-2
révéler † to reveal, to bring to light
revenir † to come back, 4-2
rêver (de + *qqch.*, **de +** *inf.*) to dream (of *st.*, of doing *st.*)
réviser to review, 1-3
revoir † to see again
au revoir good-bye, P-1
révolution *f.* revolution
revue *f.* review, journal
rez-de chaussée *m.* **(RdeCh)** ground floor, 6-1
rhume *m.* cold
rideau *m.* curtain, 6-2
rien *m.* nothing
De rien. Not at all. You're welcome., P-2
ne... rien nothing, 5-2
rigoler to joke, 10-1; to laugh (*colloq.*)
Tu rigoles ? Are you kidding?, 10-1
rire *m.* laugh
rire to laugh
risque *m.* risk
risquer (de + *inf.*) to risk, to run the risk of (doing *st.*)
rite *m.* rite, ritual
rituel *m.* ritual
rivière *f.* large stream or river (tributary), 6-3
riz *m.* rice, 5-2
robe *f.* dress, 3-3
robot *m.* robot
rock *m.* rock music, 2-2
roi *m.* king
rôle *m.* role, part
roman *m.* novel, 8-2
romanche *f.* Romansch (Romance language spoken in Switzerland)
rompre † to break, to break up
rond/e round
rosbif *m.* roast beef, 5-3
rose *f.* rose (flower)
rose *adj.* pink, 3-3
rosé *m.* rosé wine, 5-1
rôti *m.* roast, 5-3
rôti de porc pork roast, 5-3
rôtie *f.* piece of toast (*Can.*), 5-2
rouge red, 3-3
rougir to blush, 5-2
routine *f.* routine, 3-1
roux/rousse redhead, redhaired, 2-1
rue *f.* street, 6-1
rugby *m.* rugby, 2-2
rupture *f.* break, rupture
rural/e rural, 9-3
russe *m.* Russian (language)
russe *adj.* Russian, 9-2
Russie *f.* Russia, 9-2
rythme *m.* rhythm

S

sa *f. sg.* his, her, 1-1
sac *m.* bag, purse, 3-3
sac à dos backpack, 9-1
sac à main ladies' handbag
sac en plastique plastic bag
sage wise; well-behaved (for children)
Sois/Soyez sage ! Be good!
saisir to understand, to get, to grasp
saison *f.* season, 4-1
salade *f.* salad, lettuce, 5-1
salade verte green salad, 5-1
salaire *m.* salary, 8-3
salle *f.* room, P-2
salle à manger dining room, 6-1
salle de bains bathroom, 6-1
salle de classe classroom, P-2
salle de séjour living room, 6-1
salle informatique computer lab, 8-1
saluer to greet, P-1
salut hi, 'bye, P-1
samedi Saturday, 1-2
sandale *f.* sandal, 3-3
sandwich *m.* (**sandwichs** *pl.*) sandwich, 5-1
sandwich au fromage cheese sandwich, 5-1
sandwich au jambon ham sandwich, 5-1
sang *m.* blood
sang-froid *m.* composure, 7-3
sans without, P-2
sans doute undoubtedly
santé *f.* health, 7-1
sapin *m.* evergreen tree, 6-3; Christmas tree, 7-2
sardine *f.* sardine, 5-3
satellite *m.* satellite
sauce *f.* sauce
saumon *m.* salmon, 5-3
saupoudrer to sprinkle, to dust
sauter to jump, to skip
faire sauter une crêpe to flip a crêpe
sauter un repas to skip a meal, 7-1
sauvegarder (un fichier) to save (a file), 10-2
savoir † (+ *inf.*) to know (how to do *st.*), 7-3
savon *m.* soap, 3-1
savoyard/e from the region of Savoie
saxophone *m.* saxophone, 2-2
scanner *m.* scanner, 10-3
scénario *m.* screenplay, script, scenario
scène *f.* scene; stage
science *f.* science, 8-2
science-fiction *f.* science fiction, 10-1
film *m.* **de science-fiction** science fiction movie, 10-1
sciences de l'éducation education, 8-2
sciences économiques economics, 8-2
sciences humaines social sciences, 8-2
sciences naturelles natural sciences, 8-2
sciences physiques physical sciences, 8-2
sciences politiques political science, 8-2
scientifique scientific
sculpture *f.* sculpture
séance *f.* showing at a movie theater
sec/sèche dry
secondaire secondary
secrétaire *m./f.* secretary, 8-3
sécurité *f.* security
sédentaire unmoving, sedentary
seigneur *m.* lord
seize sixteen, 1-2
seizième sixteenth, 6-1
séjour *m.* living room, 6-1; stay (abroad, on vacation)
sel *m.* salt, 5-2
selon according to
semaine *f.* week, 1-3
la semaine prochaine next week, 2-3
par semaine per week
semblable *adj.* similar
sembler to appear
il me semble it seems to me, 6-3
semestre *m.* semester, 8-2
semi-voyelle *f.* semivowel, glide
semoule *f.* semolina
Sénégal *m.* Senegal, 9-2
sénégalais/e Senegalese, 9-2
sensible sensitive
sentiment *m.* feeling, 7-3
sentimental/e sentimental, 7-3
se sentir to feel
séparément separately
se séparer to separate, 7-3
sept seven, 1-2
septante seventy (*reg.*)
septembre September, 1-2
septième seventh, 6-1
séquence *f.* sequence, segment
série *f.* series, TV series, 10-1
sérieux/-euse serious, 2-1
se serrer la main to shake hands
serveur *m.*, **serveuse** *f.* server (in restaurant), 5-1
services *m. pl.* service sector, 8-3
serviette *f.* **(de toilette)** towel, 3-1
servir to serve, 3-2
se servir de (*qqch.*) to use (*st.*), 10-2
ses *pl.* his, her, 1-1
seul/e only, single, alone
seulement only, 5-1
Seychelles *f. pl.* Seychelle Islands, 9-2
shampooing *m.* shampoo, 3-1
shopping *m.* shopping, 4-2
faire † du shopping, to shop, 4-2
short *m. sg.* shorts, 3-3
si yes, 1-3; if, whether, 7-3
SIDA *m.* AIDS
siècle *m.* century
sieste *f.* nap
faire † la sieste to take a nap
sigle *m.* initials, acronym
signaler to indicate, to be a sign of, to point out
signe *m.* sign
signification *f.* meaning
signifier to mean
silence *m.* silence
s'il vous/te plaît please, P-2
similaire alike, similar
similarité *f.* likeness, similarity
simplifier to simplify
singulier/-ière singular
sinon *adv.* otherwise, or else
sirène *f.* siren
sirop *m.* syrup
sirop d'érable maple syrup
site *m.* site, 9-3
site culturel cultural site, 9-3
site historique historical site, 9-3
site Web web site, 10-2

situé/e located, situated, 6-1
situer to situate
six six, 1-2
sixième sixth, 6-1
ski *m.* skiing, 4-2
  faire † du ski to ski, 4-2
  faire † du ski nautique to water ski, 4-2
slogan *m.* slogan
smartphone *m.* smart phone, 10-2
snack-bar *m.* snack bar
sociable outgoing, 1-1
socialisme *m.* socialism
sociologie *f.* sociology, 8-2
sœur *f.* sister, 1-1
soie *f.* silk, 3-3
soif *f.* thirst, 5-1
  avoir † soif to be thirsty, 5-1
soir *m.* evening, 1-3
  ce soir tonight, 2-3
  du soir in the evening, P.M., 3-2
soirée *f.* evening, 4-3
  Bonne soirée ! Have a good evening!
sois *see* **être**
soit *conj.* that is to say
soixante sixty, 1-2
soixante-dix seventy, 1-2
soixante-et-onze seventy-one, 1-2
soixante-et-un sixty-one, 1-2
sol *m.* ground, earth
  sous-sol *m.* basement, underground, 6-1
solaire *adj.* solar
solde *f.* sale
  en solde on sale
soldé/e *adj.* on sale
soleil *m.* sun, 4-1
  Il y a du soleil. It's sunny., 4-1
solution *f.* solution
solutionner to solve, to resolve
sommaire *m.* brief table of contents
somme *f.* amount, sum
sommet *m.* top, summit
son *m. sg.* his, her, 1-1
son *m.* sound
  spectacle *m.* **son et lumière** sound and light historical production, 9-3
sondage *m.* survey, poll
sonner to ring, 3-2
sophistiqué/e sophisticated
sorte *f.* sort, kind, type
sortie *f.* outing, trip; exit
sortir to go out, 3-2
souci *m.* worry, concern
  se faire † du souci to worry, 7-3
souffler to blow out, 7-2
souhaiter to hope, to wish, 9-3
soupe *f.* soup, 5-2
souper *m.* dinner (*Can.*)
souper to have supper/dinner
source *f.* source, credit
souris *f.* mouse, 10-2
  souris sans fil wireless mouse, 10-2
sous under, below, 6-2
  sous les toits in the attic, 6-2
sous-sol *m.* basement, 6-1
sous-titre *m.* subtitle, 10-1
sous-titré/e subtitled

soutenir † to support, uphold, 8-3
souvenir *m.* memory, recollection; souvenir, memento
se souvenir de † to remember
souvent often, 3-1
soyez *see* **être**
spacieux/-euse spacious, 6-2
spécial/e peculiar, special
spécialisation *f.* **(en)** major (in), 8-2
spécialité *f.* speciality
spécifier to specify, to indicate
spectacle *m.* show, 4-3
  arts *m. pl.* **du spectacle** performing arts, 8-2
  spectacle son et lumière sound and light historical production, 9-3
spectateur *m.*, **spectatrice** *f.* audience member, onlooker, witness
  spectateurs *m. pl.* the audience
sport *m.* sport, 2-2
  faire † du sport to do/play sports, 2-2
  sport d'hiver winter sport, 4-2
sportif/-ive athletic, 2-1
stable stable
stade *m.* stadium, 2-3
standardiser to standardize
station *f.* **de métro** subway stop, 8-1
stationnement *m.* parking
  parc *m.* **de stationnement** parking lot (*Can.*), 8-1
statistique *f.* statistic
stéréotype *m.* stereotype
stratégie *f.* strategy
stress *m.* stress, 7-1
stressé/e stressed out, P-1
strophe *f.* stanza
structure *f.* structure, system, organization
studio *m.* studio apartment, 6-1
style *m.* style
stylo *m.* pen, P-2
subjonctif *m.* subjunctive mood
substantif *m.* noun
succès *m.* success
successif/-ive successive
succession *f.* sequence, succession
sucre *m.* sugar, 5-1
sucré/e sweet (for food)
sud *m.* south
suffisamment *adv.* sufficiently
suggérer † to suggest, 4-3
Suisse *f.* Switzerland, 9-2
suisse *adj.* Swiss, 9-2
suivant/e *adj.* following, next
suivi/e *adj.* consistent, continuous
  suivi/e de followed by
suivre † to follow, 8-2
  suivre † un cours to take a course, 8-2
  suivre † un régime to be on a diet, 7-1
sujet *m.* subject
super super, 3-2
superbe superb
superlatif *m.* superlative
supermarché *m.* supermarket, 5-3
superstition *f.* superstition
supplément *m.* extra or additional part
supplémentaire extra or additional
sur on, on top of, 6-2

sûr/e sure
  bien sûr of course, 2-1
  sûr de lui/ sûre d'elle self-assured, self-confident
surf *m.* surfing, 4-2
  faire † du surf to surf, 4-2
  faire † du surf des neiges to snowboard, 4-2
surfer (sur Internet) to surf (the Internet), 10-3
surgelé/e *adj.* frozen, 5-3
surgelés *m. pl.* frozen foods, 5-3
surprenant/e surprising
surprendre † to surprise
surpris/e surprised, 7-3
surtout above all, 6-2
sympa(thique) nice, 1-1
syncopé/e syncopated, irregular (rhythm)
syndicat *m.* (trade) union
  Syndicat d'initiative tourist office
système *m.* system

T

ta *f. sg.* your, 1-1
tabac *m.* tobacco; specialty shop for tobacco products, newspapers, magazines
table *f.* table
  table basse coffee table, 6-2
tableau *m.* chalkboard, P-2; painting; chart, table
  tableau blanc whiteboard, P-2
tablette : tablette *f.* **tactile** touch screen tablet, 10-2
Tahiti Tahiti, 9-2
tahitien/ne Tahitian, 9-2
taille *f.* size; waist
  de taille moyenne of medium height, 2-1
tailleur *m.* women's suit, 3-3
talon *m.* heel
  chaussure *f.* **à talons** high-heeled shoe, 3-3
  talons hauts high heels
  talons plats flat heels
tandis que while, whereas
tante *f.* aunt, 1-1
taper to type
tapis *m.* rug, 6-2
tard late, 3-1
tarte *f.* pie, 5-3
  tarte aux pommes apple pie, 5-2
tartelette *f.* small pie or tart
tartine *f.* slice of bread with butter or jam, 5-2
tasse *f.* cup, 5-1
taxi *m.* taxi, 9-1
te (t') *pron.* you, to you, 6-2
technicien *m.* **(de labo), technicienne** *f.* **(de labo)** (lab) technician, 8-3
technologie *f.* technology, 10-2
technologique technological
technophile *m.* technology-lover
technophobe *m.* technology-hater
tee-shirt *m.* T-shirt, 3-3
télé *f. see* **télévision**
téléachat : émission de téléachat *m.* infomercial, 10-1
télécharger to download, to upload, to stream, 10-2

télécommande *f.* remote control, 10-1
téléfilm *m.* made-for-TV movie, 10-1
téléphone *m.* telephone, 1-3
téléphoner (à *qqn***)** to call (*so.*), 1-3
se téléphoner to phone each other, 7-3
téléréalité *f.* reality TV, 10-1
télévisé/e : journal télévisé television news, 10-1
téléviseur *m.* television, TV set
télévision *f.* TV, television, P-2
témoin *m.* witness, 7-2
tempérament *m.* disposition, temperament
température *f.* temperature, 4-1
temps *m.* weather, 4-1; time; tense
depuis combien de temps... ? for how long . . .?, 10-3
de temps en temps from time to time, 7-1
Quel temps fait-il ? What's the weather like?, 4-1
tendance *f.* tendency
tendre tender, affectionate
tendresse *f.* tenderness
Tenez ! Here!, 3-3
tenir † to hold, 8-1
tennis *m.* tennis, 1-3; *f. pl.* tennis shoes
tension *f.* tension; tenseness
tente *f.* tent, 9-3
terme *m.* term, word
terminer to end, to finish
terrain *m.* **de sport** playing field, court, 8-1
terrasse *f.* terrace, 6-1
terre (Terre) *f.* earth (the Earth)
par terre on the floor, 6-2
terrine *f.* loaf made of ground meats, fish, and/or vegetables
territoire *m.* territory
tes *pl.* your, 1-1
tête *f.* head, 7-1
têtu/e stubborn, 1-1
texte *m.* text, passage
texto *m.* text message, 10-2
thé *m.* tea, 5-1
thé au citron tea with lemon, 5-1
thé au lait tea with milk, 5-1
thé nature tea without milk or lemon, 5-1
théâtre *m.* theater (place), 2-3; theater studies, 8-2
théâtre romain Roman theater, 9-3
thème *m.* theme
thèse *f.* thesis
thon *m.* tuna, 5-3
ticket *m.* subway ticket, 9-1; ticket (for event)
timide shy, 1-1
tirage *m.* printing, circulation in print
tirer to fire, to shoot off; to drag
tirer une conclusion to draw a conclusion
tirer un feu d'artifice to set off fireworks
tissu *m.* fabric, 3-3
titre *m.* title
toilettes *f. pl.* toilet, restroom, 6-1
articles *m. pl.* **de toilette** toiletries, 3-1
toi you, P-1
toi-même yourself
toit *m.* roof, 6-2
sous les toits in the attic, 6-2
tomate *f.* tomato, 5-3
tombe *f.* grave, tombstone
tomber to fall, 4-2
tomber amoureux/-euse (de) to fall in love (with), 7-3
ton *m. sg.* your, 1-1
ton *m.* shade, tone
tonnerre *m.* thunder, 4-1
Il y a du tonnerre. It's thundering., 4-1
tôt early, 3-1
toujours always, 3-1
tour *f.* tower
tour *m.* trip, outing, visit, 4-2; turn
faire † un tour au parc to take a walk in the park, 4-2
tourisme *m.* **: faire † du tourisme** to go sightseeing, 4-2
Office du tourisme tourism office, 9-3
tourner to turn, 9-3
tourner un film to shoot a film, 10-1
tous *m. pl.* all, 8-1
tout *m. sg.* everything, 9-1
tout, tous, toute, toutes all
Pas tout à fait ! Not quite!, 4-3
tous/toutes les... every . . ., 3-1; all (the) . . .
tous les jours every day
tout à fait completely
tout de suite right away, immediately
tout droit straight ahead, 9-3
tout le monde everyone, everybody, 10-2
trace *f.* trace
tradition *f.* tradition
traditionnel/le traditional
traduction *f.* translation
traduire to translate
tragédie *f.* tragedy
train *m.* train, 9-1
être en train de (+ *inf.***)** to be busy (doing *st.*), 3-1
traiter to treat, to deal with
tram(way) *m.* tram, street car, 9-1
tranche *f.* slice, 5-2
tranquille quiet, calm, tranquil, 6-1
transfert *m.* transfer
transports *m. pl.* **en commun** public transportation
travail *m.* work, job, 8-3
travailler to work, to study, 1-3
travailler dans le jardin to work in the garden/yard, 1-3
travailleur/-euse hard-working
travers : à travers through, across
traverser to cross, 9-3
treize thirteen, 1-2
trente thirty, 1-2
trente-et-un thirty-one, 1-2
très very, P-1
Très bien, merci. Very well, thank you., P-1
triangle *m.* triangle
trimestre *m.* trimester, quarter, 8-2
triste sad, 7-3
trois three, 1-2
troisième third, 6-1
trombone *m.* trombone
trompette *f.* trumpet
trop too, too much, 1-1
trouver to find, 3-2
Je trouve que... I find that . . .
se trouver to be located, to find oneself, 5-3
truite *f.* trout
tu you, P-1
tué/e *adj.* killed, dead
tuer to kill
tuile *f.* (roofing) tile
typique typical, 1-3
typiquement typically

U

un/e a, an, one, P-2
-unième : vingt-et-unième twenty-first, 6-1
uni/e united
uniforme *m.* uniform
uniforme *adj.* regular, uniform
union *f.* **libre** cohabitation
vivre en union libre to live together as a couple
universel/le universal
universitaire related to the university
université *f.* university, 8-1
urbain/e related to the city, urban
urgence *f.* emergency
urgent/e urgent
usager *m.* user
utile useful, 9-2
Il est utile que... It is useful (that) . . ., 9-2
utilisation *f.* use
utiliser to use

V

vacances *f. pl.* vacation, 4-2
Bonnes vacances ! Have a good vacation!, 7-2
grandes vacances summer vacation, 7-2
vaisselle *f.* tableware, dishes, 6-2
faire † la vaisselle to do the dishes
valise *f.* suitcase, 9-1
vallée *f.* valley, 6-3
valoir † to be worth
Il vaut mieux que... It is/would be better that . . ., 9-2
valse *f.* waltz
variable variable; inflected in gender/number
varié/e varied, various, diverse
variété *f.* variety, diversity
vaste vast
vaut *see* **valoir**
vedette *f.* movie star, 10-1
vélo *m.* bicycle, 2-2
faire † du vélo to ride a bicycle, to go biking, 2-2
vendeur *m.*, **vendeuse** *f.* sales clerk, 8-3
vendre to sell, 4-1
vendredi Friday, 1-3
venir † to come, 4-2
venir de (+ *inf.*) to have just (done *st.*), 8-3

vent *m.* wind, 4-1
Il y a du vent. It's windy., 4-1
ventre *m.* belly, abdomen, 7-1
verbal/e verbal
verbe *m.* verb
verglas *m.* sleet, ice on the ground, 4-1
Il y a du verglas. It's icy/slippery., 4-1
vérifier to check, to verify
verre *m.* glass, 5-1
vers around, toward, 3-2
vers *m.* line of verse
verser to pour
version *f.* **française (en VF)** dubbed in French, 10-1
version *f.* **originale (en VO)** in the original language, 10-1
vert/e green, 3-3; unripe
veste *f.* jacket, suit coat, 3-3
vêtement *m.* (an item of) clothing, 3-3
viande *f.* meat, 5-2
vidéo *f.* video
vie *f.* life, 6-3
vieux (vieil)/vieille old, 3-3
Vietnam *m.* Vietnam, 9-2
vietnamien/ne *adj.* Vietnamese, 9-2
villa *f.* detached house (not in the city); villa, 6-3
village *m.* village, 9-3
village médiéval medieval village, 9-3
village perché village perched on a hillside, 9-3
ville *f.* city, 2-3
vin *m.* wine, 5-1
vin blanc white wine, 5-1
vin rosé rosé wine, 5-1
vin rouge red wine, 5-1
vinaigre *m.* vinegar, 5-3
vingt twenty, 1-2
vingt-et-un twenty-one, 1-2
vingt-deux twenty-two, 1-2
vingtième twentieth, 6-1
violence *f.* violence, roughness, brutality
violent/e violent, rough, brutal
violet/te purple, 3-3
violon *m.* violin
violoncelle *m.* cello
virtuel *m.* virtual reality
virus *m.* virus
visage *m.* face
visite *f.* visit, 4-2
rendre visite à *qqn* to visit so., 4-1
visiter to visit a (place), 4-2
vitesse *f.* speed
vitrine *f.* display window, 3-3
Vive (la Réunion) ! Hurray for (Reunion)!, 4-2
vivre † to live (quality of life)
vœu *m.* wish, 7-2
Meilleurs vœux ! Best wishes!, 7-2
voici... here is/are . . ., P-1
voilà... here/there is/are . . ., P-2
voile *f.* sail, sailing
faire † de la voile to go sailing, 4-2
voile *m.* veil
voilé/e veiled
voir † to see, 2-3
voir † une exposition to see an exhibit, 2-3
voir † un film to see a film (in a cinema), 2-3
voir † une pièce to see a play, 2-3
Voyons ! See here!
Voyons... Let's see . . ., 9-1
voisin *m.*, **voisine** *f.* neighbor, 6-1
voiture *f.* automobile, car, 6-1
voix *f.* voice
à haute voix out loud
vol *m.* flight, 9-1
voler to fly; to steal
volley(-ball) *m.* volleyball, 2-2
volonté *f.* wish, will
de bonne volonté *adv.* willingly
Volontiers. With pleasure, gladly., 4-3
vos *pl.* your, 1-2
votre *m./f. sg.* your, 1-2
vouloir † (+ ***inf.*****)** to want, to wish (to do *st.*), 7-3
je voudrais I would like, 5-1
vous you, P-1; *pron.* to you, 6-2
vous-même yourself
vous-mêmes yourselves
voyage *m.* trip, voyage, 9-1
Bon voyage ! Have a good trip!, 7-2
faire un voyage to take a trip, 9-1
voyager † to travel, 8-3
voyelle *f.* vowel
voyons *see* **voir**
vrai/e true
C'est vrai. That's true.
Ce n'est pas vrai !/C'est pas vrai ! It can't be!, 4-2
vraiment really, 1-1
vue *f.* view
vue d'ensemble overview

W

W.-C. *m. pl.* toilet, restroom (*lit.* water closet), 6-1
webcam *f.* webcam, 10-2
week-end *m.* weekend, 1-3
ce week-end this weekend, 2-3
le week-end on weekends, every weekend, 6-3
western *m.* western (film), 10-1
wi-fi *m.* wireless network, wifi, 10-2

Y

y *pron.* there, 9-1
il y a there is/are, LP
yaourt *m.* yogurt, 5-2
yeux *m. pl. see* **œil**

Z

zapper to channel surf
zéro *m.* zero, 1-2
zoologie *f.* zoology, 8-2
Zut (alors) ! Darn!, 3-2

Appendice 4

LEXIQUE ANGLAIS-FRANÇAIS

Here is a complete list of the abbreviations used in the glossaries:

adj. adjectif/adjective
adv. adverbe/adverb
Can. canadien/Canadian usage
conj. conjonction/conjunction
fam./colloq. familier/colloquial usage
f. féminin/feminine
inf. infinitif/infinitive
inv. invariable
m. masculin/masculine
n. nom/noun
part. passé participe passé/past participle
pl. pluriel/plural
pron. pronom/pronoun
qqch./st. quelque chose/something
qqn/so. quelqu'un/someone
qqp./sw. quelque part/somewhere
reg. régional/regional usage
rel. pron. pronom relatif/relative pronoun
sg. singulier/singular
† verbe irrégulier/irregular verb

A

a, an un/e
abdomen ventre *m.*
able: to be able to pouvoir †
about de, environ, à peu près
  about ten meters away à environ dix mètres
  it is about . . . il s'agit de...
  that's about all c'est à peu près tout
above au-dessus (de)
abroad à l'étranger
absent, missing absent/e
accident accident *m.*
according to (me/you/him/her) d'après moi/toi/vous/lui/elle
accountant comptable *m./f.*
accounting comptabilité *f.*
ache mal *m.* (*pl.* des maux)
  to have a headache avoir mal à la tête
acquaintance connaissance *f.*
across from en face de
active actif/-ive
activity activité *f.*
actor/actress acteur *m.*, actrice *f.*
to add additioner, ajouter ; **(in a recipe)** incorporer
address adresse *f.*
  address book carnet *m.* d'adresses
adminstrative administratif/-ive
to adore adorer
adventure movie film *m.* d'aventures
advertisement annonce *f.*, publicité *f.* (une pub)
affected: to be affected by ressentir
affectionate affectueux/-euse
to affirm maintenir †
afraid: to be afraid avoir † peur
Africa Afrique *f.*
African africain/e
after, afterward après
  after having . . . après avoir/être (+ *part. passé*)
afternoon après-midi *m.*
  in the afternoon, P.M. de l'après-midi
again encore
age âge *m.*
  What is your age? Quel est ton/votre âge ?, Quel âge as-tu/avez-vous ?
agenda agenda *m.*
aged, old âgé/e
ago il y a...
  two days ago il y a deux jours
to (not) agree (ne... pas) être † d'accord
  I don't agree. Je ne suis pas d'accord.
air air *m.*
  air conditioning climatisation *f.*
airplane avion *m.*
airport aéroport *m.*
aisle (in a store) rayon *m.*
alarm clock réveil *m.*
alcohol alcool *m.*
Algeria Algérie *f.*
Algerian algérien/ne
alive vivant/e
all tout, tous, toute, toutes
  all alone tout/e seul/e
  all of a sudden tout d'un coup
  all right d'accord
  all the same quand même
  all the time tout le temps, toujours
to allow (so. to do st.) permettre à *qqn* de faire *qqch.*
  She allowed him to leave. Elle lui a permis de partir.
almost presque
  almost all the students presque tous les étudiants
alone seul/e
along: to get along (with him/her/them) s'entendre (avec lui/elle/eux/elles)
Alps Alpes *f. pl.*
already déjà
also aussi
always toujours
ambitious ambitieux/-euse
America Amérique *f.*
  North America Amérique du Nord
  South America Amérique du Sud
American américain/e
amphitheater amphithéâtre *m.*
to amuse oneself se distraire, s'amuser
amusing drôle, amusant/e
and et
anger colère *f.*
angry fâché/e, en colère
  to become angry with *so.* se fâcher contre qqn
animal animal *m.*
animated film film *m.* d'animation
ankle cheville *f.*
to announce annoncer
announcement (public) annonce *f.*
  birth announcement faire-part *m. inv.* de naissance
  civil union announcement faire-part *m. inv.* de pacs
  wedding announcement faire-part *m. inv.* de mariage
another un/e autre, encore un/e
answer réponse *f.*
to answer répondre
  to answer a question répondre à une question
  to answer in French répondre en français
  to answer the phone répondre au téléphone
answering machine répondeur *m.*
anthropology anthropologie *f.*
antibiotic antibiotique *m.*
antique ancien/ne
anxious anxieux/-euse ; inquiet/-ète
anyhow, anyway quand même
apartment appartement *m.*
to appear avoir † l'air (+*adj.*)
  to appear ill avoir † l'air malade
appetizer entrée *f.*
apple pomme *f.*
April avril
Arab (person) Arabe *m./f.*
Arab *adj.* arabe
Arabic (language) arabe *m.*
architect architecte *m./f.*
Argentina Argentine *f.*
Argentinian argentin/e

to argue se disputer
arm bras *m.*
armchair fauteuil *m.*
armoire armoire *f.*
around vers, autour de
  around three o'clock vers trois heures
  around the table autour de la table
to arrange ranger †
arrival arrivée *f.*
to arrive arriver
art art *m.*
  art book livre *m.* d'art
  art history histoire *f.* de l'art
article article *m.*
as comme, aussi, autant
  as always comme toujours
  as (tall) as aussi (grand/e) que
  as much (patience) as autant de (patience) que
  as many (books) as autant de (livres) que
  as soon as dès que, aussitôt que
Asia Asie *f.*
Asian asiatique
to ask demander
  to ask a question poser une question
  to ask for directions demander le chemin
asleep endormi/e
asparagus asperge *f.*
aspirin aspirine *f.*
assignment devoir *m.*
association association *f.*
astronomy astronomie *f.*
at à
  at last enfin
  at once tout de suite
  at X's house chez X
  at the same time en même temps
athletic sportif/-ive
atlas atlas *m.*
attachment pièce-jointe *f.*
to attend assister à
attention attention *f.*
attorney avocat/e *m./f.*
August août
aunt tante *f.*
Australia Australie *f.*
Australian australien/ne
author auteur *m.*
autumn automne *m.*
avenue avenue *f.*
awake réveillé/e
automobile voiture *f.*

B

baby bébé *m.*
  to babysit faire † du baby-sitting
back dos *m.*
  backpack sac *m.* à dos
back: to come back revenir †
  to come back home rentrer
bacon bacon *m.*
bad mauvais/e
  Not bad. Pas mal.
  It's too bad. C'est dommage.
badly mal
bag sac *m.*
bakery/pastry aisle rayon *m.* boulangerie-pâtisserie
balcony balcon *m.*
banana banane *f.*
baptism baptême *m.*
basement sous-sol *m.*
basket panier *m.*
basketball basket-ball *m.* (basket)
bathing suit maillot *m.* de bain (maillot)
bathroom salle *f.* de bains
to be être †
beach plage *f.*
bean *haricot *m.*
  green bean *haricot vert
beautiful beau (bel)/belle
  It's beautiful weather. Il fait beau.
because parce que
  because of à cause de (+ *n.*)
to become devenir †
bed lit *m.*
  to get out of bed se lever †
  to go to bed se coucher
  (rural) bed and breakfast gîte *m.* (rural)
bedroom chambre *f.*
beef bœuf *m.*
  ground beef bifteck *m.* haché
beer bière *f.*
to beg prier
  I'm begging you. Je t'en prie./Je vous en prie.
before avant, devant
  before (me) devant (moi) (used spatially)
  before (doing *st.*) avant de (+ *inf.*)
  before ten o'clock avant dix heures
to begin (doing *st.*) commencer † (à + *inf.*)
beginning début *m.*
behind derrière
beige beige
Belgian belge
Belgium Belgique *f.*
to believe croire † (à, en)
  I believe in God. Je crois en Dieu.
  I believe that . . . Je crois que…
  I (don't) believe so. Je (ne) crois (pas).
belly ventre *m.*
to belong to faire † partie de, appartenir † à
belongings affaires *f. pl.*
below au-dessous (de)
beside à côté (de)
best le/la meilleur/e
  my best friend mon/ma meilleur/e ami/e
  Best wishes! Meilleurs vœux !
better meilleur/e *adj.*, mieux *adv.*
  a better teacher un meilleur professeur
  (to play) better . . . than (jouer) mieux… que
  it is better to il vaut mieux (+ *inf.*)
  it is better that il vaut mieux que
between entre
beverage boisson *f.*
  alcoholic beverage boisson alcoolisée
bicycle vélo *m.*
  to go for a bike ride faire † du vélo
big gros/se, large
  It's a big dictionary. C'est un gros dictionnaire.
  These pants are too big. Ce pantalon est trop large.
bill (restaurant) addition *f.*
  bill (utilites, etc.) facture *f.*
billion milliard *m.*
biography biographie *f.*
biology biologie *f.*
bird oiseau *m.*
birthday anniversaire *m.*
  Happy Birthday! Joyeux anniversaire !
black noir/e
blackboard tableau *m.* (noir)
blond: to have blond hair avoir † les cheveux blonds, être † blond/e,
blouse chemisier *m.*
to blow souffler
  to blow out the candles souffler les bougies *f. pl.*
blue bleu/e
to blush rougir
board tableau *m.*
  board game jeu *m.* de société
  whiteboard tableau blanc
boat bateau *m.*
  sailboat bateau à voile
body corps *m.*
book livre *m.*
  art book livre *m.* d'art
to book (a seat) retenir † (une place)
bookcase étagère *f.*
bookstore librairie *f.*
boot botte *f.*
border frontière *f.*
bored ennuyé/e
  to become bored s'ennuyer †
  He bores me. Il m'ennuie.
boring ennuyeux/-euse
born: to be born naître †
  He was born in 1995. Il est né en 1995.
to borrow (from) emprunter (à)
boss patron/ne *m./f.*
botany botanique *f.*
both tous/toutes les deux
to bother gêner
  It bothers me. Ça me gêne.
bothered gêné/e
bottle bouteille *f.*
bowl bol *m.*
box boîte *f.*
boy garçon *m.*
boyfriend petit ami *m.*, copain *m.*
brand-new neuf/neuve
Brazil Brésil *m.*
Brazilian brésilien/ne
bread pain *m.*
  French bread baguette *f.*
  round loaf of bread pain de campagne
  sliced (sandwich) bread pain de mie
to break casser
  to break up rompre †, casser
breakfast petit-déjeuner *m.*
  to have breakfast prendre le petit-déjeuner
to breathe respirer
bride mariée *f.*
bridegroom marié *m.*
to bring (along) a person amener †
to bring (*st.*) apporter, emporter

brochure brochure *f.*
brother frère *m.*
  brother-in-law beau-frère *m.*
  half-brother demi-frère *m.*
  stepbrother demi-frère *m.*
brown marron *adj. inv.*
  to have brown eyes avoir † les yeux marron
  to have brown hair avoir † les cheveux bruns, être † brun/e
browser navigateur *m.*
to brush brosser
  to brush one's hair se brosser les cheveux, se coiffer
  to brush one's teeth se brosser les dents, se laver les dents
building bâtiment *m.*, immeuble *m.*, pavillon *m.*
  an apartment building immeuble *m.*
  main building pavillon principal *m.*
  tall building grand bâtiment *m.*
bus (city) bus *m.*; **(between cities)** car *m.*
business les affaires *f. pl.*, entreprise *f.*
  businessman homme *m.* d'affaires
  businesswoman femme *f.* d'affaires
busy occupé/e, pris/e
  to be busy doing *st.* être † en train de (+ *inf.*)
  I'm busy Saturday night. Je suis pris/e samedi soir.
  I'm very busy now. Je suis très occupé/e en ce moment.
but mais
butcher shop boucherie *f.*
butter beurre *m.*
to buy acheter †
by par, de
  by myself tout/e seul/e, moi-même
  by phone par téléphone
  by the door par la porte
  by Victor Hugo de Victor Hugo
  two by two deux par deux
'bye salut

C

cable cable *m.*
cafeteria cafétéria *f.*
  university cafeteria restaurant *m.* universitaire
cake gâteau *m.*
  birthday cake gâteau d'anniversaire
  chocolate cake gâteau au chocolat
calculator calculatrice *f.*
calendar calendrier *m.*
  personal calendar agenda *m.*
call appel *m.*
to call appeler †
  to be called/named s'appeler †
calm calme
  to calm down se calmer
camera appareil photo *m.*
  camcorder, video camera caméscope *m.*
  digital camera appareil photo numérique *m.* (appareil numérique)
  web camera webcam *m.*
Cameroon Cameroun *m.*
Cameroonian camerounais/e
to camp/go camping faire † du camping
camper (vehicle) caravane *f.*
campground camping *m.*
campus campus *m.*
can boîte *f.*
can (to be able to do *st.*) pouvoir † (+ *inf.*)
Canada Canada *m.*
Canadian canadien/ne
candle bougie *f.*
candy bonbon *m.*
cantaloupe melon *m.*
cap casquette *f.*
car voiture *f.*
carafe carafe *f.*
card carte *f.*
  greeting card carte de vœux
  to play cards jouer aux cartes
care: to take care of s'occuper de
  I don't care. Ça m'est égal.
  to take care of oneself se soigner
career carrière *f.*
careful prudent/e
carrot carotte *f.*
to carry apporter
  carry out (food) à emporter
cartoon (film) dessin *m.* animé; **(drawing)** dessin *m.* humoristique
cash argent *m.*; liquide *m.*
  cash register caisse *f.*
  to pay in cash payer en liquide
cashier caissier *m.*, caissière *f.*
castle château *m.*
cat chat/te *m./f.*
cathedral cathédrale *f.*
CD, compact disc CD *m. inv.*
  CD/DVD burner graveur *m.* CD/DVD
  CD/DVD player lecteur *m.* CD/DVD
to celebrate fêter
celebrity célébrité *f.*, vedette *f.*
cell phone portable *m.*
center centre *m.*
century siècle *m.*
cereal céréales *f. pl.*
ceremony cérémonie *f.*
  civil ceremony cérémonie civile
  religious ceremony cérémonie religieuse
chair chaise *f.*
  armchair fauteuil *m.*
  wheelchair fauteuil *m.* roulant
chalk (stick of) craie *f.*
change (transformation) changement *m.*; **(money)** monnaie *f.*
to change changer (de + *n.*)
  to change clothes changer de vêtements
  to change one's mind changer d'avis
change purse porte-monnaie *m.*
channel chaîne *f.*
  to channel surf zapper
character personnage *m.*
  main character personnage principal
to chat bavarder, causer
cheap bon marché *adj. inv.*
cheese fromage *m.*
chemical product produit *m.* chimique
chemistry chimie *f.*
  chemistry lab laboratoire *m.* de chimie (labo de chimie)
chess échecs *m. pl.*
chest poitrine *f.*
chicken poulet *m.*
child enfant *m./f.*
  grandchildren petits-enfants *m. pl.*
China Chine *f.*
Chinese chinois/e
chocolate chocolat *m.*
choir choeur *m.*, chorale *f.*
to choose choisir
chorus chœur *m.*, chorale *f.* ; refrain *m.*
church (Catholic) église *f.*, **(Protestant)** temple *m.*
city ville *f.*
  city bus bus *m.*
  city hall mairie *f.*
  city map plan *m.* de ville
  in the city en ville
civil servant fonctionnaire *m./f.*
civil wedding cérémonie *f.* civile
class (subject) cours *m.*
  chemistry class cours de chimie
  elective class cours facultatif
  required class cours obligatoire
class (group of people) classe *f.*
  French class (people) classe de français ; **(subject)** cours *m.* de français
classical classique
classified ad petite annonce *f.*
classmate camarade *m./f.* de classe
classroom classe *f.*, salle *f.* de classe
to clean nettoyer †
clear clair/e
climate climat *m.*
clock horloge *f.*
  clock radio radio-réveil *m.*
  three o'clock trois heures
to close fermer
  closed fermé/e
closet placard *m.*
clothing vêtements *m. pl.*
cloud nuage *m.*
  It's cloudy. Il y a des nuages. Le ciel est couvert.
coast côte *f.*
coat manteau *m.*
  parka anorak *m.*
  raincoat imperméable *m.*
  suitcoat veste *f.*
coconut noix *f.* de coco
coffee café *m.*
  coffee table table *f.* basse
  coffee with cream café crème
  coffee with milk café au lait
to cohabit vivre en union *f.* libre
cohabitation union *f.* libre
coin pièce *f.* (de monnaie)
cola coca-cola *m.* (coca)
cold rhume *m.*
  I have a cold. J'ai un rhume. / Je suis enrhumé/e.
cold froid/e
  I'm cold. J'ai froid.
  It's cold (weather). Il fait froid.
cold cuts charcuterie *f. sg.*
college faculté *f.* (fac)
  to go to college (to be a college student) être † à la fac

Colombia Colombie *f.*
Colombian colombien/ne
color couleur *f.*
comb peigne *m.*
to comb peigner
  to comb (one's hair) se peigner
to come venir †
  to come back revenir †
  to come by passer
  to come home rentrer
  to come in entrer
comedy comédie *f.*
  dark comedy comédie dramatique
community communauté *f.*
comfortable (material objects) confortable ; **(person)** à l'aise
comic strip bande *f.* dessinée (BD)
communication communication *f.*
completely tout à fait
composition rédaction *f.*
computer ordinateur *m.*
  computer file fichier *m.*
  computer lab salle *f.* informatique
  computer science informatique *f.*
  computer scientist informaticien *m.*, informaticienne *f.*
  laptop (computer) (ordinateur) portable *m.*
concentration concentration *f.*
concert concert *m.*
condiment condiment *m.*
conflict (war) conflit *m.*
conformist conformiste
Congratulations! Félicitations !
to connect relier
  to connect to the Internet se connecter sur Internet
to contaminate contaminer
continent continent *m.*
to cook faire † la cuisine
cookbook livre *m.* de cuisine
cookie biscuit *m.*
cooking cuisine *f.*
cool: It's cool weather. Il fait frais.
contrary: on the contrary au contraire
copious copieux/-euse
co-renter colocataire *m./f.*
corn maïs *m.*
  corn on the cob épi *m.* de maïs
corner coin *m.*
  at the corner (of) au coin (de)
  corner café café *m.* du coin
corridor couloir *m.*
to cost coûter
cotton coton *m.*
couch canapé *m.*
country pays *m.*
  foreign country pays étranger
  in this country dans ce pays
country(side) campagne *f.*
  in the country à la campagne
course cours *m.*
  to take a course suivre † un cours
course: of course bien sûr
courtyard cour *f.*
cousin cousin/e *m./f.*
cream crème *f.*
  whipped cream crème Chantilly
credit card carte *f.* de crédit
critic (person) critique *m.*
criticism critique *f.*
critique critique *f.*
croissant croissant *m.*
  chocolate croissant pain *m.* au chocolat
to cross traverser
cruise croisière *f.*
to cry pleurer
cucumber concombre *m.*
cuisine cuisine *f.*
culture culture *f.*
cup tasse *f.*
cupboard placard *m.*
curtain rideau *m.*
customer client/e *m./f.*
to cut couper
cute mignon/ne

D

daily quotidien/ne
  daily publication quotidien *m.*
dairy aisle rayon *m.* crèmerie
  dairy products produits *m. pl.* laitiers
dance danse *f.*
to dance faire † de la danse, danser
dangerous dangereux/-euse
dark-haired brun/e
Darn! Zut (alors) !
to date *so.* sortir avec *qqn.*
datebook agenda *m.*
daughter fille *f.*
day jour *m.*, journée *f.*
  day before yesterday avant-hier
  that day ce jour-là
  Have a good day! Bonne journée !
dead mort/e
dear cher/chère
death mort *f.*
debit card carte *f.* bancaire
deceased décédé/e
December décembre
to decide décider
deep profond/e
deeply profondément
degree (in) diplôme *m.* (en)
  to do a degree (in) préparer un diplôme (en)
  to have a degree avoir † un diplôme
delicious délicieux/-euse
deli(catessen) charcuterie *f.*
  deli counter rayon *m.* charcuterie
  deli meats charcuterie *f. sg.*
delighted enchanté/e, ravi/e
to demand exiger
dentist dentiste *m./f.*
department store grand magasin *m.*
departure départ *m.*
to depend (on) dépendre (de)
  It/That depends! Ça dépend !
to descend descendre
to describe décrire †
desert désert *m.*
to desire désirer, vouloir †
desk bureau *m.*
dessert dessert *m.*
detail détail *m.*
detective movie film *m.* policier
to detest détester
dictionary dictionnaire *m.*
to die mourir †
diet régime *m.*
  to be on a diet suivre † un régime, faire † un régime, être † au régime
different différent/e
difficult difficile
difficulty: to have difficulty doing *st.* avoir † du mal à (+ *inf.*)
dining hall restaurant universitaire *m.* (resto U)
dining room salle *f.* à manger
dinner dîner *m.*, souper *m.* (*Can.*)
  to have dinner dîner, souper (*Can.*)
  to fix dinner préparer le dîner
  Dinner's ready! À table !
directions directions *f. pl.*
  to ask directions demander le chemin
director chef *m.*, directeur *m.*, directrice *f.*
  (film) director réalisateur *m.*, réalisatrice *f.*
  (stage) director metteur *m.* en scène
to disagree ne… pas être d'accord
  I disagree. Je ne suis pas d'accord.
disagreeable désagréable
disappointed déçu/e
disciplined discipliné/e
to discuss discuter de
dish plat *m.*
  This is my favorite dish. C'est mon plat préféré.
  to do the dishes faire † la vaisselle
to disobey désobéir à
display window vitrine *f.*
disposition caractère *m.*
to divorce, to get divorced divorcer
divorced divorcé/e
to do faire †
  to carry out do-it-yourself projects bricoler, faire † du bricolage
  to not do much ne pas faire † grand-chose
  do-it-yourself projects bricolage *m.*
  do-it-yourselfer bricoleur *m.*, bricoleuse *f.*
doctor (M.D.) médecin *m.*, docteur *m.*
doctorate (Ph.D.) doctorat *m.*
documentary documentaire *m.*
dog chien/ne *m./f.*
door porte *f.*
dormitory résidence *f.*
to doubt (that) douter (que)
  without a doubt sans doute
to download télécharger
downtown centre-ville *m.*
  to go downtown descendre en ville
dozen douzaine *f.*
draftsman/woman dessinateur *m.*, dessinatrice *f.*
drama drame *m.*; comédie *f.*
  psychological drama drame psychologique
to draw dessiner
drawing dessin *m.*
dream rêve *m.*
to dream rêver
dress robe *f.*
  to get dressed s'habiller
  to get undressed se déshabiller
dressing (oil and vinegar) vinaigrette *f.*
drink boisson *f.*
  cold drink boisson rafraîchissante

hot drink boisson chaude
to drink boire †
to drive aller † en voiture, conduire †
drive: USB/flash drive clé *f.* USB
(external) hard drive disque *m.* dur (externe)
driver's license permis *m.* de conduire
drug (illegal) drogue *f.*
to take (illegal) drugs se droguer
drug (medicine) médicament *m.*
to take medication prendre † un médicament
drum set batterie *f.*
to dry essuyer †
to dry oneself off s'essuyer †
to dub doubler
dubbed doublé/e
dubbed in French en version française (en VF)
due to à cause de (+ *n.*)
dumb bête, idiot/e
during pendant
DVD, Digital Versatile Disc DVD *m. inv.*
dynamic dynamique

E

each chaque
each one chacun/e
ear oreille *f.*
early tôt
to be early être † en avance
to get up early se lever † tôt
to earn money gagner de l'argent
earth (the Earth) terre (la Terre) *f.*
east est
easy facile
to eat manger †
to eat between meals grignoter
to eat breakfast prendre † le petit-déjeuner
to eat dinner dîner, souper (*Can.*)
to eat lunch déjeuner
to eat a snack goûter, grignoter
to eat supper souper (*Can.*), dîner
e-book reader lecteur *m.* ebook
economics sciences *f. pl.* économiques, économie *f.*
edge bord *m.*
to edit retoucher
to educate oneself s'instruire †
education sciences *f. pl.* de l'éducation
egg œuf *m.*
fried egg œuf sur le plat, œuf au plat
eight huit
eighteen dix-huit
eighty quatre-vingts, huitante (*reg.*), octante (*reg.*)
elbow coude *m.*
elderly âgé/e
the elderly des personnes *f.* âgées
elective facultatif/-ive *adj.*; cours *m.* facultatif
electronic game jeu *m.* électronique
elegant élégant/e
elementary school école *f.* primaire
elevator ascenseur *m.*
eleven onze
eliminate éliminer
e-mail mail, *m.*, mél *m.*, **(as medium)** e-mail *m.*, courriel *m.* (*Can.*)
e-mail address mél *m.*
e-mail message mail *m.*, courriel *m.* (*Can.*)
embarrassed embarrassé/e, gêné/e
emphasis (in studies) concentration *f.*
employee employé/e
empty vide
to encourage encourager
encyclopedia encyclopédie *f.*
end fin *f.*
energetic énergique
engaged fiancé/e
to get engaged se fiancer
engine moteur *m.*
search engine moteur de recherche
engineer ingénieur *m.*
engineering génie *m.*
England Angleterre *f.*
English anglais/e
enough assez
enough of *st.* assez de (+ *n.*)
to enter entrer
entertainment (TV show) divertissement *m.*
enthusiastic enthousiaste
entrance entrée *f.*
environment environnement *m.*
episode épisode *m.*
equipped équipé/e
poorly equipped mal équipé/e
well-equipped bien équipé/e
errand course *f.*
to run errands faire † des courses
eraser (for a pencil) gomme *f.* ; **(for the board)** brosse *f.*
especially surtout
essay essai *m.*, devoir *m.*
Europe Europe *f.*
European européen/ne
eve veille *f.*
Christmas Eve veille de Noël
Christmas Eve dinner/party réveillon *m.* de Noël
New Year's Eve Saint-Sylvestre *f.*
New Year's Eve party réveillon *m.* du Nouvel An
even même
even numbers numéros *m.* pairs
evening soir *m.*, soirée *f.*
eight o'clock P.M. huit heures du soir
Have a good evening! Bonne soirée !
event évènement *m.*
eventually finalement
every tout, tous, toute, toutes
every day tous les jours
every evening tous les soirs
everyone tout le monde
everything tout
everywhere partout
exam examen *m.*
to study for an exam préparer un examen
to take an exam passer un examen
to pass an exam réussir un examen
example exemple *m.*
for example par exemple
except sauf, à part
everyone except him tout le monde sauf lui
except for that one à part celui-là
to exchange échanger
excited impatient/e, enthousiaste
excursion bus car *m.*
excuse excuse *f.*
Excuse me. Pardon.
exercise exercice *m.*
to exercise faire † de l'exercice
exhibit exposition *f.*
expensive cher/chère
to explain expliquer
eye œil *m.* (*pl.* yeux)

F

face figure *f.*
to face donner sur, être en face de
The window faces the street. La fenêtre donne sur la rue.
The town hall faces the market square. La mairie est en face de la Place du marché.
facing face à
Facing the town hall is a square. Face à la mairie, il y a une place.
to fail rater
fair juste
It's not fair! Ce n'est pas juste !
fairly (rather) assez (+ *adj.*)
faithful fidèle
fall automne *m.*
in the fall en automne
to fall tomber
to fall asleep s'endormir
to fall in love (with) tomber amoureux/-euse (de)
false faux/fausse
family famille *f.*
big family famille nombreuse
blended family famille recomposée
extended family famille étendue
single-parent family famille monoparentale
family relations relations *f. pl.* familiales
famous célèbre
fan fanatique *m.*
to be a fan of être † fanatique de
far (from) loin (de)
farm ferme *f.*
farmer fermier *m.*, fermière *f.*, agriculteur *m.*, agricultrice *f.*
fashion mode *f.*
to be in fashion être † à la mode
fashion designer couturier *m.*
high fashion haute couture *f.*
out of fashion démodé/e
fashionable à la mode
fast rapide *adj.*, vite *adv.*
It's a fast train. C'est un train rapide.
He runs fast. Il court vite.
to fast jeûner
to break a fast déjeûner
fat *adj.* gros/se
fat graisse *f.*
father père *m.*
father-in-law beau-père
grandfather grand-père
single father père célibataire
stepfather beau-père
favorite préféré/e

fear peur *f.*
to fear avoir † peur (de)
February février
to feel se sentir ; (*st.*) toucher *qqch.*
to feel bad aller † mal
to feel better aller † mieux
to feel good aller † bien, se sentir bien
to feel great être † en forme,
to feel like doing *st.* avoir † envie de (+ *inf.*)
feminine féminin/e
fever fièvre *f.*
few peu (de), quelques
He has few friends. Il a peu d'amis.
I have a few coins. J'ai quelques pièces.
I have a few (of them). J'en ai quelques-un/e/s.
fiancé/e fiancé *m.*, fiancée *f.*
field champ *m.*
fifteen quinze
fifty cinquante
to fight combattre †, se battre †
to fight stress pour combattre le stress
They're fighting. Ils se battent.
to fill remplir
film film *m.*
film director réalisateur *m.*, réalisatrice *f*
filmmaker cinéaste *m./f.*, réalisateur *m.*, réalisatrice *f.*
final final/e
finally finalement, enfin
to find trouver
I find that . . . Je trouve que…
fine bien
Fine, also. Bien aussi.
Fine, and you? Ça va, et toi ?
to be fine être † en forme, aller † bien
fine arts beaux-arts *m. pl.*
finger doigt *m.*
to finish finir
first *adj.* premier/-ière
first course entrée *f.*
first floor rez-de-chaussée *m.*
first *adv.* en premier
first (of all) d'abord
fish poisson *m.*
fish counter rayon *m.* poissonnerie
fishing pêche *f.*
to go fishing aller à la pêche
five cinq
to fix réparer
to fix one's hair se coiffer
fixed-price meal menu *m.*
flight vol *m.*
floor étage *m.*, terre *f.*
first (ground) floor rez-de-chaussée *m.*
second floor premier étage *m.*
on the floor par terre
flour farine *f.*
to flow couler
flower fleur *f.*
flu grippe *f.*
to fly (people) aller † en avion, prendre † l'avion ; **(birds)** voler
fog brouillard *m.*
It's foggy. Il y a du brouillard.
follow suivre †
fondue fondue *f.*
meat fondue fondue bourguignonne
cheese fondue fondue savoyarde
food provisions *f. pl.*, aliment *m.*, nourriture *f.*, cuisine *f.*
to buy food acheter des provisions
frozen foods (aliments) surgelés
I love food. J'adore la nourriture.
She prefers Italian food. Elle préfère la cuisine italienne.
foot pied *m.*
on foot à pied
football football *m.* américain
football game match *m.* de football américain
football stadium stade *m.*
for pour ; depuis (+ *time expression*) ; pendant (+ *time expression*)
I'm leaving for two weeks. Je vais partir pour quinze jours.
I'm leaving for France. Je vais partir pour la France.
I've been here for thirty minutes. Je suis ici depuis trente minutes.
I waited for thirty minutes. J'ai attendu pendant trente minutes.
foreign étranger/-ère *adj.*
foreigner étranger *m.*, étrangère *f.*
forest forêt *f.*
to forget oublier
former ancien/ne
fortunately heureusement
forty quarante
four quatre
fourteen quatorze
France France *f.*
free (a person) libre ; **(a thing)** gratuit/e
I'm not free. Je ne suis pas libre.
to freeze geler †
It's freezing. Il gèle.
French français/e
French bread (long, thin loaf) baguette *f.*
French fries frites *f.*
fresh frais/fraîche
Friday vendredi
friend ami/e, camarade *m./f.*, copain *m.*, copine *f.*
best friend meilleur/e ami/e *m./f.*
(my) boyfriend (mon) petit ami *m.*, (mon) copain *m.*, (mon) ami *m.*
(my) girlfriend (ma) petite amie *f.*, (ma) copine *f.*, (mon) amie *f.*
Your friend, Amitiés, *f. pl.*
friendly sociable
friendship amitié *f.*
from de (d')
front: in front of devant
frozen foods surgelés *m. pl.*
fruit fruit *m.*
fruit juice jus *m.* de fruit
fun: to have fun s'amuser
fun activity distraction *f.*
funny amusant/e, drôle
furious furieux/-euse
furnished meublé/e
furniture meuble *m.*
future avenir *m.*
future tense futur *m.*

G

to gain weight grossir
game jeu *m.* ; **(sports)** match *m.*
game show jeu *m.* télévisé
garage garage *m.*
garden jardin *m.*
to garden faire † du jardinage, travailler dans le jardin
garlic ail *m.*
gas gaz *m.* ; **(for a car)** essence *f.*
generous généreux/-euse
gentle doux/douce
geography géographie *f.*
geology géologie *f.*
German allemand/e
Germany Allemagne *f.*
to get obtenir †
to get a grade avoir † une note
to get along (with *so.*) s'entendre (avec *qqn*)
to get a degree obtenir † un diplôme
to get divorced divorcer
to get dressed s'habiller
to get engaged se fiancer
to get married se marier
to get ready se préparer
to get together se retrouver
to get undressed se déshabiller
to get up se lever †
Get up/Stand up! Levez-vous ! Lève-toi !
gift cadeau *m.*
girl fille *f.*, jeune fille *f.*
girlfriend petite amie *f.*, copine *f.*
to give donner, offrir †
to give advice conseiller, donner des conseils
to give back rendre
to give a present offrir †
glad content/e
glass verre *m.*
glasses lunettes *f. pl.*
sunglasses lunettes de soleil
glove gant *m.*
to go aller †
to go around faire † un tour
to go around the world faire † le tour du monde
to go back retourner
to go by passer
to go down descendre
to go home rentrer
to go in entrer
to go on/keep going continuer
to go out sortir
to go to bed se coucher
to go to the doctor aller † chez le médecin
to go up monter
God Dieu *m.*
godfather parrain *m.*
godmother marraine *f.*
golf golf *m.*
good bon/ne *adj.*,
goodbye au revoir
Good evening. Bonsoir.
Good morning. Bonjour.
Good night. Bonne nuit.
Have a good day. Bonne journée.
Have a good evening. Bonne soirée.

government gouvernement *m.*
government worker fonctionnaire *m./f.*
grade note *f.*
 to have/get a grade avoir † une note
grandchildren petits-enfants *m. pl.*
granddaughter petite-fille *f.*
grandfather grand-père *m.*
grandmother grand-mère *f.*
grandparents grands-parents *m. pl.*
grandson petit-fils *m.*
grape raisin *m.*
gray gris/e
grease graisse *f.*
Great! Génial !
green vert/e
 green bean *haricot *m.* vert
 green salad salade *f.* (verte)
grilled grillé/e
 grilled ham-and-cheese sandwich croque-monsieur *m.*
grocery store épicerie *f.*
groom marié *m.*
ground terre *f.*
 ground floor rez-de-chaussée *m.*
 on the ground par terre
to grow pousser
 to grow larger, fatter grossir
 to grow old vieillir
 to grow taller grandir
 to grow up (for children) grandir
guest invité/e *m./f.*
guide (person or book) guide *m.*
guinea pig cochon *m.* d'Inde
guitar guitare *f.*
 bass guitare guitare basse
 electric guitar guitare électrique
gym gymnase *m.*

H

hair cheveu *m.*
 to do one's hair se coiffer
 to wash one's hair se laver les cheveux
half demi/e
 half-brother demi-frère *m.*
 half-kilo demi-kilo *m.*
 half past et demi/e
hall, hallway couloir *m.*
ham jambon *m.*
hamburger *hamburger *m.*
hand main *f.*
 on the other hand, de l'autre côté, en revanche
 to raise your hand lever † le doigt, lever † la main
 handbag sac *m.* à main
 to hand in/over remettre †
handicap *handicap *m.*
to be handicapped être *handicapé/e
handsome beau (bel), belle
to happen se passer, avoir † lieu
 What's happening? Qu'est-ce qui se passe ?
happiness bonheur *m.*
happy heureux/-euse, content/e
 Happy Birthday! Joyeux anniversaire !
 Happy New Year! Bonne année !
hard (difficult) difficile
 hardworking sérieux/-euse, travailleur/-euse
harmonica harmonica *m.*
hat chapeau *m.*
 wool (knitted) hat bonnet *m.* de laine
to hate détester
to have avoir †
 to have a drink prendre † quelque chose à boire, prendre † un verre
 to have a good time s'amuser
 Have a nice day/evening/weekend! Bonne journée/soirée !/Bon week-end !
 to have just (done *st.*) venir † de (+ *inf.*)
 to have to (do *st.*) devoir † (+ *inf.*)
he il
 he and I lui et moi
head tête *f.*
 to have a headache avoir † mal à la tête
headlines gros titres *m. pl.*
health santé *f.*
 health center/clinic infirmerie *f.*
healthy (thing) bon/ne pour la santé; **(person)** en bonne santé
hear entendre
heart cœur *m.*
 heart attack crise *f.* cardiaque
hearty copieux/-euse
heavy lourd/e
 heavy jacket blouson *m.*
height taille *f.*
 of average height de taille moyenne
Hello Bonjour ; **(telephone only)** Allô
to help (*so.* do *st.*) aider (*qqn.* à + *inf.*)
her elle ; la ; son, sa, ses (+ *n.*)
 with her avec elle
 I see her. Je la vois.
 her child son enfant
 to her lui
 herself elle-même
herbal tea tisane *f.*
here ici
 Here is/are . . . Voici…
 Here/There is/are . . . Voilà…
Hi! Salut !
high *haut/e
high school lycée *m.*
hike randonnée *f.*
 to go on a hike faire † une randonnée
hill colline *f.*
him le ; lui
 I see him. Je le vois.
 to him lui
 himself lui-même
his son, sa, ses (+ *n.*)
history histoire *f.*
hockey *hockey *m.*
to hold retenir †, tenir †
 to hold in one's hand tenir dans la main
 to hold one's breath retenir † le souffle
holiday fête *f.*
 legal holiday jour *m.* férié
 religious holiday fête religieuse
home maison *f.*
homebody pantouflard/e
home owner propriétaire *m./f.*
homework devoirs *m. pl.*
 to do homework faire † les devoirs *m.*
to hope espérer †, souhaiter
horror movie film *m.* d'horreur
hors d'œuvre *hors d'œuvre *m. inv.*
horse cheval *m.*
horseback: to go horseback riding faire † du cheval
hospital (public) hôpital *m.*, **(private)** clinique *f.*
hostel (youth) auberge *f.* (de jeunesse)
hot chaud ; **(spicy)** épicé/e
 hot chocolate chocolat *m.* chaud
 I am hot. J'ai chaud.
 It's hot (weather). Il fait chaud.
hotel hôtel *m.*
hour heure *f.*
 in an hour (from now) dans une heure
house maison *f.*
 at X's house chez X
 housemate colocataire *m./f.*
 housewife/househusband femme *f.*/ homme *m.* au foyer
how comment
 How are you? Comment allez-vous ? /Comment vas-tu ?
 how many/much combien de (+ *n.*)
 How much does that cost? Ça coûte combien ?
 How old are you? Quel âge as-tu/avez-vous ?
 How's it going? Comment ça va ?
human being être *m.* humain
human body corps *m.* humain
humanities lettres *f. pl.*
humid lourd/e
 It's humid. Il fait lourd.
hundred cent
hunger faim *m.*
 to be hungry avoir † faim
Hurray for . . . ! Vive… !
to hurry up se dépêcher
 in a hurry pressé/e
 I'm always in a hurry. Je n'arrête pas de courir.
hurt blessé/e
to hurt (somewhere) avoir † mal à (+ *n.*)
to hurt (*so.*) faire † mal (à *qqn*)
husband mari *m.*
hypochondriac *m./f.* hypocondriaque

I

I je (j')
ice glace *f.*
 ice cream glace *f.*
 ice cube glaçon *m.*
 ice on the ground verglas *m.*
ID card carte *f.* d'identité
idealistic idéaliste
if si
 If I were you . . . À ta/votre place…
important important/e
in à, dans, en
 in a box dans une boîte
 in France en France
 in my room dans ma chambre
 in Paris à Paris
 in the library à la bibliothèque
 in the U.S. aux États-Unis
 in town en ville
in-laws beaux-parents *m. pl.*

included compris/e
all included tout compris
tip included service *m.* compris
utilities are included les charges *f. pl.* sont comprises
independent autonome ; indépendant/e
India Inde *f.*
Indian indien/ne
individualistic individualiste
indulgent indulgent/e
industrial industriel/le
inexpensive bon marché *adj. inv.*
infection infection *f.*
infomercial émission *f.* de téléachat
information renseignement *m.*
to get information se renseigner
injured blessé/e
inn auberge *f.*
inside dans, à l'intérieur de, dedans
inside the house dans la maison, à l'intérieur de la maison
to look inside regarder à l'intérieur, regarder dedans
instant messaging messagerie *f.* instantanée
instead of au lieu de (+ *n.*, + *inf.*)
intelligent intelligent/e
intensity intensité *f.*
interesting intéressant/e
interested: to be interested in s'intéresser à
Internet Internet *m.*
to connect to the Internet se connecter sur Internet
Internet access accès *m.* à Internet
Internet user internaute *m./f.*
on the Internet sur Internet
interview interview *f.*, **(job)** entretien *m.*
into dans
to introduce présenter
Je vous/te présente X. This is X.
invitation invitation *f.*
to invite inviter
irritable énervé/e
irritated: to become irritated s'énerver
island île *f.*
Israel Israël *m.*
Israeli israélien/ne
it ce (c') ; il ; elle ; le ; la
it is c'est ; il/elle est (+ *adj.*)
it isn't ce n'est pas ; il/elle n'est pas (+ *adj.*)
I see it. Je le/la vois.
Italian italien/ne
Italy Italie *f.*
Ivorian ivoirien/ne
Ivory Coast Côte d'Ivoire *f.*

J

jacket blouson *m.*
ski jacket anorak *m.*
(suit) jacket veste *f.*
jam confiture *f.*
January janvier
Japan Japon *m.*
Japanese japonais/e
jar pot *m.*
jazz jazz *m.*
jealous jaloux/-ouse
jeans jean *m. sg.*
job poste *m.*, travail *m.*, métier *m.*, emploi *m.*
full-time job travail à plein temps
it's my job c'est mon métier
to look for a job (as . . .) chercher un emploi (comme...)
part-time job travail à mi-temps
summer job job *m.* d'été
teaching job poste *m.* d'enseignant
What's his job? Qu'est-ce qu'il fait comme travail ?
to jog faire † du jogging
to joke plaisanter, blaguer, rigoler (*colloq.*)
You're joking! Tu rigoles !
joke histoire *f.* drôle, blague *f.*, plaisanterie *f.*
to tell a joke raconter une histoire drôle
journalism journalisme *m.*
journalist journaliste *m./f.*
July juillet
June juin

K

keyboard clavier *m.*
key clé *f.*
key word mot *m.* clé
to kid (around) rigoler (*colloq.*)
Are you kidding? Tu rigoles ?
kilo(gram) kilogramme *m.* (kilo)
kilometer kilomètre *m.*
kind gentil/le
That's kind (of you). C'est gentil à toi/vous.
king roi *m.*
king cake galette *f.* des rois
to kiss s'embrasser
kitchen cuisine *f.*
kitchen cabinet placard *m.*
(with) a kitchenette (avec) coin *m.* cuisine
knee genou *m.*
to know savoir † ; connaître †
to know a fact savoir †
to know how to do *st.* savoir † + *inf.*
to know a person/place connaître †
to know whether savoir † si

L

laboratory (lab) laboratoire *m.* (labo)
lab technician technicien *m.*, technicienne *f.* de laboratoire (de labo)
lady dame *f.*
lake lac *m.*
lamb chop côtelette *f.* d'agneau
lamp lampe *f.*
landlord/landlady propriétaire *m./f.*
language langue *f.*
in the original language en version *f.* originale (en VO)
foreign language langue étrangère
native language langue maternelle
laptop ordinateur *m.* portable, portable (*m.*)
last dernier/dernière
last month le mois dernier
last Saturday samedi dernier
last week la semaine dernière
last year l'année dernière, l'an dernier
to last durer
late tard
it's (too) late il est (trop) tard
to be late être † en retard
to laugh rire †
law droit *m.*
law school faculté *f.* de droit
lawyer avocat *m.*, avocate *f.*
lazy paresseux/-euse
to learn (to do *st.*) apprendre † (à + *inf.*)
leather cuir *m.*
to leave partir ; **(*so.*, *st.*)** quitter
to leave the lights on laisser les lumières allumées
lecture conférence *f.*
lecture hall amphithéâtre *m.*
left gauche *f.*
to the left à gauche
the (political) left la gauche
leftovers restes *m. pl.*
leg jambe *f.*
leisure activities loisirs *m. pl.*
lemon citron *m.*
lemonade citron *m.* pressé
lemon-lime soft drink limonade *f.*
to lend prêter
less moins
less (money) than . . . moins d'(argent) que...
less (handsome) than . . . moins (beau) que...
letter lettre *f.*
lettuce salade *f.*, laitue *f.*
library bibliothèque *f.* (bibli)
public library bibliothèque municipale (BM)
university library bibliothèque universitaire (BU)
license permis *m.*
driver's license permis de conduire
life vie *f.*
to lift lever †
to lift weights faire † de la musculation
light (color) clair/e ; **(weight)** léger, légère
light lumière *f.*
to leave the lights on laisser les lumières allumées
to turn on the lights allumer les lumières
to turn out the lights éteindre les lumières
lightning éclair *m.*
It's lightning. Il y a des éclairs.
likable sympathique, (sympa) *inv.*
like comme
to like aimer
to like fairly well aimer bien
to like a lot aimer beaucoup
line ligne *f.*
online en ligne
linguistics linguistique *f.*
link lien *m.*
to link relier
lip lèvre *f.*
to listen to écouter
to listen to music écouter de la musique
list liste *f.*
listing of TV programs magazine *m.* télé
liter litre *m.*
literature littérature *f.*
little petit/e (*adj.*), peu (*adv.*)

a little boy un petit garçon
He does little work. Il travaille peu.
a little bit un peu, un peu de (+ *n.*)
a little bit sad un peu triste
a little bit of money un peu d'argent
to live (location) habiter ; **(situation)** vivre †
She lives in Dijon. Elle habite Dijon.
She lives with her boyfriend. Elle vit avec son copain.
living room séjour *m.*, salle *f.* de séjour
loaf of sliced bread pain *m.* de mie
to locate trouver
to be located se trouver, être situé/e
long long/ue
a long time longtemps
For how long have you been speaking French? Depuis combien de temps est-ce que vous parlez français ?
I studied German a long time ago. Il y a longtemps que j'ai fait de l'allemand.
to look (seem) avoir † l'air (+ *adj.*)
to look after soigner, s'occuper de
to look at regarder
to look for chercher
to look good avoir † l'air bon/délicieux
to look like ressembler
to lose perdre
to lose one's composure perdre son sang-froid
to lose weight maigrir, mincir
a lot beaucoup
lots/a lot of books beaucoup de livres
to work a lot travailler beaucoup
lottery loto *m.*
to play the lottery jouer au loto
loudly fort
lovable aimable
love amour *m.*
to love aimer
to be in love (with) être † amoureux/-euse (de)
to fall in love (with) tomber amoureux/-euse (de)
luck chance *f.*
Good luck! Bonne chance !
luckily heureusement
to be lucky avoir † de la chance
unlucky malheureux/-euse
luggage bagages *m. pl.*
to carry up luggage monter les bagages
lunch déjeuner *m.*
to eat lunch déjeuner
lung poumon *m.*

M

Madam, ma'am Madame *f.* (Mme)
mad (at) faché/e (contre), en colère (avec)
magazine magazine *m.*
monthly magazine mensuel *m.*
weekly magazine hebdomadaire *m.*
mail courrier *m.*
e-mail mail *m.*, courriel (*Can.*)
mail carrier facteur *m.*, factrice *f.*
main principal/e
main building pavillon *m.* principal
main character personnage *m.* principal
main dish plat *m.* principal
major (in) spécialisation *f.* (en), majeure *f.* (en) (*Can.*)
majority plupart *f.* de (+ *n.*)
to make faire †
to make a mistake faire † une faute
makeup maquillage *m.*
to put on makeup se maquiller
man homme *m.*, monsieur *m.*
a great man un grand homme
a real gentleman un grand monsieur
mandatory obligatoire
many beaucoup de (+ *count n.*)
as many as autant de (+ *n.*)
how many? combien de ?
not many pas beaucoup
too many trop de (+ *n.*)
map carte *f.*, plan *m.*
campus map plan *m.* du campus
city map plan *m.* de ville
maple tree érable *m.*
maple syrup sirop *m.* d'érable
March mars
marital status état *m.* civil
marker (felt-tipped) feutre *m.*
market marché *m.*
flea market marché aux puces
open-air market marché en plein air
supermarket supermarché *m.*
married marié/e
to get married se marier
masculine masculin
mathematics mathématiques *f. pl.* (les maths)
May mai
maybe peut-être
mayonnaise mayonnaise *f.*
mayor maire *m.*
M.D. médecin *m.*
me moi, me
He sees me. Il me voit.
me neither moi non plus
me too moi aussi
not me pas moi
meal repas *m.*
before-meal drink apéritif *m.*
balanced meal repas équilibré
mean méchant/e
to mean vouloir † dire
What do you mean? Qu'est-ce que tu veux/vous voulez dire ?
means of transportation moyen *m.* de transport
meat viande *f.*
meat counter rayon *m.* boucherie
media médias *m. pl.*
medicine (field of study) médecine *f.* ; **(prescription drug)** médicament *m.*
mediocre médiocre
to meet se rencontrer, se retrouver, **(for the first time)** se connaître †, faire † la connaissance de qqn
to meet up (se) retrouver, se réunir
meeting rendez-vous *m.*
melon (cantaloupe) melon *m.*
Merry Christmas! Joyeux Noël !
meter mètre *m.*
Mexico Mexique *m.*
Mexican mexicain/e
microwave oven four *m.* à micro-ondes (micro-ondes)
middle: in the middle (of) au milieu (de)
middle school collège *m.*
middle-aged d'un certain âge
midnight minuit
milk lait *m.*
million million *m.*
mineral water eau *f.* minérale
minor (in) mineure *f.* (en) (*Can.*)
to minor (in) faire † une mineure (en) (*Can.*), faire † une concentration (en)
mint menthe *f.*
mint tea tisane *f.* à la menthe
minute minute *f.*
mirror miroir *m.*, glace *f.*
Miss Mademoiselle *f.* (Mlle)
to miss manquer, rater
I miss him/her. Il/Elle me manque.
I miss them. Ils/Elles me manquent.
I miss you. Tu me manques./Vous me manquez.
She just missed the bus. Elle vient de rater le bus.
missing absent/e
mistake faute *f.*, erreur *f.*
to make a mistake faire † une faute, se tromper
Mister (Mr.) Monsieur *m.* (M.)
to mix mélanger
modern moderne
moment moment *m.*
at that moment à ce moment-là
at this moment en ce moment
Monday lundi
money argent *m.*
monitor moniteur *m.*
flat-screen monitor moniteur *m.* avec un écran plat
month mois *m.*
last month le mois dernier
next month le mois prochain
moon (the Moon) lune (la Lune) *f.*
moped mobylette *f.*
more . . . than plus (+ *adv.*, + *adj.*) . . . que, plus de (+ *n.*)... que
more (expensive) than . . . plus (cher/chère) que...
more (quickly) than . . . plus (rapidement) que...
more (homework) than . . . plus de (devoirs) que...
morning matin *m.*
Moroccan marocain/e
Morocco Maroc *m.*
most la plupart *f.* des (+ *n.*)
mother mère *f.*
mother-in-law belle-mère
single mother mère célibataire
stepmother belle-mère
motorcycle moto *f.*
motorscooter mobylette *f.*
mountain montagne *f.*
to go mountain climbing faire † de l'alpinisme *m.*
mouse souris *f.*
wireless mouse souris sans fil
mouth bouche *f.*

to move (an object) bouger ; **(one's home)** déménager
movie film *m.*
  made-for-TV movie téléfilm *m.*
  movie star vedette *f.*, star *f.*
  movie theater cinéma *m.*
MP3 player baladeur *m.* MP3
Mr. Monsieur (M.)
Mrs. Madame (Mme)
Ms. Madame (Mme), Mademoiselle (Mlle)
much beaucoup de (+ *mass n.*)
  as much as autant de (+ *mass n.*)
  very much beaucoup
museum musée *m.*
  art museum musée d'art
mushroom champignon *m.*
music musique *f.*
musical comédie *f.* musicale
musician musicien *m.*, musicienne *f.*
must devoir † (+ *inf.*)
  You (One) must . . . Il faut…
  You (One) must not . . . Il ne faut pas…
mustard moutarde *f.*
my mon, ma, mes (+ *n.*)
  My name is . . . Je m'appelle…
myself moi-même

N

name (last) nom *m.*; **(first)** prénom *m.* ; **(nickname)** surnom *m.*
  My name is . . . Je m'appelle…
  What is your name? Comment vous appelez-vous/tu t'appelles ?
to name nommer
nationality nationalité *f.*
natural sciences sciences *f. pl.* naturelles
nature nature *f.*, caractère *m.*
nausea mal *m.* au cœur
  to feel nauseated avoir † mal au cœur
near (to) près (de)
  very near tout près
  nearly à peu près, presque
Neat! Chouette !
necessary nécessaire
  to be necessary falloir : il faut
neck cou *m.*
need besoin *m.*
to need avoir † besoin de (+*inf.*, + *n.*)
negative négatif/-ive
neighbor voisin/e *m./f.*
neighborhood quartier *m.*
neighboring voisin/e
neither non plus, ne… ni… ni
  me neither moi non plus
  she's neither tall nor short elle n'est ni grande, ni petite
nephew neveu *m.*
nervous agité/e, nerveux/-euse
Netherlands Pays-Bas *m. pl.*
network réseau *m.*
  social network réseau social
  wireless network réseau sans fil
never ne… jamais
new nouveau (nouvel)/nouvelle
  brand-new neuf/neuve
  What's new? Quoi de neuf ?
news informations *f. pl.* (infos), nouvelles *f. pl.*
  news broadcast journal *m.* télévisé
newsgroup forum *m.* de discussion
newspaper journal *m.*
newsstand kiosque *m.* à journaux
next prochain/e (*adj.*), ensuite (*adv.*)
  next to à côté de
nice sympathique, (sympa) (*inv.*), gentil/le, agréable
niece nièce *f.*
night nuit *f.*
  at night la nuit, le soir
nine neuf
nineteen dix-neuf
ninety quatre-vingt-dix, nonante (*reg.*)
no non
  no longer ne… plus
  no matter what n'importe quoi
  no more ne… plus
  no one ne… personne
noise bruit *m.*
  to make noise faire † du bruit
none aucun/e
  I have none of them. Je n'en ai aucun.
  None of them are here. Aucune d'entre elles sont là.
noon midi
normally normalement
north nord *m.*
  North America Amérique *f.* du Nord
nose nez *m.*
not pas, ne… pas
  not always pas toujours
  not at all pas du tout
  not bad pas mal
  not me pas moi
  not yet pas encore
notebook cahier *m.*
nothing ne… rien
novel roman *m.*
November novembre
now maintenant
number chiffre *m.*, numéro *m.*
nurse infirmier *m.*, infirmière *f.*
nut noix *f.*

O

to obey obéir à
to obtain obtenir †
obvious évident/e
occupation métier *m.*
October octobre
odd bizarre
  to do odd jobs around the house bricoler, faire † du bricolage
of de (d')
  of course bien sûr
offer offrir †
office bureau *m.*
often souvent
oil huile *f.*
  olive oil huile d'olive
OK d'accord
old vieux (vieil)/vieille ; **(former)** ancien/ne
  How old are you? Quel âge avez-vous/as-tu ?
  old-fashioned démodé/e
  older person personne *f.* âgée
  to be X years old avoir † X ans
olive olive *m.*
  olive oil huile d'olive
omelet omelette *f.*
on à, sur, en
  on foot à pied
  on purpose exprès
  on sale en solde
  on the table sur la table
  on TV à la télé
  on the contrary si, au contraire
once une fois
  once upon a time il était une fois
one un/e
onion oignon *m.*
online en ligne
  to go online aller sur Internet
only seulement ; ne… que
  He is only ten years old. Il a seulement dix ans./ Il n'a que dix ans.
open ouvert/e
to open ouvrir †
opinion opinion *f.*
  in my opinion à mon avis, d'après moi
opposite contraire *m.* ; en face (de)
  It's the opposite. C'est le contraire.
  The town hall is opposite the train station. La mairie est en face de la gare.
optimistic optimiste
optional facultatif/-ive
or ou
oral oral/e
  oral exam examen *m.* oral
  oral presentation exposé *m.*
orange (color) orange *adj. inv.*; **(fruit)** orange *f.*
  orange juice jus *m.* d'orange
  Orangina soda Orangina *m.*
order commande *f.*
to order commander
other autre (+ *n.*)
  others les autres *m./f. pl.*
our notre, nos
ourselves nous-mêmes
outdated démodé/e
outdoors en plein air, dehors
  outdoor market marché *m.* en plein air
  to play outdoors jouer dehors
outgoing sociable
outside dehors, à l'extérieur
oven four *m.*
  microwave (oven) (four à) micro-ondes *m.*
over fini/e
  It's over. C'est fini.
  over there là-bas
overcast: It's overcast. Le ciel est couvert.
overcoat manteau *m.*
to overlook donner sur
  The window overlooks the park. La fenêtre donne sur le parc.
to owe devoir † (+ *n.*)
to own posséder †, avoir †
owner propriétaire *m./f.*

P

Pacific Ocean océan *m.* Pacifique
to pack faire † les bagages
package paquet *m.*

page page *f.*
pain mal *m.* (*pl.* des maux)
 to have a pain in the leg avoir mal à la jambe
to paint peindre †
painter peintre *m.*
painting peinture *f.*, tableau *m.*
pale pâle
 to become pale pâlir
pants pantalon *m. sg.*
pantyhose collant *m.*
paper (material) papier *m.* ; **(written for a course)** dissertation *f.*, essai *m.*, devoir *m.* écrit
parent parent *m.*
park parc *m.*
to park garer
parka anorak *m.*
to participate in participer à
partner partenaire *m./f.*
part-time à mi-temps
party fête *f.*, soirée *f.*
to pass by/in front of passer devant
 to pass (an exam/a course) réussir (à)
passerby passant *m.*, passante *f.*
passport passeport *m.*
pasta pâtes *f. pl.*
pastime passe-temps *m.*
pastry (cake) pâtisserie *f.*, **(dough)** pâte *f.*
pâté pâté *m.*
path chemin *m.*
to pay payer
 to pay attention faire † attention
peach pêche *f.*
pear poire *f.*
peas petits pois *m. pl.*
pedestrian piéton *m.*
 pedestrian street rue *f.* piétonne
pen stylo *m.*
 felt-tipped pen feutre *m.*
pencil crayon *m.*
people gens *m. pl.*
pepper (spice) poivre *m.*
 green pepper poivron *m.* vert
 red pepper poivron *m.* rouge
percussion batterie *f.*
perfectly parfaitement
perhaps peut-être
permit permis *m.*
to permit (*so.* to do *st.*) permettre † (+ à *qqn*, de + *inf.*)
person personne *f.*
personality personnalité *f.*, caractère *m.*
pessimistic pessimiste
pet animal *m.* familier, animal de compagnie
pharmacist pharmacien *m.*, pharmacienne *f.*
pharmacy pharmacie *f.*
Ph.D. doctorat *m.*
philosophy philosophie *f.*
phone téléphone *m.*, **(cell)** portable *m.*, **(land line)** (téléphone) fixe *m.*
 phone number numéro *m.* de téléphone
to phone téléphoner
 to phone one another se téléphoner
photo(graph) photographie *f.* (photo)
photographer photographe *m./f.*
physical sciences sciences *f. pl.* physiques
physics physique *f.*
physiology physiologie *f.*
piano piano *m.*
 to play the piano jouer du piano
picnic pique-nique *m.*
 to have a picnic faire † un pique-nique
picture photographie *f.* (photo) ; **(painting)** tableau *m.*
pie tarte *f.*
 apple pie tarte aux pommes
piece morceau *m.*
 piece of furniture meuble *m.*
 piece of information renseignement *m.*
 piece of news nouvelle *f.*
 piece of toast pain *m.* grillé, rôtie *f.* (*Can.*), toast *m.*
piece of buttered toast with jam tartine *f*
pig cochon *m.*
pineapple ananas *m.*
pink rose
pizza pizza *f.*
place endroit *m.*, lieu *m.*
 at X's place chez X
 to take place avoir † lieu
plan projet *m.*
 to have plans être † pris/e, avoir † des projets
 to make plans faire † des projets
to plan organiser, planifier
plane avion *m.*
planner: day planner agenda *m.*
plastic plastique
plate assiette *f.*
play (theater) pièce *f.*
to play jouer
 to play an instrument jouer (de)
 to play a sport jouer (à)
 to play sports faire † du sport
 playing field terrain *m.* de sport
player joueur *m.*, joueuse *f.*
pleasant agréable
please s'il te plaît, s'il vous plaît
poem poème *m.*
poet poète *m.*
poetry poésie *f.*
police officer agent *m.* de police, agente *f.* de police
political science sciences *f. pl.* politiques
pork porc *m.*
Portugal Portugal *m.*
Portuguese portugais/e
position (job) poste *m.*
positive positif/-ive
possible possible
possibly éventuellement
post office poste *f.*
postcard carte postale *f.*
poster affiche *f.*, poster *m.*
potato pomme de terre *f.*, patate *f.* (*colloq., Can.*)
to pour verser
practical pratique
practice (music, theater) répétition *f.*, **(sports)** entraînement *m.*
to practice (music, theater) répéter †, **(sports)** s'entraîner
to prefer préférer †, aimer mieux
preparations préparatifs *m. pl.*
to prepare préparer
 prepared dish plat préparé *m.*
prescription ordonnance *f.*
present cadeau *m.*
present: to be present être présent/e
to present présenter, donner
press presse *f.*
to press presser
 to press (a button) appuyer sur (un bouton)
prestige prestige *m.*
pretty joli/e
to prevent (*so.* from doing *st.*) empêcher (à *qqn* de + *inf.*)
price prix *m.*
to print imprimer
printer imprimante *f.*
 multifunction printer imprimante multifonction
probably probablement
problem problème *m.*
produce aisle rayon *m.* fruits et légumes
profession profession *f.*
professor professeur *m.*, professeure *f.* (*Can.*) prof *m./f.* (*fam.*)
program (TV) émission *f.*
project projet *m.*
to promise (*so.* to do *st.*) promettre † (à *qqn* de + *inf.*)
psychological drama drame *m.* psychologique
psychology psychologie *f.*
public public *m.* ; public/publique *adj.*
 public transportation transports *m. pl.* en commun
pullover sweater pull(-over) *m.*
to punish punir
purple violet/te
purse sac *m.* à main
to push pousser
 to push (a button) appuyer sur (un bouton)
to put (on) mettre †; **(away)** ranger †

Q

quantity quantité *f.*
quarter quart *m.* ; trimestre *m.*
 quarter past three trois heures et quart
 quarter to three trois heures moins le quart
Quebec Québec *m.*
Quebecois québécois/e
queen reine *f.*
question question *f.*
 to ask a question poser une question
quiet réservé/e
quite assez (+ *adj.*)
quiz interrogation *f.*

R

rabbit lapin *m.*
radio radio *f.*
rail: light rail tram(way) *m.*
rain pluie *f.*
to rain pleuvoir †
 It's raining. Il pleut.

raincoat imper(méable) *m.*
to raise lever †
to raise one's hand lever † le doigt, lever † la main
to raise a child élever † un enfant
rapid rapide
rapidly vite
rarely rarement
rather assez, plutôt
raw vegetables crudités *f. pl.*
plate of raw vegetables assiette *f.* de crudités
razor rasoir *m.*
to read lire †
CD, DVD reader lecteur *m.* CD, DVD
ready prêt/e
real vrai/e
realistic réaliste
reality show émission *f.* de téléréalité
really vraiment
reason raison *f.*
reasonable raisonnable
to receive recevoir †
receptionist réceptionniste *m./f.*
recipe recette *f.*
recommendation recommandation *f.*
red rouge
redhead, redhaired roux/-sse
to reduce réduire
reference book ouvrage *m.* de référence
to reflect (on) réfléchir (à)
refrigerator réfrigérateur *m.*, frigo *m.*(*colloq.*)
region région *f.*
registrar: registrar's office bureau *m.* des incriptions
rehearsal répétition *f.*
to rehearse répéter †
to relax se détendre, se décontracter, se relaxer
relaxed décontracté/e
relative parent *m.*
remarried remarié/e
remember se rappeler †, se souvenir † de
remote control télécommande *f.*
renovated rénové/e
rent loyer *m.*
to rent louer
renter locataire *m./f.*
co-renter colocataire *m./f.*
to repeat répéter †
report (oral) exposé *m.*, **(written)** rapport *m.*, **(television/radio)** reportage *m.*
to request (that *so.* do *st.*) demander (à *qqn* de + *inf.*)
to require (*so.* to do *st.*) exiger † (à *qqn* de + *inf.*)
required obligatoire
reservation réservation *f.*
to make a reservation online faire † une réservation sur Internet
to reserve réserver, faire † une réservation
reserved réservé/e
residential résidentiel/le
residential neighborhood quartier *m.* résidentiel
resource ressource *f.*
responsibility responsabilité *f.*
responsible responsable
rest repos *m.*
to rest se reposer
restaurant restaurant *m.*
restroom toilettes *f. pl.*, W.-C. *m. pl.*
to return retourner
to return home rentrer
rice riz *m.*
to ride a bicycle faire † du vélo *m.*
right droite *f.*
It will be all right. Ça va s'arranger.
right away tout de suite
the (political) right la droite
to be right avoir † raison
to the right à droite
to ring sonner
river (flowing to sea) fleuve *m.;* **(as tributary)** rivière *f.*
roast rôti *m.*
pork roast rôti de porc
roast beef rosbif *m.*
rock music rock *m.*
role (film or theater) rôle *m.*
role play jeu *m.* de rôle
roll (bread) petit pain *m.*
roof toit *m.*
room pièce *f.*, salle *f.*
bedroom chambre *f.*
two bedroom apartment appartement *m.* trois pièces
classroom salle (de classe)
dining room salle à manger
living room salle de séjour, séjour *m.*
roommate colocataire *m./f.*, camarade de chambre *m./f.*
routine routine *f.*
rug tapis *m.*
rugby rugby *m.*
rule règle *f.*
ruler règle *f.*
to run courir †
to run errands faire † des courses *f. pl.*
RV camping-car *m.*

S

sad triste
sailboat bateau *m.* à voile
to go sailing faire † de la voile
salad salade *f.*
salary salaire *m.*
sale soldes *m. pl*
to be on sale être † en solde, soldé/e
sales clerk vendeur *m.*, vendeuse *f.*
sales representative représentant *m.*, représentante *f.* de commerce
salmon saumon *m.*
smoked salmon saumon fumé
salt sel *m.*
salty salé/e
same même
just the same quand même
the same thing la même chose *f.*
sandal sandale *f.*
sandwich (ham, cheese) sandwich *m.* (au jambon, au fromage)
Santa Claus Père Noël *m.*
Saturday samedi
to save (money) économiser ; **(a file)** sauvegarder un fichier
saxophone saxophone *m.*
to say dire †
scanner scanner *m.*
to scare faire † peur à
to be scared avoir † peur
scarf écharpe *f.*
silk scarf foulard *m.*
schedule emploi *m.* du temps
school école *f.*
elementary school école primaire
middle school collège *m.*
high school lycée *m.*
school within a university faculté *f.*
science science *f.*
science-fiction science-fiction *f.*
physical sciences sciences physiques
political science science politique
social sciences sciences humaines
screen écran *m.*
flat screen écran plat
sculpture sculpture *f.*
sea mer *f.*
seafood fruits *m. pl.* de mer
seashore bord *m.* de la mer
to search chercher
search engine moteur *m.* de recherche
season saison *f.*
seat (theater, movie) place *f.*, siège *m.*
second (measure of time) second *m.*
second (order) deuxième
second floor premier étage *m.*
secretary secrétaire *m./f.*
to see voir †
to see a doctor consulter le médecin
Let's see . . . Voyons...
See you soon! À bientôt !
See you tomorrow! À demain !
to seem (good) avoir † l'air (bon)
selfish égoïste
to sell vendre
semester semestre *m.*
to send envoyer †
Senegal Sénégal *m.*
Senegalese sénégalais/e
sensitive sensible
to separate séparer, **(couple)** se séparer
separated séparé/e
September septembre
series série *f.*
serious (person) sérieux/-euse ; **(accident, injury)** grave
to serve servir
server serveur *m.*, serveuse *f.*
service sector services *m. pl.*
to set mettre †, poser, situer
to set the table mettre † la table
seven sept
seventeen dix-sept
seventy soixante-dix, septante (*reg.*)
several plusieurs
shame honte *f.*
It's a shame. C'est dommage.
It's shameful. C'est une honte.
shampoo shampooing *m.*
shape: to be in shape être † en forme
to share partager †
to shave se raser
she elle

sheet of paper feuille *f.* de papier
shelf étagère *f.*
shirt (man's) chemise *f.* ; **(woman's)** chemisier *m.*
shoe chaussure *f.*
to shop faire † du shopping
  to shop for groceries faire † les courses *f. pl.*
shopkeeper commerçant *m.*, commerçante *f.*
shore plage *f.*, bord *m.* de la mer
short (not tall) petit/e ; **(not long)** court/e
shorts short *m. sg.*
shoulder épaule *f.*
to shout crier
show spectacle *m.*, représentation *f.*, **(TV)** émission
to show montrer
to shower se doucher, prendre † une douche
shrimp crevette *f.*
shuttle bus navette *f.*
shy timide, réservé/e
sick malade
side côté *m.*
sightseeing: to go sightseeing faire † du tourisme *m.*
silk soie *f.*
since (because) puisque ; **(time)** depuis
  Since when . . .? Depuis quand… ?
to sing chanter
singer chanteur *m.*, chanteuse *f.*
singing lesson leçon *f.* de chant
single célibataire
sink (bathroom) lavabo *m.* ; **(kitchen)** évier *m.*
Sir Monsieur *m.* (M.)
sister sœur *f.*
  half-sister demi-sœur
  sister-in-law belle-sœur
  stepsister demi-soeur
to sit down s'asseoir †
  Sit down! Asseyez-vous !/Assieds-toi !
site site *m.*
to situate situer
  to be situated at être † situé/e à
six six
sixteen seize
sixty soixante
size taille *f.*
  middle-sized de taille moyenne
to ski faire † du ski
  to water ski faire † du ski nautique
skin peau *f.*
skinny maigre
to skip (a meal) sauter (un repas)
skirt jupe *f.*
  mini-skirt mini-jupe
sky ciel *m.*
slacks pantalon *m. sg.*
to sleep dormir
  to be asleep être † endormi/e
  to fall asleep s'endormir
  to go back to sleep se rendormir
sleet verglas *m.*
slender mince
slice tranche *f.*
slim mince
slow lent
slowly lentement
small petit/e
smart intelligent/e
smart phone smartphone *m.*
smoke fumée *f.*
to smoke fumer
smoked fumé/e
snack casse-croûte *m. inv.*
  afternoon snack goûter *m.*
  snack bar snack-bar *m.*
to snack grignoter ; goûter
snake serpent *m.*
sneakers baskets *m. pl.*, tennis *m. pl.*
snow neige *f.*
to snow neiger
  It's snowing. Il neige.
to snowboard faire † du surf des neiges
snowman bonhomme *m.* de neige
so alors
  so do I moi aussi
  so what? et alors ?
soap savon *m.*
soap opera feuilleton *m.*
soccer football (foot) *m.*, soccer *m.* (*Can.*)
  soccer game match *m.* de football
sociable sociable
social sciences sciences *f. pl.* humaines
social worker assistant *m.*, assistante *f.* social/e
sociology sociologie *f.*
sock chaussette *f.*
software (program) logiciel *m.*
some du, de la, de l', des ; en ; quelques
  I have some coffee/cream/water. J'ai du café/de la crème/de l'eau.
  I have some croissants. J'ai des croissants/quelques croissants.
  I want some. J'en veux.
someone quelqu'un
something quelque chose
sometimes quelquefois
somewhere quelque part
son fils *m.*
  son-in-law gendre *m.*
  stepson beau-fils *m.*
song chanson *f.*
soon bientôt
sorry désolé/e
  to be sorry être † désolé/e, regretter
to sort trier
so-so comme ci, comme ça
sound bruit *m.*
soup soupe *f.*
south sud *m.*
  South America Amérique *f.* du Sud
souvenir souvenir *m.*
Spain Espagne *f.*
Spanish espagnol/e
to speak parler
  Speak louder! Parle/Parlez plus fort !
speciality spécialité *f.*
to spell épeler †
to spend (money) dépenser ; **(time)** passer
spice épice *f.*
  spicy épicé/e, piquant/e
spinach épinards *m. pl.*
spoon cuillère *f.*
sport sport *m.*
  sport coat veste *f.*
  sports complex centre *m.* sportif
  sports event émission *f.* sportive
  to play sports faire † du sport
  to like sports aimer le sport
spouse époux *m.*, épouse *f.*
spring printemps *m.*
  in (the) spring au printemps
spy espion *m.*, espionne *f.*
  spy movie film *m.* d'espionnage
square (in a city) place *f.*
stadium stade *m.*
staircase escalier *m.*
stairs escalier *m.*
star étoile *f.*
  movie star vedette *f.*, star *f.*
to start commencer †
  to start exercising again se remettre † à faire de l'exercice
station (train) gare *f.* ; **(subway/metro)** station *f.*
to stay rester
  to stay home rester à la maison
  to stay in a hotel loger † dans un hôtel
steak biftek *m.*, steak, *m.*
stepbrother demi-frère *m.*
stepdaughter belle-fille *f.*
stepfather beau-père *m.*
stepmother belle-mère *f.*
stepsister demi-sœur *f.*
stepson beau-fils *m.*
still encore, toujours
stomach estomac *m.*, ventre *m.*
  to have a stomach ache avoir † mal au ventre
to stop (s')arrêter
  Stop it! Arrête ! Arrêtez !
stoplight feu rouge *m.*
store magasin *m.*
storm orage *m.*
  It's storming. Il y a un orage.
story histoire *f.*
story (of a building, house) étage *m.*
  first story rez-de-chaussée *m.*
  second story premier étage
stout fort/e
stove cuisinière *f.*
straight ahead tout droit
strange bizarre, drôle
stranger étranger *m.*, étrangère *f.*
strawberry fraise *f.*
stream (large) rivière *f.*
to stream (media) télécharger
street rue *f.*
to do strength training faire † de la musculation
stress stress *m.*
stressed stressé/e
strong fort/e
stop arrêt *m.*
  bus stop arrêt *m.* de bus
  subway/metro stop station *f.* de métro
stubborn têtu/e
student étudiant *m.*, étudiante *f.*
studies études *f. pl.*
studio (apartment) studio *m.* ; **(artist's)** atelier *m.*
to study étudier, travailler

to study for an exam préparer un examen
to study (French) faire † (du français)
to study (to major in) French étudier le français
to study (tonight, this weekend) travailler (ce soir, ce week-end)
stuff affaires *f. pl.*
stupid bête
stylish chic, à la mode
subtitles sous-titres *m. pl.*
subtitled sous-titré/e ; en version originale (en VO)
to subscribe (to) s'abonner (à)
suburb banlieue *f.*
subway métro *m.*
to succeed (in doing *st.*) réussir (à + *inf.*)
sugar sucre *m.*
to suggest (doing *st.*) suggérer †, proposer (de + *inf.*)
suit (man's) costume *m.* ; **(woman's)** tailleur *m.*
suitcase valise *f.*
summer été *m.*
summer camp colonie *f.* de vacances
summer vacation grandes vacances *f. pl.*
sun soleil *m.*
It's sunny. Il y a du soleil.
sunburn coup *m.* de soleil
Sunday dimanche
sunglasses lunettes *f. pl.* de soleil
super super
supermarket supermarché *m.*
supermarket aisles rayons *m. pl.* du supermarché
to support soutenir †
sure sûr/e
to surf faire † du surf
to surf the Web surfer sur Internet
surfboard planche *f.* de surf
surfing surf *m.*
surprised étonné/e, surpris/e
sweater (cardigan) gilet *m.* ; **(pullover)** pull-over *m.*
swim nager †, faire † de la natation
swimming la natation *f.*
swimming pool piscine *f.*
swimsuit maillot *m.* de bain (maillot)
Swiss suisse
Switzerland Suisse *f.*
syrup sirop *m.*
maple syrup sirop d'érable

T

table table *f.* ; **(chart)** tableau *m.*
to set the table mettre † la table
to take prendre †
to take a nap faire † la sieste
to take a test passer un examen
to take a trip faire † un voyage
to take care of s'occuper de
to take care of oneself se soigner
to take courses suivre † des cours
to take (*so. sw.*) emmener † (*qqn qqp.*)
to take (*st. sw.*) emporter (*qqch. qqp.*)
talented doué/e
to talk (to *so.*, about *st.*) parler (à *qqn*, de *qqch.*)
tall grand/e
to tan bronzer
taste goût *m.*
to taste goûter
taxi taxi *m.*
tea thé *m.*
herbal tea tisane *f.*
tea with lemon thé au citron
tea with milk thé au lait
tea without milk or lemon thé nature
teacher professeur *m.*, prof *m./f.* (*fam.*), enseignant/e *m./f.*
team équipe *f.*
tear larme *f.*
to tease *so.* plaisanter avec *qqn*, taquiner *qqn*
technician technicien *m.*, technicienne *f.*
tedious ennuyeux/-euse
teenager adolescent *m.*, adolescente *f.*
telephone téléphone *m.* ; **(cell)** portable *m.*; **(land line)** (téléphone) fixe *m.*
telephone number numéro *m.* de téléphone
to telephone (*so.*) téléphoner à *qqn*
to telephone each other se téléphoner
television télévision *f.* (télé)
television set téléviseur *m.*
television station chaîne *f.*
to tell dire †
ten dix
tenant locataire *m./f.*
tennis tennis *m.*
tennis shoes tennis *m. pl.*
tent tente *f.*
terrace terrasse *f.*
test examen *m.*
text texte *m.*
text message texto *m.*
to thank remercier
Thank you! Merci !
that cela, ça
That's all. C'est tout.
That's it. C'est ça.
That's too bad. C'est dommage.
that (*rel. pron.*) qui, que
theater théâtre *m.*
their leur
them eux ; elles ; les ; leur
with them avec eux/elles
I see them. Je les vois.
I'm speaking to them. Je leur parle.
themselves eux-mêmes ; elles-mêmes
then alors, ensuite, puis
there là ; y
It's over there. C'est là.
She's going there tonight. Elle y va ce soir.
there is/are voilà ; il y a ; voici
therefore donc
these ces
they ils, elles, on
thin fin/e, **(person)** mince
thing chose *f.*
think penser à/de, réfléchir à
I don't think so. Je pense que non. Je (ne) pense pas.
I'm thinking about my dog. Je pense à mon chien.
I think so. Je pense que oui.
I think that . . . Je pense que...
What do you think of this film? Qu'est-ce que tu penses de ce film ?
thirst soif *f.*
to be thirsty avoir † soif
thirteen treize
thirty trente
this ce (cet), cette
this is . . . c'est/ce sont... ; voici
thousand mille
three trois
throat gorge *f.*
through par
to go through passer par
to throw (out) jeter †
thunder tonnerre *m.*
It's thundering. Il y a du tonnerre.
thunderstorm orage *m.*
Thursday jeudi
ticket billet *m.*
museum ticket entrée *f.*
subway ticket ticket *m.*
theater/concert ticket place *f.*
to tidy up ranger †
tie cravate *f.*
tights collant *m. sg.*
time temps *m.* ; l'heure *f.*
full-time à plein temps
a long time ago il y a longtemps
part-time à mi-temps
What time is it? Quelle heure est-il ?
tired fatigué/e
title titre *m.*
to (a place) à, en
today aujourd'hui
toe doigt *m.* de pied
together ensemble
toilet toilettes *f. pl.*
toiletries articles *m. pl.* de toilette
tomato tomate *f.*
tomorrow demain
the day after tomorrow après-demain
tonight ce soir
too aussi
too much trop
tooth dent *f.*
toothbrush brosse *f.* à dents
toothpaste dentifrice *m.*
touchscreen tactile *adj.*
touchscreen tablet tablette *f.* tactile
to touch up retoucher
tourism office Office *m.* du tourisme, Syndicat *m.* d'initiative
tourist touriste *m./f.*
toward vers
towel serviette *f.* (de toilette)
to towel off s'essuyer †
town ville *f.*
downtown en centre-ville
town hall mairie *f.*
traffic circulation *f.*
traffic circle rond-point *m.*
traffic jam embouteillage *m.*
train train *m.*
train station gare *f.*
transportation (means of) moyen *m.* de transport

mass transportation transports *m. pl.* en commun
to travel voyager †
tree arbre *m.*
Christmas tree sapin *m.* de Noël
family tree arbre généologique
fir tree sapin *m.*
fruit tree arbre fruitier
tremendous formidable
trimester trimestre *m.*
trip voyage *m.*
to go on a trip faire † un voyage, voyager †, partir en voyage
Have a good trip! Bon voyage !
trousers pantalon *m. sg.*
true vrai/e
That's true. C'est vrai.
truth vérité *f.*
to try (on) essayer † ; **to try to do *st.*** essayer † de + *inf.*
T-shirt tee-shirt *m.*
Tuesday mardi
Fat Tuesday Mardi gras
tuna thon *m.*
turkey dinde *f.*
to turn tourner
to turn off (the lights) éteindre (les lumières)
to turn on (an appliance) allumer (un appareil)
TV télévision *f.* (télé)
TV (or radio) station chaîne *f.* de télévision
TV remote control télécommande *f.*
TV series série *f.*
twenty vingt
twin jumeau *m.*, jumelle *f.*
two deux
typical typique

U

ugly moche, laid/e
umbrella parapluie *m.*
uncle oncle *m.*
under sous
underground au sous-sol
to understand comprendre †
undisciplined indiscipliné/e
to undress se déshabiller
uneasy inquiet/-ète
unfortunately malheureusement
unhappy malheureux/-euse
unhealthy mauvais/e pour la santé
union: civil union PACS, pacte civil de solidarité
United States États-Unis *m. pl.*
university université *f.*, fac(ulté) *f.*
university dining hall restaurant *m.* universitaire, resto U (*fam.*)
university library bibliothèque *f.* universitaire, BU *f.* (*fam.*), bibli *f.* (*Can., fam.*)
unmarried célibataire
until: until X o'clock jusqu'à X heures
up: to be up être † debout
to get up se lever †
to go up monter
to update mettre † à jour
to uphold maintenir †
to upload télécharger
upset: to be upset être † fâché/e, être † en colère
upstairs en *haut
urgent urgent/e
us nous
to use (*st.*) se servir de (*qqch*), employer †, utiliser
useful utile
usually d'habitude, habituellement
utilities charges *f. pl.*

V

vacation vacances *f. pl.*
vacation plans projets *m. pl.* de vacances
to go on vacation partir en vacances
valley vallée *f.*
vanilla vanille *f.*
vanilla ice cream glace *f.* à la vanille
variety show divertissement *m.*
VCR magnétoscope *m.*
vegan végétalien *m.*, végétalienne *f.*
vegetable légume *m.*
vegetable garden potager *m.*
cut-up raw vegetables crudités *f. pl.*
vegetarian végétarien/ne
very très
very good très bon/ne
very much beaucoup
very well, thanks très bien, merci
video vidéo *f.*
video clip clip *m.* vidéo
video game jeu *m.* électronique
Vietnam Vietnam *m.*
Vietnamese vietnamien/ne
village village *m.*
vinegar vinaigre *m.*
to visit (place, monument) visiter ; **(person)** rendre visite à
volleyball volley-ball *m.* (volley)

W

waist taille *f.*
to wait (for) attendre
waiter/waitress serveur *m.*, serveuse *f.*
to wake up se réveiller
to walk marcher, aller † à pied
to take a walk se promener †, faire † une promenade
to walk for exercise faire † de la marche
to walk the dog promener † le chien
walk promenade *f.*
wall mur *m.*
on the wall au mur
wallet portefeuille *m.*
walnut noix *f.*
to want vouloir †, avoir † envie de, désirer
war guerre *f.*
World War I la Première Guerre mondiale
World War II la Seconde Guerre mondiale
wardrobe armoire *f.*
warm chaud/e
It's warm weather. Il fait chaud. Il fait bon.
I'm warm. J'ai chaud.
warm-hearted affectueux/-euse
to wash laver
to wash one's face se laver la figure
to wash one's hands se laver les mains
to wash one's hair se laver les cheveux
wash mitt gant *m.* de toilette
to waste time perdre du temps
watch montre *f.*
to watch regarder, voir †
to watch a game voir † un match
to watch a game on TV regarder un match
to watch a movie voir † un film
to watch a movie on TV regarder un film
to watch a play voir † une pièce de théâtre (une pièce)
to watch TV regarder la télé
water eau *f.*
mineral water eau minérale
sparkling water eau gazeuse, eau pétillante
tap water eau du robinet
water skiing ski *m.* nautique
to go water skiing faire † du ski nautique
way of life manière *f.* de vivre
we nous, on
to wear porter, mettre †
weather temps *m.*
weather forecast bulletin *m.* météorologique, météo *f.*
What's the weather like? Quel temps fait-il ?
The weather's bad. Il fait mauvais.
It's nice weather. Il fait beau.
Web Web *m.*, toile *f.*,
web address adresse *f.* web
web browser navigateur *m.*
webcam webcam *f.*
web page page *f.* web
web site site *m.* web
wedding mariage *m.*
Wednesday mercredi
week semaine *f.*
weekend week-end *m.*, fin *f.* de semaine (*Can.*)
weight lifting/training musculation *f.*
to do weight training faire † de la musculation
welcome bienvenu/e ; bienvenue *f.*
You're welcome. Je t'en prie./Je vous en prie. Bienvenue. (*Can.*)
Welcome to . . . Soyez la bienvenue !
to welcome accueillir †
well bien
Well . . . Eh bien…
Well done! Bravo !
west ouest *m.*
western (film) western *m.*
What . . . ? Qu'est-ce que/qui… ?, Quel/le… ?
What? Quoi ? Comment ?
What about you? Et toi ?/Et vous ?
What color is . . .? De quelle couleur est… ?
What did you say? Comment ?
What happened? Qu'est-ce qui s'est passé ?
What is that? Qu'est-ce que c'est ?

What's the matter? Qu'est-ce que tu as/vous avez ?
What's your name? Comment tu t'appelles/vous appelez-vous ?
What sport do you prefer? Quel sport est-ce que vous préférez ?
when quand, lorsque, où (*rel. pron.*)
When do you leave? Quand est-ce que vous partez ?
lorsqu'elle était petite when she was small
It's the season when it snows. C'est la saison où il neige.
where où
I know where he is. Je sais où il se trouve.
The store where you bought it is now closed. Le magasin où tu l'as acheté est fermé actuellement.
Where did you go? Où est-ce que tu es allé/e ?
whether si
I don't know whether he is coming. Je ne sais pas s'il vient.
which quel/le (*adj.*) ; que (qu'), qui (*pron.*)
The concert, which was quite expensive, ended one hour early because of the rain. Le concert, qui coûtait assez cher, a terminé une heure en avance à cause de la pluie.
The test, which we just took, was difficult. L'examen, que nous venons de passer, était difficile.
Which book do you like best? Quel livre est-ce que tu préfères ?
while pendant que
I was working while they were swimming. Je travaillais pendant qu'elles nageaient.
white blanc/blanche
whiteboard tableau *m.* blanc
who qui
whom qui
why pourquoi
wife femme *f.*
willingly volontiers
to win gagner
wind vent *m.*
It's windy. Il y a du vent.
window fenêtre *f.*
display window vitrine *f.*
to window shop faire † du lèche-vitrine
to windsurf faire † de la planche à voile
wine vin *m.*
winner gagnant *m.*, gagnante *f.* ; vainqueur *m.*
winter hiver *m.*
winter sports sports *m. pl.* d'hiver
to wipe (off) essuyer †
to wipe oneself off s'essuyer
wireless sans fil *m.*
wireless card connexion *f.* sans fil
wireless connection connexion *f.* sans fil
wireless keyboard clavier *m.* sans fil
wireless mouse souris *f.* sans fil
to wish vouloir †, souhaiter
wish vœu *m.*
Best wishes! Meilleurs vœux !
with avec
within dans
without sans
witness témoin *m.*
woman femme *f.*
to wonder se demander
wonderful génial/e, merveilleux/-euse
wood bois *m. pl.*
wool laine *f.*
knitted wool hat bonnet *m.* de laine
word mot *m.*
work travail *m.*
to work travailler
hard-working travailleur/-euse
It'll work out. Ça va s'arranger.
to work at the computer travailler à l'ordinateur
worker travailleur *m.*, travailleuse *f.*
workplace lieu *m.* de travail
workshop atelier *m.*
to work out faire † du sport ; faire † de la gym
world monde *m.*
World War I la Première Guerre mondiale
World War II la Seconde Guerre mondiale
worn, worn out (object) abîmé/e ; **(person)** épuisé/e
worried inquiet/-ète, anxieux/-euse
to worry s'en faire †, se faire † du souci, s'inquiéter †
wounded blessé/e
wrist poignet *m.*
to write écrire †, rédiger †
writer écrivain *m.*

Y

yard jardin *m.*
year an *m.*, année *f.*
Happy New Year! Bonne année !
I am 19 years old. J'ai 19 ans.
to yell crier
yellow jaune
yes oui ; si (*after negative question*)
yesterday hier
yet encore
not yet pas encore
yogurt yaourt *m.*
you tu ; vous ; toi
to you te (t') ; vous
He sees you. Il te/vous voit.
He's speaking to you. Il te/vous parle.
with you avec toi/vous
young jeune
your ton, ta, tes ; votre, vos (+ *n.*)
yourself toi-même ; vous-même
yourselves vous-mêmes

Z

zero zéro *m.*
zoology zoologie *f.*

Sources

TEXT CREDITS

Page 18 (top): Copiepresse, Bruxelles; page 18 (middle): Copiepresse, Bruxelles; page 18 (bottom): DR / 20 ANS 67; page 19 (top left): Courtesy of Haïti en marche. www.haitienmarche.com; page 19 (top right): Used by permission of The Canadian Press; page 19 (bottom): L'Express (Neuchâtel) www.lexpress.ch; page 41: Statistique Canada, *Familles et ménages—Faits saillants en tableaux,* Recensement de 2006, catalogue 97-553-XWF2006002, Date de parution 12 septembre 2007. http://www12.statcan.ca/censusrecensement/index-fra.cfm; page 42: Source: Statistique Canada, Portrait de famille : continuité et changement dans les familles et les ménages du Canada en 2006, Recensement de 2006, catalogue 97-553-XWF2006001, Date de parution 12 septembre 2007. http://www12.statcan.ca/francais/census06/analysis/famhouse/index.cfm: page 74: Map of Pays de Richelieu used courtesy of Office de Tourisme du Pays de Richelieu; page 93: "Familiale" from *Paroles* by Jacques Prévert © Éditions Gallimard; page 123: Photo by Salomon and text from « Guide du Voyageur—Textes Comité Martiniquais du Tourisme » used courtesy of Comité Martiniquais du Tourisme; page 127: School calender © Agenda Quo Vadis; page 135: Mini Chiffres clés. Édition 2011, Ministère de la culture et de la communication/Département des études, de la prospective et des statistiques (www.culture.gouv.fr/deps); page 136: Centre Pompidou schedule of events used courtesy of the Centre National d'Art et de Culture Georges Pompidou; page 201: From "Zinna" in *Printemps et autres saisons* by J.M.G. Le Clézio © Éditions Gallimard; page 230–231: From *Je suis Cadien (suite poétique)* by Jean Arceneaux. New York: Cross Cultural Communications, 1994. Used by permission of the author; page 243: Excerpt from *Emménager à Montréal*, 2006–2007 by Jessica Murphy used courtesy of Moving To Magazines Ltd www.movingto.com; page 267 (map): Copyright SNCF. Tous droits de reproduction réservés; page 297 (left): TF1 logo used courtesy of TF1; page 297 (middle): France2 and France3 logos used courtesy of France Télévisions; page 297 (right): M6 logo used courtesy of MÉTROPOLE TÉLÉVISION; page 310: From "Profiling 2011" study by Ipsos MediaCT. Used courtesy of Ipsos France; page 317: © Étude Audence AEPM France; page 324: From *La Leçon* by Eugène Ionesco in *La Cantatrice chauve suivi de La Leçon* © Éditions Gallimard.

PHOTO CREDITS

Page 2: Simon Harris/Robert Harding World Imagery; page 5: (bottom left) Romilly Lockyer/The Image Bank/Getty Images; page 5: (bottom right) Yellow Dog Productions/The Image Bank/Getty Images; page 9: (top) cinemafestival/Shutterstock.com; page 9: (center left) cinemafestival/Shutterstock.com; page 9: (center) cinemafestival/Shutterstock.com; page 9: (center right) Entertainment Press, 2008/ Used under license from Shutterstock.com; page 9: (bottom left) Jose Gil/Shutterstock.com; page 9: (bottom center left) Debby Wong/Shutterstock.com; page 9: (bottom center right) cinemafestival/Shutterstock.com; page 9: (bottom right) Randy Miramontez/Shutterstock.com; page 10: (left) Annette Brieger/Goldpitt Films Inc./Pearson Education; page 10: (center left) Annette Brieger/Goldpitt Films Inc./Pearson Education; page 10: (center) Annette Brieger/Goldpitt Films Inc./Pearson Education; page 10: (center right) Annette Brieger/Goldpitt Films Inc./Pearson Education; page 10: (right) Annette Brieger/Goldpitt Films Inc./Pearson Education; page 12: Annette Brieger/Goldpitt Films Inc./Pearson Education; page 22: David R. Frazier/Photolibrary, Inc./Alamy; page 25: (bottom right) Chuck Pefley/Alamy; page 25: (bottom left) David R. Frazier/Photolibrary, Inc./Alamy; page 26: Réunion des Musées Nationaux/Art Resource, NY; page 31: Annette Brieger/Goldpitt Films Inc./Pearson Education; page 32: (center left) Susan Kuklin/Photo Researchers, Inc.; page 32: (bottom right) Juanmonino/iStockphoto; page 32: (top) DOZIER Marc/Hemis/Alamy; page 37: First Light/Alamy; page 47: (top left) Mary Ellen Scullen; page 47: (top right) Mary Ellen Scullen; page 48: Mary Ellen Scullen; page 51: Eastcott-Momatiuk/The Image Works; page 54: Rayes/Photodisc/Thinkstock; page 55: Mary Ellen Scullen; page 57: PHOVOIR/Alamy; page 63: (top) Courtesy of the Library of Congress; page 63: (bottom) Courtesy of the Library of Congress; page 71: Goldpitt Films Inc./Pearson Education; page 75: Annette Brieger/Goldpitt Films Inc./Pearson Education; page 80: (top) a54/ZUMA Press/Newscom; page 80: (bottom left) Icon SMI 945/Icon SMI/Newscom; page 80: (bottom right) Jack Rendulich/Icon SMI/Newscom; page 81: (bottom left) Moritz Mueller/Imago/Icon SMI/Newscom; page 81: (bottom right) Eibner/Imago/Icon SMI 429/Eibner/Imago/Icon SMI/Newscom; page 84: ERIC FEFERBERG/AFP/Getty Images; page 96: (left) Cathy Pons; page 96: (right) Cathy Pons; page 96: (top right) Cathy Pons; page 104: (bottom) VERDY/AFP/Getty Images/Newscom; page 104: (top) REUTERS/Finbarr O'Reill; page 109: Annette Brieger/Goldpitt Films Inc./Pearson Education; page 112: Bill Stevenson Photography/Purestock/SuperStock; page 114: iStockphoto/Thinkstock; page 116: (center left) ckchiu/Shutterstock.com; page 116: (center right) Kim Sayer/Dorling Kindersley; page 116: (bottom left) kkaplin/Fotolia LLC; page 116: (bottom right) Photos.com/Getty Images/Thinkstock; page 122: Robert Harding Picture Library/SuperStock; page 126: Cathy Pons; page 132: (bottom left) Annette Brieger/Goldpitt Films Inc./Pearson Education; page 132: (bottom right) Annette Brieger/Goldpitt Films Inc./Pearson Education; page 133: (bottom left) Robert Harding; page 133: (bottom right) Annette Brieger/Goldpitt Films Inc./Pearson Education; page 139: Will & Deni McIntyre/Stone/Getty Images; page 144: Catherine Karnow/Corbis; page 145: Owen Franken/Corbis; page 147: Courtesy of Andrei Campeanu; page 148: (bottom left) Eddie Linssen/Alamy; page 148: (top right) FORGET Patrick/SAGAPHOTO.COM/Alamy; page 148: (bottom right) Tom/Andia/Alamy; page 148: (top left) worldpix/Alamy; page 154: (left) GoodMood Photo/Shutterstock; page 154: (right) Megapress/Alamy; page 155: Hemis/SuperStock; page 158: Mary Ellen Scullen; page 159: Mary Ellen Scullen; page 165: (left) Annette Brieger/Goldpitt Films Inc./Pearson Education; page 165: (right) Annette Brieger/Goldpitt Films Inc./Pearson Education; page 168: (top right) Christophe Ena/

AP Images; page 168: (bottom right) Mary Ellen Scullen; page 168: (center left) Fabienne Fossez/Alamy; page 170: Mary Ellen Scullen; page 172: (bottom right) Bodo A. Schieren/Bon Appetit/Alamy; page 172: (bottom left) P.Hussenot/photocuisine/Corbis; page 173: (center right) JAPACK/Amana Images Inc./Alamy; page 173: (top right) tommiphoto/Shutterstock; page 173: (top left) Floortje/iStockphoto; page 173: (center left) SoFood/Alamy; page 176: Michael Busselle/Getty Images; page 177: (top right) Mary Ellen Scullen; page 180: Courtesy of Andrei Campeanu; page 184: Annette Brieger/Goldpitt Films Inc./Pearson Education; page 185: (top right) Mary Ellen Scullen; page 186: (top right) Annette Brieger/Goldpitt Films Inc./Pearson Education; page 186: (bottom left) Erich Lessing/Art Resource, NY; page 192: (bottom) Lonely Planet/SuperStock; page 192: (top center) guichaoua/Alamy; page 192: (top) Hemis/Alamy; page 192: (bottom center) MAISANT Ludovic/Hemis/Alamy; page 193: (top right) Photononstop/SuperStock; page 194: (top) Hemis/SuperStock; page 194: (center right) Travel Pictures Ltd/Superstock; page 194: (bottom center) Photononstop/SuperStock; page 194: (center) Photononstop/SuperStock; page 194: (bottom right) Travel Library Limited/SuperStock; page 194: (bottom left) UpperCut Images/SuperStock; page 194: (center left) Westend61/SuperStock; page 199: Peter Cade/Iconica/Getty Images; page 200: Bruno Morandi/The Image Bank/Getty Images; page 205: Teo Lannie/PhotoAlto Agency/Getty Images; page 207: (bottom) Annette Brieger/Goldpitt Films Inc./Pearson Education; page 213: Adamsmith/Purestock/SuperStock; page 214: (top left) Virginie Cassidy; page 214: (top right) Virginie Cassidy; page 214: (center left) Virginie Cassidy; page 214: (center right) Virginie Cassidy; page 214: (bottom left) Virginie Cassidy; page 214: (bottom right) Virginie Cassidy; page 215: (top left) Directphoto.org/Alamy; page 215: (top right) Directphoto.org/Alamy; page 215: (bottom right) Eric Audras/ONOKY - Photononstop/Alamy; page 221: Directphoto.org/Alamy; page 229: Philip Gould Photography; page 234: Ulrike Welsch/PhotoEdit, Inc.; page 237: (top right) Guy Schiele/Publiphoto, Inc.; page 237: (top left) Annette Brieger/Goldpitt Films Inc./Pearson Education; page 244: Megapress/Alamy; page 245: (left) Michael Krasowitz/Taxi/Getty Images; page 245: (right) Photolibrary New York; page 247: Jeff Greenberg/Alamy; page 248: Photononstop/SuperStock; page 257: Masterfile Royalty Free Division 614-807382w; page 261: Annette Brieger/Goldpitt Films Inc./Pearson Education; page 264: Chad Ehlers/Alamy; page 267: (top) G. Bowater/Corbis; page 273: Derek Croucher/Alamy; page 274: (top) A. Autenzio/Explorer/Photo Researchers, Inc.; page 274: (bottom) Rob Kavanagh/Alamy; page 275: (bottom left) ableimages/Alamy; page 275: (top left) Erik Isakson/Tetra Images/Alamy; page 275: (center right) Ton Koene/Picture Contact BV/Alamy; page 277: (left) Andalucia Plus Image bank/Alamy; page 277: (right) Walery/Getty Images; page 281: Walter Rawlings/Robert Harding World Imagery/Corbis; page 282: Mary Ellen Scullen; page 284: Vittorio Sciosia/Alamy; page 285: (center right) Directphoto.org/Alamy; page 285: (bottom right) Ian Shaw/Alamy; page 285: (bottom left) Ray Stott/The Image Works; page 289: Cathy Pons; page 291: The Granger Collection, NYC; page 296: Marc Ausset-Lacroix/WireImage; page 299: SONY PICTURE CLASSICS/UPI/Newscom; page 300: GEORGES GOBET/AFP/Getty Images/Newscom; page 307: François BAILLE/PHOTOPQR/NICE MATIN/Newscom; page 310: (center) Exactostock/SuperStock; page 315: Archives du 7ème Art/Photos 12/Alamy; page 316: Stephen Simpson/Taxi/Getty Images; page 321: Abaca/Newscom; page 322: DE MALGLAIVE ETIENNE/ZUMA Press; page 325: (left) Mary Ellen Scullen; page 325: (right) Mary Ellen Scullen.

Index

This index is divided into two parts: Part I (Structures) covers topics related to grammar and pronunciation; here you will find references for information on spelling, pronunciation, grammatical form, and language functions. Part II (Topics) includes vocabulary and cultural topics, as well as information on how to find people, places, and strategies for learning French.

Part I: Structures

Part II: Topics

Famous francophones

Francophone world

French life and culture

Learning strategies (Fiches pratiques)

Reading selections (Lisons)

Reading strategies (Lisons)

Video selections

Vocabulary

Writing strategies (Écrivons)

a France
L'ANGLETERRE
Londres
LA MER DU NORD
LES PAYS-BAS
N
L'ALLEMAGNE
Bonn
Bruxelles
LA BELGIQUE
Calais
Lille
NORD-PAS DE CALAIS
LA MANCHE
LE LUXEMBOURG
Luxembourg
Cherbourg
Amiens
HAUTE-NORMANDIE
Le Havre
Rouen
PICARDIE
Caen
BASSE-NORMANDIE
Reims
la Marne
la Seine
Paris
ÎLE-DE-FRANCE
CHAMPAGNE-ARDENNE
la Meuse
Verdun
Metz
Nancy
LORRAINE
Strasbourg
LES VOSGES
le Rhin
la Moselle
ALSACE
Mulhouse
Brest
BRETAGNE
Rennes
Le Mans
PAYS DE LA LOIRE
Angers
Troyes
Chaumont
Orléans
la Loire
Tours
Nantes
CENTRE
Dijon
BOURGOGNE
Besançon
FRANCHE-COMTÉ
Berne
LA SUISSE
le Lac Léman
Genève
Poitiers
La Rochelle
POITOU-CHARENTES
Limoges
LIMOUSIN
Vichy
Clermont-Ferrand
AUVERGNE
la Saône
Lyon
St.-Étienne
RHÔNE-ALPES
Annecy
Chamonix
Mont Blanc
Grenoble
L'ITALIE
L'OCÉAN ATLANTIQUE
Bordeaux
la Dordogne
AQUITAINE
LE MASSIF CENTRAL
le Rhône
la Garonne
Avignon
PROVENCE-ALPES-CÔTE-D'AZUR
MIDI-PYRÉNÉES
Nîmes
Nice
Cannes
Bayonne
Toulouse
Montpellier
Aix-en-Provence
Marseille
Toulon
LANGUEDOC-ROUSSILLON
Perpignan
L'ANDORRE
L'ESPAGNE
Bastia
CORSE
Ajaccio
LA MER MÉDITERRANÉE
200 kilomètres
200 milles

Le Cana
LA RUSSIE
L'OCÉAN ARCTIQUE
GROENLAND (Dan.)
L'île de Ellesmere
Les îles de la Reine-Élisabeth
L'île Victoria
L'île de Baffin
L'ALASKA
NUNAVUT
Iqaluit
TERRITOIRE DU YUKON
LES TERRITOIRES DU NORD-OUEST
Whitehorse
Yellowknife
le Grand lac de l'Ours
le Grand lac des Esclaves
Mackenzie
LES MONTAGNES ROCHEUSES
LA CHAÎNE CÔTIÈRE
le lac Athabasca
Athabasca
la Baie d'Hudson
L'OCÉAN ATLANTIQ
L'OCÉAN PACIFIQUE
L'ALBERTA
LA SASKATCHEWAN
LE MANITOBA
Nelson
Saskatchewan
LA COLOMBIE BRITANNIQUE
LE QUÉBEC
TERRE-NEUVE
L'ÎLE DU PRINCE-ÉDOUARD
St-Jean
St-Pierre-et-Miquelon (Fr.)
Edmonton
L'ONTARIO
le lac Winnipeg
l'île de Vancouver
Vancouver
Calgary
Saskatoon
Victoria
Regina
Winnipeg
Seattle
LE NOUVEAU-BRUNSWICK
Charlottetown
Moncton
Québec
Fredericton
Halifax
LA NOUVELLE-ÉCOSSE
Montréal
le lac Supérieur
1,000 kilomètres
1,000 milles
le lac Huron
Ottawa
St-Laurent
Toronto
le lac Ontario
Boston
LES ÉTATS-UNIS
le lac Michigan
Hamilton
le lac Érié
Chicago
Détroit
Le Québec
N
LA PÉNINSULE D'UNGAVA
La Baie d'Ungava
L'OCÉAN ATLANTIQUE
Arnaud
George
Rivière aux Feuilles
Koksoak
Rivière à la Baleine
Caniapiscau
La Baie d'Hudson
TERRE-NEUVE
LABRADOR
le lac à l'Eau Claire
le lac Bienville
les îles Belcher
Rivière du Petit-Mécatina
Grande Rivière de la Baleine
La Grande Rivière
Réservoir de Caniapiscau
Natashquan
LES MONTS OTISH
Eastmain
l'île d'Anticosti
Sept-Îles
QUÉBEC
Le Golfe du St-laurent
Gaspé
le lac Mistassini
Baie-Comeau
Matane
St-Pierre-et-Miquelon (Fr.)
Chibougamau
L'ÎLE DU PRINCE-EDOUARD
Rimouski
LES LAURENTIDES
le lac St-Jean
Saguenay
Harricana
Roberval
Chicoutimi
L'ONTARIO
LE NOUVEAU-BRUNSWICK
Québec
Montmagny
La Tuque
Lévis
LA NOUVELLE-ÉCOSSE
Rouyn-Noranda
Val-d'Or
Shawinigan
St-Laurent
Thetford Mines
MAINE
Sorel
St-Jérôme
St-Hyacinthe
Hull
Sherbrooke
Montréal
Granby
Ottawa
VERMONT
le lac Huron
NEW HAMPSHIRE
500 kilomètres
500 milles
NEW YORK